P9-DGM-610

IMPORTANT

HERE IS YOUR REGISTRATION CODE TO ACCESS MCGRAW-HILL PREMIUM CONTENT AND MCGRAW-HILL ONLINE RESOURCES

For key premium online resources you need THIS CODE to gain access. Once the code is entered, you will be able to use the web resources for the length of your course.

Access is provided only if you have purchased a new book.

If the registration code is missing from this book, the registration screen on our website, and within your WebCT or Blackboard course will tell you how to obtain your new code. Your registration code can be used only once to establish access. It is not transferable

To gain access to these online resources

1. **USE** your web browser to go to: **www.mhhe.com/kerin**
2. **CLICK** on "First Time User"
3. **ENTER** the Registration Code printed on the tear-off bookmark on the right
4. After you have entered your registration code, click on "Register"
5. **FOLLOW** the instructions to setup your personal UserID and Password
6. **WRITE** your UserID and Password down for future reference. Keep it in a safe place.

If your course is using WebCT or Blackboard, you'll be able to use this code to access the McGraw-Hill content within your instructor's online course.
To gain access to the McGraw-Hill content in your instructor's WebCT or Blackboard course simply log into the course with the user ID and Password provided by your instructor. Enter the registration code exactly as it appears to the right when prompted by the system. You will only need to use this code the first time you click on McGraw-Hill content.

These instructions are specifically for student access. Instructors are not required to register via the above instructions.

Thank you, and welcome to your McGraw-Hill/Irwin Online Resources.

Kerin, Hartley, Rudelius
Marketing: The Core, 2/e
ISBN-13: 978-0-07-321213-5
ISBN-10: 0-07-321213-X

FGVC-9YYN-KGRW-PTU7-4UBD

REGISTRATION CODE

REGISTRATION CODE

The McGraw·Hill Companies
McGraw-Hill Irwin

MARKETING

THE CORE

2nd EDITION

Roger A. Kerin
Southern Methodist University

Steven W. Hartley
University of Denver

William Rudelius
University of Minnesota

Boston Burr Ridge, IL Dubuque, IA Madison, WI New York San Francisco St. Louis
Bangkok Bogotá Caracas Kuala Lumpur Lisbon London Madrid Mexico City
Milan Montreal New Delhi Santiago Seoul Singapore Sydney Taipei Toronto

MARKETING: THE CORE

Published by McGraw-Hill/Irwin, a business unit of The McGraw-Hill Companies, Inc., 1221 Avenue of the Americas, New York, NY, 10020.

This book is printed on acid-free paper.

1 2 3 4 5 6 7 8 9 0 QPD/QPD 0 9 8 7 6

ISBN-13: 978-0-07-299989-1
ISBN-10: 0-07-299989-6

Editorial director: *John E. Biernat*
Publisher: *Andy Winston*
Developmental editor: *Sarah Crago/Gina Huck Siegert*
Editorial coordinator: *Amy Luck*
Executive marketing manager: *Dan Silverburg*
Senior media producer: *Damian Moshak*
Lead project manager: *Christine A. Vaughan*
Manager, New book production: *Heather D. Burbridge*
Lead designer: *Matthew Baldwin*
Photo research coordinator: *Ira C. Roberts*
Photo researcher: *Mike Hruby*
Senior media project manager: *Susan Lombardi*
Senior supplement producer: *Carol Loreth*
Cover illustration: *Ralph Kelliher*
Typeface: *10.5/12 Times Roman*
Compositor: *TechBooks/GTS Companies, York, PA*
Printer: *Quebecor World Dubuque Inc.*

Library of Congress Cataloging-in-Publication Data

Kerin, Roger A.
Marketing : the core / Roger A. Kerin, Steven W. Hartley, William Rudelius.—2nd ed.
p. cm.
Includes index.
ISBN-13: 978-0-07-299989-1 (alk. paper)
ISBN-10: 0-07-299989-6 (alk. paper)
1. Marketing. I. Hartley, Steven William. II. Rudelius, William. III. Title.
HF5415.K452 2007
658.8—dc22 2005055463

www.mhhe.com

A MESSAGE FROM THE AUTHORS

Welcome to the second edition of **Marketing: The Core!** We are truly pleased to have an opportunity to share our enthusiasm for this exciting and dynamic field with students and instructors across the United States and throughout the world.

This edition of our book is designed to reflect the many recent and extraordinary events that have changed all aspects of our economy, particularly the field of marketing. The combination of the dot-com boom then bust, the instant success of interactive and wireless technologies, the immediate and dramatic response to international terrorism, the economic recession and recovery, the shock over the ethical lapses of many of our corporate leaders, and the rapid evolution from mass marketing to micromarketing have created a completely new business environment. We've worked hard to bring you the most up-to-date text that reflects today's world of marketing for consumers, managers, and students!

This edition of **Marketing: The Core,** like its previous edition, draws upon the content of our other, longer, text entitled **Marketing.** Our goal with this text is to present the basic concepts essential to an introductory marketing course yet retain the pedagogy that has made **Marketing** a best-selling text. **Marketing: The Core** is also the result of a detailed and rigorous development process developed during the previous editions of both texts.

The process starts by building on the strengths of the active-learning approach that has evolved from our previous editions. Then we evaluate and integrate the most recent new ideas from education about how to engage today's students in learning activities. On that foundation we build a comprehensive presentation of traditional and contemporary marketing theories, concepts, approaches, and tools, based on our own expertise and the expert advice and input of many knowledgeable reviewers and users of previous editions. To bring the theories and concepts to life we use products, brands, and companies that students can relate to from their personal experiences but also less-known entrepreneurs and small businesses that may also stimulate career plans. Finally, we invest in the growing number of educational support technologies—from DVD-format videos, to web-based testing, to real-time information updates.

Feedback from students and instructors has reinforced our commitment to this approach. The first edition of **Marketing: The Core** became the best-selling first edition business text in the United States in the past several decades. In addition, it has been adapted with local cases and examples or translated for use in Canada, mainland China, Taiwan, and Ukraine. This second edition of **Marketing: The Core** represents our efforts to continue the tradition of excellence and to guarantee an exceptional learning experience for marketing students. We hope you'll enjoy reading and using the text as much as we've enjoyed preparing it.

Roger A. Kerin
Steven W. Hartley
William Rudelius

PREFACE

DISTINCTIVE FEATURES OF OUR APPROACH

The innovative pedagogical approach used in *Marketing: The Core* and its supplements is the result of our combined experiences in a variety of classroom, college, and university settings. We introduced the approach in our first edition by integrating key elements from each of our teaching styles and preferences. Of course, like most instructors, we continuously monitor the changing learning styles of students, the growth and evolution of our discipline, and the efficacy of new instructional technologies to adapt and improve the approach. Its distinctive features include:

- **Assessment-ready elements.** Learning Objectives and Chapter in Review summaries integrated to help instructors and programs address growing interest in assessment and assurance of learning.
- **High-engagement style.** An easy-to-read, high-involvement, interactive writing style that engages students through active learning techniques, timely and interesting examples, and challenging applications.
- **Personalized marketing.** A vivid and accurate description of businesses, marketing professionals, and entrepreneurs—through cases, exercises, and testimonials—that allows students to personalize marketing and identify possible career interests and role models.
- **Marketing decision making.** The use of examples, cases, and videos involving people making marketing decisions, which students can easily relate to text concepts.
- **Traditional and contemporary coverage.** Integrated coverage of traditional and contemporary concepts illustrated through relevant popular business publications.
- **Rigorous framework.** A rigorous pedagogical framework based on the use of learning objectives, concept checks, key terms, Chapter in Review summaries, and supportive supplements for instructors.
- **Comprehensive support package.** A package of support materials to accommodate a wide variety of instructor teaching styles and student learning styles.

Feedback from many of the instructors and students who have used our text and package in the past has emphasized that the synergy of these features contributes to the success of each teaching and learning experience. We focused our efforts to build on these strengths as we developed the second edition of *Marketing: The Core.*

NEW AND REVISED CONTENT

- **Integrated marketing plan activities.** Each chapter now includes an end-of-chapter section titled "Building Your Marketing Plan" that discusses an element of the strategic marketing process presented in Chapter 2 (see Figure 2–4) and the sample marketing plan presented in Appendix A. Each Building Your Marketing Plan assignment provides step-by-step activities corresponding to the topics discussed in that chapter. By completing the assignments students will have completed all of the key components of a marketing plan.
- **Assessment-ready objectives and summaries.** Each chapter (1) begins with measurable learning objectives and (2) ends with the Chapter in Review, which is a summary of chapter content related to each objective. This direct link between objectives and content facilitates now-common accreditation efforts necessary to meet assurance-of-learning requirements. The objectives are cross-referenced to specific test bank questions to allow construction of measurement instruments.
- **Increased emphasis on meeting consumer needs with new products.** Chapter 1 presents an enhanced discussion of the difficulty of introducing successful new products and provides a variety of new-product examples as engaging topics

of discussion for students. A complete update of Rollerblade's new product line and marketing program is also provided.

- **Expanded coverage of business portfolio analysis.** The Chapter 2 discussion of BCG's business portfolio analysis has been expanded and applied to Kodak's shift from film to digital technology. Students are asked to evaluate four opportunities—film, digital cameras, self-service kiosks, and printers—in terms of the BCG matrix alternatives.
- **Updated overview of the marketing environment.** Chapter 3 now includes discussions of the digital revolution taking place in the music industry, global population trends, generational cohorts (including millennials) and the transition of Gen Y to economic adults, the two new types of statistical areas used by the Census Bureau, multicultural marketing, the growth of new technologies such as VoIP and Wi-Fi, and new regulations such as the *Madrid Protocol,* the *Federal Dilution Act,* and the *CAN-SPAM Act.*
- **Addition of extended examples to ethics and social responsibility discussion.** Detailed examples of situations, products, and companies familiar to students have been added to Chapter 4. A survey showing students' attitudes toward downloading music, Xerox's efforts at green marketing through its "Design for the Environment" program, and the growth of online fraud are examples used to help students relate to the concepts presented in the chapter.
- **Updated consumer behavior coverage.** Chapter 5 includes new examples related to MP3 players, an updated discussion of the new VALS typology (including innovators, thinkers, and survivors), a description of the word-of-mouth activity called *buzz marketing,* and an update on recent debates about subliminal advertising.
- **New business-to-business content.** Chapter 6 now includes discussions of Harley-Davidson's supplier collaboration efforts, buying business services, and online business-to-business trading.
- **Updated global coverage.** Recent changes in tariffs and their cost to consumers, the latest membership of the European Union, the growing use of global brands by companies such as Coca-Cola, Gillette, L'Oréal, and McDonald's, and considerations when customizing versus standardizing marketing practices are part of the Chapter 7 discussion of global markets and global marketing.
- **New marketing research framework.** The four-step marketing research approach presented in Chapter 8 now discusses new types of census data provided annually and new idea-generation methods based on depth interviews and direct input from consumers.
- **New and updated extended examples.** Reebok, Wendy's, and Apple are used as extended examples to illustrate segmentation and typical age, gender, price, and lifestyle segments in Chapter 9. 3M, Little Remedies, and Volvo are used to explain new-product development in Chapter 10.
- **New brand management content.** The rapidly changing field of brand management includes new approaches to valuing brand equity, brand licensing, and the use of "fighting" brands now covered in Chapter 11.
- **Updated channels and supply chain discussions.** The Chapter 13 opening example uses Apple Stores to illustrate the use of a high-touch environment to distribute high-tech products. In addition, the chapter features IBM's on-demand supply chain management.
- **Updated retailing and category management coverage.** Chapter 14 provides a discussion of the growing demand for luxury products by the mass market. Other important new topics are also included, such as the replacement of bar codes with RFID technology, the trend toward self-service retailing, the new regulations affecting telemarketing, and the use of category management to determine the assortment of merchandise in a store.
- **Revised integrated marketing communications content.** Chapter 15 opens with a description of Disney's "50th Anniversary" integrated marketing campaign, which includes the popular "What's Next?" ads, TV ads, print ads, newspaper inserts, a comprehensive web campaign, a Disney Visa card, and many other

partnerships and promotions. IMC is now introduced much earlier in the chapter, and other topics such as SIMM (simultaneous media usage), direct-to-consumer marketing, and assessment of program effectiveness are included.

- **New forms of advertising and personal selling.** Important content describing the new world of advertising and personal selling have been added to Chapters 16 and 17. As more consumers learn to multitask, advertisers have turned to new attention-getting media. Internet promotions, online contests, and *advergaming* (the integration of advertising messages in a video game) are all included with recent examples. In addition, the advertising content debate sparked by Janet Jackson's Super Bowl performance is presented for student debate. More attention is given to relationship selling.
- **Updated Chapter 18: "Implementing Interactive and Multichannel Marketing."** The reviews on this chapter, introduced in the seventh edition, were extraordinary. It is now updated to include recent examples and terms, such as new descriptions of Sevencycles.com, Nike's customized product choice board, new segments of online mothers, blogs, viral marketing, and multichannel marketing initiatives.
- **New career planning appendix.** The second edition of *Marketing: The Core* includes Appendix B: "Planning a Career in Marketing." Topics include the process of marketing yourself, careers in marketing, the job search process, and sources of marketing career information.

ORGANIZATION

The second edition of *Marketing: The Core* is divided into four parts. Part 1, "Initiating the Marketing Process," looks first at what marketing is and how it creates customer value and customer relationships (Chapter 1). Then Chapter 2 provides an overview of the strategic marketing process that occurs in an organization—which provides a framework for the text. Appendix A provides a sample marketing plan as a reference for students. Chapter 3 analyzes the five major environmental factors in our changing marketing environment, and Chapter 4 provides a framework for including ethical and social responsibility considerations in marketing decisions.

Part 2, "Understanding Buyers and Markets," first describes, in Chapter 5, how individual consumers reach buying decisions. Next, Chapter 6 looks at organizational buyers and markets and how they make purchase decisions. And finally, in Chapter 7, the nature and scope of world trade and the influence of cultural differences on global marketing practices are explored.

In Part 3, "Targeting Marketing Opportunities," the marketing research function and how information about prospective consumers is linked to marketing strategy and decisions are discussed in Chapter 8. The process of segmenting and targeting markets and positioning products appears in Chapter 9.

Part 4, "Satisfying Marketing Opportunities," covers the four Ps—the marketing mix elements. The product element is divided into the natural chronological sequence of first developing new products and services (Chapter 10) and then managing existing products, services, and brands (Chapter 11). Pricing is discussed in terms of the way organizations set prices (Chapter 12). Two chapters address the place (distribution) aspects of marketing: "Managing Marketing Channels and Supply Chains" (Chapter 13) and "Retailing and Wholesaling" (Chapter 14). Chapter 15 discusses integrated marketing communications and direct marketing, topics that have grown in importance in the marketing discipline recently. The primary forms of mass market communication—advertising, sales promotion, and public relations—are covered in Chapter 16. Personal selling and sales management are covered in Chapter 17. Chapter 18 describes how interactive technologies influence customer value and the customer experience through context, content, community, customization, connectivity, and commerce.

The book closes with several useful supplemental sections. Appendix B, "Planning a Career in Marketing," discusses marketing jobs and how to get them. In addition, a detailed glossary with page references and three indexes (name, company/product, and subject) complete the book.

ACKNOWLEDGMENTS

DEVELOPMENT OF THE TEXT AND PACKAGE

This text represents a product line extension of our existing text, *Marketing*. The idea for *Marketing: The Core* was the result of many comments from McGraw-Hill sales representatives, marketing instructors throughout the world, and students who had used our and other texts in their courses. We concluded that there is a need among some instructors and students for a comprehensive, but *concise,* marketing text. As the title suggests, our plan was to create a shorter text that would enable students to understand the *central* concepts of *Marketing*. This required reducing some coverage, enhancing some explanations, keeping the vocabulary manageable, and simplifying illustrations. We also used instructor feedback to match our pedagogical elements to the target audience.

To ensure continuous improvement of our product we have utilized an extensive review and development process for this new edition of *Marketing: The Core*. The second edition development process included several phases of evaluation and a variety of stakeholder audiences (e.g., students, instructors, etc.).

- The first phase of the review process asked adopters to suggest improvements to the text and supplements through a detailed review of each component. We also surveyed students to find out what they liked about the book and what changes they would suggest.
- The second phase included symposiums across the country, including users and nonusers. These sessions focused specifically on the supplements package and its effectiveness for instructors and students.

Reviewers who were vital in the changes that were made to this edition include:

Donald Auble
Baldwin-Wallace College

Sandy Becker
Rutgers University

Mukesh Bhargava
Oakland University

Solveg Cooper
Cuesta Community College

James Cross
University of Las Vegas

Richard Davis
California State University, Chico

Kim Donahue
Indiana University

Vicki Eveland
Mercer University

Marty Flynn
Greenville Technical College

P. Renee Foster
Delta State University

James Gaubert
Clemson University

Ken Gehrt
San Jose State University

Stephen Goodwin
Illinois State University

Karen Gore
Ivy Tech State College

Cynthia Gundy
University of Central Florida

Carol Gwin
Baylor University

Randall Hansen
Stetson University

Dorothy Harpool
Wichita State University

Mary Ann Hocutt
Samford University

Rosemarie Houghton
Northwood University

James Hutton
Fairleigh Dickinson University

Jack Janosik
John Carroll University

Areti Jordan
University of Central Florida

Sungwoo Jung
State University of New York, Oneonta

Russell Lacey
University of New Orleans

Jay Lambe
Virginia Polytechnic Institute and State University

Jane Lang
East Carolina University

Kenneth Lawrence
New Jersey Institute of Technology

Rosa Lemel
Kean University

Kelly Littlefield
Northwestern Michigan College

Lynda Maddox
George Washington University

Kimberley McNeil
North Carolina A&T State University

Rajiv Mehta
New Jersey Institute of Technology

Ronald Michaels
University of Central Florida

Yuko Minowa
Long Island University

Mark Mitchell
University of South Carolina, Spartanburg

James Molinari
State University of New York, Oswego

Lester Niedell
University of Tulsa

Vanessa Gail Perry
George Washington University

Edna Ragins
North Carolina A&T State University

Stephen Ramocki
Rhode Island College

Carl Saxby
University of Southern Indiana
Darrell Scott
Idaho State University
Trina Sego
Boise State University
Ken Shaw
State University of New York, Oswego
Tom Smith
Texas Wesleyan University
Jerrod Stark
Fort Hays State University
Richard Szecsy
Our Lady of the Lake University
Frank Titlow
St. Petersburg College
Denise West
Brevard Community College

The preceding section demonstrates the amount of feedback and developmental input that went into this project, and we are deeply grateful to the numerous people who have shared their ideas with us. Reviewing a book or supplement takes an incredible amount of energy and attention. We are glad so many of our colleagues took the time to do it. Their comments have inspired us to do our best.

Reviewers who contributed to the first edition of this book include:

Chris Barnes
Lakeland Community College
Pat Bernson
County College of Morris
Al Brokaw
Michigan Technological University
Sergio Carvalho
Bernard Baruch College
John Crawford
Lipscomb University
Charlene Davis
Trinity University
Dexter Davis
Alfred State College
Beth Elam
Western New England College
Medhat Farooque
Central Arizona University
Renee Foster
Delta State University
Hershey Friedman
Brooklyn College
Connie Golden
Lakeland Community College
Susan Harmon
Middle Tennessee State University
Rosemarie Houghton
Northwood University
Jim Hutton
Fairleigh Dickinson University
Dennis Kimble
Northwood University
Anna Kwong
Santa Barbara City College
Donna Mayo
Tennessee State University
Kevin McClean
Grand Canyon University
Susan Peterson
Scottsdale Community College
Donald Roy
Tennessee State University
Marvin Shapiro
South Mountain Community College
Randy Stuart
Kennesaw State University
Lars Thording
Arizona State University—West
Sushila Umashankar
University of Arizona
Bill Wilkinson
Governor's State University

Thanks are also due to many faculty members who contributed to the text chapters and cases. They include Linda Rochford of the University of Minnesota, Duluth; Robert Hansen of the University of Minnesota; and Kenneth Goodpaster, Thomas Holloran, David Brennan, and Mark Spriggs of the University of St. Thomas. Krzysztof Przybylowski of the Warsaw School of Economics and Olga Saguinova and Irina Skorobogatykh of the Plekhanov Academy of Economics provided a number of international materials. Michael Vessey provided cases, research assistance, many special images, and he led our efforts on the Integrated Resource Manual. Rick Armstrong, Bruce McLean, Chris Cole, and Jennifer Cole produced the videos. Carol Johnson of the University of Denver was responsible for the revision of the test bank.

Many businesspeople also provided substantial assistance by making available information that appears in the text and supplements, much of it for the first time in college materials. Thanks are due to Jeremy Stonier and Nicholas Skally of Rollerblade; Carol Watzke of CNS; David Ford of Ford Consulting Group; Maureen Cahill of Mall of America; Jack McKeon and Frank Lynch of Golden Valley Microwave Foods; Wayne Johansen of HOM Furniture; Donald Dunham of BP plc; Dr. George Dierberger and David Windorski of 3M; and Keith Nowak of Nokia. We also acknowledge the special help of Fred Senn and Kim Eskro of Fallon Worldwide; Mathew Kornberg of Little Remedies; Kirk Hodgdon and Mary Brown of Bolin; and Dan Stephenson of the Philadelphia Phillies.

Several businesses provided product samples and props that are contained in the Mini-Instructor's Survival Kit. We gratefully acknowledge the assistance and support of Karolyn Warfel and Betsy Boyer of Victor Mousetraps; George Dierberger of 3M (3M Pet Care Liquid Bandage); David Windorski of 3M (Flag Highlighter); Cynthia Harvell and Joselynne Little of ACT II Microwave Popcorn; Kimberly Crews of the Census Bureau; Barbara Davis of Ken Davis Products; Nicholas Skally of Rollerblade;

Leonard Fuld of Fuld & Company; Karen McCall of Panasonic; Stacie Barrett of Valassis; Mary Brown of Bolin Marketing; and Triestina Greco of Nutella-Ferrero.

Staff support from the Southern Methodist University, the University of Denver, and the University of Minnesota was essential. We gratefully acknowledge the help of Wanda Hanson, Louise Holt, Jeanne Milazzo, Gloria Valdez, and Nancy Mulder for their many contributions.

Finally, we acknowledge the professional efforts of the McGraw-Hill/Irwin staff. Completion of our book and its many supplements required the attention and commitment of many editorial, production, marketing, and research personnel. Our Burr Ridge–based team included John Biernat, Andy Winston, Barrett Koger, Sarah Crago, Amy Luck, Sue Lombardi, Christine Vaughan, Ira Roberts, Heather Burbridge, Dan Silverburg, Dave Kapoor, and many others. In addition, we relied on Michael Hruby for constant attention regarding photo elements of the text. Finally, our developmental editor, Gina Huck Siegert of Imaginative Solutions, Inc., provided outstanding assistance, advice, coordination, editing, and guidance with extraordinary professionalism and enthusiasm. Handling the countless details of our text, supplements, and support technologies has become an incredibly complex challenge. We thank these valuable team members for their efforts.

Roger A. Kerin
Steven W. Hartley
William Rudelius

A STUDENT'S GUIDE TO *MARKETING: THE CORE*, 2/e

Marketing: The Core, 2/e offers an array of pedagogical features to help you learn and apply the concepts.

Chapter-Opening Vignettes

Chapter-opening vignettes introduce you to the chapter concepts ahead, using a recognizable and interesting company example. For instance, in Chapter 1, the authors use 3M's Post-it® Note technology to grab your interest while introducing the concepts of marketing. The chapter-opening discussion is then integrated into parts of the narrative and exhibits throughout the chapter.

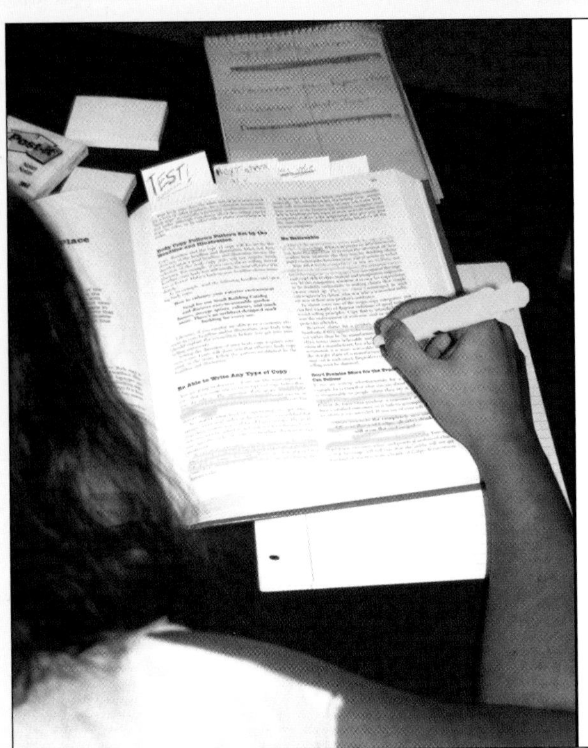

CHAPTER 1

CREATING CUSTOMER RELATIONSHIPS AND VALUE THROUGH MARKETING

LEARNING OBJECTIVES

After reading this chapter you should be able to:

1 Define marketing and identify the requirements for marketing to occur.

2 Explain how marketing discovers and satisfies consumer needs.

3 Distinguish between marketing mix elements and environmental forces.

4 Explain how organizations build strong customer relationships and customer value through marketing.

5 Describe how today's customer era differs from prior eras oriented to production and selling.

A MARKETING AND PRODUCT PUZZLE: HOW DO COLLEGE STUDENTS STUDY?

3M inventor David Windorski faced a curious challenge—trying to understand how college students study! And then designing a useful product that helps improve their studying.

But that was only part of his challenge. True, he needed useful details on how college students do their day-to-day studying, including preparing for exams. But he also wanted to identify ways to convert his knowledge about student study habits into a product they would find useful and that could use 3M's technology and be manufactured and marketed by 3M.

Sound simple? Perhaps! But David Windorski spent several years of his life moving the idea gleaned from marketing research on students to an actual product.[1]

After a quick look at how the original Post-it® Notes came to be, let's follow Windorski's winding path through the marketing research, technical research and development, manufacturing, and marketing that resulted in his innovative Post-it® brand products.

The Legend: The Product Nobody Seemed to Want In a surprising, oft-told success story, 25 years ago another 3M inventor, Art Fry, discovered a curious adhesive in his laboratory. It was an adhesive that would stick temporarily with finger pressure, unstick with a simple tug without leaving a mark, and restick when wanted. 3M, the world leader in adhesive technology,

5

Dynamic Graphics

Exhibits throughout the book are given a fresh, new look with the addition of creative frames and drawings designed to present important information in an interesting yet easy-to-understand layout.

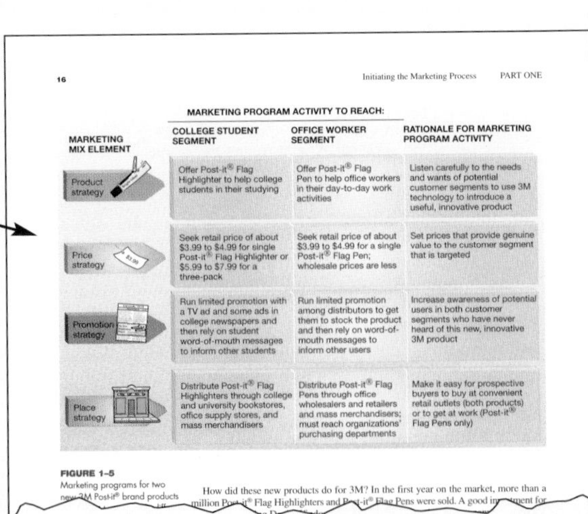

16 Initiating the Marketing Process PART ONE

MARKETING MIX ELEMENT	MARKETING PROGRAM ACTIVITY TO REACH: COLLEGE STUDENT SEGMENT	OFFICE WORKER SEGMENT	RATIONALE FOR MARKETING PROGRAM ACTIVITY
Product strategy	Offer Post-it® Flag Highlighter to help college students in their studying	Offer Post-it® Flag Pen to help office workers in their day-to-day work activities	Listen carefully to the needs and wants of potential customer segments to use 3M technology to introduce a useful, innovative product
Price strategy	Seek retail price of about $3.99 to $4.99 for single Post-it® Flag Highlighter or $5.99 to $7.99 for a three-pack	Seek retail price of about $3.99 to $4.99 for a single Post-it® Flag Pen; wholesale prices are less	Set prices that provide genuine value to the customer segment that is targeted
Promotion strategy	Run limited promotion with a TV ad and some ads in college newspapers and then rely on student word-of-mouth messages to inform other students	Run limited promotion among distributors to get them to stock the product and then rely on word-of-mouth messages to inform other users	Increase awareness of potential users in both customer segments who have never heard of this new, innovative 3M product
Place strategy	Distribute Post-it® Flag Highlighters through college and university bookstores, office supply stores, and mass merchandisers	Distribute Post-it® Flag Pens through office wholesalers and retailers and mass merchandisers; must reach organizations' purchasing departments	Make it easy for prospective buyers to buy at convenient retail outlets (both products) or to get at work (Post-it® Flag Pens only)

FIGURE 1–5
Marketing programs for two new 3M Post-it® brand products

How did these new products do for 3M? In the first year on the market, more than a million Post-it® Flag Highlighters and Post-it® Flag Pens were sold.

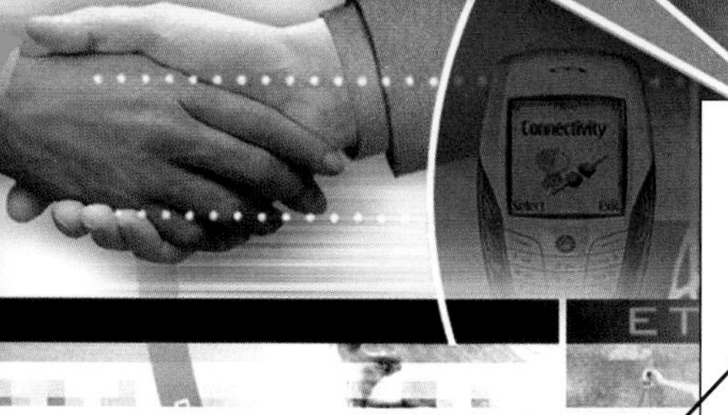

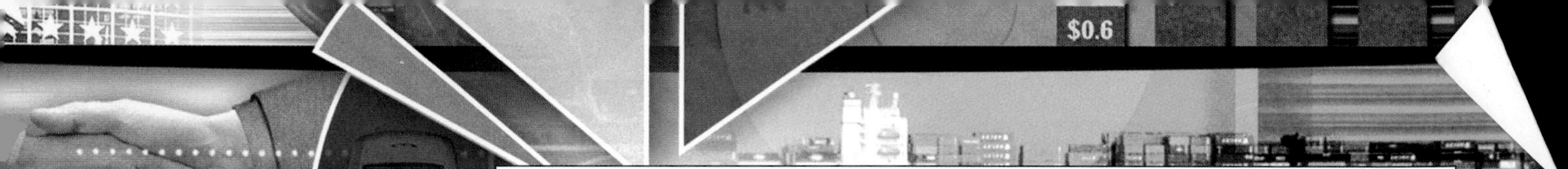

Marketing NewsNet

This boxed feature provides exciting, current examples of marketing applications in action, organized around the following themes: technology and e-commerce, customer value, global, and cross functional.

144 Understanding Buyers and Markets PART TWO

MARKETING NEWSNET The Global Teenager—A Market of 500 Million Consumers with $100 Billion to Spend

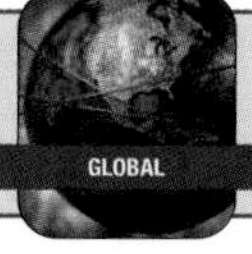

The "global teenager" market consists of 500 million 13- to 19-year-olds in Europe, North and South America, and industrialized nations of Asia and the Pacific Rim who have experienced intense exposure to television (MTV broadcasts in 166 countries), movies, travel, the Internet, and global advertising by companies such as Benetton, Sony, Nike, and Coca-Cola. The similarities among teens across these countries are greater than their differences. For example, a global study of middle-class teenagers' rooms in 25 industrialized

apparel, Levi's blue jeans, Nike athletic shoes, Swatch watches, and Procter & Gamble Clearasil facial medicine.

Teenagers around the world appreciate fashion and music, and desire novelty and trendier designs and images. They also acknowledge an Americanization of fashion and culture based on another study of 6,500 teens in 26 countries. When asked what country had the most influence on their attitudes and purchase behavior, 54 percent of teens from the United States, 87 percent of those from Latin America, 80 per-

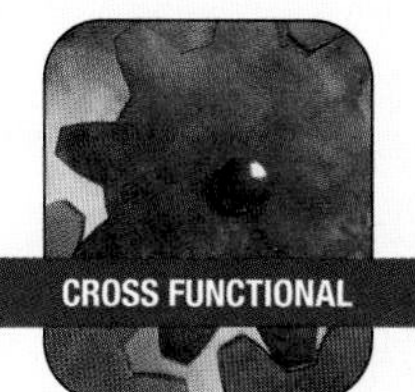

Ethics and Social Responsibility Alert

These boxes increase your awareness and assessment of current topics of ethical and social concern.

CHAPTER 16 Advertising, Sales Promotion, and Public Relations 357

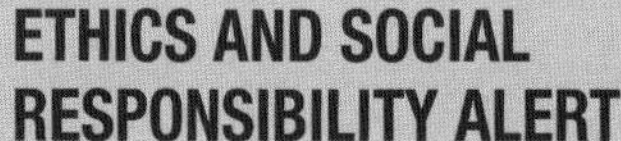

ETHICS AND SOCIAL RESPONSIBILITY ALERT Who Decides What Is "Appropriate" Advertising?

The controversy created by Janet Jackson's halftime performance in Super Bowl XXXVIII has sparked a complicated debate about what is appropriate content for media and advertising and who should decide what is appropriate. The Federal Communications Commission is legally responsible for policing the airwaves. Congress can also influence the industry with laws such as the recently proposed Clean Airwaves Act. Large media and retailing companies are also weighing in: Wal-Mart banned some magazines such as *Maxim* and *Stuff* from its stores, and six Clear Channel radio

and Abercrombie & Fitch is dropping its suggestive quarterly catalog.

For each group, the difficulty is in trying to match content with consumer preferences, because preferences vary from segment to segment. The FCC, Congress, and large and small companies have all received complaints about advertising content from conservative segments of the population. At the same time, a recent survey reported that 74 percent of consumers ages 12–20 think that many people have overreacted to the issue. Some experts are anticipating that the result will be a continuum of media and content

Concept Checks

Found at the end of each major chapter section, these checkpoints offer critical thinking and memory recall questions, helping you reflect on the text and test your comprehension of the material before reading on.

Concept Check

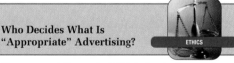

1. You see the same ad in *Time* and *Fortune* magazines and on billboards and TV. Is this an example of reach or frequency?
2. Why has the Internet become a popular advertising medium?
3. Describe three approaches to scheduling advertising.

Cultural Diversity

cross-cultural analysis
Study of similarities and differences among consumers in two or more nations or societies

values
Socially preferable modes of conduct or states of existence that tend to persist over time

Marketers must be sensitive to the cultures of different societies if they are to develop successful exchange relationships with global consumers. A necessary step in this process is **cross-cultural analysis**, which involves the study of similarities and differences among consumers in two or more nations or societies.[10] A thorough cross-cultural analysis involves an understanding of and an appreciation for the values, customs, symbols, and language of other societies.

Values A society's **values** represent socially preferable modes of conduct or states of existence that tend to persist over time. Understanding and working with these aspects of a society are important factors in global marketing. For example,

- McDonald's does not sell hamburgers in its restaurants in India because the cow is considered sacred by almost 85 percent of the population. Instead, McDonald's sells the McMaharajah: two all-mutton patties, special sauce, lettuce, cheese, pickles, onions on a sesame-seed bun.
- Germans have not responded to the promotion of credit cards such as Visa or MasterCard, nor to the idea of borrowing to purchase goods and services. Indeed, the German word for "debt," *schuld,* is the same as the German word for "guilt."

customs
Norms and expectations about the way people do things in a specific country

Customs **Customs** are what is considered normal and expected about the way people do things in a specific country. Clearly, customs can vary significantly from country to country. Some customs may seem unusual to Americans. Consider, for example, that in France men wear twice the number of cosmetics that women do and that Japanese women give Japanese men chocolates on Valentine's Day.

The custom of giving token business gifts is popular in many countries where they are expected and accepted. However, bribes, kickbacks, and payoffs offered to entice someone to commit an illegal or improper act on behalf of the giver for economic gain

Helpful Margin Definitions

Brief definitions of the key terms contained in the text are placed in the margin for quick reference and review.

Going Online Exercises

These end-of chapter exercises ask you to go online and think critically about a specific company's use of the Internet—helping you apply your knowledge of key chapter concepts, terms, and topics, as well as evaluate the success or failure of the company's efforts.

CHAPTER 14 Retailing and Wholesaling **327**

GOING ONLINE Consumers Can Now "Shop with Their Bot"

www.mhhe.com/Kerin

For many consumers, comparison shopping is not appealing because of the inconvenience of traveling to multiple locations. Even on the Internet, finding and searching multiple websites can be tedious. One solution is a form of software called an *intelligent agent,* or *bot* (derived from robot), which automatically searches for the best price. Try each of the following shopping bots—www.mysimon.com and www.shopping.com—to find the best price for one of the following products:

1. Wilson tennis racket
2. Sony TV
3. Guess jeans

How did the two bots differ? What range of prices did you obtain? What shipping and handling charges would apply to each purchase? Why are different recommendation made by the agents?

Video Case Studies

This end-of-chapter feature provides an up-close look at a company example—reinforcing the chapter content, while bringing the material to life. Nokia, 3M, and the Philadelphia Phillies are just a few of the exciting video cases now available with *Marketing: The Core,* 2/e.

groups throughout the world. The approach is reflected in the company's business strategy:

> We intend to exploit our leadership role by continuing to target and enter segments of the communications market that we believe will experience rapid growth or grow faster than the industry as a whole and that cater to the diverse needs, lifestyles, and preferences of our customers.

In fact, Nowak believes that "to be successful in the mobile phone business of today and tomorrow, Nokia has to fully understand the fundamental nature and rationale of segmentation."

THE COMPANY

Nokia started in 1865, when a mining engineer built a wood-pulp mill in southern Finland to manufacture paper. Over the next century, the company diversified into industries ranging from paper to chemicals and rubber. In the 1960s, Nokia ventured into telecom-

are combining digital audio, video, and data technologies into third generation (3G) communication devices that reach consumers globally. The convergence of the mobile phone (audio), digital camera (video), personal digital assistant (PDA), Internet and e-mail services (data), and other multimedia technologies will usher in the fourth generation (4G) of global communication devices.

The annual global demand for mobile phones has increased significantly over the years—from more than 400 million units in 2000 to about 650 million units shipped in 2004. In 2008, mobile phone shipments could exceed 950 million units. Marketers of 1G and 2G mobile phones used a geographic segmentation strategy as wireless communication networks were developed. Most started with the United States and then proceeded to Europe and Asia. However, each market grew at different rates. In 2004, Asia was the largest mobile phone market with 240 million, or 37 percent of all handsets sold that year. Europe was second with 240 million ... ed by ... ents

merchandisers for a suggested retail price of $11.95 to $15.95. And now it's also being stocked by golf retailers across the country like Golfsmith, Austad's, Golf Galaxy, and Target. The golf glove is available in both men's and women's left hand versions and in small, medium, medium/large, large, and extra-large hand sizes. A right hand version for both genders appeared in 2005. 3M projected first year sales of $1 million in the United States.

THE GOLF MARKET

Several socioeconomic and demographic trends impact the golf glove market favorably. First, the huge baby boomer population (those born between 1946 and 1964) has matured, reaching its prime earning potential. This allows for greater discretionary spending on leisure activities, such as golf. According to the National Golf Foundation (NGF), most spending on golf equipment (clubs, bags, balls,

sporting good superstores. However, mass merchandisers have recently increased their shares due to the typically lower prices offered by these retailers. FootJoy and Titleist, both owned by Acushnet, are the top two golf glove market share leaders. Nike, which recently entered the golf equipment market with Tiger Woods as its spokesperson, has a measurable share of the golf glove market. These golf glove marketers focus on technology and comfort to create points of difference from its competitors, such as the recently introduced FootJoy F3™ glove ($16), the Titleist Players-Tech™ glove ($22), and the Custom Crested Tech Xtreme glove ($22).

3M'S NEW PRODUCT PROCESS

Since about half of 3M's products are less than five years old, the process used by 3M to develop new product innovations is critical to its success and continued growth. Every

VIDEO CASE 11 Philadelphia Phillies, Inc.: Sports Marketing 101

"Bring everyone in closer. Have fans feel 'I'm not alone here; lots of others are in the seats. This is a *happening*!'" chuckles David Montgomery, president and chief executive officer of the Philadelphia Phillies, Inc.

He continues, "Old Veterans Stadium had too big an inventory of seats for baseball. The new facility and the fact that it's a game played in summer out in the open air really takes you to a much broader audience. Our challenge is to appeal to all the segments in that audience." What Montgomery is referring to is the Phillies' new world-class Citizens Bank Park baseball stadium that opened in 2004. It is a baseball-only ballpark, seating 43,500 fans, where every seat is angled toward home plate to give fans the best view of the action. This contrasts the 62,000-seat Veterans Stadium that both the Phillies and the Philadelphia Eagles football team shared from 1971 to 2003 where sightlines were always a compromise for the two sports.

The new fan-friendly Phillies stadium is just one element in today's complex strategy to market the Philadelphia Phillies effectively to many different segments of fans—a far different challenge than in the past. A century ago

ballplayers. You printed tickets—hoping and praying a winning team would bring in fans and sell those tickets. And your advertising consisted of printing the team's home schedule in the local paper.

THE PHILLIES TODAY: APPEALS, SEGMENTS, AND ACTIVITIES

Marketing a major-league baseball team is far different today.

"How do you market a product that is all over the board?" asks David Buck, the Phillies' vice president of marketing. He first gives a general answer to his question: "The ballpark experience is the key. As long as you project an image of a fun ballpark experience in everything you do, you're going to be in good shape. Our best advertising is word-of-mouth from happy fans."

Next come the specifics. Marketing the appeal of a fun ballpark experience to all segments of fans is critical because the Phillies can't promise a winning baseball team. Every team, even the New York Yankees, has its ups and downs. The Phillies are no different. Reaching the different segments of

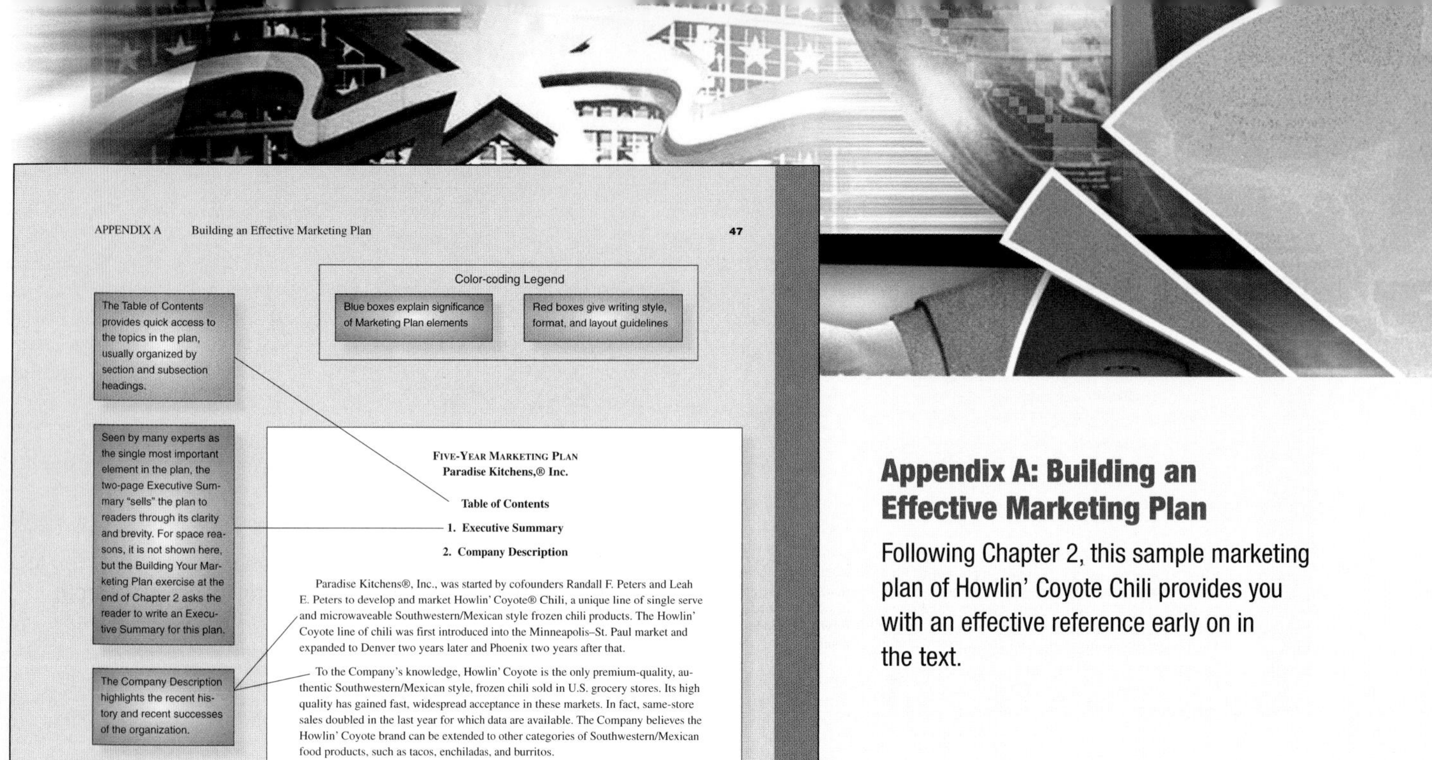

APPENDIX A Building an Effective Marketing Plan 47

Color-coding Legend

Blue boxes explain significance of Marketing Plan elements

Red boxes give writing style, format, and layout guidelines

The Table of Contents provides quick access to the topics in the plan, usually organized by section and subsection headings.

Seen by many experts as the single most important element in the plan, the two-page Executive Summary "sells" the plan to readers through its clarity and brevity. For space reasons, it is not shown here, but the Building Your Marketing Plan exercise at the end of Chapter 2 asks the reader to write an Executive Summary for this plan.

The Company Description highlights the recent history and recent successes of the organization.

The Strategic Focus and Plan sets the strategic direction for the entire organization, a direction with which proposed actions of the marketing plan must be consistent. This section is not included in all marketing plans. See Chapter 2.

The qualitative Mission/Vision statement focuses the activities of Paradise Kitchens for the stakeholder groups to be served. See Chapter 2.

Five-Year Marketing Plan
Paradise Kitchens,® Inc.

Table of Contents

1. Executive Summary

2. Company Description

Paradise Kitchens®, Inc., was started by cofounders Randall F. Peters and Leah E. Peters to develop and market Howlin' Coyote® Chili, a unique line of single serve and microwaveable Southwestern/Mexican style frozen chili products. The Howlin' Coyote line of chili was first introduced into the Minneapolis–St. Paul market and expanded to Denver two years later and Phoenix two years after that.

To the Company's knowledge, Howlin' Coyote is the only premium-quality, authentic Southwestern/Mexican style, frozen chili sold in U.S. grocery stores. Its high quality has gained fast, widespread acceptance in these markets. In fact, same-store sales doubled in the last year for which data are available. The Company believes the Howlin' Coyote brand can be extended to other categories of Southwestern/Mexican food products, such as tacos, enchiladas, and burritos.

Paradise Kitchens believes its high-quality, high-price strategy has proven successful. This marketing plan outlines how the Company will extend its geographic coverage from 3 markets to 20 markets by the year 2010.

3. Strategic Focus and Plan

This section covers three aspects of corporate strategy that influence the marketing plan: (1) the mission/vision, (2) goals, and (3) core competence/sustainable competitive advantage of Paradise Kitchens.

Mission/Vision

The mission and vision of Paradise Kitchens is to market lines of high-quality Southwestern/Mexican food products at premium prices that satisfy consumers in this fast-growing food segment while providing challenging career opportunities for employees and above-average returns to stockholders.

Appendix A: Building an Effective Marketing Plan

Following Chapter 2, this sample marketing plan of Howlin' Coyote Chili provides you with an effective reference early on in the text.

Building Your Marketing Plan

Each chapter ends with an activity that allows you to build a marketing plan, step-by-step.

20 Initiating the Marketing Process PART ONE

BUILDING YOUR MARKETING PLAN

If your instructor assigns a marketing plan for your class, don't make a face and complain about the work—for two special reasons. First, you will get insights into trying to actually "do marketing" that often go beyond what you can get by simply reading the textbook. Second, thousands of graduating students every year get their first job by showing prospective employers a "portfolio" of samples of their written work from college—often a marketing plan if they have one. This can work for you.

This "Building Your Marketing Plan" section at the end of each chapter gives you suggestions to improve and focus your marketing plan. You will use the sample marketing plan in Appendix A as a guide, and this section after each chapter will help you apply those Appendix A ideas to your own marketing plan.

The first step in writing a good marketing plan is to have a business or product that enthuses you and for which you can get detailed information, so you can avoid glittering generalities. We offer these additional bits of advice in selecting a topic:

- *Do* pick a topic that has personal interest for you—a family business, a business or product you or a friend might want to launch, or a student organization needing marketing help.
- *Do not* pick a topic that is so large it can't be covered adequately or so abstract it will lack specifics.

1 Now to get you started on your marketing plan, list four or five possible topics and compare these with the criteria your instructor suggests and those shown above. Think hard, because your decision will be with you all term long and may influence the quality of the resulting marketing plan you show to a prospective employer.

2 When you have selected your marketing plan topic, whether the plan is for an actual business, a possible business, or a student organization, write the "company description" in your plan, as shown in Appendix A.

APPENDIX

PLANNING A CAREER IN MARKETING

GETTING A JOB: THE PROCESS OF MARKETING YOURSELF

Getting a job is usually a lengthy process, and it is exactly that—a *process* that involves careful planning, implementation, and control. You may have everything going for you: a respectable grade point average (GPA), relevant work experience, several extracurricular activities, superior communication skills, and demonstrated leadership qualities. Despite these, you still need to market yourself systematically and aggressively; after all, even the best products lie dormant on the retailer's shelves unless marketed effectively.

The process of getting a job involves the same activities marketing managers use to develop and introduce products into the marketplace.[1] The only difference is that you are marketing yourself, not a product. You need to conduct marketing research by analyzing your personal qualities (performing a self-audit) and by identifying job opportunities. Based on your research results, select a target market—those job opportunities that are compatible with your interests, goals, skills, and abilities—and design a marketing mix around that target market. *You* are the "product";[2] you must decide how to "position" yourself in the job market. The price component of the marketing mix is the salary range and job benefits (such as health and life insurance, vacation time, and retirement benefits) that you hope to receive. Promotion involves communicating with prospective employers through written and electronic correspondence (advertising) and job interviews (personal selling). The place element focuses on how to reach prospective employers—a ... fairs, for example.

such as athletic teams, law firms, and banks, and nonprofit organizations such as universities, the performing arts, and government agencies, has added to the numerous opportunities offered by traditional employers such as manufacturers, retailers, and advertising agencies. In addition, e-commerce has created a variety of new opportunities such as product development managers for application service providers, data miners, and permission marketing managers for graduates with marketing skills.[3]

Recent studies of career paths and salaries suggest that marketing careers can also provide excellent opportunities for advancement and substantial pay. For example, about one of every five chief executive officers (CEOs) of the nation's 500 most valuable publicly held companies have a career history that is heaviest in marketing.[4] Similarly, reports of average starting salaries of college graduates indicate that salaries in marketing compare favorably with those in many other fields. The average starting salary of new marketing undergraduates in 2004 was $34,712, compared with $26,758 for journalism majors and $29,543 for advertising majors.[5] The future is likely to be even better. The U.S. Department of Labor reports that marketing and sales will be one of the fastest-growing occupations through 2012.[6]

Figure B–1 describes marketing occupations in six major categories: product management and physical distribution, advertising and promotion, retailing, sales, marketing research, and nonprofit marketing. One of these may be

PRODUCT MANAGEMENT AND PHYSICAL DISTRIBUTION

Product development manager creates a road map for new products by working with customers to determine their needs and with designers to create the product.
Product manager is responsible for integrating all aspects of a product's marketing program including research, sales, sales promotion, advertising, and pricing.
Supply chain manager oversees the part of a company that transports products to consumers and handles customer service.
Operations manager supervises warehousing and other physical distribution functions and often is directly involved in moving goods on the warehouse floor.
Inventory control manager forecasts demand for goods, coordinates production with plant managers, and tracks shipments to keep customers supplied.
Physical distribution specialist is an expert in the transportation and distribution of goods and also evaluates the costs and benefits of different types of transportation.

SALES

Direct or retail salesperson sells directly to consumers in the salesperson's office, the consumer's home, or a retailer's store.
Trade salesperson calls on retailers or wholesalers to sell products for manufacturers.
Industrial or semitechnical salesperson sells supplies and services to businesses.
Professional salesperson sells complicated or custom-designed products to businesses. This requires understanding of the product technology.
Customer service manager maintains good relations with customers by coordinating the sales staff, marketing management, and physical distribution management.

NONPROFIT MARKETING

Marketing manager develops and directs marketing campaigns, fundraising, and public relations.

ADVERTISING AND PROMOTION

Account executive maintains contact with clients while coordinating the creative work among artists and copywriters. Account executives work as partners with the client to develop marketing strategy.
Media buyer deals with media sales representatives in selecting advertising media and analyzes the value of media being purchased.
Copywriter works with art director in conceptualizing advertisements and writes the text of print or radio ads or the storyboards of television ads.
Art director handles the visual component of advertisements.
Sales promotion manager designs promotions for consumer products and works at an ad agency or a sales promotion agency.
Public relations manager develops written or filmed messages for the public and handles contacts with the press.
Internet marketing manager develops and executes the e-business marketing plan and manages all aspects of the advertising, promotion, and content for the online business.

RETAILING

Buyer selects products a store sells, surveys consumer trends, and evaluates the past performance of products and suppliers.
Store manager oversees the staff and services at a store.

MARKETING RESEARCH

Project manager for the supplier coordinates and oversees the market studies for a client.
Account executive for the supplier serves as a liaison between client and market research firm, like an advertising agency account executive.
In-house project director acts as project manager (see above) for the market studies conducted by the firm for which he or she works.
Competitive intelligence researcher uses new information technologies to monitor the competitive environment.
Data miner compiles and analyzes consumer data to identify behavior patterns, preferences, and user profiles for personalized marketing programs.

SOURCE: Adapted from David W. Rosenthal and Michael A. Powell, *Careers in Marketing*, ©1984, pp. 352–54.

FIGURE B–1
Marketing occupations

Several other jobs related to product management deal with physical distribution issues such as storing the manufactured product (inventory), moving the product from ...

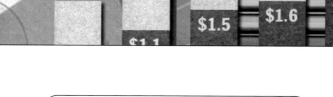

Appendix B: Planning a Career in Marketing

This appendix describes marketing careers and a marketing process to use during your job search.

AN INSTRUCTOR'S GUIDE TO SUPPLEMENTS

With this greatly enhanced package, you and your students are covered from the basic supplements to the latest in educational technologies. Check it out for yourself.

LECTURE PREPARATION TOOLS

Integrated Resource Manual. This thoroughly revised and expanded Integrated Resource Manual for *Marketing: The Core,* 2/e provides instructors with a wide range of materials to bring real-world excitement to the classroom and enhance student learning. This Integrated Resource Manual is offered in three user friendly formats: (1) as a printed version, (2) on CD-ROM disks in both an uneditable Adobe Acrobat pdf document containing all the PowerPoint thumbnail slide images in the left margin and in an editable Microsoft Word format without the extra complexity of the PowerPoint materials, and (3) on the www.mhhe.com/kerin website in both formats contained in the CD-ROM disks.

The Integrated Resource Manual contains these elements for each of the 18 chapters in *Marketing: The Core,* 2/e:

- Detailed lecture notes with accompanying PowerPoint materials on figures and photos from the textbook and supplemental print ads, TV ads, and short lecturettes (called Supplemental Lecture Notes, or SLNs).
- Answers to Concept Checks and Discussion and Application Questions.
- Suggestions for Going Online and Building Your Marketing Plan exercises.
- Teaching note for the end-of-chapter video case.
- In-class activities (ICAs) often tied to one of the props provided in the Mini-Instructor's Survival Kit (discussed below in more detail).

In addition, the Integrated Resource Manual contains these other valuable teaching aids:

- A guide to using and adapting the PowerPoint materials.
- Suggestions for helping students analyze cases.
- Ideas and student handouts for teaching large classes and marketing plans.
- Specific teaching techniques.

Instructor's Resource CD-ROM (IRCD). The CD-ROM includes the print and electronic supplements, so you have access to all of the supplements on one disk. It also contains the EZTest package.

E-Newsletter. The field of marketing evolves every day. Stay current with our unique adopter service, a bimonthly e-newsletter. Each issue contains the latest marketing news with photos and graphics. Every article is keyed to relevant discussions in text chapters and concludes with discussion questions you can use in class or add to tests. Back issues are archived in a searchable database on the Instructor's Center of the Online Learning Center (www.mhhe.com/kerin). Sign up through the Online Learning Center or contact your McGraw-Hill/Irwin sales representative.

Mini-Instructor's Survival Kit (ISK). This is a small box containing a dozen product samples and brochures—or "props"—to help bring real-world marketing examples into the classroom. These props are intended to be used with the in-class activities (ICAs) and accompanying PowerPoint materials appearing in the Integrated Resource Manual. However, they can be used separately or sometimes with a related video case.

LECTURE PRESENTATION TOOLS

Video case studies. A unique series of 18 contemporary marketing cases is available in VHS and DVD formats. Each video case corresponds with chapter-specific topics and an end-of-chapter case in the text.

PowerPoint presentation and digital assets. This comprehensive tool includes figure slides, commercials, product shots, advertisements, and video segments from the video package.

ASSESSMENT TOOLS

3,000+ question test bank. The test bank contains 3,000 questions categorized by topic and level of learning (definitional, conceptual, or application), and correlated to the Learning Objectives and Chapter in Review within each chapter of the text. The instructor-friendly format allows easy selection of questions from any part of the text, boxed materials, and cases.

EZTest software. This supplement contains all of the multiple-choice questions and the short essay questions from the test bank, and questions from the web quizzes. The EZTest program allows you to select any of the questions, make changes if desired, or add new questions—and quickly print out a finished set customized to your course.

PageOut quizzes with instructor gradebook. Assign quizzes in PageOut to give students incentive to read the text and prepare for class. Grades for each student will automatically post to your class gradebook.

Web quizzes. These quizzes are available to help prepare students for taking tests and can be found at www.mhhe.com/kerin. Fifty percent of the questions in each web quiz are also in the test bank to reward students who utilize this study aid.

ONLINE TECHNOLOGY

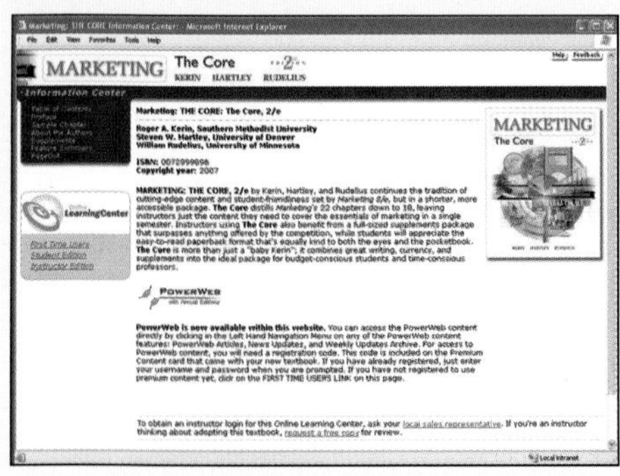

Online Learning Center

This robust book-specific website includes resources for both instructors and students. Through the Instructor Edition link we offer downloadable supplement materials and continuous updates. Through the Student Edition link students have a 24–7 study center to keep them up-to-date, to provide examples for application, and to prepare for a test. The Online Learning Center also provides a link to PageOut.

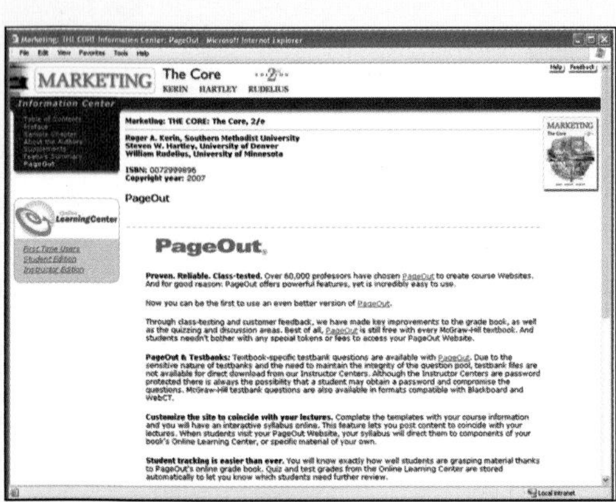

Create a course website in no time!

PageOut

This unique point-and-click course website tool enables you to create a high-quality course website without knowing HTML coding. With PageOut you can post your syllabus online, assign McGraw-Hill Online Learning Center or e-Book content, add links to important off-site resources, and maintain student results in the online gradebook.

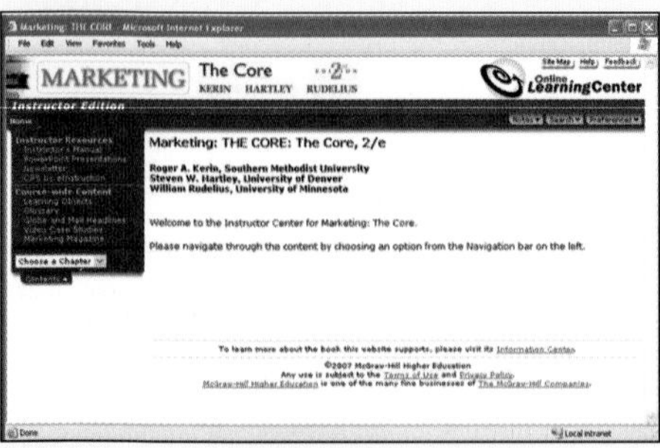

Online Learning Center—Instructor Edition

- **"Ask the Authors"**
- **Integrated Resource Manual**
- **PowerPoint.** Includes concept screens and art from the text and notes on other digital assets available in the PowerPoint Presentation Assembly Guide.
- **Classroom Performance System (CPS).** CPS is a revolutionary system that brings ultimate interactivity to the lecture hall or classroom. CPS is a wireless response system that gives you immediate feedback from every student in the class. CPS units include easy-to-use software for creating and delivering questions and assessments to your class. With CPS you can ask subjective and objective questions. Then every student simply responds with their individual, wireless response pad, providing instant results. CPS is the perfect tool for engaging students while gathering important assessment data.
- **Test bank.** This is available through PageOut.

Online Learning Center—Student Edition with PowerWeb

- **Key term flash cards**
- **Self-quizzes with feedback**
- **Online video cases**
- **Chapter summaries and outlines**
- **PowerPoint**
- **Career Section**

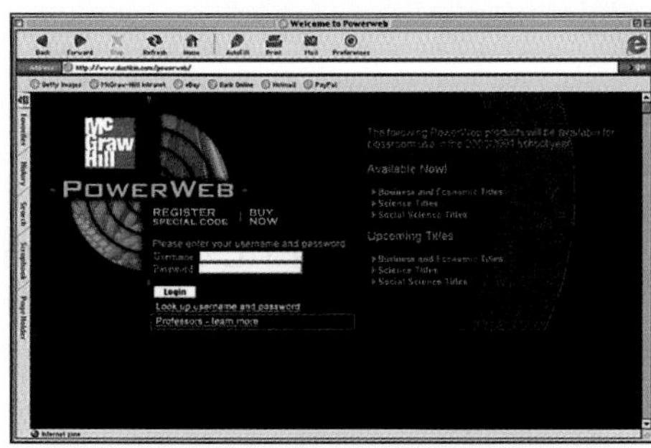

PowerWeb

- **Daily news feed.** Headlines with annotations from the leading periodicals and news sources—searchable by topic.
- **Weekly case updates.** Each week a new short case dealing with a company in the headlines is presented.
- ***Readings in Marketing.*** A collection of important articles selected by a team of marketing professors provides deeper topical study.
- **PowerSearch current journals and periodicals.** Search engine powered by Northern Lights.
- **Career resources**
- **Web research**
- **Study tips**

WebCT/Blackboard/eCollege/TopClass

You can use *Marketing: The Core,* 2/e online material with any online platform—including Blackboard, WebCT, and eCollege—to expand the reach of your course and open up distance learning options.

Blackboard
www.blackboard.com

WebCT courses · campus · community

eCollege.com

TopClass

BRIEF CONTENTS

DETAILED CONTENTS

Part 1 Initiating the Marketing Process 2

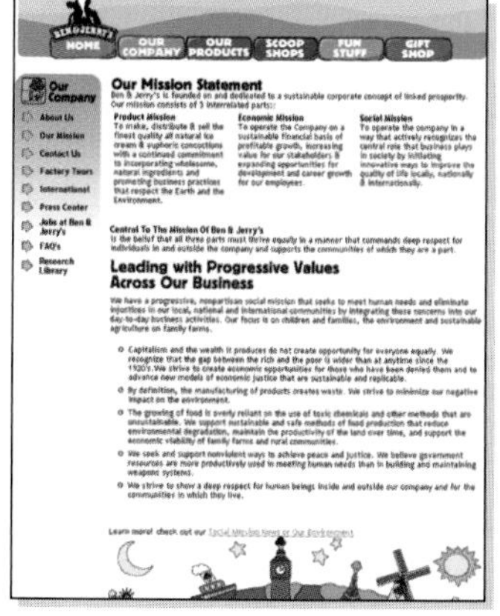

iPod
10,000 songs in your pocket. Works with Mac or PC. The new iPod.

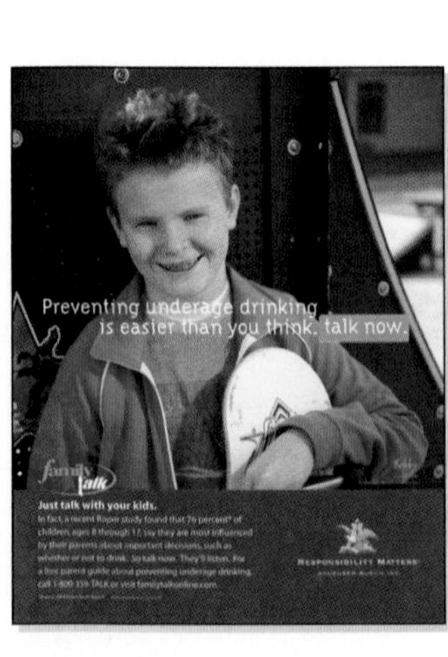
Preventing underage drinking is easier than you think. talk now.
family talk
Just talk with your kids.

Part 2 Understanding Buyers and Markets 96

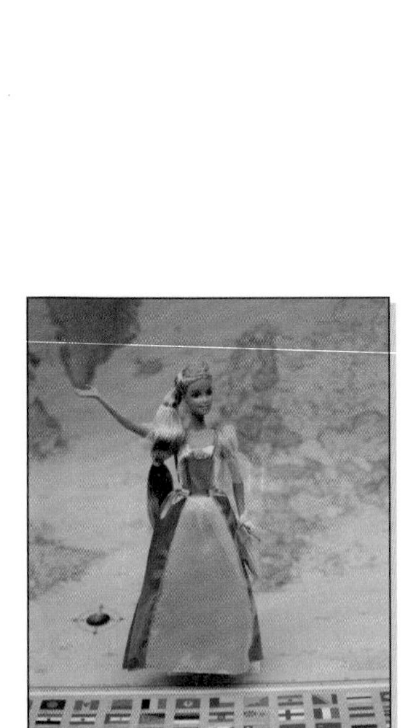

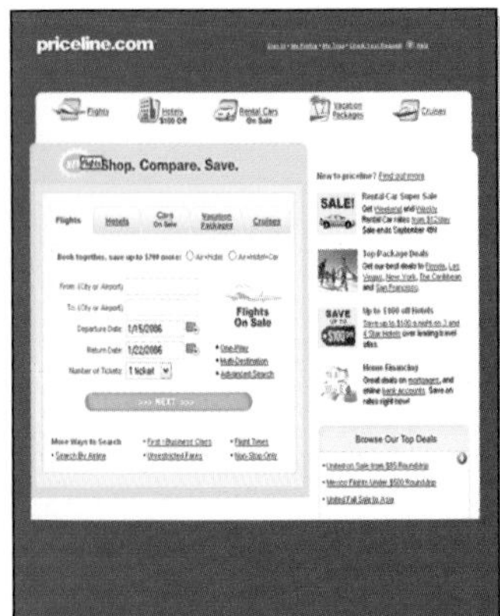

SUPER BOWL
HERO

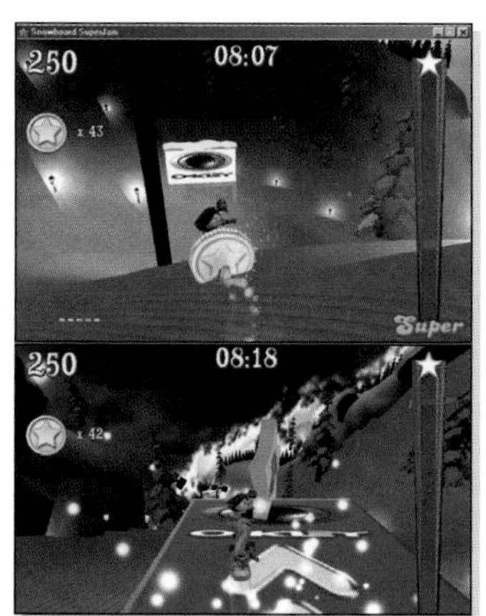
250
08:07
250
08:18
Super

17 PERSONAL SELLING AND SALES MANAGEMENT 374

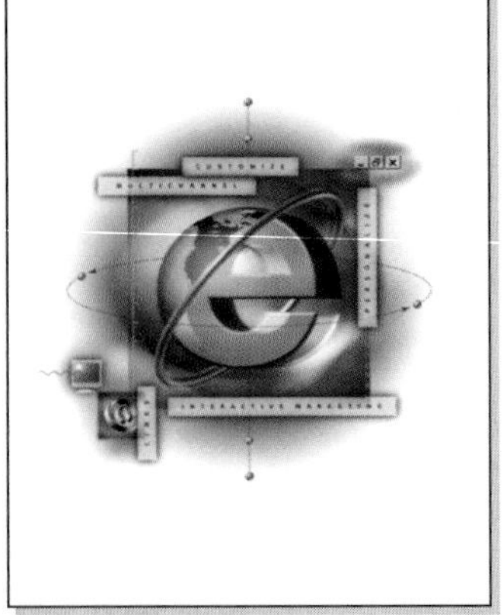

18 IMPLEMENTING INTERACTIVE AND MULTICHANNEL MARKETING 396

MARKETING

THE CORE

PART

PART 1
Initiating the Marketing Process

PART 2
Understanding Buyers and Markets

PART 3
Targeting Marketing Opportunities

PART 4
Satisfying Marketing Opportunities

1

INITIATING THE MARKETING PROCESS

HOW PART 1 FITS INTO THE BOOK

Laying the foundation for the entire book, chapters in Part 1 explain what marketing and the strategic marketing process are, and relate the importance of environmental, ethical, and social responsibility factors to a manager's marketing actions.

TEST!
NEXT WEEK
Body Copy Follows Pattern Set by the Headline and Illustration
Be Believable
Be Able to Write Any Type of Copy

Chapter 1

Creating Customer Relationships and Value through Marketing

LEARNING OBJECTIVES

After reading this chapter you should be able to:

1. Define marketing and identify the requirements for marketing to occur.
2. Explain how marketing discovers and satisfies consumer needs.
3. Distinguish between marketing mix elements and environmental forces.
4. Explain how organizations build strong customer relationships and customer value through marketing.
5. Describe how today's customer era differs from prior eras oriented to production and selling.

A MARKETING AND PRODUCT PUZZLE: HOW DO COLLEGE STUDENTS STUDY?

3M inventor David Windorski faced a curious challenge—trying to understand how college students study! And then designing a useful product that helps improve their studying.

But that was only part of his challenge. True, he needed useful details on how college students do their day-to-day studying, including preparing for exams. But he also wanted to identify ways to convert his knowledge about student study habits into a product they would find useful and that could use 3M's technology and be manufactured and marketed by 3M.

Sound simple? Perhaps! But David Windorski spent several years of his life moving the idea gleaned from marketing research on students to an actual product.[1]

After a quick look at how the original Post-it® Notes came to be, let's follow Windorski's winding path through the marketing research, technical research and development, manufacturing, and marketing that resulted in his innovative Post-it® brand products.

The Legend: The Product Nobody Seemed to Want In a surprising, oft-told success story, 25 years ago another 3M inventor, Art Fry, discovered a curious adhesive in his laboratory. It was an adhesive that would stick temporarily with finger pressure, unstick with a simple tug without leaving a mark, and restick when wanted. 3M, the world leader in adhesive technology,

3M Post-it® Notes or Post-it® Flags

+

Felt Tip Highlighters

=

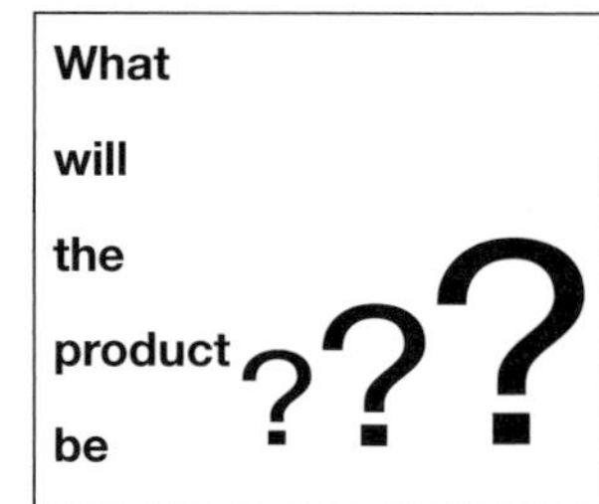

3M Product that will combine Post-it® Notes or Post-it® Flags and highlighters

For the creative way a student project helped lead to a new product for college students using 3M's technology, see the text.

manufactures and markets hundreds of adhesive products from Scotch® brand Magic™ Tape to Nexcare™ Tattoo™ Waterproof Bandages for kids.

What was the problem with Art Fry's "restickable" adhesive technology? He used his restickable slips to mark hymns for him to sing with his church choir. But problems existed for his restickable slips because no one at 3M could figure out:

1. Who might use the restickable slips.
2. How, when, and where they might be used.

Finally, 3M got the idea to mail some of these slips to the secretaries of the chief executive officers of the 500 largest corporations in the United States to see if they wanted and could use them. The resounding "Yes, we love them" answers resulted in today's 3M Post-it® Notes—and the 3M division that generates the largest revenues and profits in the company.

Discovering Student Studying Needs Fast-forward to David Windorski's challenge in late 2001. As an inventor of Post-it® brand products, Windorski was seeking ways to design new products for college students. He had some creative "thinking time" under 3M's "15% Rule" in which inventors can use up to 15 percent of their time to do initially unfunded research that might lead to marketable 3M products. Working with a team of four college students, Windorski and the team observed and questioned dozens of students about how they studied—how they used their textbooks, how they wrote and used their lecture notes, how they did research and wrote papers, how they reviewed for exams, and so on.

3M inventor David Windorski holds some of his early models that combined Post-it® brand products and highlighters.

Let's listen to Windorski describe what college students were telling him about their studying habits that might lead to a new Post-it® product:

> The basic idea for the product comes from students' studying behavior. What they often do is highlight a page in their book or their notes and then they can't find the important page after they highlighted it. So it's kind of natural behavior to highlight a passage and then mark the page with a Post-it® Note or Post-it® Flag of some kind. So it's reasonable to put Post-it® products together with a highlighter to have two functions in one.

Satisfying Student Studying Needs OK, but then how do you enhance a highlighter to be useful for students in their studying? This is exactly the question David Windorski had to solve with his inventive mind.

Designing a marketable product for students was not done overnight. In fact, it took Windorski a few years of creativity, hard work, and attention to countless details. He started by trying to attach a pad of small Post-it® Flags to the top of a highlighter. This design combined the two products but had a giant drawback: The combination was awkward and the Post-it® Flags would probably tear off when bouncing around in students' backpacks.

So Windorski went back to his drawing board—or more literally, to wood blocks and modeling clay. Some of his early models are shown in the photo. A wooden mock-up—a nonworking model—showed Windorski how the 2-in-1

Besides the college student segment, can 3M use its technology to reach the office segment? 3M's marketing programs for these two segments appear later in the chapter.

product would feel. Then he modeled the product in clay, which featured two revolutionary ideas: (1) using *small* Post-it® Flags rather than the larger Post-it® Notes and (2) putting the Post-it® Flags *inside* the barrel of the highlighter.

Was this the finished product? Not at all! There were many more breakthroughs and dead ends in Windorski's search for the 2-in-1 highlighter plus Post-it® Flags before he had a 3M product that students could actually use in studying. And he had a lot more work to produce a few hundred working products that students could actually try and tell him what they liked and didn't like about the product.

But Windorski had taken some giant steps in trying not only (1) to discover students' needs for his product but also (2) to satisfy those needs for a practical, useful product. He was also starting to wonder if his ideas might be extended to apply to a possible product for office workers. Later in the chapter we'll see both what products resulted from his innovative thinking and 3M's marketing plan that gets his products into the hands of students and other consumers.

3M's Technology, Marketing, and You What marketing strategy is the 3M Post-it® marketing team using today? By the time you reach the end of this chapter, you will know some of the answers to this question.

One key to how well 3M succeeds lies in the subject of this book: marketing. In this chapter and in the rest of the book we'll introduce you to many of the people, organizations, ideas, and activities in marketing that have spawned the products and services that have been towering successes, shattering failures, or something in between. And who knows? Somewhere in the pages of this textbook you may find a career.

WHAT IS MARKETING?

Here's some good news: In many respects you are a marketing expert already because you do many marketing activities every day. For example, would you sell more high-definition 42-inch plasma Panasonic TVs for $3,999 or $999 each? You answered $999, right? And because of your good experiences with your past Panasonic TVs, you'd seriously consider the plasma Panasonic TV.[2] So your experience in shopping for products already gives you great insights into the world of marketing. As a consumer, you've already been involved in thousands of marketing decisions—but mainly on the buying, not the selling, side. But just to test your expertise, try the "marketing expert" questions in Figure 1–1. You'll find the answers in the next few pages.

The bad news is, good marketing isn't always easy. In 3M's case, it's easy to talk about finding new applications for 3M's technologies but not so simple to do. One of 3M's strategies is to market Post-it® brand products designed for the special needs of different groups, or segments, of users. What special features might 3M build into a Post-it® product for (1) the college student segment and (2) the office worker segment? Give some thought to this. We'll analyze 3M's strategies for these two segments later in the chapter.

FIGURE 1–1
The see-if-you're-really-a-marketing-expert test

Answer the questions below. The correct answers are given later in the chapter.

1. True or false. You can now buy a robotic floor washer that scrubs your hard-surface floor better than you can mop it—even when you're not there!
2. Eating, talking on a cell phone, changing a CD, and other distracted driving behaviors account for what percentage of auto accidents each year according to the National Highway Traffic Safety Administration? (*a*) 5%, (*b*) 10%, (*c*) 30%, (*d*) 50%.
3. True or false. The 60-year lifetime value of a loyal Kleenex customer is $994.
4. To be socially responsible, 3M puts what recycled material into its very successful ScotchBrite® Never Rust™ Soap Pads? (*a*) aluminum cans, (*b*) steel-belted tires, (*c*) plastic bottles, (*d*) computer screens.

Marketing: Using Exchanges to Satisfy Needs

marketing
Provides value to customers through close relationships with them to benefit the organization and those closely related to it

The American Marketing Association, representing marketing professionals, states that "**marketing** is an organizational function and a set of processes for creating, communicating, and delivering value to customers and for managing customer relationships in ways that benefit the organization and its stakeholders."[3] Many people incorrectly believe that marketing is the same thing as advertising or personal selling; this definition shows marketing to be a far broader activity. This definition stresses the importance of delivering genuine value in the goods, services, and ideas marketed to customers. Also, note that the organization doing the marketing and the stakeholders affected—such as customers, employees, suppliers, and shareholders—should both benefit.

To serve both buyers and sellers, marketing seeks (1) to discover the needs and wants of prospective customers and (2) to satisfy them. These prospective customers include both individuals buying for themselves and their households, and organizations that buy for their own use (such as manufacturers) or for resale. The key to achieving these two objectives is the idea of **exchange**, which is the trade of things of value between buyer and seller so that each is better off after the trade.

exchange
Trade of things of value between buyer and seller so that each is better off

The Diverse Forces Influencing Marketing Activities

Although an organization's marketing activity focuses on assessing and satisfying consumer needs, countless other people, groups, and forces interact to shape the nature of that activity (Figure 1–2). Foremost is the organization itself, whose mission and objectives determine what business it is in and what goals it seeks to achieve. Within the organization, management is responsible for establishing these goals. The marketing department works closely with a network of other departments and employees to help provide the customer-satisfying products required for the organization to survive and prosper.

Figure 1–2 also shows the key people, groups, and forces outside the organization that influence marketing activities. The marketing department is responsible for developing relationships with the organization's customers, shareholders, suppliers, and other organizations. Environmental forces, which consist of social, technological,

FIGURE 1–2
An organization's marketing department relates to many people, groups, and forces

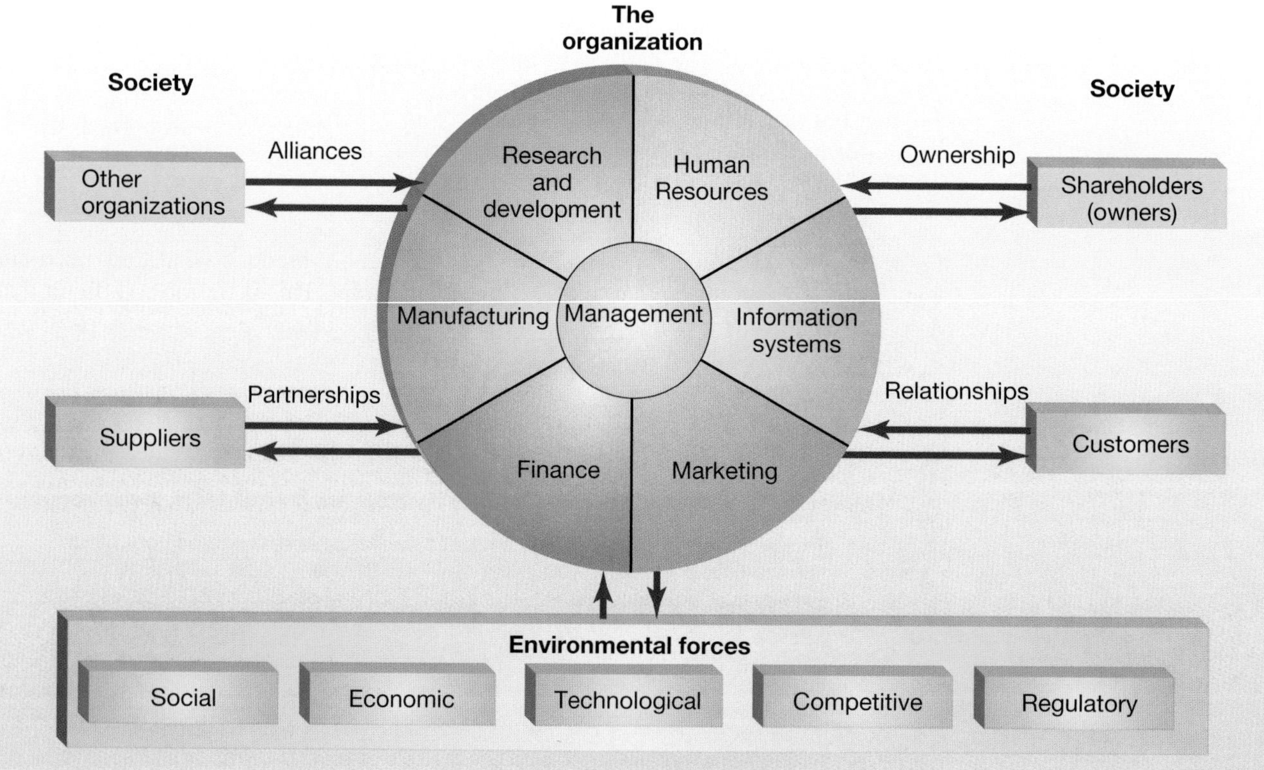

economic, competitive, and regulatory forces, also shape an organization's marketing activities. Finally, an organization's marketing decisions are affected by and also impact society as a whole.

The organization must strike a continual balance among the sometimes differing interests of these individuals and groups. For example, it is not possible to simultaneously provide the lowest-priced and highest-quality products to customers and pay the highest prices to suppliers, highest wages to employees, and maximum returns to shareholders.

Concept Check

1. What is marketing?
2. Marketing focuses on ________________ and ________________ consumer needs.

HOW MARKETING DISCOVERS AND SATISFIES CONSUMER NEEDS

The importance of discovering and satisfying consumer needs is so critical to understanding marketing that we look at each of these two steps in detail next.

Discovering Consumer Needs

The first objective in marketing is discovering the needs of prospective consumers. This is far more difficult than it sounds.

Discovering consumer needs may look easy, but when you get down to the specifics of developing new products, problems crop up. For one thing, consumers may not always know or be able to describe what they need and want. When Apple built its first Apple II personal computer and started a new industry, consumers didn't really know what the benefits would be. So they had to be educated and to learn how to use personal computers. Also, Bell, a U.S. bicycle helmet maker, has listened to its customers, collected hundreds of their ideas, and put several into its new products.[4] This is where effective marketing research, the topic of Chapter 8, can help.

The Challenge of Meeting Consumer Needs with New Products New-product experts generally estimate that up to 94 percent of the more than 33,000 new consumable products (food, beverage, health, beauty, and other household and pet products) introduced in the United States annually "don't succeed in the long run."[5] Robert M. McMath, who has studied more than 70,000 of these new-product launches, has two key suggestions: (1) focus on what the customer benefit is, and (2) learn from the past.[6]

The solution to preventing such product failures seems embarrassingly obvious. First, find out what consumers need and want. Second, produce what they need and want, and don't produce what they don't need and want. This is far more difficult than it sounds. The four products shown on the next page illustrate just how hard it is to achieve new-product success, a topic covered in more detail in Chapter 10.

Without reading further, think about the potential benefits to customers and possible "showstoppers"—factors that might doom the product—for each of the four products pictured. Some of the products may come out of your past, and others may be on your horizon. Here's a quick analysis of the four new products, sometimes with comments adapted from McMath:

- *Dr. Care Toothpaste*. As a result of extensive research, Dr. Care family toothpaste in its aerosol container was introduced two decades ago. The vanilla-mint-flavored product's benefits were advertised as being easy to use and sanitary. Pretend for a minute that you are five years old and left alone in the bathroom to brush your teeth using your Dr. Care toothpaste. Hmm! Apparently, surprised parents were not enthusiastic about the bathroom wall paintings by their future Rembrandts—a showstopper that doomed this creative product.[7]

For these four products, identify (1) what benefits the product provides buyers and (2) what "showstoppers" might kill the product in the marketplace. Answers are discussed in the text.

Vanilla-mint-flavored toothpaste in an aerosol container

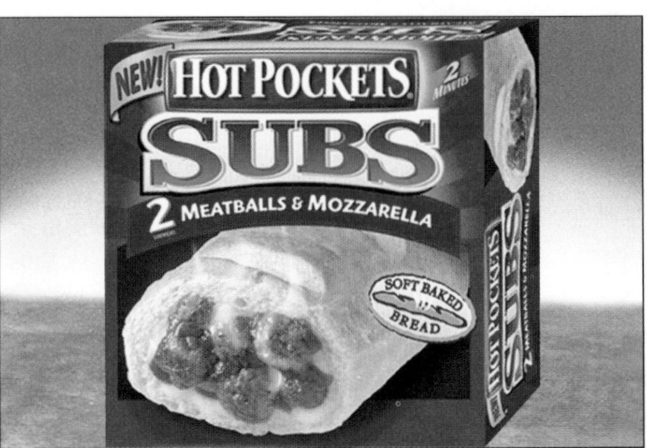

Meat and cheese microwaveable sandwiches

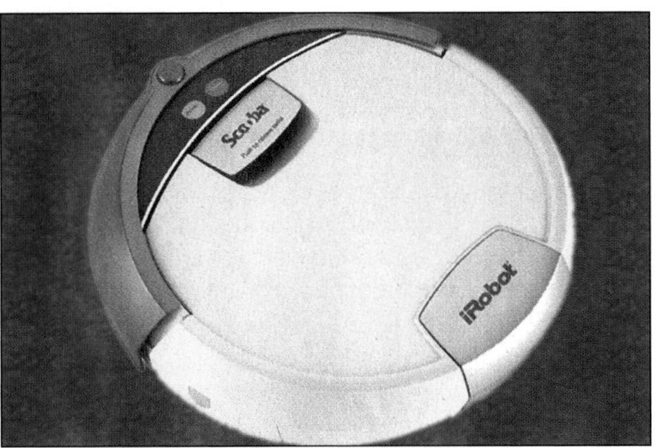

Robotic floor washer

Reduced-carb cola with some sugar

- *Hot Pockets*. Introduced in 1983, these convenient meat and cheese microwaveable sandwiches are a favorite brand among students. More than 20 varieties have been introduced, from Hot Pockets Pizza Snacks to Hot Pockets subs. A none-too-serious potential showstopper: Excessive ice crystals can form on the product due to variations in freezer temperatures; if this happens and the sandwich is thawed before eaten, it may not taste as good.[8]
- *iRobot's Scooba™ Robotic Floor Washer.* Introduced during the 2005 Holiday season, the Scooba robotic floor washer vacuums, washes, scrubs, and dries a hard-surface floor in a single operation (question 1, Figure 1-1). At $259.99 the Scooba does a better job than a mop, which just spreads the dirt around according to Scooba's manufacturer. Possible showstoppers: Because the Scooba has limited "robotic intelligence," it can get stuck under furniture until the consumer releases it and dirt in corners is a problem.[9]
- *Coca-Cola's C2*. In summer 2003, Coca-Cola spent $50 million to launch C2, a reduced-carb cola that still contained some sugar to add taste. The company's biggest new product since Diet Coke two decades earlier, C2 was targeted to 20- to 40-year-olds wanting some sugar in their cola while also watching the calories. C2 was sometimes priced 60 percent higher at retail than Coke, a devastating concern to buyers. But the big showstopper: Many cola drinkers were disappointed in C2's taste, complaining it was flat or had an unpleasant aftertaste.[10]

Firms spend billions of dollars annually on marketing and technical research that significantly reduces, but doesn't eliminate, new-product failure. So meeting

ETHICS AND SOCIAL RESPONSIBILITY ALERT

Cell Phones and Distracted Driving—Just as Dangerous as Drunk Driving

Using a cell phone, eating a burger, changing a CD, or reading a newspaper—normally, marketers want to encourage these behaviors. However, if done while driving a car, they can have disastrous consequences. Cell phones are an especially critical problem. In a recent study, researchers found that the distracting effect of using a cell phone exceeded that of a person with a 0.08 blood-alcohol level, the legal limit for drunk driving in most states.

Why do drivers engage in these dangerous behaviors? In 2002, they spent an average of 300 hours on the road and want that time to be productive. According to a recent study, more than 50 percent of drivers who have a cell phone admit to using it while driving. And a more sobering study from the National Highway Traffic Safety Administration estimated that distracted drivers accounted for almost 30 percent of all automobile crashes, or 1.2 million accidents a year—many of them fatal (question 2, Figure 1–1).

Many states and most European nations have enacted legislation to reduce or eliminate cell phone use. Some organizations have developed public service announcements (PSAs) and driver-training videos to educate consumers on the dangers of distracted driving. Some states have created billboards to inform drivers of their moral if not legal obligation to drive attentively.[11]

Do you use your cell phone while driving? Should states be encouraged to restrict cell phone use by drivers? Are states restricting your individual rights? Or are these laws making you safer on the highway?

the changing needs of consumers is a continuing challenge for firms around the world.

Consumer Needs and Consumer Wants Should marketing try to satisfy consumer needs or consumer wants? The answer is both. Heated debates rage over this question, depending on the definitions of needs and wants and the amount of freedom given to prospective customers to make their own buying decisions.

A *need* occurs when a person feels deprived of basic necessities such as food, clothing, and shelter. A *want* is a need that is shaped by a person's knowledge, culture, and personality. So if you feel hungry, you have developed a basic need and desire to eat something. Let's say you then want to eat an apple or a candy bar because, based on your past experience and personality, you know these will satisfy your hunger need. Effective marketing, in the form of creating an awareness of good products at convenient locations, can clearly shape a person's wants.

At issue is whether marketing persuades prospective customers to buy the "wrong" things—say, a candy bar rather than an apple to satisfy hunger pangs. Of increasing concern, as described in the Ethics and Social Responsibility Alert, is the distracting effect of cell phones used by drivers, which significantly increases highway accidents.

Certainly, marketing tries to influence what we buy. A question then arises: At what point do we want government and society to step in to protect consumers? Most consumers would say they want government to protect us from harmful drugs and unsafe cars but not from candy bars and soft drinks. To protect vehicle drivers and their passengers, should government restrict the use of cell phones by drivers? Such questions have no clear-cut answers, which is why legal and social issues are central to marketing. Because even psychologists and economists still debate the exact meanings of *need* and *want,* we shall use the terms interchangeably throughout the book.

As shown in Figure 1–3 on the next page, discovering needs involves looking carefully at prospective customers, whether they are children buying M&M's candy, college students buying Rollerblade in-line skates, or firms buying Xerox photocopying machines. A principal activity of a firm's marketing department is to scrutinize carefully its consumers to understand what they need and want and the trends and factors that shape them.

market
People with desire and ability to buy a specific product

What a Market Is Potential consumers make up a **market**, which is people with both the desire and the ability to buy a specific product. All markets ultimately are people. Even when we say a firm bought a Xerox copier, we mean one or several people in the firm decided to buy it. People who are aware of their unmet needs may

FIGURE 1–3
Marketing's first task: discovering consumer needs

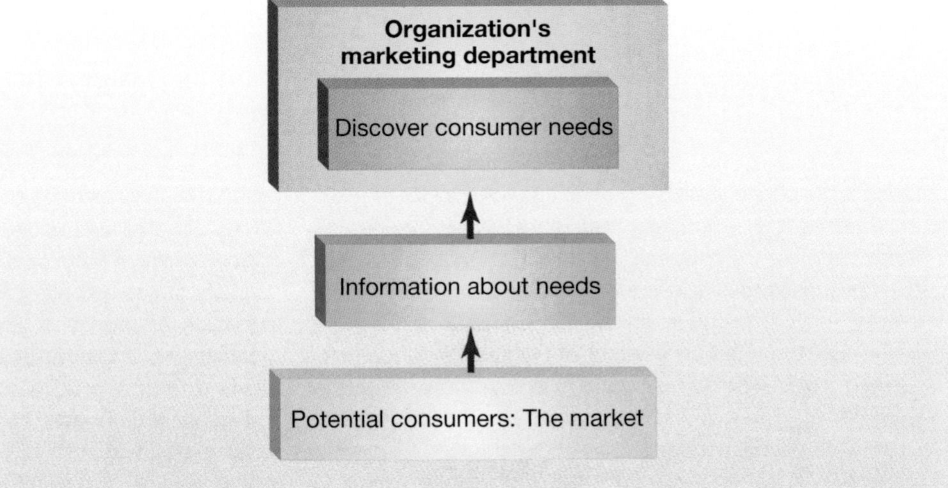

have the desire to buy the product, but that alone isn't sufficient. People must also have the ability to buy, such as the authority, time, and money. People may even "buy" an idea that results in an action, such as having their blood pressure checked annually or turning down their thermostat to save energy.

Satisfying Consumer Needs

Marketing doesn't stop with the discovery of consumer needs. Because the organization obviously can't satisfy all consumer needs, it must concentrate its efforts on certain needs of a specific group of potential consumers. This is the **target market**—one or more specific groups of potential consumers toward which an organization directs its marketing program.

> **target market**
> *Specific group of potential consumers toward which an organization directs its marketing program*

The Four Ps: Controllable Marketing Mix Factors Having selected its target market consumers, the firm must take steps to satisfy their needs. Someone in the organization's marketing department, often the marketing manager, must take action and develop a complete marketing program to reach consumers by using a combination of four tools, often called the four Ps—a useful shorthand reference to them first published by Professor E. Jerome McCarthy:[12]

- *Product.* A good, service, or idea to satisfy the consumer's needs.
- *Price.* What is exchanged for the product.
- *Promotion.* A means of communication between the seller and buyer.
- *Place.* A means of getting the product to the consumer.

We'll define each of the four Ps more carefully later in the book, but for now it's important to remember that they are the elements of the **marketing mix**, the marketing manager's controllable factors—product, price, promotion, and place—that can be used to solve a marketing problem. For example, when a company puts a product on sale, they are changing one element of the marketing mix—namely, the price.

> **marketing mix**
> *The marketing manager's controllable factors—product, price, promotion, and place—that can be used to solve a marketing problem*

> **environmental forces**
> *Uncontrollable marketing factors such as social, economic, technological, competitive, and regulatory forces*

The Uncontrollable, Environmental Forces While marketers can control their marketing mix factors, other factors are mostly beyond their control (see Figure 1–2). These are the **environmental forces** in a marketing decision, the uncontrollable factors involving social, economic, technological, competitive, and regulatory forces. Examples are what consumers themselves want and need, changing technology, the state of the economy in terms of whether it is expanding or contracting, actions that competitors take, and government restrictions. These five environmental factors are discussed in Chapter 3.

Costco and Starbucks provide customer value using two very different approaches. For their strategies, see the text.

STARBUCKS COFFEE
'Half-Caf'
While you might think this refers to milk made from really small cows, 'Half-Caf' actually means half regular and half decaf. Customize Your Cup.

THE MARKETING PROGRAM: HOW CUSTOMER RELATIONSHIPS ARE BUILT

A firm's marketing program connects the firm to its customers. To clarify this link, we shall first discuss the critically important concepts of customer value, customer relationships, and relationship marketing, and then illustrate these concepts with 3M's marketing program for its new product for students.

Customer Value and Customer Relationships

Intense competition in today's fast-paced domestic and global markets has caused massive restructuring of many American industries and businesses. American managers are seeking ways to achieve success in this new, more intense level of global competition.[13]

This has prompted many successful U.S. firms to focus on "customer value." That firms gain loyal customers by providing unique value is the essence of successful marketing. What is new, however, is a more careful attempt at understanding how a firm's customers perceive value. For our purposes, **customer value** is the unique combination of benefits received by targeted buyers that includes quality, price, convenience, on-time delivery, and both before-sale and after-sale service. Firms now actually try to place a dollar value on a loyal, satisfied customer. For example, loyal Kleenex customers average 6.7 boxes a year, about $994 over 60 years in today's dollars (question 3, Figure 1–1).[14]

customer value
Buyers' benefits including quality, price, convenience, on-time delivery, and before- and after-sale service

Research suggests that firms cannot succeed by being all things to all people.[15] Instead, firms must find ways to build long-term customer relationships to provide unique value that they alone can deliver to targeted markets. Many successful firms have chosen to deliver outstanding customer value with one of three value strategies: best price, best product, or best service.

Companies such as Wal-Mart, Southwest Airlines, Costco, and Dell Computer have all been successful offering consumers the best price. Other companies such as Starbucks, Nike, Microsoft, and Johnson & Johnson claim to provide the best products on the market. Finally, companies such as Lands' End and Home Depot deliver value by providing exceptional service.

Relationship Marketing and the Marketing Program

A firm achieves meaningful customer relationships by creating connections with its customers through careful coordination of the product, its price, the way it's promoted, and how it's placed.

Relationship Marketing: Easy to Understand, Hard to Do The hallmark of developing and maintaining effective customer relationships is today called **relationship marketing**. Successful relationship marketing links an organization to its individual customers, employees, suppliers, and other partners for their mutual long-term benefits. In terms of selling a product, relationship marketing involves a personal, ongoing relationship between the organization and its individual customers that begins before and continues after the sale.

relationship marketing
Linking the organization to its individual customers, employees, suppliers, and other partners for their mutual long-term benefit

Huge manufacturers find this rigorous standard of relationship marketing difficult to achieve. Today's information technology, along with cutting-edge manufacturing and marketing processes, have led to tailoring goods or services to the tastes of individual customers in high volumes at a relatively low cost. Thus, you can place an Internet order for all the components of a Dell or Apple computer and have it delivered in four or five days—in a configuration tailored to your unique wants. But with today's Internet purchases, you will probably have difficulty achieving the same personal, tender-loving-care connection that you once had with your own local computer store, bookstore, or other retailer.

The Marketing Program Effective relationship marketing strategies help marketing managers discover what prospective customers need. They must translate this information into concepts for products the firm might develop to satisfy these needs (Figure 1–4). These concepts must then be converted into a tangible **marketing program**—a plan that integrates the marketing mix to provide a good, service, or idea to prospective buyers. These consumers then react to the offering favorably (by buying) or unfavorably (by not buying), and the process is repeated. As shown in Figure 1–4, this process is continuous in an effective organization: Consumer needs trigger product concepts that are translated into actual products that stimulate further discovery of consumer needs.

marketing program
Plan that integrates the marketing mix to provide a good, service, or idea to prospective buyers

A 3M Product and Marketing Program to Help Students Study

To see some specifics of an actual marketing program, let's return to our earlier example of 3M's inventor David Windorski and his search for a way to combine felt-tip highlighters and 3M's Post-it® Notes or Post-it® Flags to help college students in their studying. We will look at how Windorski worked with 3M: (1) to move his invention from simply ideas and crude mock-ups to a useful highlighter product, (2) to add a new product that extends the product line, and (3) to undertake an actual marketing program for the resulting products.

FIGURE 1–4
Marketing's second task: satisfying consumer needs

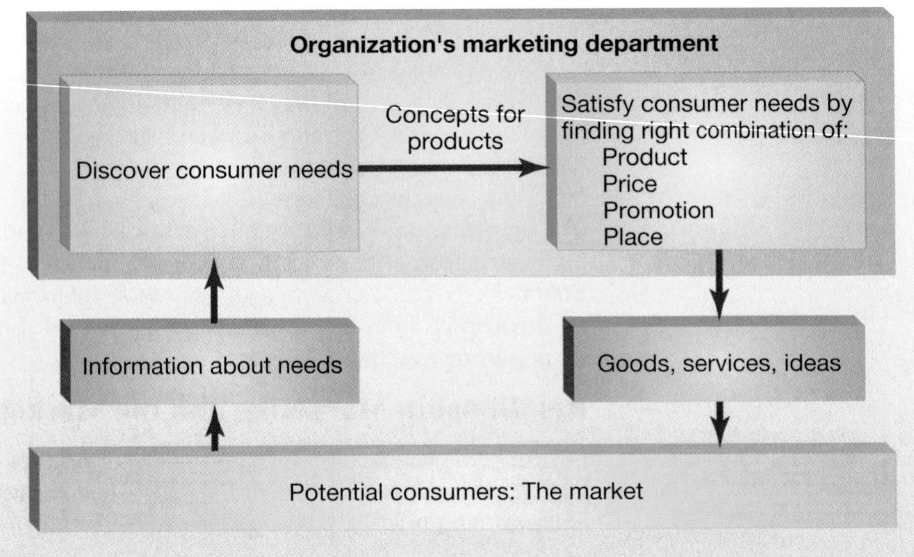

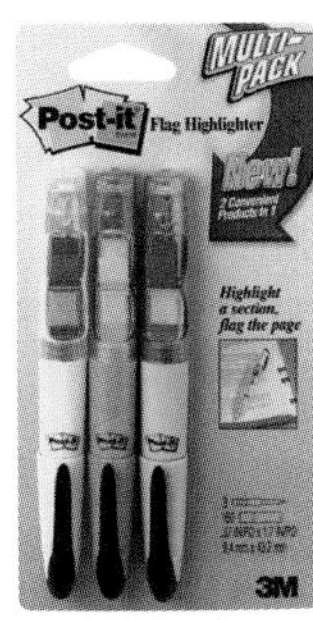

What David Windorski's wood and clay models led to: 3M Post-it® Flag Highlighters in many colors.

Moving from Ideas to a Marketable Highlighter Product After working on 15 or 20 wood and clay models, Windorski concluded he had to build a highlighter product that would dispense 3M Post-it® Flags because the Post-it® Notes were simply too large to put inside the barrel of a highlighter.

Hundreds of the initial workable highlighter product with Post-it® Flags inside were produced and given to students—and also office workers—to get their reactions. Two suggestions from users quickly emerged:

- Because of the abuse the product will take in students' pockets and backpacks, the product needs a convenient, reliable cover to protect the Post-it® Flags when it isn't being used.
- Although the new highlighter would have 50 Post-it® Flags inside the barrel, students wanted to make sure refills are available.

This customer feedback, while very useful, also caused special challenges for Windorski. For example, he soon discovered that to address the two suggestions above, he had to design a rotating cover that would enclose the Post-it® Flags and not pinch them when rotated.

Listening to students, Windorski and 3M packaged the Post-it® Flag Highlighters two ways: (1) singly with refills in the package and (2) in three-packs in favorite student colors—yellow, pink, and blue—with separate packages of refills.

Extending the Product Line Most of David Windorski's initial design energies under 3M's 15% Rule had gone into his Post-it® Flag Highlighter research and development. But Windorski also considered other related products. Many people in offices need immediate access to Post-it® Flags while writing longhand with pens. Students are a potential market for this product, too, but probably a smaller market segment than office workers.

Marketing research among North American office workers refined the design and showed the existence of a sizable market for a 3M Post-it® Flag Pen. Even here, however, Windorski encountered surprises: Consumers in one country may prefer blue ink while those in the country next door prefer black ink. The same is true of the width of line the pen produces.

A Market Program for the Post-it® Flag Highlighter and Pen After several years of research, development, and production engineering to make sure the product could be manufactured at reasonable cost, 3M took the product to market in 2002. Figure 1–5 on the next page outlines the strategies for each of the four marketing mix elements in 3M's marketing program to market its Post-it® Flag Highlighters and Post-it® Flag Pens. Though similar, we can compare the marketing program for each of the two products:

3M's product line of Post-it® Flag Highlighters and Post-it® Flag pens.

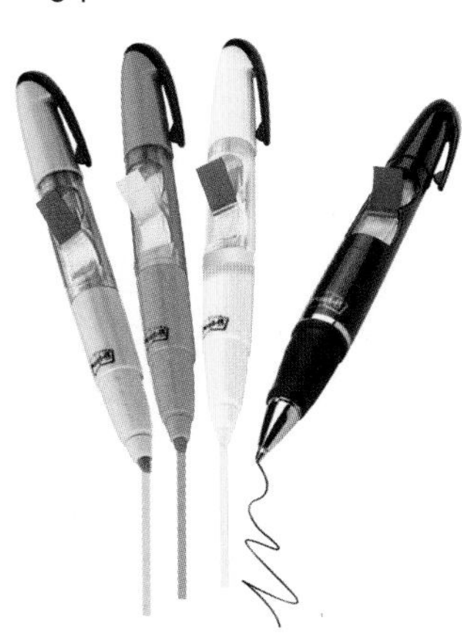

- *Post-it® Flag Highlighter*. The target market is mainly college students. So 3M's initial challenge was to build student awareness of a product that they didn't know existed and had never seen. 3M used a mix of print ads in college newspapers and TV ads, and then relied on student word-of-mouth advertising—one student telling his or her roommate how great the product is. Gaining distribution in bookstores and having attractive packaging was also critical. 3M charged a price to distributors that it hoped would result in a reasonable retail price to students and also provide 3M and its distributors with an acceptable profit.
- *Post-it® Flag Pen*. The primary target market is people working in offices. However, as with the Post-it® Flag Highlighter, there is overlap in the market segments, so 3M gained distribution in some college bookstores of Post-it® Flag Pens, too. But as shown in Figure 1–5, the Post-it® Flag Highlighter is primarily purchased by ultimate consumers—mostly students. In contrast, the Post-it® Flag Pens are mainly business products—bought by the purchasing department in an organization and stocked as office supplies for employees to use. So the marketing program in Figure 1–5 reflects the different distribution or "place" strategies for the two products.

MARKETING MIX ELEMENT	MARKETING PROGRAM ACTIVITY TO REACH: COLLEGE STUDENT SEGMENT	OFFICE WORKER SEGMENT	RATIONALE FOR MARKETING PROGRAM ACTIVITY
Product strategy 	Offer Post-it® Flag Highlighter to help college students in their studying	Offer Post-it® Flag Pen to help office workers in their day-to-day work activities	Listen carefully to the needs and wants of potential customer segments to use 3M technology to introduce a useful, innovative product
Price strategy 	Seek retail price of about $3.99 to $4.99 for single Post-it® Flag Highlighter or $5.99 to $7.99 for a three-pack	Seek retail price of about $3.99 to $4.99 for a single Post-it® Flag Pen; wholesale prices are less	Set prices that provide genuine value to the customer segment that is targeted
Promotion strategy 	Run limited promotion with a TV ad and some ads in college newspapers and then rely on student word-of-mouth messages to inform other students	Run limited promotion among distributors to get them to stock the product and then rely on word-of-mouth messages to inform other users	Increase awareness of potential users in both customer segments who have never heard of this new, innovative 3M product
Place strategy 	Distribute Post-it® Flag Highlighters through college and university bookstores, office supply stores, and mass merchandisers	Distribute Post-it® Flag Pens through office wholesalers and retailers and mass merchandisers; must reach organizations' purchasing departments	Make it easy for prospective buyers to buy at convenient retail outlets (both products) or to get at work (Post-it® Flag Pens only)

FIGURE 1–5
Marketing programs for two new 3M Post-it® brand products targeted at two distinctly different customer segments: college students and office workers

How did these new products do for 3M? In the first year on the market, more than a million Post-it® Flag Highlighters and Post-it® Flag Pens were sold. A good investment for 3M in encouraging David Windorski to think creatively under the company's 15% Rule!

Concept Check

1. An organization can't satisfy the needs of all consumers, so it must focus on one or more subgroups, which are its ________________.
2. What are the four marketing mix elements that make up the organization's marketing program?
3. What are environmental forces?

HOW MARKETING BECAME SO IMPORTANT

To understand why marketing is a driving force in the modern global economy, let us look at the (1) evolution of the market orientation, (2) ethics and social responsibility in marketing, and (3) breadth and depth of marketing activities.

Evolution of the Market Orientation

Many American manufacturers have experienced four distinct stages in the life of their firms. The first stage, the *production era,* covers the early years of the United States up until the 1920s. Goods were scarce and buyers were willing to accept virtually any goods that were available and make do with them. In the *sales era* from the 1920s to the 1960s, manufacturers found they could produce more goods than buyers could consume. Competition grew. Firms hired more salespeople to find new buyers. This sales era continued into the 1960s for many American firms.

marketing concept
Idea that an organization should strive to satisfy the needs of consumers while also trying to achieve the organization's goals

In the 1960s, marketing became the motivating force among many American firms and the *marketing concept era* dawned. The **marketing concept** is the idea that an organization should (1) strive to satisfy the needs of consumers (2) while also trying to achieve the organization's goals. General Electric probably launched the marketing concept and its focus on consumers when its 1952 annual report stated: "The concept introduces . . . marketing . . . at the beginning rather than the end of the production cycle and integrates marketing into each phase of the business."[16]

market orientation
Focusing organizational efforts to collect and use information about customers' needs to create customer value

Firms such as General Electric, Marriott, and Toyota have achieved great success by putting huge effort into implementing the marketing concept, giving their firms what has been called a *market orientation.* An organization that has a **market orientation** focuses its efforts on (1) continuously collecting information about customers' needs, (2) sharing this information across departments, and (3) using it to create customer value.[17] The result is today's *customer era*, in which firms seek continuously to satisfy the high expectations of customers.

This focus on customers has led to *customer relationship management (CRM),* the process of identifying prospective buyers, understanding them intimately, and developing favorable long-term perceptions of the organization and its offerings so that buyers will choose them in the marketplace.[18] This requires the commitment of managers and employees throughout the organization.

Ethics and Social Responsibility: Balancing Interests

Today, the standards of marketing practice have shifted from an emphasis on producers' interests to consumers' interests. Organizations increasingly consider the social and environmental consequences of their actions for all parties.

Ethics Many marketing issues are not specifically addressed by existing laws and regulations. Should information about a firm's customers be sold to other organizations? Should consumers be on their own to assess the safety of a product? These questions raise difficult ethical issues. Many companies, industries, and professional associations have developed codes of ethics to assist managers.

societal marketing concept
View that organizations should satisfy the needs of consumers in a way that provides for society's well-being

Social Responsibility While many ethical issues involve only the buyer and seller, others involve society as a whole. A manufacturer dumping toxic wastes into streams has an impact on the environment and society. This example illustrates the issue of social responsibility, the idea that individuals and organizations are accountable to a larger society. The well-being of society at large should be recognized in an organization's marketing decisions. In fact, some marketing experts stress the **societal marketing concept**, the view that an organization should discover and satisfy the needs of its consumers in a way that also provides for society's well-being.[19] For example, Scotchbrite Never Rust Wool Soap Pads from 3M—which are made from recycled plastic bottles—are more expensive than competitors' (SOS and Brillo) but superior because they don't rust or scratch (question 4, Figure 1–1).

The Breadth and Depth of Marketing

Marketing affects every person and organization. To understand this, let's analyze (1) who markets, (2) what they market, (3) who buys and uses what is marketed, (4) who benefits from these marketing activities, and (5) how they benefit.

Who Markets? Every organization markets. It's obvious that business firms involved in manufacturing (Heinz), retailing (Toys "Я" Us), and providing services (America Online) market their offerings. And nonprofit organizations such as your local hospital, your college, places (cities, states, countries), and even special causes (Stop Smoking!) also engage in marketing. Finally, individuals such as political candidates often use marketing to gain attention and preference.[20]

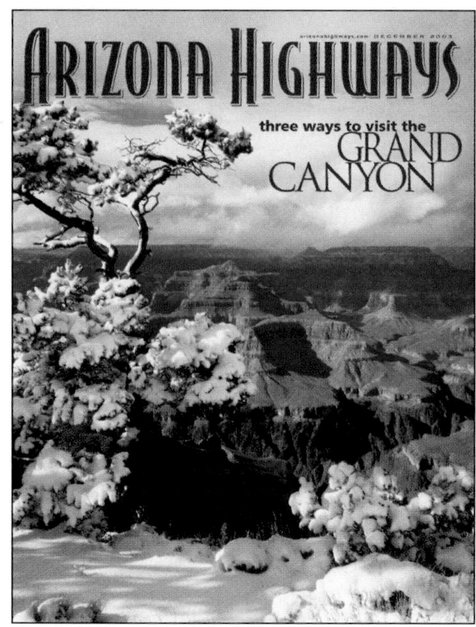

Marketing is used by nonprofit organizations, causes, and places, as well as businesses.

What Is Marketed? Goods, services, and even ideas are marketed. *Goods* are physical objects such as iron ore, apples, or a computer. *Services* are intangible items such as airline trips, financial advice, or telephone calls. *Ideas* are intangibles involving thoughts about actions or causes.

Ideas are most often marketed by nonprofit organizations or the government. For example, your local library may market the idea of developing improved reading skills. Charities market the idea that it's worthwhile for you to donate your time or money, and orchestras market fine music. States like Arizona market themselves as attractive places for tourists to visit.

Who Buys and Uses What Is Marketed? Both individuals and organizations buy and use goods and services that are marketed. **Ultimate consumers** are the people—whether 80 years or eight months old—who use the goods and services purchased for a household. In contrast, **organizational buyers** are those manufacturers, retailers, or government agencies that buy goods and services for their own use or for resale. Although the terms *consumers, buyers,* and *customers* are sometimes used for both ultimate consumers and organizations, there is no consistency on this. In this book you will be able to tell from the example whether the buyers are ultimate consumers, organizations, or both.

ultimate consumers
People who use the goods and services purchased for a household

organizational buyers
Manufacturers, wholesalers, retailers, and government agencies that buy goods and services for their own use or for resale

utility
Benefits or customer value received by users of the product

Who Benefits? In our free-enterprise society there are three specific groups that benefit from effective marketing: consumers who buy, organizations that sell, and society as a whole. True competition between products and services in the marketplace ensures that we consumers can find value from the best products, the lowest prices, or exceptional service. Providing choices leads to the consumer satisfaction and quality of life that we have come to expect from our economic system.

Organizations that provide need-satisfying products with effective marketing programs—for example, Target, IBM, and Avon—have blossomed. But competition creates problems for ineffective competitors, such as eToys and hundreds of other dot-com businesses that failed in the last few years.

Finally, effective marketing benefits society. It enhances competition, which, in turn, both improves the quality of products and services and lowers their prices. This makes countries more competitive in world markets and provides jobs and a higher standard of living for their citizens.

How Do Consumers Benefit? Marketing creates **utility**, the benefits or customer value received by users of the product. This utility is the result of the marketing exchange process. There are four different utilities: form, place, time, and possession. The production of the good or service constitutes *form utility. Place utility* means having the offering available where consumers need it, whereas *time utility* means having it available when needed. *Possession utility* is the value of making an item easy to purchase through the provision of credit cards or financial arrangements. Marketing creates its utilities by bridging space (place utility) and hours (time utility) to provide products (form utility) for consumers to own and use (possession utility).

Concept Check

1. What are the two key characteristics of the marketing concept?
2. What is the difference between goods and services?

CHAPTER IN REVIEW

1 *Define marketing and identify the requirements for marketing to occur.*
Marketing is an organizational function and a set of processes for creating, communicating, and delivering value to customers and for managing customer relationships in ways that benefit the organization and its stakeholders. This definition relates to two primary goals of marketing: (*a*) assessing the needs of consumers and (*b*) satisfying them.

2 *Explain how marketing discovers and satisfies consumer needs.*
The first objective in marketing is discovering the needs of prospective consumers. This is not an easy task because consumers may not always know or be able to describe what they need and want. The second objective in marketing is satisfying the needs of targeted consumers. Because an organization obviously can't satisfy all consumer needs, it must concentrate its efforts on certain needs of a specific group of potential consumers or target market—one or more specific groups of potential consumers toward which an organization directs its marketing program. Having selected its target market consumers, the organization then takes action to satisfy their needs by developing a unique marketing program to reach them.

3 *Distinguish between marketing mix elements and environmental forces.*
Four elements in a marketing program designed to satisfy customer needs are product, price, promotion, and place. These elements are called the marketing mix, the four Ps, or the controllable variables because they are under the general control of the marketing department. Environmental forces, also called uncontrollable variables, are largely beyond the organization's control. These include social, economic, technological, competitive, and regulatory forces.

4 *Explain how organizations build strong customer relationships and customer value through marketing.*
The essence of successful marketing is to provide sufficient value to gain loyal, long-term customers. Customer value is the unique combination of benefits received by targeted buyers that usually includes quality, price, convenience, on-time delivery, and both before-sale and after-sale service. Marketers do this by using one of three value strategies: best price, best product, or best service.

5 *Describe how today's customer era differs from prior eras oriented to production and selling.*
U.S. business history can be divided into four periods: the production era, the sales era, the marketing concept era, and the current customer era. The production era covers the period to the 1920s when buyers were willing to accept virtually any goods that were available. The central notion was that products would sell themselves. The sales era lasted from the 1920s to the 1960s. Manufacturers found they could produce more goods than buyers could consume, and competition grew, so the solution was to hire more salespeople to find new buyers. In the 1960s, the marketing concept era dawned, when organizations began to integrate marketing into each phase of the business. In today's customer era, organizations focus their efforts on (*a*) continuously collecting information about customers' needs, (*b*) sharing this information across departments, and (*c*) using it to create customer value.

FOCUSING ON KEY TERMS

customer value p. 13
environmental forces p. 12
exchange p. 8
market p. 11
marketing p. 8
marketing concept p. 17
marketing mix p. 12
marketing program p. 14
market orientation p. 17
organizational buyers p. 18
relationship marketing p. 14
societal marketing concept p. 17
target market p. 12
ultimate consumers p. 18
utility p. 18

DISCUSSION AND APPLICATION QUESTIONS

1 What consumer wants (or benefits) are met by the following products or services? (*a*) Carnation Instant Breakfast, (*b*) Adidas running shoes, (*c*) Hertz Rent-A-Car, and (*d*) television home shopping programs.

2 Each of the four products, services, or programs in question 1 has substitutes. Respective examples are (*a*) a ham and egg breakfast, (*b*) regular tennis shoes, (*c*) taking a bus, and (*d*) a department store. What consumer benefits might these substitutes have in each case that some consumers might value more highly than those mentioned in question 1?

3 A college in a metropolitan area wishes to increase its evening-school offerings of business-related courses such as marketing, accounting, finance, and management. Who are the target market customers (students) for these courses?

4 What actions involving the four marketing mix elements might be used to reach the target market in question 3?

5 What environmental forces (uncontrollable variables) must the college in question 3 consider in designing its marketing program?

6 3M is now trying to sell its Post-it® Notes globally. What are the advantages and disadvantages of trying to reach new global markets?

GOING ONLINE Your Personal Mechanized "Transporter"

"It!" "Ginger!" "Jetson's scooter!" These were early names given the revolutionary Segway™ Human Transporter (HT), a technology shrouded in secrecy until it was launched in 2001. The Segway HT relies on computers and gyroscopes to control its speed, balance, and direction. It can travel up to 15 miles on a six-hour battery charge.

Go to the Segway HT website (www.segway.com). View both the consumer and business models.

1 What do you see as the advantages and disadvantages of the Segway HT?

2 For businesses, what applications could the Segway HT be used for?

3 Why would consumers want to buy a Segway HT?

BUILDING YOUR MARKETING PLAN

If your instructor assigns a marketing plan for your class, don't make a face and complain about the work—for two special reasons. First, you will get insights into trying to actually "do marketing" that often go beyond what you can get by simply reading the textbook. Second, thousands of graduating students every year get their first job by showing prospective employers a "portfolio" of samples of their written work from college—often a marketing plan if they have one. This can work for you.

This "Building Your Marketing Plan" section at the end of each chapter gives you suggestions to improve and focus your marketing plan. You will use the sample marketing plan in Appendix A as a guide, and this section after each chapter will help you apply those Appendix A ideas to your own marketing plan.

The first step in writing a good marketing plan is to have a business or product that enthuses you and for which you can get detailed information, so you can avoid glittering generalities. We offer these additional bits of advice in selecting a topic:

- *Do* pick a topic that has personal interest for you—a family business, a business or product you or a friend might want to launch, or a student organization needing marketing help.
- *Do not* pick a topic that is so large it can't be covered adequately or so abstract it will lack specifics.

1 Now to get you started on your marketing plan, list four or five possible topics and compare these with the criteria your instructor suggests and those shown above. Think hard, because your decision will be with you all term long and may influence the quality of the resulting marketing plan you show to a prospective employer.

2 When you have selected your marketing plan topic, whether the plan is for an actual business, a possible business, or a student organization, write the "company description" in your plan, as shown in Appendix A.

VIDEO CASE 1 Rollerblade: Benefits beyond Expectations

4D, ABT, TRS, TFS . . . and SIS! Does this look like a spoonful of alphabet soup?

Perhaps. But it really refers to Rollerblade's technologies, programs, and commitment to providing in-line skaters with the best quality of skates and skating experiences possible. Or "by providing benefits beyond what people are expecting to have," as Jeremy Stonier, Rollerblade's vice president and general manager, describes it. In fact, Rollerblade's leading-edge technology is covered by more than 265 patents, with more on the way, such as the new adjustable 4D™ frame and the Crossfire™ Shell, TFS Power, and Air Power.

ROLLERBLADE'S LAUNCH

At Rollerblade's launch two decades ago only one in-line skate manufacturer existed—Rollerblade. The company had only a single skate line and there were few sales. No one had even heard of in-line skating! So Rollerblade used a "guerrilla marketing" campaign to get the word out. It used a tiny budget to develop attention-getting promotions to make people aware of the skates and to try them. Promotions ranged from "Demo Vans" in supermarket parking lots, where prospects could try the skates for a half hour, to putting Rollerblade skates on Minnesota Viking cheerleaders at a football game or Arnold Schwarzenegger. Marketing research was almost limited to what skaters told the Demo Van drivers.

A SKATE LINE FOR EACH SEGMENT

From the outset in-line skaters have been united by a common experience: the thrill and fun of the speed and freedom that comes from almost frictionless wheels on their feet. "As the market has matured, it has settled into four core groups of users," says Stonier. Each requires a number of unique skate features.

"The trickiest segment we sell to is probably the Street/Vert and Urban skaters—the 14- to 22-year-old in your neighborhood who is doing tricks you might see on ESPN's X Games," says Stonier. Members of Team Rollerblade, a skating group that gives demonstrations around the country, suggest and test new technologies that find their way first into skates for this segment. The TRS Team Skate (TRS for Team Rollerblade Series), designed for the Street/Vert subsegment, contains a radically new "walkable" and Specialized Fit foot liner to keep the skater's feet cool, dry, and comfortable. The new Urban subsegment—skaters who want to cruise down city streets—has the Twister II Pro skate that has a new hard shell for added protection and support, wide profile wheels for stability, and a shorter aluminum frame for power transmission and maneuverability.

Skate buyers overlap somewhat in the Fitness/Recreation segment. The Fitness group skates two or three times a week, at high speeds, and may even aspire to skate in an in-line marathon. As a result, Rollerblade developed the Crossfire 4D for men and the Activa 4D for women series of skates. "No other skate in the industry combines this level of form, function, fit, and aesthetics," exclaims Ronnie Kuliecza, director of product development. The 4D refers to an innovative, adjustable frame that when shorter allows for tighter turns and longer permits more speed. These skates also incorporate the new Crossfire Shell for stability and control for turning and 90mm wheels for speed. Finally, these skates use the revolutionary TFS (Total Fit System) Power closure system. Pulling on the TFS disc provides an effortless, quick, and customized fit.

Since most adult skaters are Recreational skaters, Rollerblade designed the new Spiritblade ABT (Active Braking Technology) skate for this larger subsegment. With this skate, both beginner and intermediate skaters get the comfort, reliability, and safety they want. ABT allows the skater to keep all wheels on the ground: moving the foot forward lowers the brake for a controlled stop.

With the Junior segment, parents are always concerned about having to buy their children new shoes or skates as their feet grow. Not only does the Micro TFS extendable skate adjust four sizes with a push of a button, but it also has the new TFS Micro closure system. With a simple push of a button and a turn of a dial, a thin cable provides quick closure.

The Race segment is just what the name implies—expert speed skaters wanting the maximum in technical features and performance. The Pro-Blade World Champion Limited Edition with its carbon fiber shell, and the Lightning TF Air with the new Air Power that inflates several small chambers around both sides of the ankle for a secure fit, are two models that meet the needs of this segment.

The segments don't stop there. Besides its flagship Rollerblade brand marketed through sporting goods and skate specialty stores, Rollerblade has a lower-priced Bladerunner line sold through mass merchant and sporting goods chain stores. Finally, the global market has enormous potential. With China and South Korea showing high growth today, who knows what new segments could be next?

A FOCUS ON EACH CONSUMER

"One of the big differences between marketing today and in the future is that we will be able to reach each person, such as designing your own personal workout program," says Nicholas Skally, Rollerblade's manager of marketing and public relations. Rollerblade's website (www.rollerblade.com) is a step in that direction. "An important benefit of the website is our ability to acquire marketing research data on individual consumers inexpensively," says Skally. This enables Rollerblade to get feedback and ideas directly from its end users. Website topics include everything from helping you choose which skate is right for you (Skate Selector) to helping you brush up on your braking technique.

In the past, Rollerblade often sent out millions of direct-mail pieces or bought commercials on national TV networks. Today, Skally points out that Rollerblade now focuses more narrowly by selecting magazines that link directly to the user segments or grassroots programs like Skate-in-School (SIS) that offer physical education class options to students in more than 900 schools.

ROLLERBLADE'S FIRSTS

"If you're going to buy a pair of in-line skates, it only makes sense to buy from us," says Stonier, "because we're the ones who started it, perfected it, and continue to push the innovation." As evidence of Rollerblade's innovation, he points to a number of firsts, such as the use of polyurethane boots and wheels, metal frames, dual bearings, and heel brakes. Other firsts include breathable liners, push-button adjustable children's skates, and more importantly, skates designed specifically for women *by women*. Rollerblade employed an engineering team composed of women to develop in-line skates with specially designed lines, cuffs, and footbeds that meets the unique needs of women skaters.

Questions

1 What trends in the environmental forces (social, economic, technological, competitive, and regulatory) (*a*) work for and (*b*) work against Rollerblade's potential growth in the twenty-first century?

2 Compare the likely marketing goals for Rollerblade (*a*) in 1986 when Rollerblade was launched and (*b*) today.

3 What kind of focused communication and promotion actions might Rollerblade take to reach the (*a*) Fitness/Recreation and (*b*) Junior market segments? For some starting ideas, visit rollerblade.com.

4 In searching for global markets to enter, (*a*) what are some criteria that Rollerblade should use to select countries to enter, and (*b*) what three or four countries meet these criteria best and are the most likely candidates?

BEN&JERRY'S

HOME | OUR COMPANY | OUR PRODUCTS | SCOOP SHOPS | FUN STUFF | GIFT SHOP

- About Us
- Our Mission
- Contact Us
- Factory Tours
- International
- Press Center
- Jobs at Ben & Jerry's
- FAQ's
- Research Library

Our Mission Statement

Ben & Jerry's is founded on and dedicated to a sustainable corporate concept of linked prosperity. Our mission consists of 3 interrelated parts::

Product Mission
To make, distribute & sell the finest quality all natural ice cream & euphoric concoctions with a continued commitment to incorporating wholesome, natural ingredients and promoting business practices that respect the Earth and the Environment.

Economic Mission
To operate the Company on a sustainable financial basis of profitable growth, increasing value for our stakeholders & expanding opportunities for development and career growth for our employees.

Social Mission
To operate the company in a way that actively recognizes the central role that business plays in society by initiating innovative ways to improve the quality of life locally, nationally & internationally.

Central To The Mission Of Ben & Jerry's
is the belief that all three parts must thrive equally in a manner that commands deep respect for individuals in and outside the company and supports the communities of which they are a part.

Leading with Progressive Values Across Our Business

We have a progressive, nonpartisan social mission that seeks to meet human needs and eliminate injustices in our local, national and international communities by integrating these concerns into our day-to-day business activities. Our focus is on children and families, the environment and sustainable agriculture on family farms.

- Capitalism and the wealth it produces do not create opportunity for everyone equally. We recognize that the gap between the rich and the poor is wider than at anytime since the 1920's.We strive to create economic opportunities for those who have been denied them and to advance new models of economic justice that are sustainable and replicable.
- By definition, the manufacturing of products creates waste. We strive to minimize our negative impact on the environment.
- The growing of food is overly reliant on the use of toxic chemicals and other methods that are unsustainable. We support sustainable and safe methods of food production that reduce environmental degradation, maintain the productivity of the land over time, and support the economic viability of family farms and rural communities.
- We seek and support nonviolent ways to achieve peace and justice. We believe government resources are more productively used in meeting human needs than in building and maintaining weapons systems.
- We strive to show a deep respect for human beings inside and outside our company and for the communities in which they live.

Learn more! check out our Social Mission News or Our Environment

CHAPTER 2

DEVELOPING SUCCESSFUL MARKETING AND CORPORATE STRATEGIES

LEARNING OBJECTIVES

After reading this chapter you should be able to:

1 Describe the three organizational levels of strategy.

2 Describe why business, mission, organizational culture, and goals are important in organizations.

3 Explain how organizations set strategic directions by assessing where they are now and seek to be in the future.

4 Describe the strategic marketing process and its three key phases: planning, implementation, and control.

5 Explain how the marketing mix elements are blended into a cohesive marketing program.

WHERE CAN AN "A" IN ICE CREAM MAKING LEAD?

These two entrepreneurs aren't just your typical Tom, Dick, or Harry! Consider some facts about the company they founded:

- It launched a program letting customers send "Ice Cream by Mail" via its website.
- It contributes a minimum of $1.1 million annually to charities.
- Its PartnerShops help not-for-profit organizations provide training and job opportunities for people such as at-risk youth.[1]

By now you know the company: Ben & Jerry's, or more formally, Ben & Jerry's Homemade, Inc. Its website (opposite page) reflects its creative, funky approach to business—linked to a genuine concern for social causes.

Ben & Jerry's is proof that the American dream is still alive and well. Ben Cohen and Jerry Greenfield were grade school classmates on Long Island. In 1978 they headed north to Vermont and started an ice cream parlor in a renovated gas station.[2] Buoyed with enthusiasm, $12,000 they had borrowed and saved, and ideas from the $5 they spent on a Penn State correspondence course in ice cream making (with perfect scores on their open-book tests!) they were off and running.[3]

Today, Ben & Jerry's Homemade, Inc., now owned by Unilever, has more than $200 million in annual sales

worldwide—mainly from selling its incredibly rich ice cream. Ben & Jerry's has also been a leader with its social mission. For example, the company is committed to paying its employees a "livable wage" and providing top-quality benefits, as well as purchasing supplies from other socially responsible companies.[4] Customers love Cherry Garcia and One Sweet Whirled ice cream flavors, but many also want to support Ben & Jerry's social mission and environmental concerns, too. The company has international sales in Europe, the Mideast, and Asia.

Chapter 2 describes how organizations set their mission and overall direction and link these activities to marketing strategies. As consumers become more concerned about a company's impact on society, marketing strategy may need to be linked to the social goals of the company's mission statement.

ORGANIZATIONS AND THEIR LEVELS OF STRATEGY

Large organizations today are extremely complex. All of us deal in some way with huge organizations every day, so it is useful to understand (1) the two basic kinds of organizations and (2) the levels that exist in them and their link to marketing.

Today's organizations can be divided into business firms and not-for-profit organizations. A *business firm* is a privately owned organization that serves its customers in order to earn a profit. **Profit** is the reward to a business firm for the risk it undertakes in offering a product for sale. It's the money left over after a firm's total expenses are subtracted from its total sales. In contrast to business firms, a *nonprofit organization* is a nongovernmental organization that serves its customers but does not have profit as an organizational goal. For simplicity in the rest of the book, however, the terms *firm, company, corporation,* and *organization* are used to cover both business and not-for-profit operations.

profit
Reward to a business firm for the risk it undertakes in offering a product for sale

Levels in Organizations and How Marketing Links to Them

All organizations have a strategic direction. That is, they have an idea of what they hope to achieve and how they plan to achieve it. Marketing not only helps set this direction but must also help the organization move there. Figure 2–1 summarizes the three levels of strategy in an organization.

FIGURE 2–1
The three levels of strategy in organizations: corporate, business unit, and functional

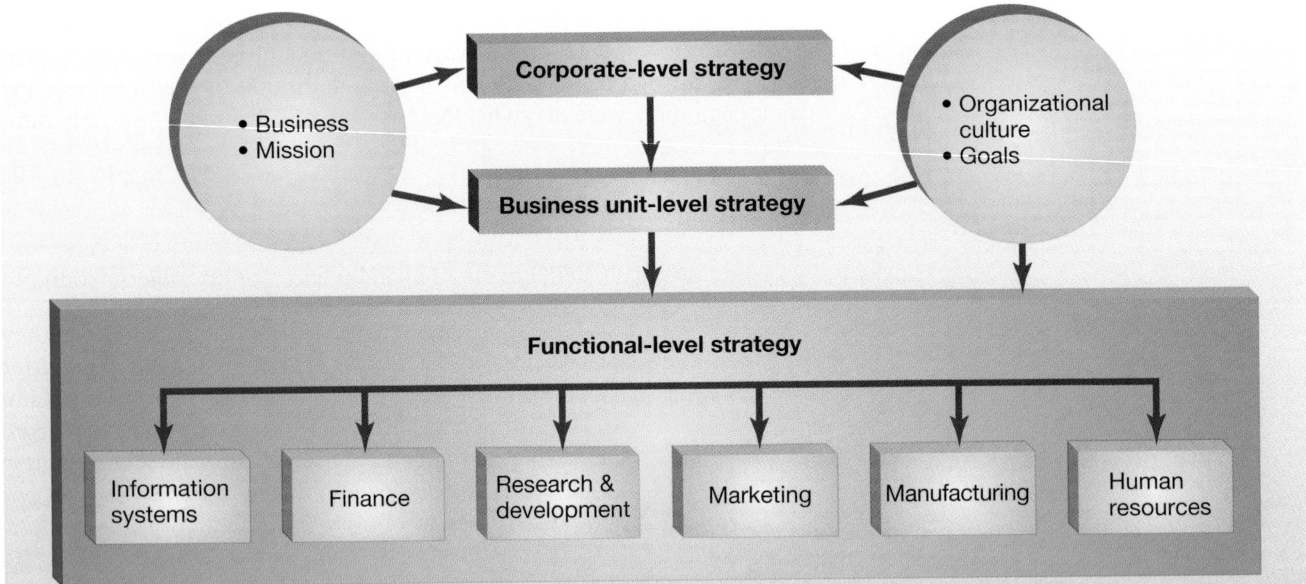

The *corporate level* is where top management directs overall strategy for the entire organization. Multimarket, multiproduct firms such as General Electric or Johnson & Johnson really manage a group of different businesses, variously termed *strategic business units* (SBUs), strategic business segments, or product-market units (PMUs).[5] Each of these units markets a set of related products to a clearly defined group of customers. While the corporate level creates value for the shareholders of the firm, as measured by stock performance and profitability, the *business unit level* is where business unit managers set the direction for individual products and markets. Strategic direction is more specific at the business unit level of an organization. For less complex firms with a single business focus, such as Ben & Jerry's, the corporate and business unit levels may merge.

Each business unit has marketing and other specialized activities (such as finance, research and development, or human resources) at the *functional level*. This is where groups of specialists *actually* create value for the organization. The name of a *department* generally refers to its specialized function, such as the marketing department or information systems department. At the functional level, the strategic direction becomes more specific and focused. In a large corporation with multiple business units, marketing may be called on to assess consumer trends as an aid to corporate planning. At the business unit level, marketing may be asked to provide leadership in developing a new, integrated customer service program across all business units.

Strategy Issues in Organizations

Organizations need a reason for their existence—and a direction. This is where their business, mission, organizational culture, and goals converge. We'll discuss each below. As shown in Figure 2–1, business and mission apply to the corporate and business unit levels, while goals relate to all three levels.

The Business Organizations like Ben & Jerry's, the Red Cross, and your college exist for a purpose—to accomplish something for someone. At birth, most organizations have clear ideas about what "something" and "someone" mean. But as the organization grows over time, often its purpose gets fuzzy, unclear.

This is where the organization repeatedly asks some of the most difficult questions it ever faces: What is our business? Who are our customers? What offerings should we provide to give these customers value? One guideline in defining the company's business: Try to understand the people served by the organization and the value they receive, which emphasizes the critical customer-driven focus that successful organizations have.

In a now-famous article, Harvard professor Theodore Levitt cited American railroads as organizations that had a narrow, production-oriented statement of their business: "We are in the railroad business!" This narrow definition of their business lost sight of who their customers were and what their needs were. Railroads saw only other railroads as competitors and failed to design strategies to compete with airlines, barges, pipelines, trucks, bus lines, and cars. Railroads would probably have fared better over the past century by recognizing they are in "the transportation business."[6]

With this focus on the customer, Disney *is not* in the movie and theme park business, but rather it *is* in the business of creating fun and fantasy for customers. Similarly, as we'll see shortly, Medtronic is *the* world leader in developing, producing, and marketing heart pacemakers and other implantable medical devices. Yet Medtronic *is not* in the medical device business. It *is* in the business of alleviating pain, restoring health, and extending life. In this respect Medtronic's business somewhat overlaps its mission, the next topic.

mission
Statement of the organization's scope

The Mission By understanding its business, an organization can take steps to define its **mission**, a statement of the organization's scope, often identifying its customers, markets, products, technology, and values. Today, often used interchangeably with *vision*, the *mission statement* frequently has an inspirational theme—something

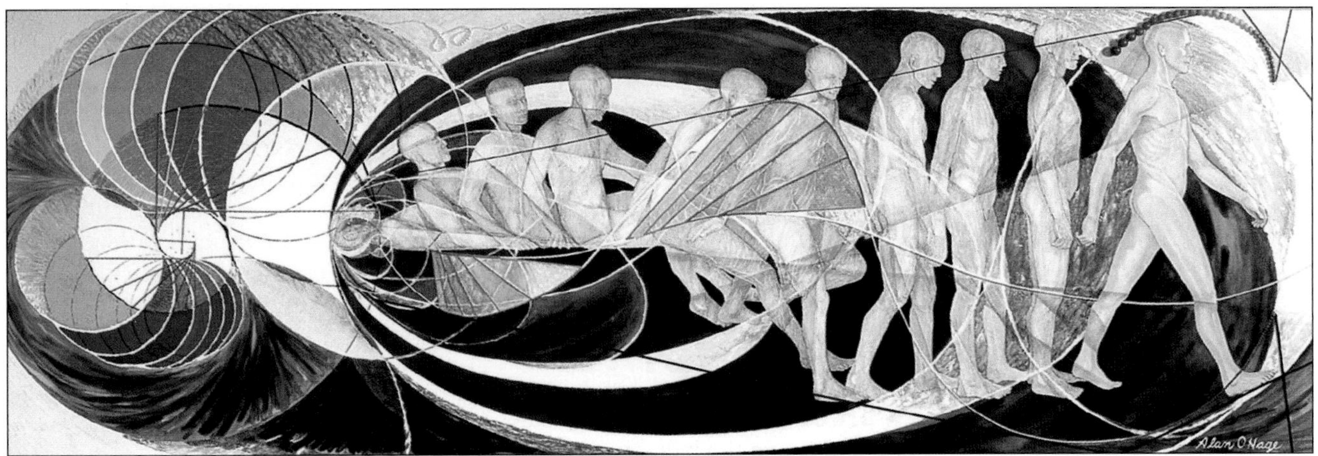

People see this "rising figure" mural in the headquarters of a world-class corporation. What does it tell about its mission? For some insights and why it is important, see the text.

that can ignite the loyalty of employees and others with whom the organization comes in contact. This is probably the best-known mission statement in America:

> To explore strange new worlds, to seek out new life and new civilizations, to boldly go where no one has gone before.

This continuing mission for the starship *Enterprise,* as Gene Roddenberry wrote it for the *Star Trek* adventure series, is inspirational and focuses the advanced technology, strong leadership, and skilled crew of the *Enterprise* on what is to be accomplished.

This inspiration and focus appears in the mission of many organizations, like the American Red Cross:

> To improve the quality of human life; to enhance self-reliance and concern for others; and to help people avoid, prepare for, and cope with emergencies.

Or like this first sentence from Medtronic's mission statement:

> To contribute to human welfare by application of biomedical engineering in the research, design, manufacture, and sale of instruments or appliances that alleviate pain, restore health, and extend life.

Organizational Culture Organizations must connect not just with their customers but with all their *stakeholders,* who are the people who are affected by what the company does and how well it performs. This group includes employees, owners, and board members, as well as suppliers, distributors, unions, local communities, and, of course, customers. Communicating the mission statement is an important corporate-level marketing function. The "rising figure" wall painting at Medtronic's corporate headquarters powerfully communicates the inspiration and focus of its mission to employees, doctors, and patients alike.[7]

organizational culture
Set of values, ideas, and attitudes that is learned and shared among the members of an organization

Whether at the corporate, business, or functional level, every unit has an **organizational culture**, which is a set of values, ideas, and attitudes that is learned and shared among the members of an organization. At Medtronic, a corporate officer presents each new employee with a medallion with the "rising figure" on one side and the mission on the other. Each December five or six patients, accompanied by their physicians, describe to a large employee holiday celebration how Medtronic products have changed their lives. These activities send clear messages to employees and other stakeholders about Medtronic's cohesive organizational culture.

When corporations merge or are acquired, organizational cultures can collide, often resulting from conflicts in missions and goals. Ben & Jerry's is an example. When Unilever acquired Ben & Jerry's in April 2000, it had 180 times the annual sales of Ben & Jerry's and dozens of well-known brands (Wisk, Dove, Lipton). This really makes Ben & Jerry's only a small business unit in Unilever. How will Ben & Jerry's fare in its new corporate setting? Time will tell.

goals (objectives)
Targets of performance to be achieved, often by a specific time

Goals **Goals** or **objectives** (terms used interchangeably in this textbook) convert the mission into targeted levels of performance to be achieved, often by a specific time. These goals measure how well the mission is being accomplished. As shown in Figure 2–1, goals exist at the corporate, business unit, and functional levels. All lower-level goals must contribute to achieving goals at the next, higher level.

Business firms can pursue several different types of goals:

- *Profit.* Classic economic theory assumes a firm seeks to get as high a financial return on its investment—profit—as possible.
- *Sales.* If profits are acceptable, a firm may elect to maintain or increase its sales level even though profitability may not be maximized.
- *Market share.* A firm may choose to maintain or increase its market share, sometimes at the expense of greater profits if industry status or prestige is at stake. **Market share** is the ratio of sales revenue of the firm to the total sales revenue of all firms in the industry, including the firm itself.
- *Quality.* A firm may target the highest quality as Medtronic does with its implantable medical devices.
- *Customer satisfaction.* Customers are the reason the organization exists, so their perceptions and actions are of vital importance. Their satisfaction can be measured directly with surveys or tracked with proxy measures like number of customer complaints or percentage of orders shipped within 24 hours of receipt.
- *Employee welfare.* A firm may recognize the critical importance of its employees by having an explicit goal stating its commitment to good employment opportunities and working conditions for them.
- *Social responsibility.* A firm may seek to balance conflicting goals of consumers, employees, and stockholders to promote overall welfare of all these groups, even at the expense of profits. U.S. firms manufacturing products abroad increasingly seek to be "good global citizens" by paying reasonable wages and reducing pollution from their manufacturing plants.

market share
Ratio of a firm's sales to the total sales of all firms in the industry

Many private organizations that do not seek profits also exist. Examples are museums, symphony orchestras, and private hospitals. These organizations strive to serve consumers as efficiently as possible. Government agencies also perform marketing activities in trying to achieve their goal of serving the public good.

Concept Check

1. What are the three levels in today's large organizations?
2. What is the meaning of an organization's mission?
3. How do an organization's goals relate to its mission?

SETTING STRATEGIC DIRECTIONS

Setting strategic directions involves answering two other difficult questions: (1) Where are we now? and (2) Where do we want to go?

A Look Around: Where Are We Now?

Asking an organization where it is at the present time involves identifying its customers, competencies, and competitors. More detailed approaches of assessing "where are we now?" include SWOT analysis, discussed later in this chapter, and environmental scanning (Chapter 3). Both may be done at each of the three levels in the organization.

Customers Ben & Jerry's customers are ice cream and frozen yogurt eaters. But they are not all the same, because they have different flavor preferences, fat preferences,

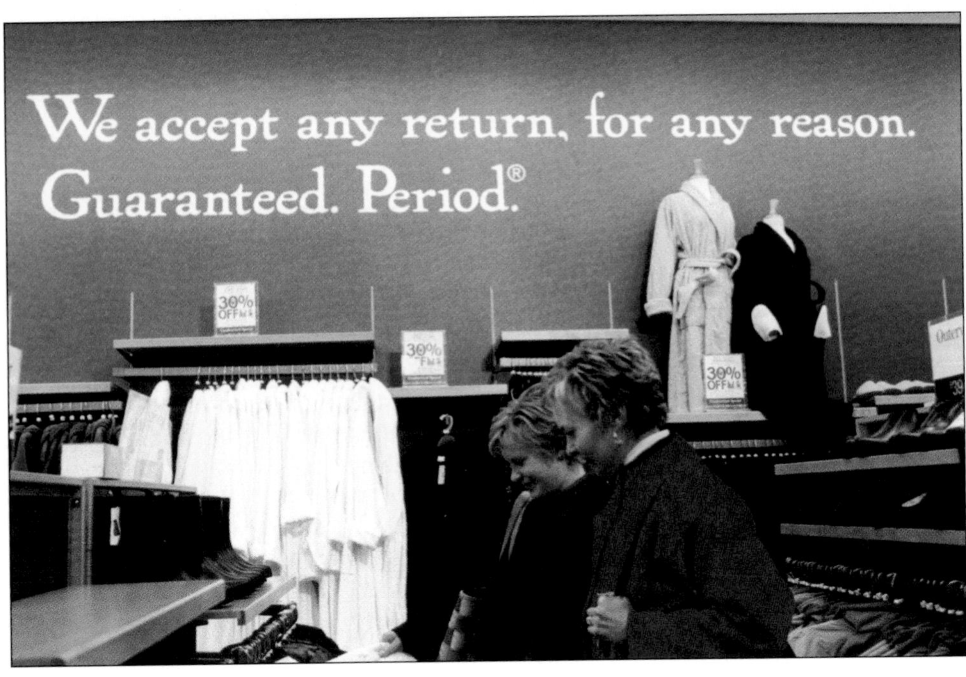

Lands' End's unconditional guarantee for its products highlights its focus on its customers.

convenience preferences, and so on. Medtronic's "customers" are cardiologists and heart surgeons who serve patients.

Lands' End provides an example of a clear focus on customers. Its stores and website give a remarkable statement about its commitments to customer relationships and quality of its products with these unconditional words:

GUARANTEED. PERIOD.®

Its website points out the Lands' End guarantee has always been an unconditional one and it has read: "If you are not completely satisfied with any item you buy from us, at any time during your use of it, return it and we will refund your full purchase price." But to get the message across more clearly to its customers, it put it in the two-word guarantee above.

The crucial point: Strategic directions must be customer-focused and provide genuine value and benefits to present and prospective customers. This Lands' End customer focus was apparent to Sears, Roebuck & Co., which bought Lands' End in 2002. By early 2004. Sears had handed over much of its retail apparel operations to executives of Lands' End.[8]

Competencies "What do we do best?" asks about our organization's capabilities or competencies. *Competencies* are an organization's special capabilities, including skills, technologies, and resources that distinguish it from other organizations. Exploiting these competencies can lead to success.[9] In Medtronic's case its competencies include world-class technology plus training, service, and marketing activities that respond to life-threatening medical needs. *BusinessWeek* magazine calls Medtronic "the standard setter for quality."[10] Competencies should be distinctive enough to provide a *competitive advantage,* a unique strength relative to competitors, often based on quality, time, cost, or innovation.[11] In 2005, Dell's low-cost, direct-sales model has made it not only no. 1 in personal computer sales but enabled it to move into the servers, printers, and peripherals markets as well.[12]

Competitors In today's global competition the lines among competitive sectors are increasingly blurred. Lands' End started as a catalog retailer. But defining its competitors simply as other catalog retailers is a huge oversimplification. Lands' End now competes not only with other catalog retailers of clothing but with traditional department stores, mass merchandisers, and specialty shops. Even well-known clothing brands like Liz Claiborne now have their own chain stores. Although only some of the clothing in any of these store types competes directly with Lands' End products, all the stores have websites for Internet selling. Which means there's a lot of competition out there!

Now part of the merged Sears-Kmart operations, Lands' End operates not only its separate retail stores but also departments within Sears, both of which complement its catalog and Internet operations. Like all Internet retailers, it has a goal of increasing its "conversion rate," the percentage of browsers who actually buy something on visits to the website.

Compared to other big name e-tailers—or Internet retailers—Lands' End's conversion rate is among the best. This is because it has invested heavily in technology to make its site more consumer friendly, such as having a "virtual model" of a customer to let him or her "try things on" online. So successful firms like Lands' End continuously assess both who the competitors are and how they are changing in order to respond with their own strategies.

Growth Strategies: Where Do We Want to Go?

Knowing where the organization is at the present time enables managers to set a direction for the firm and start to allocate resources to move toward that direction. Two techniques to aid in these decisions are (1) business portfolio and (2) market-product analyses.

Business Portfolio Analysis The Boston Consulting Group's (BCG) *business portfolio analysis* uses quantified performance measures and growth targets to analyze a firm's business units (called strategic business units, or SBUs, in the BCG analysis) as though they were a collection of separate investments.[13] While used at the strategic business unit level here, this BCG analysis has also been applied at the product line or individual product or brand level. More than 75 percent of the largest U.S. firms have used it in some form. BCG, a nationally known management consulting firm, advises its clients to locate the position of each of its SBUs on a portfolio analysis matrix (Figure 2–2 on the next page).

Kodak today must make a series of difficult marketing decisions. From what you know about cameras and photos, assess Kodak's sales opportunities for the four products shown here. For some possible answers and a way to show these opportunities graphically, see the text and Figure 2–2.

Kodak digital cameras

Kodak printers (to print digital photos at home)

Kodak film sold in the U.S., Canada, and Western Europe

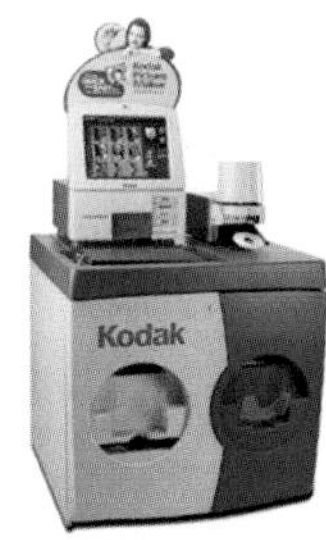

Kodak self-service kiosks in retail outlets

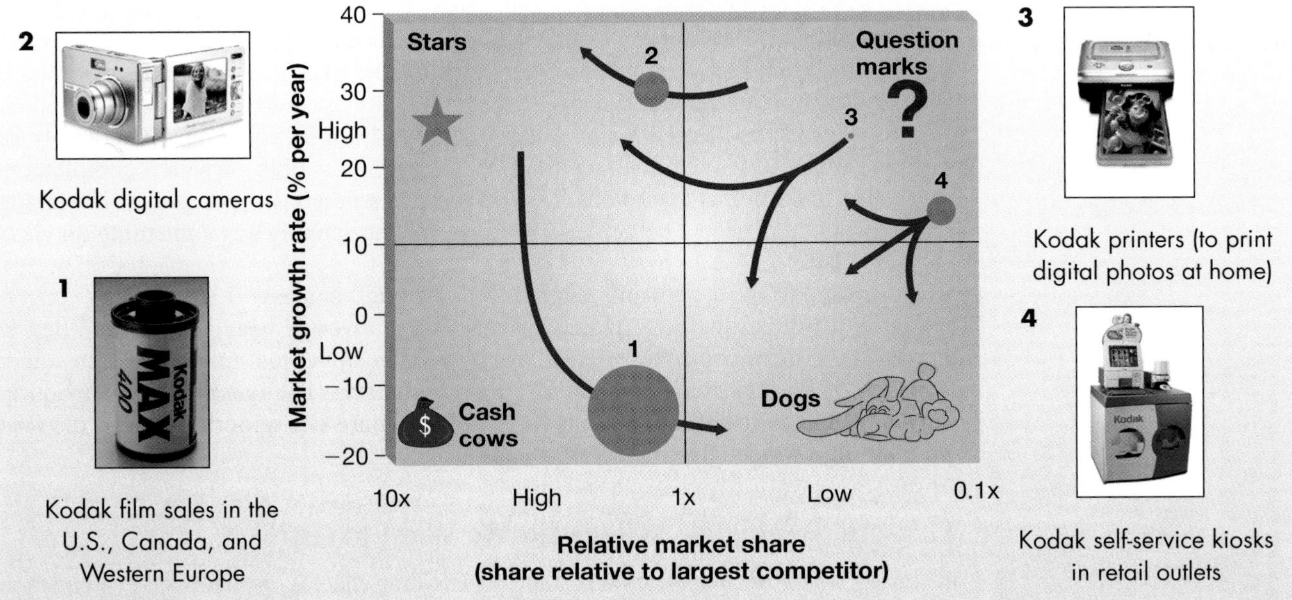

FIGURE 2–2
Boston Consulting Group business portfolio analysis for Kodak, as it might appear in 2006

The vertical axis is the *market growth rate,* which is the annual rate of growth of the specific market or industry in which a given SBU is competing. The horizontal axis is the *relative market share,* defined as the sales of the SBU divided by the sales of the largest firm in the industry. A relative market share of 10× (at the left end of the scale) means that the SBU has 10 times the *share* of its largest competitor, whereas a share of 0.1× (at the right end of the scale) means it has only 10 percent of the *sales* of its largest competitor.

BCG has given specific names and descriptions to the four resulting quadrants in its business portfolio analysis matrix based on the amount of cash they generate for or require from the firm:

- *Cash cows* are SBUs that typically generate large amounts of cash, far more than they can invest profitably in their own product line. They have a dominant share of a slow-growth market and provide cash to pay large amounts of company overhead and to invest in other SBUs.
- *Stars* are SBUs with a high share of high-growth markets that may need extra cash to finance their own rapid future growth. When their growth slows, they are likely to become cash cows.
- *Question marks* or *problem children* are SBUs with a low share of high-growth markets. They require large injections of cash just to maintain their market share, much less increase it. Their name implies management's dilemma for these SBUs: choosing the right ones to invest in and phasing out the rest.
- *Dogs* are SBUs with a low share of low-growth markets. Although they may generate enough cash to sustain themselves, they do not hold the promise of ever becoming real winners for the firm. Dropping SBUs that are dogs may be required, except when relationships with other SBUs, competitive considerations, or potential strategic alliances exist.[14]

A firm's SBUs often start as question marks and go counterclockwise around Figure 2–2 to become stars, then cash cows, and finally dogs. Because most firms have limited influence on the market growth rate, their main alternative in a business portfolio analysis framework is to try to change the relative market share. To accomplish this, management makes conscious decisions on what role each SBU should have in the future and either injects or removes cash from it.

Four Kodak SBUs are shown as they appeared in 2006 and can serve as an example of BCG analysis. The area of each circle in Figure 2–2 is roughly proportional to the corresponding SBU's 2006 sales revenue. In a more complete analysis, its other SBUs would be included. This Kodak example also shows the agonizing strategic decisions Kodak faces in the camera and film business with the arrival of digital technology.

More than a century ago, Kodak virtually invented the photography industry. Nicknamed "Big Yellow" for its film packages, until about 2000 Kodak relied not on its cameras for the bulk of its revenues and profits but on its film for the billions of photographs taken every year. Two factors changed that: (1) more competition from film manufacturers like Fuji and (2) the popularization of digital cameras that need no conventional film.

So in late 2003, Kodak announced a shift in its strategic priorities from film to digital technology. We'll briefly compare Kodak's position in 2003 when it commited to digital technology with that in early 2006. One thing, however, is eminently clear. The success of Kodak's strategy and its product lines shown in Figure 2–2 depends on how millions of consumers like you take pictures and convert your pictures into useful images over the next decade. Here is a snapshot of the sales opportunities of the four product lines reflected in the comments of analysts:

1. *Kodak film sales in the United States, Canada, and Western Europe*. An $8 billion per year "cash cow" in 2003, Kodak film sales are still its biggest single source of revenue. In its "death throes," Kodak worldwide film sales were projected to decline 10 to 12 percent per year through 2006.[15]

2. *Kodak digital cameras*. A $1 billion business in 2003, Kodak expects its "filmless imaging market" to grow from 30 percent of its 2003 revenues to 60 percent in 2006.[16] By 2006, Kodak had become a serious player in the digital camera market, ranking no. 1 in the United States with a 22 percent market share and ranking no. 3 in the world.[17] Kodak clearly expects its digital cameras to be a "star" soon. The challenge: New rivals are emerging, like Nokia, which is putting advanced cameras in its cell phones.
3. *Kodak printers (to print digital photos at home)*. With 82 percent of digital prints made this way in 2003, this might look like a clear BCG star with Kodak's expected new line of home printers. But with Kodak competing with established printer manufacturers like Hewlett-Packard, Canon, and now Dell, the future of this "question mark" could range from being a "dog" to a "star."[18]
4. *Kodak self-service kiosks in retail outlets*. With only about 1 percent of the market in printed pictures in 2003, these self-service machines used to take up to four minutes to make an 8 × 10 photo from film. But by 2006 consumers are increasingly turning to kiosks in retail shops to make prints from their digital cameras.[19] As shown in Figure 2–2, an innovative technology (the kiosks) faces big unknowns, also because Japanese copiers are well entrenched in these outlets.[20]

Are these BCG projections valid? How you use digital cameras and make their prints hold the answer. Recent Kodak strategies are discussed later in the chapter.

The primary strength of business portfolio analysis lies in forcing a firm to place each of its SBUs in the growth-share matrix, which in turn suggests which SBUs will be cash producers and cash users in the future. Weaknesses are that it is often difficult (1) to get the needed information and (2) to incorporate competitive information into business portfolio analysis.[21]

Market-Product Analysis Firms can also view growth opportunities in terms of markets and products. Let's think of it this way: For any product there is both a current market (consisting of existing customers) and a new market (consisting of potential customers). And for any market, there is a current product (what they're now using) and a new product (something they might use if it were developed). These four market-product strategies are shown in Figure 2–3 on the next page.[22]

As Unilever attempts to increase sales revenues of its Ben & Jerry's business, it must consider all four of the alternative market-product strategies shown in Figure 2–3. For example, it can try to use *market penetration*—a marketing strategy of increasing

FIGURE 2–3
Four market-product strategies: alternative ways to expand sales revenues for Ben & Jerry's

Markets	PRODUCTS: Current	PRODUCTS: New
Current	**Market penetration** Selling more Ben & Jerry's super premium ice cream to Americans	**Product development** Selling a new product such as children's clothing under the Ben & Jerry's brand to Americans
New	**Market development** Selling more Ben & Jerry's super premium ice cream in South American markets for the first time	**Diversification** Selling a new product such as children's clothing in South American markets for the first time

sales of present products in existing markets, in this case by increasing sales of Ben & Jerry's present ice cream products to U.S. consumers. There is no change in either the basic product line or the market served, but increased sales are possible—either by selling more ice cream (through better promotion or distribution) *or* by selling the same amount of ice cream at a higher price to its existing customers.

Market development, a marketing strategy of selling existing products to new markets, is a reasonable alternative for Ben & Jerry's. South America, for example, is a good possible new market. There is good news and bad news for this marketing strategy: As the income of South American households increases, consumers may be able to buy more ice cream, but the Ben & Jerry's brand is relatively unknown.

Product development is a marketing strategy of selling new products to existing markets. Figure 2–3 shows that the firm could try leveraging the Ben & Jerry's brand, as mentioned earlier, by selling its own Ben & Jerry's brand of children's clothing in the United States. This, of course, has dangers because Americans may not be able to see a clear connection between the company's expertise in ice cream and, say, children's clothing.

Diversification is a marketing strategy of developing new products and selling them in new markets. This is a potentially high-risk strategy for Ben & Jerry's, and for most firms, because the company has neither previous production experience nor marketing experience on which to draw. For example, in trying to sell a Ben & Jerry's brand of children's clothing in South America, the company has expertise neither in producing children's clothing nor in marketing to South American consumers.

Which strategies will Ben and Jerry's follow? Keep your eyes, ears, and taste buds working to discover the marketing answers.

Concept Check

1. What are competencies and why are they important?
2. What is business portfolio analysis?
3. What are the four market-product strategies?

THE STRATEGIC MARKETING PROCESS

After the organization assesses where it's at and where it wants to go, other questions emerge:

1. How do we allocate our resources to get where we want to go?
2. How do we convert our plans to actions?
3. How do our results compare with our plans, and do deviations require new plans?

How can Ben & Jerry's identify new ice cream flavors and social responsibility programs that contribute to its mission? The text describes how the strategic marketing process and its SWOT analysis can help.

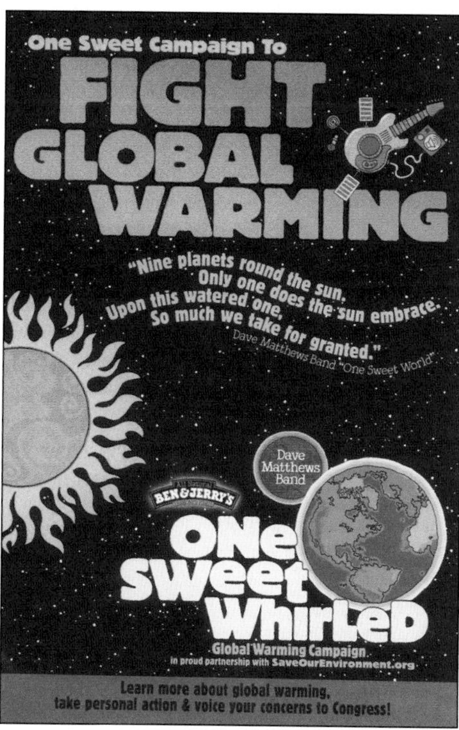

strategic marketing process
Approach whereby an organization allocates its marketing mix resources to reach its target markets

marketing plan
Road map for the marketing activities of an organization for a specified future period of time

This same approach is used in the **strategic marketing process**, whereby an organization allocates its marketing mix resources to reach its target markets. Figure 2–4 on the next page shows this process is divided into three phases—planning, implementation, and control—and it identifies the chapters covering each topic.

The strategic marketing process is so central to the activities of most organizations that they formalize it as a **marketing plan**, which is a road map for the marketing activities of an organization for a specified future period of time, such as one year or five years.

The following section gives an overview of the strategic marketing process that places Chapters 3 through 18 in perspective.

Strategic Marketing Process: The Planning Phase

As shown in Figure 2–4, the planning phase of the strategic marketing process consists of the three steps shown at the top of the figure: (1) situation analysis, (2) market-product focus and goal setting, and (3) the marketing program. Let's use the recent marketing planning experiences of several companies to look at each of these steps.

situation analysis
Taking stock of where a firm or product has been recently, where it is now, and where it is headed

SWOT analysis
Organization's appraisal of its internal strengths and weaknesses and its external opportunities and threats

Step 1: Situation (SWOT) Analysis The essence of **situation analysis** is taking stock of where the firm or product has been recently, where it is now, and where it is headed in terms of the organization's plans and the external factors and trends affecting it. The situation analysis box in Figure 2–4 is the first of the three steps in the planning phase.

An effective shorthand summary of the situation analysis is a **SWOT analysis**, an acronym describing an organization's appraisal of its internal **S**trengths and **W**eaknesses and its external **O**pportunities and **T**hreats. Both the situation and SWOT analyses can be done at the level of the entire organization, the business unit, the product line, or the specific product. As an analysis moves from the level of the entire organization to the specific product, it, of course, gets far more detailed. For small firms or those with basically a single product line, an analysis at the firm or product level is really the same thing.

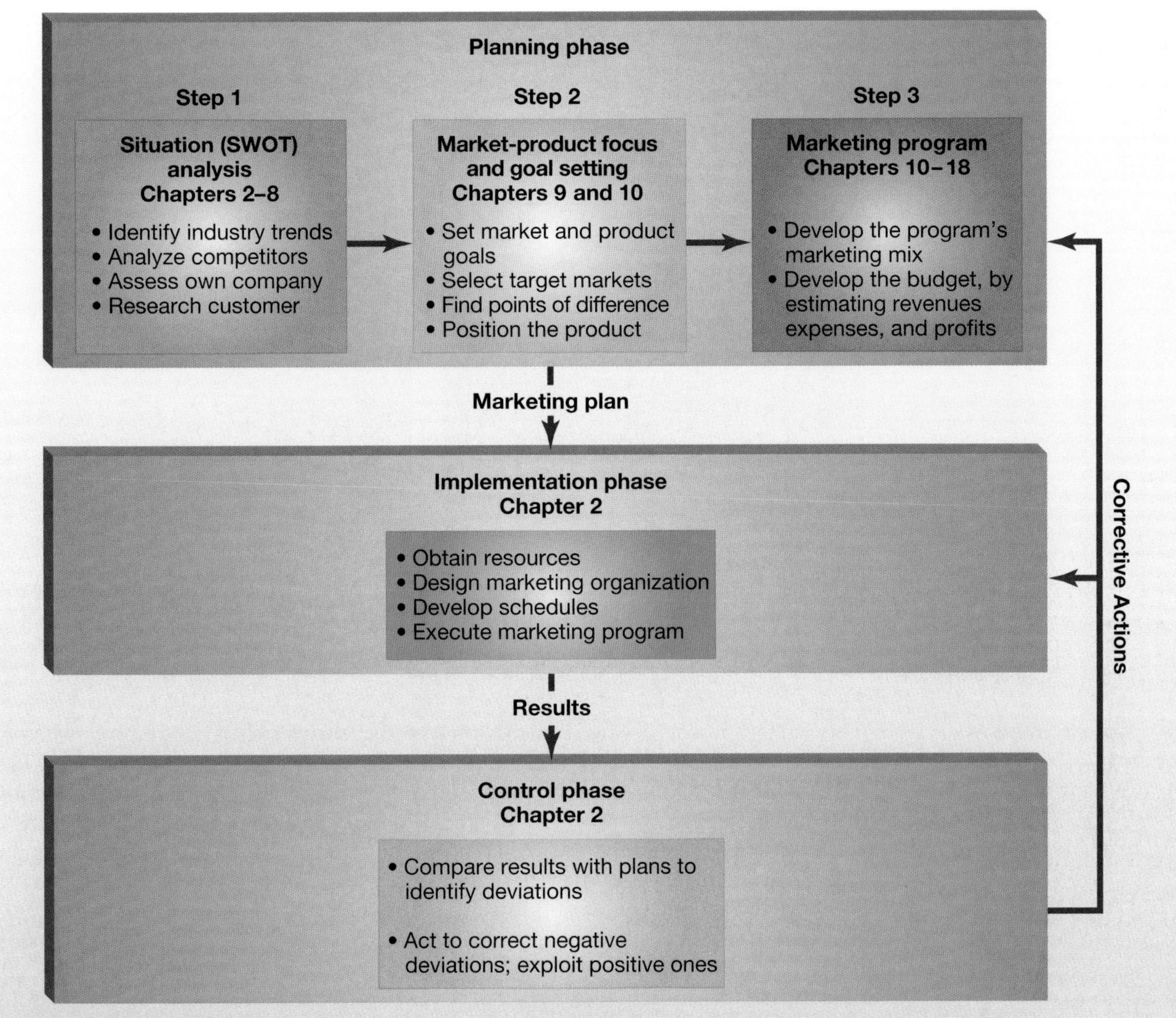

FIGURE 2–4
The strategic marketing process

The SWOT analysis is based on an exhaustive study of the four areas shown in step 1 of the planning phase of the strategic marketing process (Figure 2–4). Knowledge of these areas forms the foundation on which the firm builds its marketing program:

- Identifying trends in the firm's industry.
- Analyzing the firm's competitors.
- Assessing the firm itself.
- Researching the firm's present and prospective customers.

Let's assume you are the Unilever vice president responsible for integrating Ben & Jerry's into Unilever's business. You might do the SWOT analysis shown in Figure 2–5. Note that your SWOT table has four cells formed by the combination of internal versus external factors (the rows) and favorable versus unfavorable factors (the columns) that summarize Ben & Jerry's strengths, weaknesses, opportunities, and threats.

A SWOT analysis helps a firm identify the strategy-related factors in these four cells that can have a major effect on the firm. The goal is not simply to develop the SWOT analysis but to translate the results of the analysis into specific actions to help the firm grow and succeed. The ultimate goal is to identify the *critical* factors affecting the firm and then build on vital strengths, correct glaring weaknesses, exploit significant opportunities, and avoid disaster-laden threats. That is a big order.

FIGURE 2–5
Ben & Jerry's: a SWOT analysis to get it growing again

Location of Factor	TYPE OF FACTOR	
	Favorable	**Unfavorable**
Internal	**Strengths** • Prestigious, well-known brand name among U.S. consumers • 40 percent share of the U.S. super premium ice cream market • Can complement Unilever's existing ice cream brands • Widely recognized for its social responsibility actions	**Weaknesses** • Danger that B&J's social responsibility actions may add costs, reduce focus on core business • Need for experienced managers to help growth • Flat sales and profits in recent years
External	**Opportunities** • Growing demand for quality ice cream in overseas markets • Increasing U.S. demand for frozen yogurt and other low-fat desserts • Success of many U.S. firms in extending successful brand in one product category to others	**Threats** • Consumer concern with fatty desserts; B&J customers are the type who read new government-ordered nutritional labels • Competes with giant Pillsbury and its Häagen-Dazs brand • International downturns increase the risks for B&J in European and Asian markets

The Ben and Jerry's SWOT analysis in Figure 2–5 can be the basis for these kinds of specific actions. An action in each of the four cells might be:

- *Build on a strength.* Find specific efficiencies in distribution with Unilever's existing ice cream brands.
- *Correct a weakness.* Recruit experienced managers from other consumer product firms to help stimulate growth.
- *Exploit an opportunity.* Develop a new line of low-fat frozen yogurts to respond to consumer health concerns.
- *Avoid a disaster-laden threat.* Focus on less risky international markets, such as Canada and Mexico.

Examples of more in-depth study in these four areas appear in the SWOT analysis in Figure 1 in the marketing plan in Appendix A and the chapters in this textbook cited in that plan.

Step 2: Market-Product Focus and Goal Setting Determining which products will be directed toward which customers (step 2 of the planning phase in Figure 2–4) is essential for developing an effective marketing program (step 3). This decision is often based on **market segmentation**, which involves aggregating prospective buyers into groups, or segments, that (1) have common needs and (2) will respond similarly to a marketing action. Ideally, a firm can use market segmentation to identify the segments on which it will focus its efforts—its target market segments—and develop one or more marketing programs to reach them.

market segmentation
Sorting potential buyers into groups that have common needs and will respond similarly to a marketing action

As always, understanding the customer is essential. In the case of Medtronic, executives researched a potential new market in Asia by talking extensively with doctors in India and China. They learned that these doctors saw some of the current state-of-the-art features of heart pacemakers as unnecessary and too expensive. Instead, they wanted an affordable pacemaker that was reliable and easy to implant. This information led Medtronic to develop and market a new product, the Champion heart pacemaker, directed at the needs of this Asian market segment.

The Champion: Medtronic's high-quality, long-life, low-cost heart pacemaker for an Asian market segment.

Goal setting involves setting measurable marketing objectives to be achieved. Such objectives would be different depending on the level of marketing involved. For a specific market, the goal may be to introduce a new product, such as Medtronic's Champion pacemaker in Asia or Toyota's launch of its hybrid car, the Prius. For a specific brand or product, the goal may be to create a promotional campaign or pricing strategy that will get more consumers to purchase. For an entire marketing program, the objective is often a series of actions to be implemented over several years.

Using the strategic marketing process shown in Figure 2–4, let's examine Medtronic's five-year plan to reach the "affordable and reliable" segment of the pacemaker market:[23]

- *Set marketing and product goals.* The chances of new-product success are increased by specifying both market and product goals. Based on their market research showing the need for a reliable yet affordable pacemaker, Medtronic executives set the following as their goal: Design and market such a pacemaker in the next three years that could be manufactured in China for the Asian market.
- *Select target markets.* The Champion pacemaker will be targeted at cardiologists and medical clinics performing heart surgery in India, China, and other Asian countries.
- *Find points of difference.* **Points of difference** are those characteristics of a product that make it superior to competitive substitutes. Just as a competitive advantage is a unique strength of an entire organization compared to its competitors, points of difference are unique characteristics of one of its products that make it superior to competitive products it faces in the marketplace. For the Champion pacemaker, the key points of difference are *not* the state-of-the-art features that drive up production costs and are important to only a minority of patients. Instead, they are high quality, long life, reliability, ease of use, and low cost.
- *Position the product.* The pacemaker will be "positioned" in cardiologists' and patients' minds as a medical device that is high quality and reliable with a long, nine-year life. The name Champion is selected after testing acceptable names among doctors in India, China, Pakistan, Singapore, and Malaysia.

points of difference
Those characteristics of a product or service that make it superior to competitive substitutes

Details in these four elements of step 2 provide a solid foundation to use in developing the marketing program, the next step in the planning phase of the strategic marketing process.

Step 3: Marketing Program Activities in step 2 tell the marketing manager which customers to target and which customer needs the firm's product offerings can satisfy—the *who* and *what* aspects of the strategic marketing process. The *how* aspect—step 3 in the planning phase—involves developing the program's marketing mix and its budget.

Figure 2–6 shows components of each marketing mix element that are combined to provide a cohesive marketing program. For the five-year marketing plan of Medtronic, these marketing mix activities include the following:

- *Product strategy.* Offer a Champion brand heart pacemaker with features needed by Asian patients at an affordable price.
- *Price strategy.* Manufacture the Champion to control costs so that it can be priced below $1,000 (in U.S. dollars)—a fraction of the price of the state-of-the-art pacemakers offered in Western markets.
- *Promotion strategy.* Feature demonstrations at cardiologist and medical conventions across Asia to introduce the Champion and highlight the device's features and application.

FIGURE 2–6
Elements of the marketing mix that comprise a cohesive marketing program

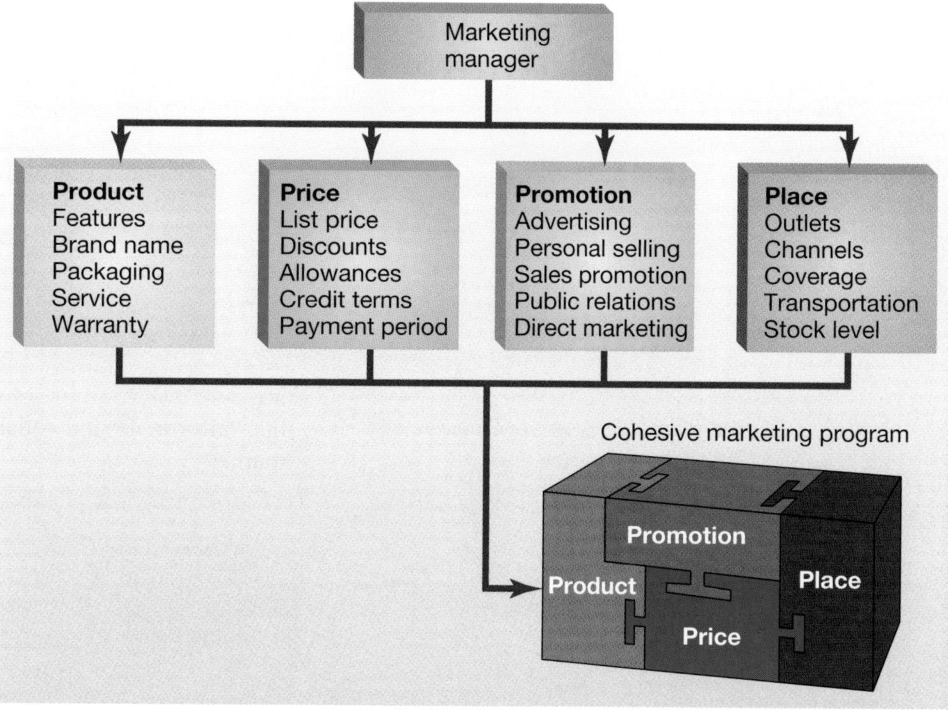

- *Place (distribution) strategy.* Search out, utilize, and train reputable medical distributors across Asia to call on cardiologists and medical clinics.

Putting this marketing program into effect requires that the firm commit time and money to it in the form of a sales forecast and budget that must be approved by top management.

Concept Check

1. What is the difference between a strength and an opportunity in a SWOT analysis?
2. What is market segmentation?
3. What are points of difference and why are they important?

Strategic Marketing Process: The Implementation Phase

As shown in Figure 2–4, the result of the tens or hundreds of hours spent in the planning phase of the strategic marketing process is the firm's marketing plan. Implementation, the second phase of the strategic marketing process, involves carrying out the marketing plan that emerges from the planning phase. If the firm cannot put the marketing plan into effect—in the implementation phase—the planning phase was a waste of time. Figure 2–4 also shows the four components of the implementation phase: (1) obtaining resources, (2) designing the marketing organization, (3) developing schedules, and (4) actually executing the marketing program designed in the planning phase. Eastman Kodak provides a case example.

Obtaining Resources In late 2003, Kodak announced a bold plan (discussed earlier) to reenergize the filmmaker for the new age of digital cameras and prints. Kodak needed money to implement the plan, so it cut shareholder dividends by 72 percent to invest the $3 billion saved in Kodak's digital technologies.[24] And in early 2004,

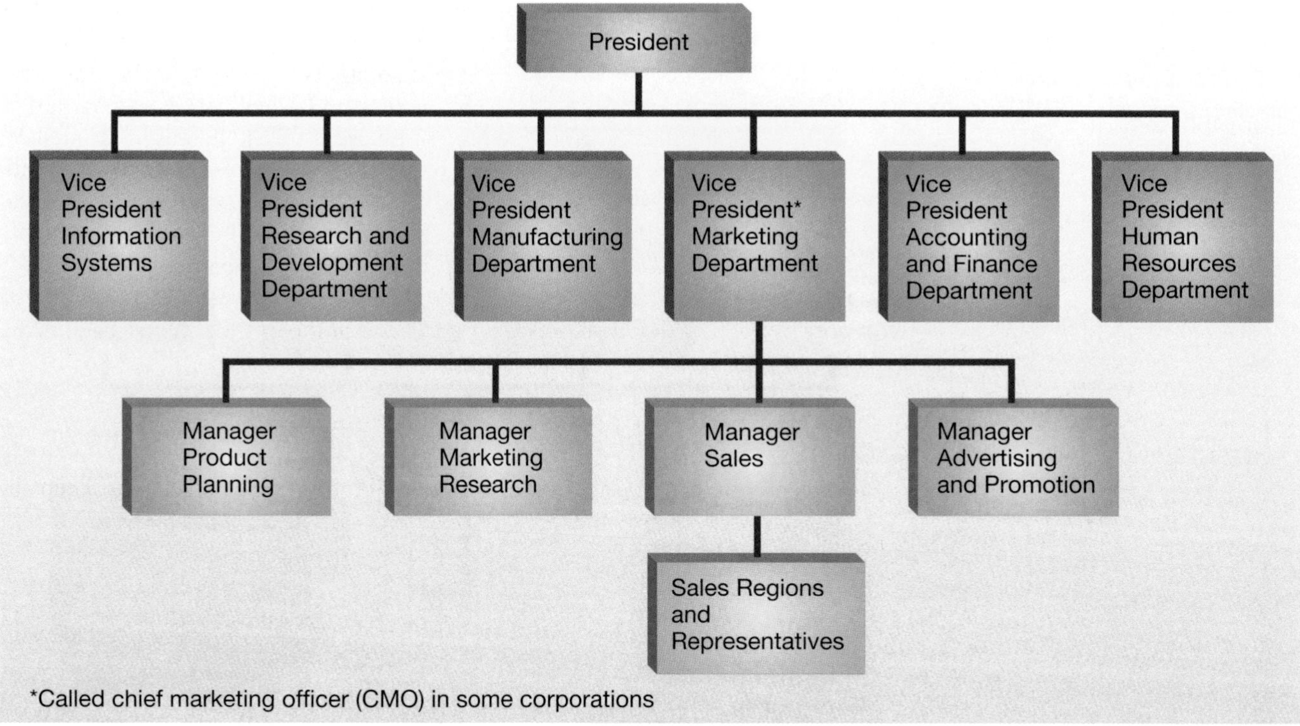

FIGURE 2–7
Organization of a typical manufacturing firm, showing a breakdown of the marketing department

Kodak announced a painful cut of up to 15,000 jobs over the next three years to add more money to invest in Kodak's digital future.[25]

Designing the Marketing Organization A marketing program needs a marketing organization to implement it. Figure 2–7 shows the organization chart of a typical manufacturing firm, giving some details of the marketing department's structure. Four managers of marketing activities are shown to report to the vice president of marketing. Regional sales managers and an international sales manager may report to the manager of sales. This marketing organization is responsible for converting marketing plans to reality as a part of the corporate team.

In the 1990s a number of large consumer products firms changed the title of the head of the marketing department from "vice president of marketing" to "chief marketing officer" (CMO), but the responsibilities have stayed largely the same.[26]

Developing Schedules Effective implementation requires goals, deadlines, and schedules. To implement Kodak's plan to focus on its digital business opportunities, Kodak set some key goals:[27]

- Boost sales from $13 billion in 2003 to $16 billion in 2006 and $20 billion in 2010.
- Increase the share of Kodak's revenues from its digital businesses from 30 percent in 2003 to 60 percent in 2006.

To achieve these goals, Kodak acquired and partnered with firms having digital expertise, and launched new lines of digital cameras.

Executing the Marketing Program Marketing plans are meaningless pieces of paper without effective execution of those plans. This effective execution requires attention to detail for both marketing strategies and marketing tactics. A **marketing strategy** is the means by which a marketing goal is to be achieved, usually characterized by a specified target market and a marketing program to reach it. Although the term *marketing strategy* is often used loosely, it implies both the end sought (target market) and

marketing strategy
Means by which a marketing goal is to be achieved

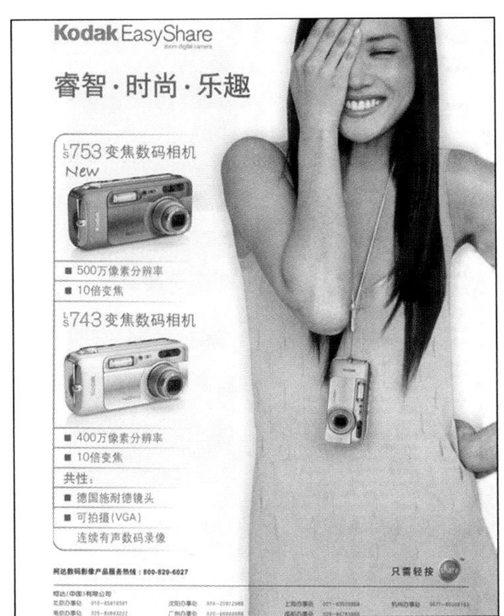

Kodak is pursuing opportunities for sales of digital cameras—along with sales of film cameras and film—in China.

the means to achieve it (marketing program). At this marketing strategy level, Kodak will seek to increase sales not only of digital cameras but also of film cameras and film in emerging markets like India, China, and Eastern Europe where low prices, simplicity, and convenience are important.[28]

To implement a marketing program successfully, hundreds of detailed decisions are often required. These decisions, called **marketing tactics**, are detailed day-to-day operational decisions essential to the overall success of marketing strategies. At Kodak, writing ads and setting prices for its new lines of digital cameras are examples of marketing tactics.

marketing tactics
Detailed day-to-day operational decisions essential to the overall success of marketing strategies

Marketing strategies and marketing tactics shade into each other. Effective marketing program implementation requires excruciating concern for both.

Strategic Marketing Process: The Control Phase

The control phase of the strategic marketing process seeks to keep the marketing program moving in the direction set for it (see Figure 2–4). Accomplishing this requires the marketing manager (1) to compare the results of the marketing program with the goals in the written plans to identify deviations and (2) to act on these deviations—correcting negative deviations and exploiting positive ones.

Comparing Results with Plans to Identify Deviations In late 2003, as Kodak executives looked at the company's sales revenues from 1998 through 2003, they didn't like what they saw: the very flat trend, or AB in Figure 2–8. Extending the 1998–2003 trend to 2010 along BC continues the flat sales revenues, a totally unacceptable, no-growth strategy.

Kodak set a growth target of 6 percent annually, the line BD in Figure 2–8 that will give sales revenues of $16 billion in 2006 and $20 billion in 2010. This reveals a wedge-shaped shaded gap in the figure. Planners call this the *planning gap,* the difference between the projection of the path to reach a new goal (line BD) and the projection of the path of the results of a plan already in place (line BC).

The ultimate purpose of the firm's marketing program is to "fill in" this planning gap—in Kodak's case, to move its future sales revenue line from the no-growth line BC up to the challenging target of line BD. But poor performance can result in actual sales revenues being far less than the targeted levels. This is the essence of evaluation: comparing actual results with planned objectives.

FIGURE 2–8
Evaluation and control of Kodak's marketing program, showing Kodak's planning gap

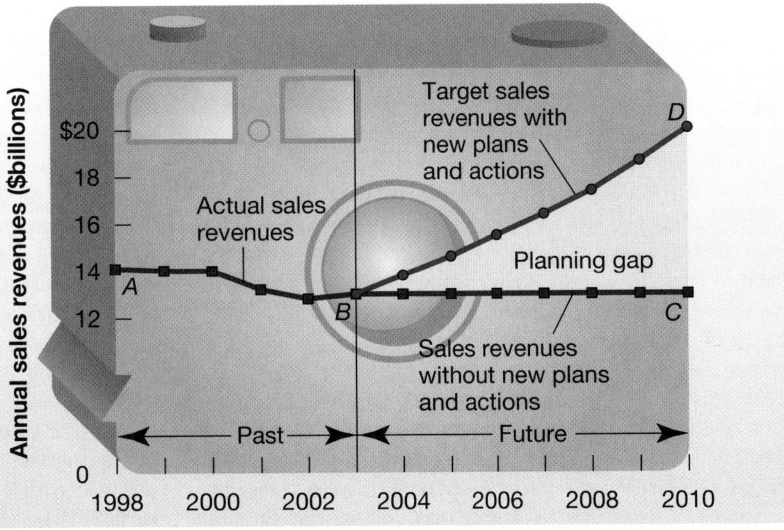

Acting on Deviations When evaluation shows that actual performance fails to meet expectations, managers need to take corrective actions. And when actual results are far better than the plan called for, creative managers find ways to exploit the situation. Two possible Kodak midcourse corrections for both positive and negative deviations from targets illustrate these management actions:

- *Exploiting a positive deviation.* If Kodak's film strategy in India and China shows promise, it might partner with more local companies to produce cameras and film and to process film.[29]
- *Correcting a negative deviation.* However, if Indian and Chinese consumers choose to skip film cameras and jump directly to digital ones, Kodak will likely need to develop a digital camera strategy for these consumers.

The Kodak ad for digital cameras on the previous page directed at Chinese consumers suggests it is rethinking its Asian strategy that stresses film cameras.

Concept Check

1. What is the control phase of the strategic marketing process?
2. How do the objectives set for a marketing program in the planning phase relate to the control phase of the strategic marketing process?

CHAPTER IN REVIEW

1 *Describe the three organizational levels of strategy.*
Most large business firms and nonprofit organizations are divided into three levels of strategy: (*a*) the corporate level, where top management directs overall strategy for the entire organization; (*b*) the business unit level, where business unit managers set the direction for their products and markets to exploit value-creating opportunities; and (*c*) the functional level, where groups of specialists actually create value for the organization.

2 *Describe why business, mission, organizational culture, and goals are important in organizations.*
Organizations exist to accomplish something for someone. To give organizations direction and focus, they continuously assess their business, mission, organizational culture, and goals. First, an organization defines what its business is—the set of customer needs, such as transportation, it wants to satisfy. Next, an organization defines its mission, which is a statement that describes its customers, markets, and products and inspires loyalty from its stakeholders. An organization's culture serves to connect it with its stakeholders based on a set of shared values, ideas, and attitudes. Finally, the organization's goals measure how well it accomplishes its mission at each organizational level by providing specific targeted levels of performance to be achieved, such as sales and profits, by a specific time period.

3 *Explain how organizations set strategic directions by assessing where they are now and seek to be in the future.*
Managers of an organization ask two key questions to set a strategic direction. The first question, Where are we now?, requires an organization to (*a*) assess its customers to determine whether its direction must be modified based on changes in consumer trends; (*b*) reevaluate its competencies to ensure that its special capabilities still provide a competitive advantage; and (*c*) analyze its current and potential competitors from a global perspective to determine whether any business definition modifications are needed. The second question, Where do we want to go?, requires an organization to actually set a direction and allocate resources to move it in that direction. Business portfolio and market-product analyses are two useful techniques to do this.

4 *Describe the strategic marketing process and its three key phases: planning, implementation, and control.*
An organization uses the strategic marketing process to allocate its marketing mix resources to reach its target markets. This process consists of three phases, which are usually formalized in a marketing plan. The planning phase consists of (*a*) a situation (SWOT) analysis of the organization's strengths, weaknesses, opportunities, and threats; (*b*) a market-product focus through market segmentation, points of difference analysis, and goal setting; and (*c*) a marketing program that specifies the budget and activities (marketing strategies and tactics) for each marketing mix element. The implementation phase carries out the marketing plan that emerges from the planning phase. It has four key elements: obtaining resources, designing the marketing organization, developing schedules, and executing the marketing program. The control phase compares the results from the implemented marketing program with the marketing plan's goals to identify the "planning gaps" and take actions to exploit positive deviations or correct negative ones.

5 *Explain how the marketing mix elements are blended into a cohesive marketing program.*
A marketing manager uses information obtained during the SWOT analysis, market-product focus, and goal-setting steps in the planning process to develop marketing strategies and marketing tactics for each marketing mix element for a given product, which are then implemented, as specified in the marketing plan, as a marketing program.

FOCUSING ON KEY TERMS

goals p. 27
marketing plan p. 33
marketing strategy p. 38
marketing tactics p. 39
market segmentation p. 35
market share p. 27
mission p. 25
objectives p. 27
organizational culture p. 26
points of difference p. 36
profit p. 24
situation analysis p. 33
strategic marketing process p. 33
SWOT analysis p. 33

DISCUSSION AND APPLICATION QUESTIONS

1 (*a*) Explain what a mission statement is. (*b*) Using Medtronic as an example from the chapter, explain how it gives a strategic direction to its organization. (*c*) Create a mission statement for your own career.

2 What competencies best describe (*a*) your college or university, (*b*) your favorite restaurant, and (*c*) the company that manufactures the computer you own or use most often?

3 Why does a product often start as a question mark and then move counterclockwise around BCG's growth-share matrix shown in Figure 2–2?

4 What is the main result of each of the three phases of the strategic marketing process? (*a*) planning, (*b*) implementation, and (*c*) control.

5 Select one strength, one weakness, one opportunity, and one threat from the SWOT analysis for Ben & Jerry's shown in Figure 2–5, and suggest a specific possible action that Unilever might take to exploit or address each one.

6 The goal-setting step in the planning phase of the strategic marketing process sets quantified objectives for use in the control phase. What actions are suggested for a marketing manager if measured results are below objectives? Above objectives?

GOING ONLINE Medtronic's Mission Statement

Medtronic is the global leader in developing and marketing medical technology solutions, generating over $9 billion in sales by 2005. Every six seconds, someone in over 120 countries benefits from a Medtronic product or therapy, such as a cardiac pacemaker, a pain management system, or implantable insulin pump. Go to Medtronic's website (www.medtronic.com/corporate/mission.html) and assess its mission.

1 What stakeholders are specifically mentioned or implied in Medtronic's mission? What values are associated with each stakeholder?

2 What is the scope of Medtronic's mission? Why does Medtronic limit its scope?

3 Why does Medtronic NOT define itself as being in the "medical device" business?

BUILDING YOUR MARKETING PLAN

1 Read Appendix A, "Building an Effective Marketing Plan." Then write a 600-word executive summary for the Paradise Kitchens marketing plan using the numbered headings shown in the plan. When you have completed your own marketing plan, write a 600-word executive summary to go in the front of it.

2 Give focus to your marketing plan by (*a*) writing your mission statement in 25 words or less, (*b*) listing three nonfinancial goals and three financial goals, (*c*) writing your competitive advantage in 35 words or less, and (*d*) doing a SWOT analysis table.

3 Draw a simple organization chart for your organization.

4 Develop a Gantt chart to schedule the key activities to implement your marketing plan.

5 In terms of the control, list (*a*) four or five critical factors (such as revenues and number of customers) and (*b*) how frequently (monthly, quarterly) you will monitor them to determine if special actions are needed.

VIDEO CASE 2 BP: Allocating Resources to Bring You Gasoline *and* Fresh Bread!

"You never have enough time, you never have enough money, and you never have enough people to do everything you want to do," explains Louis Sierra, vice president and performance unit leader at BP plc. When it comes to resources we "ask ourselves where can we invest or where should we invest," he continues.

Sierra is describing the situation managers at BP typically face as they try to decide where to allocate their resources. The answers are developed through the evaluation of many possible opportunities and the development of strategic plans. In fact, he relies on the plans to determine "what it is you do and, just as importantly, what it is you don't do"!

THE COMPANY

BP plc—often shortened to simply BP—is one of the world's largest producers and marketers of petroleum products. The company's mission, sometimes described as its brand promise, is:

> In all our activities we seek to display some unchanging, fundamental qualities—integrity, honest dealing, treating everyone with respect and dignity, striving for mutual advantage, and contributing to human progress.

To help translate the mission into practical action, BP also specifies four brand values. These values express the way BP does business; they provide the foundation on which decisions are based; and they enable the presentation of a consistent message to all stakeholders. Sierra explains that they "permeate BP anywhere it works, anywhere in the world." The values are:

- **Performance:** BP sets the global standards of performance on financial and environmental dimensions, and safety, growth, and customer and employee satisfaction.
- **Innovation:** Through the creative approaches of employees, and the development and application of cutting-edge technology, BP seeks breakthrough solutions for its customers.
- **Progress:** BP is always looking for new and better ways of doing business.
- **Green:** BP is committed to the proactive and responsible treatment of the planet's natural resources.

As BP evaluates opportunities for growth it considers many options. Market penetration options involve increasing sales of existing products to current customers. Product development options involve providing new products, such as BP's latest clean fuel called BP Ultimate, to current customers. Market development involves taking existing products to new consumers, beyond those in the 100 countries BP already serves. Finally, diversification options include new businesses such as BP Solar, a solar electricity producer, to serve new markets.

One of the opportunities for growth recently evaluated by BP is the convenience and fuel store concept called BP Connect. Through \$120 billion in acquisitions, BP added Amoco, ARCO, and Castrol to its organization to become the largest retailer of petroleum products in the world. Its 28,500 retail sites, including 15,900 stations in the United States, serve 13 million customers per day. BP used its strategic planning process to assess the situation, set goals, and develop the marketing tactics for BP Connect.

TRENDS IN CONVENIENCE STORE AND GASOLINE RETAILING

Several major trends currently affect both traditional convenience store and petroleum retailing worldwide:

- *Mergers and acquisitions.* During the past several years, BP and other major oil firms, such as Exxon (Mobil) and Total (PetroFina & Elf), have merged with or acquired one or more of their competitors.
- *Convergence.* Since 1977, the percentage of gasoline stations in the United States that are also convenience stores has gone from 5 percent to about 50 percent. To improve profitability, convenience stores and gasoline retailers have encroached on each other's domain by offering products and services typically sold by the other.

- *Competition.* In the United States, large supermarket chains (such as Albertson's, in partnership with ARCO, which is owned by BP), mass merchandisers (such as Wal-Mart), and membership organizations (such as Costco or Sam's Club), have added retail petroleum operations that are located on their parking lots.
- *Convenience.* Changes in lifestyle and shopping behavior have resulted in a greater demand for time and place convenience by consumers. Gasoline retailers have replaced the old "gas and cigarettes" strategy with a "scrambled merchandising" strategy that offers consumers several unrelated product lines in a single retail outlet, such as food, car washes, ATM banking, and new payment technologies (such as ExxonMobil's Speedpass) to speed up the transactions.
- *Branding.* A growing number of petroleum retailers are using brand management to create a consistent, global, and proprietary image that enables firms to differentiate their offerings from those of competitors to gain a competitive advantage.
- *Co-branding.* Co-branding involves the pairing of brand names into a coherent image from two or more marketers to capitalize on the strengths of each that appeals to a firm's target consumers. Convenience store and petroleum marketers have developed relationships with fast-food restaurants (such as Taco Bell, Blimpie's, etc.) to satisfy consumer needs immediately, instead of having them buy the same brand elsewhere.

THE BP CONNECT CONCEPT

To discover exactly what consumers wanted in a convenience and fuel store, BP conducted extensive marketing research. For example, it constructed a full-scale prototype of a 4,200-square-foot convenience food-gasoline station in an Atlanta warehouse. Reactions of U.S. consumers touring the Atlanta prototype were overwhelmingly positive. Based on the situation analysis and the results of the research, BP decided to invest $4.4 billion to update old or build new BP Connect stations worldwide. The research also helped BP decide that BP Connect stores will feature:

- *A new logo.* The BP shield and Amoco torch will be replaced by a new "helios" logo that BP hopes will enhance its corporate image as a "green," environmentally friendly company.
- *Solar panels.* BP is the world's largest producer of solar power, so BP Connect will use renewable electricity generated from solar panels in its curved canopy to provide 10 to 20 percent of the power needed to operate the station.
- *High-tech pumps and twenty-first century information technology.* Instead of traditional rectangular pumps, BP Connect stations will have curved ones that include an 8-inch touch screen to display news, weather, sports scores, and promotions; enable consumers to order food inside while pumping gas and to pay with a debit/credit card; and print travel maps from in-store Internet kiosks.
- *Sectional design.* Using a wide, open-aisle design, BP Connect will be divided into five sections: food service, beverage, impulse-buying with snacks, convenience-store, and Internet kiosk. Lighting will change with each section. In-store offerings will include fresh fruit and produce, a bakery, and a Wild Bean Coffee quick-serve restaurant. Some stores will have attached car washes.

BP plans on spending $200 million to let its BP Connect stores link to the Internet, which will let drivers check traffic congestion at the gas pumps or go inside and—for a fee—use the Web at a kiosk. The goal: Help BP generate half its retail sales from nonfuel items within five years.

THE MARKETING ISSUES

The initial implementation of the BP Connect marketing plan introduced the first BP Connect outlets in London, England, and Lisbon, Portugal, to enthusiastic reviews. The first BP Connect stations in the United States, opened in Indianapolis, Cleveland, and Atlanta. As the BP Connect rollout continues, BP also continues to watch industry trends. Not only is there huge competition from other petroleum companies, but convenience store, supermarket, and mass-merchandiser chains are moving into the gasoline business. BP will need to use the control phase of the process to compare results with goals and make any modifications, if necessary.

Questions

1 How does BP use its strategic marketing process to allocate resources to opportunities such as the BP Connect concept? Is BP Connect consistent with BP's mission and values? Explain.

2 Conduct a SWOT (strengths, weaknesses, opportunities, threats) analysis for the BP Connect concept—looking forward globally to the next three years.

3 In addition to features such as high-tech pumps and twenty-first century information technology, what other marketing mix activities would you recommend as part of Step 3 of the planning phase?

APPENDIX

A BUILDING AN EFFECTIVE MARKETING PLAN

"New ideas are a dime a dozen," observes Arthur R. Kydd, "and so are new products and new technologies." Kydd should know. As chief executive officer of St. Croix Venture Partners, he and his firm have provided the seed money and venture capital to launch more than 60 startup firms in the last 25 years. Today, those firms have more than 5,000 employees. Kydd explains:

> I get 200 to 300 marketing and business plans a year to look at, and St. Croix provides startup financing for only two or three. What sets a potentially successful idea, product, or technology apart from all the rest is markets and marketing. If you have a real product with a distinctive point of difference that satisfies the needs of customers, you may have a winner. And you get a real feel for this in a well-written marketing or business plan.[1]

This appendix (1) describes what marketing and business plans are, including the purposes and guidelines in writing effective plans, and (2) provides a sample marketing plan.

MARKETING PLANS AND BUSINESS PLANS

After explaining the meanings, purposes, and audiences of marketing plans and business plans, this section describes some writing guidelines for them and what external funders often look for in successful plans.

Meanings, Purposes, and Audiences

A marketing plan is a road map for the marketing activities of an organization for a specified future period of time, such as one year or five years.[2] It is important to note that no single "generic" marketing plan applies to all organizations and all situations. Rather, the specific format for a marketing plan for an organization depends on the following:

- *The target audience and purpose.* Elements included in a particular marketing plan depend heavily on (1) who the audience is and (2) what its purpose is. A marketing plan for an internal audience seeks to point the direction for future marketing activities and is sent to all individuals in the organization who must implement the plan or who will be affected by it. If the plan is directed to an external audience, such as friends, banks, venture capitalists, or potential investors, for the purpose of raising capital, it has the additional function of being an important sales document. In this case, it contains elements such as the strategic plan/focus, organization, structure, and biographies of key personnel that would rarely appear in an internal marketing plan. Also, the financial information is far more detailed when the plan is used to raise outside capital. The elements of a marketing plan for each of these two audiences are compared in Figure A–1.
- *The kind and complexity of the organization.* A small neighborhood restaurant has a somewhat different marketing plan than Nestlé, which serves international markets. The restaurant's plan would be relatively simple and directed at serving customers in a local market. In Nestlé's case, because there is a hierarchy of marketing plans, various levels of detail would be used—such as the entire organization, the business unit, or the product/product line.
- *The industry.* Both the restaurant serving a local market and Medtronic, selling heart pacemakers globally, analyze competition. Not only are their geographic thrusts far different, but the complexities of their offerings and, hence, the time periods likely to be covered by their plans also differ. A one-year marketing plan may be adequate for the restaurant, but Medtronic may need a five-year planning horizon because product-development cycles for complex, new medical devices may be three or four years.

In contrast to a marketing plan, a **business plan** is a road map for the entire organization for a specified future period of time, such as one year or five years.[3] A key difference between a marketing plan and a business plan is that the business plan contains details on the research and development (R&D)/operations/manufacturing activities of the organization. Even for a manufacturing business, the marketing plan is probably 60 or 70 percent of the entire business plan. For businesses like a small restaurant

Element of the plan	Marketing plan		Business plan	
	For internal audience (to direct the firm)	For external audience (to raise capital)	For internal audience (to direct the firm)	For external audience (to raise capital)
1. Executive summary	✓	✓	✓	✓
2. Description of company		✓		✓
3. Strategic plan/focus		✓		✓
4. Situation analysis	✓	✓	✓	✓
5. Market-product focus	✓	✓	✓	✓
6. Marketing program strategy and tactics	✓	✓	✓	✓
7. R&D and operations program			✓	✓
8. Financial projections	✓	✓	✓	✓
9. Organization structure		✓		✓
10. Implementation plan	✓	✓	✓	✓
11. Evaluation and control	✓		✓	
Appendix A: Biographies of key personnel		✓		✓
Appendix B, etc.: Details on other topics	✓	✓	✓	✓

FIGURE A–1
Elements in typical marketing and business plans targeted at different audiences

or an auto repair shop, their marketing and business plans are virtually identical. The elements of a business plan typically targeted at internal and external audiences appear in the two right-hand columns in Figure A–1.

The Most-Asked Questions by Outside Audiences

Lenders and prospective investors reading a business or marketing plan that is used to seek new capital are probably the toughest audiences to satisfy. Their most-asked questions include the following:

1. Is the business or marketing idea valid?
2. Is there something unique or distinctive about the product or service that separates it from substitutes and competitors?
3. Is there a clear market for the product or service?
4. Are the financial projections realistic and healthy?
5. Are the key management and technical personnel capable, and do they have a track record in the industry in which they must compete?
6. Does the plan clearly describe how those providing capital will get their money back and make a profit?

Rhonda M. Abrahms, author of *The Successful Business Plan,* observes that "within the first five minutes of reading your . . . plan, readers must perceive that the answers to these questions are favorable."[4] While her comments apply to plans seeking to raise capital, the first five questions just listed apply equally well to plans for internal audiences.

Writing and Style Suggestions

There are no magic one-size-fits-all guidelines for writing successful marketing and business plans. Still, the following writing and style guidelines generally apply:[5]

- Use a direct, professional writing style. Use appropriate business terms without jargon. Present and future tenses with active voice ("I will write an effective marketing plan.") are generally better than past tense and passive voice ("An effective marketing plan was written by me.").

- Be positive and specific to convey potential success. At the same time, avoid superlatives ("terrific," "wonderful"). Specifics are better than glittering generalities. Use numbers for impact, justifying projections with reasonable quantitative assumptions, where possible.
- Use bullet points for succinctness and emphasis. As with the list you are reading, bullets enable key points to be highlighted effectively.
- Use A-level (the first level) and B-level (the second level) headings under the numbered section headings to help readers make easy transitions from one topic to another. This also forces the writer to organize the plan more carefully. Use these headings liberally, at least one every 200 to 300 words.
- Use visuals where appropriate. Photos, illustrations, graphs, and charts enable massive amounts of information to be presented succinctly.
- Shoot for a plan 15 to 35 pages in length, not including financial projections and appendixes. An uncomplicated small business may require only 15 pages, while a high-technology start-up may require more than 35 pages.
- Use care in layout, design, and presentation. Laser printers give a more professional look than ink-jet printers do. Use 11- or 12-point type (you are now reading 10.5-point type) in the text. Use a serif type (with "feet," like that you are reading now) in the text because it is easier to read, and sans serif (without "feet") in graphs and charts like Figure A–1. A bound report with a nice cover and clear title page adds professionalism.

These guidelines are used, where possible, in the sample marketing plan that follows.

SAMPLE FIVE-YEAR MARKETING PLAN FOR PARADISE KITCHENS,® INC.

To help interpret the marketing plan for Paradise Kitchens, Inc., that follows, we will describe the company and suggest some guidelines in interpreting the plan.

Background on Paradise Kitchens, Inc.

With a degree in chemical engineering, Randall F. Peters spent 15 years working for General Foods and Pillsbury with a number of diverse responsibilities: plant operations, R&D, restaurant operations, and new business development. His wife Leah, with degrees in both molecular cellular biology and food science, held various Pillsbury executive positions in new category development and packaged goods, and restaurant R&D. In the company's start-up years, Paradise Kitchens survived on the savings of Randy and Leah, the cofounders. With their backgrounds, they decided Randy should serve as president and CEO of Paradise Kitchens, and Leah should focus on R&D and corporate strategy.

Interpreting the Marketing Plan

The marketing plan on the next pages, based on an actual Paradise Kitchens plan, is directed at an external audience (see Figure A–1). To protect proprietary information about the company, some details and dates have been altered, but the basic logic of the plan has been kept.

Notes in the margins next to the Paradise Kitchens plan fall into two categories:

1. *Substantive notes* are in blue boxes. These notes elaborate on the significance of an element in the marketing plan and are keyed to chapter references in this textbook.
2. *Writing style, format, and layout notes* are in red boxes and explain the editorial or visual rationale for the element.

A closing word of encouragement: Writing an effective marketing plan is hard, but challenging and satisfying, work. Dozens of the authors' students have used effective marketing plans they wrote for class in their interviewing portfolio to show prospective employers what they could do and to help them get their first job.

Color-coding Legend

Blue boxes explain significance of Marketing Plan elements

Red boxes give writing style, format, and layout guidelines

The Table of Contents provides quick access to the topics in the plan, usually organized by section and subsection headings.

Seen by many experts as the single most important element in the plan, the two-page Executive Summary "sells" the plan to readers through its clarity and brevity. For space reasons, it is not shown here, but the Building Your Marketing Plan exercise at the end of Chapter 2 asks the reader to write an Executive Summary for this plan.

The Company Description highlights the recent history and recent successes of the organization.

The Strategic Focus and Plan sets the strategic direction for the entire organization, a direction with which proposed actions of the marketing plan must be consistent. This section is not included in all marketing plans. See Chapter 2.

The qualitative Mission/Vision statement focuses the activities of Paradise Kitchens for the stakeholder groups to be served. See Chapter 2.

FIVE-YEAR MARKETING PLAN
Paradise Kitchens,® Inc.

Table of Contents

1. Executive Summary

2. Company Description

Paradise Kitchens®, Inc., was started by cofounders Randall F. Peters and Leah E. Peters to develop and market Howlin' Coyote® Chili, a unique line of single serve and microwaveable Southwestern/Mexican style frozen chili products. The Howlin' Coyote line of chili was first introduced into the Minneapolis–St. Paul market and expanded to Denver two years later and Phoenix two years after that.

To the Company's knowledge, Howlin' Coyote is the only premium-quality, authentic Southwestern/Mexican style, frozen chili sold in U.S. grocery stores. Its high quality has gained fast, widespread acceptance in these markets. In fact, same-store sales doubled in the last year for which data are available. The Company believes the Howlin' Coyote brand can be extended to other categories of Southwestern/Mexican food products, such as tacos, enchiladas, and burritos.

Paradise Kitchens believes its high-quality, high-price strategy has proven successful. This marketing plan outlines how the Company will extend its geographic coverage from 3 markets to 20 markets by the year 2010.

3. Strategic Focus and Plan

This section covers three aspects of corporate strategy that influence the marketing plan: (1) the mission/vision, (2) goals, and (3) core competence/sustainable competitive advantage of Paradise Kitchens.

<u>Mission/Vision</u>

The mission and vision of Paradise Kitchens is to market lines of high-quality Southwestern/Mexican food products at premium prices that satisfy consumers in this fast-growing food segment while providing challenging career opportunities for employees and above-average returns to stockholders.

The Goals section sets both the nonfinancial and financial targets—where possible in quantitative terms—against which the company's performance will be measured. See Chapter 2.

Lists use parallel construction to improve readability—in this case a series of infinitives starting with "To . . ."

Photos or sample ads can illustrate key points effectively, even if they are not in color as they appear here.

A brief caption on photos and sample ads ties them to the text and highlights the reason for being included.

Goals

For the coming five years Paradise Kitchens seeks to achieve the following goals:

- Nonfinancial goals
  1. To retain its present image as the highest-quality line of Southwestern/ Mexican products in the food categories in which it competes.
  2. To enter 17 new metropolitan markets.
  3. To achieve national distribution in two convenience store or supermarket chains by 2005 and five by 2006.
  4. To add a new product line every third year.
  5. To be among the top five chili lines—regardless of packaging (frozen or canned) in one-third of the metro markets in which it competes by 2006 and two-thirds by 2008.
- Financial goals
  1. To obtain a real (inflation-adjusted) growth in earnings per share of 8 percent per year over time.
  2. To obtain a return on equity of at least 20 percent.
  3. To have a public stock offering by the year 2006.

Core Competency and Sustainable Competitive Advantage

In terms of core competency, Paradise Kitchens seeks to achieve a unique ability to (1) provide distinctive, high-quality chilies and related products using Southwestern/Mexican recipes that appeal to and excite contemporary tastes for these products and (2) deliver these products to the customer's table using effective manufacturing and distribution systems that maintain the Company's quality standards.

In keeping with the goal of achieving national distribution through chains, Paradise Kitchens recently obtained distribution through a convenience store chain where it uses this point-of-purchase ad that adheres statically to the glass door of the freezer case.

To translate these core competencies into a sustainable competitive advantage, the Company will work closely with key suppliers and distributors to build the relationships and alliances necessary to satisfy the high taste standards of our customers.

To improve readability, each numbered section usually starts on a new page. (This is not done in this plan to save space.)

The Situation Analysis is a snapshot to answer the question, "Where are we now?" See Chapter 2.

The SWOT Analysis identifies strengths, weaknesses, opportunities, and threats to provide a solid foundation as a springboard to identify subsequent actions in the marketing plan. See Chapter 2.

Each long table, graph, or photo is given a figure number and title. It then appears as soon as possible after the first reference in the text, accommodating necessary page breaks. This also avoids breaking long tables like this one in the middle. Short tables or graphs that are less than 1 ½ inches are often inserted in the text without figure numbers because they don't cause serious problems with page breaks.

Effective tables seek to summarize a large amount of information in a short amount of space.

4. Situation Analysis

This situation analysis starts with a snapshot of the current environment in which Paradise Kitchens finds itself by providing a brief SWOT (strengths, weaknesses, opportunities, threats) analysis. After this overview, the analysis probes ever-finer levels of detail: industry, competitors, company, and consumers.

SWOT Analysis

Figure 1 shows the internal and external factors affecting the market opportunities for Paradise Kitchens. Stated briefly, this SWOT analysis highlights the great strides taken by the company since its products first appeared on grocers' shelves. In the

Figure 1. SWOT Analysis for Paradise Kitchens

Internal Factors	**Strengths**	**Weaknesses**
Management	Experienced and entrepreneurial management and board	Small size can restrict options
Offerings	Unique, high-quality, high-price products	Many lower-quality, lower-price competitors
Marketing	Distribution in three markets with excellent acceptance	No national awareness or distribution; restricted shelf space in the freezer section
Personnel	Good workforce, though small; little turnover	Big gap if key employee leaves
Finance	Excellent growth in sales revenues	Limited resources may restrict growth opportunities when compared to giant competitors
Manufacturing	Sole supplier ensures high quality	Lack economies of scale of huge competitors
R&D	Continuing efforts to ensure quality in delivered products	Lack of canning and microwavable food processing expertise
External Factors	**Opportunities**	**Threats**
Consumer/Social	Upscale market, likely to be stable; Southwestern/Mexican food category is fast-growing segment due to growth in Hispanic American population and desire for spicier foods	Premium price may limit access to mass markets; consumers value a strong brand name
Competitive	Distinctive name and packaging in its markets	Not patentable; competitors can attempt to duplicate product; others better able to pay slotting fees
Technological	Technical breakthroughs enable smaller food producers to achieve many economies available to large competitors	Competitors have gained economies in canning and microwavable food processing
Economic	Consumer income is high; convenience important to U.S. households	More households "eating out," and bringing prepared take-out into home
Legal/Regulatory	High U.S. Food & Drug Admin. standards eliminate fly-by-night competitors	Mergers among large competitors being approved by government

The text discussion of Figure 1 (the SWOT Analysis table) elaborates on its more important elements. This "walks" the reader through the information from the vantage of the plan's writer.

The Industry Analysis section provides the backdrop for the subsequent, more detailed analysis of competition, the company, and the company's customers. Without an in-depth understanding of the industry, the remaining analysis may be misdirected. See Chapter 2.

Sales of Mexican entrees are significant and provide a variety of future opportunities for Paradise Kitchens.

Even though relatively brief, this in-depth treatment of sales of Mexican foods in the United States demonstrates to the plan's readers the company's understanding of the industry in which it competes.

As with the Industry Analysis, the Competitors Analysis demonstrates that the company has a realistic understanding of its major chili competitors and their marketing strategies. Again, a realistic assessment gives confidence that subsequent marketing actions in the plan rest on a solid foundation. See Chapters 2, 3, 8, 9, and 18.

Company's favor internally are its strengths of an experienced management team and board of directors, excellent acceptance of its lines in the three metropolitan markets in which it competes, and a strong manufacturing and distribution system to serve these limited markets. Favorable external factors (opportunities) include the increasing appeal of Southwestern/Mexican foods, the strength of the upscale market for the Company's products, and food-processing technological breakthroughs that make is easier for smaller food producers to compete.

Among unfavorable factors, the main weakness is the limited size of Paradise Kitchens relative to its competitors in terms of the depth of the management team, available financial resources, and national awareness and distribution of product lines. Threats include the danger that the Company's premium prices may limit access to mass markets and competition from the "eating-out" and "take-out" markets.

Industry Analysis: Trends in Frozen and Mexican Foods

Frozen Foods. According to *Grocery Headquarters,* consumers are flocking to the frozen food section of grocery retailers. The reasons: hectic lifestyles demanding increased convenience and an abundance of new, tastier, and nutritious products.[6] By 2004, total sales of frozen food in supermarkets, drugstores, and mass merchandisers, such as Target and Costco (excluding Wal-Mart) reached $27.6 billion. Prepared frozen meals, which are defined as meals or entrees that are frozen and require minimal preparation, accounted for $7.3 billion, or 26 percent of the total frozen food market.

Sales of Mexican entrees totaled $506 million.[7] Heavy consumers of frozen meals, those who eat five or more meals every two weeks, tend to be kids, teens, and young adults 35–44 years old.[8]

Mexican Foods. Currently, Mexican foods such as burritos, enchiladas, and tacos are used in two-thirds of American households. These trends reflect a generally more favorable attitude on the part of all Americans toward spicy foods that include red chili peppers. The growing Hispanic population in the U.S., about 36 million and almost $600 billion in purchasing power in 2004, partly explains the increasing demand for Mexican food.[9]

Competitors in the Chili Market

The chili market represents over $500 million in annual sales. On average, consumers buy five to six servings annually, according to the NPD Group. The products fall primarily into two groups: canned chili (70 percent of sales) and dry chili (25 percent of sales). The remaining 5 percent of sales go to frozen chili products. Besides Howlin' Coyote, Stouffer's offers a frozen chili product (Slowfire Classic's Chunky Beef & Bean Chili) as part of its broad line of frozen dinners and entrees.[10]

This page uses a "block" style and does *not* indent each paragraph, although an extra space separates each paragraph. Compare this page with page 50, which has indented paragraphs. Most readers find indented paragraphs in marketing plans and long reports are easier to follow.

The Company Analysis provides details of the company's strengths and marketing strategies that will enable it to achieve the mission, vision, and goals identified earlier. See Chapter 2.

The higher-level "A heading" of Customer Analysis has a more dominant typeface and position than the lower-level "B heading" of Customer Characteristics. These headings introduce the reader to the sequence and level of topics covered. The organization of this textbook uses this kind of structure and headings.

Satisfying customers and providing genuine value to them is why organizations exist in a market economy. This section addresses the question of "Who are the customers for Paradise Kitchens's products?" See Chapters 5, 6, 7, 8, and 9.

Bluntly put, the major disadvantage of the segment's dominant product, canned chili, is that it does not taste very good. A taste test described in an issue of *Consumer Reports* magazine ranked 26 canned chili products "poor" to "fair" in overall sensory quality. The study concluded, "Chili doesn't have to be hot to be good. But really good chili, hot or mild, doesn't come out of a can."

Company Analysis

The husband-and-wife team that cofounded Paradise Kitchens, Inc., has 44 years of experience between them in the food-processing business. Both have played key roles in the management of the Pillsbury Company. They are being advised by a highly seasoned group of business professionals, who have extensive understanding of the requirements for new product development.

The Company now uses a single outside producer with which it works closely to maintain the consistently high quality required in its products. The greater volume has increased production efficiencies, resulting in a steady decrease in the cost of goods sold.

Customer Analysis

In terms of customer analysis, this section describes (1) the characteristics of customers expected to buy Howlin' Coyote products and (2) health and nutrition concerns of Americans today.

Customer Characteristics. Demographically, chili products in general are purchased by consumers representing a broad range of socioeconomic backgrounds. Howlin' Coyote chili is purchased chiefly by consumers who have achieved higher levels of education and whose income is $50,000 and higher. These consumers represent 50 percent of canned and dry mix chili users.

The household buying Howlin' Coyote has one to three people in it. Among married couples, Howlin' Coyote is predominantly bought by households in which both spouses work. While women are a majority of the buyers, single men represent a significant segment.

Because the chili offers a quick way to make a tasty meal, the product's biggest users tend to be those most pressed for time. Howlin' Coyote's premium pricing also means that its purchasers are skewed toward the higher end of the income range. Buyers range in age from 25 to 54 and often live in the western United States, where spicy foods are more readily eaten.

The five Howlin' Coyote entrees offer a quick, tasty meal with high-quality ingredients.

This section demonstrates the company's insights into a major trend that has a potentially large impact.

Health and Nutrition Concerns. Coverage of food issues in the U.S. media is often erratic and occasionally alarmist. Because Americans are concerned about their diets, studies from organizations of widely varying credibility frequently receive significant attention from the major news organizations. For instance, a study of fat levels of movie popcorn was reported in all the major media. Similarly, studies on the healthfulness of Mexican food have received prominent "play" in print and broadcast reports. The high caloric levels of much Mexican and Southwestern-style food have been widely reported and often exaggerated. Some Mexican frozen food competitors, such as Don Miguel, Mission Foods, Ruiz Foods, and Jose Ole, plan to offer or have recently offered more "carb-friendly" and "fat-friendly" products in response to this concern.

Howlin' Coyote is already lower in calories, fat, and sodium than its competitors, and those qualities are not currently being stressed in its promotions. Instead, in the space and time available for promotions, Howlin' Coyote's taste, convenience, and flexibility are stressed.

Size of headings should give a professional look to the report and not overwhelm the reader. These two headings are too large.

5. Market-Product Focus

This section describes the five-year marketing and product objectives for Paradise Kitchens and the target markets, points of difference, and positioning of its lines of Howlin' Coyote chilies.

Marketing and Product Objectives

Howlin' Coyote's marketing intent is to take full advantage of its brand potential while building a base from which other revenue sources can be mined—both in and out of the retail grocery business. These are detailed in four areas below:

As noted in Chapter 10, the chances of success for a new product are significantly increased if objectives are set for the product itself and if target market segments are identified for it. This section makes these explicit for Paradise Kitchens. The objectives also serve as the planned targets against which marketing activities are measured in program implementation and control.

- Current markets. Current markets will be grown by expanding brand and flavor distribution at the retail level. In addition, same-store sales will be grown by increasing consumer awareness and repeat purchases, thereby leading to the more efficient broker/warehouse distribution channel.
- New markets. By the end of Year 5, the chili, salsa, burrito, and enchilada business will be expanded to a total of 20 metropolitan areas. This will represent 70 percent of U.S. food store sales.
- Food service. Food service sales will include chili products and smothering sauces. Sales are expected to reach $693,000 by the end of Year 3 and $1.5 million by the end of Year 5.
- New products. Howlin' Coyote's brand presence will be expanded at the retail

A heading should be spaced closer to the text that follows (and that it describes) than the preceding section to avoid confusion for the reader. This rule is not followed for the Target Markets heading, which now unfortunately appears to "float" between the preceding and following paragraphs.

This section identifies the specific niches or target markets toward which the company's products are directed. When appropriate and when space permits, this section often includes a market-product grid. See Chapter 9.

An organization cannot grow by offering only "me-too products." The greatest single factor in a new product's failure is the lack of significant "points of difference" that sets it apart from competitors' substitutes. This section makes these points of difference explicit. See Chapter 10.

A positioning strategy helps communicate the company's unique points of difference of its products to prospective customers in a simple, clear way. This section describes this positioning. See Chapters 9 and 10.

level through the addition of new products in the frozen-foods section. This will be accomplished through new product concept screening in Year 1 to identify new potential products. These products will be brought to market in Years 2 and 3.

Target Markets

The primary target market for Howlin' Coyote products is households with one to three people, where often both adults work, with individual income typically above $50,000 per year. These households contain more experienced, adventurous consumers of Southwestern/Mexican food and want premium quality products.

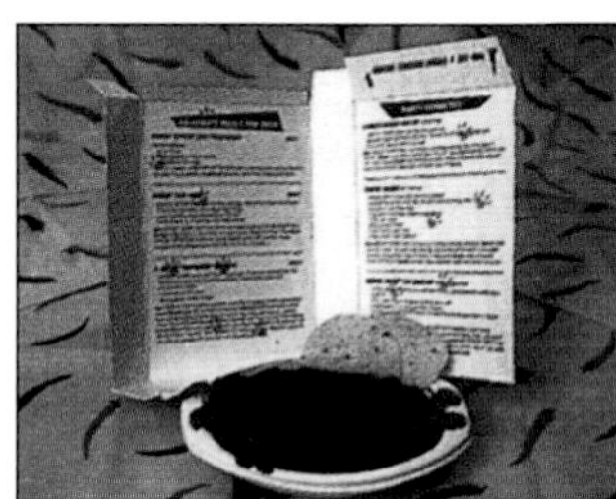

To help buyers see the many different uses for Howlin' Coyote chili, recipes are even printed on the *inside* of the packages.

Points of Difference

The "points of difference"—characteristics that make Howlin' Coyote chilies unique relative to competitors—fall into three important areas:

- Unique taste and convenience. No known competitor offers a high-quality, "authentic" frozen chili in a range of flavors. And no existing chili has the same combination of quick preparation and home-style taste that Howlin' Coyote does.
- Taste trends. The American palate is increasingly intrigued by hot spices. In response to this trend, Howlin' Coyote brands offer more "kick" than most other prepared chilies.
- Premium packaging. Howlin' Coyote's packaging graphics convey the unique, high-quality product contained inside and the product's nontraditional positioning.

Positioning

In the past chili products have been either convenient or tasty, but not both. Howlin' Coyote pairs these two desirable characteristics to obtain a positioning in consumers' minds as very high-quality "authentic Southwestern/Mexican tasting" chilies that can be prepared easily and quickly.

Everything that has gone before in the marketing plan sets the stage for the marketing mix actions—the 4 Ps—covered in the marketing program. See Chapters 10 through 18.

The section describes in detail three key elements of the company's product strategy: the product line, its quality and how this is achieved, and its "cutting edge" packaging. See Chapters 10 and 11.

This Price Strategy section makes the company's price point very clear, along with its price position relative to potential substitutes. When appropriate and when space permits, this section might contain a break-even analysis. See Chapter 12.

This "introductory overview" sentence tells the reader the topics covered in the section—in this case in-store demonstrations, recipes, and cents-off coupons. While this sentence may be omitted in short memos or plans, it helps readers see where the text is leading. These sentences are used throughout this plan. This textbook also generally utilizes these introductory overview sentences to aid your comprehension.

6. Marketing Program

The four marketing mix elements of the Howlin' Coyote chili marketing program are detailed below. Note that "chile" is the vegetable and "chili" is the dish.

Product Strategy

After first summarizing the product line, the approach to product quality and packaging are covered.

Product Line. Howlin' Coyote chili, retailing for $3.99 for an 11-ounce serving, is available in five flavors. The five are Green Chile Chili, Red Chile Chili, Beef and Black Bean Chili, Chicken Chunk Chili, and Mean Bean Chili.

Unique Product Quality. The flavoring systems of the Howlin' Coyote chilies are proprietary. The products' tastiness is due to extra care lavished upon the ingredients during production. The ingredients used are of unusually high quality. Meats are low-fat cuts and are fresh, not frozen, to preserve cell structure and moistness. Chilies are fire-roasted for fresher taste. Tomatoes and vegetables are select quality. No preservatives or artificial flavors are used.

Packaging. Reflecting the "cutting edge" marketing strategy of its producers, Howlin' Coyote bucks conventional wisdom in packaging. It avoids placing predictable photographs of the product on its containers. Instead, Howlin' Coyote's package shows a Southwestern motif that communicates the product's out-of-the-ordinary positioning.

The Southwestern motif makes Howlin' Coyote's packages stand out in a supermarket's freezer case.

Price Strategy

Howlin' Coyote Chili is, at $3.99 for an 11-ounce package, priced comparably to the other frozen offerings and higher than the canned and dried chili varieties. However, the significant taste advantages it has over canned chilies and the convenience advantages over dried chilies justify this pricing strategy.

Promotion Strategy

Key promotion programs feature in-store demonstrations, recipes, and cents-off coupons.

Elements of the Promotion Strategy are highlighted in terms of the three key promotional activities the company is emphasizing: in-store demonstrations, recipes, and cents-off coupons. For space reasons the company's online strategies are not shown in the plan. See Chapters 15, 16, 17, and 18.

In-Store Demonstrations. In-store demonstrations enable consumers to try Howlin' Coyote products and discover their unique qualities. Demos will be conducted regularly in all markets to increase awareness and trial purchases.

Recipes. Because the products' flexibility of use is a key selling point, recipes are offered to consumers to stimulate use. The recipes are given at all in-store demonstrations, on the back of packages, through a mail-in recipe book offer, and in coupons sent by direct-mail or free-standing inserts.

Another bulleted list adds many details for the reader, including methods of gaining customer awareness, trial, and repeat purchases as Howlin' Coyote enters new metropolitan areas.

Cents-Off Coupons. To generate trial and repeat-purchase of Howlin' Coyote products, coupons are distributed in four ways:

- In Sunday newspaper inserts. These inserts are widely read and help generate awareness.
- In-pack coupons. Each box of Howlin' Coyote chili will contain coupons for $1 off two more packages of the chili. These coupons will be included for the first three months the product is shipped to a new market. Doing so encourages repeat purchases by new users.
- Direct-mail chili coupons. Those households that fit the Howlin' Coyote demographics described previously will be mailed coupons.
- In-store demonstrations. Coupons will be passed out at in-store demonstrations to give an additional incentive to purchase.

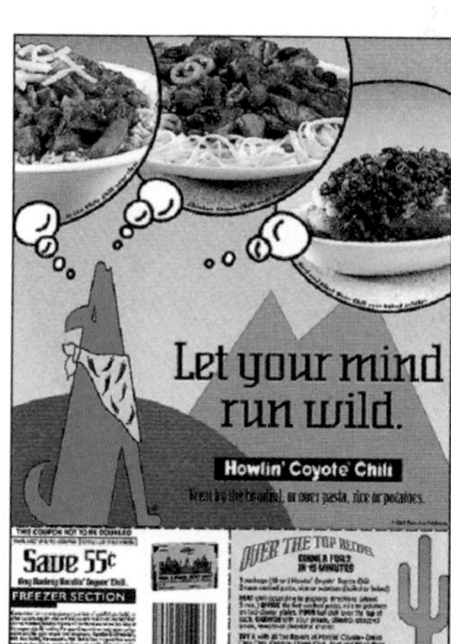

Sunday newspaper inserts encourage consumer trial and provide recipes to show how Howlin' Coyote chili can be used in summer meals.

The Place Strategy is described here in terms of both (1) the present method and (2) the new one to be used when the increased sales volume makes it feasible. See Chapters 13 and 14.

Place (Distribution) Strategy

Howlin' Coyote is distributed in its present markets through a food distributor. The distributor buys the product, warehouses it, and then resells and delivers it to grocery retailers on a store-by-store basis. As sales grow, we will shift to a more efficient system using a broker who sells the products to retail chains and grocery wholesalers.

All the marketing mix decisions covered in the just-described marketing program have both revenue and expense effects. These are summarized in this section of the marketing plan.

7. Financial Data and Projections

Note that this section contains no introductory overview sentence. While the sentence is not essential, many readers prefer to see it to avoid the abrupt start with Past Sales Revenues.

Past Sales Revenues

Historically, Howlin' Coyote has had a steady increase in sales revenues since its introduction in 1997. In 2001, sales jumped spectacularly, due largely to new

The graph shows more clearly the dramatic growth of sales revenue than data in a table would do.

The Five-Year Financial Projections section starts with the judgment forecast of cases sold and the resulting net sales. Gross profit and then operating profit—critical for the company's survival—are projected. An actual plan often contains many pages of computer-generated spreadsheet projections, usually shown in an appendix to the plan.

Because this table is very short, it is woven into the text, rather than given a figure number and title.

Because the plan proposes to enter 17 new metropolitan markets in the coming five years (for a total of 20), it is not possible to simply extrapolate the trend in Figure 2. Instead, management's judgment must be used. Methods of making sales forecasts—including the "lost horse" technique used here—are discussed in Chapter 8.

The Organization of Paradise Kitchens appears here. It reflects the bare-bones organizational structure of successful small businesses. Often a more elaborate marketing plan will show the new positions expected to be added as the firm grows.

Figure 2. Sales Revenues for Paradise Kitchens, Inc.

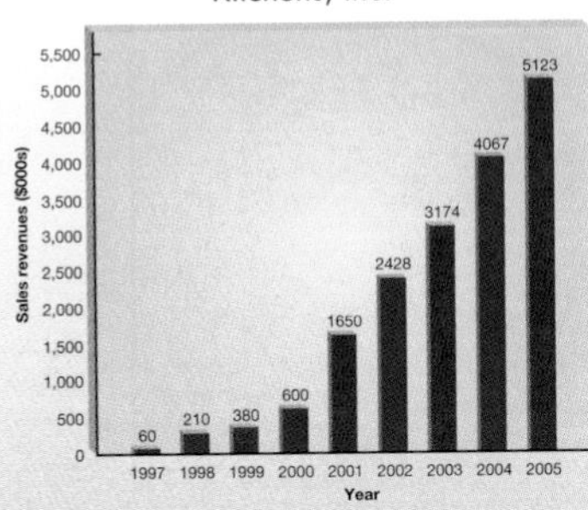

promotion strategies. Sales have continued to rise, but at a less dramatic rate. The trend in sales revenues appears in Figure 2.

Five-Year Projections

Five-year financial projections for Paradise Kitchens appear below:

			Projections				
Financial Element	Units	Actual 2005	Year 1 2006	Year 2 2007	Year 3 2008	Year 4 2009	Year 5 2010
Cases sold	1,000	353	684	889	1,249	1,499	1,799
Net sales	$1,000	5,123	9,913	12,884	18,111	21,733	26,080
Gross profit	$1,000	2,545	4,820	6,527	8,831	10,597	12,717
Operating profit (loss)	$1,000	339	985	2,906	2,805	3,366	4,039

These projections reflect the continuing growth in number of cases sold (with 8 packages of Howlin' Coyote chili per case) and increasing production and distribution economies of scale as sales volume increases.

8. Organization

Paradise Kitchens's present organization appears in Figure 3. It shows the four people reporting to the President. Below this level are both the full-time and part-time employees of the Company.

Figure 3. The Paradise Kitchens Organization

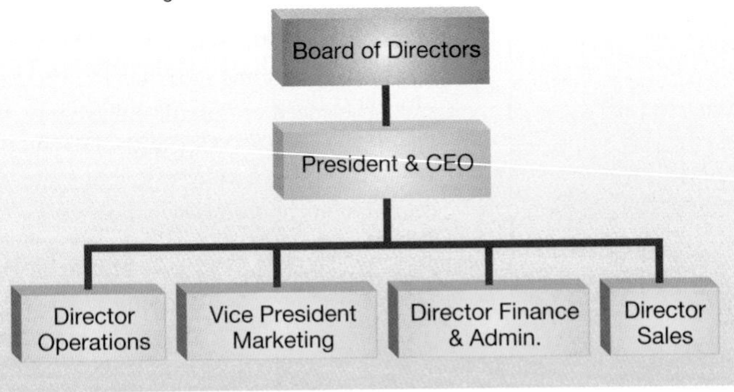

The Implementation Plan shows how the company will turn plans into results. Gantt charts are often used to set deadlines and assign responsibilities for the many tactical marketing decisions needed to enter a new market.

At present Paradise Kitchens operates with full-time employees in only essential positions. It now augments its full-time staff with key advisors, consultants, and subcontractors. As the firm grows, people with special expertise will be added to the staff.

9. Implementation Plan

Introducing Howlin' Coyote chilies to 17 new metropolitan areas is a complex task and requires that creative promotional activities gain consumer awareness and initial trial among the target market households identified earlier. The anticipated rollout schedule to enter these metropolitan markets appears in Figure 4.

Figure 4. Rollout Schedule to Enter New U.S. Markets

Year	New Markets Added	Cumulative Markets	Cumulative Percentage of U.S. Market
Today (2005)	2	5	16
Year 1 (2006)	3	8	21
Year 2 (2007)	4	12	29
Year 3 (2008)	2	14	37
Year 4 (2009)	3	17	45
Year 5 (2010)	3	20	53

The essence of Evaluation and Control is comparing actual sales with the targeted values set in the plan and taking appropriate actions. Note that the section briefly describes a contingency plan for alternative actions, depending on how successful the entry into a new market turns out to be.

The diverse regional tastes in chili will be monitored carefully to assess whether minor modifications may be required in the chili recipes. As the rollout to new metropolitan areas continues, Paradise Kitchens will assess manufacturing and distribution trade-offs. This is important in determining whether to start new production with selected high-quality regional contract packers.

10. Evaluation and Control

Monthly sales targets in cases have been set for Howlin' Coyote chili for each metropolitan area. Actual case sales will be compared with these targets and tactical marketing programs modified to reflect the unique sets of factors in each metropolitan area. The speed of the roll-out program will increase or decrease, depending on Paradise Kitchens's performance in the successive metropolitan markets it enters.

Various appendixes may appear at the end of the plan, depending on the purpose and audience for them. For example, resumes of key personnel or detailed financial spreadsheets often appear in appendixes. For space reasons these are not shown here.

Appendix A. Biographical Sketches of Key Personnel

Appendix B. Detailed Financial Projections

iPod
10,000 songs* in your pocket. Works with Mac® or PC. The new iPod™.
TM & ©2003 Apple Computer, Inc. All rights reserved. *40GB model only. For more information, call 1-800-MY-APPLE or visit www.apple.com/ipod.

CHAPTER 3

SCANNING THE MARKETING ENVIRONMENT

LEARNING OBJECTIVES

After reading this chapter you should be able to:

1 Explain how environmental scanning provides information about social, economic, technological, competitive, and regulatory forces.

2 Describe how social forces such as demographics and culture and economic forces such as macroeconomic conditions and consumer income affect marketing.

3 Describe how technological changes can affect marketing.

4 Discuss the forms of competition that exist in a market, key components of competition, and the impact of competition on corporate structures.

5 Explain the major legislation that ensures competition and regulates the elements of the marketing mix.

IT'S SHOW TIME!

Don't blink, because the world of entertainment is changing faster than anyone imagined possible. Online music, high-definition televisions, digital photography, computer-based media centers, and software for making movies are just some of the many products new to the entertainment industry. The revolution began with the combination of Apple's iPod music player, which can store 10,000 songs in a device smaller than a deck of cards, and its iTunes Music Store, which sells more than 10,000,000 songs each month for just $.99 each. Other new forms of digital entertainment products include digital video recorders (DVRs), which record TV shows on hard drives instead of tape, and home entertainment "hubs," which utilize wireless networks to link digital devices from around the home.

Suddenly the music, television, photography, movie, and computer industries are converging. Musicians, recording companies, television networks, camera companies, movie studios, computer companies, retail stores, and consumers like you are part of a completely different entertainment marketplace. How did this happen? The marketing environment changed!

First, consumers changed. They gradually made it clear that they prefer more convenient and customer-friendly approaches to purchasing music, television programming, movies, and photographs. Second, technology changed. High-speed Internet became available to millions of users, computers with improved storage capabilities and CD burners were introduced, high-resolution displays became smaller and less expensive, and file-transfer software was developed. Third, the regulatory environment changed. You may remember the first file-sharing service, Napster, was sued by the Recording Industry Association of America (RIAA) and ordered to stop helping users exchange copyrighted material. The ruling led to new agreements between music labels and services like iTunes and sparked a worldwide debate about copyright protection. Finally, competitive forces have changed. Companies such as Disney, Pixar, Apple, Hewlett-Packard, Sony, Napster, A&M Records, and many others are now in an environment where they might be competitors or partners. Apple, for example, has created a partnership with Motorola to produce a cell phone that can play iTunes music downloads, but it is competing with Microsoft, Sony, and RealNetworks to become the industry standard in the music-downloading business. All of these changes, and the trends they suggest, led one expert to predict that "how we watch movies, look at photos, listen to music, even read a book promises to change profoundly in the next decade."[1]

Many businesses operate in environments where important forces change. Anticipating and responding to changes such as those experienced by the entertainment industry often means the difference between marketing success and failure. This chapter describes how the marketing environment has changed in the past and how it is likely to change in the future.

ENVIRONMENTAL SCANNING IN THE NEW MILLENNIUM

environmental scanning *Process of acquiring information on events outside the organization to identify and interpret potential trends*

Changes in the marketing environment are a source of opportunities and threats to be managed. The process of continually acquiring information on events occurring outside the organization to identify and interpret potential trends is called **environmental scanning**. Environmental trends typically arise from five sources: social, economic, technological, competitive, and regulatory forces. As shown in Figure 3–1 and described later in this chapter, these forces affect the marketing activities of a firm in numerous ways.

An Environmental Scan of Today's Marketplace

What trends might affect marketing in the future? A firm conducting an environmental scan of the marketplace might uncover key trends such as those listed in Figure 3–2 for each of the five environmental factors.[2] Although the list of trends is far from complete, it reveals the breadth of an environmental scan—from the growing diversity of the U.S. population, to the shift of white-collar work to offshore locations, to the increasing

FIGURE 3–1
Environmental forces affecting the organization, as well as its suppliers and customers

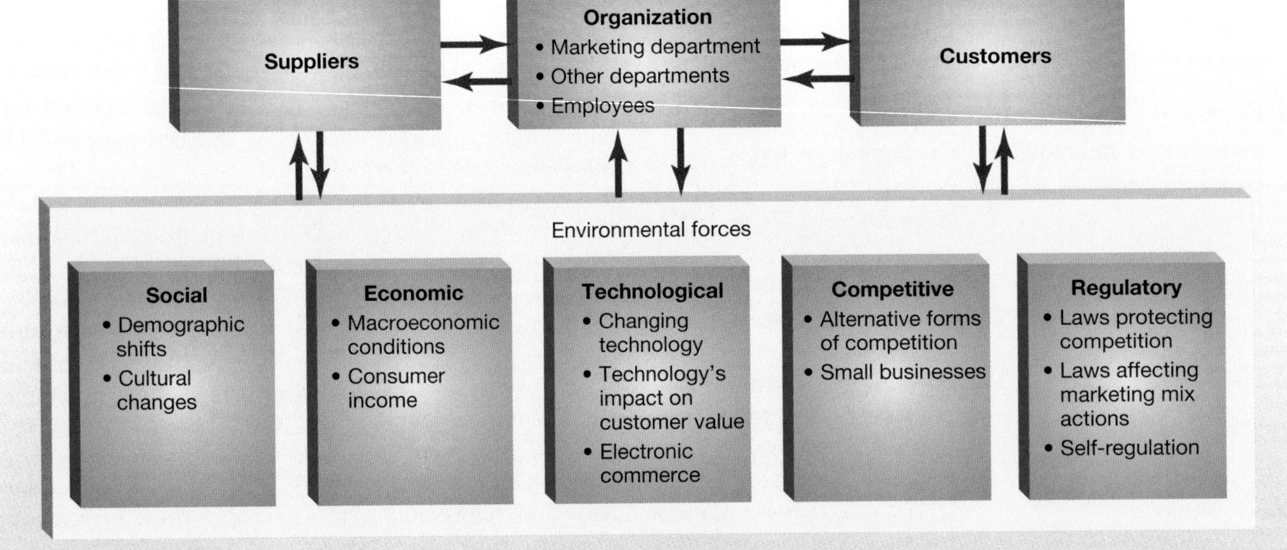

ENVIRONMENTAL FORCE	TREND IDENTIFIED BY AN ENVIRONMENTAL SCAN
Social	• Declining differences in gender roles and buying patterns • Growing diversity of the U.S. population • Decline in smoking and tobacco use throughout the world
Economic	• Increasing military and humanitarian expenditures related to the war on terrorism • The shift of white-collar work to offshore locations • Increase in money management as many workers approach retirement
Technological	• Increasing use of wireless broadband technology • The dramatic growth of the open source (free) software movement, started by Linux • Advances in biotechnology, cosmetic surgery, and cancer drugs
Competitive	• The growing influence of China as the world leader in technology manufacturing • The development of corporate competitive intelligence departments and relationships with federal security agencies • Increased focus on empowering workers to improve performance
Regulatory	• New legislation related to digital copyright and intellectual property protection • Greater concern for privacy and personal information collection • New legislation on Internet taxation, e-mail spam, and domain names

FIGURE 3–2
An environmental scan of today's marketplace

use of wireless technology. These trends affect consumers and the businesses and organizations that serve them. Trends such as these are covered as the five environmental forces are described in the following pages.

SOCIAL FORCES

social forces
Demographic characteristics of the population and its values

The **social forces** of the environment include the demographic characteristics of the population and its values. Changes in these forces can have a dramatic impact on marketing strategy.

Demographics

demographics
Description of a population according to characteristics such as age, gender, ethnicity, income, and occupation

Describing a population according to selected characteristics such as age, gender, ethnicity, income, and occupation is referred to as **demographics**. Several organizations such as the Population Reference Bureau and the United Nations monitor the world population profile, while many other organizations such as the U.S. Census Bureau provide information about the American population.

The World Population at a Glance The most recent estimates indicate that there are 6.4 billion people in the world today, and that the population is likely to grow to 9 billion by 2050. While this growth has led to the term *population explosion,* the increases have not occurred worldwide—they are primarily in the developing countries of Africa, Asia, and Latin America. In fact, India is predicted to have the world's largest population in 2050 with 1.6 billion people, and China will be a close second with 1.4 billion people.[3] Another important global trend is the shifting age structure of the world population. It is expected that the number of people older than 65 will more than double in the coming decades, while the number of youth will grow at a much lower rate. Global income levels and living standards have also been increasing, although the averages across countries are very different.

For marketers, global trends such as these have many implications. Obviously, the relative size of countries such as India and China will mean they represent huge markets for many product categories. Elderly populations in developed countries are likely to save less and begin spending their funds on health care, travel, and other retirement-related products and services. Economic progress in developing countries will lead to growth in entrepreneurship, new markets for infrastructure related to manufacturing, communication, and distribution, and the growth of exports.[4]

The U.S. Population Studies of the demographic characteristics of the U.S. population suggest several important trends. Generally, the population is becoming larger, older, and more diverse. In 2005, the U.S. population was estimated to be 297 million people. If current trends in life expectancy, birthrates, and immigration continue, by 2025 the U.S. population will exceed 350 million people. This growth suggests that niche markets based on age, life stage, family structure, geographic location, and ethnicity will become increasingly important. The global trend toward an older population is particularly true in the United States. Today, there are approximately 35 million people 65 and older. By 2025, this age group will include more than 70 million people, or 20 percent of the population. You may have noticed companies trying to attract older consumers without alienating younger ones. Pepsi, for example, ran an ad featuring a teenage boy at a rock concert who discovers his father is at the same concert. Finally, the term *minority* as it is currently used is likely to become obsolete as the size of most ethnic groups will double by 2025.[5]

baby boomers
Generation of children born between 1946 and 1964

Generation X
Members of the U.S. population born between 1965 and 1976

Generational Cohorts A major reason for the graying of America is that the **baby boomers**—the generation of children born between 1946 and 1964—are growing older. As the 78 million boomers have aged, their participation in the workforce and their earnings have increased, making them an important consumer market. It has been estimated that this group accounts for 56 to 58 percent of the purchases in most consumer product and service categories. In the future, boomers' interests will reflect concern for their children and grandchildren, their own health, and their retirement, and companies will need to position products to respond to these interests. Generally, baby boomers are receptive to anything that makes them feel younger. Olay's Total Effects product line, for example, includes anti-aging moisturizers, cleansing cloths, and restoration treatments designed for this age group.

The baby boom cohort is followed by **Generation X**, which includes the 15 percent of the population born between 1965 and 1976. This period is also known as the baby

Which generational cohorts are these advertisers trying to reach?

MARKETING NEWSNET

After Seeing 23 Million Ads, Generation Y Is Turning 21

There are 72 million members of the Generation Y cohort. About 20 percent of them have already reached the age of 21, and the rest are not far behind. Why is this important? Because much more than legal privileges begin when someone turns 21. This transition to adulthood signals a period when many people graduate from college, look for their first full-time job, start forming their own households, purchase their first new car and home, and select savings and retirement funds. They also begin developing brand loyalties that could last a lifetime. As a result, 21-year-olds are just beginning a path of extraordinary influence on the marketplace.

Generation Y is known as a savvy, demanding, and sometimes marketing-skeptical group, so marketers are eager to better understand them. Would you have guessed any of the following facts about 21-year-olds?

- Number of advertisements received in the past 21 years: 23 million
- Amount a 21-year-old will spend in his or her lifetime: $2,241,141
- Years until a 21-year-old will buy a vacation home: 22
- Percentage of 21-year-olds who have a credit card: 93%
- Hours each week a 21-year-old spends online: 10

Of course, there is a lot more to know about 21-year-olds, but if you watch closely you'll start seeing unique product and service offerings—and maybe a few more ads—designed with just that age in mind.

bust, because the number of children born each year was declining. This is a generation of consumers who are self-reliant, entrepreneurial, supportive of racial and ethnic diversity, and better educated than any previous generation. They are not prone to extravagance and are likely to pursue lifestyles that are a blend of caution, pragmatism, and traditionalism. For example, Generation X is saving, planning for retirement, and taking advantage of 401(k) plans much earlier than the boomer generation. As the baby boomers move into grandparenthood, Generation X is becoming the new parent market. In response, some brands that Generation X helped popularize are expanding their offerings. Tommy Hilfiger and DKNY, for example, have launched children's lines for the babies of Generation X parents.[6]

Generation Y
The 72 million Americans born between 1977 and 1994

The generational cohort labeled **Generation Y** includes the 72 million Americans born between 1977 and 1994. This was a period of increasing births, which resulted from baby boomers having children, and it is often referred to as the echo boom or baby boomlet. Generation Y exerts influence on music, sports, computers, videogames, and especially cell phones. Generation Y views wireless communication as a lifeline to friends and family and has been the first to use text messaging, cell phone games, and built-in cameras. This is also the group that includes recent and future 21-year-olds—the beginning of adult responsibilities and many new consumer activities. The accompanying Marketing NewsNet describes some of the important changes that many "Gen Ys" face.[7] The term *millennials* is also used, with inconsistent definitions, to refer to younger members of Generation Y and sometimes to Americans born since 1994.

Because the members of each generation are distinctive in their attitudes and consumer behavior, marketers have been studying the many groups or cohorts that make up the marketplace and have developed *generational marketing* programs for them. In addition, global marketers have discovered that many of the American generational differences also exist outside of the United States.[8]

Population Shifts A major regional shift in the U.S. population toward western and southern states is underway. During the period from 1995 to 2025, California, New Mexico, Hawaii, Arizona, and Nevada are expected to grow at the fastest rates. Three states—California, Texas, and Florida—will account for 45 percent of the population change in the United States, gaining more than 6 million people in each state.[9]

To assist marketers in gathering data on the population, the Census Bureau has developed a classification system to describe the varying locations of the population. The system consists of two types of *statistical areas*:

- A *metropolitan statistical area* has at least one urbanized area of 50,000 or more people, and adjacent territory that has a high degree of social and economic integration.
- A *micropolitan statistical area* has at least one urban cluster of at least 10,000 but less than 50,000 people, and adjacent territory that has a high degree of social and economic integration.

If a metropolitan statistical area contains a population of 2.5 million or more, it may be subdivided into smaller areas called *metropolitan divisions*. In addition, adjacent metropolitan statistical areas and micropolitan statistical areas may be grouped into *combined statistical areas*.[10] There are currently 362 metropolitan statistical areas, which include 83 percent of the population, and 573 micropolitan areas, which include 10 percent of the population.

Racial and Ethnic Diversity A notable trend is the changing racial and ethnic composition of the U.S. population. Approximately one in four U.S. residents is African American, American Indian, Asian, Pacific Islander, or a representative of another racial or ethnic group. Diversity is further evident in the variety of peoples that make up these groups. For example, Asians consist of Asian Indians, Chinese, Filipinos, Japanese, Koreans, and Vietnamese. For the first time, the 2000 Census allowed respondents to choose more than one of the six race options, and more than 6 million reported more than one race. Hispanics, who may be from any race, currently make up 12 percent of the U.S. population and are represented by Mexicans, Puerto Ricans, Cubans, and others of Central and South American ancestry. The United States is becoming more diverse; but Figure 3–3 suggests that the racial and ethnic groups tend to be concentrated in geographic regions.[11]

While the growing size of these groups has been identified through new Census data, their economic impact on the marketplace is also very noticeable. By 2007, Hispanics, African Americans, and Asians will spend $900 billion, $850 billion, and

FIGURE 3–3
Racial and ethnic concentrations in the United States (excluding whites)

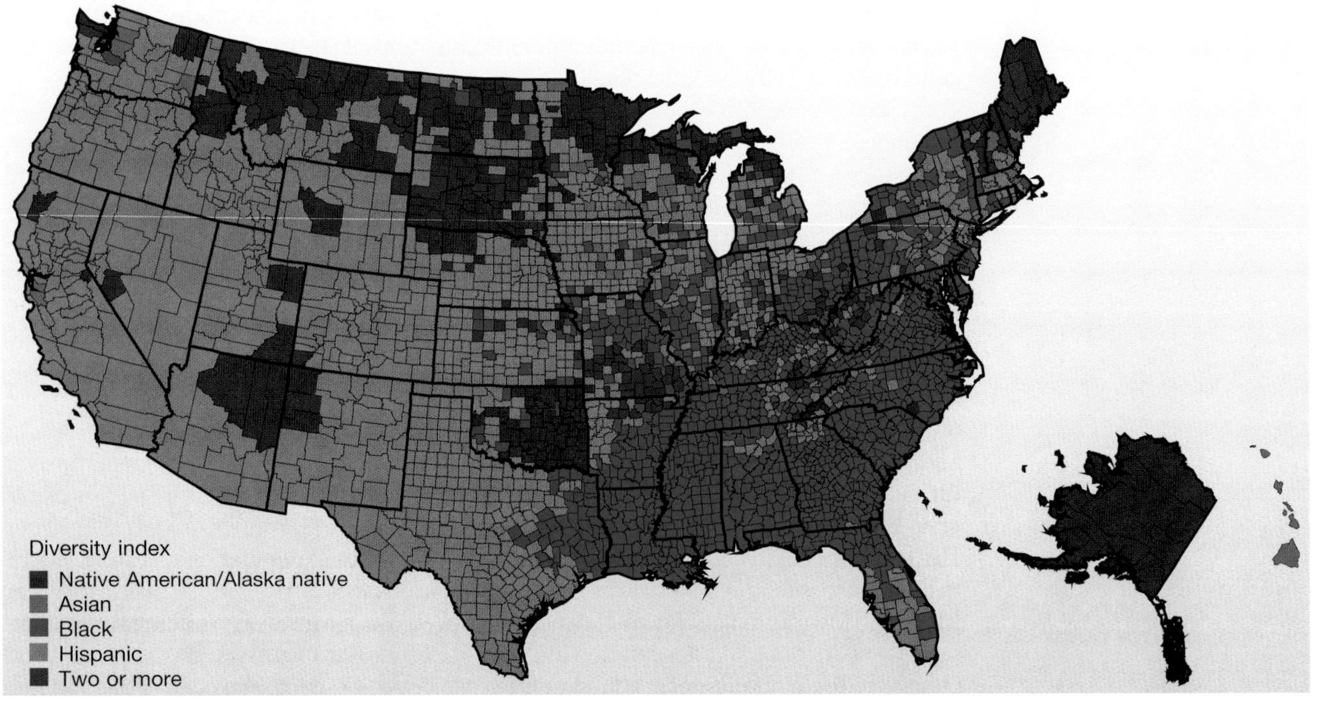

SOURCE: *American Demographics,* November 2002.

multicultural marketing
Marketing programs that reflect unique aspects of different races

$455 billion each year, respectively. To adapt to this new marketplace, many companies are developing **multicultural marketing** programs, which are combinations of the marketing mix that reflect the unique attitudes, ancestry, communication preferences, and lifestyles of different races. Because businesses must now market their products to a consumer base with many racial and ethnic identities, in-depth marketing research that allows an accurate understanding of each culture is essential.[12]

Culture

culture
Set of values, ideas, and attitudes that are learned and shared among the members of a group

A second social force, **culture**, incorporates the set of values, ideas, and attitudes that are learned and shared among the members of a group. Because many of the elements of culture influence consumer buying patterns, monitoring national and global cultural trends is important for marketing. Cross-cultural analysis needed for global marketing is discussed in Chapter 7.

Culture includes values, which vary with age but tend to be very similar for men and women. All age groups, for example, rank "protecting the family" and "honesty" as the most important values. Consumers under 20 rank "friendship" third, while the 20 to 29 and 30 to 39 age groups rank "self-esteem" and "health and fitness" as their third most important values, respectively. These values are reflected in the growth of products and services that consumers believe are consistent with their values. Concern for health and fitness is one reason 51 million people in the United States report that they are trying to control their weight. But they are less likely to "diet" than they are to create a healthy and balanced lifestyle. Stouffer's Lean Cuisine is trying to respond to the trend by suggesting that health-conscious consumers don't have to sacrifice taste for nutrition with its "Do something good for yourself" campaign. Similarly, Jenny Craig's primary market is 35- to 55-year-old people who are interested in a healthier lifestyle. Other products related to this trend include vitamins, exercise equipment, fitness drinks, and magazines such as *Fitness, Runner's World,* and *Walking.*[13]

Concept Check

1. Describe three generational cohorts.
2. Why are many companies developing multicultural marketing programs?
3. How are important values such as "health and fitness" reflected in the marketplace today?

ECONOMIC FORCES

economy
Income, expenditures, and resources that affect the cost of running a business or household

The second component of the environmental scan, the **economy**, pertains to the income, expenditures, and resources that affect the cost of running a business and household. We'll consider two aspects of these economic forces: a macroeconomic view of the marketplace and a microeconomic perspective of consumer income.

Macroeconomic Conditions

Of particular concern at the macroeconomic level is the inflationary or recessionary state of the economy, whether actual or perceived by consumers or businesses. In an inflationary economy, the cost to produce and buy products and services escalates as prices increase. From a marketing standpoint, if prices rise faster than consumer incomes, the number of items consumers can buy decreases. This relationship is evident in the cost of a college education. Today, the average cost of one year of college is approximately 16 percent of the annual income of an average middle-class family, compared with 9 percent in 1976.[14]

Whereas inflation is a period of price increases, recession is a time of slow economic activity. Businesses decrease production, unemployment rises, and many consumers have less money to spend. The U.S. economy experienced recessions in the early 1970s, early 1980s, and early 1990s. From 1998 through early 2000 the U.S. economy grew rapidly as businesses invested in "new economy" technology and as consumers spent their stock market gains. Following this period of growth, however, the economy again entered a slow-growth recessionary period from 2001 through 2003.[15]

Consumer Income

The microeconomic trends in terms of consumer income are also important issues for marketers. Having a product that meets the needs of consumers may be of little value if they are unable to purchase it. A consumer's ability to buy is related to income, which consists of gross, disposable, and discretionary components.

Gross Income The total amount of money made in one year by a person, household, or family unit is referred to as *gross income* (or "money income" at the Census Bureau). While the typical U.S. household earned only about $8,700 of income in 1970, it earned about $43,318 in 2003. When gross income is adjusted for inflation, however, income of that typical U.S. household was relatively stable from 1970 to 2002 (e.g., adjusted for inflation the 1970 salary was $40,338). Figure 3–4 shows the distribution of annual income among U.S. households.[16]

Disposable Income The second income component, *disposable income,* is the money a consumer has left after paying taxes to use for food, shelter, clothing, and transportation. Thus, if taxes rise at a faster rate than does income, consumers must economize. In recent years, consumers' allocation of income has shifted. As the marketplace has become more efficient, producing products that are more durable and use less energy, consumers have increased their disposable income. Car maintenance costs, for example, have declined 28 percent since 1985, because automobile quality has improved. Much of the money is being spent on new categories of "necessities" such as vitamins and supplements; antibacterial bodywashes, lotions, and deodorants; antiwrinkle creams; and children's shampoos, toothpaste, and bath products.[17]

Discretionary Income The third component of income is *discretionary income,* the money that remains after paying for taxes and necessities. Discretionary income is used for luxury items such as a cruise on the Queen Mary 2. An obvious problem in defining discretionary versus disposable income is determining what is a luxury and what is a necessity.

FIGURE 3–4
Income distribution of U.S. households

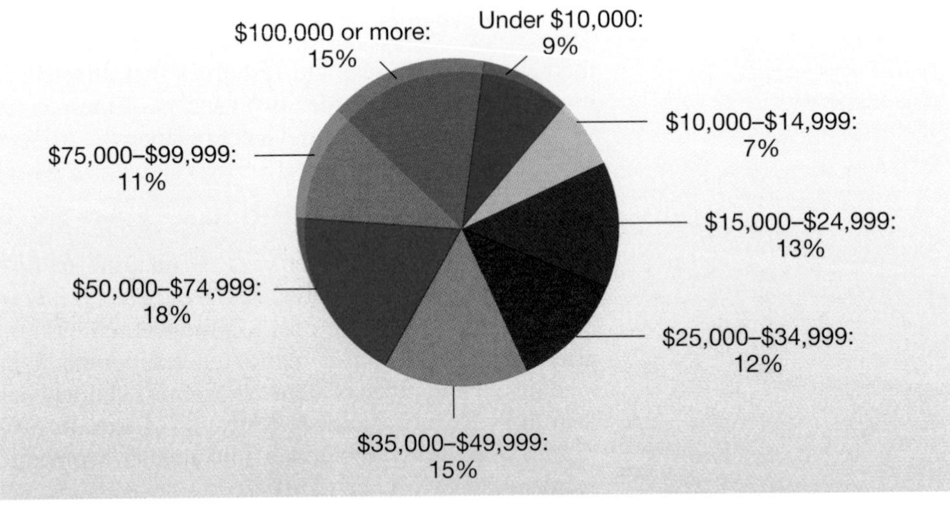

As consumers' discretionary income increases, so does the enjoyment of pleasure travel.

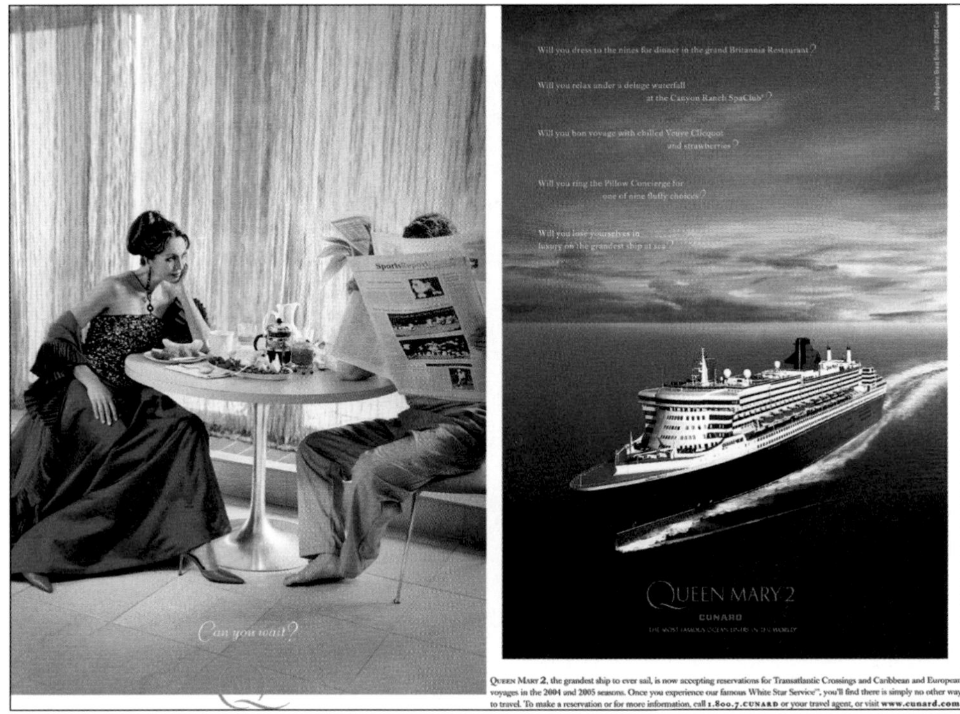

The Department of Labor monitors consumer expenditures through its annual Consumer Expenditure Survey. In 2002, consumers spent approximately 13 percent of their income on food, 33 percent on housing, and 4 percent on clothes. While an additional 36 percent is often spent on transportation, health care, and insurance, the remainder is generally viewed as discretionary. The percentage of income spent on food and housing typically declines as income increases, which can provide an increase in discretionary income. Discretionary expenditures can also be increased by reducing savings. The Bureau of Labor Statistics has observed that the percentage of income put into savings has been steadily declining and is expected to be only 2.7 percent in 2012, compared with 3.7 percent today.[18]

TECHNOLOGICAL FORCES

technology
Inventions from applied science or engineering research

Our society is in a period of dramatic technological change. **Technology**, the third environmental force, refers to inventions or innovations from applied science or engineering research. Each new wave of technological innovation can replace existing products and companies. Do you recognize the items pictured on the next page and what they may replace?

Technology of Tomorrow

Technological change is the result of research, so it is difficult to predict. Some of the most dramatic technological changes occurring now, however, include the following:

1. Advances in nanotechnology, the science of unimaginably small electronics, will lead to smaller microprocessors, efficient fuel cells, and cancer-detection sensors.
2. High-definition televisions and programming will become the industry standard.
3. In the next five years as much as 50 percent of all telephone calls could be made over the Internet.
4. Companies will begin building software databases so that lines of code can be "reused."

These trends in technology are already seen in today's marketplace. Cablevision recently launched a high-definition-only service called Voom, which carries 25 HD

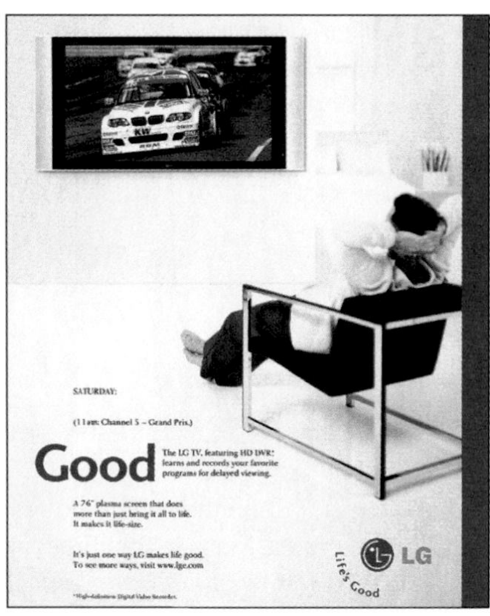

Technological change leads to new products. What products might be replaced by these innovations?

channels. Voice over Internet Protocol (VoIP) companies such as Vonage offer very low-cost, over-the-Internet telephone services, and Xerox has already saved $30 million in two years by "reusing" software. Other technologies such as flash memory, music downloading services, and plasma screen televisions are likely to replace or substitute for existing products and services such as floppy disks or CDRs, music stores and CDs, and televisions with CRT or projection screens.[19]

Technology's Impact on Customer Value

Advances in technology are having important effects on marketing. First, the cost of technology is plummeting, causing the customer value assessment of technology-based products to focus on other dimensions such as quality, service, and relationships. When Plaxo introduced its address book software, it gave the product away at no charge, reasoning that satisfied customers would later buy upgrades and related products. A similar approach is now used by many cellular telephone vendors, who charge little for the telephone if the purchase leads to a telephone service contract.[20]

Technology also provides value through the development of new products. Many automobile manufacturers now offer customers a navigation system that uses satellite signals to help the driver reach any destination. Under development are radarlike collision avoidance systems that disengage cruise control, reduce the engine speed, and even apply the brakes.[21] Other new products likely to be available soon include a "smart ski" with an embedded microprocessor that will adjust the flexibility of the ski to snow conditions; injectable health monitors that will send glucose, oxygen, and other clinical information to a wristwatch-like monitor; and electronic books that will allow you to download any volume and view it on pages coated with electronic "ink" and embedded electrodes.[22]

Electronic Business Technologies

marketspace
Information- and communication-based electronic exchange environment occupied by digitized offerings

The transformative power of technology may be best illustrated by the rapid growth of the **marketspace**, an information- and communication-based electronic exchange environment mostly occupied by sophisticated computer and telecommunication technologies and digitized offerings. Any activity that uses some form of electronic communication in the inventory, exchange, advertisement, distribution, and payment of goods and services is often called *electronic commerce.* Network technologies are now used for everything from filing expense reports, to monitoring daily sales, to sharing information with employees, to communicating instantly with suppliers.

Many companies have adapted Internet-based technology internally to support their electronic business strategies. An *intranet,* for example, is an Internet-based network used within the boundaries of an organization. It is a private Internet that may or may

MARKETING NEWSNET

Where Can You Go When You Are Wireless? Anywhere!

Electronic technologies are going through an incredible transformation. It started when network engineers were looking for a way to transmit an Internet connection without wires. The concept of "wireless fidelity" soon became "Wi-Fi," and businesses were eager to use it. Then two New York City residents started a free Wi-Fi node in midtown Manhattan's Bryant Park, and consumer demand skyrocketed. Soon there were nodes throughout the country: Levi Strauss Plaza in San Francisco, Tryst Coffeehouse in Washington, D.C., O'Hare Airport in Chicago, all Starbucks in Seattle, and the lobbies of Sheraton Four Points hotels around the nation. Currently, industry experts estimate that there are more than 12,000 nodes worldwide.

But this is just the beginning. Wi-Fi will soon grow beyond Internet connections and be found in most consumer electronics devices, including videogames, televisions, music players, cell phones, PDAs, digital cameras, and PCs. Then central servers will be able to record and store television programs, music, and video and play it back on any screen in the network.

Why is this revolution taking place so quickly? First, it is inexpensive: An access point is about $100 and a wireless card for a computer is about $60. Second, the technology is fast and powerful. Finally, it works. These three attributes combine to create an alluring option. At the current growth rate there will be more than 99 million people on Wi-Fi networks by 2007.

Several companies are working on devices that will hang on your key chain and glow when you are in signal range of an access point. So where can you go when you are wireless? Soon the answer will truly be anywhere!

not be connected to the public Internet. *Extranets,* which use Internet-based technologies, permit communication between a company and its supplier, distributors, and other partners (such as advertising agencies). The Marketing NewsNet describes how the latest Internet development—the Wi-Fi revolution—is transforming how companies do business.[23]

COMPETITIVE FORCES

competition
Alternative firms that could provide a product to satisfy a specific market's needs

The fourth component of the environmental scan, **competition**, refers to the alternative firms that could provide a product to satisfy a specific market's needs. There are various forms of competition, and each company must consider its present and potential competitors in designing its marketing strategy.

Alternative Forms of Competition

There are four basic forms of competition that form a continuum from pure competition to monopolistic competition to oligopoly to pure monopoly.

At one end of the continuum is *pure competition,* in which every company has a similar product. Companies that deal in commodities common to agribusiness (for example, wheat, rice, and grain) often are in a pure competition position in which distribution (in the sense of shipping products) is important but other elements of marketing have little impact.

In the second point on the continuum, *monopolistic competition,* the many sellers compete with their products on a substitutable basis. For example, if the price of coffee rises too much, consumers may switch to tea. Coupons or sales are frequently used marketing tactics.

Oligopoly, a common industry structure, occurs when a few companies control the majority of industry sales. For example, AT&T, MCI, Verizon, and Sprint control approximately 80 percent of the $16 billion international long-distance telephone service market. Similarly, the entertainment industry in the United States is dominated by

Viacom, Disney, and Time Warner, and the major firms in the U.S. defense contractor industry are Boeing, United Technologies, and Lockheed Martin. Critics of oligopolies suggest that because there are few sellers, price competition among firms is not desirable because it leads to reduced profits for all producers.[24]

The final point on the continuum, *pure monopoly,* occurs when only one firm sells the product. Monopolies are common for producers of goods considered essential to a community: water, electricity, and telephone service. Typically, marketing plays a small role in a monopolistic setting because it is regulated by the state or federal government. Government control usually seeks to ensure price protection for the buyer, although deregulation in recent years has encouraged price competition in the electricity market.[25] Concern that Microsoft's 86 percent share of the PC operating system market is a monopoly has led to lawsuits and consent decrees from the U.S. Justice Department and fines from the European Union.[26]

Small Businesses as Competitors

While large companies provide familiar examples of the forms and components of competition, small businesses make up the majority of the competitive landscape for most businesses. Consider that there are approximately 23 million small businesses in the United States, which employ half of all private sector employees. In addition, small businesses generate 60 to 80 percent of all new jobs annually and 50 percent of the gross domestic product (GDP). Research has shown that there is a strong correlation between national economic growth and the level of new small business activity in the previous years.[27]

Concept Check

1. What is the difference between a consumer's disposable and discretionary income?
2. How does technology impact customer value?
3. In pure competition there are a ______________ number of sellers.

REGULATORY FORCES

regulation
Restrictions state and federal laws place on business

For any organization, the marketing and broader business decisions are constrained, directed, and influenced by regulatory forces. **Regulation** consists of restrictions state and federal laws place on business with regard to the conduct of its activities. Regulation exists to protect companies as well as consumers. Much of the regulation from the federal and state levels is the result of an active political process and has been passed to ensure competition and fair business practices. For consumers, the focus of legislation is to protect them from unfair trade practices and ensure their safety.

Protecting Competition

Major federal legislation has been passed to encourage competition, which is deemed desirable because it permits the consumer to determine which competitor will succeed and which will fail. The first such law was the *Sherman Antitrust Act* (1890). Lobbying by farmers in the Midwest against fixed railroad shipping prices led to the passage of this act, which forbids (1) contracts, combinations, or conspiracies in restraint of trade and (2) actual monopolies or attempts to monopolize any part of trade or commerce. Because of vague wording and government inactivity, however, there was only one successful case against a company in the nine years after the act became law, and the Sherman Act was supplemented with the *Clayton Act* (1914). This act forbids certain actions that are likely to lessen competition, although no actual harm has yet occurred.

In the 1930s, the federal government had to act again to ensure fair competition. During that time, large chain stores appeared, such as the Great Atlantic & Pacific Tea Company (A&P). Small businesses were threatened, and they lobbied for the

Robinson-Patman Act (1936). This act makes it unlawful to discriminate in prices charged to different purchasers of the same product, where the effect may substantially lessen competition or help to create a monopoly.

Product-Related Legislation

Various federal laws in existence specifically address the product component of the marketing mix. Some are aimed at protecting the company, some at protecting the consumer, and at least one at protecting both.

Company Protection A company can protect its competitive position in new and novel products under the patent law, which gives inventors the right to exclude others from making, using, or selling products that infringe the patented invention. The federal copyright law is another way for a company to protect its competitive position in a product. The copyright law gives the author of a literary, dramatic, musical, or artistic work the exclusive right to print, perform, or otherwise copy that work. Copyright is secured automatically when the work is created. However, the published work should bear an appropriate copyright notice, including the copyright symbol, the first year of publication, and the name of the copyright owner, and it must be registered under the federal copyright law. Digital technology has necessitated new copyright legislation, called the *Digital Millenium Copyright Act* (1998), to improve protection of copyrighted digital products. In addition, producers of DVD movies, music recordings, and software want protection from devices designed to circumvent antipiracy elements of their products.[28]

Consumer Protection There are many consumer-oriented federal laws regarding products. The various laws include more than 30 amendments and separate laws relating to food, drugs, and cosmetics, such as the *Infant Formula Act* (1980), the *Nutritional Labeling and Education Act* (1990), new labeling requirements for dietary supplements (1997), and proposed labeling guidelines for trans fats (2006).[29] Various other consumer protection laws have a broader scope, such as the *Fair Packaging and Labeling Act* (1966), the *Child Protection Act* (1966), and the *Consumer Product Safety Act* (1972), which established the Consumer Product Safety Commission to monitor product safety and establish uniform product safety standards. Many of these laws came about because of **consumerism**, a grassroots movement started in the 1960s to increase the influence, power, and rights of consumers in dealing with institutions. This movement continues and is reflected in growing consumer demands for ecologically safe products, and ethical and socially responsible business practices. One hotly debated issue concerns liability for environmental abuse.

consumerism
A movement started to increase the influence, rights, and power of consumers

Both Company and Consumer Protection Trademarks are intended to protect both the firm selling a trademarked product and the consumer buying it. A Senate report states

> The purposes underlying any trademark statute [are] twofold. One is to protect the public so that it may be confident that, in purchasing a product bearing a particular trademark which it

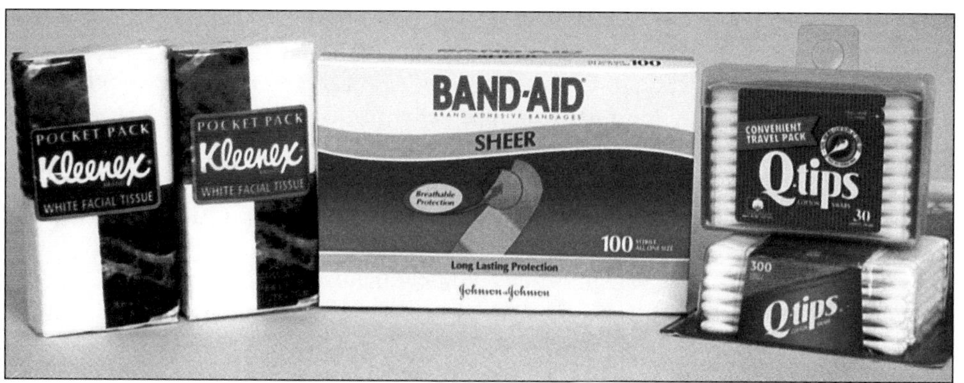

These products are identified by protected trademarks. Are any of these trademarks in danger of becoming generic?

> favorably knows, it will get the product which it asks for and wants to get. Secondly, where the owner of a trademark has spent energy, time, and money in presenting to the public the product, he is protected in this investment from misappropriation in pirates and cheats.

This statement was made in connection with another product-related law, the *Lanham Act* (1946), which provides for registration of a company's trademarks. Historically, the first user of a trademark in commerce had the exclusive right to use that particular word, name, or symbol in its business. Registration under the Lanham Act provides important advantages to a trademark owner that has used the trademark in interstate or foreign commerce, but it does not confer ownership. A company can lose its trademark if it becomes generic, which means that it has primarily come to be merely a common descriptive word for the product. Coca-Cola, Whopper, and Xerox are registered trademarks, and competitors cannot use these names. Aspirin and escalator are former trademarks that are now generic terms in the United States and can be used by anyone. In 1988, the *Trademark Law Revision Act* resulted in a major change to the Lanham Act, allowing a company to secure rights to a name before actual use by declaring an intent to use the name.[30] In 2003, the United States agreed to participate in the *Madrid Protocol,* which is a treaty that facilitates the protection of U.S. trademark rights throughout the world.[31]

One of the most recent changes in trademark law is the U.S. Supreme Court's ruling that companies may obtain trademarks for colors associated with their products. The reason is that, over time, consumers may begin to associate a particular color with a specific brand. Examples of products that may benefit from the new law include NutraSweet's sugar substitute in pastel blue packages and Owens-Corning Fiberglas Corporation's pink insulation.[32] Another recent addition to trademark law is the *Federal Dilution Act* (1995), which is used to prevent someone from using a trademark on a noncompeting product (e.g., "Cadillac" brushes).[33]

Pricing-Related Legislation

The pricing component of the marketing mix is the focus of regulation from two perspectives: price fixing and price discounting. Although the Sherman Act did not outlaw price fixing, the courts view this behavior as *per se illegal* (*per se* means "through or of itself"), which means the courts see price fixing itself as illegal.

Certain forms of price discounting are allowed. Quantity discounts are acceptable; that is, buyers can be charged different prices for a product provided there are differences in manufacturing or delivery costs. Promotional allowances or services may be given to buyers on an equal basis proportionate to volume purchased. Also, a firm can meet a competitor's price "in good faith." Legal and regulatory aspects of pricing are covered in more detail in Chapter 12.

Distribution-Related Legislation

The government has four concerns with regard to distribution—earlier referred to as "place" actions in the marketing mix—and the maintenance of competition. The first, *exclusive dealing,* is an arrangement a manufacturer makes with a reseller to handle only its products and not those of competitors. This practice is only illegal under the Clayton Act when it substantially lessens competition.

Requirement contracts require a buyer to purchase all or part of its needs for a product from one seller for a period of time. These contracts are not always illegal but depend on the court's interpretation of their impact on distribution.

Exclusive territorial distributorships are a third distribution issue often under regulatory scrutiny. In this situation, a manufacturer grants a distributor the sole rights to sell a product in a specific geographical area. The courts have found few violations with these arrangements.

The fourth distribution strategy is a *tying arrangement,* whereby a seller requires the purchaser of one product to also buy another item in the line. These contracts may be

ETHICS AND SOCIAL RESPONSIBILITY ALERT

Is Telemarketing a First Amendment Right?

The Federal Trade Commission is responsible for managing the National Do Not Call Registry (www.donotcall.gov), the list of telephone numbers that telemarketers must not call. Proponents of the list argue that it will give consumers relief from unwanted telephone solicitations. Others have suggested that the registry violates free speech rights protected under the Constitution. A District Court ruled that the do-not-call list was not legal because it prevented calls from businesses but not charities. More recently, however, the Circuit Court of Appeals ruled that the registry does not violate the First Amendment. Meanwhile, more than 64 million people have placed their numbers on the registry, and 66 million people made purchases in response to telemarketing calls. Many experts believe the Supreme Court will eventually rule on the law. What is your opinion? Is your number on the "do-not-call" or the "call" list?

illegal when the seller has such economic power in the tying product that the seller can restrain trade in the tied product.

Advertising- and Promotion-Related Legislation

Promotion and advertising are aspects of marketing closely monitored by the Federal Trade Commission (FTC), which was established by the *FTC Act of 1914.* The FTC has been concerned with deceptive or misleading advertising and unfair business practices and has the power to (1) issue cease and desist orders and (2) order corrective advertising. In issuing a *cease and desist order,* the FTC orders a company to stop practices it considers unfair. With *corrective advertising,* the FTC can require a company to spend money on advertising to correct previous misleading ads. The enforcement powers of the FTC are so significant that often just an indication of concern from the commission can cause companies to revise their promotion.

A landmark legal battle regarding deceptive advertising involved the Federal Trade Commission and Campbell Soup Co. It had been Campbell's practice to insert clear glass marbles into the bottom of soup containers used in print advertisements to bring the soup ingredients (e.g., noodles or chicken) to the surface. The FTC ruled that the advertising was deceptive because it misrepresented the amount of solid ingredients in the soup, and it issued a cease and desist order. Campbell and its advertising agency agreed to discontinue the practice. Future ads used a ladle to show the ingredients.[34]

Other laws have been introduced to regulate promotion practices. The *Deceptive Mail Prevention and Enforcement Act* (1999), for example, provides specifications for direct-mail sweepstakes, such as the requirement that the statement "No purchase is necessary to enter" is displayed in the mailing, in the rules, and on the entry form. Similarly, the *Telephone Consumer Protection Act* (1991) provides requirements for telemarketing promotions, including fax promotions. Telemarketing is also subject to a law that created the *National Do Not Call Registry,* which is a list of consumer phone numbers of people who do not want to receive unsolicited telemarketing calls. See the accompanying Ethics and Social Responsibility Alert for more information about the registry.[35] Finally, new laws such as the *Children's Online Privacy Protection Act* (1998) and the *Controlling the Assault of Non-Solicited Pornography and Marketing (CAN-SPAM) Act* (2004) are designed to restrict information collection and unsolicited e-mail promotions on the Internet.[36]

self-regulation
Alternative to government control where an industry attempts to police itself

Control through Self-Regulation

The government has provided much legislation to create a competitive business climate and protect the consumer. An alternative to government control is **self-regulation,**

where an industry attempts to police itself. The major television networks, for example, have used self-regulation to set their own guidelines for TV ads for children's toys. These guidelines have generally worked well. There are two problems with self-regulation, however: noncompliance by members and enforcement. In addition, if attempts at self-regulation are too strong, they may violate the Robinson-Patman Act. The best-known self-regulatory group is the Better Business Bureau (BBB). This agency is a voluntary alliance of companies whose goal is to help maintain fair practices. Although the BBB has no legal power, it does try to use "moral suasion" to get members to comply with its ruling. The BBB recently developed a reliability assurance program, called BBB Online, to provide objective consumer protection for Internet shoppers. Before they display the BBB Online logo on their website, participating companies must be members of their local Better Business Bureau, have been in business for at least one year, have agreed to abide by BBB standards of truth in advertising, and have committed to work with the BBB to resolve consumer disputes that arise over goods or services promoted or advertised on their site.[37]

Concept Check

1. The ______________________ Act was punitive toward monopolies, whereas the ______________________ Act was preventive.
2. Describe some of the recent changes in trademark law.
3. How does the Better Business Bureau encourage companies to follow its standards for commerce?

CHAPTER IN REVIEW

1 *Explain how environmental scanning provides information about social, economic, technological, competitive, and regulatory forces.*
Many businesses operate in environments where important forces change. Environmental scanning is the process of acquiring information about these changes to allow marketers to identify and interpret trends. There are five environmental forces businesses must monitor: social, economic, technological, competitive, and regulatory. By identifying trends related to each of these forces businesses can develop and maintain successful marketing programs. Several trends that most businesses are monitoring include the growing diversity of the U.S. population, the increasing use of wireless technology, and new legislation related to intellectual property and privacy.

2 *Describe how social forces such as demographics and culture and economic forces such as macroeconomic conditions and consumer income affect marketing.*
Demographic information describes the world population, the U.S. population, generational cohorts such as baby boomers, Generation X, and Generation Y, geographic shifts of the population, and the racial and ethnic diversity of the population that has led to multicultural marketing programs. Cultural factors include the impact of values such as "health and fitness" on consumer preferences. Economic forces include macroeconomic conditions related to the inflationary or recessionary state of the economy. Gross income has remained stable for more than 30 years although the rate of saving has been declining.

3 *Describe how technological changes can affect marketing.*
Technological innovations can replace existing products and services. Digital cameras, for example, have reduced the need for film, and music downloading services are changing how consumers buy music. Changes in technology can also have an impact on customer value by reducing the cost of products, improving the quality of products, and providing new products that were not previously feasible. Electronic commerce, including the Wi-Fi revolution, is transforming how companies do business.

4 *Discuss the forms of competition that exist in a market, key components of competition, and the impact of small businesses as competitors.*
There are four forms of competition: pure competition, monopolistic competition, oligopoly, and monopoly. While large companies are often used as examples of marketplace competitors, there are 23 million small businesses in the United States, which have a significant impact on the economy.

5 *Explain the major legislation that ensures competition and regulates the elements of the marketing mix.*
Regulation exists to protect companies and consumers. Legislation that ensures a competitive marketplace includes the Sherman Antitrust Act. Product-related legislation includes copyright and trademark laws that protect companies and packaging and labeling laws that protect consumers. Pricing- and distribution-related laws are designed to create a competitive marketplace with fair prices and availability. Regulation related to promotion and advertising reduces deceptive practices and provides enforcement through the Federal Trade Commission. Self-regulation through organizations such as the Better Business Bureau provides an alternative to federal and state regulation.

FOCUSING ON KEY TERMS

baby boomers p. 62
competition p. 69
consumerism p. 71
culture p. 65
demographics p. 61
economy p. 65
environmental scanning p. 60
Generation X p. 62
Generation Y p. 63
marketspace p. 68
multicultural marketing p. 65
regulation p. 70
self-regulation p. 73
social forces p. 61
technology p. 67

DISCUSSION AND APPLICATION QUESTIONS

1 For many years Gerber has manufactured baby food in small, single-sized containers. In conducting an environmental scan, identify three trends or factors that might significantly affect this company's future business, and then propose how Gerber might respond to these changes.

2 Describe the new features you would add to an automobile designed for consumers in the 55+ age group. In what magazines would you advertise to appeal to this target market?

3 New technologies are continuously improving and replacing existing products. Although technological change is often difficult to predict, suggest how the following companies and products might be affected by the Internet and digital technologies: (*a*) Kodak cameras and film, (*b*) American Airlines, and (*c*) the Metropolitan Museum of Art.

4 In recent years in the brewing industry, a couple of large firms that have historically had most of the beer sales (Anheuser-Busch and Miller) have faced competition from many small "micro" brands. In terms of the continuum of competition, how would you explain this change?

5 Why would Xerox be concerned about its name becoming generic?

6 Develop a "Code of Business Practices" for a new online vitamin store. Does your code address advertising? Privacy? Use by children? Why is self-regulation important?

GOING ONLINE Using the Web to Scan the Environment

There are many sources of information that might be useful in an environmental scan. Two particularly useful websites include FEDSTATS (www.fedstats.gov) and the United Nations (www.un.org). The FEDSTATS page links 100 federal agencies, including the U.S. Census Bureau, the Department of Commerce, and the Bureau of Labor Statistics. The United Nations page provides links to its Economic and Social Development division, which supports programs related to population, development trends, statistics, and others.

Use the sites to help answer the following questions:

1 What is the current (to the minute) population of the United States? What is the projected population of the United States in 2050?

2 What population or social trends can be identified with UN information?

BUILDING YOUR MARKETING PLAN

Your marketing plan will include a situation analysis based on internal and external factors that are likely to affect your marketing program.

1 To summarize information about external factors, create a table similar to Figure 3–2 and identify three trends related to each of the five forces (social, economic, technological, competitive, and regulatory) that relate to your product or service.

2 When your table is completed, describe how each of the trends represents an opportunity or a threat for your business.

VIDEO CASE 3 Flyte Tyme Productions, Inc.: The Best Idea Wins

"Terry was looking for a keyboard player to be in the band he was just starting," remembers Jimmy Jam of Flyte Tyme Productions, Inc. "I had sort of rebelled because I had first thought of myself as a drummer," says Jam. But after he listened and heard how good the drummer was, he told Terry, "I'll be the keyboard player."

The conversation took place a few weeks after Terry Lewis and Jimmy Jam met at a summer math program for gifted junior high school students, sponsored by a local university. The two came to prominence in the early 1980s as members of the funk band "The Time" that appeared as the opener on many of Prince's early tours. The pair still credit Prince for much of their tenacious work ethic and eclectic musical tastes. After leaving the band, Terry and Jimmy started a music production company—Flyte Tyme—creating the new name by adapting the old one. Now in their early 40s, the two have worked together for 20 years, most of it in Flyte Tyme Productions (www.flytetyme.com), where their clients include Mary J. Blige, Boyz II Men, Mariah Carey, Aretha Franklin, Janet Jackson, Patti LaBelle, Usher, TLC, and many others.

THE MUSIC

Sunglasses, fedoras, and sharp suits are Jam and Lewis's signature image, but—curiously—they have no signature sound. Instead, their approach is to tailor tunes for each artist. Janet Jackson's steamy ballads don't sound anything like Patti LaBelle's big Diane Warren ballads. They also work in a wide variety of music genres—from gospel (Yolanda Adams) and country (Rissi Palmer) to jazz (Herb Alpert) and pop (Mariah Carey).

Flyte Tyme's successes are impressive. They produced Usher's no. 1 pop hit "U Remind Me," which held the top spot on the charts for four weeks. They also produced an album for Japanese pop star Hikaru Utada, which climbed to the top of Japan's pop charts, selling 4 million copies in two weeks. And then there are projects like creating music for the NBA All-Star game!

These and other hits put Flyte Tyme in extraordinary company. Having produced 16 no. 1 singles on *Billboard*'s pop chart, they are second only to the producer for the Beatles (with 23) and tied with the producer for Elvis Presley. Flyte Tyme has also produced more than 40 Top-10 hits and more than 100 albums that have reached gold, platinum, and multiplatinum status. They are three-time Grammy winners for Producer of the Year, Best R&B Song, and Best Dance Recording. Most recently they have been nominated for the fourth consecutive year for Producer of the Year. In an industry where consumers' preferences, technology, competition, and the regulatory environment change at an extraordinary pace, Flyte Tyme has managed to stay on top for more than 20 years.

THE TEAM AND ITS FORMULA FOR SUCCESS

How have Jam and Lewis stayed at the top of the music game so long? Janet Jackson's answer: "There are no egos involved." Terry Lewis echoes this and says about his relationship with Jam: "He's the best partner a person could have. We've never had a contract—we've never had one argument in twenty-something years, not saying we don't disagree about things but our attitudes are the *best* idea wins. Not the right, not the wrong, but the *best*!"

"What we try to do is get everybody relaxed—check the egos at the door, that kind of thing. We find that we do it a lot more with new artists than with the older, more established artists," explains Jam. "Psychology is a big part of producing. Some artists like to work right away, others like to play pool, have lunch, talk on the phone, then they mosey in and record," he says. "If you think of Janet Jackson or Mariah Carey—the people who you would think of as superstars, you would think that they would bring a superstar ego with them. But it's almost the opposite," says Jam. "New artists often come to Flyte Tyme with a feeling they have to prove something. And what happens is, you don't really get a natural performance," says Jam.

Another of Flyte Tyme's special strengths: adapting the music and lyrics to an artist's unique talents, not the other way around. Their interest in many types of music and their experience with many artists allow them to add new ideas to the creative process. Still, Flyte Tyme may work on several different versions based on its perceptions of what radio stations or MTV will play.

Jam and Lewis work on both the music and lyrics for many of their songs, but Jam leans slightly more toward the melodies and Lewis toward the vocals and lyrics. In fact, Lewis keeps "The Book of Titles," and any time someone says something clever or in an interesting way it goes into the book. "Music is the soundtrack of life," says Lewis. "The inspiration for words I just take from watching people, and life has a lot of verses in it," he adds.

MARKETING, DISTRIBUTION, COMPETITION

Selecting the best music ideas requires an instinct to find the right blend of art and business. The elements of the art include a huge respect for and understanding of the artists, an interest in a broad palette of musical sounds, and a good ear for melodies and vocals. The business components of their formula include understanding many of the factors—such as consumers, technology, and competition—that influence their business.

Music artists walking in the door of Flyte Tyme receive an array of services: a studio facility with Jam, Lewis, and an experienced staff providing ideas, direction, and focus—"trying to get things out of them they didn't know they had in them," says Lewis. Flyte Tyme Records, the marketing arm, develops the artist's image, the marketing plan, advertising, and distribution—everything to get the record or CD on the rack to be sold. "If you have $100,000 to spend on promotion, you can do a nice music video and then you can spend a lot of time trying to get it played on MTV or BET or VH1 or any of the appropriate video channels," says Jam. Or sometimes the music calls for a different strategy, Flyte Tyme's "groundhog approach." For example, in the early 1990s with one of its bands, Flyte Tyme piled the band in a Winnebago and hit college campuses.

Today, Flyte Tyme creates a lot of that same groundhog buzz with its website, where the music audience can learn about Flyte Tyme's artists and activities. Jam and Lewis note that the new fee-based online music services are a great tool for providing the public access to music. In addition, while the delivery system—buying a CD at a retail store, downloading music from the Internet, or burning a CD—doesn't affect the process of Flyte Tyme's making the music in the studio, adapting to the environmental changes is important. "Change doesn't frighten us," says Lewis, "and we change with time."

Questions

1 Based on the case information and what you know about today's music industry, conduct an environmental scan for Flyte Tyme to identify key trends. For each of the five environmental forces (social, economic, technological, competitive, and regulatory), identify trends likely to influence it in the near future.

2 About 80 percent of start-up businesses fail within five years. What reasons explain Flyte Tyme's continuing success?

3 What marketing factors and actions must Jimmy Jam and Terry Lewis consider in developing music (*a*) for a new, unknown artist and (*b*) an established artist like Janet Jackson?

4 What promotional and distribution strategies should Flyte Tyme use to get its music in front of prospective buyers?

CHAPTER 4

ETHICS AND SOCIAL RESPONSIBILITY IN MARKETING

LEARNING OBJECTIVES

After reading this chapter you should be able to:

1. Explain the differences between legal and ethical behavior in marketing.
2. Identify factors that influence ethical and unethical marketing decisions.
3. Describe the different concepts of social responsibility.
4. Recognize unethical and socially irresponsible consumer behavior.

THERE IS MORE BREWING AT ANHEUSER-BUSCH THAN BEER

Why would a company spend more than a half-billion dollars since 1982 trying to convince people not to abuse its products and millions more to decrease litter and solid waste? Ask Anheuser-Busch, the world's largest brewer.

Anheuser-Busch has been an advocate for responsible drinking for more than two decades. The company began an aggressive campaign to fight alcohol abuse and underage drinking with its landmark "Know When to Say When" campaign in 1982. In 1989, a Consumer Awareness and Education Department was established within the company. This department was charged with developing and implementing programs, advertising and partnerships that promote responsible drinking, helping prevent alcohol abuse, and helping stop underage drinking before it starts. For example, more than 5.6 million copies of the company's *Family Talk about Drinking* guidebook have been distributed free to parents and educators in the past decade. In 2004, the brewer began a new chapter in its awareness and education efforts with the launch of its "Responsibility Matters" campaign. This effort emphasizes and implements effective education and awareness programs that promote responsibility and responsible behaviors, such as parents talking with their children about underage drinking, adults being designated drivers, retailers checking IDs to prevent sales to minors, and more. Anheuser-Busch believes these efforts are partly responsible for the sizable decline in the incidents of drunk-driving accidents, underage drinking, and other forms of alcohol abuse since 1982.

Responsibility at Anheuser-Busch is broader than its successful alcohol awareness and education initiatives. The company is an advocate and sponsor of numerous efforts to preserve the natural environment. A notable example is its massive recycling effort through

Anheuser-Busch Recycling Corporation (ABRC). ABRC is the world's largest recycler of aluminum cans. ABRC recycles over 800 million pounds of aluminum annually—the equivalent of about 130 percent of the beer cans Anheuser-Busch ships worldwide. The rationale for founding ABRC was simple: Voluntary recycling reduces litter and solid waste while conserving natural resources.

Anheuser-Busch acts on what it views as an ethical obligation to its customers and the general public with its alcohol awareness and education programs. At the same time, the company's efforts to protect the environment reflect its broader social responsibility.[1]

NATURE AND SIGNIFICANCE OF MARKETING ETHICS

ethics
Moral principles and values that govern the actions and decisions of an individual or a group

Ethics are the moral principles and values that govern the actions and decisions of an individual or group. They serve as guidelines on how to act rightly and justly when faced with moral dilemmas.

Ethical/Legal Framework in Marketing

laws
Society's standards and values that are enforceable in court

A good starting point for understanding the nature and significance of ethics is the distinction between legality and ethicality of marketing decisions. Whereas ethics deal with personal moral principles and values, **laws** are society's values and standards that are enforceable in the courts. This distinction can sometimes lead to the rationalization that if a behavior is within reasonable ethical and legal limits, then it is not really illegal or unethical. When a recent survey asked the question, "Is it OK to get around the law if you don't actually break it?" 61 percent of businesspeople who took part responded "yes."[2] How would you answer this question?

There are numerous situations in which judgment plays a large role in defining ethical and legal boundaries. Consider the following situations.[3]

1. More than 70 percent of the physicians in the Maricopa County (Arizona) Medical Society agreed to establish a maximum fee schedule for health services to curb rising medical costs. All physicians were required to adhere to this schedule as a condition for membership in the society. The U.S. Supreme Court ruled that this agreement to set prices violated the Sherman Act and represented price fixing, which is illegal.
2. A company in California sells a computer program to auto dealers showing that car buyers should finance their purchase rather than paying cash. The program omits the effect of income taxes and misstates the interest earned on savings over the loan period. The finance option always provides a net benefit over the cash option. Company employees agree that the program does mislead buyers, but say the company will "provide what [car dealers] want as long as it is not against the law."

Would you be able to describe these situations as clearly ethical and legal or unethical and illegal? Probably not. As you read further in this chapter, you will be asked to consider other ethical dilemmas.

Current Perceptions of Ethical Behavior

There has been a public outcry about the ethical practices of businesspeople.[4] Public opinion surveys show that 58 percent of U.S. adults rate the ethical standards of business executives as only "fair" or "poor"; 90 percent think white-collar crime is "very common" or "somewhat common"; 76 percent say the lack of ethics in businesspeople contributes to tumbling societal moral standards; only the U.S. government is viewed as less trustworthy than corporations among institutions in the United States; and advertising practitioners, telemarketers, and car salespeople are thought to be among the least ethical occupations. Surveys of corporate employees generally confirm this public

perception. When asked if they were aware of ethical problems in their companies, a third say, "yes."

There are at least three possible reasons the state of perceived ethical business conduct is at its present level. First, there is increased pressure on businesspeople to make decisions in a society characterized by diverse value systems. Second, there is a growing tendency for business decisions to be judged publicly by groups with different values and interests. Finally, and most disturbing, ethical business conduct may have declined.

Concept Check

1. What are ethics?
2. What are three possible reasons for the present state of ethical conduct in the United States?

UNDERSTANDING ETHICAL MARKETING BEHAVIOR

Researchers have identified numerous factors that influence ethical marketing behavior. Figure 4–1 presents a framework that shows these factors and their relationships.

Societal Culture and Norms

As described in Chapter 3, *culture* refers to the set of values, ideas, and attitudes that are learned and shared among members of a group. Culture also serves as a socializing force that dictates what is morally right and just. This means that moral standards can be different in different cultures. Sometimes differences in moral standards, particularly between societies with different cultures, can create moral dilemmas. For example, Levi Strauss decided to end much of its business dealings in China because of what the company called "pervasive human rights abuses." According to its vice president for corporate marketing: "There are wonderful commercial opportunities in China. But when ethical issues collide with commercial appeal, we try to ensure ethics as the trump card. For us, ethical issues precede all others."[5]

Societal values and attitudes also affect ethical and legal relationships among individuals, groups, and business institutions and organizations. Consider the copying of another's copyright, trademark, or patent. These are viewed as intellectual property. Unauthorized use, reproduction, or distribution of intellectual property is illegal in the United States and most countries and can result in fines and prison terms of perpetrators.

FIGURE 4–1
A framework for understanding ethical behavior

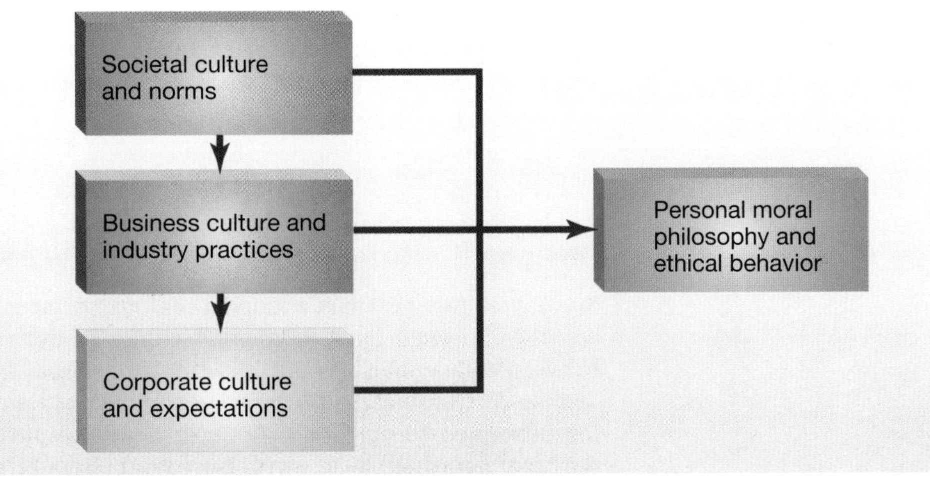

MARKETING NEWSNET Internet Piracy and Campus Pirates

Have you ever downloaded music or a movie from the Internet or from a peer-to-peer file-sharing program such as Kazaa or Morpheus without paying for it? This question was recently posed to a random sample of 1,000 U.S. college and university students. The findings described below may or may not surprise you.

Not surprisingly, most students (69 percent) download music. A smaller number (26 percent) download movies. For those students who download music, 92 percent admit to never or seldom paying for the copies they made. For students who download movies, 96 percent say they never or seldom pay for the copies made. In a related finding, 76 percent of students say it is okay to download music and movies from unauthorized sources to save money.

Downloading music and movies from unauthorized sources is illegal and unethical. The cost of a CD or the price of a movie ticket or rental seems small compared with the legal and ethical ramifications.

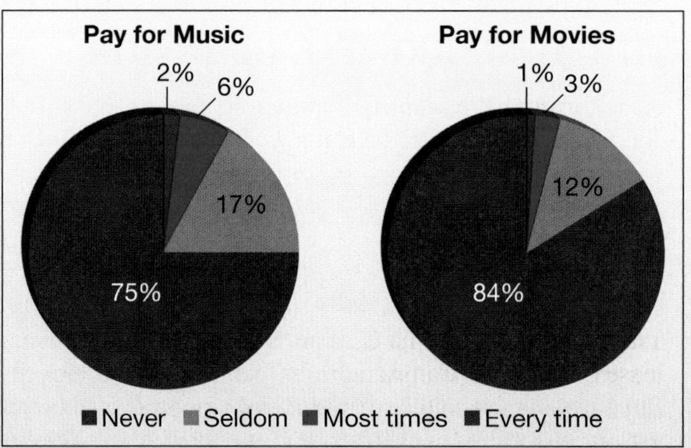

Q. How often do you pay for the music that you download? *Asked only of those who have downloaded music from the Internet.*

Q. How often do you pay for the movies that you download? *Asked only of those who have downloaded a movie from the Internet.*

The owners of intellectual property also lose. For example, annual lost sales from the theft of intellectual property amount to $22 billion in the music industry, $3.5 billion in the movie industry, and $15 billion in the software industry.[6] Lost sales, in turn, result in lost jobs, royalties, wages, and tax revenue. But what about a person downloading copyrighted music and movies over the Internet or from peer-to-peer file-sharing programs, without paying the owner of this property? Is this an ethical or unethical act? It depends on who you ask. Surveys of the U.S. public indicate that the majority consider such acts unethical. The accompanying Marketing NewsNet describes college student views on downloading music and movies.[7]

Business Culture and Industry Practices

Societal culture provides a foundation for understanding moral behavior in business activities. *Business cultures* "comprise the effective rules of the game, the boundaries between competitive and unethical behavior, [and] the codes of conduct in business dealings."[8] Consumers have witnessed numerous instances where business cultures in the brokerage (inside trading), insurance (deceptive sales practices), and defense (bribery) industries went awry. Business culture affects ethical conduct both in the exchange relationship between sellers and buyers and in the competitive behavior among sellers.

Ethics of Exchange The exchange process is central to the marketing concept. Ethical exchanges between sellers and buyers should result in both parties being better off after a transaction.

Prior to the 1960s, most American business culture believed in the legal concept of *caveat emptor,* which means "let the buyer beware." In other words, it was the responsibility of the buyer, not the seller, to ensure the integrity of an exchange. This changed in 1962 when President John F. Kennedy outlined a **Consumer Bill of Rights** that codified the ethics of exchange between buyers and sellers. These were the right (1) to safety, (2) to be informed, (3) to choose, and (4) to be heard. Consumers expect and often demand that these rights be protected, as have American businesses.

Consumer Bill of Rights *Codified the ethics of exchange between buyers and sellers, including right to safety, to be informed, to choose, and to be heard*

The right to safety manifests itself in industry and federal safety standards for most products sold in the United States. In fact, the U.S. Consumer Product Safety Commission routinely monitors the safety of 15,000 consumer products. However, even the most vigilant efforts to ensure safe products cannot foresee every possibility. Mattel's experience with its Cabbage Patch Snacktime Kids doll is a case in point.[9] The doll was designed to "eat" plastic french fries, celery, and other tidbits by drawing them into its motorized mouth. Despite exhaustive laboratory and in-home testing, Mattel executives did not consider that a child's hair might get caught in the doll's mouth and cause harm. It did! Mattel immediately informed buyers of the safety issue, pulled the dolls from store shelves, refunded buyers, and discontinued the product.

The right to be informed means that marketers have an obligation to give consumers complete and accurate information about products and services, but this is not always the case.[10] For example, three U.S. advertising agencies recently agreed to settle Federal Trade Commission (FTC) claims that they failed to disclose the actual costs of car leases and credit transactions in their advertising for three Japanese carmakers. This right also applies to the solicitation of personal information over the Internet and its subsequent use by marketers. An FTC survey of websites indicated that 92 percent collect personal information such as consumer e-mail addresses, telephone numbers, shopping habits, and financial data. Yet, only two-thirds of websites inform consumers of what is done with this information once obtained. The FTC wants more than posted privacy notices that merely inform consumers of a company's data-use policy, which critics say are often vague, confusing, or too legalistic to be understood. This view is shared by two-thirds of consumers who worry about protecting their personal information online. The consumer right to be informed has spawned numerous federal legislation, such as the *Children's Online Privacy Protection Act* (1998), and self-regulation initiatives restricting disclosure of personal information.

The Federal Trade Commission plays an active role in educating consumers and businesses about the importance of personal information privacy on the Internet. FTC initiatives are detailed on its website.

Relating to the right to choose, today many supermarket chains demand "slotting allowances" from manufacturers, in the form of cash or free goods, to stock new products. This practice could limit the number of new products available to consumers and interfere with their right to choose. One critic of this practice remarked, "If we had had slotting allowances a few years ago, we might not have had granola, herbal tea, or yogurt."

Finally, the right to be heard means that consumers should have access to public-policy makers regarding complaints about products and services. This right is illustrated in limitations put on telemarketing practices. Consumer complaints about latenight and repeated calls resulted in the *Telephone Consumer Protection Act* of 1991. The FTC established the Do Not Call Registry in

2003 for consumers who do not want to receive unsolicited telemarketing calls. More than 64 million consumers have their telephone numbers listed in the registry, which is managed by the FTC. A telemarketer can be fined $11,000 for each call made to a telephone number posted on the registry.

Ethics of Competition Business culture also affects ethical behavior in competition with other businesses. Two kinds of unethical behavior are most common: (1) economic espionage and (2) bribery.

Economic espionage is the clandestine collection of trade secrets or proprietary information about a company's competitors. This practice is illegal and unethical and carries serious criminal penalties for the offending individual or business. Espionage activities include illegal trespassing, theft, fraud, misrepresentation, wiretapping, the search of a competitor's trash, and violations of written and implicit employment agreements with noncompete clauses. About 56 percent of the largest firms in the United States have uncovered espionage in some form, costing them $200 billion annually in lost sales.[11]

Economic espionage is most prevalent in high-technology industries, such as electronics, specialty chemicals, industrial equipment, aerospace, and pharmaceuticals, where technical know-how and trade secrets separate industry leaders from followers. But espionage can occur anywhere—even in the ready-to-eat cookie industry. Procter & Gamble charged that competitors photographed its plants and production lines, stole a sample of its cookie dough, and infiltrated a confidential sales presentation to learn about its technology, recipe, and marketing plan. The competitors paid Procter & Gamble $120 million in damages after a lengthy dispute.[12]

The second form of unethical competitive behavior is giving and receiving bribes and kickbacks. Bribes and kickbacks are often disguised as gifts, consultant fees, and favors. This practice is more common in business-to-business and government marketing than in consumer marketing. For example, two American Honda Motor Company executives were fined and sentenced to prison for extracting $15 million in kickbacks from Honda dealers and advertising agencies, and a series of highly publicized trials uncovered widespread bribery in the U.S. Defense Department's awarding of $160 billion in military contracts.[13]

In general, bribery is most evident in industries experiencing intense competition and in countries in earlier stages of economic development. According to a recent United Nations' study, 15 percent of all companies in industrialized countries have to pay bribes to win or retain business. In Asia, this figure is 40 percent. In Eastern Europe, 60 percent of all companies must pay bribes to do business. A recent poll of senior executives engaged in global marketing revealed that Bangladesh and Nigeria were the most likely countries to evidence bribery to win or retain business. Iceland and Finland were the least likely.[14]

The prevalence of economic espionage and bribery in international marketing has prompted laws to curb these practices. Two significant laws, the *Economic Espionage Act* (1996) and the *Foreign Corrupt Practices Act* (1977), address these practices in the United States. Both are detailed in Chapter 7.

Corporate Culture and Expectations

A third influence on ethical practices is corporate culture. *Corporate culture* reflects the shared values, beliefs, and purpose of employees that affect individual and group behavior. The culture of a company demonstrates itself in the dress (business casual versus business suits), how the working environment is structured (cubicles versus closed offices), and how employees are compensated (stock options versus overtime). Culture is also apparent in the expectations for ethical behavior present in formal codes of ethics and the ethical actions of top management and co-workers.

code of ethics
Formal statement of ethical principles and rules of conduct

Codes of Ethics A **code of ethics** is a formal statement of ethical principles and rules of conduct. It is estimated that 80 percent of U.S. companies have some sort

What does 3M's Scotchgard have to do with ethics? Read the text to find out.

of ethics code and one of every five large companies has corporate ethics officers. At United Technologies, for example, 160 corporate ethics officers distribute the company's ethics code, translated into 24 languages, to employees who work for this defense and engineering giant around the world.[15] Ethics codes and committees typically address contributions to government officials and political parties, relations with customers and suppliers, conflicts of interest, and accurate recordkeeping. For example, General Mills provides guidelines for dealing with suppliers, competitors, and customers, and recruits new employees who share these views. However, an ethics code is rarely enough to ensure ethical behavior. Coca-Cola has an ethics code and emphasizes that its employees be ethical in their behavior. But that did not stop some Coca-Cola employees from rigging the results of a test market for a frozen soft drink to win Burger King's business. Coca-Cola subsequently agreed to pay Burger King and its operators more than $20 million to settle the matter.[16]

The lack of specificity is one of the major reasons for the violation of ethics codes. Employees must often judge whether a specific behavior is really unethical. The American Marketing Association has addressed this issue by providing a detailed code of ethics, which all members agree to follow. This code can be found at the American Marketing Association website (www.marketingpower.com).

Ethical Behavior of Top Management and Co-Workers Workers sometimes violate ethics codes because of how they perceive the behavior of top management and co-workers. How an employee evaluates the company's response to unethical behavior plays an important role in his or her actions. A study of business executives reported that 40 percent had been implicitly or explicitly rewarded for engaging in ethically troubling behavior. Moreover, 31 percent of those who refused to engage in unethical behavior were penalized, either through outright punishment or a diminished status in the company.[17] Clearly, ethical dilemmas often bring personal and professional conflict. For this reason, numerous states have laws protecting **whistle-blowers**, employees who report unethical or illegal actions of their employers. Some firms, such as General Dynamics and Dun & Bradstreet, have appointed ethics officers responsible for safeguarding these individuals from recrimination.

whistle-blowers
Employees who report unethical or illegal actions of their employers

Personal Moral Philosophy and Ethical Behavior

Ultimately, ethical choices are based on the personal moral philosophy of the decision maker. Moral philosophy is learned through the process of socialization with friends and family and by formal education. It is also influenced by the societal, business, and corporate culture in which a person finds him- or herself. Two prominent personal moral philosophies have direct bearing on marketing practice: (1) moral idealism and (2) utilitarianism.

Moral Idealism **Moral idealism** is a personal moral philosophy that considers certain individual rights or duties as universal, regardless of the outcome. This philosophy exists in the Consumer Bill of Rights and is favored by moral philosophers and consumer interest groups. For example, the right to know applies to probable defects in an automobile that relate to safety.

moral idealism
Moral philosophy that considers certain individual rights or duties as universal, regardless of the outcome

This philosophy also applies to ethical duties. A fundamental ethical duty is to do no harm. Adherence to this duty prompted the recent decision by 3M executives to phase out production of a chemical 3M had manufactured for nearly 40 years. The substance, used in far-ranging products from pet food bags, candy wrappers, carpeting, and 3M's popular Scotchgard fabric protector, had no known harmful health or environmental effect. However, the company discovered that the chemical appeared in miniscule amounts in humans and animals around the world and accumulated in tissue. Believing that the substance could be possibly harmful in large doses, 3M voluntarily stopped its production acknowledging that the outcome of this action was a potential loss of $500 million in annual sales.[18]

utilitarianism
Moral philosophy that focuses on the "greatest good for the greatest number"

Utilitarianism An alternative perspective on moral philosophy is **utilitarianism**, which is a personal moral philosophy that focuses on "the greatest good for the greatest number," by assessing the costs and benefits of the consequences of ethical behavior. If the benefits exceed the costs, then the behavior is ethical. If not, then the behavior is unethical. This philosophy underlies the economic tenets of capitalism and, not surprisingly, is embraced by many business executives and students.

Utilitarian reasoning was apparent in Nestlé Food Corporation's marketing of Good Start infant formula, sold by Nestlé's Carnation Company. The formula, promoted as hypoallergenic, was designed to prevent or reduce colic caused by an infant's allergic reaction to cow's milk, a condition suffered by 2 percent of babies. However, some severely milk-allergic infants experienced serious side effects after using Good Start, including convulsive vomiting. Physicians and parents charged that the hypoallergenic claim was misleading, and the Food and Drug Administration investigated the matter. A Nestlé vice president defended the claim and product, saying, "I don't understand why our product should work in 100 percent of cases. If we wanted to say it was foolproof, we would have called it allergy-free. We call it hypo-, or less, allergenic."[19] Nestlé officials seemingly believed that most allergic infants would benefit from Good Start—"the greatest good for the greatest number." However, other views prevailed, and the claim was dropped from the product label.

An appreciation for the nature of ethics, coupled with a basic understanding of why unethical behavior arises, alerts a person to when and how ethical issues exist in marketing decisions. Ultimately, ethical behavior rests with the individual, but the consequences affect many.

Concept Check

1. What rights are included in the Consumer Bill of Rights?
2. What is meant by moral idealism?

UNDERSTANDING SOCIAL RESPONSIBILITY IN MARKETING

social responsibility
Idea that organizations are part of a larger society and are accountable to that society for their actions

As we saw in Chapter 1, the societal marketing concept stresses marketing's social responsibility by not only satisfying the needs of consumers but also providing for society's welfare. **Social responsibility** means that organizations are part of a larger society and are accountable to that society for their actions. Like ethics, agreement on the nature and scope of social responsibility is often difficult to come by, given the diversity of values present in different societal, business, and corporate cultures.

Concepts of Social Responsibility

Figure 4–2 shows three concepts of social responsibility: (1) profit responsibility, (2) stakeholder responsibility, and (3) societal responsibility.

Profit Responsibility *Profit responsibility* holds that companies have a simple duty: to maximize profits for their owners or stockholders. This view is expressed by Nobel laureate Milton Friedman, who said, "There is one and only one social responsibility of business—to use its resources and engage in activities designed to increase its profits so long as it stays within the rules of the game, which is to say, engages in open and free competition without deception or fraud."[20] Nonetheless, there are concerns about *profiteering*. Profiteering occurs when a company makes excessive profits usually by taking advantage of a shortage of supply to charge extremely high prices. But where to draw the line? Genzyme, the maker of Cerezyme,

FIGURE 4–2
Three concepts of social responsibility

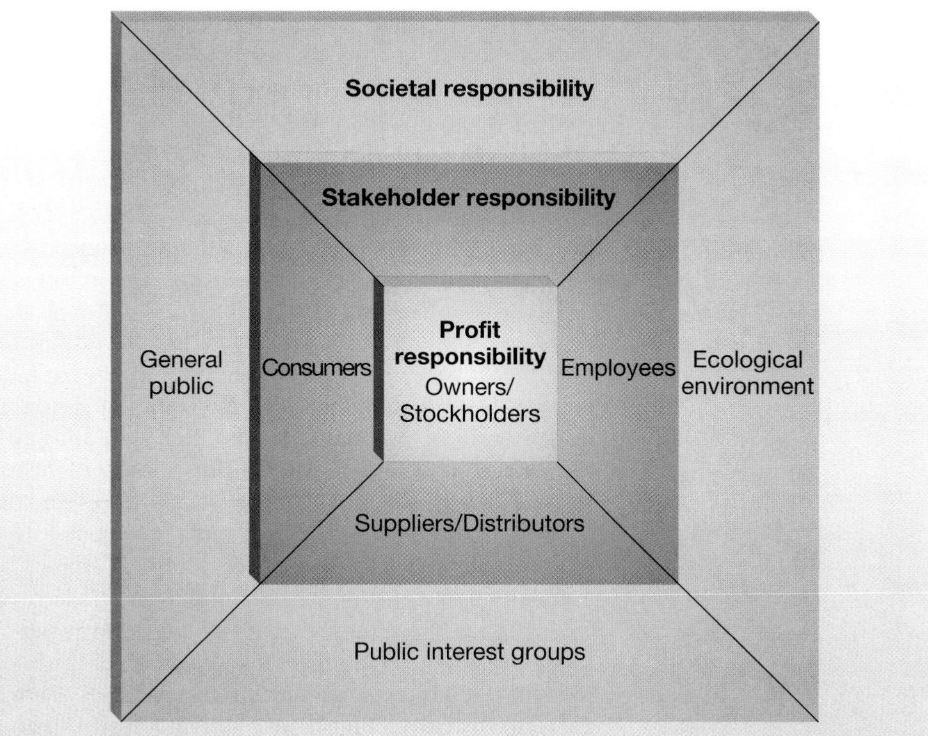

a drug that treats a genetic illness called Gaucher's disease that affects 20,000 people worldwide, has been criticized for apparently adopting this view in its pricing practices. Genzyme charges up to $170,000 for a year's worth of Cerezyme. A Genzyme spokesperson responded saying the company spends about $150 million annually to manufacture Cerezyme and freely gives the drug to patients without insurance. Also, the company invested considerable dollars in research over several years to develop Cerezyme, and the drug's profits are reinvested in ongoing R&D programs.[21]

Stakeholder Responsibility Criticism of the profit view has led to a broader concept of social responsibility. *Stakeholder responsibility* focuses on the obligations an organization has to those who can affect achievement of its objectives. These constituencies include consumers, employees, suppliers, and distributors. Source Perrier S.A., the supplier of Perrier bottled water, exercised this responsibility when it recalled 160 million bottles of water in 120 countries after traces of a toxic chemical were found in 13 bottles. The recall cost the company $35 million, and $40 million more in lost sales. Even though the chemical level was not harmful to humans, Source Perrier's president believed he acted in the best interests of the firm's consumers, distributors, and employees by removing "the least doubt, as minimal as it might be, to weigh on the image of the quality and purity of our product"—which it did.[22]

Failure to consider a company's broader constituencies can have negative consequences. For example, Bridgestone/Firestone, Inc., executives were widely criticized for how they responded to complaints about the safety of selected Firestone-brand tires. These tires had been linked to crashes that killed at least 174 people and injured more than 700 in the United States. In 2000, the company recalled 6.5 million tires under pressure from the National Highway Traffic Administration. After the recall, Firestone tire sales fell by nearly one-half, which affected Firestone employees, suppliers, and distributors as well. Ford Motor Company, a large buyer of Firestone tires, ended its exclusive contract with the tire producer.[23]

Societal Responsibility An even broader concept of social responsibility has emerged in recent years. *Societal responsibility* refers to obligations that organizations have (1) to the preservation of the ecological environment and (2) to the general public. Concerns about the environment and public welfare are represented by interest and advocacy groups such as Greenpeace, an international environmental organization.

Chapter 3 detailed the importance of ecological issues in marketing. Companies have responded to this concern through what is termed **green marketing**—marketing efforts to produce, promote, and reclaim environmentally sensitive products.

green marketing
Marketing efforts to produce, promote, and reclaim environmentally sensitive products

Green marketing takes many forms.[24] At 3M, product development opportunities emanate both from consumer research and its "Pollution Prevention Pays" program. This program solicits employee suggestions on how to reduce pollution and recycle materials. Since 1975, this program has generated almost 5,000 ideas that eliminated more than 1.7 billion pounds of air, water, and solid-waste pollutants from the environment. Xerox's "Design for the Environment" program focuses on ways to make its equipment recyclable and remanufacturable. Today, 90 percent of Xerox-designed products are remanufacturable. This effort has kept more than 1.4 billion pounds of equipment from being discarded in U.S. landfills since 1991. Boise Cascade, a leading North American timber manufacturer, and Lowe's and Home Depot, two home-and-garden center retail chains, have discontinued the sale of wood products from the world's endangered forests. FedEx and UPS are converting their delivery trucks with standard diesel engines to more fuel-efficient and cleaner technologies, such as hybrid electric vehicles. These vehicles can cut fuel costs by half and lower fuel emissions by 90 percent. These voluntary responses to environmental issues have been implemented with little or no additional cost to consumers and actually resulted in cost savings to companies.

cause marketing
Tying the charitable contributions of a firm directly to sales produced through the promotion of one of its products

Socially responsible efforts on behalf of the general public are becoming more common. A formal practice is **cause marketing**, which occurs when the charitable contributions of a firm are tied directly to the customer revenues produced through the promotion of one of its products.[25] This definition distinguishes cause marketing from a firm's standard charitable contributions, which are outright donations. For example, Procter & Gamble raises funds for the Special Olympics when consumers purchase selected company products, and MasterCard International links usage of its card with fund raising for institutions that combat cancer, heart disease, child abuse, drug abuse, and muscular dystrophy. Barnes & Noble promotes literacy, and Coca-Cola sponsors local Boys and Girls Clubs. Avon Products, Inc., focuses on different issues in different countries: breast cancer in the United States, Canada, Philippines, Mexico, Venezuela, Malaysia, and Spain; programs for women who care for senior citizens in Japan; emotional and financial support for mothers in Germany; and AIDS in Thailand. Cause marketing programs incorporate all three concepts of social responsibility by addressing public concerns and satisfying customer needs. They can also enhance corporate sales and profits as described in the accompanying Marketing NewsNet.[26]

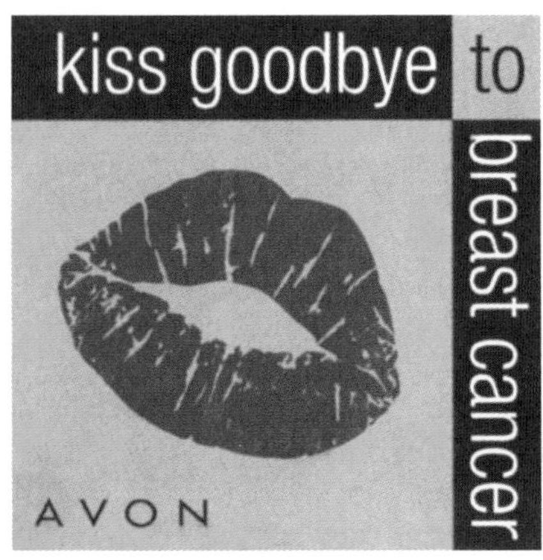

Avon Products, Inc., employs cause marketing programs in the fight against breast cancer.

The Social Audit: Doing Well by Doing Good

Converting socially responsible ideas into actions involves careful planning and monitoring of programs. Many companies develop, implement, and evaluate their social responsibility efforts by means of a **social audit**, which is a systematic assessment of a firm's objectives, strategies, and performance in terms of social responsibility. Frequently, marketing and social responsibility programs are integrated, as is the case with McDonald's. The company's concern for the needs of families with children who are chronically or terminally ill was converted into some 212 Ronald McDonald Houses around the world. These facilities, located near treatment centers, enable families to stay together during the child's care. In this case, McDonald's is contributing to the welfare of a portion of its target market.

social audit
Systematic assessment of a firm's objectives, strategies, and performance in the domain of social responsibility

MARKETING NEWSNET

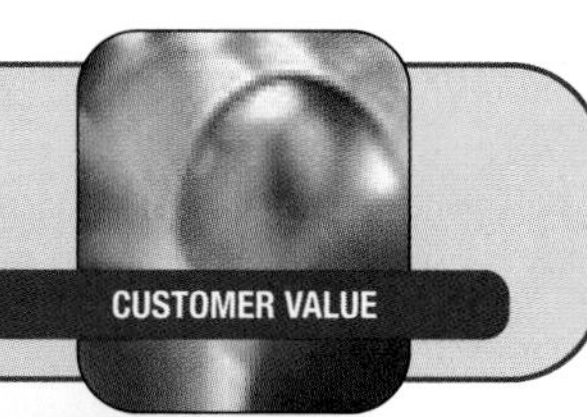

Will Consumers Switch Brands for a Cause? Yes, If . . .

American Express Company pioneered cause marketing when it sponsored the renovation of the Statue of Liberty. This effort raised $1.7 million for the renovation, increased card usage among cardholders, and attracted new cardholders. In 2002, U.S. companies raised more than $5 billion for causes they champion. It is estimated that cause marketing will raise over $10 billion in 2008.

Cause marketing benefits companies as well as causes. Research indicates that 92 percent of U.S. consumers say they have a more favorable opinion of companies that support causes. Also, 84 percent of consumers say they will switch to a brand or retailer that supports a good cause if the price and quality of brands or retailers are equal. In short, cause marketing may be a valued point of difference for brands and companies, all other things being equal.

For more information, including news, links, and case studies, visit the Cause Marketing Forum website at www.causemarketingforum.com.

A social audit consists of five steps:[27]

1. Recognition of a firm's social expectations and the rationale for engaging in social responsibility endeavors.
2. Identification of social responsibility causes or programs consistent with the company's mission.
3. Determination of organizational objectives and priorities for programs and activities it will undertake.
4. Specification of the type and amount of resources necessary to achieve social responsibility objectives.
5. Evaluation of social responsibility programs and activities undertaken and assessment of future involvement.

Corporate attention to social audits will increase as companies seek to achieve sustainable development and improve the quality of life in a global economy. *Sustainable development* involves conducting business in a way that protects the natural environment while making economic progress. Ecologically responsible programs such as green marketing represent one such initiative. Other programs focus on working conditions at overseas manufacturing sites that produce goods for U.S. companies. Public opinion surveys show that 90 percent of U.S. citizens are concerned about working conditions under which products are made in Asia and Latin America. Companies such as Reebok, Nike, Liz Claiborne, Levi Strauss, and Mattel have responded by imposing codes of conduct to reduce harsh or abusive working conditions at overseas manufacturing facilities.[28] Reebok, for example, now monitors production of its sporting apparel and equipment to ensure that no child labor is used in making its products.

Companies that show societal responsibility have been rewarded for their efforts. Research has shown that these companies (1) benefit from favorable word-of-mouth among consumers and (2) typically outperform less responsible companies on financial performance.[29]

Marketing and social responsibility programs are often integrated, as is the case with McDonald's. Its concern for ill children is apparent in the opening of another Ronald McDonald House for children and their families.

Turning the Table: Consumer Ethics and Social Responsibility

Consumers also have an obligation to act ethically and responsibly in the exchange process and use of products. Unfortunately, consumer behavior is somewhat spotty.

Unethical practices of consumers are a serious concern to marketers.[30] These practices include filing warranty claims after the claim period, misredeeming coupons, making fraudulent returns of merchandise, providing inaccurate information on credit applications, tampering with utility meters, tapping cable TV lines, pirating music, movies, and software from the Internet, and submitting phony insurance claims. Consumers also act unethically toward each other. According to the FBI, consumer complaints about online auction fraud, in which consumers misrepresent their goods to others, outnumbers all reports of online crime. The cost to marketers of such behavior in lost sales and prevention expenses is huge. For example, consumers who redeem coupons for unpurchased products or use coupons for other products cost manufacturers $1 billion each year. Fraudulent automobile insurance claims cost insurance companies more than $10 billion annually. Unauthorized downloading of music, movies, and software from the Internet cost companies about $40 billion per year in lost sales. Electrical utilities lose between 1 and 3 percent of yearly revenues because of meter tampering. In addition, retailers lose about $30 billion yearly from shoplifting.

Research on unethical consumer behavior indicates that these acts are rarely motivated by economic need. This behavior appears to be influenced by (1) a belief that a consumer can get away with the act and it is worth doing and (2) the rationalization that the act is justified or driven by forces outside the individual—"everybody does it." These reasons were vividly expressed by a 24-year-old who pirated a movie, *The Hulk,* and was sentenced to six months of house arrest, three years of probation, and a $7,000 fine. He said, "I didn't like paying for movies," and added, "so many people do it, you never think you're going to get caught."[31]

Consumer purchase, use, and disposition of environmentally sensitive products relate to consumer social responsibility. Research indicates that consumers are sensitive to ecological issues. However, research also shows that consumers (1) may be unwilling to sacrifice convenience and pay potentially higher prices to protect the environment and (2) lack the knowledge to make informed decisions dealing with the purchase, use, and disposal of products.[32]

Consumer confusion over which products are environmentally safe is also apparent, given marketers' rush to produce "green products." For example, few consumers realize

Reebok has been a leader in improving workplace conditions in factories that produce its sporting apparel and equipment.

that nonaerosol "pump" hairsprays are the second-largest cause of air pollution, after drying paint. In California alone, 27 tons of noxious hairspray fumes are expelled every day. And "biodegradable" claims on a variety of products, including trash bags, have not proven to be accurate, thus leading to buyer confusion. The FTC has drafted guidelines that describe the circumstances when environmental claims can be made and would not constitute misleading information. For example, an advertisement or product label touting a package as "50 percent more recycled content than before" could be misleading if the recycled content has increased from 2 percent to 3 percent.[33]

Ultimately, marketers and consumers are accountable for ethical and socially responsible behavior. The twenty-first century will prove to be a testing period for both.

Concept Check

1. What is meant by social responsibility?
2. Marketing efforts to produce, promote, and reclaim environmentally sensitive products are called ______________.
3. What is a social audit?

CHAPTER IN REVIEW

1 *Explain the differences between legal and ethical behavior in marketing.*
A good starting point for understanding the nature and significance of ethics is the distinction between legality and ethicality of marketing decisions. Whereas ethics deal with personal moral principles and values, laws are society's values and standards that are enforceable in the courts. This distinction can lead to the rationalization that if a behavior is within reasonable ethical and legal limits, then it is not really illegal or unethical. Judgment plays a large role in defining ethical and legal boundaries in marketing. Ethical dilemmas arise when acts or situations are not clearly ethical and legal or unethical and illegal.

2 *Identify factors that influence ethical and unethical marketing decisions.*
Four factors influence ethical marketing behavior. First, societal culture and norms serve as socializing forces that dictate what is morally right and just. Second, business culture and industry practices affect ethical conduct both in the exchange relationships between buyers and sellers and the competitive behavior among sellers. Third, corporate culture and expectations are often defined by corporate ethics codes and the ethical behavior of top management and co-workers. Finally, an individual's personal moral philosophy, such as moral idealism or utilitarianism, will dictate ethical choices. Ultimately, ethical behavior rests with the individual, but the consequences affect many.

3 *Describe the different concepts of social responsibility.*
Social responsibility means that organizations are part of a larger society and are accountable to that society for their actions. There are three concepts of social responsibility. First, profit responsibility holds that companies have a simple duty: to maximize profits for their owners or stockholders. Second, stakeholder responsibility focuses on the obligations an organization has to those who can affect achievement of its objectives. Those constituencies include consumers, employees, suppliers, and distributors. Finally, societal responsibility focuses on obligations that organizations have to the preservation

of the ecological environment and the general public. Companies are placing greater emphasis on societal responsibility today and are reaping the rewards of positive word-of-mouth from their consumers and favorable financial performance.

4 *Recognize unethical and socially irresponsible consumer behavior.*

Consumers, like marketers, have an obligation to act ethically and responsibly in the exchange process and in the use and disposition of products. Unfortunately, consumer behavior is spotty on both counts. Unethical consumer behavior includes filing warranty claims after the claim period, misredeeming coupons, pirating music, movies, and software from the Internet, and submitting phony insurance claims, among other behaviors. Unethical behavior is rarely motivated by economic need. Rather, research indicates that this behavior is influenced by (*a*) a belief that a consumer can get away with the act and it is worth doing and (*b*) the rationalization that such acts are justified or driven by forces outside the individual—"everybody does it." Consumer purchase, use, and disposition of environmentally sensitive products relate to consumer social responsibility. Even though consumers are sensitive to ecological issues they (*a*) may be unwilling to sacrifice convictions and pay potentially higher prices to protect the environment and (*b*) lack the knowledge to make informed decisions dealing with the purchase, use, and disposal of products.

FOCUSING ON KEY TERMS

cause marketing p. 88
code of ethics p. 84
Consumer Bill of Rights p. 83
ethics p. 80
green marketing p. 88
laws p. 80
moral idealism p. 85
social audit p. 88
social responsibility p. 86
utilitarianism p. 86
whistle-blowers p. 85

DISCUSSION AND APPLICATION QUESTIONS

1 What concepts of moral philosophy and social responsibility are applicable to the practices of Anheuser-Busch described in the introduction to this chapter? Why?

2 Compare and contrast moral idealism and utilitarianism as alternative personal moral philosophies.

3 How would you evaluate Milton Friedman's view of the social responsibility of a firm?

4 Cause marketing programs have become popular. Describe two such programs with which you are familiar.

GOING ONLINE Doing Well By Doing Good

Business for Social Responsibility (BSR) is a membership organization for companies seeking to sustain their commercial success in ways that demonstrate respect for ethical values, people, communities, and the environment. As part of its mission, BSR scans numerous publications and news services each month to identify what is new in corporate social responsibility.

Choose a topic from Chapter 4 pertaining to ethics or social responsibility that interests you, such as economic espionage, current perceptions of ethical behavior, sustainable development, or green marketing. Visit the BSR website at www.bsr.org and go to the "Issue Areas in CSR." Can you update at least one example in the text related to your chosen topic?

BUILDING YOUR MARKETING PLAN

Consider these potential stakeholders that may be affected in some way by the marketing plan on which you are working: shareholders (if any), suppliers, employees, customers, and society in general. For each group of stakeholders,

1 Identify what, if any, ethical and social responsibility issues might arise.

2 Describe, in one or two sentences, how your marketing plan addresses each potential issue.

VIDEO CASE 4 Starbucks Corporation: Serving More than Coffee

Wake up and smell the coffee—Starbucks is everywhere! As the world's number one specialty coffee retailer, Starbucks serves more than 25 million customers in its stores every week. The concept of Starbucks goes far beyond being a coffeehouse or coffee brand. It represents the dream of its founder, Howard Schultz, who wanted to take the experience of an Italian—specifically, Milan—espresso bar to every corner of every city block in the world. So what is the *Starbucks experience*? According to the company,

> You get more than the finest coffee when you visit Starbucks. You get great people, first-rate music, a comfortable and upbeat meeting place, and sound advice on brewing excellent coffee at home. At home you're part of a family. At work you're part of a company. And somewhere in between there's a place where you can sit back and be yourself. That's what a Starbucks store is to many of its customers—a kind of "third place" where they can escape, reflect, read, chat, or listen.

But there is more. Starbucks has embraced corporate social responsibility like few other companies. A recent Starbucks Corporate Social Responsibility Annual Report described the company's views on social responsibility:

> Starbucks defines corporate social responsibility as conducting our business in ways that produce social, environmental, and economic benefits to the communities in which we operate. In the end, it means being responsible to our stakeholders.
>
> There is a growing recognition of the need for corporate accountability. Consumers are demanding more than "product" from their favorite brands. Employees are choosing to work for companies with strong values. Shareholders are more inclined to invest in business with outstanding corporate reputations. Quite simply, being socially responsible is not only the right thing to do; it can distinguish a company from its industry peers.

Starbucks not only recognizes the central role that social responsibility plays in its business. It also takes constructive action to be socially responsible.

THE COMPANY

Starbucks is the leading retailer, roaster, and brand of specialty coffee in the world, with more than 7,500 retail locations in North America, Latin America, Europe, the Middle East, and the Pacific Rim. Beginning in 1971 with a single retail location in Seattle, Washington, Starbucks became a Fortune 500 company in 2003 with annual sales exceeding $4 billion. In addition, Starbucks is ranked as one of the "Ten Most Admired Companies in America" and one of the "100 Best Companies to Work For" by *Fortune* magazine. It has been recognized as one of the "Most Trusted Brands" by *Ad Week* magazine. *Business Ethics* magazine placed Starbucks twenty-first in its list of the "100 Best Citizens" in 2003. Starbucks' performance can be attributed to a passionate pursuit of its mission and adherence to six guiding principles. Both appear in Figure 1.

COMMITMENT TO CORPORATE SOCIAL RESPONSIBILITY

Starbucks continually emphasizes its commitment to corporate social responsibility. Speaking at the annual shareholders meeting in March 2004, Howard Schultz said,

> From the beginning, Starbucks has built a company that balances profitability with a social conscience. Starbucks business practices are even more relevant today as consumers take a cultural audit of the goods and services they use. Starbucks is known not only for serving the highest quality coffee, but for enriching the daily lives of its people, customers, and coffee farmers. This is the key to Starbucks ongoing success and we are pleased to report our positive results to shareholders and partners (employees).

Each year, Starbucks makes public a comprehensive report on its corporate social responsibility initiatives. A central feature of this annual report is the alignment of the

FIGURE 1
Starbucks Mission Statement and Guiding Principles

Establish Starbucks as the premier purveyor of the finest coffee in the world while maintaining our uncompromising principles as we grow.

The following six principles will help us measure the appropriateness of our decisions:

1. Provide a great work environment and treat each other with respect and dignity.
2. Embrace diversity as an essential component in the way we do business.
3. Apply the highest standards of excellence to the purchasing, roasting, and fresh delivery of our coffee.
4. Develop enthusiastically satisfied customers all the time.
5. Contribute positively to our communities and our environment.
6. Recognize that profitability is essential to our future success.

company's social responsibility decisions and actions with Starbucks Mission Statement and Guiding Principles. The Starbucks 2003 Corporate Social Responsibility Report, titled "Living Our Values," focused on six topical areas: (*a*) partners, (*b*) diversity, (*c*) coffee, (*d*) customers, (*e*) community and environment, and (*g*) profitability.

Partners

Starbucks employs some 74,000 people around the world. The company considers its employees as partners following the creation of Starbucks stock option plan in 1991, called "Bean Stock." The company believes that giving eligible full- and part-time employees an ownership in the company and sharing the rewards of Starbucks' financial success has made the sense of partnership real. In addition, the company has one of the most competitive employee benefits and compensation packages in the retail industry. Ongoing training, career advancement opportunities, partner recognition programs, and diligent efforts to ensure a healthy and safe work environment have all contributed to the fact that Starbucks has one of the lowest employee turnover rates within the restaurant and fast food industry.

Diversity

Starbucks strives to mirror the customers and communities it serves. On a quarterly basis, the company monitors the demographics of its workforce to determine whether they reflect the communities in which Starbucks operates. In 2003, Starbucks' U.S. workforce was comprised of 63 percent women and 24 percent people of color. The company also is engaged in a joint venture called Urban Coffee Opportunities (UCO) created to bring Starbucks stores to diverse neighborhoods. There were 52 UCO locations employing almost 1,000 Starbucks partners at the end of 2003.

Supplier diversity is also emphasized. To do business with Starbucks as a diverse supplier, that company must be 51 percent owned, operated, and managed by women, minorities, or socially disadvantaged individuals and meet Starbucks requirements of quality, service, value, stability, and sound business practice. The company spent $80 million with diverse suppliers in 2003 and expects to spend $95 million with diverse suppliers in 2004.

Coffee

Starbucks attention to quality coffee extends to its coffee growers located in more than 20 countries. Sustainable development is emphasized. This means that Starbucks pays coffee farmers a fair price for the beans; that the coffee is grown in an ecologically sound manner; and that Starbucks invests in the farming communities where its coffees are produced.

One long-standing initiative is Starbucks' partnership with Conservation International, a nonprofit organization dedicated to protecting soil, water, energy, and biological diversity worldwide. Starbucks is particularly focused on environmental protection and helping local farmers earn more for their crops. In 2003, Starbucks invested more than $1 million in social programs, notably health and education projects, that benefited farming communities in nine countries, from Columbia to Indonesia.

Customers

Starbucks serves customers in 32 countries. The company and its partners are committed to providing each customer the optimal Starbucks experience every time they visit a store. For very loyal Starbucks customers, that translates into 18 visits per month on average.

Making a connection with customers at each store and building the relationship a customer has with Starbucks *baristas,* or coffee brewers, is important in creating the Starbucks experience. Each barista receives 24 hours of training in customer service and basic retail skills, as well as "Coffee Knowledge" and "Brewing the Perfect Cup" classes. Baristas are taught to anticipate the customers' needs and to make eye contact while carefully explaining the various coffee flavors and blends. Starbucks also enhances the customer relationship by soliciting feedback and responding to patrons' experiences and concerns. Starbucks Customer Relations reviews and responds to every inquiry or comment, often within 24 hours for telephone calls and e-mails.

Community and Environment

Efforts to contribute positively to the communities it serves and the environments in which it operates are emphasized in Starbucks' guiding principles. "We aren't in the coffee business, serving people. We are in the people business, serving coffee," says Howard Schultz. Starbucks and its partners have been recognized for volunteer support and financial contributions to a wide variety of local, national, and international social, economic, and environmental initiatives. For example, the "Make Your Mark" program rewards partners' gifts of time for volunteer work with charitable donations from Starbucks. In addition, Starbucks is a supporter of CARE International, a nonprofit organization dedicated to fighting global poverty.

Starbucks is also committed to environmental responsibility. Starbucks has a longtime involvement with Earth Day activities. It has instituted companywide energy and water conservation programs and waste reduction, recycling, and reuse initiatives proposed by partner *Green Teams.*

Profitability

At Starbucks, profitability is viewed as essential to its future success. When Starbucks' guiding principles were conceived, profitability was included but intentionally placed last on the list. This was done not because profitability was the least important. Instead, it was believed that adherence to the five other principles would ultimately lead to good financial performance. In fact, it has.

Questions

1 How does Starbucks' approach to social responsibility relate to the three concepts of social responsibility described in the text?

2 What role does sustainable development play in Starbucks' approach to social responsibility?

PART

PART 1
Initiating the Marketing Process

PART 2
Understanding Buyers and Markets

PART 3
Targeting Marketing Opportunities

PART 4
Satisfying Marketing Opportunities

2 UNDERSTANDING BUYERS AND MARKETS

HOW PART 2 FITS INTO THE BOOK

Chapters in Part 2 stress how marketing seeks to serve the needs and wants of potential buyers, whether they are individuals and household consumers, organizations, or global customers.

IS IT A VOLVO?

CHAPTER 5

CONSUMER BEHAVIOR

LEARNING OBJECTIVES

After reading this chapter you should be able to:

1. Describe the stages in the consumer purchase decision process.
2. Distinguish among three variations of the consumer purchase decision process: routine, limited, and extended problem solving.
3. Identify major psychological influences on consumer behavior.
4. Identify the major sociocultural influences on consumer behavior.

GETTING TO KNOW THE AUTOMOBILE CUSTOM(H)ER AND INFLUENC(H)ER

Who buys about 67 percent of new cars and light trucks? Who spends about $100 billion on new and used cars and trucks and automotive accessories? Who influences 85 percent of all vehicle buying decisions? Women. Yes, women.

Women are a driving force in the U.S. automotive industry. Enlightened automakers such as Volvo have hired women designers, engineers, and marketing executives to better understand and serve this valuable automobile consum(h)er and influenc(h)er of purchase decisions. What have they learned? First, women cast the deciding vote in the family-car purchase and, of course, make the final decision in all of their own purchase decisions. Second, sleek exteriors and interior designs that fit a driver's proportions as well as easy vehicular entry and exit, minimal maintenance, good visibility, storage space, and effortless parking are important to women . . . and men. "We have found that by meeting women's expectations, we exceeded those of most men," says Hans-Olov Olsson, president and CEO of Volvo Cars, a unit of Ford Motor Company. Not surprisingly, 54 percent of Volvo buyers in North America are women.

Third, women approach car buying in a deliberate manner. They frequently visit auto-buying websites and scan car advertisements to gather information, but recommendations of friends and relatives matter most. Women shop an average of three dealerships before making a purchase decision—one more than men. While only a third of women say that price is the most influential factor when they shop for a car, 73 percent say price determines their final decision. Finally, automakers have learned that the great majority of women dislike the car-buying process.

Recognition of women as purchasers and influencers in car and truck buying has also altered the behavior of dealers. Many dealers now use a one-price policy and have stopped negotiating a vehicle's price. Industry research indicates that 68 percent of new-car buyers dread the price negotiation process involved in buying a car, and women often refuse to do it at all.[1]

consumer behavior
Actions a person takes in purchasing and using products and services

This chapter examines **consumer behavior**, the actions a person takes in purchasing and using products and services, including the mental and social processes that come before and after these actions. This chapter shows how the behavioral sciences help answer questions such as why people choose one product or brand over another, how they make these choices, and how companies use this knowledge to provide value to consumers.

CONSUMER PURCHASE DECISION PROCESS

purchase decision process
Stages a buyer passes through in making choices about which products or services to buy

Behind the visible act of making a purchase lies an important decision process that must be investigated. The stages a buyer passes through in making choices about which products and services to buy is the **purchase decision process**. This process has the five stages shown in Figure 5–1: (1) problem recognition, (2) information search, (3) alternative evaluation, (4) purchase decision, and (5) postpurchase behavior.

Problem Recognition: Perceiving a Need

Problem recognition, the initial step in the purchase decision, is perceiving a difference between a person's ideal and actual situations big enough to trigger a decision.[2] This can be as simple as finding an empty milk carton in the refrigerator; noting, as a first-year college student, that your high school clothes are not in the style that other students are wearing; or realizing that your laptop computer may not be working properly.

In marketing, advertisements or salespeople can activate a consumer's decision process by showing the shortcomings of competing (or currently owned) products. For instance, an advertisement for a portable MP3-capable CD player could stimulate problem recognition because it emphasizes "maximum music from one device."

Information Search: Seeking Value

After recognizing a problem, a consumer begins to search for information about what product or service might satisfy the newly discovered need. First, you may scan your memory for previous experiences with products or brands.[3] This action is called *internal search.* For frequently purchased products such as shampoo and conditioner, this may be enough. Or a consumer may undertake an *external search* for information.[4] This is especially needed when past experience or knowledge is insufficient, the risk of making a bad decision is high, and the cost of gathering information is low. The primary sources of external information are (1) *personal sources,* such as relatives and friends whom the consumer trusts; (2) *public sources,* including various product-rating organizations such as *Consumer Reports,* government agencies, and TV "consumer programs"; and (3) *marketer-dominated sources,* such as information from sellers that include advertising, company websites, salespeople, and point-of-purchase displays in stores.

Suppose you consider buying a portable MP3-capable CD player. You will probably tap several of these information sources: friends and relatives, portable MP3-capable

FIGURE 5–1
Purchase decision process

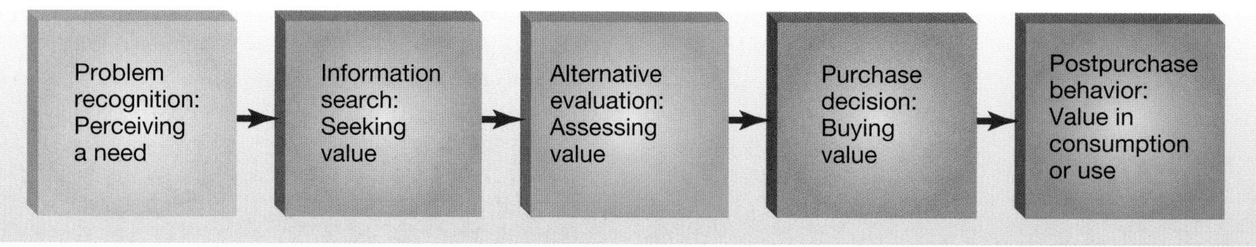

BRAND	MODEL	PRICE	SOUND QUALITY	BUMP IMMUNITY	BATTERY LIFE (HOURS) CD	BATTERY LIFE (HOURS) MP3	EASE OF USE
Sony	D-CJ01	$130	Excellent	Good	30	23	Very Good
Philips	EXP503/17	180	Excellent	Fair	17	15	Excellent
Panasonic	SL-MP50	100	Excellent	Good	29	11	Very Good
Philips	EXP203	100	Excellent	Fair	7	11	Excellent
RCA	RP-2415	120	Good	Fair	6	8	Good
Samsung	MCD-SM60	80	Fair	Good	17	15	Excellent
SonicBlue	Rio Volt SP90	100	Very Good	Fair	6	15	Very Good
SonicBlue	Rio Volt SP250	180	Good	Good	5	13	Very Good

Rating: Excellent, Very Good, Good, Fair, Poor

FIGURE 5–2
Consumer Reports' evaluation of portable MP3-capable CD players (abridged)

advertisements, brand and company websites, and stores carrying these CD players (for demonstrations). You might study the comparative evaluation of portable MP3-capable CD players that appeared in *Consumer Reports,* a portion of which appears in Figure 5–2.[5]

Alternative Evaluation: Assessing Value

The information search stage clarifies the problem for the consumer by (1) suggesting criteria, or points to consider, for the purchase, (2) providing brand names that might meet the criteria, and (3) developing consumer value perceptions. Given only the information shown in Figure 5–2, what selection criteria would you use in buying a portable MP3-capable CD player? Would you use price, sound quality, ease of use, or some other combination of these and other criteria?

For some of you, the information provided may be inadequate because it does not contain all the factors you might consider when evaluating portable MP3-capable CD players. These factors are a consumer's *evaluative criteria,* which represent both the objective attributes of a brand (such as the locate speed) and the subjective ones (such as prestige) you use to compare different products and brands. Firms try to identify and make the most of both types of criteria to create the best value for the money sought by you and other consumers. These criteria are often displayed in advertisements.

Consumers often have several criteria for evaluating brands. (Didn't you in the preceding exercise?) Knowing this, companies seek to identify the most important evaluative criteria that consumers use when judging brands. For example, among the evaluative criteria shown in the columns of Figure 5–2, suppose you use three in considering brands of portable MP3-capable CD players: (1) a list price under $150, (2) sound quality, and (3) battery life of more than 10 hours. These criteria establish the brands in your *consideration set*—the group of brands that a consumer would consider acceptable from among all the brands in the product class of which he or she is aware.[6] Your evaluative criteria result in five models and five brands (Panasonic, Philips, Samsung, SonicBlue, and Sony) in your consideration set. If these alternatives don't satisfy you, you can change your evaluative criteria to create a different consideration set of models and brands. For example, bump immunity might join the list of evaluative criteria if you are a jogger.

Purchase Decision: Buying Value

Having examined the alternatives in the consideration set, you are almost ready to make a purchase decision. Two choices remain: (1) from whom to buy and (2) when to buy. The choice of which seller to buy from will depend on such considerations as the terms of sale, your past experience buying from the seller, and the return policy.

Deciding when to buy is frequently determined by a number of factors. For instance, you might buy sooner if one of your preferred brands is on sale or its manufacturer offers a rebate. Other factors such as the store atmosphere, pleasantness of the shopping experience, salesperson persuasiveness, time pressure, and financial circumstances could also affect whether a purchase decision is made or postponed.[7]

Use of the Internet to gather information, evaluate alternatives, and make buying decisions adds a technological dimension to the consumer purchase decision process. Consumer benefits and costs associated with this technology and its marketing implications are detailed in Chapter 18.

A satisfactory or unsatisfactory consumption or use experience is an important factor in postpurchase behavior. Marketer attention to this stage can pay huge dividends as described in the text.

Postpurchase Behavior: Value in Consumption or Use

After buying a product, the consumer compares it with his or her expectations and is either satisfied or dissatisfied. A company's sensitivity to a customer's consumption experience strongly affects the value a customer perceives after the purchase. Studies show that satisfaction or dissatisfaction affects consumer communications and repeat-purchase behavior. Satisfied buyers tell three other people about their experience. Dissatisfied buyers complain to nine people.[8] Satisfied buyers also tend to buy from the same seller each time a purchase occasion arises. The financial impact of repeat-purchase behavior is significant.

Accordingly, firms such as General Electric (GE), Johnson & Johnson, Coca-Cola, and British Airways focus attention on postpurchase behavior to maximize customer satisfaction and retention. These firms, among many others, now provide toll-free telephone numbers, offer liberalized return and refund policies, and engage in staff training to handle complaints, answer questions, and record suggestions.

Often a consumer is faced with two or more highly attractive alternatives, such as a Panasonic or Sony portable MP3-capable CD player. If you choose the Panasonic, you may think, Should I have purchased the Sony? This feeling of postpurchase anxiety is called *cognitive dissonance.* To alleviate it, consumers often applaud themselves for making the right choice. So after your purchase, you may seek information to confirm your choice by asking friends questions like, "Don't you like my new CD player?" or by reading ads of the brand you chose. You might even look for negative features about the brand you didn't buy and decide that the Philips headphones didn't feel right. Firms often use ads or follow-up calls from salespeople in this postpurchase stage to comfort buyers that they made the right decision. For many years, Buick ran an advertising campaign with the message, "Aren't you really glad you bought a Buick?"

Involvement and Problem-Solving Variations

involvement
Personal, social, and economic significance of a purchase to the consumer

Sometimes consumers don't engage in the five-step purchase decision process. Instead, they skip or minimize one or more steps depending on the level of **involvement**. The level of involvement that a consumer has in a particular purchase depends on the personal, social, and economic consequences of that purchase to the consumer.[9] Item such as soap or toothpaste may have such a low level of involvement for consumers that they may skip or minimize one or more steps in the process. But they may do just the opposite for a high-involvement purchase like an audio-video system or an automobile.

High-involvement purchase occasions typically have at least one of three characteristics: the item to be purchased (1) is expensive, (2) can have serious personal

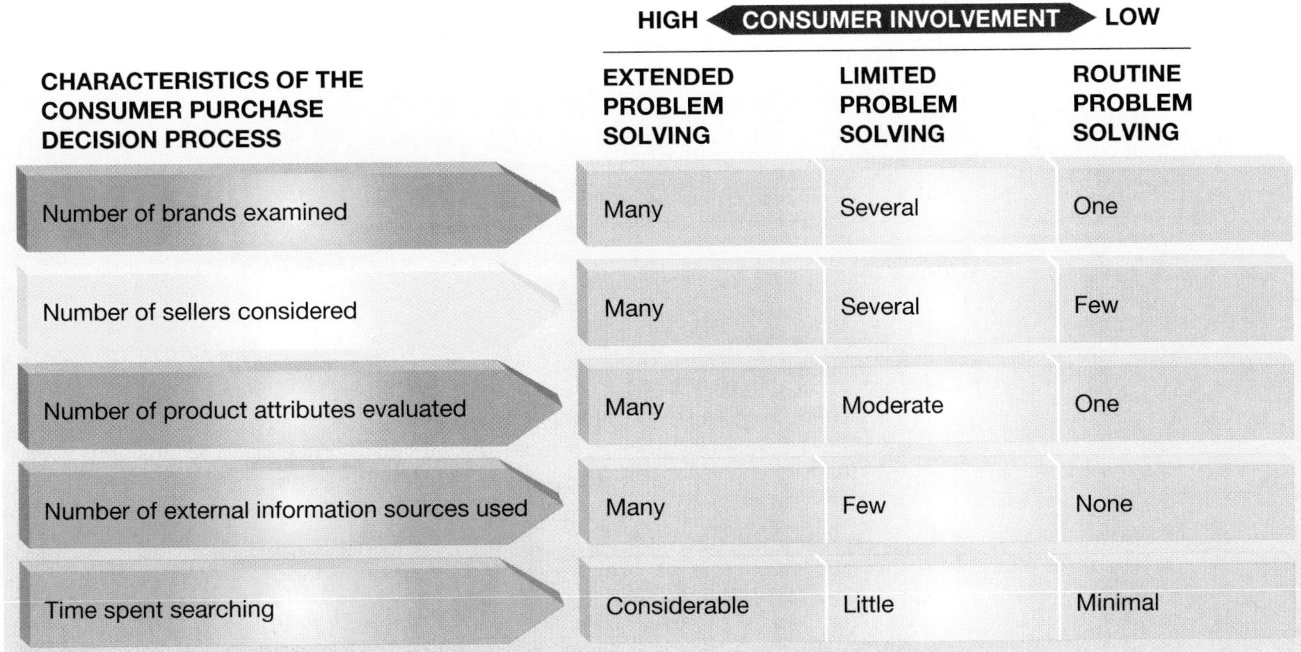

HIGH ◄ CONSUMER INVOLVEMENT ► LOW			
CHARACTERISTICS OF THE CONSUMER PURCHASE DECISION PROCESS	EXTENDED PROBLEM SOLVING	LIMITED PROBLEM SOLVING	ROUTINE PROBLEM SOLVING
Number of brands examined	Many	Several	One
Number of sellers considered	Many	Several	Few
Number of product attributes evaluated	Many	Moderate	One
Number of external information sources used	Many	Few	None
Time spent searching	Considerable	Little	Minimal

FIGURE 5–3
Comparison of problem-solving variations

consequences, or (3) could reflect on one's social image. For these occasions, consumers engage in extensive information search, consider many product attributes and brands, form attitudes, and participate in word-of-mouth communication. Researchers have identified three general variations in the consumer purchase process based on consumer involvement and product knowledge. Figure 5–3 summarizes some of the important differences between the three problem-solving variations.[10]

Extended Problem Solving In extended problem solving, each of the five stages of the consumer purchase decision process is used in the purchase, including considerable time and effort on external information search and in identifying and evaluating alternatives. Several brands are in the consideration set, and these are evaluated on many attributes. Extended problem solving exists in high-involvement purchase situations for items such as automobiles, houses, and financial instruments.

Limited Problem Solving In limited problem solving, consumers typically seek some information or rely on a friend to help them evaluate alternatives. In general, several brands might be evaluated using a moderate number of different attributes. You might use limited problem solving in choosing a toaster, a restaurant for lunch, and other purchase situations in which you have little time or effort to spend researching options.

Routine Problem Solving For products such as table salt and milk, consumers recognize a problem, make a decision, and spend little effort seeking external information and evaluating alternatives. The purchase process for such items is virtually a habit and typifies low-involvement decision making. Routine problem solving is typically the case for low-priced, frequently purchased products.

Situational Influences

Often the purchase situation will affect the purchase decision process. Five *situational influences* have an impact on your purchase decision process: (1) the purchase task, (2) social surroundings, (3) physical surroundings, (4) temporal effects, and (5) antecedent states.[11] The purchase task is the reason for engaging in the decision in the first place. Information searching and evaluating alternatives may differ depending on whether the purchase is a gift, which often involves social visibility, or for the buyer's own use. Social surroundings, including the other people present when a purchase decision is made, may also affect what is purchased. Physical surroundings such as decor,

FIGURE 5–4
Influences on the consumer purchase decision process

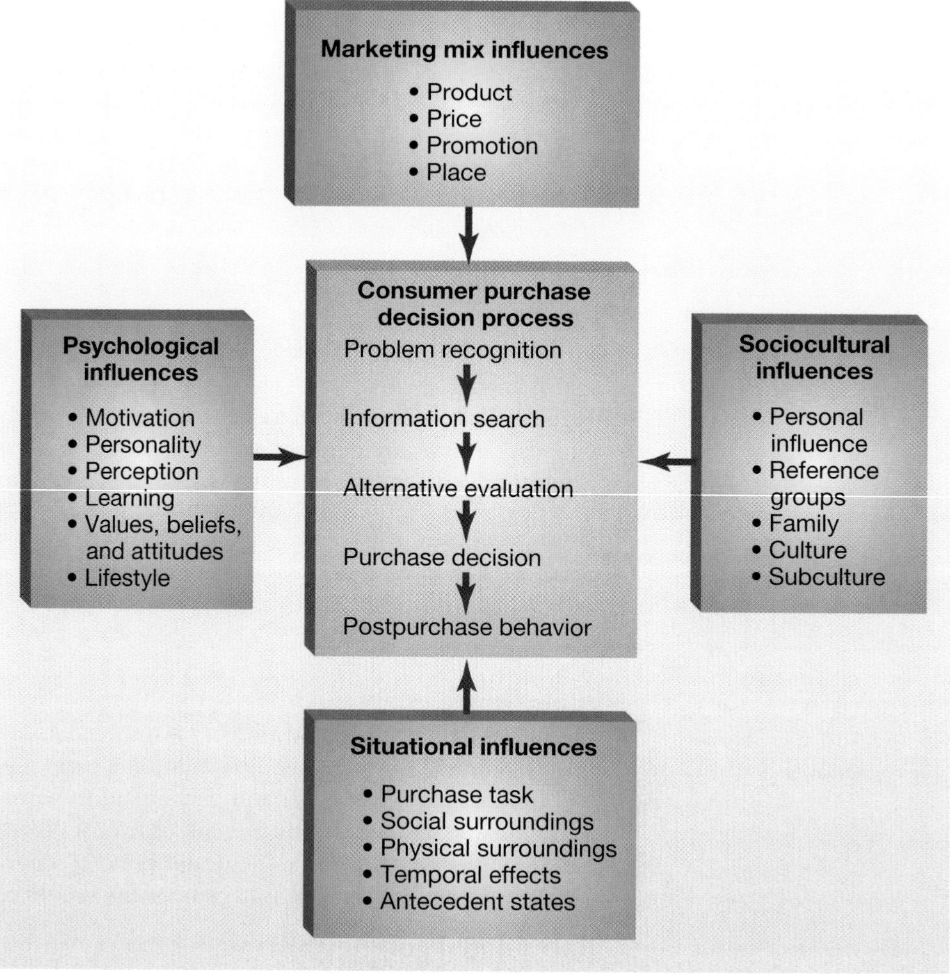

music, and crowding in retail stores may alter how purchase decisions are made. Temporal effects such as time of day or the amount of time available will influence where consumers have breakfast and lunch and what is ordered. Finally, antecedent states, which include the consumer's mood or the amount of cash on hand, can influence purchase behavior and choice.

Figure 5–4 shows the many influences that affect the consumer purchase decision process. The decision to buy a product also involves important psychological and sociocultural influences, the two important topics discussed during the remainder of this chapter. Marketing mix influences are described later in Part 4 of the book.

Concept Check

1. What is the first stage in the consumer purchase decision process?
2. The brands a consumer considers buying out of the set of brands in a product class of which the consumer is aware is called the ________________.

PSYCHOLOGICAL INFLUENCES ON CONSUMER BEHAVIOR

Psychology helps marketers understand why and how consumers behave as they do. In particular, psychological concepts such as motivation and personality; perception; learning; values, beliefs, and attitudes; and lifestyle are useful for interpreting buying processes and directing marketing efforts.

Motivation and Personality

Motivation and personality are two familiar psychological concepts that have specific meanings and marketing implications. They are both used frequently to describe why people do some things and not others.

motivation
Energizing force that stimulates behavior to satisfy a need

Motivation **Motivation** is the energizing force that stimulates behavior to satisfy a need. Because consumer needs are the focus of the marketing concept, marketers try to arouse these needs.

An individual's needs are boundless. People possess physiological needs for basics such as water, shelter, and food. They also have learned needs, including esteem, achievement, and affection. Psychologists point out that these needs are hierarchical; that is, once physiological needs are met, people seek to satisfy their learned needs. Figure 5–5 shows one need hierarchy and classification scheme that contains five need classes.[12] *Physiological needs* are basic to survival and must be satisfied first. A Red Lobster advertisement featuring a seafood salad attempts to activate the need for food. *Safety needs* involve self-preservation and physical well-being. Smoke detector and burglar alarm manufacturers focus on these needs. *Social needs* are concerned with love and friendship. Dating services such as e-harmony.com and match.com try to arouse these needs. *Personal needs* include the need for achievement, status, prestige, and self-respect. The American Express Gold Card and Brooks Brothers Clothiers appeal to these needs. Sometimes firms try to arouse multiple needs to stimulate problem recognition. Michelin combined safety with parental love to promote tire replacement for automobiles. *Self-actualization needs* involve personal fulfillment. For example, a long-running U.S. Army recruiting program invited enlistees to "Be all you can be."

personality
Someone's consistent behaviors or responses to recurring situations

Personality While motivation is the energizing force that makes consumer behavior purposeful, a consumer's personality guides and directs behavior. **Personality** refers to a person's consistent behaviors or responses to recurring situations. Although many personality theories exist, most identify key traits such as assertiveness, extroversion, compliance, dominance, and aggression, among others. Research suggests that compliant people prefer known brand names and use more mouthwash and toilet soaps. In contrast, aggressive types use razors, not electric shavers, apply more cologne

FIGURE 5–5
Hierarchy of needs

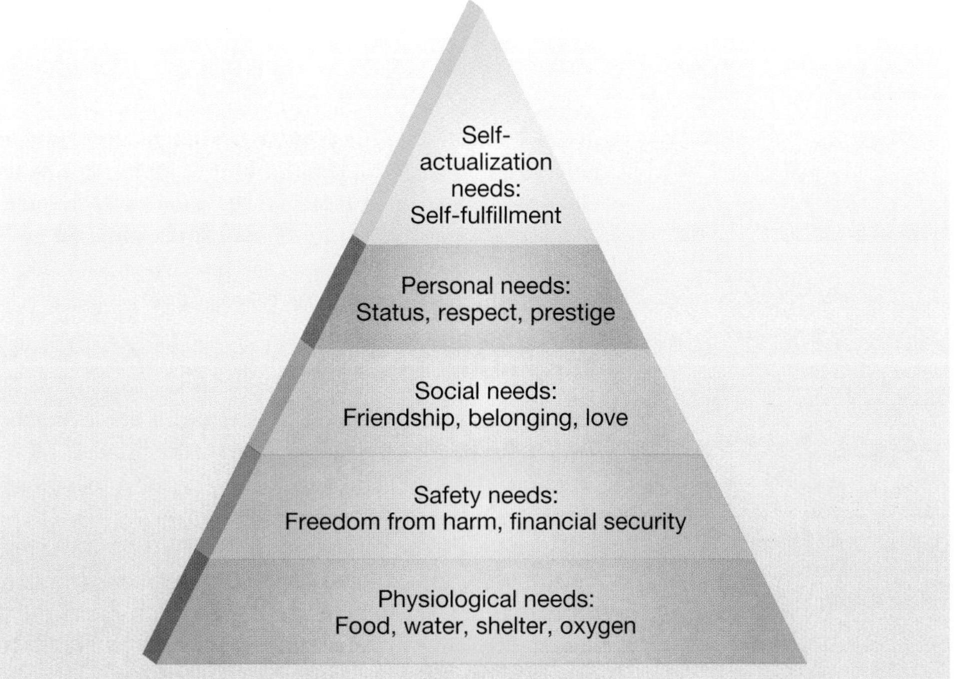

ETHICS AND SOCIAL RESPONSIBILITY ALERT

The Ethics of Subliminal Messages

For about 50 years, the topic of subliminal perception and the presence of subliminal messages and images embedded in commercial communications has sparked heated debate. In fact, the Federal Communications Commission has denounced subliminal messages as deceptive. Still, consumers spend $50 million a year for audiotapes with subliminal messages designed to help them raise their self-esteem, quit smoking, or lose weight. Almost two-thirds of U.S. consumers think subliminal messages are present in commercial communications; about half are convinced that this practice can cause them to buy things they don't want.

Subliminal messages are not illegal in the United States, however, and marketers are often criticized for pursuing opportunities to create these messages in both electronic and print media. A recent book by August Bullock, *The Secret Sales Pitch: An Overview of Subliminal Advertising,* is devoted to this topic. Bullock identifies images and advertisements that he claims contain subliminal messages and describes techniques that can be used for conveying these messages.

Do you believe that attempts to implant subliminal messages in electronic and print media are a deceptive practice and unethical, regardless of their intent?

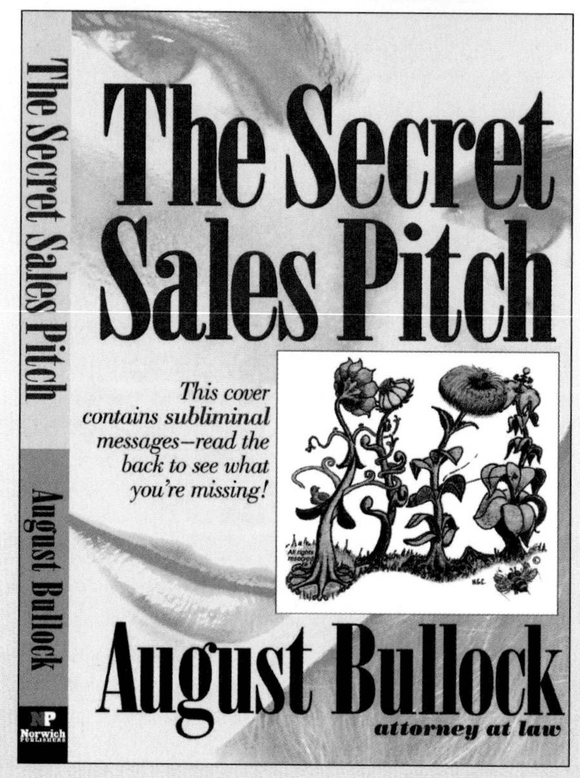

and after-shave lotions, and purchase signature goods such as Gucci, Yves St. Laurent, and Donna Karan as an indicator of status.[13]

Personality characteristics often reveal a person's *self-concept,* which is the way people see themselves and the way they believe others see them. Marketers recognize that people have an actual self-concept and an ideal self-concept. The actual self refers to how people actually see themselves. The ideal self describes how people would like to see themselves. These two self-images are reflected in the products and brands a person buys, including automobiles, home appliances and furnishings, magazines, clothing, grooming and leisure products, and frequently, the stores in which a person shops. The importance of self-concept is summed up by a senior executive at Barnes & Noble: "People buy books for what the purchase says about them—their taste, their cultivation, their trendiness."[14]

Perception

One person sees a Cadillac as a mark of achievement; another sees it as showing off. This is the result of **perception**—the process by which an individual selects, organizes, and interprets information to create a meaningful picture of the world.

perception
Process by which someone selects, organizes, and interprets information to create a meaningful picture of the world

Selective Perception The average consumer operates in a complex, information-rich environment. The human brain organizes and interprets all this information with a process called *selective perception,* which filters the information so that only some of it is understood or remembered or even available to the conscious mind. *Selective exposure* occurs when people pay attention to messages that are consistent with their attitudes and beliefs and ignore messages that are inconsistent. Selective exposure

Why does the Good Housekeeping seal for Clorox's new Fresh Step Crystals cat litter appear in the ad, and why does Mary Kay, Inc., offer a free sample of its new Velocity brand fragrance through its mkvelocity.com website? The answer appears in the text.

often occurs in the postpurchase stage of the consumer decision process, when consumers read advertisements for the brand they just bought. It also occurs when a need exists—you are more likely to "see" a McDonald's advertisement when you are hungry rather than after you have eaten a pizza.

Selective comprehension involves interpreting information so that it is consistent with your attitudes and beliefs. A marketer's failure to understand this can have disastrous results. For example, Toro introduced a small, lightweight snowblower called the Snow Pup. Even though the product worked, sales failed to meet expectations. Why? Toro later found out that consumers perceived the name to mean that Snow Pup was a toy or too light to do any serious snow removal. When the product was renamed Snow Master, sales increased sharply.[15]

Selective retention means that consumers do not remember all the information they see, read, or hear, even minutes after exposure to it. This affects the internal and external information search stage of the purchase decision process. This is why furniture and automobile retailers often give consumers product brochures to take home when they leave the showroom.

Because perception plays an important role in consumer behavior, it is not surprising that subliminal perception is a popular topic for discussion. *Subliminal perception* means that you see or hear messages without being aware of them. The presence and effect of subliminal perception on behavior is a hotly debated issue, with more popular appeal than scientific support.[16] If these messages did influence behavior, would their use be an ethical practice? (See the accompanying Ethics and Social Responsibility Alert.[17])

perceived risk
Anxiety felt when a consumer cannot anticipate possible negative outcomes of a purchase

Perceived Risk Perception plays a major role in the perceived risk in purchasing a product or service. **Perceived risk** represents the anxieties felt because the consumer cannot anticipate the outcomes of a purchase but believes that there may be negative consequences. Examples of possible negative consequences are the size of the financial outlay required to buy the product (Can I afford $500 for those skis?), the risk of physical harm (Is bungee jumping safe?), and the performance of the product (Will the hair coloring work?). A more abstract form is psychosocial (What will my friends say if I wear that sweater?). Perceived risk affects information search, because the greater the perceived risk, the more extensive the external search stage is likely to be.

Recognizing the importance of perceived risk, companies develop strategies to reduce the consumer's risk and encourage purchases. These strategies and examples of firms using them include the following:

- *Obtaining seals of approval:* the Good Housekeeping seal for Fresh Step Crystals cat litter.
- *Securing endorsements from influential people:* the National Fluid Milk Processor Promotion Board "Got Milk" advertising campaign.
- *Providing free trials of the product:* samples of Mary Kay's Velocity fragrance.
- *Giving extensive usage instructions:* Clairol hair coloring.
- *Providing warranties and guarantees:* Cadillac's four-year, 50,000-mile, Gold Key Bumper-to-Bumper warranty.

Learning

learning
Behaviors that result from repeated experience or reasoning

Much consumer behavior is learned. Consumers learn which information sources to consult for information about products and services, which evaluative criteria to use when assessing alternatives, and, more generally, how to make purchase decisions. **Learning** refers to those behaviors that result from (1) repeated experience or (2) reasoning.

Behavioral Learning *Behavioral learning* is the process of developing automatic responses to a situation built up through repeated exposure to it. Four variables are central to how consumers learn from repeated experience: drive, cue, response, and reinforcement. A *drive* is a need that moves an individual to action. Drives, such as hunger, might be represented by motives. A *cue* is a stimulus or symbol perceived by consumers. A *response* is the action taken by a consumer to satisfy the drive, whereas a *reinforcement* is the reward. Being hungry (drive), a consumer sees a cue (a billboard), takes action (buys a sandwich), and receives a reward (it tastes great!).

Marketers use two concepts from behavioral learning theory. *Stimulus generalization* occurs when a response elicited by one stimulus (cue) is generalized to another stimulus. Using the same brand name for different products is an application of this concept, such as Tylenol Cold & Flu and Tylenol P.M. *Stimulus discrimination* refers to a person's ability to perceive differences in stimuli. Consumers' tendency to perceive all light beers as being alike led to Budweiser Light commercials that distinguished between many types of "lights" and Bud Light.

Cognitive Learning Consumers also learn through thinking, reasoning, and mental problem solving without direct experience. This type of learning, called *cognitive learning,* involves making connections between two or more ideas or simply observing the outcomes of others' behaviors and adjusting your own accordingly. Firms also influence this type of learning. Through repetition in advertising, messages such as "Advil is a headache remedy" attempt to link a brand (Advil) and an idea (headache remedy) by showing someone using the brand and finding relief.

brand loyalty
Favorable attitude toward and consistent purchase of a single brand over time

Brand Loyalty Learning is also important to marketers because it relates to habit formation. Developing habits means that a consumer is solving problems (such as what to do when she's hungry) routinely and consistently, without much thought. Not surprisingly, there is a close link between habits and **brand loyalty**, which is a favorable attitude toward and consistent purchase of a single brand over time. Brand loyalty results from positive reinforcement. If a consumer is satisfied with a product, he reduces his risk and saves time by consistently purchasing that same brand.

Values, Beliefs, and Attitudes

Values, beliefs, and attitudes play a central role in consumer decision making.

Attitudes toward Colgate Total toothpaste and Extra Strength Bayer aspirin were successfully changed by these ads. How? Read the text to find out how marketers can change consumer attitudes toward products and brands.

attitude
Tendency to respond to something in a consistently favorable or unfavorable way

beliefs
Consumer's perceptions of how a product or brand performs

Attitude Formation An **attitude** is a "learned predisposition to respond to an object or class of objects in a consistently favorable or unfavorable way."[18] Attitudes are shaped by our values and beliefs, which we develop in the process of growing up. For example, we speak of American core values, including material well-being and humanitarianism. We also have personal values, such as thriftiness and ambition. Marketers are concerned with both but focus mostly on personal values. Personal values affect attitudes by influencing the importance assigned to specific product attributes, or features. Suppose thriftiness is one of your personal values. When you evaluate cars, fuel economy (a product attribute) becomes important. If you believe a specific car has this attribute, you are likely to have a favorable attitude toward it.

Beliefs also play a part in attitude formation. In consumer terms, **beliefs** are one's perception of how a product or brand performs on different attributes. Beliefs are based on personal experience, advertising, and discussions with other people. Beliefs about product attributes are important because, along with personal values, they create the favorable or unfavorable attitude the consumer has toward certain products and services.

Attitude Change Marketers use three approaches to try to change consumer attitudes toward products and brands, as shown in the following examples.[19]

1. *Changing beliefs about the extent to which a brand has certain attributes.* To allay consumer concern that aspirin use causes an upset stomach, Bayer Corporation successfully promoted the gentleness of its Extra Strength Bayer Plus aspirin.
2. *Changing the perceived importance of attributes.* Pepsi-Cola made freshness an important product attribute when it stamped freshness dates on its cans. Prior to doing so, few consumers considered cola freshness an issue. After Pepsi spent about $25 million on advertising and promotion, a consumer survey found that 61 percent of cola drinkers believed freshness dating was an important attribute.
3. *Adding new attributes to the product.* Colgate-Palmolive included a new antibacterial ingredient, tricloson, in its Colgate Total toothpaste and spent $100 million marketing the brand. The result? Colgate replaced Crest as the market leader for the first time in 25 years.

Lifestyle

Lifestyle is a mode of living that is identified by how people spend their time and resources, what they consider important in their environment, and what they think of themselves and the world around them. The analysis of consumer lifestyles, called *psychographics,* provides insights into consumer behavior. Psychographics, the practice of combining psychology, lifestyle, and demographics, is often used to uncover consumer motivations for buying and using products and services. A prominent psychographic system is VALS from SRI Consulting Business Intelligence (SRIC-BI).[20] The VALS system identifies eight consumer segments based on (1) their primary motivation for buying and having certain products and services and (2) their resources. According to SRIC-BI researchers, consumers are motivated to buy products and services and seek experiences that give shape, substance, and satisfaction to their lives. But not all consumers are alike. Consumers are inspired by one of three primary motivations—ideals, achievement, and self-expression—that give meaning to their self or the world and governs their activities. The different levels of resources enhance or constrain a person's expression of his or her primary motivation. A person's resources include psychological, physical, demographic, and material capacities such as income, self-confidence, and risk-taking.

The VALS system seeks to explain why and how consumers make purchase decisions. Consumers motivated by ideals are guided by knowledge and principle. These consumers divide into two segments. *Thinkers* are mature, reflective, and well-educated people who value order, knowledge, and responsibility. They are practical consumers, deliberate information-seekers, who value durability and functionality in products over styling and newness. *Believers,* with fewer resources, are conservative, conventional people with concrete beliefs based on traditional, established codes: family, religion, community, and the nation. They choose familiar products and brands, favor American-made products, and are generally brand loyal.

Do you wish to know your VALS profile? If you do, simply respond to the questions on the VALS survey at www.sric-bi.com/vals.

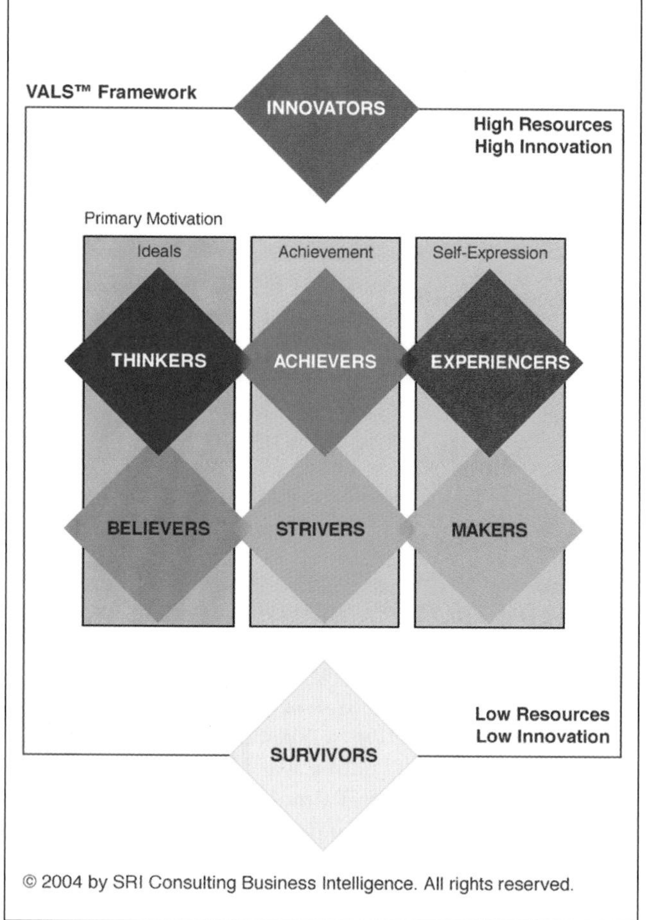

Consumers motivated by achievement look for products and services that demonstrate success to their peers or to a peer group they aspire to. These consumers include *Achievers,* who have a busy, goal-directed lifestyle and a deep commitment to career and family. Image is important to them. They prefer established, prestige products and services and are interested in time-saving devices given their hectic schedules. *Strivers* are trendy, fun-loving, and less self confident than achievers. They also have lower levels of education and household income. Money defines success for them. They favor stylish products and are as impulsive as their financial circumstances permit.

Consumers motivated by self-expression desire social or physical activity, variety, and risk. *Experiencers* are young, enthusiastic, and impulsive consumers who become excited about new possibilities but are equally quick to cool. They savor the new, the offbeat, and the risky. Their energy finds an outlet in exercise, sports, outdoor recreation, and social activities. Much of their income is spent on fashion items, entertainment, and socializing and particularly on looking good and having the latest things. *Makers,* with fewer resources, express themselves and experience the world by working on it—building a house, raising children, or fixing a car. They are practical people who have constructive skills, value self-sufficiency, and are unimpressed by material possessions except those with a practical or functional purpose.

Two segments stand apart. *Innovators* are successful, sophisticated, take-charge people with high self-esteem and abundant resources of all kinds. Image is important to them, not as evidence of power or status, but as an expression of cultivated tastes, independence, and character. They are receptive to new ideas and technologies and their lives are characterized by variety. *Survivors,* with the least resources of any segment, focus on meeting basic needs (safety and security) rather than fulfilling desires. They represent a very modest market for most products and services and are loyal to favorite brands, especially if they can be purchased at a discount.

Concept Check

1. The problem with the Toro Snow Pup was an example of selective __________.
2. What three attitude-change approaches are most common?

SOCIOCULTURAL INFLUENCES ON CONSUMER BEHAVIOR

Sociocultural influences, which evolve from a consumer's formal and informal relationships with other people, also have an impact on consumer behavior. These include personal influence, reference groups, the family, culture, and subculture.

Personal Influence

A consumer's purchases are often influenced by the views, opinions, or behaviors of others. Two aspects of personal influence are important to marketing: opinion leadership and word-of-mouth activity.

opinion leaders
Individuals who have social influence over others

Opinion Leadership Individuals who have social influence over others are called **opinion leaders**. Opinion leaders are more likely to be important for products that provide a form of self-expression. Automobiles, clothing, and club memberships are products affected by opinion leaders, but appliances are not.

About 10 percent of U.S. adults—from influential community leaders and business executives to movie stars—are opinion leaders.[21] Identifying, reaching, and influencing opinion leaders is a major challenge for companies. Some firms use sports figures or celebrities as spokespersons to represent their products, such as actor Pierce Brosnan and tennis player Anna Kournikova for Omega watches, in the hope that they are opinion leaders. Others promote their products in media believed to reach opinion leaders.

Firms use actors or athletes as spokespersons to represent their products, such as Pierce Brosnan and Anna Kournikova for Omega watches, in the hope that they are opinion leaders.

MARKETING NEWSNET BzzAgent—The Business of Buzz

Have you recently heard about a new product, movie, website, book, or restaurant from someone you know . . . or a complete stranger? If so, you may have been buzzed.

Marketers recognize the power of word of mouth. The challenge has been to harness that power. BzzAgent LLC does just that. Its nationwide volunteer army of 90,000 natural-born talkers channel their chatter toward products and services they deem authentically worth talking about. "Our goal is to capture honest word of mouth," says David Bolter, BzzAgent's founder, "and to build a network that turns passionate customers into brand evangelists."

BzzAgent's method is simple. Once a client signs on with BzzAgent, the company searches its "agent" database for those who match the demographic and psychographic profile of the target market for a client's offering. Agents then can sign up for a buzz campaign and receive a sample product and a training manual for buzz-creating strategies. Each time an agent completes an activity, he or she is expected to file an online report describing the nature of the buzz and its effectiveness. BzzAgent coaches respond with encouragement and feedback on additional techniques.

Agents keep the products they promote. They also earn points redeemable for books, CDs, and other items by filing detailed reports. Who are the agents? About 65 percent are older than 25, 60 percent are women, and two are Fortune 500 CEOs. All are gregarious and genuinely like the product or service, otherwise they wouldn't participate in the buzz campaign.

Estée Lauder, Monster.com, Anheuser-Busch, Penguin Books, Lee jeans, and Rock Bottom Restaurants have used BzzAgent. But BzzAgent's buzz isn't cheap, and not everything is buzz worthy. Deploying 1,000 agents on a 12-week campaign can cost a company $100,000, exclusive of product samples. BzzAgent researches a product or service before committing to a campaign and rejects about 80 percent of the companies that seek its service. It also refuses campaigns for politicians, religious groups, and certain products, like firearms. Interested in BzzAgent? Visit its website at www.bzzagent.com.

word of mouth
People influencing each other in personal conversations

Word of Mouth People influencing others during conversations is called **word of mouth**. Word of mouth is the most powerful and authentic information source for consumers because it typically involves friends viewed as trustworthy. According to a recent study, 67 percent of U.S. consumer product sales are directly based on word-of-mouth activity among friends, family, and colleagues.[22]

The power of personal influence has prompted firms to promote positive and retard negative word of mouth. For instance, "teaser" advertising campaigns are run in advance of new-product introductions to stimulate conversations. Other techniques such as advertising slogans, music, and humor also heighten positive word of mouth. Increasingly, companies recruit and deploy people to produce *buzz*—popularity created by consumer word of mouth. Read the accompanying Marketing NewsNet to learn how this is done by BzzAgent.[23]

On the other hand, rumors about Kmart (snake eggs in clothing), McDonald's (worms in hamburgers), Corona Extra beer (contaminated beer), and Snickers candy bars in Russia (a cause of diabetes) have resulted in negative word of mouth, none of which was based on fact. Firms have found that supplying factual information, providing toll-free numbers for consumers to call the company, and giving appropriate product demonstrations have proven helpful.

The power of word of mouth has been magnified by the Internet through online forums, blogs, chat rooms, bulletin boards, and websites. In fact, Ford uses special software to monitor online messages and find out what consumers are saying about its vehicles. Chapter 18 describes how companies initiate and manage word of mouth in an online environment using viral marketing techniques.

Reference Groups

reference groups
People to whom an individual looks as a basis for self-appraisal or as a source of personal standards

Reference groups are people to whom an individual looks as a basis for self-appraisal or as a source of personal standards. For example, you might consider the other students in your school, or your family, as a reference group. Reference groups affect consumer purchases because they influence the information, attitudes, and aspiration levels that help set a consumer's standards. Reference groups have an important influence on the purchase of luxury products but not of necessities—reference groups exert a strong influence on the brand chosen when its use or consumption is highly visible to others.

Consumers have many reference groups, but three groups have clear marketing implications. A *membership group* is one to which a person actually belongs, including fraternities and sororities, social clubs, and the family. Such groups are easily identifiable and are targeted by firms selling insurance, insignia products, and charter vacations. An *aspiration group* is one that a person wishes to be a member of or wishes to be identified with, such as a professional society. Firms frequently rely on spokespeople or settings associated with their target market's aspiration group in their advertising. A *dissociative group* is one that a person wishes to maintain a distance from because of differences in values or behaviors.

Family Influence

Family influences on consumer behavior result from three sources: consumer socialization, passage through the family life cycle, and decision making within the family or household.

Consumer Socialization The process by which people acquire the skills, knowledge, and attitudes necessary to function as consumers is *consumer socialization*.[24] Children learn how to purchase (1) by interacting with adults in purchase situations and (2) through their own purchasing and product usage experiences. Research demonstrates that children show signs of brand preferences as early as age two, and these preferences often last a lifetime. This knowledge has prompted Sony to introduce My First Sony, a line of portable audio equipment for children; Time, Inc., to launch *Sports Illustrated for Kids;* and Polaroid to develop the Cool Cam camcorder for children between ages 9 and 14.

family life cycle
Family's progression from formation to retirement, each phase bringing with it distinct purchasing behaviors

Family Life Cycle Consumers act and purchase differently as they go through life. The **family life cycle** concept describes the distinct phases that a family progresses through from formation to retirement, each phase bringing with it identifiable purchasing behaviors.[25] Today, the traditional family—married couples with children younger than 18 years—constitutes just 23.5 percent of all U.S. households. The remaining 76.5 percent of U.S. households include single parents, unmarried couples, divorced, never-married, or widowed individuals, and older married couples whose children no longer live at home.

Young singles' buying preferences are for nondurable items, including prepared foods, clothing, personal care products, and entertainment. They represent a target market for recreational travel, automobile, and consumer electronics firms. Young married couples without children are typically more affluent than young singles because usually both spouses are employed. These couples exhibit preferences for furniture, housewares, and gift items for each other. Young marrieds with children are driven by the needs of their children. They make up a sizable market for life insurance, various children's products, and home furnishings. Single parents with children are the least financially secure of households with children. Their buying preferences are affected by a limited economic status and tend toward convenience foods, child care services, and personal care items.

Middle-aged married couples with children are typically better off financially than their younger counterparts. They are a significant market for leisure products and home improvement items. Middle-aged couples without children typically have a large amount of discretionary income. These couples buy better home furnishings, status automobiles, and financial services. Persons in the last two phases—older married and

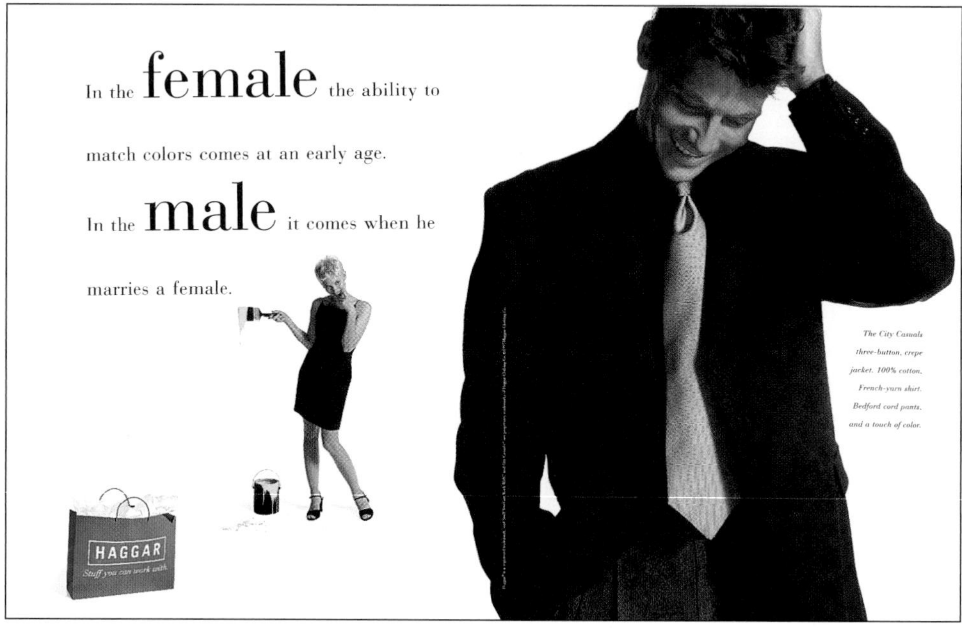

The Haggar Clothing Co. recognizes the important role women play in the choice of men's clothing. The company directs a large portion of its advertising toward women because they influence and purchase men's clothing.

older unmarried—make up a sizable market for prescription drugs, medical services, vacation trips, and gifts for younger relatives.

In the **female** the ability to
match colors comes at an early age.
In the **male** it comes when he
marries a female.
HAGGAR
The City Casuals
three-button, crepe
jacket. 100% cotton.
French-yarn shirt.
Bedford cord pants,
and a touch of color.

Family Decision Making A third family-based influence on consumer decision making occurs in the context of the relationship dynamics of the household. Two decision-making styles exist: spouse-dominant and joint decision making. With a joint decision-making style, most decisions are made by both husband and wife. Spouse-dominant decisions are those for which either the husband or the wife is responsible. Research indicates that wives tend to have the most say when purchasing groceries, children's toys, clothing, and medicines. Husbands tend to be more influential in home and car maintenance purchases. Joint decision making is common for cars, vacations, houses, home appliances and electronics, and medical care. As a rule, joint decision making increases with the education of the spouses.[26]

Roles of individual family members in the purchase process are another element of family decision making. Five roles exist: (1) information gatherer, (2) influencer, (3) decision maker, (4) purchaser, and (5) user. Family members assume different roles for different products and services.[27] For example, 89 percent of wives either influence or make outright purchases of men's clothing. Knowing this, Haggar Clothing, a menswear marketer, now advertises in women's magazines such as *Vanity Fair* and *Redbook*. Even though women are often the grocery decision maker, they are not necessarily the purchaser. More than 40 percent of all food-shopping dollars are spent by male customers. Increasingly, preteens and teenagers are the information gatherers, influencers, decision makers, and purchasers of products and services items for the family, given the prevalence of working parents and single-parent households. Children under 12 directly influence about $300 billion in annual family purchases. Teenagers influence another $450 billion. These figures help explain why, for example, Nabisco, Johnson & Johnson, Apple Computer, Kellogg, P&G, Sony, and Oscar Mayer, among countless other companies, spend more than $32 billion annually in media that reach preteens and teens.

Culture and Subculture

As described in Chapter 3, culture refers to the set of values, ideas, and attitudes that are learned and shared among the members of a group. Thus we often refer to the American culture, the Latin American culture, or the Japanese culture.

subcultures
Subgroups within a larger culture that have unique values, ideas, and attitudes

Subgroups within the larger, or national, culture with unique values, ideas, and attitudes are referred to as **subcultures**. Various subcultures exist within the American

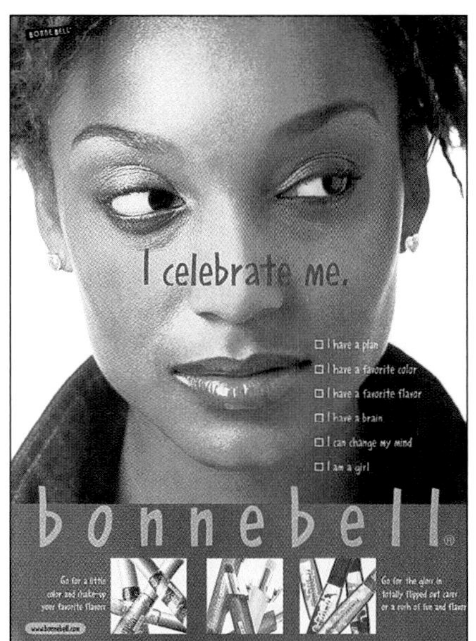

African American women represent a large market for health and beauty products. Cosmetic companies such as Bonne Bell Cosmetics, Inc., actively seek to serve this market.

culture. The three largest racial/ethnic subcultures in the United States are African Americans, Hispanics, and Asians Americans. Collectively, they annually spend about $2.5 trillion for goods and services.[28] Each of these groups exhibits sophisticated social and cultural behaviors that affect their buying patterns.

African American Buying Patterns African Americans have the largest spending power of the three racial/ethnic subcultures in the United States. Consumer research on African American buying patterns have focused on similarities and differences with whites'. Even though similarities outweigh differences, there are consumption patterns that do differ between African Americans and whites.[29] For example, African Americans spend far more than whites on children's apparel, footware, and telephone services. African American women spend three times more on health and beauty products than white women. Furthermore, the typical African American family is five years younger than the typical white family. This factor alone accounts for some of the observed differences in preferences for clothing, music, shelter, cars, and many other products, services, and activities.

Recent research indicates that while African Americans are price conscious, they are strongly motivated by quality and choice. Regardless of socioeconomic status, they respond more to products and advertising that appeal to their African American pride and heritage, as well as address their ethnic features and needs.

Hispanic Buying Patterns Hispanics represent the largest racial/ethnic subculture in the United States in terms of population. About 50 percent of Hispanics in the United States are immigrants, and the majority are under the age of 25.

Research on Hispanic buying practices has uncovered several consistent patterns:[30]

1. Hispanics are quality and brand conscious. They are willing to pay a premium price for premium quality and are often brand loyal.
2. Hispanics prefer buying American-made products, especially those offered by firms that cater to Hispanic needs.
3. Hispanic buying preferences are strongly influenced by family and peers.
4. Hispanics consider advertising a credible product information source, and U.S. firms spend $3 billion annually on advertising to Hispanics.
5. Convenience is not an important product attribute to Hispanic homemakers with respect to food preparation or consumption, nor is low caffeine in coffee and soft drinks, low fat in dairy products, and low cholesterol in packaged foods.

The Hershey Company recently launched a line of candy items tailored to Hispanic taste preferences.

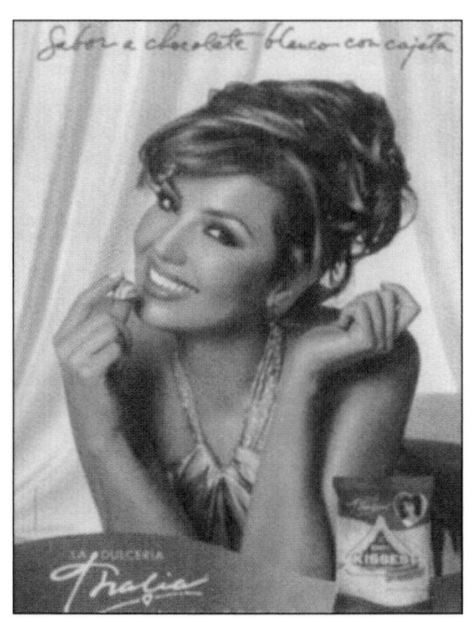

Despite some consistent buying patterns, marketing to Hispanics has proven to be a challenge for two reasons. First, the Hispanic subculture is highly diverse and composed of Mexicans, Puerto Ricans, Cubans, and others of Central and South American ancestry. Cultural differences among these nationalities often affect product preferences. For example, Campbell Soup Company sells its Casera line of soups, beans, and sauces using different recipes to appeal to Puerto Ricans on the East Coast and Mexicans in the Southwest. Second, a language barrier exists, and commercial messages are frequently misinterpreted when translated into Spanish. Volkswagen learned this lesson when the Spanish translation of its "Driver's Wanted" slogan suggested "chauffeurs wanted." The Spanish slogan is now *Agarra calle,* a slang expression that can be loosely translated as "let's hit the road."[31] Campbell Soup has overcome the language issue. It provides Spanish and English labels on its soups in parts of the western and southwestern United States.

Asian American Buying Patterns About 70 percent of Asians Americans in the United States are immigrants, and most are under the age of 30. Recent U.S. census figures indicate that Asian Americans are a fast-growing racial/ethnic subculture in the United States.

The Asian American subculture is composed of Chinese, Japanese, Filipinos, Koreans, Asian Indians, people from Southeast Asia, and Pacific Islanders. The diversity of the Asian American subculture is so great that generalizations about buying patterns of this group are difficult to make.[32] Consumer research on Asian Americans suggests that individuals and families divide into two groups. *Assimilated* Asian Americans are conversant in English, highly educated, hold professional and managerial positions, and exhibit buying patterns very much like the typical American consumer. *Nonassimilated* Asian Americans are recent immigrants who still cling to their native languages and customs. The diversity of Asian Americans evident in language, customs, and tastes requires marketers to be sensitive to different Asian nationalities. For example, Anheuser-Busch's agricultural products division sells eight different varieties of California-grown rice, each with a different Asian label to cover a range of nationalities and tastes. The company's advertising also addresses the preferences of Chinese, Japanese, and Koreans for different kinds of rice bowls.

Concept Check

1. What are the two primary forms of personal influence?
2. What two challenges must marketers overcome when marketing to Hispanics?

CHAPTER IN REVIEW

1 *Describe the stages in the consumer purchase decision process.*

The consumer purchase decision process consists of five stages. They are problem recognition, information search, alternative evaluation, purchase decision, and postpurchase behavior. Problem recognition is perceiving a difference between a person's ideal and actual situation big enough to trigger a decision. Information search involves remembering previous purchase experiences (internal search) and external search behavior such as seeking information from other sources. Alternative evaluation clarifies the problem for the consumer by (*a*) suggesting the evaluative criteria to use for the purchase, (*b*) yielding brand names that might meet the criteria, and (*c*) developing consumer value perceptions. The purchase decision involves the choice of an alternative, including from whom to buy and when to buy. Postpurchase behavior involves the comparison of the chosen alternative with a consumer's expectations, which leads to satisfaction or dissatisfaction and subsequent purchase behavior.

2 *Distinguish among three variations of the consumer purchase decision process: routine, limited, and extended problem solving.*

Consumers don't always engage in the five-stage purchase decision process. Instead, they skip or minimize one or more stages depending on the level of involvement—the personal, social, and economic significance of the purchase. For low-involvement purchase occasions, consumers engage in routine problem solving. They recognize a problem, make a decision, and spend little effort seeking external information and evaluating alternatives. For high-involvement purchase occasions, each of the five stages of the consumer purchase decision process is used, including considerable time and effort on external information search and in identifying and evaluating alternatives. With limited problem solving, consumers typically seek some information or rely on a friend to help them evaluate alternatives.

3 *Identify major psychological influences on consumer behavior.*

Psychology helps marketers understand why and how consumers behave as they do. In particular, psychological concepts such as motivation and personality; perception; learning; values, beliefs, and attitudes; and lifestyle are useful for interpreting buying processes. Motivation is the energizing force that stimulates behavior to satisfy a need. Personality refers to a person's consistent behaviors or responses to recurring situations. Perception is the process by which an individual selects, organizes, and interprets information to create a meaningful picture of the world. Consumers filter information through selective exposure, comprehension, and retention.

Much consumer behavior is learned. Learning refers to those behaviors that result from (*a*) repeated experience and (*b*) reasoning. Brand loyalty results from learning. Values, beliefs, and attitudes are also learned and influence how consumers evaluate products, services, and brands. A more general concept is lifestyle. Lifestyle, also called *psychographics,* combines psychology and demographics and focuses on how people spend their time and resources, what they consider important in their environment, and what they think of themselves and the world around them.

4 *Identify major sociocultural influences on consumer behavior.*

Sociocultural influences, which evolve from a consumer's formal and informal relationships with other people, also affect consumer behavior. These involve personal influence, reference groups, the family, social class, culture, and subculture. Opinion leadership and word-of-mouth behavior are two major sources of personal influence on consumer behavior. Reference groups are people to whom an individual looks as a basis for self-approval or as source of personal standards. Family influences on consumer behavior result from three sources: consumer socialization; passage through the family life cycle; and decision making within the family or household. A more subtle influence on consumer behavior than direct contact with others is the social class to which people belong. Persons within social classes tend to exhibit common values, attitudes, beliefs, lifestyles, and buying behaviors. Finally, a person's culture and subculture have been shown to influence product preferences and buying patterns.

FOCUSING ON KEY TERMS

attitude p. 109
beliefs p. 109
brand loyalty p. 108
consumer behavior p. 100
family life cycle p. 113
involvement p. 102
learning p. 108
motivation p. 105
opinion leaders p. 111
perceived risk p. 107
perception p. 106
personality p. 105
purchase decision process p. 100
reference groups p. 113
subcultures p. 114
word of mouth p. 112

DISCUSSION AND APPLICATION QUESTIONS

1 Review Figure 5–2 in the text, which shows the MP3-capable CD player attributes identified by *Consumer Reports*. Which attributes are important to you? What other attributes might you consider? Which brand would you prefer?

2 Assign one or more levels of the hierarchy of needs and the motives described in Figure 5–5 to the following products: (*a*) life insurance, (*b*) cosmetics, (*c*) *The Wall Street Journal,* and (*d*) hamburgers.

3 Which social class would you associate with each of the following items or actions: (*a*) tennis club membership, (*b*) an arrangement of plastic flowers in the kitchen, (*c*) *True Romance* magazine, (*d*) *Smithsonian* magazine, (*e*) formally dressing for dinner frequently, and (*f*) being a member of a bowling team?

4 With which stage in the family life cycle would the purchase of the following products and services be most closely identified: (*a*) bedroom furniture, (*b*) life insurance, (*c*) a Caribbean cruise, (*d*) a house mortgage, and (*e*) children's toys?

GOING ONLINE Tracking Buying Power of Multicultural Consumers

The size and economic significance of racial/ethnic subcultures in the United States has been documented by the U.S. Census. Population statistics supplied by the U.S. Census are readily accessible at www.census.gov. These statistics coupled with data useful for marketing purposes offer valuable insights into the growing diversity of the U.S. population.

The Selig Center for Economic Growth at the University of Georgia provides useful information on the buying power of African Americans, Hispanics, and Asian Americans, the three largest racial/ethnic subcultures in the United States. Visit the Center's website at www.selig.uga.edu for answers to the following questions.

1 What is the most recent estimate of the buying power of African Americans, Hispanics, and Asian Americans in the United States?

2 In which states is African American buying power the highest? Which states have the highest Hispanic and Asian American buying power?

BUILDING YOUR MARKETING PLAN

To do a consumer analysis for the product—the good, service, or idea—in your marketing plan:

1 Identify the consumers who are most likely to buy your product—the primary target market—in terms of (*a*) their demographic characteristics and (*b*) any other kind of characteristics you believe are important.

2 Describe (*a*) the main points of difference of your product for this group and (*b*) what problem they help solve for the consumer, in terms of the first stage in the consumer purchase decision process in Figure 5–1.

3 Identify the one or two key influences for each of the four outside boxes in Figure 5–4: (*a*) marketing mix, (*b*) psychological, (*c*) sociocultural, and (*d*) situational influences.

This consumer analysis will provide the foundation for the marketing mix actions you develop later in your plan.

VIDEO CASE 5 Ken Davis Products, Inc.: Sauces for All Tastes

"Cooking is a lot like music," explains Barbara Jo Davis. "There are musicians who are excellent musicians and they can play any of the classical music to perfection, but they don't know how to improvise. And then there are the jazz musicians who can do both of these things."

"The same thing is true of cooks," continues Barbara. "There are the cooks who can follow a recipe . . . and will be the best cooks in the world as long as they have a recipe. But if they have to improvise, then they're lost. So what we want to do is help those who aren't the improvisers."

THE COMPANY

Barbara Jo Davis is president of Ken Davis® Products, Inc., a small regional business that develops and markets barbecue sauces. "We position Ken Davis Bar-B-Q Sauces, not as something you use for grilling, but as something that adds flavor to ordinary food—a 'spice kit in a jar'," explains Barbara Davis.

The company was founded by Barbara Davis's late spouse Ken Davis. Ken owned a restaurant where he served his grandmother's recipe for barbecue sauce, and he received such positive feedback from his customers he decided to write the recipe down to ensure it would taste the same every time he made it. He called in Barbara, then a home economist for a large consumer foods corporation, to help him do it. Shortly afterward, Ken closed the restaurant, married Barbara, and began marketing his barbecue sauce full-time. Barbara Davis stayed with the consumer foods corporation, becoming a manager for the test kitchens and for the cookbooks, until 1988 when she left to work for Ken Davis Products full-time.

While Ken Davis Products is a market leader in its region, it has not expanded nationwide. Barbara Davis explains, "What I hear consumers say again and again is the reason they buy Ken Davis Bar-B-Q Sauces is because it's a local company. I think the reason we're the market leaders is because it's a personal product. People know who the person is. They can see me driving around in my car."

PRODUCTS, BRAND NAMES, AND PACKAGING

As president of a small, regional business, Barbara Davis has her hands in almost everything from testing new barbeque sauces and recipes in the Ken Davis test kitchen (see photo) to personally promoting Ken Davis Bar-B-Q Sauces on a 90-second radio show. Let's look at some of her product, brand name, and packaging decisions.

Today Ken Davis Products markets four barbeque sauces:

- Original Bar-B-Q Sauce: The original "secret recipe" Ken Davis got from his grandmother that has been a regional favorite for over 30 years.
- 2 Carb Original Bar-B-Q Sauce: Same great flavor as the Original but with only 2 grams of carbohydrates (compared to 10 in the Original) and no sugar in each serving.
- Smooth 'n Spicy Bar-B-Q Sauce: A smooth blend of cumin, spices, and Jalapeno peppers with just a touch of heat.
- Sweet & Smoky Bar-B-Q Sauce: Introduced in 2005, a sauce that's sweet (but with only 5 grams of carbohydrates per serving), and a tiny bit spicier than the Original but has a definite smoky flavor.

Coming out of the test kitchen, the new smoky barbeque sauce needed a name. What to call it? Early candidates: Original, Part II; Smoky Campfire; Test Batch #19; Sweet Roast; and Crazy Woman Creek. "Give me a break," says Barbara Davis. "Finally, we decided *not* to be cutesy, but to simply describe the flavor." So Ken Davis Sweet & Smoky Bar-B-Q Sauce was born—introduced with a label that looks fun and inviting in a sassy purple color.

She has talked to consumers who used Ken Davis Bar-B-Q Sauces everywhere from in the kitchen to an outdoor grill to over a campfire. This convinced Barbara Davis that the original cylindrical plastic bottle wasn't easy to grip in all these places. So in 2004 the new plastic bottle with its easy-to-hold squared shape appeared, as shown on the opposite page. The new bottle has "Ken Davis" embossed in the plastic. Long-time fans of Ken Davis Bar-B-Q Sauce can still purchase the original mayonnaise-style jar in two sizes—quarts and pints.

LISTENING TO CONSUMERS

Barbara Davis has discovered through consumer interviews that the barbeque buying decision is still made by the female head of the household, but everybody in the family seems to participate in the decision. "Kids especially like our sauce a lot," explains Barbara Davis, "and elderly people like the Original Recipe because it's got a lot of flavor but it's not hot or spicy." The other flavors appeal to segments of consumers who do like spicier or smokier flavors or who have nutrition concerns.

Ken Davis Products prides itself on staying abreast of changing consumer tastes and trends. In addition to conducting formal interviews, Barbara Davis solicits informal feedback from current and potential Ken Davis customers. She will talk to testers at an in-store sampling or even walk up to shoppers in the barbecue sauce aisle and ask them about their purchases. Barbara Davis believes, "You have to listen to your consumer because you're not in this business to please yourself. You're in business to please your consumer." In addition to discovering the latest tastes, she has learned from her customers that the primary promotional vehicle used to spread the word about Ken Davis Products is word of mouth.

COMMUNICATING WITH CONSUMERS

To make the most of this word-of-mouth strategy, Ken Davis Products participates in event marketing and in-store sampling. Ken Davis used to always say, "The best way to sell a food product is to get people to taste it, because it's ultimately the taste that will keep them as customers." Barbara Davis has found that another successful strategy to get people talking about Ken Davis Products is to become involved in the community. She regularly talks to groups of young entrepreneurs or invites school children to her test kitchen to learn how to cook. "You do all of these little things just to get people thinking Ken Davis. And they don't even know they're thinking Ken Davis half the time. But it's so ingrained that when they go to the grocery store, why would they look at those other brands?" Ken Davis Products also uses some more traditional promotional vehicles. These include its website, newsletters, radio ads, and a morning radio show.

Barbara Davis sends out a newsletter twice a year to Ken Davis Product users with new recipe ideas and stories about the company. Today's busy family is always on the lookout for quick and easy recipes. The newsletter also contains other practical articles ranging from eating healthy and organizing your grocery and shopping list to the most common mistake in grilling steak.

The radio ads reflect the local, homegrown differentiation strategy used by Ken Davis Products. Barbara Davis does the commercials herself, which are completely unrehearsed. "That way I don't have to pay talent," she chuckles.

The morning radio show also reflects her friendly, helpful style. Known as "Ms. Barbara," Barbara Davis appears on a segment called "The 90-Second Chef" on a three-times-a-week morning radio show. Her cell phone rings at about 8:40 A.M. Mondays, Wednesdays, and Fridays, and Barbara Davis goes on the air regardless of where she's at—even when she's eating a hot dog in New York's Grand Central Station. She then gives cooking tips or a recipe or answers questions from the program's husband-and-wife co-hosts. Nearly a show-stopper: "Barbara, can you make anything with bananas and Ken Davis Bar-B-Q Sauce?" But after some research Barbara found an answer—a recipe for Jamaican Cream of Banana Soup. "A dollop of Ken Davis Bar-B-Q Sauce makes it a little smoky with a hint of molasses flavor, and so there!" laughs "Ms. Barbara."

THE MULTIPLE ROLES OF A SMALL BUSINESSPERSON

After working for a large corporation and then becoming a small business entrepreneur, Barbara Davis is in a unique position to comment on the satisfactions and hardships of owning your own business. She stresses that you have to know everything about your business—you can't specialize as in a large corporation. You also get to make all the decisions and have the satisfaction of being a part of the process every step of the way. "But," Barbara adds, "you have to work harder than you have ever worked in your life. You have to always be working. When I was working for a corporation, I resented working all those hours because it wasn't for me. But now when I'm working all these hours I love it because I am doing it for myself. That's the reward—it's all for you."

Questions

1 In what ways have American eating habits changed over the past decade that affect a barbecue sauce manufacturer?

2 What are the two or three main (*a*) objective evaluative criteria and (*b*) subjective evaluative criteria consumers of Ken Davis Bar-B-Q Sauces might use?

3 How can Ken Davis Products do marketing research on consumers to find out what they eat, to learn how they use barbecue sauces, and to get ideas for new products?

4 (*a*) Do you think a small, regional company such as Ken Davis Products should have entered the market as a premium-priced product or a low-priced product? (*b*) What should its pricing strategy be today?

5 What do you see are the (*a*) satisfactions and (*b*) concerns of being in business for yourself?

it's all inside.™

JCPenney

catalog | .com

1.800.222.6161 jcpenney.com

CHAPTER 6

ORGANIZATIONAL MARKETS AND BUYER BEHAVIOR

LEARNING OBJECTIVES

After reading this chapter you should be able to:

1. Distinguish among industrial, reseller, and government organizational markets.
2. Describe the key characteristics of organizational buying that make it different from consumer buying.
3. Explain how buying centers and buying situations influence organizational purchasing.
4. Recognize the importance and nature of online buying in industrial, reseller, and government organizational markets.

BUYING PAPER IS A STRATEGIC BUSINESS DECISION AT JCPENNEY

Kim Nagele views paper differently than most people do. As the senior procurement agent at JCPMedia, he and a team of purchasing professionals buy more than 260,000 tons of paper annually at a cost of hundreds of millions of dollars.

JCPMedia is the print and paper purchasing arm for JCPenney, the fifth-largest retailer in the United States and the largest catalog merchant of general merchandise in the Western Hemisphere. Paper is serious business at JCPMedia, which buys paper for JCPenney catalogs (see opposite page), newspaper inserts, and direct-mail pieces. Some 10 companies from around the world, including International Paper in the United States, Stora Enso in Sweden, and UPM-Kymmene, Inc., a Finnish paper company, supply paper to JCPMedia.

The choice of paper and suppliers is a strategic business decision given its revenue and expense consequences. Therefore, JCPMedia paper buyers work closely with JCPenney marketing personnel and within budget constraints to assure that the right quality and quantity of paper is purchased at the right price point for merchandise featured in the millions of catalogs, newspaper inserts, and direct-mail pieces distributed every year. In addition to paper quality and price, buyers formally evaluate supplier capabilities. These include a supplier's capacity to deliver selected grades of paper from specialty items to magazine papers, the availability of specific types of paper to meet printing deadlines, and ongoing environmental programs. For example, a supplier's forestry management and antipollution practices are considered in the JCPMedia buying process.[1]

Purchasing paper for JCPMedia is one example of organizational buying. This chapter examines the types of organizational buyers; key characteristics of organizational buying, including online buying; and some typical buying decisions in organizational markets.

THE NATURE AND SIZE OF ORGANIZATIONAL MARKETS

business marketing
Marketing to firms, governments, or not-for-profit organizations

organizational buyers
Manufacturers, wholesalers, retailers, and government agencies that buy goods and services for their own use or for resale

Understanding organizational markets and buying behavior is a necessary prerequisite for effective business marketing. **Business marketing** is the marketing of goods and services to companies, governments, or not-for-profit organizations for use in the creation of goods and services that they can produce and market to others. So many firms engage in business marketing that it is important to understand the characteristics of organizational buyers and their buying behavior.

Organizational buyers are those manufacturers, wholesalers, retailers, and government agencies that buy goods and services for their own use or for resale. For example, these organizations buy computers and telephone services for their own use. However, manufacturers buy raw materials and parts that they reprocess into the finished goods they sell. Wholesalers and retailers resell the goods they buy without reprocessing them. Organizational buyers include all buyers in a nation except ultimate consumers. These organizational buyers purchase and lease large volumes of capital equipment, raw materials, manufactured parts, supplies, and business services. In fact, because they often buy raw materials and parts, process them, and sell the upgraded product several times before it is purchased by the final organizational buyer or ultimate consumer, the total annual purchases of organizational buyers are far greater than those of ultimate consumers.

Organizational buyers are divided into three different markets: (1) industrial, (2) reseller, and (3) government markets (Figure 6–1).[2]

Industrial Markets

There are about 12 million firms in the industrial, or business, market. These *industrial firms* in some way reprocess a product or service they buy before selling it again to the next buyer. This is certainly true of Corning, Inc., which transforms an exotic blend of materials to create optical fiber capable of carrying much of the telephone traffic in the United States at once on a single strand. It is also true (if you stretch your imagination) of a firm selling services, such as a bank that takes money from its depositors, reprocesses it, and "sells" it as loans to borrowers.

FIGURE 6–1
Type and number of organizational customers in the United States

KIND OF MARKET	TYPE OF ORGANIZATION	NUMBER
Industrial (business) markets—11,967,000	Manufacturers	355,000
	Mining	25,000
	Construction	710,000
	Farms, timber, and fisheries	2,054,000
	Service	7,707,000
	Finance, insurance, and real estate	724,000
	Transportation, communications, and public utilities	336,000
	Not-for-profit associations	56,000
Reseller markets—3,810,000	Wholesalers	860,000
	Retailers	2,950,000
Government markets—88,000	Government units	88,000

The importance of services in the United States today is emphasized by the composition of the industrial markets shown in Figure 6–1. The first four types of industrial firms (manufacturers; mining; construction; and farms, timber, and fisheries) sell physical products and represent 26 percent of all the industrial firms, or about 3.1 million. The services market sells diverse services such as legal advice, auto repair, and dry cleaning. Along with finance, insurance, and real estate businesses, and transportation, communication, and public utility firms, these service firms represent about 73 percent of all industrial firms, or about 8.8 million.

Reseller Markets

Wholesalers and retailers that buy physical products and resell them again without any reprocessing are *resellers*. In the United States there are almost 3 million retailers and 860,000 wholesalers. In this chapter we look at these resellers mainly as organizational buyers in terms of (1) how they make their own buying decisions and (2) which products they choose to carry.

Government Markets

Government units are the federal, state, and local agencies that buy goods and services for the constituents they serve. There are about 88,000 of these government units in the United States. Their annual purchases vary in size from the $898 million the Federal Aviation Administration intends to spend for 3,000 computerized workstations for 22 major air traffic control centers in the United States to lesser amounts spent by local school or sanitation districts.[3]

MEASURING INDUSTRIAL, RESELLER, AND GOVERNMENT MARKETS

North American Industry Classification System (NAICS)
Provides common industry definitions for Canada, Mexico, and the United States

The measurement of industrial, reseller, and government markets is an important first step for a firm interested in gauging the size of one, two, or all three of these markets in the United States and around the world. This task has been made easier with the **North American Industry Classification System (NAICS)**.[4] The NAICS provides common industry definitions for Canada, Mexico, and the United States, which makes easier the measurement of economic activity in the three member countries of the North American Free Trade Agreement (NAFTA). The NAICS replaced the Standard Industrial Classification (SIC) system, a version of which has been in place for more than 50 years in the three NAFTA member countries. The SIC neither permitted comparability across countries nor accurately measured new or emerging industries. Furthermore, the NAICS is consistent with the International Standard Industrial Classification of All Economic Activities, published by the United Nations, to facilitate measurement of global economic activity.

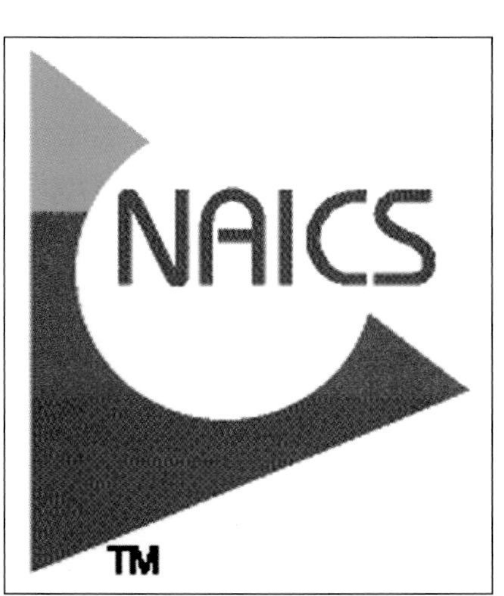

The NAICS groups economic activity to permit studies of market share, demand for goods and services, import competition in domestic markets, and similar studies. It designates industries with a numerical code in a defined structure. A six-digit coding system is used. The first two digits designate a sector of the economy, the third digit designates a subsector, and the fourth digit represents an industry group. The fifth digit designates a specific industry and is the most detailed level at which comparable data is available for Canada, Mexico, and the United States. The sixth digit designates individual country-level national industries. Figure 6–2 on the next page presents an abbreviated breakdown within the information industries sector (code 51) to illustrate the classification scheme.

The NAICS permits a firm to find the NAICS codes of its present customers and then obtain NAICS-coded lists for similar firms. Also, it is possible to monitor NAICS categories to determine the growth in various sectors and industries

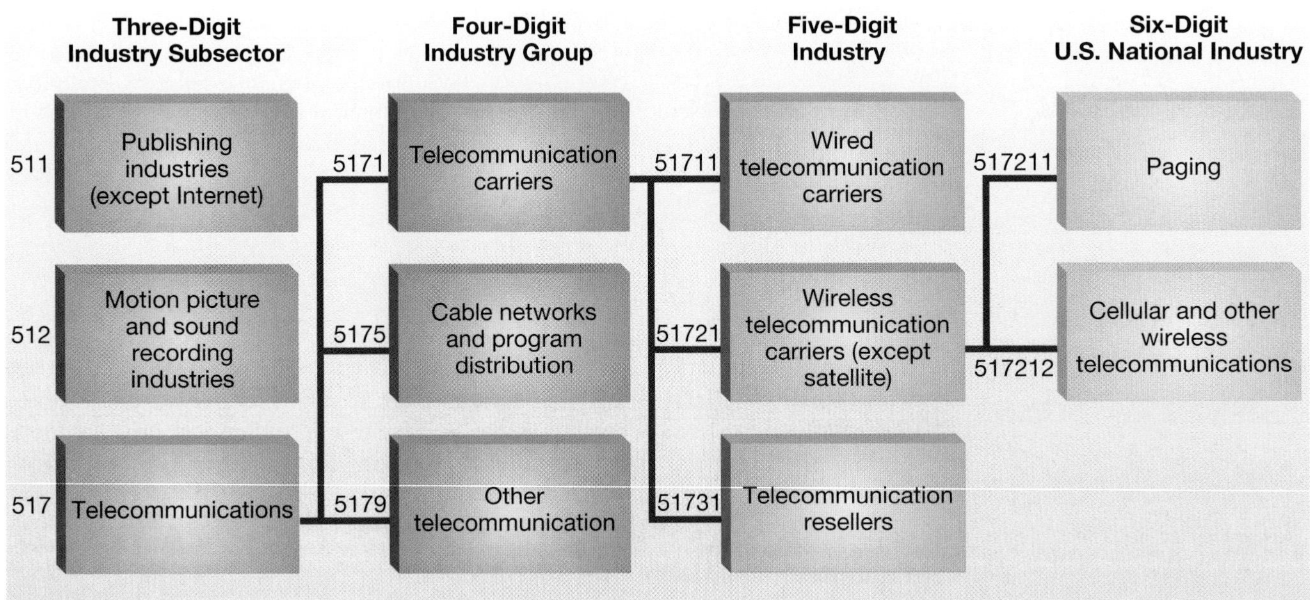

FIGURE 6–2
NAICS breakdown for information industries sector: NAICS code 51 (abbreviated)

to identify promising marketing opportunities. However, NAICS codes, like the earlier SIC codes, have important limitations. The NAICS assigns one code to each organization based on its major economic activity, so large firms that engage in many different activities are still given only one NAICS code. A second limitation is that five-digit national industry codes are not available for all three countries because the respective governments will not reveal data when too few organizations exist in a category.

Concept Check

1. What are the three main types of organizational buyers?
2. What is the North American Industry Classification System (NAICS)?

CHARACTERISTICS OF ORGANIZATIONAL BUYING

Organizations are different from individuals, so buying for an organization is different from buying for yourself or your family. True, in both cases the objective in making the purchase is to solve the buyer's problem—to satisfy a need or want. But unique objectives and policies of an organization put special constraints on how it makes buying decisions. Understanding the characteristics of organizational buying is essential in designing effective marketing programs to reach these buyers. Key characteristics of organizational buying appear in Figure 6–3 and are discussed next.[5]

Demand Characteristics

derived demand
Demand for industrial products and services driven by demand for consumer products and services

Consumer demand for products and services is affected by their price and availability and by consumers' personal tastes and discretionary income. By comparison, industrial demand is derived. **Derived demand** means that the demand for industrial products and services is driven by, or derived from, demand for consumer products and services. For example, the demand for Weyerhaeuser's pulp and paper products is based on consumer demand for newspapers, Domino's "keep warm" pizza-to-go boxes, FedEx packages, and disposable diapers. Derived demand is based on expectations of future consumer demand. For instance, Whirlpool purchases parts for its washers and dryers

CHARACTERISTICS	DIMENSIONS
Market characteristics	• Demand for industrial products and services is derived. • Few customers typically exist, and their purchase orders are large.
Product or service characteristics	• Products or services are technical in nature and purchased on the basis of specifications. • Many of goods purchased are raw and semifinished. • Heavy emphasis is placed on delivery time, technical assistance, and postsale service.
Buying process characteristics	• Technically qualified and professional buyers follow established purchasing policies and procedures. • Buying objectives and criteria are typically spelled out, as are procedures for evaluating sellers and their products or services. • There are multiple buying influences, and multiple parties participate in purchase decisions. • There are reciprocal arrangements, and negotiation between buyers and sellers is commonplace. • Online buying over the Internet is widespread.
Marketing mix characteristics	• Direct selling to organizational buyers is the rule, and distribution is very important. • Advertising and other forms of promotion are technical in nature. • Price is often negotiated, evaluated as part of broader seller and product or service qualities, and frequently affected by quantity discounts.

FIGURE 6–3
Key characteristics of organizational buying behavior

in anticipation of consumer demand, which is affected by the replacement cycle for these products and by consumer income.

Size of the Order or Purchase

The size of the purchase involved in organizational buying is typically much larger than that in consumer buying. The dollar value of a single purchase made by an organization often runs into the thousands or millions of dollars. For example, Motorola was paid $63 million to install a cellular phone system in Brazil.[6] With so much money at stake, most organizations place constraints on their buyers in the form of purchasing policies or procedures. Buyers must often get competitive bids from at least three prospective suppliers when the order is above a specific amount, such as $5,000. When the order is above an even higher amount, such as $50,000, it may require the review and approval of a vice president or even the president of the company. Knowing how the size of the order affects buying practices is important in determining who participates in the purchase decision and makes the final decision, and also the length of time required to arrive at a purchase agreement.

Number of Potential Buyers

Firms selling consumer products or services often try to reach thousands or millions of individuals or households. For example, your local supermarket or bank probably serves thousands of people, and Kellogg tries to reach 80 million American households with its breakfast cereals and probably succeeds in selling to a third or half of these in any given year. In contrast, firms selling to organizations are often restricted to far fewer buyers. Gulfstream Aerospace Corporation can sell its business jets to a few

MARKETING NEWSNET The Airbus A380 Superjumbo Jet Takes Flight

Rapidly expanding demand for intercontinental passenger air traffic and the growth of the global air freight industry bodes well for aircraft manufacturers. Europe's Airbus expects to transport future air travelers and cargo in the largest airplane ever built—its A380 superjumbo jet. The A380 features passenger models seating more than 555 people, spread over two full decks, and a freightliner model capable of delivering 331,000 pounds of cargo. The A380 has a list price of about $250 million.

The demand for the A380 will depend on prospective buyers' expectation of future air transport traffic. If initial orders are an indication, the future is bright for superjumbo jet aircraft. Airbus has already taken orders for the A380 from buyers on five continents, including Singapore Airlines, Qantas Airways, Lufthansa, Virgin Atlantic Airways, Air France, Emirates Airlines, UPS, and FedEx.

thousand organizations throughout the world, and B. F. Goodrich sells its original equipment tires to fewer than 10 car manufacturers.

Derived demand, the size of the purchase order, and the number of potential buyers will play a part in the commercial success of the new A380 superjumbo jet developed by Europe's Airbus. Read the accompanying Marketing NewsNet to learn more about the largest airplane ever built.[7]

Organizational Buying Objectives

Organizations buy products and services for one main reason: to help them achieve their objectives. For business firms the buying objective is usually to increase profits through reducing costs or increasing sales. 7-Eleven buys automated inventory systems to increase the number of products that can be sold through its convenience stores and to keep them fresh. Nissan Motor Company switched its advertising agency because it expects the new agency to devise a more effective ad campaign to help it sell more cars. To improve executive decision making, many firms buy advanced computer systems to process data. The objectives of nonprofit firms and government agencies are usually to meet the needs of the groups they serve. Thus, a hospital buys a high-technology diagnostic device to serve its patients better. Understanding buying objectives is a necessary first step in marketing to organizations.

Many companies today have broadened their buying objectives to include an emphasis on buying from minority- and women-owned suppliers and vendors. Companies such as Pitney Bowes, PepsiCo, Coors, and JCPenney report that sales, profits, and customer satisfaction have increased because of their minority- and women-owned supplier and vendor initiatives. Other companies include environmental initiatives. For example, Lowe's and Home Depot, two home-and-garden center chains, no longer purchase lumber from companies that harvest timber from the world's endangered forests.[8]

Organizational Buying Criteria

In making a purchase, the buying organization must weigh key buying criteria that apply to the potential supplier and what it wants to sell. *Organizational buying criteria* are the objective attributes of the supplier's products and services and the capabilities of the supplier itself. These criteria serve the same purpose as the evaluative criteria

MARKETING NEWSNET

Harley-Davidson's Supplier Collaboration Creates Customer Value . . . and a Great Ride

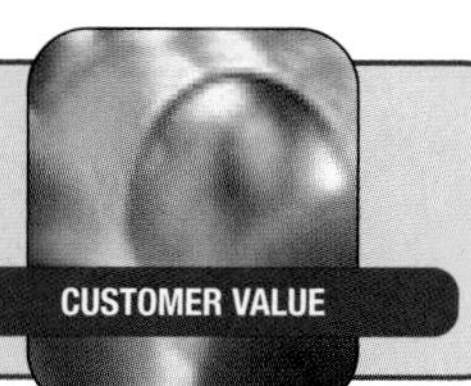

It's nice to be admired. Harley-Davidson's well-deserved reputation for innovation, product quality, and talented management and employees has made it a perennial member of *Fortune* magazine's list of "America's Most Admired Companies."

Harley-Davidson is also respected by suppliers for the way it collaborates with them in product design. According to Jeff Bluestein, the company's chairman and CEO, "We involve our suppliers as much as possible in future products, new-product development, and get them working with us." Emphasis is placed on quality benchmarks, cost control, delivery schedules, and technological innovation as well as building mutually beneficial, long-term relationships. Face-to-face communication is encouraged, and many suppliers have personnel officed at Harley-Davidson's Product Development Center.

The relationship between Harley-Davidson and Milsco Manufacturing is a case in point. Milsco has been the sole source of original equipment motorcycle seats and a major supplier of aftermarket parts and accessories, such as saddlebags, for Harley-Davidson since 1934. Milsco engineers and designers work closely with their Harley counterparts in the design of each year's new products. The notion of a mutually beneficial relationship is expressed by Ron Priem, Milsco's manager of industrial design: "Harley-Davidson refers to us as stakeholders, someone who can win or lose from a successful or failed program. We all share responsibility toward one another." Priem also notes that Harley-Davidson is not Milsco's only customer. It is simply the customer that he most respects.

used by consumers and described in Chapter 5. Seven of the most commonly used criteria are (1) price, (2) ability to meet the quality specifications required for the item, (3) ability to meet required delivery schedules, (4) technical capability, (5) warranties and claim policies in the event of poor performance, (6) past performance on previous contracts, and (7) production facilities and capacity.[9] Suppliers that meet or exceed these criteria create customer value.

Many organizational buyers today are transforming their buying criteria into specific requirements that are communicated to prospective suppliers. This practice, called *reverse marketing,* involves the deliberate effort by organizational buyers to build relationships that shape suppliers' products, services, and capabilities to fit a buyer's needs and those of its customers.[10] Consider Deere & Company, the maker of John Deere farm, construction, and lawn-care equipment. Deere employs 94 supplier-development engineers who work full-time with the company's suppliers to improve their efficiency and quality and reduce their costs. According to a Deere senior executive, "Their quality, delivery, and costs are, after all, our quality, delivery, and costs."[11] Read the accompanying Marketing NewsNet to learn how Harley-Davidson emphasizes supplier collaboration in its product design.[12]

Buyer–Seller Relationships and Supply Partnerships

Another distinction between organizational and consumer buying behavior lies in the nature of the relationship between organizational buyers and suppliers. Specifically, organizational buying is more likely to involve complex negotiations concerning delivery schedules, price, technical specifications, warranties, and claim policies. These negotiations also can last for more than a year. This was the case when the Lawrence

Livermore National Laboratory recently acquired two IBM supercomputers—each with capacity to perform 360 trillion mathematical operations per second—at a cost of $290 million.[13]

Reciprocal arrangements also exist in organizational buying. *Reciprocity* is an industrial buying practice in which two organizations agree to purchase each other's products and services. The U.S. Justice Department frowns on reciprocal buying because it restricts the normal operation of the free market. However, the practice exists and can limit the flexibility of organizational buyers in choosing alternative suppliers.

Long-term contracts are also prevalent.[14] As an example, the U.S. Department of Defense recently announced it intends to spend $6.9 billion over five years for computer and computer technology provided by Electronic Data Systems. Hewlett-Packard is engaged in a 10-year, $3 billion contract to manage Procter & Gamble's information technology in 160 countries.

supply partnership
Relationship between a buyer and supplier that adopt mutually beneficial objectives, policies, and procedures

In some cases, buyer–seller relationships evolve into supply partnerships.[15] A **supply partnership** exists when a buyer and its supplier adopt mutually beneficial objectives, policies, and procedures for the purpose of lowering the cost or increasing the value of products and services delivered to the ultimate consumer. Intel, the world's largest manufacturer of microprocessors and the "computer inside" most personal computers, is a case in point. Intel supports its suppliers by offering them quality management programs and by investing in supplier equipment that produces fewer product defects and boosts supplier productivity. Suppliers, in turn, provide Intel with consistent high-quality products at a lower cost for its customers, the makers of personal computers, and finally you, the ultimate customer. Retailers, too, have forged partnerships with their suppliers. Wal-Mart has such a relationship with Procter & Gamble for ordering and replenishing P&G's products in its stores. By using computerized cash register scanning equipment and direct electronic linkages to P&G, Wal-Mart can tell P&G what merchandise is needed, along with how much, when, and to which store to deliver it on a daily basis.

THE ORGANIZATIONAL BUYING PROCESS AND THE BUYING CENTER

organizational buying behavior
Process by which organizations determine the need for goods and then choose among alternative suppliers

Organizational buyers, like consumers, engage in a decision process when selecting products and services. **Organizational buying behavior** is the decision-making process that organizations use to establish the need for products and services and identify, evaluate, and choose among alternative brands and suppliers. There are important similarities and differences between the two decision-making processes. To better understand the nature of organizational buying behavior, we first compare it with consumer buying behavior. We then describe a unique feature of organizational buying—the buying center.

Stages in the Organizational Buying Process

As shown in Figure 6–4, the five stages a student might use in buying a portable MP3-capable CD player also apply to organizational purchases. However, comparing the two right-hand columns in Figure 6–4 reveals some key differences. For example, when a portable MP3-capable CD player manufacturer buys earphones for its units from a supplier, more individuals are involved, supplier capability becomes more important, and the postpurchase evaluation behavior is more formal. The earphone-buying decision process is typical of the steps made by organizational buyers.

The Buying Center: A Cross-Functional Group

For routine purchases with a small dollar value, a single buyer or purchasing manager often makes the purchase decision alone. In many instances, however, several

STAGE IN THE BUYING DECISION PROCESS	CONSUMER PURCHASE: PORTABLE MP3-CAPABLE CD PLAYER FOR A STUDENT	ORGANIZATIONAL PURCHASE: EARPHONES FOR A PORTABLE MP3-CAPABLE CD PLAYER
Problem recognition	Student doesn't like the features of the portable CD player now owned and desires a new one.	Marketing research and sales departments observe that competitors are improving the earphones on their portable CD models. The firm decides to improve the earphones on their own new models, which will be purchased from an outside supplier.
Information search	Student uses past experience, that of friends, ads, the Internet, and *Consumer Reports* to collect information and uncover alternatives.	Design and production engineers draft specifications for earphones. The purchasing department identifies suppliers of portable CD player earphones.
Alternative evaluation	Alternative portable CD players are evaluated on the basis of important attributes desired in a portable CD player, and several stores are visited.	Purchasing and engineering personnel visit with suppliers and assess (1) facilities, (2) capacity, (3) quality control, and (4) financial status. They drop any suppliers not satisfactory on these factors.
Purchase decision	A specific brand of portable CD player is selected, the price is paid, and the student leaves the store.	They use (1) quality, (2) price, (3) delivery, and (4) technical capability as key buying criteria to select a supplier. Then they negotiate terms and award a contract.
Postpurchase behavior	Student reevaluates the purchase decision, may return the player to the store if it is unsatisfactory.	They evaluate suppliers using a formal vendor rating system and notify a supplier if earphones do not meet their quality standard. If the problem is not corrected, they drop the firm as a future supplier.

FIGURE 6–4
Comparing the stages in consumer and organizational purchases

buying center
Group of people in an organization who participate in the buying process

people in the organization participate in the buying process. The individuals in this group, called a **buying center**, share common goals, risks, and knowledge important to purchase decisions. For most large multistore chain resellers, such as Sears, 7-Eleven convenience stores, Target, or Safeway, the buying center is very formal and is called a *buying committee*. However, most industrial firms or government units use informal groups of people or call meetings to arrive at buying decisions.

A firm marketing to industrial firms and government units must understand the structure, technical and business functions represented, and the behavior of the buying center. One researcher has suggested four questions to provide guidance in understanding the buying center in these organizations:[16] Which individuals are in the buying center for the product or service? What is the relative influence of each member of the group? What are the buying criteria of each member? How does each member of the group perceive our firm, our products and services, and our salespeople?

People in the Buying Center Who makes up the buying center in a given organization depends on the specific item being bought. Although a buyer or purchasing manager is almost always a member of the buying center, individuals from other functional areas are included depending on what is to be purchased. In buying a million-dollar machine tool, the president (because of the size of the purchase)

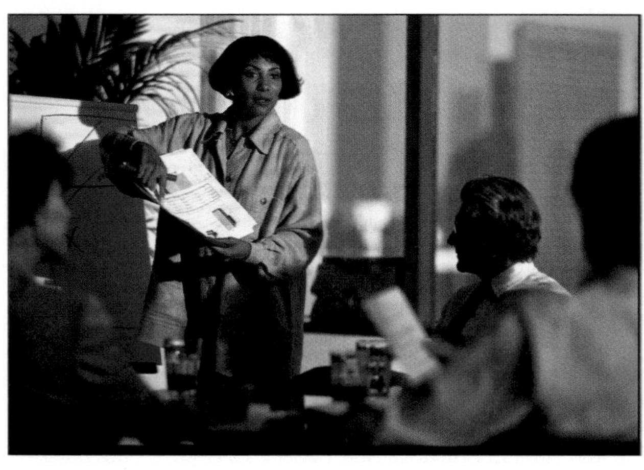

and the production vice president would probably be members. For key components to be included in a final manufactured product, a cross-functional group of individuals from research and development (R&D), engineering, and quality control are likely to be added. For new word-processing equipment, experienced secretaries who will use the equipment would be members. Still, a major question in understanding the buying center is finding and reaching the people who will initiate, influence, and actually make the buying decision.

Roles in the Buying Center Researchers have identified five specific roles that an individual in a buying center can play. In some purchases the same person may perform two or more of these roles.

- *Users* are the people in the organization who actually use the product or service, such as a secretary who will use a new word processor.
- *Influencers* affect the buying decision, usually by helping define the specifications for what is bought. The information systems manager would be a key influencer in the purchase of a new mainframe computer.
- *Buyers* have formal authority and responsibility to select the supplier and negotiate the terms of the contract. The purchasing manager probably would perform this role in the purchase of a mainframe computer.
- *Deciders* have the formal or informal power to select or approve the supplier that receives the contract. Whereas in routine orders the decider is usually the buyer or purchasing manager, in important technical purchases it is more likely to be someone from R&D, engineering, or quality control. The decider for a key component being included in a final manufactured product might be any of these three people.
- *Gatekeepers* control the flow of information in the buying center. Purchasing personnel, technical experts, and secretaries can all help or prevent salespeople (or information) from reaching people performing the other four roles.

Buying Situations and the Buying Center The number of people in the buying center largely depends on the specific buying situation. Researchers who have studied organizational buying identify three types of buying situations, called **buy classes**. These buy classes vary from the routine reorder, or *straight rebuy,* to the completely new purchase, termed *new buy.* In between these extremes is the *modified rebuy.* Some examples will clarify the differences.[17]

buy classes
Three types of organizational buying situations: new buy, straight rebuy, or modified rebuy

- *Straight rebuy.* Here the buyer or purchasing manager reorders an existing product or service from the list of acceptable suppliers, probably without even checking with users or influencers from the engineering, production, or quality control departments. Office supplies and maintenance services are usually obtained as straight rebuys.
- *Modified rebuy.* In this buying situation the users, influencers, or deciders in the buying center want to change the product specifications, price, delivery schedule, or supplier. Although the item purchased is largely the same as with the straight rebuy, the changes usually necessitate enlarging the buying center to include people outside the purchasing department.
- *New buy.* Here the organization is a first-time buyer of the product or service. This involves greater potential risks in the purchase, so the buying center is enlarged to include all those who have a stake in the new buy. Procter & Gamble's recent purchase of a multimillion-dollar fiber-optic network from Corning, Inc., linking its corporate offices in Cincinnati, represented a new buy.[18]

BUYING CENTER DIMENSION	NEW BUY	STRAIGHT REBUY	MODIFIED REBUY
	BUY-CLASS SITUATION		
People involved	Many	One	Two to three
Decision time	Long	Short	Moderate
Problem definition	Uncertain	Well-defined	Minor modifications
Buying objective	Good solution	Low-priced supplier	Low-priced supplier
Suppliers considered	New/present	Present	Present
Buying influence	Technical/operating personnel	Purchasing agent	Purchasing agent and others

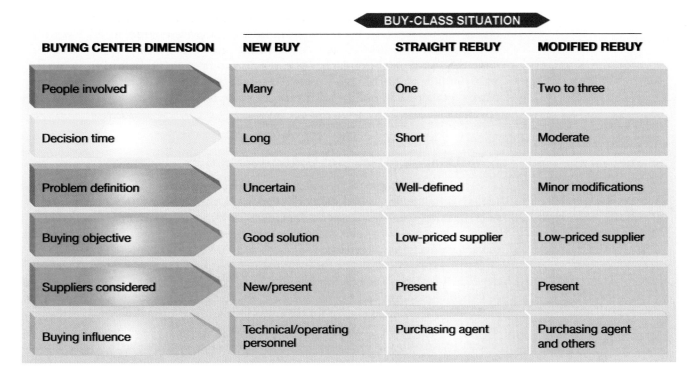

FIGURE 6–5
How the buying situation affects buying center behavior

Figure 6–5 summarizes how buy classes affect buying center tendencies in different ways.[19]

Concept Check

1. What one department is almost always represented by a person in the buying center?
2. What are the three types of buying situations or buy classes?

ONLINE BUYING IN ORGANIZATIONAL MARKETS

Organizational buying behavior and business marketing continues to evolve with the application of Internet technology. Organizations dwarf consumers both in terms of online transactions made and purchase volume.[20] In fact, organizational buyers account for about 80 percent of the total worldwide dollar value of all online transactions. Organizational buyers in the United States account for about 60 percent of these purchases.

Prominence of Online Buying in Organizational Markets

Online buying in organizational markets is prominent for three major reasons.[21] First, organizational buyers depend heavily on timely supplier information that describes product availability, technical specifications, application uses, price, and delivery schedules. This information can be conveyed quickly via Internet technology. Second, this technology has been shown to substantially reduce buyer order processing costs. At General Electric, online buying has cut the cost of a transaction from $50 to $100 per purchase to about $5. Third, business marketers have found that Internet technology can reduce marketing costs, particularly sales and advertising expense, and broaden their potential customer base for many types of products and services. For these reasons, online buying is popular in all three kinds of organizational markets. For example, airlines electronically order over $400 million in spare parts from the Boeing Company each year. Customers of W. W. Grainger, a large U.S. wholesaler of maintenance, repair, and operating supplies, buy more than $425 million worth of these products annually online. Supply and service purchases totaling $650 million each year are made online by the Los Angeles County government.

E-Marketplaces: Virtual Organizational Markets

e-marketplaces
Online trading communities that bring together buyers and supplier organizations

A significant development in organizational buying has been the creation of online trading communities, called **e-marketplaces**, that bring together buyers and supplier organizations. These online communities go by a variety of names, including B2B exchanges and e-hubs, and make possible the real-time exchange of information, money, products, and services.

E-marketplaces can be independent trading communities or private exchanges. Independent e-marketplaces act as a neutral third-party and provide an Internet technology trading platform and a centralized market that enable exchanges between buyers and sellers. They charge a fee for their service and exist in settings that have one or more of the following features: (1) thousands of geographically dispersed buyers and sellers, (2) volatile prices caused by demand and supply fluctuations, (3) time sensitivity due to perishable offerings and changing technologies, and (4) easily comparable offerings between a variety of suppliers. Well-known independent e-marketplaces include PlasticsNet (plastics), FreeMarkets (industrial parts, raw material, and commodities), and XSAg.com (agricultural products). Small business buyers and sellers, in particular, benefit from independent e-marketplaces. These e-marketplaces offer them an economical way to expand their customer base and reduce the cost of products and services. eBay recently launched eBayBusiness to serve the small businesses market in the United States.

Large companies tend to favor private exchanges that link them with their network of qualified suppliers and customers. Private exchanges focus on streamlining a company's purchase transactions with its suppliers and customers. Like independent e-marketplaces, they provide a technology trading platform and central market for buyer–seller interactions. They are not a neutral third party, however, but represent the interests of their owners. For example, Worldwide Retail Exchange performs the buying function for its 62 retail members, including Best Buy, The Gap, Radio Shack, Safeway, Target, and Walgreen. The Global Healthcare Exchange engages in the buying and selling of health care products for 1,400 hospitals and more than 100 health care suppliers, such as Abbott Laboratories, Johnson & Johnson, and U.S. Surgical. Each of these private exchanges has saved their members $1 billion due to efficiencies in purchase transactions.

Online Auctions in Organizational Markets

Online auctions have grown in popularity among organizational buyers and business marketers. Many e-marketplaces offer this service. Two general types of auctions are common: (1) a traditional auction and (2) a reverse auction.[22] Figure 6–6 shows how buyer and seller participants and price behavior differ by type of auction. Let's look at each auction type to understand the implications of each for buyers and sellers.

traditional auction
Occurs when a seller puts an item up for sale and would-be buyers bid in competition with each other

In a **traditional auction** a seller puts an item up for sale and would-be buyers are invited to bid in competition with each other. As more would-be buyers become involved, there is an upward pressure on bid prices. Why? Bidding is sequential—that is, bidders bid in order, one at a time. Prospective buyers observe the bids of others and decide whether or not to increase the bid price. The auction ends when a single bidder

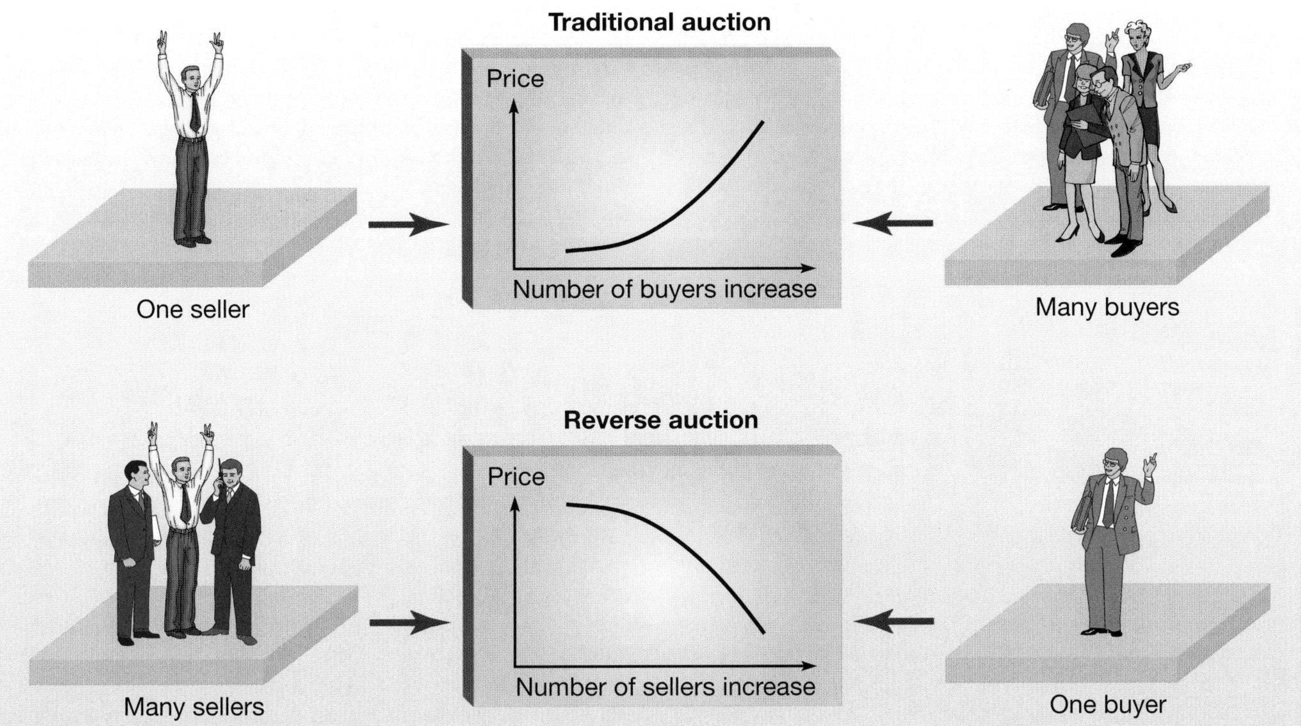

FIGURE 6–6
How buyer and seller participants and price behavior differ by type of online auction

reverse auction
Occurs when a buyer communicates a need for something and would-be suppliers bid in competition with each other

remains and "wins" the item with its highest price. Traditional auctions are often used to dispose of excess merchandise. For example, Dell Inc. sells surplus, refurbished, or closeout computer merchandise at its dellauction.com website.

A reverse auction works in the opposite direction from a traditional auction. In a **reverse auction**, a buyer communicates a need for a product or service and would-be suppliers are invited to bid in competition with each other. As more would-be suppliers become involved, there is a downward pressure on bid prices for the buyer's business. Why? Like traditional auctions, bidding is sequential and prospective suppliers observe the bids of others and decide whether or not to decrease the bid price. The auction ends when a single bidder remains and "wins" the business with its lowest price. Reverse auctions benefit organizational buyers by reducing the cost of their purchases. As an example, General Electric's Global eXchange Services unit, which runs online reverse auctions for the company, claims it recently saved $780 million on the purchase of $6 billion worth of products and services.

Clearly, buyers welcome the lower prices generated by reverse auctions. Some suppliers also favor reverse auctions because they give them a chance to capture business that they might not have otherwise had because of a long-standing purchase relationship between the buyer and another supplier. On the other hand, suppliers say that reverse auctions put too much emphasis on prices, discourage consideration of other important buying criteria, and threaten supply partnership opportunities.[23]

Concept Check

1. What are e-marketplaces?
2. In general, which type of online auction creates upward pressure on bid prices and which type creates downward pressure on bid prices?

CHAPTER IN REVIEW

1 *Distinguish among industrial, reseller, and government organizational markets.*
There are three different organizational markets: industrial, reseller, and government. Industrial firms in some way reprocess a product or service they buy before selling it to the next buyer. Resellers—wholesalers and retailers—buy physical products and resell them again without any reprocessing. Government agencies, at the federal, state, and local levels, buy goods and services for the constituents they serve. The North American Industry Classification System (NAICS) provides common industry definitions for Canada, Mexico, and the United States, which facilitates the measurement of economic activity for these three organizational markets.

2 *Describe the key characteristics of organizational buying that make it different from consumer buying.*
Seven major characteristics of organizational buying make it different from consumer buying. These include demand characteristics, size of the order or purchase, number of potential buyers, buying objectives, buying criteria, buyer–seller relationships and supply partnerships, and multiple buying influences within organizations. The organizational buying process itself is more formalized, more individuals are involved, supplier capability is more important, and the postpurchase evaluation behavior often includes performance of the supplier and the item purchased. Figure 6–4 details how the purchase of an MP3-capable CD player differs between a consumer and organizational purchase.

3 *Explain how buying centers and buying situations influence organizational purchasing.*
Buying centers and buying situations have an important influence on organizational purchasing. A buying center consists of a group of individuals who share common goals, risks, and knowledge important to a purchase decision. A buyer or purchasing manager is almost always a member of a buying center. However, other individuals may affect organizational purchasing due to their unique roles in a purchase decision. Five specific roles that a person may play in a buying center include users, influencers, buyers, deciders, and gatekeepers. The specific buying situation will influence the number of people in and the different roles played in a buying center. For a routine reorder of an item—a straight rebuy situation—a purchasing manager or buyer will typically act alone in making a purchasing decision. When an organization is a first-time purchaser of a product or service—a new buy situation—a buying center is enlarged and all five roles in a buying center often emerge. A modified rebuy buying situation lies between these two extremes. Figure 6–5 offers additional insights into how buying centers and buying situations influence organization purchasing.

4 *Recognize the importance and nature of online buying in industrial, reseller, and government organizational markets.*
Organizations dwarf consumers in terms of online transactions made and purchase volume. Online buying in organizational markets is popular for three reasons. First, organizational buyers depend on timely supplier information that describes product availability, technical specifications, application uses, price, and delivery schedules. This information can be conveyed quickly via Internet technology. Second, this technology substantially reduces buyer order processing costs. Third, business marketers have found that Internet technology can reduce marketing costs, particularly sales and advertising expense, and broaden their customer base. Two developments in online buying have been the creation of e-marketplaces and online auctions. E-marketplaces provide a technology trading platform and a centralized market for buyer–seller transactions and make possible the real-time exchange of information, money, products, and services. These e-marketplaces can be independent trading communities, such as FreeMarkets, or private exchanges such as the Worldwide Retail Exchange. Online traditional and reverse auctions represent a second major development. With traditional auctions, the highest-priced bidder "wins." Conversely, the lowest-priced bidder "wins" with reverse auctions.

FOCUSING ON KEY TERMS

business marketing p. 122
buy classes p. 130
buying center p. 129
derived demand p. 124
e-marketplaces p. 132
North American Industry Classification System (NAICS) p. 123
organizational buyers p. 122
organizational buying behavior p. 128
reverse auction p. 133
supply partnership p. 128
traditional auction p. 132

DISCUSSION AND APPLICATION QUESTIONS

1 Describe the major differences among industrial firms, resellers, and government units in the United States.

2 List and discuss the key characteristics of organizational buying that make it different from consumer buying.

3 What is a buying center? Describe the roles assumed by people in a buying center and what useful questions should be raised to guide any analysis of the structure and behavior of a buying center.

4 A firm that is marketing multimillion-dollar wastewater treatment systems to cities has been unable to sell a new type of system. This setback has occurred even though the firm's systems are cheaper than competitive systems and meet U.S. Environmental Protection Agency (EPA) specifications. To date, the firm's marketing efforts have been directed to city purchasing departments and the various state EPAs to get on approved bidder's lists. Talks with city-employed personnel have indicated that the new system is very different from current systems and therefore city sanitary and sewer department engineers, directors of these two departments, and city council members are unfamiliar with the workings of the system. Consulting engineers, hired by cities to work on the engineering and design features of these systems and paid on a percentage of system cost, are also reluctant to favor the new system. (*a*) What roles do the various individuals play in the purchase process for a wastewater treatment system? (*b*) How could the firm improve the marketing effort behind the new system?

GOING ONLINE Navigating the NAICS

The North American Industrial Classification System (NAICS) structures industrial sectors into their component industries. The NAICS can be accessed at www.census.gov by clicking "NAICS." Industry information can be obtained by navigating through the codes.

You have been hired as a market analyst by a snack food company that is looking for opportunities outside its normal business. The vice president of marketing has asked you to look into the dog and cat food manufacturing industry to determine its size. She suggests that a good place to start is the NAICS, beginning with the two-digit manufacturing sectors (codes 31–33).

1 What is the three-digit industry subsector code for food manufacturing?
2 What is the six-digit U.S. code for dog and cat food manufacturing?
3 How many establishments exist and what is the value of shipments sold by the U.S. dog and cat food manufacturing industry based on the latest government statistics? (*Hint:* You will need to click "Economic Census" to get this information.)

BUILDING YOUR MARKETING PLAN

Your marketing plan may need an estimate of the size of the market potential or industry potential (see Chapter 9) for a particular product-market in which you compete. Use these steps:

1 Define the product-market precisely, such as ice cream.
2 Visit the NAICS website at www.census.gov.
3 Click "NAICS" and enter a keyword that describes your product-market (e.g., ice cream).
4 Follow the instructions to the specific NAICS code and economic census data that details the dollar sales and provides the estimate of market or industry potential.

VIDEO CASE 6 Lands' End: Where Buyers Rule

Organizational buying is a part of the marketing effort that influences every aspect of business at Lands' End. As senior vice president of operations Phil Schaecher explains, "When we talk about purchasing at Lands' End, most people think of the purchase of merchandise for resale, but we buy many other things aside from merchandise, everything from the simplest office supply to the most sophisticated piece of material-handling equipment." As a result, Lands' End has developed a sophisticated approach to organizational buying, which is one of the keys to its incredible success.

THE COMPANY

The company started by selling sailboat equipment, duffle bags, rainsuits, and sweaters from a basement location in Chicago's old tannery district. In its first catalog, the company name was printed with a typing error—the apostrophe in the wrong place—but the fledgling company couldn't afford to correct and reprint it. So ever since, the company name has been Lands' End—with the misplaced apostrophe.

When the company outgrew its Chicago location, founder Gary Comer relocated it to Dodgeville, Wisconsin, where he had fallen in love with the rolling hills and changing seasons. The original business ideas were simple: "Sell only things we believe in, ship every order the day it arrives, and unconditionally guarantee everything." Over time, the company developed eight principles of doing business:

1 Never reduce the quality of a product to make it cheaper.
2 Price products fairly and honestly.
3 Accept any return for any reason.

4 Ship items in stock the day after the order is received.
5 What is best for the customer is best for Lands' End.
6 Place contracts with manufacturers who are cost-conscious and efficient.
7 Operate efficiently.
8 Keep overhead low.

These principles became the guidelines for the company's dedicated local employees and helped create extraordinary expectations from Lands' End customers.

Today, Lands' End is one of the world's largest direct merchants, with annual sales of traditionally styled clothing, luggage, and home products exceeding $1.4 billion. The products are offered through catalogs, the Internet, and retail stores. Last year, Lands' End distributed more than 260 million catalogs designed for specific segments, including *The Lands' End Catalog, Lands' End Men, Lands' End Women, Lands' End Kids, Lands' End for School, Lands' End Home,* and *Lands' End Corporate*. In a typical day, catalog shoppers place more than 40,000 telephone calls to the company. The Lands' End website (www.landsend.com) also offers every Lands' End product and a wide variety of Internet shopping innovations such as a 3-D model customized to each customer (called My Virtual Model™); a "personal shopper," to suggest products that match the consumer's preferences; and a feature that allows customers to "chat" online directly with a customer service representative. Lands' End also operates stores in the United States, the United Kingdom, and Japan. Selected Lands' End merchandise is also sold at Sears following the purchase of Lands' End by Sears in 2002.

The company's goal is to please customers with the highest levels of quality and service in the industry. Lands' End maintains the high quality of its products through several important activities. For example, the company works directly with mills and manufacturers to retain control of quality and design. "The biggest difference between Lands' End and some other retailers or catalog businesses is that we actually design all the product here and we do all the specifications. Therefore, the manufacturer is building that product directly to our specs, we are not buying off of somebody else's line," explains Joan Mudget, vice president of quality assurance. In addition, Lands' End tests its products for comfort and fit by paying real people (local residents and children) to "wear-test" and "fit-test" all types of garments.

Service has also become an important part of the Lands' End reputation. Customers expect prompt, professional service at every step—initiating the order, making selections, shipping, and follow-up (if necessary). Some of the ways Lands' End meets these expectations include offering the simplest guarantee in the industry—"Guaranteed. Period."—toll-free telephone lines open 24 hours a day, 364 days a year, continuous product training for telephone representatives, and two-day shipping. Lands' End operators even send personal responses to all e-mail messages, approximately 230,000 per year.

ORGANIZATIONAL BUYING AT LANDS' END

The sixth Lands' End business principle (described above) is accomplished through the company's organizational buying process. First, its buyers specify fabric quality, construction, and sizing standards, which typically exceed industry standards, for current and potential Lands' End products. Then the buyers literally search around the world for the best possible source of fabrics and products. Once a potential supplier is identified, one of the company's 150 quality assurance personnel makes an information-gathering visit. The purpose of the visit is to understand the supplier's values, to assess four criteria (economic, quality, service, and vendor), and to determine if the Lands' End standards can be achieved.

Lands' End evaluations of potential suppliers lead to the selection of what the company hopes will become long-term partners. As Mudget explains, "When we're looking for new manufacturers we are looking for the long term. I think one of the most interesting things is we're not out there looking for new vendors every year to fill the same products." In fact, Lands' End believes that the term *supplier* does not adequately describe the importance the company places on the relationships. Lands' End suppliers are viewed as allies, supporters, associates, colleagues, and stakeholders in the future of the company. Once an alliance is formed the product specifications and the performance on those specifications are regularly evaluated.

Lands' End buyers face a variety of buying situations. Straight rebuys involve reordering an existing product—such as shipping boxes—without evaluating or changing specifications. Modified rebuys involve changing some aspect of a previously ordered product—such as the collar of a knit shirt—based on input from consumers, retailers,

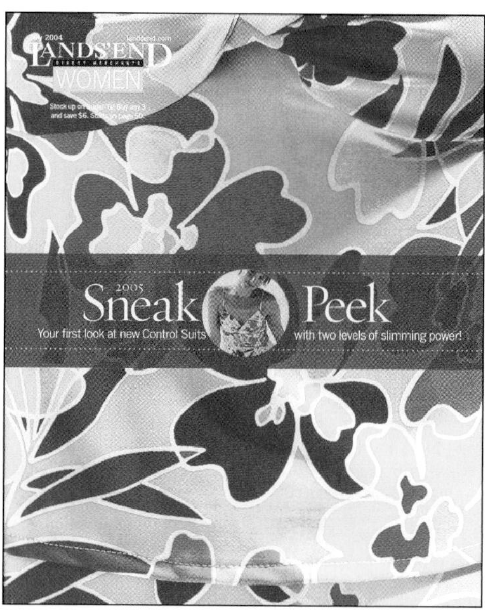

or other people involved in the purchase decision. Finally, new buys involve first-time purchases—such as Lands' End addition of men's suits to its product line. The complexity of the process can vary with the type of purchase. Schaecher explains, "As you get more complicated in the purchase there are more things you look at to decide on a vendor."

FUTURE CHALLENGES FOR LANDS' END

Lands' End faces several challenges as it pursues improvements in its organizational buying process. First, new technologies offer opportunities for fast, efficient, and accurate communication with suppliers. Ed Smidebush, general inventory manager, describes a new system at Lands' End: "Our quick response system is a computerized system where we transmit electronically to our vendors each Sunday night, forecast information as well as stock positions and purchase order information so that on Monday morning this information will be incorporated directly into their manufacturing reports so that they can prioritize their production." Occasionally Lands' End must work with its suppliers to improve their technology and information system capabilities.

Another challenge for Lands' End is to anticipate changes in consumer interests. While it has many years of experience with retail consumers, preferences for colors, fabrics, and styles change frequently, requiring buyers to constantly monitor the marketplace. In addition, Lands' End's more recent offerings to corporate customers require constant attention "because business customers' wants and incentives, and the environment in which they're shopping, are very different from consumers at home," explains marketing manager Hilary Kleese.

Finally, Lands' End must anticipate the quantities of each of its products consumers are likely to order. To do this, historical information is used to develop forecasts. One of the best tests of their forecast accuracy is the holiday season, when Lands' End receives more than 100,000 calls each day. Having the right products available is important because, as every employee knows from Principle 4, every order must be shipped the day after it is received.

Questions

1 Who is likely to comprise the buying center in the decision to select a new supplier for Lands' End? Which of the buying center members are likely to play the roles of users, influencers, buyers, deciders, and gatekeepers?

2 Which stages of the organizational buying decision process does Lands' End follow when it selects a new supplier? What selection criteria does the company utilize in the process?

3 Describe purchases Lands' End buyers typically face in each of the three buying situations: straight rebuy, modified rebuy, new buy.

CHAPTER 7

REACHING GLOBAL MARKETS

LEARNING OBJECTIVES

After reading this chapter you should be able to:

1. Identify the major trends that have influenced the landscape of global marketing in the past decade.
2. Identify the environmental factors that shape global marketing efforts.
3. Name and describe the alternative approaches companies use to enter global markets.
4. Explain the distinction between standardization and customization when companies craft worldwide marketing programs.

MATTEL'S GLOBAL MARKETING IS MORE THAN CHILD'S PLAY

Mattel is rewriting the rules for toy marketing on a global scale. As the worldwide leader in the design, manufacture, and marketing of toys and family products, Mattel successfully markets its best-selling Barbie®, Hot Wheels®, Fisher-Price®, and American Girl® brands in more than 150 countries.

Mattel's global marketing success can be linked to its new-product development effort. Toy developers are encouraged to think globally from the moment a new toy is conceived, with an eye to developing products that are likely to have universal appeal. Why? Mattel's research with children in dozens of countries has yielded a novel insight: Children are more alike than they are different in their product preferences. Today, Mattel markets as much as 80 percent of its product offerings to a global audience, with just 20 percent geared to individual country markets. Mattel's product introductions as well are global in scope. For example, Mattel recently launched Rapunzel Barbie on the same day in 59 countries supported by a televised advertising campaign broadcast in 35 languages. The widening international reach of retailing giants such as Wal-Mart, Target, and French-based Carrefour SA (the world's second-largest retailer) also permits Mattel to coordinate its store merchandising campaigns on a global scale.

Mattel's global marketing orientation has paid huge dividends. About 40 percent of the company's sales come from outside the United States. One Barbie is sold every three seconds somewhere in the world.[1]

This chapter describes the global marketing environment at the dawn of the twenty-first century. It also highlights the many ways successful companies like Mattel engage in global marketing.

DYNAMICS OF WORLD TRADE

The dollar value of world trade has more than doubled in the past decade. Manufactured goods and commodities account for 75 percent of world trade. Service industries, including telecommunications, transportation, insurance, education, banking, and tourism, represent the other 25 percent of world trade.

Four trends in the past decade have significantly affected world trade:

Trend 1: Gradual decline of economic protectionism by individual countries.

Trend 2: Formal economic integration and free trade among nations.

Trend 3: Global competition among global companies for global customers.

Trend 4: Development of networked global marketspace.

Decline of Economic Protectionism

protectionism
Practice of shielding one or more industries of a country's economy from foreign competition through the use of tariffs or quotas

tariffs
Government tax on goods or services entering a country, primarily serving to raise prices on imports

Protectionism is the practice of shielding one or more industries within a country's economy from foreign competition, usually through the use of tariffs or quotas. The economic argument for protectionism is that it preserves jobs, protects a nation's political security, discourages economic dependency on other countries, and encourages the development of domestic industries.

A **tariff** is a tax on goods or services entering a country. Because a tariff raises the price of an imported product, tariffs give a price advantage to domestic products competing in the same market. The effect of tariffs on world trade and consumer prices is substantial.[2] Consider U.S. rice exports to Japan. The U.S. Rice Millers' Association claims that if the Japanese rice market were opened to imports by lowering tariffs, lower prices would save Japanese consumers $6 billion annually, and the United States would gain a large share of the Japanese rice market. Similarly, tariffs imposed on bananas by Western European countries cost consumers $2 billion a year.

quota
Restriction placed on the amount of a product allowed to enter or leave a country

A **quota** is a restriction placed on the amount of a product allowed to enter or leave a country. By limiting supply of foreign products, an import quota helps domestic industries retain a certain percentage of the domestic market. For consumers, however, the limited supply may mean higher prices for domestic products. The best-known quota concerns the limits of foreign automobile sales in many countries. Quotas imposed by European countries make European cars 25 percent more expensive than similar models in the United States or Japan, costing European customers $40 billion per year. Less visible quotas apply to the importation of mushrooms, heavy motorcycles, textiles, color TVs, and sugar. For example, U.S. sugar import quotas have existed for over 50 years and preserve about half of the U.S. sugar market for domestic producers. American consumers pay almost $2 billion annually in extra food costs because of this quota.

World Trade Organization
Institution that sets rules governing trade between its members through a panel of trade experts

Both tariffs and quotas discourage world trade (Figure 7–1). As a result, the major industrialized nations of the world formed the **World Trade Organization** (WTO) in 1995 to address a broad array of world trade issues. The 148 member countries of the WTO, which include the United States, account for more than 90 percent of world trade.[3] The WTO sets rules governing trade between its members through panels of trade experts who decide on trade disputes between members and issue binding decisions. The WTO reviews more than 200 disputes annually. For instance, it denied Eastman Kodak's multimillion-dollar damage claim that the Japanese government protected Fuji Photo from import competition.

Rise of Economic Integration

In recent years, a number of countries with similar economic goals have formed transnational trade groups or signed trade agreements for the purpose of promoting free trade among member nations and enhancing their individual economies. Three of

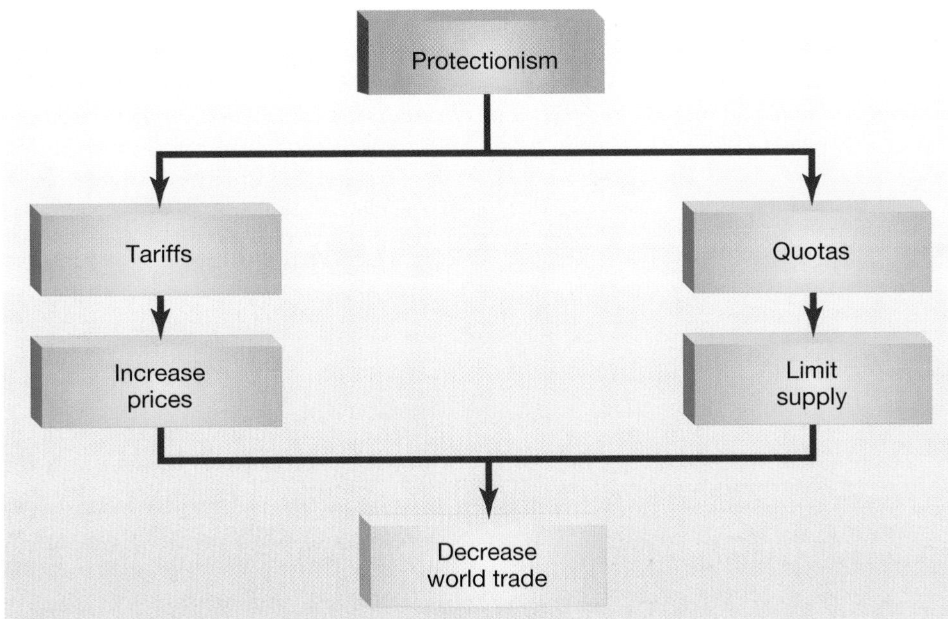

FIGURE 7–1
How protectionism affects world trade

the best-known examples are the European Union (or simply EU), the North American Free Trade Agreement (NAFTA), and Asian Free Trade Areas.

European Union The European Union consists of 25 member countries that have eliminated most barriers to the free flow of goods, services, capital, and labor across their borders (see Figure 7–2 on the next page).[4] Bulgaria and Romania are expected to join the EU in 2007. This single market houses about 500 million consumers with a combined gross domestic product larger than that of the United States. In addition, 12 countries have adopted a common currency called the *euro*. Adoption of the euro has been a boon to electronic commerce in the EU by eliminating the need to continually monitor currency exchange rates.

The EU creates abundant marketing opportunities because firms no longer find it necessary to market their products and services on a nation-by-nation basis. Rather, pan-European marketing strategies are possible due to greater uniformity in product and packaging standards; fewer regulatory restriction on transportation, advertising, and promotion imposed by countries; and removal of most tariffs that affect pricing practices. For example, Colgate-Palmolive Company now markets its Colgate toothpaste with one formula and package across EU countries at one price. Similarly, Black & Decker—the maker of electrical hand tools, appliances, and other consumer products—now produces 8, not 20, motor sizes for the European market, resulting in production and marketing cost savings. These practices were previously impossible because of different government and trade regulations. Europeanwide distribution from fewer locations is also feasible given open borders. French tire maker Michelin has closed 180 of its European distribution centers and now uses just 20 to serve all EU countries.

North American Free Trade Agreement The North American Free Trade Agreement lifted many trade barriers between Canada, Mexico, and the United States and created a marketplace with more than 435 million consumers.[5] NAFTA has stimulated trade flows among member nations as well as cross-border retailing, manufacturing, and investment. For example, NAFTA paved the way for Wal-Mart to move to Mexico and Mexican supermarket giant Gigante to move into the United States. Whirlpool Corporation's Canadian subsidiary stopped making washing machines in Canada and moved that operation to Ohio. Whirlpool then shifted the

FIGURE 7–2
The 25 countries of the European Union in 2006; Bulgaria and Romania are expected to join in 2007

production of kitchen ranges and compact dryers to Canada. Ford invested $60 million in its Mexico City manufacturing plant to produce smaller cars and light trucks for global sales.

Asian Free Trade Agreements Efforts to liberalize trade in East Asia—from Japan and the four "Little Dragons" (Hong Kong, Singapore, South Korea, and Taiwan) through Thailand, Malaysia, and Indonesia—are also growing. Although the trade agreements are less formal than those underlying the EU and NAFTA, they have reduced tariffs among countries and promoted trade.

A New Reality: Global Competition among Global Companies for Global Consumers

The emergence of a largely borderless economic world has created a new reality for marketers of all shapes and sizes. Today, world trade is driven by global competition among global companies for global consumers.

global competition
Occurs when firms originate, produce, and market their products and services worldwide

Global Competition **Global competition** exists when firms originate, produce, and market their products and services worldwide. The automobile, pharmaceutical, clothing, electronics, aerospace, and telecommunication fields represent well-known industries with sellers and buyers on every continent. Other industries that are increasingly global in scope include soft drinks, cosmetics, ready-to-eat cereals, snack chips, and retailing.

Pepsi-Cola is available in more than 190 countries and territories and accounts for a quarter of all soft drinks sold internationally. This Brazilian ad—"How to make jeans last 10 years"—features the popular Diet Pepsi brand targeted at weight-conscious consumers.

Global competition broadens the competitive landscape for marketers. The familiar "cola war" waged by Pepsi-Cola and Coca-Cola in the United States has been repeated around the world, including India, China, and Argentina. Procter & Gamble's Pampers and Kimberly-Clark's Huggies have taken their disposable diaper rivalry from the United States to Western Europe. Boeing and Europe's Airbus vie for lucrative commercial aircraft contracts on virtually every continent.

Global Companies Three types of companies compete in the global marketplace: (1) international firms, (2) multinational firms, and (3) transnational firms. All three employ people in different countries, and many have administrative, marketing, and manufacturing operations (often called *divisions* or *subsidiaries*) around the world. However, a firm's strategy for global markets and marketing defines the type of company it is.

An *international firm* markets its existing products and services in other countries the same way it does at home. Avon, for example, successfully distributes its product line through direct selling in Asia, Europe, and South America, using nearly the same marketing strategy used in the United States.

multidomestic marketing strategy
A multinational firm's offering as many different product variations, brand names, and advertising programs as countries in which it does business

global marketing strategy
Practice of standardizing marketing activities when there are cultural similarities and adapting them when cultures differ

A *multinational firm* views the world as consisting of unique parts and markets to each part differently. Multinationals use a **multidomestic marketing strategy**, which means that they have as many different product variations, brand names, and advertising programs as countries in which they do business. For example, Unilever markets its fabric softener known as Snuggle in the United States in 10 different European countries under seven brand names, including Kuschelweich in Germany, Coccolino in Italy, and Mimosin in France. These products have different packages, different advertising programs, and occasionally different formulas. Procter & Gamble markets Mr. Clean, its multipurpose cleaner, in North America and Asia. But you won't find Mr. Clean in other parts of the world. In Latin America, Mr. Clean is Mastro Limpio. Mr. Clean is Mr. Proper in Europe, Africa, and the Middle East.

A *transnational firm* views the world as one market and emphasizes universal consumer needs and wants more than differences among cultures. Transnational marketers employ a **global marketing strategy**—the practice of standardizing marketing activities when there are cultural similarities and adapting them when cultures differ.

MARKETING NEWSNET

The Global Teenager—A Market of 500 Million Consumers with $100 Billion to Spend

The "global teenager" market consists of 500 million 13- to 19-year-olds in Europe, North and South America, and industrialized nations of Asia and the Pacific Rim who have experienced intense exposure to television (MTV broadcasts in 166 countries), movies, travel, the Internet, and global advertising by companies such as Benetton, Sony, Nike, and Coca-Cola. The similarities among teens across these countries are greater than their differences. For example, a global study of middle-class teenagers' rooms in 25 industrialized countries indicated it was difficult, if not impossible, to tell whether the rooms were in Los Angeles, Mexico City, Tokyo, Rio de Janeiro, Sidney, or Paris. Why? Teens spend $100 billion annually for a common gallery of products: Sony video games, Tommy Hilfiger apparel, Levi's blue jeans, Nike athletic shoes, Swatch watches, and Procter & Gamble Clearasil facial medicine.

Teenagers around the world appreciate fashion and music, and desire novelty and trendier designs and images. They also acknowledge an Americanization of fashion and culture based on another study of 6,500 teens in 26 countries. When asked what country had the most influence on their attitudes and purchase behavior, 54 percent of teens from the United States, 87 percent of those from Latin America, 80 percent of the Europeans, and 80 percent of those from Asia named the United States. This phenomenon has not gone unnoticed by parents. As one parent in India said, "Now the youngsters dress, talk, and eat like Americans."

Global marketing strategies are popular among many business-to-business marketers such as Caterpillar and Komatsu (heavy construction equipment) and Texas Instruments, Intel, Hitachi, and Motorola (semiconductors). Consumer goods marketers such as Timex, Seiko, and Swatch (watches), Coca-Cola and Pepsi-Cola (cola soft drinks), Mattel and LEGO (children's toys), Gillette (personal care products), L'Oréal and Shiseido (cosmetics), and McDonald's (quick-service restaurants) successfully execute this strategy. Each of these companies markets a **global brand**—a brand marketed under the same name in multiple countries with similar and centrally coordinated marketing programs.[6] Global brands have the same product formulation or service concept, deliver the same benefits to consumers, and use consistent advertising across multiple countries and cultures. This isn't to say that global brands are not sometimes tailored to specific cultures or countries. However, adaptation is only used when necessary to better connect the brand to consumers in different markets. Consider McDonald's.[7] This global marketer has adapted its proven formula of "food, fun, and families" across 119 countries. Although the Golden Arches and Ronald McDonald appear worldwide, McDonald's tailors other aspects of its marketing program. It serves beer in Germany, wine in France, and coconut, mango, and tropical mint shakes in Hong Kong. Hamburgers are made with different meat and spices in Japan, Thailand, India, and the Philippines. But McDonald's world-famous French fry is standardized. Its French fry in Beijing, China, tastes like the one in Paris, France, which tastes like the one in your neighborhood.

global brand
A brand marketed under the same name in multiple countries with similar and centrally coordinated marketing programs

Global Consumers Global competition among global companies often focuses on the identification and pursuit of global consumers as described in the accompanying Marketing NewsNet.[8] **Global consumers** consist of customer groups living in

global consumers
Customers living around the world who have similar needs or seek similar benefits from products or services

many different countries who have similar needs or seek similar features and benefits from products or services. Evidence suggests the presence of a global middle-income class, a global youth market, and a global elite segment. Each consumes a common assortment of products and services regardless of geographic location. A variety of companies have capitalized on the global consumer. Whirlpool, Sony, and IKEA have benefited from the growing global middle-income class desire for kitchen appliances, consumer electronics, and home furnishings, respectively. Levi's, Nike, Coca-Cola, and Benetton have tapped the global youth market. DeBeers, Rolls Royce, Chanel, and Gucci cater to the elite segment for luxury goods worldwide.

Emergence of a Networked Global Marketspace

The use of Internet technology as a tool for exchanging goods, services, and information on a global scale is the fourth trend affecting world trade. The broad reach of this technology suggests that its potential for promoting world trade is huge. In fact, sales arising from electronic commerce are projected to represent 11 percent of world trade in 2008, up from about 1 percent in 2001.

The promise of a networked global marketspace is that it enables the exchange of goods, services, and information from companies *anywhere* to customers *anywhere* at *any time* and at a lower cost. This promise has become a reality for buyers and sellers in industrialized countries that possess the telecommunications infrastructure necessary to support Internet technology. In particular, companies engaged in business-to-business marketing have spurred the growth of global electronic commerce. Ninety percent of global electronic commerce revenue arises from business-to-business transactions among a dozen countries in North America, Western Europe, and the Asia/Pacific Rim region. Industries that have benefited from this technology include industrial chemicals and controls, maintenance, repair, and operating supplies, computer and electronic equipment and components, aerospace parts, and agricultural and energy products. The United States, Canada, United Kingdom, Germany, Sweden, Japan, and Taiwan are among the most active participants in worldwide business-to-business electronic commerce.[9]

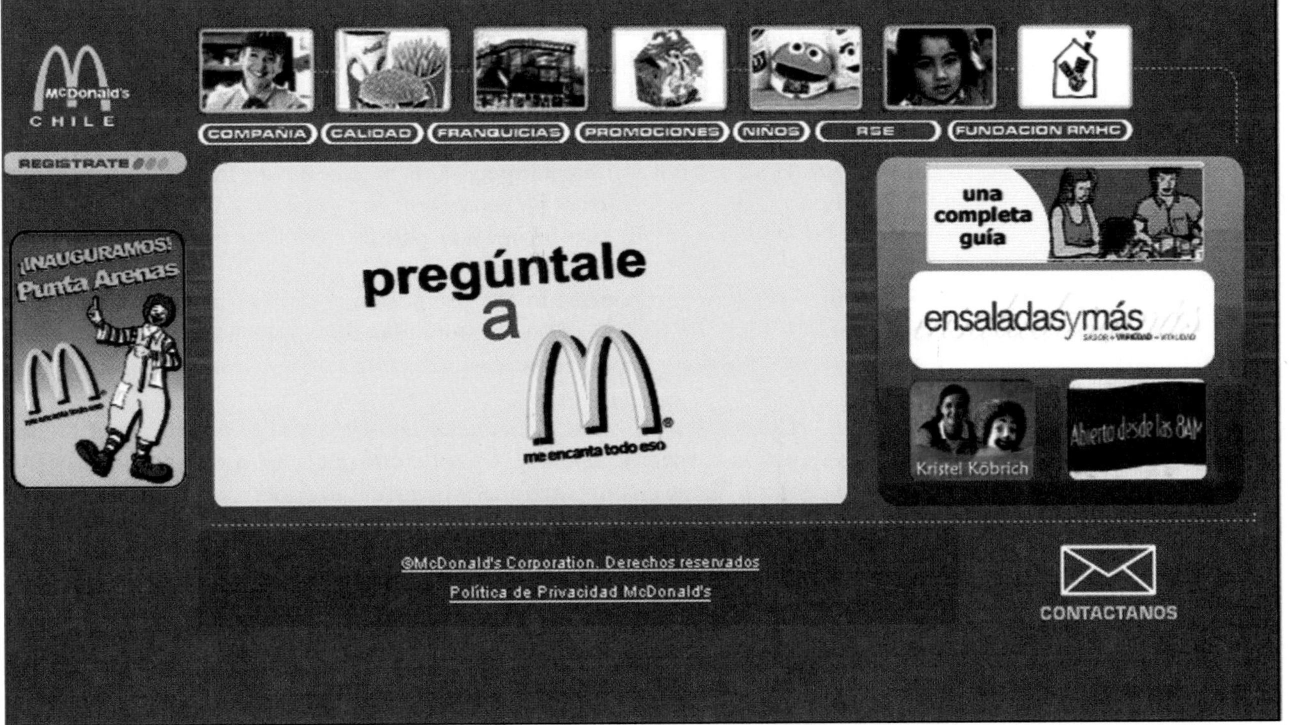

McDonald's features multiple country and language websites that customize content and communicate with consumers in their native tongue. The website for Chile shown here is an example.

Marketers recognize that the networked global marketspace offers unheard of access to prospective buyers on every continent. Companies that have successfully taken advantage of this access manage multiple country and language websites that customize content and communicate with consumers in their native tongue. Nestlé, the world's largest packaged food manufacturer, coffee roaster, and chocolate maker is a case in point. The company operates 31 individual country websites in 16 languages that span five continents.

Concept Check

1. What is protectionism?
2. What is the difference between a multidomestic marketing strategy and a global marketing strategy?

A GLOBAL ENVIRONMENTAL SCAN

Global companies conduct continuing environmental scans of the five sets of environmental factors described earlier in Figure 3–1 (social, economic, technological, competitive, and regulatory forces). This section focuses on three kinds of uncontrollable environmental variables—cultural, economic, and political–regulatory variables—that affect global marketing practices in strikingly different ways than those in domestic markets.

Cultural Diversity

cross-cultural analysis
Study of similarities and differences among consumers in two or more nations or societies

values
Socially preferable modes of conduct or states of existence that tend to persist over time

Marketers must be sensitive to the cultures of different societies if they are to develop successful exchange relationships with global consumers. A necessary step in this process is **cross-cultural analysis**, which involves the study of similarities and differences among consumers in two or more nations or societies.[10] A thorough cross-cultural analysis involves an understanding of and an appreciation for the values, customs, symbols, and language of other societies.

Values A society's **values** represent socially preferable modes of conduct or states of existence that tend to persist over time. Understanding and working with these aspects of a society are important factors in global marketing. For example,

- McDonald's does not sell hamburgers in its restaurants in India because the cow is considered sacred by almost 85 percent of the population. Instead, McDonald's sells the McMaharajah: two all-mutton patties, special sauce, lettuce, cheese, pickles, onions on a sesame-seed bun.
- Germans have not responded to the promotion of credit cards such as Visa or MasterCard, nor to the idea of borrowing to purchase goods and services. Indeed, the German word for "debt," *schuld,* is the same as the German word for "guilt."

customs
Norms and expectations about the way people do things in a specific country

Customs **Customs** are what is considered normal and expected about the way people do things in a specific country. Clearly, customs can vary significantly from country to country. Some customs may seem unusual to Americans. Consider, for example, that in France men wear twice the number of cosmetics that women do and that Japanese women give Japanese men chocolates on Valentine's Day.

The custom of giving token business gifts is popular in many countries where they are expected and accepted. However, bribes, kickbacks, and payoffs offered to entice someone to commit an illegal or improper act on behalf of the giver for economic gain is considered corrupt in most cultures. The widespread use of bribery in global marketing has led to an agreement among the world's major exporting nations to make

What cultural lesson did Coca-Cola executives learn when they used the Eiffel Tower and the Parthenon in its global advertising campaign?

bribery of foreign government officials a criminal offense. This agreement is patterned after the **Foreign Corrupt Practices Act (1977)**, which makes it a crime for U.S. corporations to bribe an official of a foreign government or political party to obtain or retain business in a foreign country. Bribery paid to foreign companies is another matter. In France and Greece, bribes paid to foreign companies are a tax-deductible expense!

Foreign Corrupt Practices Act (1977)
Law that makes it a crime for U.S. corporations to bribe an official of a foreign government or political party to obtain or retain business

cultural symbols
Things that represent ideas or concepts

Cultural Symbols **Cultural symbols** are things that represent ideas or concepts. Symbols and symbolism play an important role in cross-cultural analysis because different cultures attach different meanings to things. By cleverly using cultural symbols, global marketers can tie positive symbolism to their products and services to enhance their attractiveness to consumers. However, improper use of symbols can spell disaster. A culturally sensitive global marketer will know that

- North Americans are superstitious about the number 13, and Japanese feel the same way about the number 4. *Shi,* the Japanese word for "four," is also the word for "death." Knowing this, Tiffany & Company sells its fine glassware and china in sets of five, not four, in Japan.
- "Thumbs-up" is a positive sign in the United States. However, in Russia and Poland, this gesture has an offensive meaning when the palm of the hand is shown, as AT&T learned. The company reversed the gesture depicted in ads, showing the back of the hand, not the palm.

Cultural symbols stir up deep feelings. Consider how executives at Coca-Cola Company's Italian office learned this lesson. In a series of advertisements directed at Italian vacationers, the Eiffel Tower, Empire State Building, and the Tower of Pisa were turned into the familiar Coca-Cola bottle. However, when the white marble columns in the Parthenon that crowns Athens's Acropolis were turned into Coca-Cola bottles, the Greeks were outraged. Greeks refer to the Acropolis as the "holy rock," and a government official said the Parthenon is an "international symbol of excellence" and that "whoever insults the Parthenon insults international culture." Coca-Cola apologized for the ad.[11]

Language Global marketers should know not only the basics of the native tongues of countries in which they market their products and services but also the subtleties and unique expressions of the language. About 100 official languages exist in the world, but anthropologists estimate that at least 3,000 different languages are actually spoken. There are 20 official languages spoken in the European Union, and Canada has two official languages (English and French). Seventeen major languages are spoken in India alone.

English, French, and Spanish are the principal languages used in global diplomacy and commerce. However, the best language with which to communicate with consumers is their own, as any seasoned global marketer will agree. Unintended meanings of brand names and messages have ranged from the absurd to the obscene:

- When the advertising agency responsible for launching Procter & Gamble's successful Pert shampoo in Canada realized that the name means "lost" in French, it substituted the brand name Pret, which means "ready."
- The Vicks brand name common in the United States is German slang for sexual intimacy; therefore, Vicks is called Wicks in Germany.

back translation
Retranslating a word or phrase back into the original language by a different interpreter to catch errors

Experienced global marketers use **back translation**, where a translated word or phrase is retranslated back into the original language by a different interpreter to catch errors.[12] For example, IBM's first Japanese translation of its "Solution for a small planet" advertising message yielded "Answers that make people smaller." The error was caught by back translation and corrected.

Economic Considerations

Global marketing is also affected by economic considerations. Therefore, a scan of the global marketplace should include (1) an assessment of the economic infrastructure in different countries, (2) measurement of consumer income in different countries, and (3) recognition of a country's currency exchange rates.

Economic Infrastructure The *economic infrastructure*—a country's communications, transportation, financial, and distribution systems—is a critical consideration in determining whether to try to market to a country's consumers and organizations. Parts of the infrastructure that North Americans or Western Europeans take for granted can be huge problems elsewhere. This is true not only in developing nations but even in countries of the former Soviet Union, Eastern Europe, the Indian subcontinent, and China where such an infrastructure is assumed to be in place.

The communication infrastructures in these countries also differ. Their telecommunication systems and networks in use—such as telephones, cable television, broadcast radio and television, computers and the Internet, satellite, and wireless telephone—are often limited or outdated compared with that of developed countries. But notable exceptions exist. China has the most Internet users in the world.

Even the financial and legal systems can cause problems. Formal operating procedures among financial institutions and private companies did not exist under communism and are still limited. As a consequence, it is estimated that two-thirds of the commercial transactions in Russia involve nonmonetary forms of payment.[13] The legal red tape involved in obtaining titles to buildings and land for manufacturing, wholesaling, and retailing operations also has been a huge problem. Nevertheless, the Coca-Cola Company has invested more than $750 million to build bottling and distribution facilities in Russia. Allied Lyons spent $30 million to build a plant to make Baskin-Robbins ice cream.

Consumer Income and Purchasing Power A global marketer selling consumer goods must also consider what the average per capita income or what the average household income is within a country and how the income is distributed to determine a nation's purchasing power. Per capita income varies greatly between nations. Average yearly per capita income in EU countries is $20,000 and is less than $200 in some developing countries such as Vietnam. A country's income distribution is important because it gives a more reliable picture of a country's purchasing power. Generally speaking, the greater the number of middle-income households in a country, the greater a nation's purchasing power tends to be.

Seasoned global marketers recognize that people in developing countries often have government subsidies for food, housing, and health care that supplement their income. Accordingly, people with seemingly low incomes are actually promising customers for

The Coca-Cola Company has made a huge financial investment in bottling and distribution facilities in Russia.

a variety of products.[14] For example, a consumer in South Asia earning the equivalent of $250 per year can afford Gillette razors. When that consumer's income rises to $1,000, a Sony television becomes affordable, and a new Volkswagen or Nissan can be bought with an annual income of $10,000. In developing countries of Eastern Europe, a $1,000 annual income makes a refrigerator affordable, and $2,000 brings an automatic washer within reach—good news for Whirlpool, the world's leading manufacturer and marketer of major home appliances.

currency exchange rate
Price of one country's currency expressed in terms of another country's currency

Currency Exchange Rates A **currency exchange rate** is the price of one country's currency expressed in terms of another country's currency. As economic conditions change, so can the exchange rate between countries. One day the U.S. dollar may be worth 121.7 Japanese yen or 1.5 Swiss francs. But the next day it may be worth 120.5 Japanese yen or 1.3 Swiss francs.

Fluctuations in exchange rates among the world's currencies can affect everyone from international tourists to global companies. For example, when the U.S. dollar is "strong" against the euro, it takes fewer dollars to purchase goods in the EU. As a result, more U.S. tourists will travel to Europe. This is great news for Europe's travel industry, but bad news for European consumers who want to buy U.S. goods, as they will have to pay more for them. And they may choose not to buy. Mattel learned this lesson the hard way. The company was recently unable to sell its popular Holiday Barbie doll and accessories in many international markets because they were too expensive. Why? Barbie prices, expressed in U.S. dollars, were set without regard for how they would translate into other currencies and were too high for many foreign buyers.[15]

Political–Regulatory Climate

Assessing the political and regulatory climate for marketing in a country or region of the world means not only in identifying the current climate but determining how long a favorable or unfavorable climate will last. An assessment of a country or regional political–regulatory climate includes an analysis of political stability and trade regulations.

Political Stability Trade among nations or regions depends on political stability. Billions of dollars have been lost in the Middle East and Africa as a result of internal political strife, terrorism, and war. Losses such as these encourage careful selection of politically stable countries and regions of the world for trade.

Political stability in a country is affected by numerous factors, including a government's ideas about foreign companies and trade with other countries. These factors combine to create a political climate that is favorable or unfavorable for foreign marketing and financial investment.

Trade Regulations Countries have a variety of rules that govern business practices within their borders. These rules often serve as trade barriers. For example, Japan has some 11,000 trade regulations. Japanese car safety rules effectively require all automobile replacement parts to be Japanese and not American or European; public health rules make it illegal to sell aspirin or cold medicine without a pharmacist present. The Malaysian government has advertising regulations stating that "advertisements must not project or promote an excessively aspirational lifestyle," Greece bans toy advertising, and Sweden outlaws all advertisements to children.

Concept Check

1. Cross-cultural analysis involves the study of ______________.
2. When foreign currencies can buy more U.S. dollars, are U.S. products more or less expensive for a foreign consumer?

GLOBAL MARKET-ENTRY STRATEGIES

Once a company has decided to enter the global marketplace, it must select a means of market entry. Four general options exist: (1) exporting, (2) licensing, (3) joint venture, and (4) direct investment.[16] As Figure 7–3 demonstrates, the amount of financial commitment, risk, marketing control, and profit potential increases as the firm moves from exporting to direct investment.

Exporting

exporting
Producing goods in one country and selling them in another country

Exporting is producing goods in one country and selling them in another country. This entry option allows a company to make the least number of changes in terms of its product, its organization, and even its corporate goals.

FIGURE 7–3
Alternative global market-entry strategies

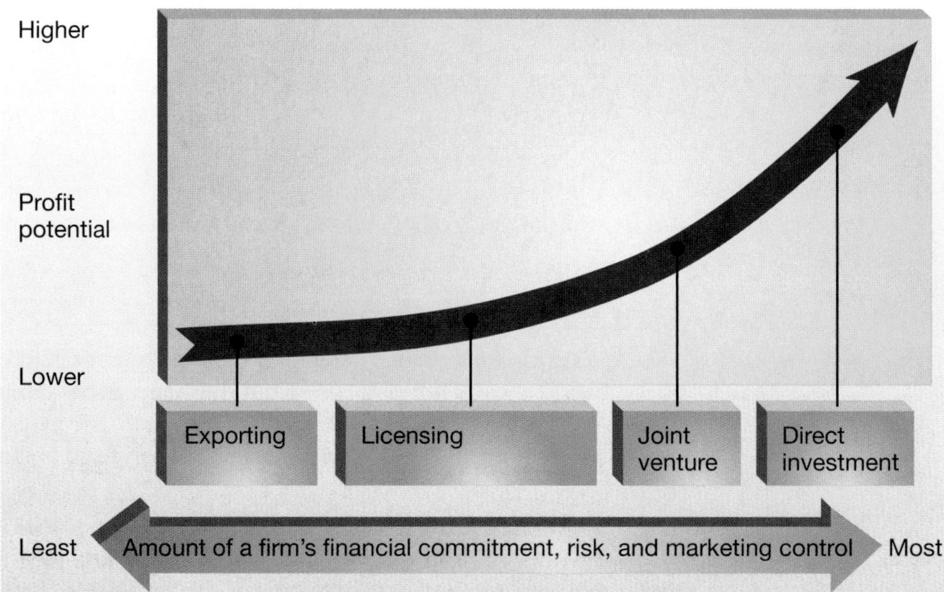

MARKETING NEWSNET

Creative Cosmetics and Creative Export Marketing in Japan

How does a medium-sized U.S. cosmetics firm sell 1.5 million tubes of lipstick in Japan annually? Fran Wilson Creative Cosmetics can attribute its success to a top-quality product, effective advertising, and a novel export marketing program. The firm's Moodmatcher lip coloring comes in green, orange, silver, black, and six other hues that change to a shade of pink, coral, or red, depending on a woman's chemistry when it's applied.

The company does not sell to department stores. According to a company spokesperson, "Shiseido and Kanebo [two large Japanese cosmetics firms] keep all the other Japanese or import brands out of the major department stores." Rather, the company sells its Moodmatcher lipstick through Japanese distributors that reach Japan's 40,000 beauty salons. The result? The company, with its savvy Japanese distributors, accounts for 20 percent of the $4.3 million of lipsticks exported annually to Japan by U.S. companies.

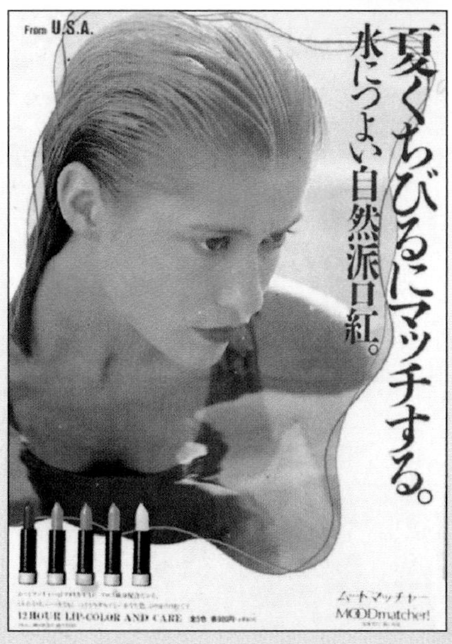

Indirect exporting is when a firm sells its domestically produced goods in a foreign country through an intermediary. This kind of exporting is ideal for the company that has no overseas contacts but wants to market abroad. The intermediary is often a distributor that has the marketing know-how and the resources necessary for the effort to succeed. Fran Wilson Creative Cosmetics of New York uses an indirect exporting approach to sell its products in Japan. Read the Marketing NewsNet to find out how this innovative marketer and its Japanese distributors sell 20 percent of the lipsticks exported to Japan by U.S. companies.[17]

Direct exporting is when a firm sells its domestically produced goods in a foreign country without intermediaries. Most companies become involved in direct exporting when they believe their volume of sales will be sufficiently large and easy to obtain so that they do not require intermediaries. Direct exporting involves more risk than indirect exporting for the company but also opens the door to increased profits. The Boeing Company applies a direct exporting approach. Boeing is not only the world's largest aerospace company, it is also the largest U.S. exporter, generating almost one-half of its total revenue from export sales.

Even though exporting is commonly employed by large firms, it is the prominent global market-entry strategy among small- and medium-sized companies.

Licensing

Under licensing, a company offers the right to a trademark, patent, trade secret, or other similarly valued items of intellectual property in return for a royalty or a fee. The advantages to the company granting the license, the licensor, are low risk and the chance to enter a foreign market at little cost. The licensee gains information that allows it to start with a competitive advantage. The foreign country gains employment by having the product manufactured locally. Yoplait yogurt is licensed from Sodima, a French cooperative, by General Mills for sales in the United States.

Nestlé has made a sizable direct investment in ice cream manufacturing in China to produce its global brands such as Drumstick.

There are some serious drawbacks to this mode of entry, however. The licensor gives up control of its product. In addition, some licensees are able to modify the product somehow and enter the market with product and marketing knowledge gained at the expense of the company that got them started. To offset this disadvantage to the licensor, many companies strive to keep the licensee dependent on them for improvements and successful operation. Finally, should the licensee prove to be a poor choice, the name or reputation of the company may be harmed.

A variation of licensing is *franchising*. Franchising, in which a company contracts with an individual to set up an operation to provide products or services under the company's established brand name, is one of the fastest-growing market-entry strategies. More than 35,000 franchises of U.S. firms are located in countries throughout the world. Franchises include soft-drink, motel, retailing, fast-food, and car rental operation and a variety of business services. McDonald's is a premier global franchiser: more than 70 percent of the company's stores are franchised, and over 60 percent of the company's sales come from non-U.S. operations.

Joint Venture

When a foreign company and a local firm invest together to create a local business, it is called a **joint venture**. These two companies share ownership, control, and profits of the new company. For example, Elite Foods is a joint venture between Elite Industries and PepsiCo created to market Frito-Lay's Cheetos, Ruffles, and Doritos and other snacks in Israel.

joint venture
Occurs when a foreign company and a local firm invest together to create a local business, sharing ownership, control, and profits of the new company

The advantages of this option are twofold. First, one company may not have the necessary financial, physical, or managerial resources to enter a foreign market alone. The joint venture between Ericsson, a Swedish telecommunications firm, and CGCT, a French switch maker, enabled them together to obtain a $100 million French contract. Ericsson's money and technology combined with CGCT's knowledge of the French market helped them to win the contract that neither of them could have won alone. Second, a government may require or encourage a joint venture before it allows a foreign company to enter its market. This is the case in China, where thousands of Chinese–foreign joint ventures operate.

The disadvantages arise when the two companies disagree about policies or courses of action for their joint venture or when governmental bureaucracy bogs down the effort. For example, U.S. firms often prefer to reinvest earnings gained, whereas some foreign companies may want to spend those earnings. Or a U.S. firm may want to return profits earned to the United States, while the local firm or its government may oppose this—the problem now faced by many potential joint ventures in Eastern Europe, Russia, Latin America, and South Asia.

Direct Investment

direct investment
Occurs when a domestic firm actually invests in and owns a foreign subsidiary or division

The biggest commitment a company can make when entering the global market is **direct investment**, which entails a domestic firm actually investing in and owning a foreign subsidiary or division. Examples of direct investment are Nissan's Smyrna, Tennessee, plant that produces pickup trucks and the DaimlerChrysler factory in Vance, Alabama, that makes the M-class sport utility vehicle. Many U.S.-based global companies use this mode of entry. Reebok entered Russia by creating a subsidiary known as Reebok Russia, Motorola formed a Chinese subsidiary that manufactures mobile phones and other telecommunication equipment, and Ford built a $1.9 billion automobile plant in Brazil.

For many firms, direct investment often follows one of the other three market-entry strategies. For example, Harley-Davidson now operates marketing and sales subsidiaries in Germany, Italy, the United Kingdom, and Japan, among other countries, following on the success of its European and Asian exporting strategy.

The advantages to direct investment include cost savings, better understanding of local market conditions, and fewer local restrictions. Firms entering foreign markets using direct investment believe that these advantages outweigh the financial commitments and risks involved.

Concept Check

1. What mode of entry could a company follow if it has no previous experience in global marketing?
2. How does licensing differ from a joint venture?

CRAFTING A WORLDWIDE MARKETING PROGRAM

The choice of a market-entry strategy is a necessary first step for a marketer when joining the community of global companies. The next step involves designing, implementing, and controlling marketing programs worldwide.

Successful global marketers standardize global marketing programs whenever possible and customize them wherever necessary. The extent of standardization and customization is often rooted in a careful global environment scan supplemented with judgment based on experience and marketing research.

Product and Promotion Strategies

Global companies have five strategies for matching products and their promotion efforts to global markets. As Figure 7–4 on the next page shows, the strategies focus on whether a company extends or adapts its product and promotion message for consumers in different countries and cultures.

A product may be sold globally in one of three ways: (1) in the same form as in its home market, (2) with some adaptations, or (3) as a totally new product:[18]

1. *Product extension.* Selling virtually the same product in other countries is a product extension strategy. It works well for products such as Coca-Cola, Gillette razors, Mattel's Barbie, Wrigley's gum, Levi's jeans, Sony consumer electronics, Harley-Davidson motorcycles, and Nokia cell phones. As a general rule, product extension seems to work best when the consumer market target for the product is alike across countries and cultures—that is, consumers share the same desires, needs, and uses for the product.

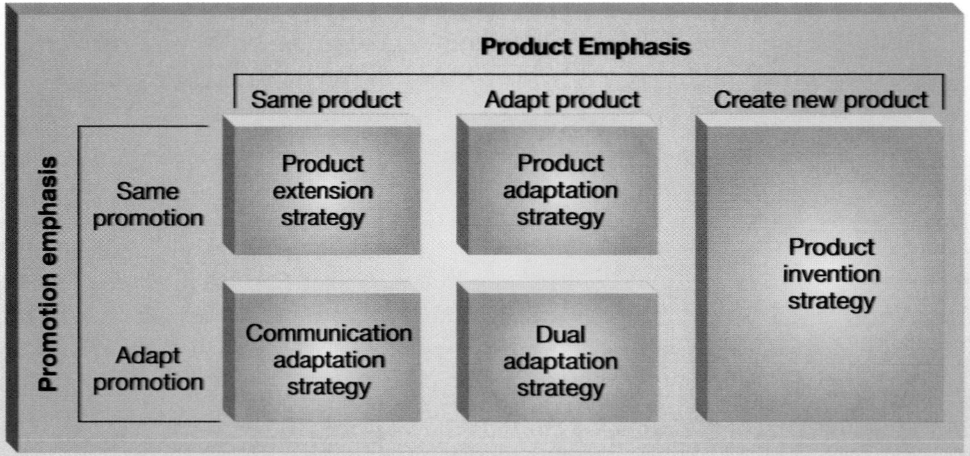

FIGURE 7–4
Five product and promotion strategies for global marketing

2. *Product adaptation.* Changing a product to make it more appropriate for a country's climate or consumer preferences is a product adaptation strategy. Exxon sells different gasoline blends based on each country's climate. Gerber baby food comes in different varieties in different countries. Vegetable and Rabbit Meat is a favorite food in Poland. Freeze-Dried Sardines and Rice is popular in Japan. Maybelline's makeup is formulaically adapted in labs to local skin types and weather across the globe, including an Asia-specific mascara that doesn't run during the rainy season.
3. *Product invention.* Alternatively, companies can invent totally new products designed to satisfy common needs across countries. Black & Decker did this with its Snake Light Flexible Flashlight. Created to address a global need for portable lighting, the product became a best seller in North America, Europe, Latin America, and Australia and is the most successful new product developed by Black & Decker. Similarly, Whirlpool developed a compact, automatic clothes washer specifically for households in developing countries with annual household incomes of $2,000. The washer features bright colors because washers are often placed in home living areas, not hid in laundry rooms (which don't exist in many homes in developing countries).

Gillette delivers the same global message whenever possible, as shown in the Gillette for Women Venus ads from Greece, Germany, and the United States.

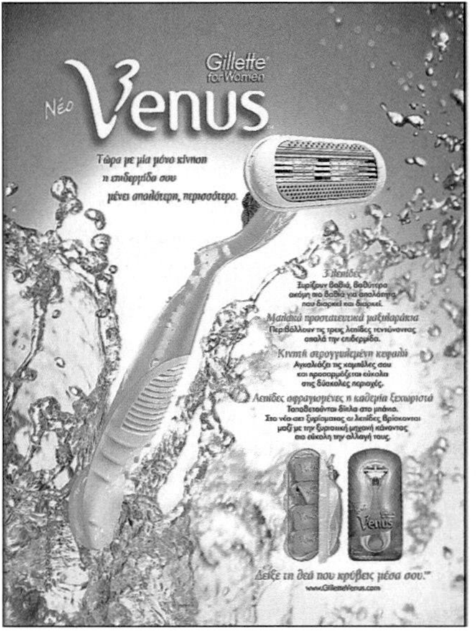

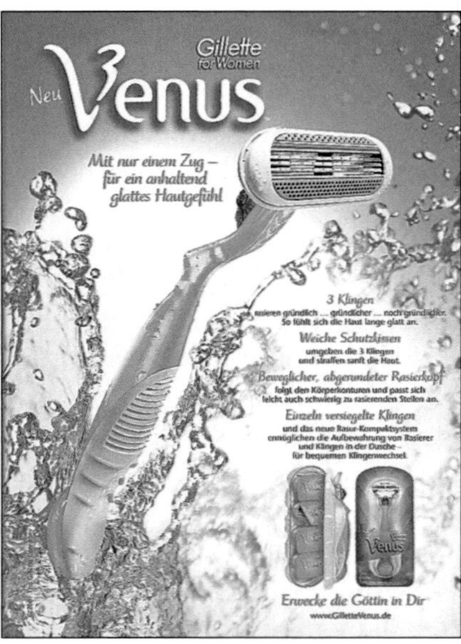

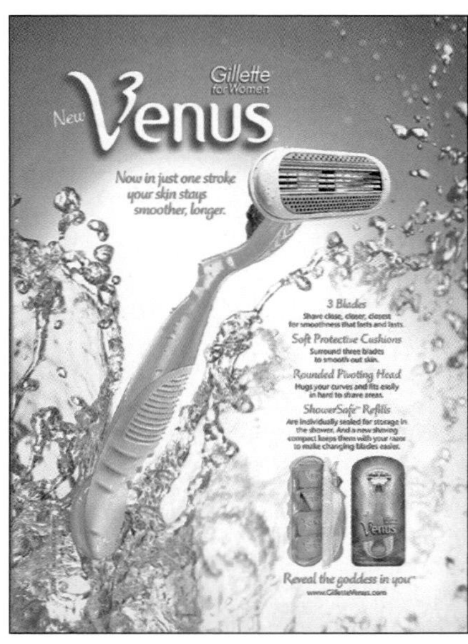

An identical promotion message is used for the product extension and product adaptation strategies around the world. Gillette uses the same global message for its men's toiletries: "Gillette, the Best a Man Can Get." Even though Exxon adapts its gasoline blends for different countries based on climate, the promotion message is unchanged: "Put a Tiger in Your Tank."

Global companies may also adapt their promotion message. For instance, the same product may be sold in many countries but advertised differently. As an example, L'Oréal, a French health and beauty products marketer, introduced its Golden Beauty brand of sun care products through its Helena Rubenstein subsidiary in Western Europe with a communication adaptation strategy. Recognizing that cultural and buying motive differences related to skin care and tanning exist, Golden Beauty advertising features dark tanning for northern Europeans, skin protection to avoid wrinkles among Latin Europeans, and beautiful skin for Europeans living along the Mediterranean Sea, even though the products are the same.

Other companies use a dual adaptation strategy by modifying both their products and promotion messages. Nestlé does this with Nescafé coffee. Nescafé is marketed using different coffee blends and promotional campaigns to match consumer preferences in different countries.

These examples illustrate the simple rule applied by global companies: Standardize product and promotion strategies whenever possible and customize them wherever necessary. This is the art of global marketing.[19]

Distribution Strategy

Distribution is of critical importance in global marketing. The availability and quality of retailers and wholesalers as well as transportation, communication, and warehousing facilities are often determined by a country's stage of economic development. Figure 7–5 outlines the channel through which a product manufactured in one country must travel to reach its destination in another country. The first step involves the seller; its headquarters is the starting point and is responsible for the successful distribution to the ultimate consumer.

The next step is the channel between two nations, moving the product from one country to another. Intermediaries that can handle this responsibility include resident buyers in a foreign country, independent merchant wholesalers who buy and sell the product, or agents who bring buyers and sellers together.

Once the product is in the foreign nation, that country's distribution channels take over.[20] These channels can be very long or surprisingly short, depending on the product. In Japan, fresh fish go through three intermediaries before getting to a retail outlet. Conversely, shoes only go through one intermediary. In other cases, the channel does not even involve the host country. Procter & Gamble sells its soap door to door in the Philippines because there are no other alternatives in many parts of that country. The sophistication of a country's distribution channels increase as its economic infrastructure develops. Supermarkets facilitate selling products in many nations, but they are not popular or available in many others where culture and lack of refrigeration dictate shopping on a daily rather than a weekly basis. For example, when Coke and Pepsi entered China, both created direct-distribution channels, investing in refrigerator units for small retailers.

FIGURE 7–5
Channels of distribution in global marketing

Pricing Strategy

Global companies face many challenges in determining a pricing strategy as part of their worldwide marketing effort. Individual countries, even those with free trade agreements, may place competitive, political, and legal constraints on the pricing flexibility of global companies. For example, Wal-Mart was told by German antitrust authorities that the prices in its stores were too low, relative to competitors, and faced a fine for violating the country's trade practices if the prices weren't raised![21]

Pricing too low or too high can have dire consequences. When prices appear too low in one country, companies can be charged with "dumping," a practice subject to severe penalties and fines. **Dumping** is when a firm sells a product in a foreign country below its domestic price or below its actual cost. A recent trade dispute involving U.S. apple growers and Mexico is a case in point. Mexican trade officials claimed that U.S. growers were selling their red and golden delicious apples in Mexico below the actual cost of production. They imposed a 101 percent tariff on U.S. apples, and a severe drop in U.S. apple exports to Mexico resulted. Later negotiations set a price floor on the price of U.S. apples sold to Mexico.[22]

dumping
Occurs when a firm sells a product in a foreign country below its domestic prices or below its actual cost

When companies price their products very high in some countries but competitively in others, they face a gray market problem. A **gray market**, also called *parallel importing,* is a situation where products are sold through unauthorized channels of distribution. A gray market comes about when individuals buy products in a lower-priced country from a manufacturer's authorized retailer, ship them to higher-priced countries, and then sell them below the manufacturer's suggested retail price through unauthorized retailers. Many well-known products have been sold through gray markets, including Olympus cameras, Seiko watches, and Mercedes-Benz cars. Parallel importing is legal in the United States. It is illegal in the European Union.

gray market
Situations where products are sold through unauthorized channels of distribution

Concept Check

1. Products may be sold globally in three ways. What are they?
2. What is dumping?

CHAPTER IN REVIEW

1 *Identify the major trends that have influenced the landscape of global marketing in the past decade.*
Four major trends have influenced the landscape of global marketing in the past decade. First, there has been a gradual decline of economic protectionism by individual countries, leading to a reduction in tariffs and quotas. Second, there is growing economic integration and free trade among nations, reflected in the creation of the European Union and the North American Free Trade Agreement. Third, there is increased global competition among global companies for global consumers, resulting in firms adopting global marketing strategies and promoting global brands. And finally, a networked global marketspace has emerged using Internet technology as a tool for exchanging goods, services, and information on a global scale.

2 *Identify the environmental factors that shape global marketing efforts.*
Three major environmental factors shape global marketing efforts. First, there are cultural factors, including values, customs, cultural symbols, and language. Economic factors also shape global marketing efforts. These include a country's stage of economic development and economic infrastructure, consumer income and purchasing power, and currency exchange rates. Finally, political-regulatory factors in a country or region of the world create a favorable or unfavorable climate for global marketing efforts.

3 *Name and describe the alternative approaches companies use to enter global markets.*
Companies have four alternative approaches for entering global markets. These are exporting, licensing, joint venture, and direct investment. Exporting involves producing goods in one country and selling them in another country. Under licensing, a company offers the right to a trademark, patent, trade secret, or similarly valued items of intellectual property in return for a royalty or fee. In a joint venture, a foreign company and a local firm invest together to create a local business. Direct investment entails a domestic firm actually investing in and owning a foreign subsidiary or division.

4 *Explain the distinction between standardization and customization when companies craft worldwide marketing programs.*
Companies distinguish between standardization and customization when crafting worldwide marketing programs.

Standardization means that all elements of the marketing program are the same across countries and cultures. Customization means that one or more elements of the marketing program are adapted to meet the needs or preferences of consumers in a particular country or culture. Global marketers apply a simple rule when crafting worldwide marketing programs: Standardize marketing programs whenever possible and customize them wherever necessary.

FOCUSING ON KEY TERMS

back translation p. 148
cross-cultural analysis p. 146
cultural symbols p. 147
currency exchange rate p. 149
customs p. 146
direct investment p. 153
dumping p. 156
exporting p. 150
Foreign Corrupt Practices Act (1977) p. 147
global brand p. 144
global competition p. 142
global consumers p. 144
global marketing strategy p. 143
gray market p. 156
joint venture p. 152
multidomestic marketing strategy p. 143
protectionism p. 140
quota p. 140
tariffs p. 140
values p. 146
World Trade Organization p. 140

DISCUSSION AND APPLICATION QUESTIONS

1 What is meant by this statement: "Quotas are a hidden tax on consumers, whereas tariffs are a more obvious one"?
2 How successful would a television commercial in Japan be if it featured a husband surprising his wife in her dressing area on Valentine's Day with a small box of chocolates containing four candies? Why?
3 As a novice in global marketing, which alternative for global market-entry strategy would you be likely to start with? Why? What other alternatives do you have for a global market entry?
4 Coca-Cola is sold worldwide. In some countries, Coca-Cola owns the bottling facilities; in others, it has signed contracts with licensees or relies on joint ventures. When selecting a licensee in each country, what factors should Coca-Cola consider?

GOING ONLINE Getting to Know the WTO

The World Trade Organization is the only international organization dealing with the global rules of trade between nations. Its intended function is to ensure that trade flows as smoothly, predictably, and freely as possible. Understanding how the WTO operates is a necessary prerequisite for global marketing.

Visit the WTO website at www.wto.org to learn more about how this organization functions and the issues it faces. A useful starting point for familiarizing yourself with the WTO is to find answers to the following questions:

1 Countries are constantly seeking WTO membership. How many countries are now members of this organization? Which country is the newest member?
2 What are the 10 most common misunderstandings about the WTO identified by this organization?

BUILDING YOUR MARKETING PLAN

Does your marketing plan involve reaching global customers outside the United States? If the answer is no, read no further and do not include a global element in your plan.

If the answer is yes, try to identify:

1 What features of your product are especially important to potential customers.
2 In which countries these potential customers live.
3 Special marketing issues that are involved in trying to reach them.

Answers to these questions will help in developing more detailed marketing mix strategies described in later chapters.

VIDEO CASE 7 CNS Breathe Right Strips: Going Global

"It's naive to treat 'international' as one big market—particularly within OTC," explains Marti Morfitt, president and CEO of CNS, the company that manufactures Breathe Right® nasal strips. "There are many discrete, unique markets, and local expertise is needed to understand the dynamics within each and address them effectively."

"OTC" refers to over-the-counter medical products like aspirin or cough syrup that customers can buy without a doctor's prescription. Breathe Right nasal strips qualify as an OTC product. But, that doesn't mean there isn't a lot of technology and medical science behind it.

Breathe Right nasal strips are innovative adhesive strips with patented dual flex bars inside. When attached to the nose, they gently lift and hold open nasal passages, making it easier to breathe. Breathe Right strips are used for a variety of reasons, all to help breathe better through the nose: athletes hoping to play their best (particularly when wearing mouth guards); snorers (and their spouses) hoping for a quiet night's sleep; and allergy, sinusitis, and cold sufferers looking for drug-free relief from nasal congestion.

HOW IT ALL BEGAN

Breathe Right strips were invented by Bruce Johnson, a chronic nasal congestion sufferer. At times Johnson put straws or paper clips in his nose at night to keep his nasal passages open. He eventually came up with a prototype for Breathe Right strips. He brought his invention to CNS, Inc., which recognized its market potential. CNS took the strips to the Food and Drug Administration for approval of claims for relief of snoring and nasal congestion.

CNS, a small company, had a limited marketing budget. However, it got a big public relations break when Jerry Rice, the legendary wide receiver for the San Francisco 49ers, wore a Breathe Right strip on national TV and scored two touchdowns during the 49ers' 1995 Super Bowl victory. Demand for the strips soared.

"What really helped sales of Breathe Right strips was that CNS had done a very effective job of getting press kits in the hands of news and sports media," says Morfitt. "When people on television asked, 'What is that funny looking thing on his nose?' the reporters could talk about how the strip was an effective consumer product for everyone. And a $1.4 million business turned into a $45 million business in just one year," she explains.

THE DECISION TO GO GLOBAL

As awareness and trial in the United States was building, CNS began to get inquiries from people in other countries asking where they could buy strips. In 1995 CNS decided to take advantage of global interest and introduce Breathe Right strips internationally.

What countries did CNS choose to enter with its Breathe Right strips? "Countries we focus on are those with a large OTC market, high per-capita spending in the OTC market, and future prospects for growth," says Kevin McKenna, vice president for international at CNS. All these factors relate to market size. "But the real key to success in a market is a local partner that is entrepreneurial and has an ability to execute in terms of achieving distribution and sales."

IMPORTANCE OF LOCAL PARTNERS

Dynamic world market changes in the last 30 years have influenced opportunities for global sales of Breathe Right strips. Key trends include increased availability of OTC products formerly available only by prescription and a global push toward self-care, spurred by the increasing cost of health and medical care. Additionally, OTC products have extended beyond the traditional boundary of the pharmacy and into grocery and other channels; and the role of the pharmacist has expanded from that of medical professional to one that includes selling and marketing OTC products to consumers.

At the same time, changes were taking place within CNS. When Morfitt joined CNS in 1998, she began pulling together a new management group with extensive experience in marketing consumer packaged goods, both in the United States and abroad. CNS began seeking "hungry" international partners who would bring greater localized market expertise and direct-selling capabilities than past partners. Morfitt also wanted partners with demonstrated entrepreneurial spirit to match that of the new management team.

The company's partner in Italy, BluFarm Group, uses its local knowledge and direct-selling skills to partner with pharmacists to teach them how to increase sales of Breathe Right strips in their stores. In Italy, as throughout much of Europe, OTC products such as antacids, aspirin, and nasal strips are typically placed behind pharmacy counters and therefore not visible to customers. The only way to sell a product is for a customer to ask for it by name. BluFarm Group recognized the importance of in-store advertising and sales execution to build awareness and created point-of-sale materials such as window and counter displays (see photo) to let customers know that Breathe Right strips were available in the store. "BluFarm's ability to capture consumers' awareness of Breathe Right strips as they walk in the retailer's door has beneficial results for CNS, BluFarm, pharmacists, and consumers," says McKenna.

"Working with an experienced local partner helps overcome surprises in global markets," says Nick Naumann, senior marketing communications manager at CNS. One surprise: universal product codes (UPC) on packaging aren't "universal"—they are used only in the United States and Canada. "Different forms of those codes in other countries can take a few weeks to six months or more of government review to obtain," he says.

Even the same packaging colors don't work around the globe. Research with U.S. consumers revealed they wanted darker packaging to suggest the strips' use at night by snorers and those with stuffed noses. "'Too grim and negative' Asian and European consumers told us," says Naumann. Breathe Right strips in those countries have a lighter, airier look than in the United States to convey the open feeling one gets from the nasal strips.

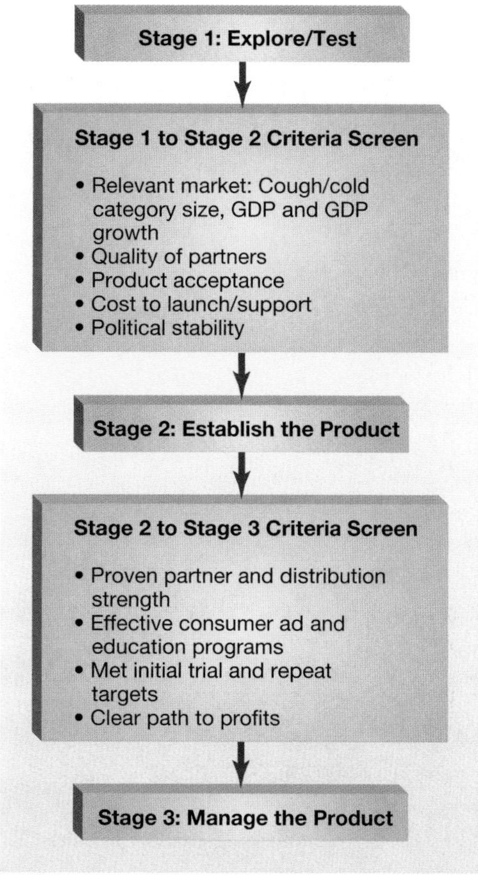

MANAGING GLOBAL GROWTH

Today, Breathe Right strips are sold in more than 25 countries. To ensure the Breathe Right brand continues to meet growth expectations, CNS now uses a three-stage approach to penetrate and develop new markets:

- Stage 1: Explore/test the concept
  - — Use screening criteria to identify high-potential markets
  - — Identify potential partners
  - — Validate concept with research
  - — Develop strategy and launch test market
- Stage 2: Establish the product
  - — Penetrate the marketplace
  - — Refine messages for local market
  - — Evaluate partnership and marketing strategies
- Stage 3: Manage the product
  - — Achieve sustainability/profitability
  - — Exploit new product and new use opportunities

Stage 1: Explore/Test

↓

Stage 1 to Stage 2 Criteria Screen

- Relevant market: Cough/cold category size, GDP and GDP growth
- Quality of partners
- Product acceptance
- Cost to launch/support
- Political stability

↓

Stage 2: Establish the Product

↓

Stage 2 to Stage 3 Criteria Screen

- Proven partner and distribution strength
- Effective consumer ad and education programs
- Met initial trial and repeat targets
- Clear path to profits

↓

Stage 3: Manage the Product

Overall, this approach starts with what works in the United States and extends it into new markets, paying close attention to local needs and customs. Throughout the three stages CNS conducts market research and makes financial projections.

As shown in the figure, at each stage of the market development process, performance must be met for the product to enter the next stage. Once success with Breathe Right nasal strips is established in a country, the groundwork is laid and international partners have the ability to introduce other Breathe Right products.

LOOKING FORWARD

"We believe the Breathe Right brand has great potential, both domestically and around the world," says Morfitt. "Growth will come both from further expansion of Breathe Right nasal strips and from other drug-free, better-breathing line extensions," says Morfitt.

Questions

1 What are the advantages and disadvantages for CNS taking Breathe Right strips into international markets?

2 What are the advantages to CNS of (*a*) using its three-stage process to enter new global markets and (*b*) having specific criteria to move through the stages?

3 Using the CNS criteria, with what you know, which countries should have highest priority for CNS?

4 Which single segment of potential Breathe Right strip users would you target to enter new markets?

5 Which marketing mix variables should CNS emphasize the most to succeed in a global arena? Why?

PART

PART 1
Initiating the Marketing Process

PART 2
Understanding Buyers and Markets

PART 3
Targeting Marketing Opportunities

PART 4
Satisfying Marketing Opportunities

3 Targeting Marketing Opportunities

HOW PART 3 FITS INTO THE BOOK

The two chapters in Part 3 discuss key marketing methods—techniques to help discover potential buyers of a product and determine their needs and wants; then focusing marketing efforts on those key segments most likely to buy the product.

CHAPTER 8
Marketing Research: From Information to Action

CHAPTER 9
Identifying Market Segments and Targets

STAR WARS
EPISODE III
DIE RACHE DER SITH
DAS OFFIZIELLE SPIEL ZUM FILM -
JETZT IM HA

PlayStation 2
EPISODE III

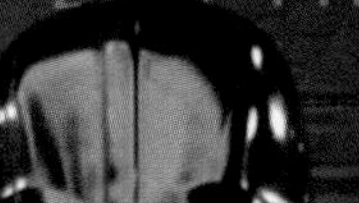

Bild

CHAPTER

8 MARKETING RESEARCH: FROM INFORMATION TO ACTION

LEARNING OBJECTIVES

After reading this chapter you should be able to:

1 Identify the reason for doing marketing research.

2 Describe the four-step marketing research approach leading to marketing actions.

3 Describe how secondary and primary data are used in marketing, including the uses of questionnaires, observations, experiments, and panels.

4 Describe three approaches to developing a sales forecast for a company.

TEST SCREENINGS: LISTENING TO CONSUMERS TO REDUCE MOVIE RISKS

Blockbuster movies are essential for today's fiercely competitive world of filmmaking, examples being *Star Wars: Episode III—Revenge of the Sith, Shoeless Joe,* and *Rope Burns.*

What's in a Movie Name? Can't remember those last two movies, even after scratching your head? Well, test screenings by the studios—a form of marketing research—found that moviegoers had problems with those titles, too. Here's what happened:

- *Shoeless Joe* became *Field of Dreams* because audiences thought Kevin Costner might be playing a homeless person.
- *Rope Burns* became *Million Dollar Baby* because audiences didn't like the original name. The movie won the 2005 Academy Award for Best Picture starring Hillary Swank as a woman boxer and Clint Eastwood as her trainer.

Filmmakers want movie titles that are concise, are attention-getting, capture the essence of the film, and have no legal restrictions—basically, the same factors that make a good brand name.[1]

The Risks in Today's Blockbuster Movies Bad titles, poor scripts, temperamental stars who stomp off the set, and too-costly special effects are just some of the nightmares faced by movie producers. Today's films average more than $103 million to produce and market,[2] movie studios use market research to reduce their risk of losses by tracking, and adapting to, the ever-changing tastes of moviegoers. This includes conducting test screenings.

For test screenings, 300 to 400 prospective viewers are recruited to attend a "sneak preview" of a film before its release. After viewing the movie, the audience fills out an exhaustive survey to critique the title, plot, characters, music, and ending as well as the marketing program (posters, trailers, etc.) to identify improvements to make in the final edit of the movie.[3]

Virtually every major U.S. movie produced today uses test screenings to obtain the key reactions of consumers likely to be in the target audience. Test screenings resulted in *Fatal Attraction* having probably the most commercially successful "ending-switch" of all time. In its sneak previews, audiences liked everything but the ending, which had Alex (Glenn Close) committing suicide and managing to frame Dan (Michael Douglas) as her murderer by leaving his fingerprints on the knife she used. The studio shot $1.3 million of new scenes for the ending that audiences eventually saw.[4]

George Lucas and his six-film *Star Wars* epic is a huge movie success story—as witnessed in the $9 billion of *Star Wars* merchandise sold around the globe by mid-2005. But it was not always this easy for George Lucas.[5] For his first *Star Wars* movie in 1977, Lucas had to go back to his budget people to beg for an extra $10,000 for some better rubber masks for Chewbocca and other characters so they could actually move their mouths.[6] With today's digital technology that's no problem. However, budgets are still a concern: At $115 million for making *Star Wars Episode III—Revenge of the Sith* and $95 million for marketing and printing it, costs far exceeded those for the average Hollywood movie.

These examples show how marketing research is the link between marketing strategy and decisive actions, the main topic of this chapter. Also, marketing research is often used to help a firm develop sales forecasts, the final topic in the chapter.

THE ROLE OF MARKETING RESEARCH

To place marketing research in perspective, we can describe (1) what it is, (2) some of the difficulties in conducting it, and (3) the four steps marketing executives can use in conducting marketing research.

What Is Marketing Research?

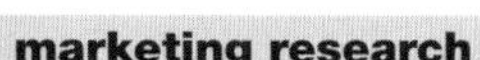

marketing research
Process of collecting and analyzing information in order to recommend actions

Marketing research is the process of defining a marketing problem and opportunity, systematically collecting and analyzing information, and recommending actions.[7] Although marketing research isn't perfect at predicting consumer reaction, it can reduce risk and uncertainty to help marketing managers take more effective marketing actions.

Why Good Marketing Research Is Difficult

Ask a moviegoer if she liked the title for a film she just saw and you'll probably get a straightforward answer. But often marketing researchers face difficulties in asking consumers questions about new, unknown products. For example,

- Suppose your company is developing a brand new product, never before seen by consumers. Would consumers really know whether they are likely to buy a particular product that they probably have never thought about before?

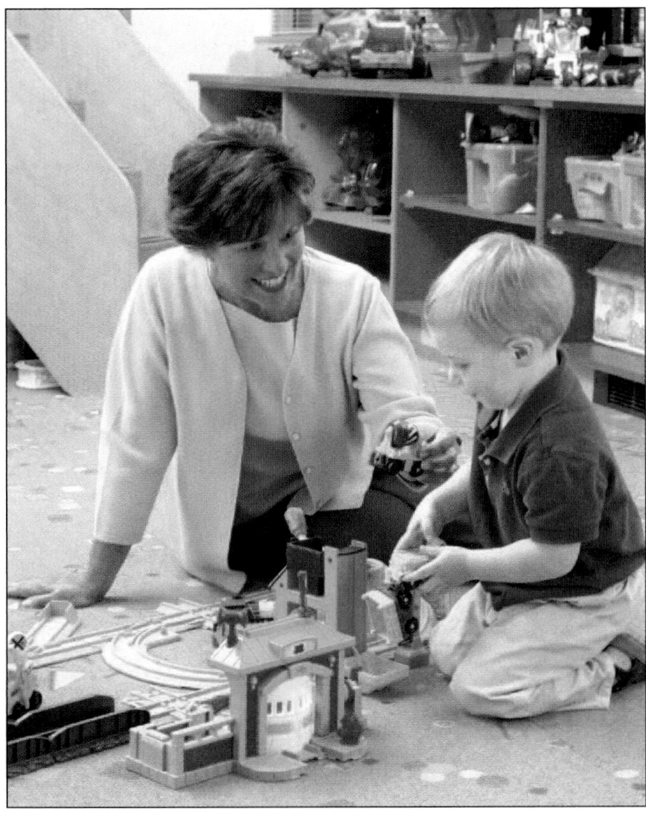

How can Fisher-Price do marketing research on young children who can't even fill out a questionnaire? For the answer, see the text.

- Imagine if you, as a consumer, were asked about your personal hygiene habits. Even though you know the answer, would you reveal it? When personal or status questions are involved, will people give honest answers?
- Will consumers' actual purchase behavior be the same as their stated interest or intentions? Will they buy the same brand they say they will?

A task of marketing research is to overcome these difficulties and obtain as much information as needed to make reasonable estimates about what consumers will or won't buy.

Four-Step Marketing Research Approach

Marketers have tried to improve the results of their research by using more formal, systematic approaches such as that shown in Figure 8–1. This four-step sequence starts with defining the problem carefully (step 1) and developing a research plan for collecting the most appropriate information to try to solve the problem (step 2). It then concludes by actually collecting the relevant data (step 3) and developing a report to management that converts the data into findings and recommendations (step 4). The following pages examine each step in more detail. Problems in marketing can also represent opportunities. Furthermore, market research often performs the valuable role of testing new ideas for products or services before large amounts of time and money are spent actually creating and offering them.

Concept Check

1. What is marketing research?
2. What are the four steps marketing researchers use to help develop marketing actions?

FIGURE 8–1
Four-step marketing research approach leading to better marketing actions

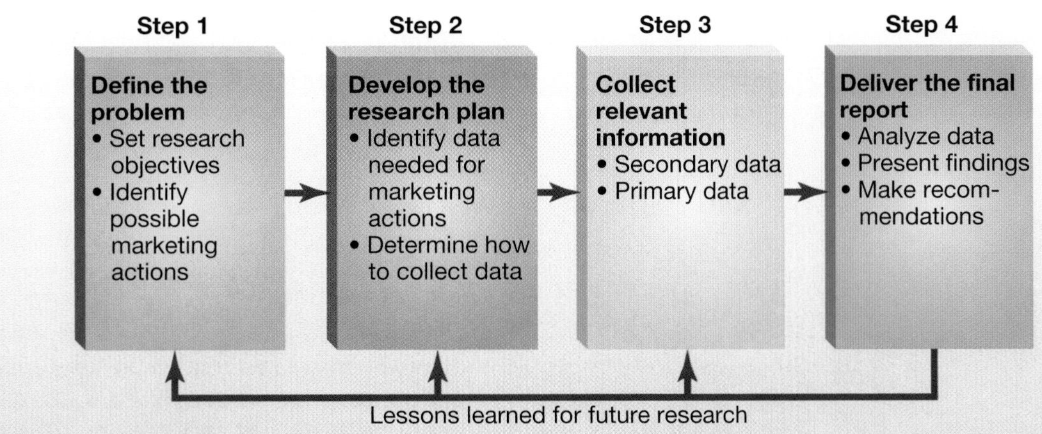

STEP 1: DEFINE THE PROBLEM

Designers at Fisher-Price, the nation's top marketer of infant and preschool toys, seek to develop toys they think kids will like, but the problem is: How can they be certain kids will like the toys? As part of their market research, Fisher-Price gets children to play at its state-licensed nursery school in East Aurora, New York. From behind one-way mirrors, Fisher-Price designers and marketing researchers watch the children use, and abuse, the toys to develop better products.

The original model of a classic Fisher-Price toy, the Chatter Telephone™, was simply a wooden phone with a dial that rang a bell. Observers noted, however, that the children kept grabbing the receiver like a handle to pull the phone along behind them, so a designer added wheels, a noisemaker, and eyes that bobbed up and down.

Fisher-Price's toy testing shows how to define the problem and its two key elements: setting the research objectives and identifying possible marketing actions suggested by the research.

Set the Research Objectives

In undertaking marketing research, *objectives* are specific, measurable goals the decision maker—in this case, an executive at Fisher-Price—seeks to achieve in solving a problem. Typical marketing objectives are increasing sales and profits, discovering what consumers are aware of and want, and finding out why a product isn't selling well. For Fisher-Price, the immediate research objective was to decide whether to market the old or new telephone design.

Identify Possible Marketing Actions

measures of success
Criteria or standards used in evaluating proposed solutions to a problem

Effective decision makers develop specific **measures of success**, which are criteria or standards used in evaluating proposed solutions to the problem. Different research outcomes—based on the measure of success—lead to different marketing actions. For the Fisher-Price problem, if a measure of success were the total time children spent playing with each of the two telephone designs, the results of observing them would lead to clear-cut actions as follows:

Measure of Success: Playtime	Possible Marketing Action
• Children spent more time playing with old design.	• Continue with old design; don't introduce new design.
• Children spent more time playing with new design.	• Introduce new design; drop old design.

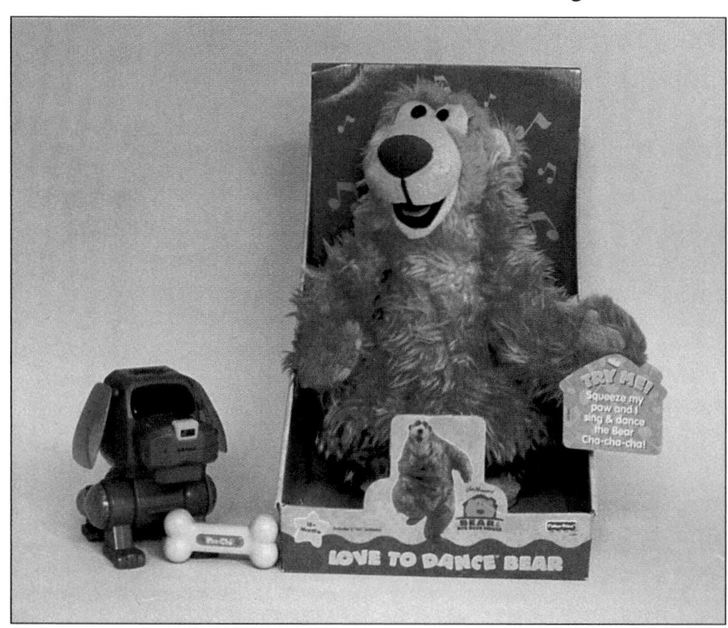

Marketing research turned up Fisher-Price's Love to Dance Bear "toy of the year" but missed Tiger Electronic's Poo-Chi, the robotic puppy.

One test of whether marketing research should be done is if different outcomes will lead to different marketing actions. If all the research outcomes lead to the same action—such as top management sticking with the older design regardless of what the observed children liked—the research is useless and a waste of money. In this case, research results showed that kids liked the new design, so Fisher-Price introduced its noisemaking pull-toy Chatter Telephone, which became a toy classic and sold millions.

Toy marketing research goes beyond manufacturers such as Fisher-Price. Every summer Digital Research, Inc., a marketing research firm, evaluates almost 500 new toys from more than 160 toy manufacturers to select *Family Fun* magazine's Toy of the Year award. More than 700 children "toy testers" are involved. And they've been right on the money in selecting

Barney the TV dinosaur, Tickle Me Elmo, Sing & Snore Ernie, and Fisher-Price's Love to Dance Bear™ as hot toys—ones that jumped off retailers' shelves. But they missed Tiger Electronic's robotic puppy, Poo-Chi.[8] Forecasting which toys are hot is critical for retailers, which must place orders to manufacturers 8 to 10 months before Christmas shoppers walk into their stores. Bad forecasts can lead to lost sales for understocks and severe losses for overstocks.

Most marketing researchers would agree with the saying that "a problem well-defined is half-solved," but they know that defining a problem is an incredibly difficult task. For example, if the objectives are too broad, the problem may not be researchable. If they are too narrow, the value of the research results may be seriously lessened. This is why marketing researchers spend so much time in defining a marketing problem precisely and writing a formal proposal that describes the research to be done.[9]

STEP 2: DEVELOP THE RESEARCH PLAN

The second step in the marketing research process involves (1) identifying the data needed for marketing decisions and (2) determining how to collect the data.

Identify Data Needed for Marketing Actions

Often marketing research studies wind up collecting a lot of data that are interesting but irrelevant for marketing decisions. In the Fisher-Price Chatter Telephone case, it might be nice to know the children's favorite colors, whether they like wood or plastic toys better, and so on. In fact, knowing answers to these questions might result in later modifications of the toy, but right now the problem is to select one of two toy designs. So this study must focus on collecting data that help managers make a clear choice between the two telephone designs.

Determine How to Collect Data

Determining how to collect useful marketing research data is often as important as actually collecting the data—step 3 in the process, which is discussed later. Two key elements in deciding how to collect the data are (1) concepts and (2) methods.

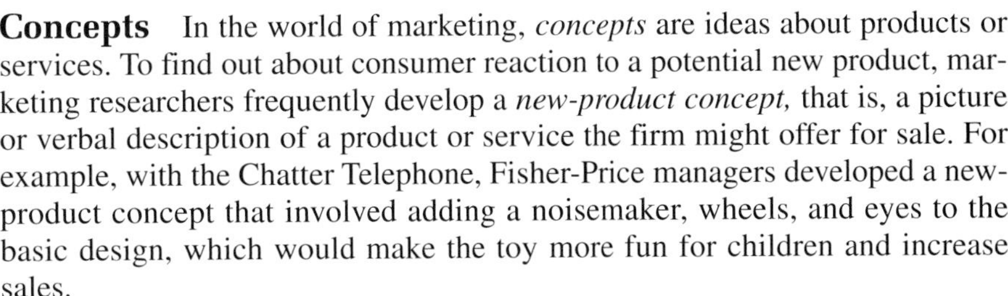

Concepts In the world of marketing, *concepts* are ideas about products or services. To find out about consumer reaction to a potential new product, marketing researchers frequently develop a *new-product concept,* that is, a picture or verbal description of a product or service the firm might offer for sale. For example, with the Chatter Telephone, Fisher-Price managers developed a new-product concept that involved adding a noisemaker, wheels, and eyes to the basic design, which would make the toy more fun for children and increase sales.

Methods *Methods* are the approaches that can be used to collect data to solve all or part of a problem. For example, if you are the marketing researcher at Fisher-Price responsible for the Chatter Telephone, you face a number of methods issues in developing your research plan, including the following:

- Can we actually ask three- or four-year-olds meaningful questions they can answer about their liking or disliking of the two designs?
- Are we better off not asking them questions but simply observing their behavior?

- If we simply observe the children's behavior, how can we do this in a way to get the best information without biasing the results?

Millions of other people have asked similar questions about millions of other products and services. How can you find and use the methodologies that other marketing researchers have found successful? Information on useful methods is available in tradebooks, textbooks, and handbooks that relate to marketing and marketing research. Some periodicals and technical journals, such as the *Journal of Marketing* and the *Journal of Marketing Research* published by the American Marketing Association, summarize methods and techniques valuable in addressing marketing problems.

Special methods vital to marketing are (1) sampling and (2) statistical inference. For example, marketing researchers often use *sampling* by selecting a group of distributors, customers, or prospects, asking them questions, and treating their answers as typical of all those in whom they are interested. They may then use *statistical inference* to generalize the results from the sample to much larger groups of distributors, customers, or prospects to help decide on marketing actions.

Concept Check

1. How do measures of success relate to marketing actions?
2. What is the difference between concepts and methods?

STEP 3: COLLECT RELEVANT INFORMATION

Collecting enough relevant information to make a rational, informed marketing decision sometimes simply means using your knowledge to decide immediately. At other times it entails collecting an enormous amount of information at great expense.

Figure 8–2 shows how the different kinds of marketing information fit together. **Data**, the facts and figures related to the problem, are divided into two main parts: secondary data and primary data. **Secondary data** are facts and figures that have already been recorded before the project at hand, whereas **primary data** are facts and figures that are newly collected for the project.

data
Facts and figures related to a problem

secondary data
Facts and figures that have already been recorded before the project at hand

primary data
Facts or figures that are newly collected for a project

Secondary Data: Internal

Secondary data divide into two parts—internal and external secondary data—depending on whether the data come from inside or outside the organization needing the research.

Data that have already been collected and exist inside the business firm or other organization are internal secondary data. These include product sales data, and sales reports on customer calls.

Secondary Data: External

Published data from outside the organization are external secondary data. The U.S. Census Bureau publishes a variety of useful reports. Best known is the Census 2000, which is a count of the U.S. population in the year 2000. This population census is conducted every 10 years. It contains detailed information on American households, such as the number of people per household and their age, sex, race/ethnic background, income, occupation, and education. Marketers use these

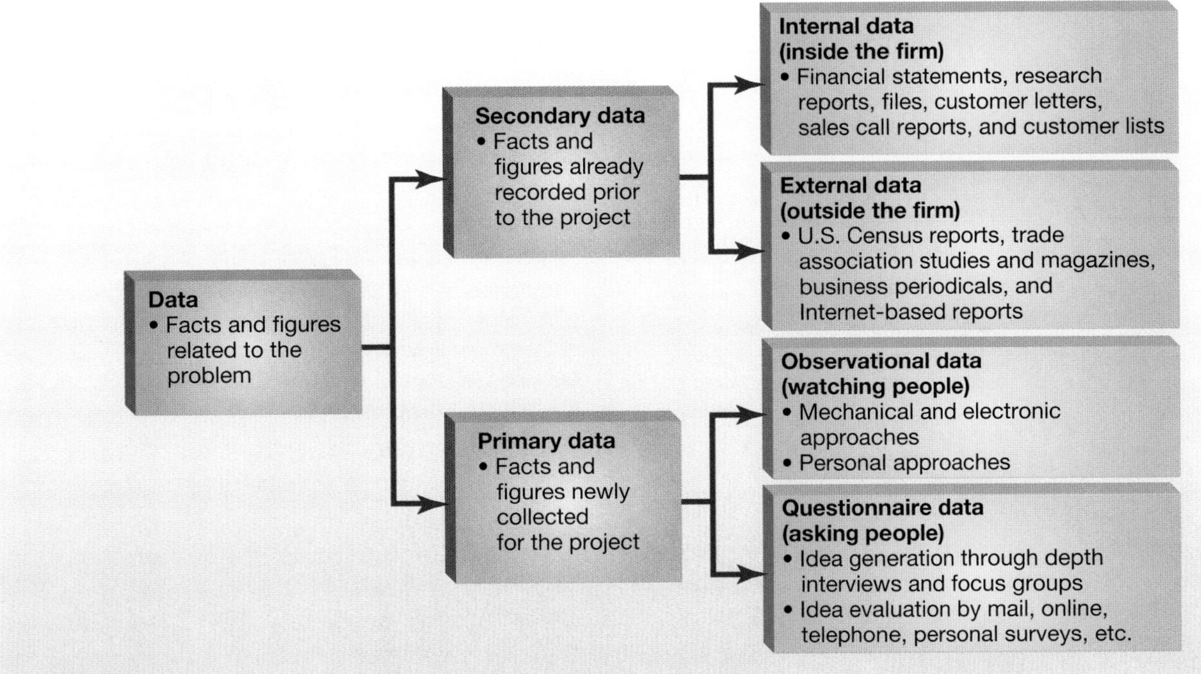

FIGURE 8–2
Types of marketing information

data to identify characteristics and trends of ultimate consumers. Because the traditional every-10-year Census has the problem of timeliness, starting in 2006 it will be supplemented by the American Community Survey that will provide annual data for communities with more than 65,000 people and less frequently for smaller communities.[10]

The Census Bureau also publishes other reports that are vital to business firms selling products and services to organizations. The Economic Census, which now encompasses the former U.S. Census of Manufacturers, U.S. Census of Retail Trade, and others, is conducted every five years. The 2002 Economic Census contains data on the number and size of establishments in the United States that produce a good or service on the basis of its North American Industry Classification (NAICS).

Finally, trade associations, universities, and business periodicals provide detailed data of value to market researchers and planners. These data are now available online via the Internet and can be identified and located using a search engine like Google. The Marketing NewsNet on the next page provides examples.

Advantage and Disadvantages of Secondary Data

A general rule among marketing people is to obtain secondary data first and then collect primary data. Two important advantages of secondary data are (1) the tremendous time savings if the data have already been collected and published or exist internally and (2) the low cost, such as free or inexpensive census reports. Furthermore, a greater level of detail is often available through secondary data, especially U.S. Census Bureau data.

However, these advantages must be weighed against some significant disadvantages. First, the secondary data may be out of date, especially if they are U.S. Census population data collected only every 10 years. Second, the definitions or categories might not be quite right for your project. For example, the age groupings might be wrong for your project. Finally, because the data are collected for another purpose, they may not be specific enough for your project. In such cases it may be necessary to collect primary data.

MARKETING NEWSNET

Online Databases and Internet Resources Useful for Marketers

Information contained in online databases available via the Internet consists of indexes to articles in periodicals and statistical or financial data on markets, products, and organizations that are accessed either directly or via Internet search engines or portals through key word searches.

Online databases of indexes, abstracts, and full-text information from periodicals include

- LexisNexis™ Academic (www.lexisnexis.com), which provides full-text documents from more than 5,600 news, business, legal, and reference publications.
- ProQuest databases (www.proquest.com), which provide summaries of management, marketing, and other business articles from more than 8,500 publishers.

Statistical and financial data on markets, products, and organizations include

- Bloomberg (www.bloomberg.com), *Investor's Business Daily* (www.investors.com), and *The Wall Street Journal* (www.wsj.com), all providing up-to-the-minute business news and security prices plus research reports on companies, industries, and countries.
- FISonline (www.fisonline.com), which has created a database that contains information on more than 28,000 companies worldwide (15,000 U.S. public companies and 20,000 non-U.S. public companies).
- STAT-USA (www.stat-usa.gov) from the Department of Commerce, which provides information on U.S. business, economic, and trade activity collected by the federal government.

Portals and search engines include

- Firstgov.gov (www.firstgov.gov), a portal to all U.S. government websites. Users click on links to browse by topic or enter keywords for specific searches.
- Google (www.google.com), a portal to the entire Internet. Users click on links to browse by topic or enter key words for specific searches.

Some of these websites are accessible only if your educational institution has paid a subscription fee. To see if you can access these sites for free, check with your institution's website.

Concept Check

1. What is the difference between secondary and primary data?
2. What are some advantages and disadvantages of secondary data?

Primary Data: Observing Behavior

The two principal ways to collect new or primary data for a marketing study are by (1) observing people and (2) asking them questions.

observational data
Facts and figures obtained by watching, either mechanically or in person, how people behave

Facts and figures obtained by watching—either mechanically, electronically, or in person—how people actually behave is the way marketing researchers collect **observational data**. National TV ratings, such as those of Nielsen Media Research shown in Figure 8–3, are an example of mechanical observational data collected by a "people meter." The people meter is a box that (1) is attached to TV sets, VCRs, cable boxes, and satellite dishes in more than 9,000 homes across the country; (2) has a remote that operates the meter when a viewer begins and finishes watching a TV program; and (3) stores and then transmits the viewing information each night to Nielsen Media Research.

Nielsen also employs separate local samples in each of the 210 local markets. Ten of the nation's largest markets use the same people meter technology to provide demographic viewing information daily. In an additional 46 local markets, electronic set-meters are used every day to record what channel is being tuned and for how long, resulting in household-level ratings that are produced daily throughout the year. In all nonpeople meter markets demographic data are collected through TV

FIGURE 8–3
Nielsen ratings of the top 10 network primetime television series for the 2004–2005 season through September 18, 2005

RANK	PROGRAM	NETWORK	RATING	SHARE
1	*American Idol*—Tuesday	Fox	15.7	24
2	*American Idol*—Wednesday	Fox	15.3	23
3	*CSI*	CBS	13.8	22
4	*Survivor: Palau*	CBS	12.2	20
5	*Survivor: Vanuatu*	CBS	11.7	18
6	*CSI: Miami*	CBS	11.1	18
6	*Dancing with the Stars*	ABC	11.1	18
8	*NFL Monday Night Football*	ABC	10.9	18
8	*Without a Trace*	CBS	10.9	18
10	*Desperate Housewives*	ABC	10.7	17

SOURCE: Copyright 2005 Nielsen Media Research.

diaries or booklets (not a mechanical but a manual measurement system) during as many as seven months. All nonpeople meter markets use this measurement in February, May, July, and November, which are known as "the sweeps."[11]

On the basis of all this observational data, Nielsen Media Research then calculates the "rating" and "share" of each TV program. With 110.2 million TV households in the United States based on the 2000 U.S. Census, a single ratings point equals 1 percent, or 1,102,000 TV households.[12] In TV viewing a share point is the percentage of TV sets in use tuned to a particular program. Because TV networks and cable sell more than $32 billion annually in advertising and set advertising rates to advertisers on the basis of those data, precision in the Nielsen data is critical. Thus, a change of one percentage point in a rating can mean gaining or losing up to $50 million in advertising revenue because advertisers pay rates on the basis of the size of the audience for a TV program. So from Figure 8–3, we might expect to pay more for a 30-second TV ad on *American Idol* than one on *Survivor: Vanuatu.* Broadcast and cable networks may change the time slot or even cancel a TV program if its ratings are consistently poor and advertisers are unwilling to pay a rate based on a higher guaranteed rating.

What determines if *American Idol* stays on the air? For the importance of the TV "ratings game," see the text.

The people meter's limitations—as with all observational data collected mechanically (or manually)—relate to how the measurements are taken. In 2003, Nielsen reported a 7 to 12 percent annual decline from 2002 in the prime-time TV watched by men in the important 18 to 34 market segment. This is the very group most likely to watch TV at sports bars, on the treadmill at their athletic club, or on DVDs, or skip regular TV entirely to play videogames or surf the Web. So to get more accurate viewing data, Nielsen is putting more technology into its people meter and increasing the sample of homes to 10,000 by 2006.[13]

Nielsen//NetRatings also uses an electronic meter to record Internet user behavior. These data are collected by tracking the actual mouse clicks made by users from more than 100,000 individuals in 13 countries as they surf the Internet via a meter installed on their home or work computers. Nielsen//NetRatings identifies the top websites that have the largest unique audiences, the top advertising banners viewed, the top Internet advertisers,

FIGURE 8–4
Nielsen//NetRatings of the top 10 Internet websites for September 2005

RANK	PROPERTY	UNIQUE AUDIENCE (000s)	REACH %	HOURS AND MINUTES PER PERSON PER WEEK
1	Yahoo	88,732	60.73	2:47
2	MSN	88,630	60.66	1:39
3	Microsoft	84,581	57.88	0:40
4	AOL	70,487	48.24	6:48
5	Google	61,897	42.36	0:29
6	eBay	45,386	31.06	1:45
7	MapQuest	31,142	21.31	0:12
8	Amazon	29,868	20.44	0:19
9	Weather Channel	29,730	20.35	0:21
10	Real	29,428	20.14	0:38

SOURCE: Nielsen/NetRatings.

and global Internet usage for selected European and Asian countries. Figure 8–4, showing the top 10 Internet websites, gives interesting comparisons about Internet usage. For example, while eBay reaches about one-fourth fewer users than Google in a month, the typical eBay user spends more than three times the minutes per week than a Google user.

Observational data can take some strange twists. Jennifer Voitle, a laid-off investment bank employee with four advanced degrees, responded to an Internet ad and found a new career: *mystery shopper*. Companies pay her to check on the quality of their products and services and write a detailed report on what she finds. She gets paid to travel to Mexican and Hawaiian hotels, eat at restaurants, play golf, test-drive new cars at auto dealerships, shop for groceries and clothes, and play arcade games. But her role posing as a customer gives her client unique marketing research information that can be obtained in no other way. Says Jennifer, "Can you believe they call this work?"[14]

Is this *really* marketing research? A *mystery shopper* at work.

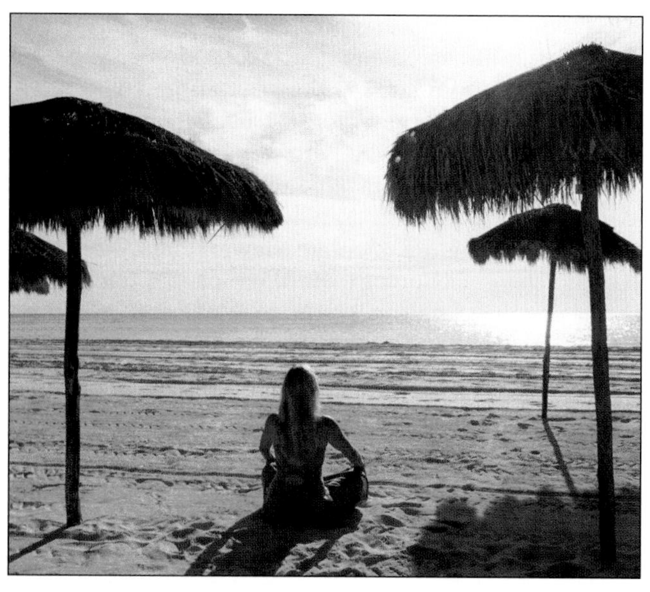

Watching consumers in person and videotaping them are other observational approaches. For example, Aurora Foods observes how consumers bake cakes in its test kitchens to see if baking instructions on the cake box are understood and followed correctly. Gillette marketing researchers actually videotaped consumers brushing their teeth in their own bathrooms to see how they really brush—not just how they *say* they brush. The new-product result: Gillette's new Oral-B CrossAction toothbrush that's supposed to do a better job, at $4.99 each.[15]

Personal observation is both useful and flexible, but it can be costly and unreliable when different observers report different conclusions in watching the same event. Also, although observation can reveal what people do, it cannot easily determine why they do it, such as why they are buying or not buying a product. This is the principal reason for using questionnaires.

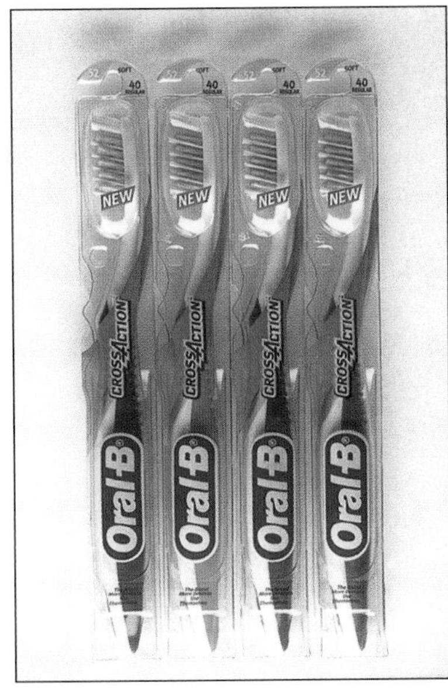

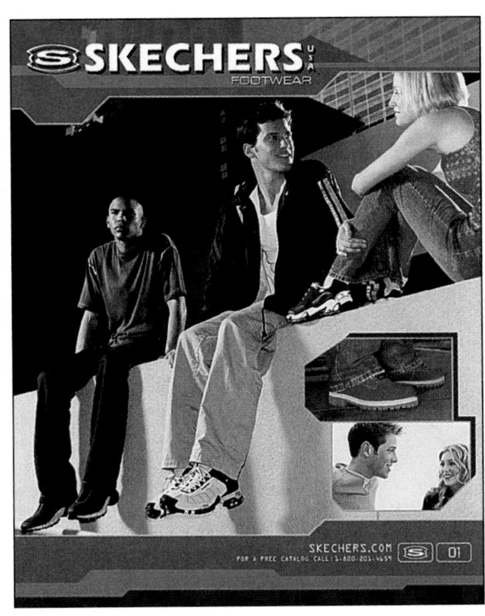

How do you do marketing research on things as diverse as toothbrushes, soap pads, and fashion products for teenagers? For some creative answers, see the text.

Primary Data: Questioning Consumers

How many dozens of times have you filled out some kind of a questionnaire? Maybe at school to find out what kind of outside activities you might like. Or at the store where you shop to see if you are pleased with the kind of help and service you receive. Or by telephone or e-mail to get some ideas about your clothing preferences.

These are examples of the second principal way of gathering information from past, present, or potential consumers—which is by asking them questions and recording their answers. We can divide these questioning techniques into (1) idea generation methods and (2) idea evaluation methods, although the dividing line between them is often fuzzy and there are a number of special kinds of techniques in each category.[16] But all these questioning methods result in valuable **questionnaire data**, which are facts and figures obtained by asking people about their attitudes, awareness, intentions, and behaviors.

questionnaire data
Facts or figures obtained by asking people about their attitudes, awareness, intentions, and behaviors

Idea Generation Methods—Coming Up with Ideas "Oh, Dad, you *so* don't get it," is the kind of marketing research feedback Daniel Kranzler often gets when he conducts his *individual interviews* (a single researcher asking questions of one respondent). His company, Mforma, makes games and ringtones for cell phones. With teenagers' ideas often driving the leading-edge designs and features in cell phones, Kranzler wants to connect with their latest thoughts. So to whom does he turn for *very direct* input but his 18-year-old daughter, Kat, who tells it like she sees it.[17]

Mforma's approach to getting design ideas from today's cutting-edge cell phone users—teenagers.

General Mills sought ideas about why Hamburger Helper didn't fare too well with consumers when introduced. Initial instructions called for cooking a half pound of hamburger separately from the noodles or potatoes, which were later mixed with the hamburger. So General Mills researchers used a special kind of individual interview called *depth interviews* in which researchers ask lengthy, free-flowing kinds of questions to probe for underlying ideas and feelings. These depth interviews showed that consumers (1) didn't think it contained enough meat and (2) didn't want the hassle of cooking in two different pots. So the Hamburger Helper product manager changed the recipe to call for a full pound of

Marketing research by Teenage Research Unlimited involves having teenagers complete a drawing describing themselves.

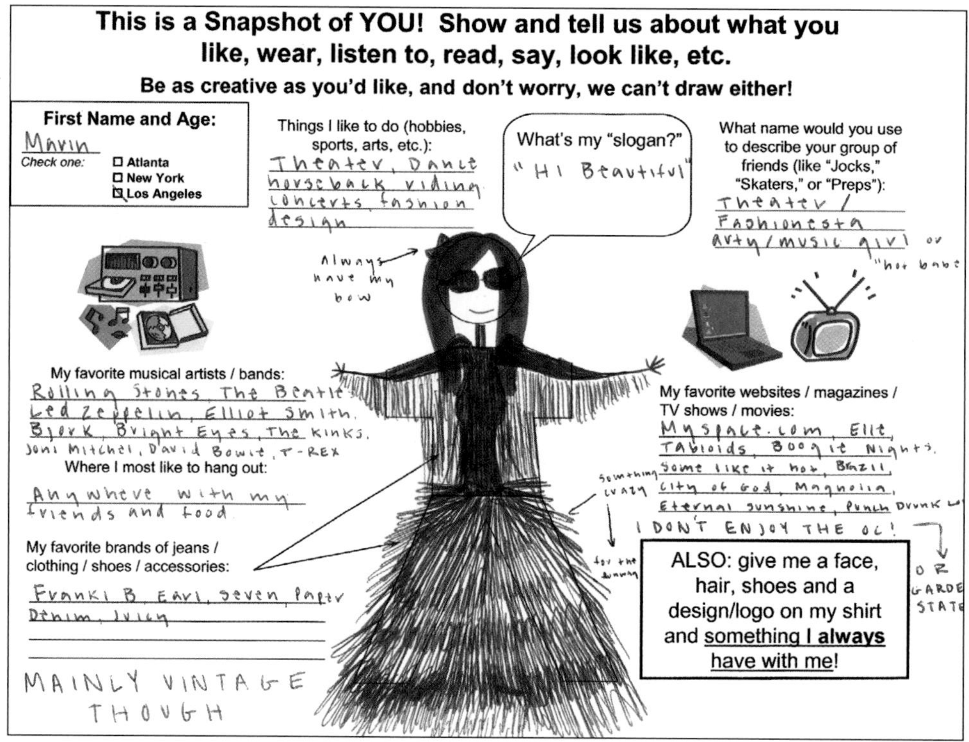

meat and to allow users to prepare it in one dish; this converted a potential failure into a success.[18]

Focus groups are informal sessions of 6 to 10 past, present, or prospective customers in which a discussion leader, or moderator, asks their opinions about the firm's and its competitors' products, how they use these products, and special needs they have that these products don't address. Often video-recorded and conducted in special interviewing rooms with a one-way mirror, these groups enable marketing researchers and managers to hear and watch consumer reactions. The informality and peer support in an effective focus group uncover ideas that are often difficult to obtain with individual interviews.

In the mid-1990s, 3M sought ways to push further into the home-care business and decided to target the wool soap pads niche, which was dominated by giants SOS and Brillo. 3M ran eight focus groups around the United States and heard consumers complain that standard wool pads scratched their expensive cookware. These interviews led to 3M's internationally successful Scotch-Brite® Never Scratch wool soap pad.[19]

Finding "the next big thing" for consumers has become the obsession not only for consumer product firms but also for firms in many other industries. The result is that marketing researchers have come to rely on techniques that are far more basic—many would say bizarre—than more traditional individual or focus group interviews. These "fuzzy front end" methods attempt to identify elusive consumer tastes or trends far before typical consumers have recognized them themselves. Three examples of unusual ways to collect consumer data and their results include the following:

- Having consumers take a photo of themselves every time they snack. This resulted in General Mills' Homestyle Pop Secret popcorn, which delivers the real butter and bursts of salt in microwave popcorn that consumers thought they could only get from the stovetop variety.[20]
- Having teenagers complete a drawing. This is used by researchers at Teenage Research Unlimited (TRU) to help discover what teenagers like, wear, listen to, read, and watch. TRU surveys 2,000 teens twice a year to identify their lifestyles, attitudes, trends, and behaviors. With its Coolest Brand Meter™, TRU asks teens to specify the coolest brands within specific product categories, such as sneakers and clothing.[21]

- Hiring "cool hunters," people with tastes far ahead of the curve. This is used to identify the next big things likely to sweep popular teen culture. Many marketers consult Look-Look, a marketing research firm that can call on up to 20,000 "field correspondents" who specialize in hunting for "trendsetters" for ideas, products, and fashions that are deemed to be "cool" in large cities around the world. Look-Look provides these teenage field correspondents with digital cameras to send back uploaded images from parties, concerts, and sporting events.[22] For example, Wet Seal uses this method to anticipate teenage girls' fashions while Skechers uses it to spot footwear trends.

Idea Evaluation—Testing an Idea In idea evaluation, the marketing researcher tries to test ideas discovered earlier to help the marketing manager recommend marketing actions. This often involves more conventional questionnaires using personal, mail, telephone, e-mail, fax, or Internet surveys of a large sample of past, present, or prospective consumers.

In choosing between these alternatives, the marketing researcher must balance cost against the expected quality of information obtained. Personal interview surveys have a major advantage of enabling the interviewer to be flexible in asking probing questions or getting reactions to visual materials, but are very costly to conduct. Mail surveys are usually biased because those most likely to respond have had especially positive or negative experiences with the product or brand. While telephone interviews allow flexibility, unhappy respondents may hang up on the interviewer, even with the efficiency of computer-assisted telephone interviewing (CATI). E-mail, fax, and Internet surveys are restricted to respondents having the technologies but are expanding rapidly.[23]

Figure 8–5 shows typical problems to guard against in wording questions to obtain meaningful answers from respondents. For example, in a question of whether you eat at fast-food restaurants regularly, the word *regularly* is ambiguous. Two people might answer yes to the question, but one might mean "once a day" while the other means "once or twice a month." Both answers appear as yes to the researcher who tabulates them, but they suggest that dramatically different marketing actions be directed to each of these two prospective consumers. Therefore, it is essential that marketing research questions

FIGURE 8–5
Typical problems in wording questions

PROBLEM	SAMPLE QUESTION	EXPLANATION OF PROBLEM
Leading question	Why do you like Wendy's fresh meat hamburgers better than those of competitors?	Consumer is led to make statement favoring Wendy's hamburgers.
Ambiguous question	Do you eat at fast-food restaurants regularly? ☐ Yes ☐ No	What is meant by word *regularly*—once a day, once a month, or what?
Unanswerable question	What was the occasion for eating your first hamburger?	Who can remember the answer? Does it matter?
Two questions in one	Do you eat Wendy's hamburgers and chili? ☐ Yes ☐ No	How do you answer if you eat Wendy's hamburgers but not chili?
Nonmutually exclusive answers	What is your age? ☐ Under 20 ☐ 20–40 ☐ 40 and over	What answer does a 40-year-old check?

How might Wal-Mart have done early marketing research to help develop its supercenters, which have achieved international success? For its unusual research, see the text.

be worded precisely so that all respondents interpret the same question similarly.

Primary Data: Panels and Experiments

Two special ways that observations and questionnaires are sometimes used are panels and experiments.

Marketing researchers often want to know if consumers change their behavior over time, and so they take successive measurements of the same people. A *panel* is a sample of consumers or stores from which researchers take a series of measurements. For example, the NPD Group collects data about consumer purchases such as apparel, food, and electronics from its Online Panel, which consists of more than 2.5 million individuals worldwide. So a firm like General Mills can use descriptive research—counting the frequency of consumer purchases—to measure switching behavior from one brand of its breakfast cereal (Wheaties) to another (Cheerios) or to a competitor's (Kellogg's Special K). A disadvantage of panels is that the marketing research firm needs to recruit new members continually to replace those who drop out. These new recruits must match the characteristics of those they replace to keep the panel representative of the marketplace.

An *experiment* involves obtaining data by manipulating factors under tightly controlled conditions to test cause and effect, an example of causal research. The interest is in whether changing one of the independent variables (a cause) will change the behavior of the dependent variable that is studied (the result). In marketing experiments, the independent variables of interest—sometimes called the marketing *drivers*—are often one or more of the marketing mix elements, such as a product's features, price, or promotion (like advertising messages or coupons). The ideal dependent variable usually is a change in purchases (incremental unit or dollar sales) of individuals, households, or organizations. For example, food companies often use *test markets,* which is offering a product for sale on a limited basis in a defined area to help decide the likely effectiveness of potential marketing actions. So a test market is really a kind of marketing experiment to reduce risks. In 1988, Wal-Mart opened three experimental stand-alone supercenters to gauge consumer acceptance before deciding to open others. Today, Wal-Mart operates more than 1,000 supercenters in the United States and around the globe.[24]

A potential difficulty with experiments is that outside factors (such as actions of competitors) can distort the results of an experiment and affect the dependent variable (such as sales). A researcher's task is to identify the effect of the marketing variable of interest on the dependent variable when the effects of outside factors in an experiment might hide it.

Advantages and Disadvantages of Primary Data

Compared with secondary data, primary data have the advantage of being more specific to the problem being studied. The main disadvantages are that primary data are usually far more costly and time consuming to collect than secondary data.

Concept Check

1. What is the difference between observational and questionnaire data?
2. Which survey provides the greatest flexibility for asking probing questions: mail, telephone, or personal interview?
3. What is the difference between a panel and an experiment?

At 10 P.M. what is this man likely to buy besides these diapers? For the curious answer data mining gives, see the text.

Making the Most of Information Technology

The Internet and the PC provide a gateway to exhaustive sources of information on the competition, the market, and the consumer. Sources feeding this database range from internal data about sales and customers to external data from marketing research services such as TV ratings. Today's marketing managers, who are responsible for increasing the sales of their product or brand, can be drowned in an ocean of marketing data like those shown in Figure 8–6. So they need to adopt strategies for dealing with it all. The marketer's task is to convert this data ocean into useful analyses on which to base informed decisions.

Information technology involves operating computer networks that can store and process data. Such systems make data accessible to those who can query a system to analyze information to make better decisions. Generally speaking, time is scarce and the available information is incredibly complex. Professionals must organize and interpret data clearly, quickly, and simply—and information technology can make the job much easier.

Today information technology is used to extract hidden information from large databases such as consumer purchases or treatment effectiveness on millions of medical patients.[25] Marketing research services now offer the ability to track household demographics and lifestyle *and* combine this information with those households' product purchases, TV viewing behavior, and responses to coupon or free-sample promotions. Firms such as Information Resources' InfoScan and AC Nielsen's ScanTrack collect this information through the bar-code scanners at the checkout counters in supermarket, drug, convenience, and mass merchandise retailers in the United States and abroad.[26] Campbell Soup, maker of Swanson frozen dinners, used the information from one of these services to shift a TV ad campaign from a serious to a light theme, which increased sales of Swanson dinners by 14 percent.[27]

Retail stores also use a technique called *data mining* to find statistical links using large databases that suggest marketing opportunities. You may not need a computer analysis to tell you that peanut butter and grape jelly purchases are linked. But would

FIGURE 8–6
Today's marketing managers use information from many marketing factors to increase the sales of their products or brands

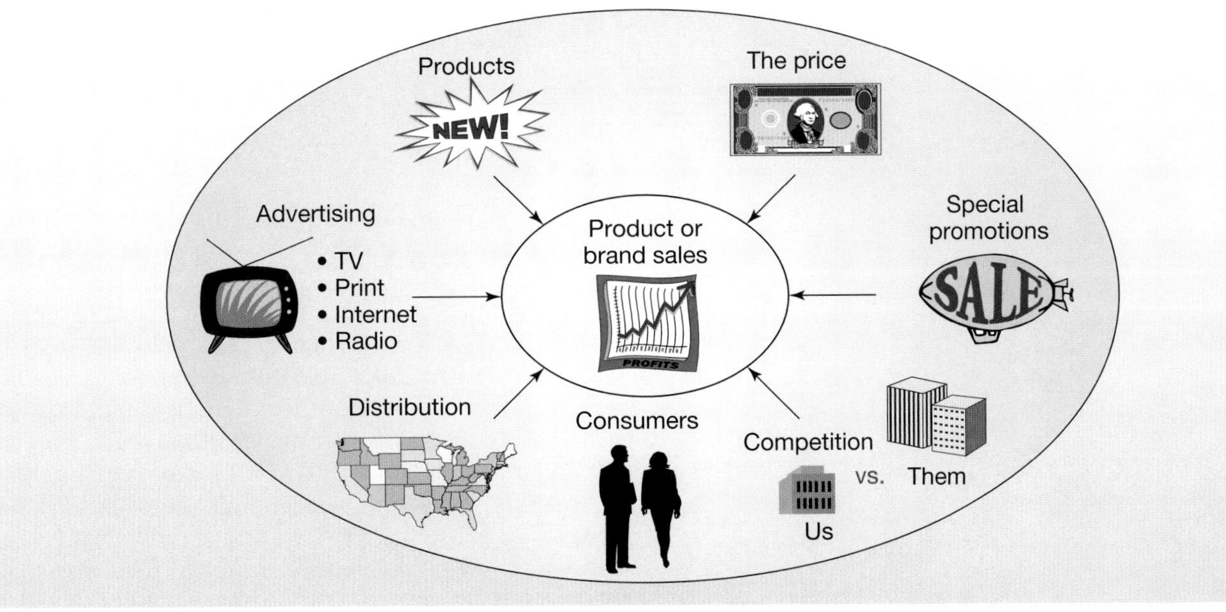

SOURCE: Ford Consulting Group, Inc.

you have expected that men buying diapers in the evening sometimes buy a six-pack of beer as well? This is exactly what supermarkets discovered when they mined checkout data from scanners. So they placed diapers and beer near each other, then placed potato chips between them—and increased sales on all three items! On the near horizon: Radio-frequency identification (RFID) technology using a "smart tag" microchip on the diapers and beer to tell whether they wind up in the same shopping bag—at 10 P.M. in the evening.[28]

STEP 4: DELIVER THE FINAL REPORT

Marketing data and information have little value unless they are translated into findings and recommendations that lead to marketing actions for the marketing managers. How do we prepare the work so that managers can use it to support actions? Step 4 in the marketing research approach involves delivering a useful report to marketing managers by (1) analyzing the data, (2) presenting the findings, and (3) making recommendations.[29]

Analyzing the Data

Let's consider the case of Tony's Pizza and Teré Carral, the marketing manager responsible for the Tony's brand.

Teré is concerned about the limited growth in the Tony's brand over the past four years. She hires a consultant to collect and analyze data to explain what's going on with her brand and to recommend ways to improve its growth. Teré asks the consultant to put together a proposal that includes the answers to two key questions:

1. How are Tony's sales doing on a household basis? For example, are fewer households buying Tony's pizzas, *or* is each household buying fewer Tony's? Or both?
2. What factors might be contributing to Tony's very flat sales over the past four years?

Facts uncovered by the consultant are vital. For example, is the average household consuming more or less Tony's pizza than in previous years? Is Tony's flat sales performance related to a specific factor? With answers to these questions Teré can identify actions in her marketing plan and implement them over the coming year.

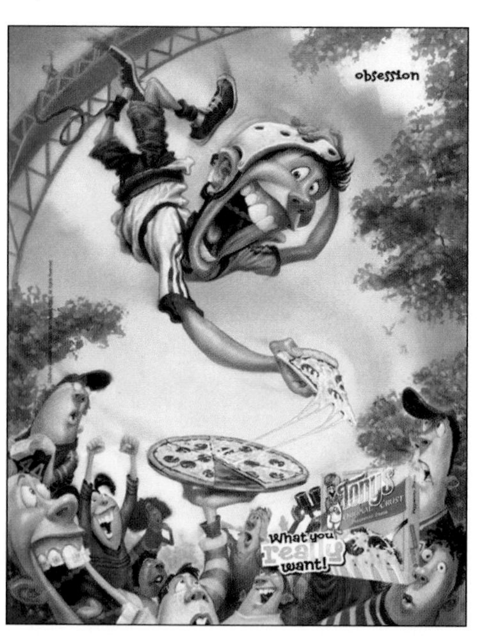

How are sales doing? To see how marketers at Tony's Pizza assessed this question and the reasons they came up with this ad, read the text.

Presenting the Findings

Findings should be clear and understandable from the way the data are presented. Managers are responsible for *actions*. Often it means delivering the results in clear pictures and, if possible, in a single page.

The consultant gives Teré the answers to her questions using Figure 8–7, a creative way to present findings graphically. Let's look over the shoulders of Teré and the consultant while they interpret these findings:

- Figure 8–7A, the chart showing annual sales. This shows the annual growth of the Tony's Pizza brand is stable but virtually flat from 2002 through 2005.
- Figure 8–7B, the chart showing average annual sales per household. Look closely at this graph. At first glance, it may seem like sales in 2005 are *half* what they were in 2002, right? But be careful to read the numbers on the vertical axis. They show that household purchases of Tony's have been steadily declining over the past four years, from an average of 3.4 pizzas per household in 2002 to 3.1 pizzas per household in 2005. (Significant, but hardly a 50 percent drop.) Now the question is, if Tony's annual sales are stable, yet the average individual household is buying fewer Tony's pizzas, what's going on? The answer is, more households are buying pizzas—it's just that each household is buying fewer Tony's pizzas. That households aren't choosing Tony's is

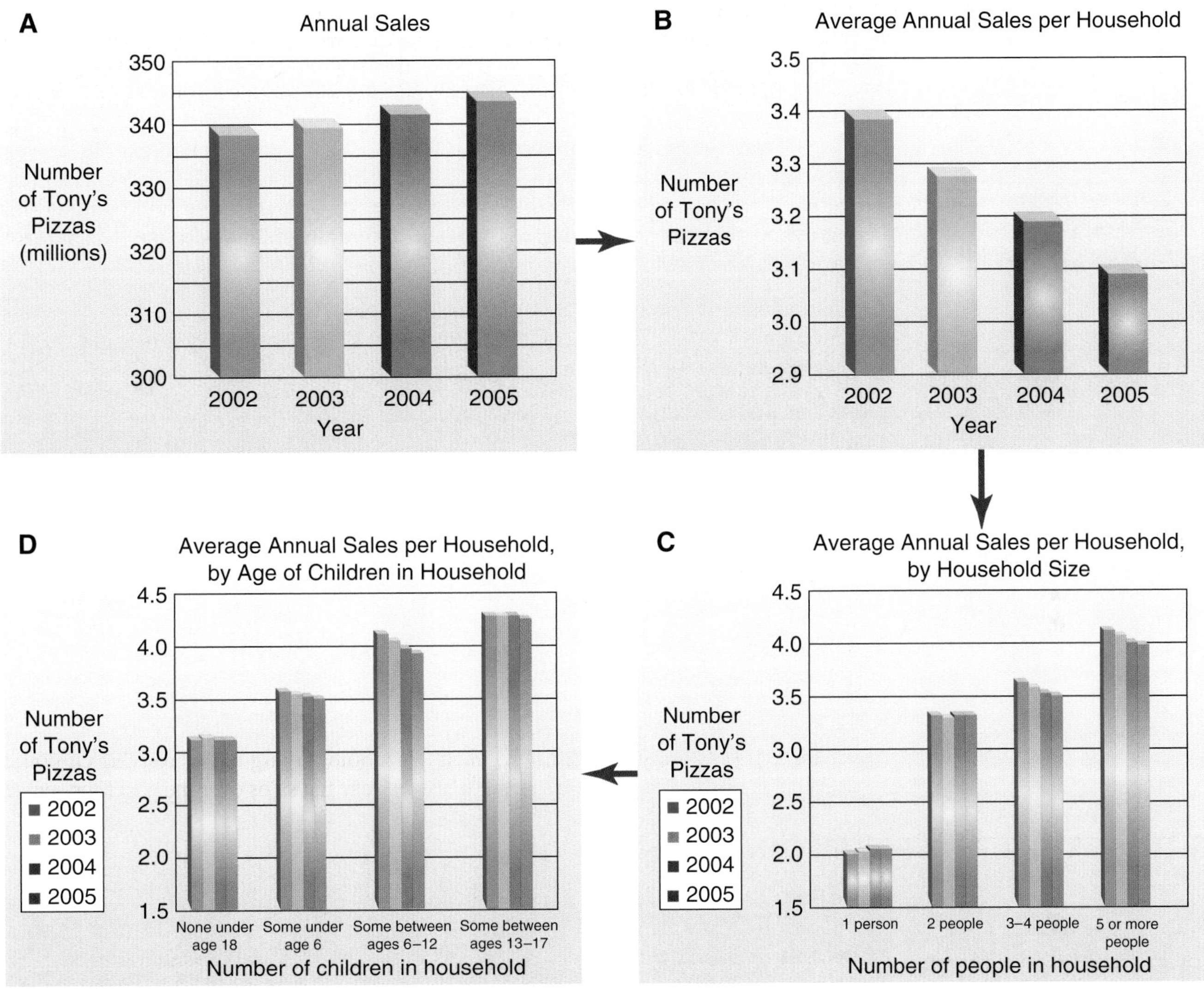

SOURCE: Teré Carral, Tony's Pizza.

FIGURE 8–7
Presenting findings to Tony's marketing manager that lead to recommendations and actions

a genuine source of concern. But again, here's a classic example of a marketing problem representing a marketing opportunity. The number of households buying pizza is *growing,* and that's good news for Tony's.

- Figure 8–7C, the chart showing average annual sales per household, by household size. Oh, oh! This chart starts to show a source of the problem: Even though average sales of pizza to households with only one or two people is stable, households with three or four people and those with five or more are declining in average annual pizza consumption. Which households tend to have more than two people? Answer: Households *with children.* Therefore, we should look more closely at the pizza-buying behavior of households with children.
- Figure 8–7D, the chart showing average annual sales per household, by age of children in the household. Oh, oh, oh! The picture is becoming very clear now: The real problem is in the serious decline in average consumption in the households with younger children, especially in households with children in the 6- to 12-year-old age group.

Identifying a sales problem in households with children 6- to 12-years-old is an important discovery, as Tony's sales are declining in a market segment that is known to be one of the heaviest in buying pizzas.

Making Recommendations

Effective marketing research doesn't stop with data analysis and findings. Instead, the data analysis and findings must lead to recommendations that trigger marketing actions.

Teré Carral, the marketing manager for Tony's Pizza, met with her team to convert the market research findings into specific marketing recommendations with a clear objective: Target families with children ages 6 to 12 to reverse the trend among this segment and gain strength in one of the most important segments in the frozen pizza category. This will be done through developing

- An advertising campaign that will target children 6 to 12.
- A monthly promotion calendar with this 6 to 12 age group target in mind.
- A special event program reaching children 6 to 12.

As her first marketing action, Teré undertakes advertising research to develop ads that appeal to children in the 6 to 12 age group and their families and develops the ad on page 178.

Concept Check

1. What is data mining?
2. In the marketing research for Tony's Pizza, what is an example of (*a*) a finding and (*b*) a recommendation?

SALES FORECASTING TECHNIQUES

sales forecast
Total sales of a product that a firm expects to sell during a specified time period under specified conditions

Forecasting or estimating potential sales is often a key goal in a marketing research study. Good sales forecasts are important for a firm as it schedules production. The term **sales forecast** refers to the total sales of a product that a firm expects to sell during a specified time period under specified environmental conditions and its own marketing efforts. For example, Betty Crocker might develop a sales forecast of 4 million cases of cake mix for U.S. consumers in 2008, assuming consumers' dessert preferences remain constant and competitors don't change prices.

Three main sales forecasting techniques are often used: (1) judgments of the decision maker, (2) surveys of knowledgeable groups, and (3) statistical methods.

Judgments of the Decision Maker

Probably 99 percent of all sales forecasts are simply the judgment of the person who must act on the results of the forecast—the individual decision maker. A *direct forecast* involves estimating the value to be forecast without any intervening steps. Examples appear daily: How many quarts of milk should I buy? How much money should I get out of the ATM?

You probably get the same cash withdrawal most times you use the ATM. But if you need to withdraw more than the usual amount, you would probably make some intervening steps (such as counting the cash in your pocket or estimating what you'll need for special events this week) to obtain your direct estimate.

A *lost-horse forecast* involves starting with the last known value of the item being forecast, listing the factors that could affect the forecast, assessing whether they have a positive or negative impact, and making the final forecast. The technique gets its name from how you'd find a lost horse: go to where it was last seen, put yourself in its shoes, consider those factors that could affect where you might go (to the pond if you're thirsty, the hayfield if you're hungry, and so on), and go there. For example, a

How might a marketing manager for Wilson tennis rackets forecast sales through 2009? Use a lost-horse forecast, as described in the text.

product manager for Wilson's tennis rackets in early 2006 who needed to make a sales forecast through 2009 would start with the known value of 2005 sales and list the positive factors (more tennis courts, more TV publicity) and the negative ones (competition from other sports, high prices of graphite and ceramic rackets) to arrive at the final series of annual sales forecasts.

Surveys of Knowledgeable Groups

If you wonder what your firm's sales will be next year, ask people who are likely to know something about future sales. Two common groups that are surveyed to develop sales forecasts are prospective buyers and the firm's salesforce.

A *survey of buyers' intentions forecast* involves asking prospective customers if they are likely to buy the product during some future time period. For industrial products with few prospective buyers, this can be effective. There are only a few hundred customers in the entire world for Boeing's largest airplanes, so Boeing surveys them to develop its sales forecasts and production schedules.

A *salesforce survey forecast* involves asking the firm's salespeople to estimate sales during a coming period. Because these people are in contact with customers and are likely to know what customers like and dislike, there is logic to this approach. However, salespeople can be unreliable forecasters—painting too rosy a picture if they are enthusiastic about a new product and too grim a forecast if their sales quota and future compensation are based on it.

Statistical Methods

The best-known statistical method of forecasting is *trend extrapolation,* which involves extending a pattern observed in past data into the future. When the pattern is described with a straight line, it is *linear trend extrapolation.* Suppose that in early 2000 you were a sales forecaster for the Xerox Corporation and had actual sales running from 1988 to 1999 (Figure 8–8). Using linear trend extrapolation, you draw a line to fit the past data and project it into the future to give the forecast values shown for 2000 to 2006.

If in 2004 you want to compare your forecasts with actual results, you are in for a surprise—illustrating the strength and weakness of trend extrapolation. Trend extrapolation assumes that the underlying relationships in the past will continue into the future, which is the basis of the method's key strength: simplicity. If this assumption

FIGURE 8–8
Linear trend extrapolation of sales revenues of Xerox, made at the start of 2000

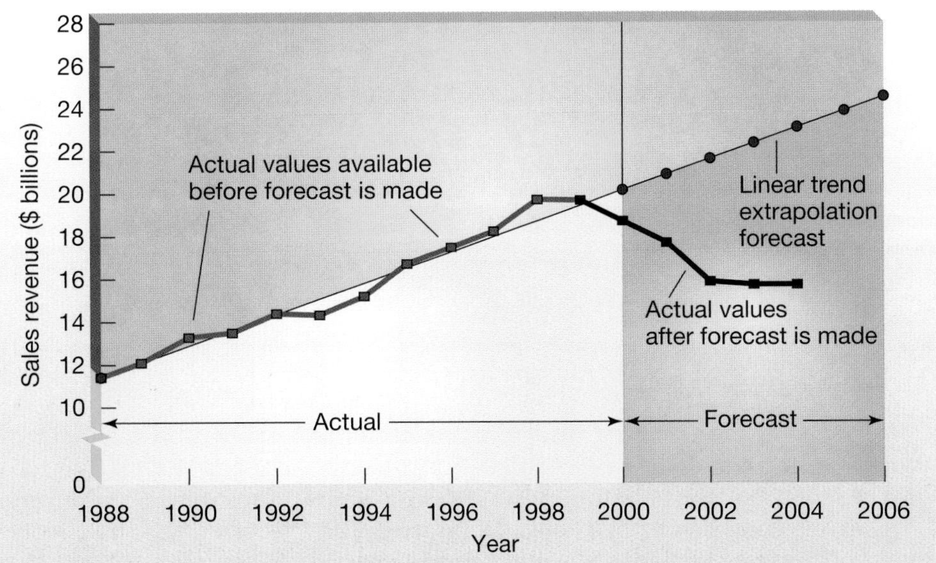

proves correct, you have an accurate forecast. However, if this proves wrong, the forecast is likely to be wrong. In this case your forecasts from 2001 through 2003 were too high, as shown in Figure 8–8, largely because of fierce competition in the photocopying industry.

Concept Check

1. What are the three kinds of sales forecasting techniques?
2. How do you make a lost-horse forecast?
3. What is linear trend extrapolation?

CHAPTER IN REVIEW

1 *Identify the reason for doing marketing research.*
To be successful, products and marketing programs must meet the wants and needs of potential customers. So marketing research reduces risk by providing the vital information to help marketing managers understand those wants and needs and translate them into actions in their marketing activities.

2 *Describe the four-step marketing research approach leading to marketing actions.*
The first step of the four-step marketing research approach involves defining the problem, which requires setting the research objectives and identifying possible marketing actions. The second step, developing the research plan, involves identifying data needed and determining how to collect the data. The third step involves collecting the relevant information, which includes considering pertinent secondary and primary data. Analyzing the data, presenting findings, and making recommendations is the fourth step.

3 *Describe how secondary and primary data are used in marketing, including the uses of questionnaires, observations, experiments, and panels.*
Secondary data have been recorded prior to the project. Internal secondary data come from within the organization, such as sales reports and customer comments. The most widely used external secondary data are reports from the U.S. Bureau of the Census on characteristics of the country's population, manufacturers, and retailers. Primary data are collected specifically for the project and are obtained by either observing or questioning people. Observing people in marketing is done in various ways, including electronically with Nielsen people meters to measure TV viewing habits or personally, say, with mystery shoppers. Questionnaires involve asking people questions—in person, by telephone or fax, in a printed survey, or by Internet. Panels involve a sample of consumers or stores that are measured repeatedly through time to see if behavior changes. Experiments, such as test markets, involve measuring the effect of marketing variables like price or advertising on sales.

4 *Describe three approaches to developing a sales forecast for a company.*
One approach uses subjective judgments of the decision maker, such as direct or lost-horse forecasts. Surveys of knowledgeable groups is a second method. It involves obtaining information such as the intentions of potential buyers or estimates of the salesforce. Statistical methods involving extending a pattern observed in past data into the future is a third example. The best-known statistical method is linear trend extrapolation.

FOCUSING ON KEY TERMS

data p. 168
marketing research p. 164
measures of success p. 166
observational data p. 170
primary data p. 168
questionnaire data p. 173
sales forecast p. 180
secondary data p. 168

DISCUSSION AND APPLICATION QUESTIONS

1 (*a*) Why might a marketing researcher prefer to use secondary data rather than primary data in a study? (*b*) Why might the reverse be true?

2 Suppose your dean of admissions is considering surveying high school seniors about their perceptions of your school to design better informational brochures for them. What are the advantages and disadvantages of doing (*a*) telephone interviews and (*b*) an Internet survey of seniors who have requested information on the school?

3 Nielsen Media Research obtains ratings of local TV stations by having households fill out diary questionnaires. These give information on (*a*) who is watching TV and (*b*) what program. What are the limitations of this questionnaire method?

4 Right out of school you get your dream job that relates to your favorite sport: You're the marketing manager for a small company that gives flying lessons in ultralight planes to college students. A summer intern shows you the questionnaire below. In terms of Figure 8–5, (*i*) identify the problem with each question and (*ii*) correct it. *Note:* Some questions may have more than one problem.

a. Have you ever flown in commercial airliners and in ultralight planes? ☐ Yes ☐ No

b. Why do you think ultralights are so much safer than hang gliders?

c. At what age did you first know you liked to fly?
☐ Under 10 ☐ 10 to 20 ☐ 21 to 30 ☐ Over 30

d. How much did you spend on recreational activities last year?
☐ $100 or less ☐ $801 to $1,201
☐ $101 to $400 ☐ $1,201 to $1,600
☐ $401 to $800 ☐ $1,600 or more

e. How much would you pay for ultralight flying lessons?

f. Would you sign up for a class that met regularly?
☐ Yes ☐ No

5 Wisk detergent decides to run a test market to see the effect of coupons and in-store advertising on sales. The index of sales is as follows:

ELEMENT IN TEST MARKET	WEEKS BEFORE COUPON	WEEK OF COUPON	WEEK AFTER COUPON
Without in-store ads	100	144	108
With in-store ads	100	268	203

What are your conclusions and recommendations?

6 Suppose Fisher-Price wants to run a simple experiment to evaluate a proposed chatter telephone design. It has two different groups of children on which to run its experiment for one week each. The first group has the old toy telephone, whereas the second group is exposed to the newly designed pull toy with wheels, a noisemaker, and bobbing eyes. The dependent variable is the average number of minutes during the two-hour play period that one of the children is playing with the toy, and the results are as follows:

ELEMENT IN EXPERIMENT	FIRST GROUP	SECOND GROUP
Independent variable	Old design	New design
Dependent variable	13 minutes	62 minutes

Should Fisher-Price introduce the new design? Why?

GOING ONLINE What's New in Marketing Research?

WorldOpinion calls its website "The World's Market Research Web Site." To check out the latest marketing research news, job opportunities, and directories of more than 8,500 research locations in 99 countries, go to www.worldopinion.com and do the following:

1 Click on the "News" link on WorldOpinion's home page to read about the current news and issues facing the market research industry.

2 Click on the "The Frame" link, a set of online articles published by Survey Sampling, International.

BUILDING YOUR MARKETING PLAN

To help you collect the most useful data for your marketing plan, develop a three-column table:

1 In column 1, list the information you would ideally like to have to fill holes in your marketing plan.

2 In column 2, identify the source for each bit of information in column 1, such as a Web search, talking to prospective customers, looking at internal data, and so forth.

3 In column 3, set a priority on information you will have time to spend collecting by ranking them: 1 = most important; 2 = next most important, and so forth.

VIDEO CASE 8 Ford Consulting Group, Inc.: From Data to Actions

"The fast pace of working as a marketing professional isn't getting any easier," agrees David Ford, as he talks with Mark Rehborg, Tony's Pizza brand manager. "The speed of communication, the availability of real-time market information, and the responsibility for a brand's profit make marketing one of the most challenging professional jobs today."

Mark responds, "Ten years ago, we could reach 80 percent of our target market with 3 television spots—but today, to reach the same 80 percent, we would have to buy 97 spots. We haven't the luxury to be complacent—our core consumer, the 6- to 12-year-old 'big kid,' is part of a savvy, wired culture that is changing rapidly."

THE COMPANY AND ITS CLIENTS

David Ford, president of Ford Consulting Group (FCG), assists clients such as Tony's in translating the market and sales information into marketing actions. Mark executes ideas that will draw consumers to Tony's and manages sales and profit performance. He distributes budgeted funds to promote the product. Feedback from the sales force requesting promotion funds is a common occurrence.

The information that FCG consultants and Tony's use most often for this analysis comes from places like AC Nielsen's ScanTrack and Information Resources' InfoScan (IRI) that summarize sales data from grocery stores and other outlets that scan purchases at the checkout.

FCG's typical consulting project involves helping clients make sense of their existing information, *not* in helping clients collect more information. Most often the client has a critical time deadline for FCG's data analysis and action recommendations: The client "wants" the answer a week ago, about four days *before* it hires FCG!

The project that follows is typical of the work Ford Consulting Group (www.fordconsultinggroup.com) undertakes for a client. The data are hypothetical, but the situation is a very typical one in the grocery products industry. Here's a snapshot of some of the terms in the case:

- "You" have just come on the job, as the new marketing person.
- "NE" is the Northeastern sales region of Tony's.
- "SE, NW, SW" are the other sales regions.

PART 1: A TYPICAL QUESTION, ON A TYPICAL DAY

Let's dive into the background of a typical question you might face, on a typical day. On the opposite page are some memos you are given (one from Mark to you) as background.

You dig into Lauretta's data files and develop Table 1 that shows how Tony's is doing in the company's four sales regions and the entire United States on key marketing dimensions. Without reading further, take a deep breath and try to answer question 1 below.

PART 2: UNCOVERING THE TRUTH

Let's assume your analysis (question 1) shows NE is a problem, so we need to understand what's going on in the NE. You dig into the data and develop Table 2. It shows the situation for the four largest supermarket chains in the Northeast sales region that carry Tony's. Now answer question 2.

Questions

1 Study Table 1. (*a*) How does the situation in the Northeast compare with the other regions in the United States? (*b*) What appears to be the reason(s) that sales are soft? (*c*) Write a 150-word e-mail with attachments to Mark Rehborg, your boss, giving your answers to *b*.

2 Study Table 2. (*a*) What do you conclude from this information? (*b*) Summarize your conclusions in a 150-word e-mail with attachments to Mark, who needs them for a meeting tomorrow with Margaret, the Northeast sales region manager. (*c*) What marketing actions might your memo suggest?

TO: Mark Rehborg, Tony's Brand Manager
FROM: Steve Quam, Tony's Field Sales
CC: Margaret Loiaza, NE Sales Region Manager

RE: Feedback on Sales Call at Food-Fast

Hi Mark—

Our sales call at Food-Fast wasn't so great. They don't see how our Tony's is going to sell well enough to justify the additional shelf-space. I also talked to Margaret and she said that second quarter may be weaker than planned across all the NE, and I should give you a heads-up. (She's on vacation this week, Aruba!) She's planning to schedule some time with you to talk about additional promotion money to do catch-up in the third quarter. She'll be there next week.

Steve

TO: You, the New Marketing Person
FROM: Mark Rehborg, Tony's Brand Manager (Your Boss)

RE: Small Project due Friday

Hi You,

Can you help out here? I've got a meeting with Margaret on Friday afternoon, and she's concerned that Food-Fast and the whole NE is going to need some additional promotion dollars.

Lauretta started the analysis and was hurt in a kick-boxing accident yesterday and won't be back to work for a week. Her files are attached. Can you look through her files and summarize what's going on in the NE and the rest of the U.S.? Does Margaret need more promotion money?

Let's discuss Friday AM.

Mark

TA E COMPARISON O TONY S PER ORMANCE Y REGION

REGION	QUARTER Y CHANGE IN O UME (%)	DISTRI UTION (%)	PRICE ( )	PRICE GAP ( )	PROMOTION SUPPORT (%)	PROMOTION O UME (%)
NE	3%	93%	$1.29	+8	7%	14%
SE	5	95	1.11	−1	9	16
NW	8	98	1.19	+1	8	15
SW	6	96	1.25	0	8	15
U.S.	6	97	1.19	0	8	15

[a] % of outlets carrying Tony's.
[b] Price gap = (Our price) − (Competitor's price).
[c] Promotion support = % of the time brand was promoted.
[d] Promotion volume = % of the volume sold on promotion.

TA E COMPARISON O MA OR SUPERMARKET CHAINS IN THE NORTHEAST

SUPER MARKET CHAIN	QUARTER Y CHANGE IN O UME (%)	DISTRI UTION (%)	PRICE ( )	PRICE GAP ( )	PROMOTION SUPPORT (%)	PROMOTION O UME (%)
Save-a-lot	5%	95%	$1.39	+10	10%	19%
Food-Fast	0	90	1.28	−1	3	4
Get-Fresh	0	90	1.30	+1	3	4
Dollars-Off	7	97	1.34	+5	7	14

DENVER
JAY-
Rbk
R-99
FOUNDED
1999
PATENT PENDING

CHAPTER 9 IDENTIFYING MARKET SEGMENTS AND TARGETS

LEARNING OBJECTIVES

After reading this chapter you should be able to:

1 Explain what market segmentation is and when to use it.

2 Identify the five steps involved in segmenting and targeting markets.

3 Recognize the different factors used to segment consumer and organizational markets.

4 Know how to develop a market-product grid to identify a target market and recommend resulting actions.

5 Explain how marketing managers position products in the marketplace.

SNEAKERS MARKETING WARS: JAY-Z, YAO MING, AND A "SWOOSHLESS" NIKE LINE FOR WAL-MART

In today's annual $16 billion U.S. sneakers war among Reebok, Nike, Adidas, and others, a new shoe introduction can have the effect of a toy pop gun—or a salvo across a battleship's bow. That's how serious the competition is. And Reebok recently launched a marketing strategy featuring music stars like Jay-Z (opposite page) that challenges conventional wisdom.

How Do You *Stand Out* on "Sneaker Walls"?

What do you need in the sneaker business to stand out from the pack when consumers are faced with hundreds of athletic shoe choices, often on "sneaker walls" in sporting goods stores? The answer: All sneaker manufacturers—large and small—are searching for new market segments of consumers and ways to differentiate their products from their global competitors. Some examples of reaching narrow, often new, segments:[1]

- Nike's "swooshless" starter line. In spring 2005, Nike introduced its low-price ($40) "Starter" brand exclusively in Wal-Mart—without its signature "swoosh" or the Nike brand name.
- The Adidas 1, with in-sole computer. The Adidas 1 appeared also in spring 2005, with a thin sensor that monitors shock to the shoe, adjusting the footbed in the runner's shoe 1,000 times per second—at $250 a pair.
- Puma and teenagers. Puma targets teenagers with a fashion, coolness, low-tech strategy in its sneakers sold only through hipper stores.
- New Balance and the older folks. Stressing it is "Endorsed by No One," New Balance quietly sells countless widths of shoes for the wider and narrower feet of America's "mature" segment.

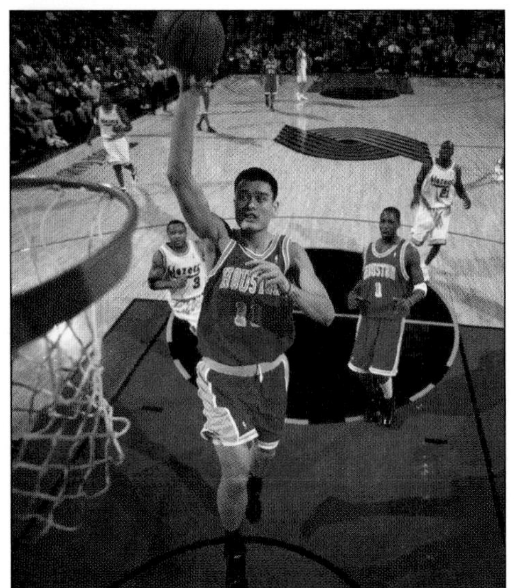

New Segments and Strategies Reebok is reaching a new market segment and getting publicity for its entire sneaker line by signing endorsements with popular rappers and hip-hop music stars. Example: S. Carter Collection by Rbk. Don't recognize the S. Carter name? The street-inspired S. Carter Collection is named for hip-hop star Jay-Z, who was originally known as Shawn Carter. S. Carter low tops (on page 186) are a long way from the look of Reebok's traditional "performance" athletic shoes, but their $100 million in sales make them the fastest-selling shoes in Reebok's history.[2]

The look is not all that's unusual about Jay-Z's endorsement agreement with Reebok. Basketball star Yao Ming and tennis star Venus Williams have endorsement agreements with Reebok not only for their own footwear lines but also to promote its entire line and not to wear products from competitors. Yao Ming's $70 million contract with Reebok also will help it market its sports lines in his native China. But Jay-Z agrees to promote *only* his line of Reebok shoes designed for a street-fashion market segment. This means he is allowed to wear competing brands in public and can also promote Rocawear, the clothing company he co-founded. Can you imagine Tiger Woods wearing a Reebok hat in the U.S. Open golf tournament—and his Nike sponsor being happy about it? Reebok says the "standard, more restrictive deal would have risked tagging its rapper allies as walking billboards for the corporation, hurting their countercultural appeal."[3]

Competitive Trends Reebok also signed deals with the NBA ($175 million) and the NFL ($250 million) to be their exclusive team uniform providers while offering branded apparel to consumers. And beginning in 2005, Reebok was the provider of footwear to Major League Baseball players not under contract with other manufacturers. The Sporting Goods Manufacturers Association (SGMA) and the NPD Group identified the following U.S. trends to consider in planning for the sneaker wars for 2006 and beyond:[4]

- *Age segments.* Teenagers/college-aged consumers comprise more than 32 percent of total sales, are the largest segment, and spend more for sneakers than older consumers.
- *Gender segments.* Both men and women are important segments—women because their sales growth is higher than men, and men because they still buy more in total (double) at higher average prices.
- *Price segments.* More than 62 percent of sneakers purchased today cost less than $50 per pair.
- *Sport segments.* In the United States, running shoes are number one ($4.5 billion today and 29 percent market share); basketball shoes are number two ($3.2 billion and 21 percent); and cross-training shoes number three ($2.0 billion and 13 percent). Basketball sales are up, but cross-training is down slightly.
- *Lifestyle segments.* Most recent sales growth in sneakers is due to casual styles that have a strong fashion component, where the retro look is prominent. Almost three-fourths of all sneakers are purchased for casual rather than for sports or fitness purposes. However, sales of higher-priced performance shoes have risen dramatically in the last few years.

The strategies sneaker manufacturers use to satisfy needs of different customers illustrate successful market segmentation, the main topic of this chapter. After discussing why markets need to be segmented, this chapter covers the steps a firm uses in segmenting and targeting a market and positioning its offering to the marketplace.

WHY SEGMENT MARKETS?

A business firm segments its markets so it can respond more effectively to the wants of groups of potential buyers and thus increase its sales and profits. Not-for-profit organizations also segment the clients they serve to satisfy client needs more effectively while achieving the organization's goals. Let's use the dilemma of sneaker buyers finding their ideal Reebok shoes to describe (1) what market segmentation is and (2) when it is necessary to segment markets.

What Market Segmentation Means

market segmentation
Sorting potential buyers into groups that have common needs and will respond similarly to a marketing action

market segments
Groups of prospective buyers that result from market segmentation

product differentiation
Strategy of using different marketing mix activities, such as product features and advertising, to help consumers perceive a product as being different and better than competing products

People have different needs and wants, even though it would be easier for marketers if they didn't. **Market segmentation** involves aggregating prospective buyers into groups that (1) have common needs and (2) will respond similarly to a marketing action. **Market segments** are the relatively homogeneous groups of prospective buyers that result from the market segmentation process. Each market segment consists of people who are relatively similar to each other in terms of their consumption behavior.

The existence of different market segments has caused firms to use a marketing strategy of **product differentiation**. This strategy involves a firm's using different marketing mix activities, such as product features and advertising, to help consumers perceive the product as being different and better than competing products. The perceived differences may involve physical features or nonphysical ones, such as image or price. The Reebok example discussed below shows how the company is using market segmentation, product differentiation, and market-product grids to develop effective marketing strategies.

Segmentation: Linking Needs to Actions The process of segmenting a market and selecting specific segments as targets is the link between the various buyers' needs and the organization's marketing program (Figure 9–1). Market segmentation is only a means to an end: to lead to tangible marketing actions that can increase sales and profitability.

Market segmentation first stresses the importance of grouping people or organizations in a market according to the similarity of their needs and the benefits they are looking for in making a purchase. Second, such needs and benefits must be related to specific marketing actions the organization can take. These actions may involve separate products or other aspects of the marketing mix such as price, advertising, or distribution strategies.

How Reebok's Segmentation Strategy Developed In 1979, Paul Fireman, who had dropped out of college to run his family's business, wandered through an international trade fair and saw Reebok's custom track shoes. He bought the U.S. license from the British manufacturer and started selling running shoes in 1981.

In a brilliant marketing decision, Fireman introduced soft-leather aerobic dance shoes in flamboyant colors—the Reebok Freestyle—in 1982. Figure 9–2 on the next page shows the first year that Reebok introduced a variety of shoes—from tennis and basketball shoes in 1984 to cross-training shoes in 1988, golf shoes in 1997 and the S. Carter line of shoes in 2003. For simplicity, Figure 9–2 covers only shoes and does not show nonshoe lines, like fitness water (2001) and NBA/NFL apparel (2002).

FIGURE 9–1
Market segmentation—linking market needs to an organization's marketing program

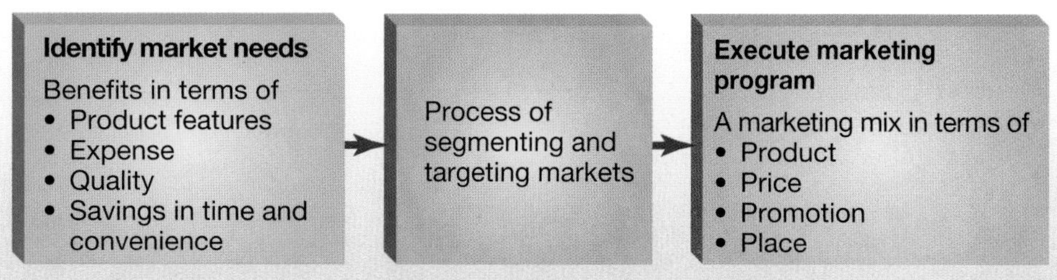

Reebok's $3 billion-a-year sneaker business has a huge need to generate sales from new opportunities. As a result, Reebok has expanded both the markets it targets and the products it develops to satisfy this need, as detailed in Figure 9–2.

market-product grid
Framework relating the segments of a market to products or marketing actions of the firm

Using Market-Product Grids A **market-product grid** is a framework to relate the market segments of potential buyers to products offered or potential marketing actions by the firm. The market-product grid in Figure 9–2 shows different market segments of sneaker users as rows in the grid, whereas the columns show the different shoe product lines chosen by Reebok. In a complete market-product grid analysis, each cell in the grid can show the estimated market size of a given product sold to a specific market segment.

The cells with red boxes in Figure 9–2, labeled P, represent Reebok's primary target market segment when it introduced each type of shoe. The blue boxes, labeled S, represent the secondary target market segments that also bought these products. In some cases, Reebok discovered that large numbers of people in a segment not originally targeted for a particular shoe style bought it anyway. Today, Reebok products are purchased by two types of segments: performance-oriented consumers (30 percent), who buy sneakers and apparel for athletic purposes; and nonathletic-oriented consumers (70 percent), who buy sneakers and apparel for comfort, style, price, or other nonathletic reasons. But as Figure 9–2 depicts, two segments of consumers in the nonathletic-oriented category, comfort/style conscious and walker, bought running, aerobic, and cross-trainer shoes not initially targeted at their respective segments. When this trend became apparent to Reebok in 1986, it introduced its walking shoe line directly at the walker segment.

What segmentation strategy will Reebok use in the future? Only Reebok knows, but it will certainly involve trying to differentiate its products more clearly from its competitors and targeting new global consumers. The Marketing NewsNet describes how Reebok, Nike, and Vans have succeeded in using market segmentation and product differentiation strategies to reach special groups of customers.[5]

FIGURE 9–2
Market-product grid showing how different Reebok shoes reach segments of customers with different needs

MARKET SEGMENT		PRODUCT								
GENERAL	GROUP WITH NEED	RUNNING SHOES (1981)	AEROBIC SHOES (1982)	TENNIS SHOES (1984)	BASKETBALL SHOES (1984)	KIDS SHOES (1984)	WALKING SHOES (1986)	CROSS-TRAINING SHOES (1988)	GOLF SHOES (1997)	S. CARTER SHOES (2003)
Performance-oriented 30%	Runners	P						P		
	Aerobic/fitness exercisers		P					P		
	Tennis players			P				P		
	Basketball players				P			P		
	Golfers								P	
	Adventure seekers							P		
Nonathletic-oriented 70%	Walkers	S	S	S	S		P	P		
	Children					P				
	Comfort/style-conscious	S	S	S	S		S	S		
	Street fashion									P

Key: P = Primary market S = Secondary market

MARKETING NEWSNET Sneaker Strategies—Who's Doing What

Special lacing systems, shock absorbers, and cushions. Off-the-shelf versus design-your-own-shoe on a website. These are some of the innovative technologies and strategies used by sneaker manufacturers to attract new consumers and differentiate their products from those offered by competitors.

Reebok

Reebok's Premier Series of shoes targets the specific needs of runners and features the new DMX Shear and Foam cushioning and Play Dry™ moisture management technologies. Because one style does not fit all, Reebok designed the Premier Control ($100) for runners whose feet tend to turn outward and the Premier Road ($85) with extra cushioning for pavement runners, two of several in the Premier line. And working with Yao Ming, Reebok has developed its $100 High Post that includes a special lacing system for added ankle support.

Nike

The "Michael-inspired" Air Jordan basketball shoe was originally launched in 1985. Today's Air Jordan XIX ($165) basketball shoe incorporates the latest Zoom Air cushioning technology. It also features the radically new "Tech-Flex" lace cover for instep support, a carbon fiber midfoot shank plate for lateral support, and an adjustable strap for a more snug fit. Nike also lets you design your own running or basketball shoes at www.nikeid.com. Nike's MJ replacement? Basketball phenom LeBron James, with his new Zoom LeBron II shoes and accessories.

Vans

Vans has targeted the rising wave of skateboard, snowboard, biking, and outdoor enthusiasts. To reach skateboarders, Vans relies on its endorsing athletes to design and market its signature lines and promote its skateboard events. Vans had a breakthrough when Foot Locker carried its shoes in more than 2,700 retail outlets.

When to Segment Markets

Compared to 30 or 40 years ago, the one-size-fits-all mass markets—like that for Tide laundry detergent—no longer exist. The global marketing officer at Procter & Gamble, which markets Tide, says, "Every one of our brands is targeted." Welcome to today's era of market segmentation and target marketing.[6]

A business firm goes to the trouble and expense of segmenting its markets when it expects that this will increase its sales, profit, and return on investment. When expenses are greater than the potentially increased sales from segmentation, a firm should not attempt to segment its market. The specific situations that illustrate this point are the cases of (1) one product and multiple market segments, (2) multiple products and multiple market segments, and (3) "segments of one," or mass customization.

Does Harry Potter appeal only to the kids' segment? See the text for the answer to this amazing publishing success.

Examples of Successful Market Segmentation Movies, magazines, and books are single products frequently directed to two or more distinct market segments. Movie companies often run different TV commercials or magazine ads featuring different aspects of a newly released film (love, or drama, or spectacular scenery) that are targeted to different market segments. *Time* magazine now publishes more than 200 different U.S. editions and more than 100 international editions, each targeted at unique geographic and demographic segments using a special mix of advertisements. As shown on the next page, Street & Smith's baseball yearbook issue uses different covers in different regions of the United States, featuring a professional baseball star from that region on the cover.

Harry Potter's phenomenal success is based both on author J. K. Rowling's fiction-writing wizardry and her publisher's creativity in marketing globally to preteen, teen, and adult segments of readers. By

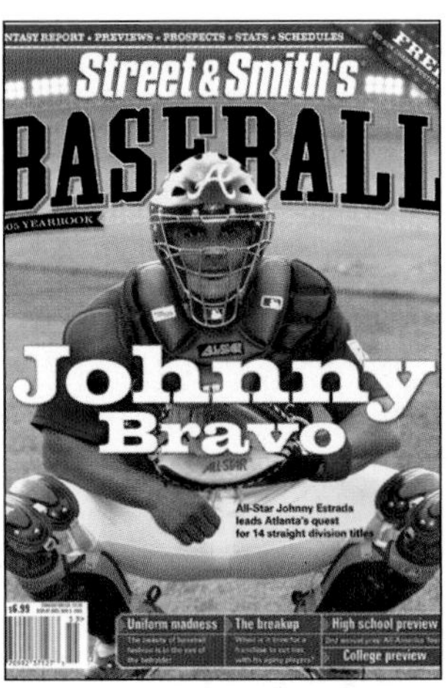

mid-2005 when *Harry Potter and the Half-Blood Prince* appeared, more than 260 million Harry Potter books in 62 languages had been sold worldwide, and the books were often at the top of the *New York Times* fiction best-seller list—for *adults.*[7] Although multiple TV commercials for movies and separate covers or advertisements for magazines or books are expensive, they are minor compared with the costs of producing an entirely new movie, magazine, or book for another market segment.

Reebok's different styles of shoes, each targeted at a different type of user, are an example of multiple products aimed at multiple markets. Designing and manufacturing these different styles of shoes is clearly more expensive than producing only a single style but seems worthwhile if it serves customers' needs better, doesn't reduce quality or increase price, and adds to the sales revenues and profits.

American marketers are rediscovering today what their ancestors running the corner general store knew a century ago: Every customer is unique, has unique wants and needs, and desires special tender loving care from the seller—the essence of *customer relationship management* (CRM). Efficiencies in manufacturing and marketing during the past century made mass-produced goods so affordable that most customers were willing to compromise their individual tastes and settle for standardized products. Today's Internet ordering and flexible manufacturing and marketing processes have made *mass customization* possible, tailoring goods or services to the tastes of individual customers on a high-volume scale.

Mass customization is the next step beyond *build-to-order* (BTO), manufacturing a product only when there is an order from a customer. Dell Computer uses BTO systems that trim work-in-progress inventories and shorten delivery times to customers. Dell's three-day deliveries are made possible by restricting its computer line to only a few basic modules and stocking a variety of each. This gives customers a good choice with quick delivery. Dell PCs can be assembled in four minutes. Most Dell customization comes from spending 90 minutes loading the unique software each customer selects. But even this system falls a bit short of total mass customization with virtually unlimited specification of features by customers.[8]

The Segmentation Trade-Off: CRM versus Synergies The key to successful product differentiation and market segmentation strategies is finding the ideal balance between satisfying a customer's individual wants and achieving organizational **synergy**, the increased customer value achieved through performing organizational functions more efficiently. The "increased customer value" can take many forms: more products, improved quality on existing products, lower prices, easier access to product through improved distribution, and so on. So the ultimate criterion for an organization's marketing success in customer relationship management is that customers should be better off as a result of the increased synergies.

synergy
Increased customer value achieved through performing organizational functions more efficiently

Ann Taylor Stores Corp.'s Loft chain tries to reach trendy, casual consumers while its flagship Ann Taylor chain targets a more sophisticated woman. Do these ads from their separate catalogs convey this difference? For the potential dangers of this two-segment strategy, see the text.

Ann Taylor

Ann Taylor Loft

The firm should also achieve increased revenues and profits from the product differentiation and market segmentation strategies it uses. When the increased customer value involves adding new products or a new chain of stores, the product differentiation-market segmentation trade-off raises a critical issue: Are the new products or new chain simply stealing customers and sales from the older, existing ones?

For example, Ann Taylor Stores, Gap, and Abercrombie & Fitch are examples of specialty retailers struggling with how to keep the original chain of stores fresh without having their newcomer chain of stores cannibalize sales from the original chain.[9] The flagship Ann Taylor chain targets a segment of polished, sophisticated women while its sister Ann Taylor Loft chain seeks to reach women wanting moderately priced, trendy, casual clothes they can wear to the office. The potential nightmare: From 2002 to 2004 annual sales revenues of the Loft stores doubled and passed those of the Ann Taylor flagship chain, which was struggling to reach its target customers.

Other retail chains have the same cannibalization problem. Is Gap's appeal to the 20s and 30s segment it targets really distinct from its Old Navy chain, which is trying to reach moms shopping for families and teens? Or is Abercrombie & Fitch's young adult segment really different enough from its Hollister chain, which is trying to reach high schoolers, or are they simply stealing sales from each other?

Concept Check

1. Market segmentation involves aggregating prospective buyers into groups that have two key characteristics. What are they?
2. When should a firm segment its markets?

STEPS IN SEGMENTING AND TARGETING MARKETS

The process of segmenting a market and then selecting and reaching the target segments is divided into the five steps discussed in this section, as shown in Figure 9–3 on the next page. Segmenting a market is not an exact science—it requires large doses of common sense and managerial judgment.

Let's have you put on your entrepreneur's hat to use the market segmentation process to choose target markets and take useful marketing actions. Suppose you own

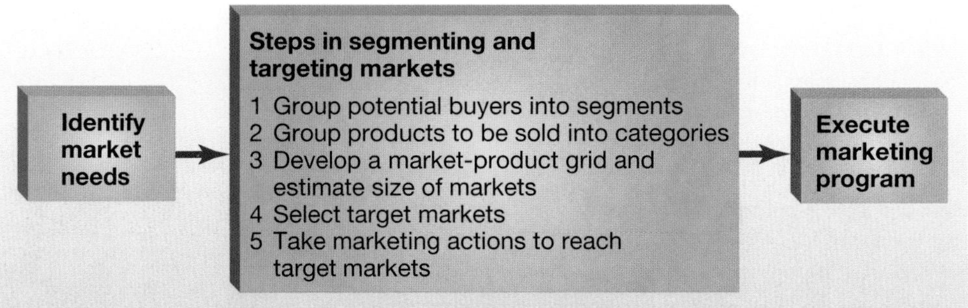

FIGURE 9–3
The five key steps in segmenting and targeting markets link market needs of customers to the organization's marketing program

a Wendy's fast-food restaurant next to a large urban university that offers both day and evening classes. Your restaurant specializes in the Wendy's basics: hamburgers, french fries, Frosty desserts, and chili. Even though you are part of a chain and have some restrictions on menu and decor, you are free to set your hours of business and to undertake local advertising. How can market segmentation help?

Step 1: Group Potential Buyers into Segments

It's not always a good idea to segment a market. Grouping potential buyers into meaningful segments involves meeting some specific criteria that answer the question, Would segmentation be worth doing and is it possible? If so, the next step is to find specific variables that can be used to create the various segments.

Criteria to Use in Forming the Segments A marketing manager should develop segments for a market that meet five main criteria:

- *Potential for increased profit.* The best segmentation approach is the one that maximizes the opportunity for future profit and ROI. If this potential is maximized without segmentation, don't segment. For not-for-profit organizations, the criterion is the potential for serving client users more effectively.
- *Similarity of needs of potential buyers within a segment.* Potential buyers within a segment should be similar in terms of a marketing action, such as product features sought or advertising media used.
- *Difference of needs of buyers among segments.* If the needs of the various segments aren't very different, combine them into fewer segments. A different segment usually requires a different marketing action that, in turn, means greater costs. If increased sales don't offset extra costs, combine segments and reduce the number of marketing actions.
- *Potential of a marketing action to reach a segment.* Reaching a segment requires a simple but effective marketing action. If no such action exists, don't segment.
- *Simplicity and cost of assigning potential buyers to segments.* A marketing manager must be able to put a market segmentation plan into effect. This means being able to recognize the characteristics of potential buyers and then assigning them to a segment without encountering excessive costs.

The global market for chicken is an example of how the five criteria can be used effectively to segment a market. While Americans (one segment) tend to prefer the white chicken meat, Russians (another segment) prefer the dark. Because it's easy to separate the white and dark meat portions of the chicken, it made sense—and increased profits—to market the dark meat to Russia. Today, about one-fourth of all U.S. chicken legs are eaten by Russians.[10]

Ways to Segment Consumer Markets A number of variables can be used to segment U.S. consumer markets, many based on those from the 2000 U.S. Census.

MicroFridge
PROGRAMS FROM MAC-GRAY MAKE COLLEGE LIFE EASIER.
Your students aren't just hungry for knowledge. They're hungry, period. That's why genuine MicroFridge units are used in residence halls across the country to increase occupancy rates and student satisfaction. A MicroFridge program is a safe way to improve the quality of on-campus life and make residence hall rooms feel more like home. Plus, it can provide a new revenue stream for you.
To learn all the ways Mac-Gray can make college life easier for you and your students—including our flexible financing options, laundry programs and copier and laser printer programs—call 1-800-298-1022, ext. 374, or visit www.mac-gray.com.
YOU feed THEIR MINDS. WE'LL TAKE CARE OF THE REST.
MAC-GRAY
Life just got easier
1-800-298-1022 • www.mac-gray.com

What special benefit does a MicroFridge offer, and to which market segment might this appeal? The answer appears in the text.

They generally divide into two categories: (1) customer characteristics and (2) buying situations. Here are some examples of how certain *customer characteristics* can be used to segment specific markets:

- *Geographic customer characteristic: Region.* Campbell's found that its canned nacho cheese sauce, which could be heated and poured directly onto nacho chips, was too hot for Americans in the East and not hot enough for those in the West and Southwest. The result: Today, Campbell's plants in Texas and California produce a hotter nacho cheese sauce than that produced in the other plants to serve their regions better.
- *Demographic customer characteristic: Household size.* More than half of all U.S. households are made up of only one or two persons, so Campbell's packages meals with only one or two servings—from Great Starts breakfasts to L'Orient dinners.
- *Psychographic customer characteristic: Lifestyle.* Claritas provides lifestyle segmentation services to marketers. Claritas's lifestyle segmentation is based on the belief that people of similar lifestyle characteristics tend to live near one another, have similar interests, and buy similar products and services. One of its services classifies every *household* in the United States into one of 48 unique market segments.

Buying situations are another way to segment consumer markets. These buying situations include benefits sought (product features, quality, service, warranty) and usage (heavy user, light user, nonuser). Two examples show how these buying situations can be used in developing consumer segments:

- *Benefits sought: Product features.* Understanding what benefits are important to different customers is often a useful way to segment markets because it can lead directly to specific marketing actions, such as a new product, ad campaign, or distribution system. For example, MicroFridge targets its combination microwave/refrigerator/freezer at college dorm residents, who are often woefully short of space. Busy, convenience-oriented consumers are beginning to use online grocery shopping and delivery from services like Peapod, which is currently located in Chicago, Boston, Washington, D.C., among other markets.
- *Usage/patronage: Usage rate.* **Usage rate** is the quantity consumed or patronage—store visits—during a specific period. It varies significantly among different customer groups. Airlines have developed frequent-flier programs to encourage passengers to use the same airline repeatedly, a technique sometimes called *frequency marketing,* which focuses on usage rate.

usage rate
Quantity consumed or times visited during a specific period

One key conclusion emerges about usage: In market segmentation studies, some measure of usage by, or sales obtained from, various segments is central to the analysis.

To obtain usage rate data, the Simmons Market Research Bureau semiannually surveys about 33,000 adults 18 years of age and older to discover how the products and services they buy and the media they watch relate to their lifestyle and demographic characteristics.

80/20 rule
Idea that 80 percent of a firm's sales are obtained from 20 percent of its customers

Usage rate is sometimes referred to in terms of the **80/20 rule**, a concept that suggests 80 percent of a firm's sales are obtained from 20 percent of its customers. The percentages in the 80/20 rule are not really fixed at exactly 80 percent and 20 percent but suggest that a small fraction of customers provides a large fraction of a firm's sales. For example, the Simmons survey shows that the 17.7 percent of the U.S. population who are heavy users of fast-food restaurants provide 37.9 percent of the consumption volume, or more than twice the consumption of the average customer. Thus, as a Wendy's restaurant owner you want to keep the heavy-user segment constantly in mind.

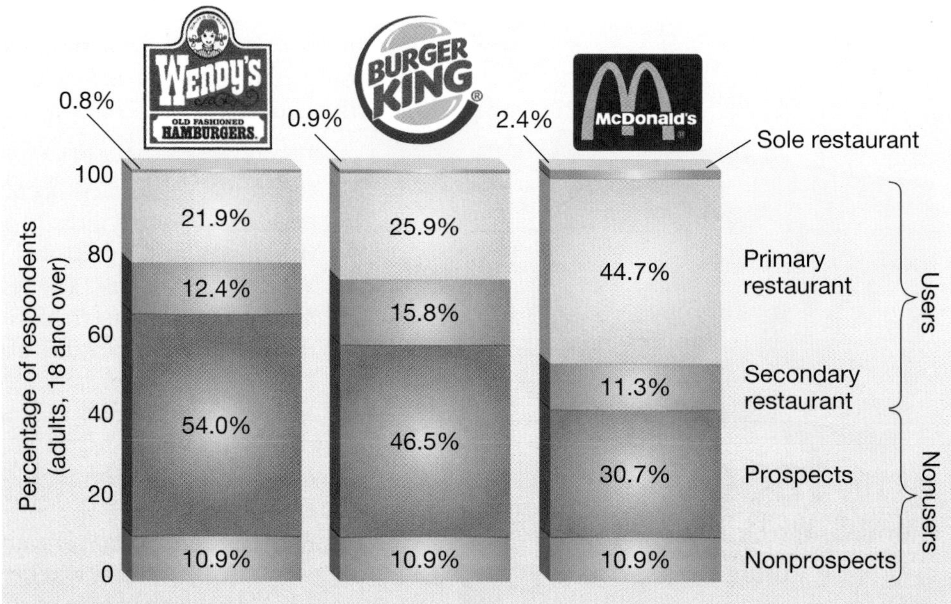

FIGURE 9–4
Comparison of various kinds of users and nonusers for Wendy's, Burger King, and McDonald's fast-food restaurants

As part of the Simmons fast-food survey, restaurant patrons were asked if each restaurant was (1) the only restaurant they went to, (2) the primary one, or (3) one of several secondary ones. This national information, shown in Figure 9–4, might give you, as a Wendy's owner, some ideas in developing your local strategy. The Wendy's bar in Figure 9–4 shows that your sole (0.8 percent), primary (21.9 percent), and secondary (12.4 percent) restaurant segments are somewhat behind Burger King and far behind McDonald's, so a natural strategy is to look at these two competitors and devise a marketing program to win customers from them.[11]

The nonusers part of your own bar in Figure 9–4 also provides ideas. It shows that 10.9 percent of adult Americans don't go to fast-food restaurants in a typical month and are really nonprospects—unlikely to ever go to your restaurant. But the 54.0 percent of the Wendy's bar shown as prospects may be worth detailed thought. These adults use the product category (fast-food restaurants) but *do not* go to Wendy's. New menu items or new promotional strategies might succeed in converting these prospects into users.

Variables to Use in Forming Segments In determining one or two variables to segment the market for your Wendy's restaurant, very broadly we find two main markets: students and nonstudents. To segment the students, we could try a variety of demographic variables, such as age, sex, year in school, or college major, or psychographic variables, such as personality characteristics, attitudes, or interests. But none of these variables really meets the five criteria listed previously—particularly, the fourth criterion about leading to a doable marketing action to reach the various segments. Four student segments that *do* meet these criteria include the following:

- Students living in dormitories (college residence halls, sororities, fraternities).
- Students living near the college in apartments.
- Day commuter students living outside the area.
- Night commuter students living outside the area.

These segmentation variables are really a combination of where the student lives and the time he or she is on campus (and near your restaurant). For nonstudents who might be customers, similar variables might be used:

- Faculty and staff members at the university.
- People who live in the area but aren't connected with the university.
- People who work in the area but aren't connected with the university.

JACKPOT
$1
SCRATCH THREE 2 WIN!
PRINT
SCAN
COPY
437
It's a win-win-win. Print, copy and scan in brilliant color, at amazing speed. The Xerox WorkCentre® C2424. Finally, a 24 ppm networked color multifunction for under $3,000.
Xerox Color. It makes business sense.
Lucky you. Introducing the Xerox WorkCentre C2424 Color Multifunction. It's the most versatile color multifunction you can get for under $3,000. Print, copy and scan in crisp black and white, or brilliant color with Xerox Solid Ink Technology. It's clean, versatile and incredibly fast at up to 24 pages per minute, with an industry-leading first-page-out time of just six seconds. Its speed and performance increase productivity by saving end-user time and maintenance. Easy to use, compact enough for any office, completely integrated and with a superior image quality of 2400 dpi, the Xerox WorkCentre C2424 Color Multifunction is the winning ticket.
PRINT COPY SCAN
XEROX.
xerox.com/office/1982
1-800-ASK-XEROX ext. 1982
Technology | Document Management | Consulting Services

What variables might Xerox use to segment the organizational markets for its answer to color copying problems? For the possible answer and related marketing actions, see the text.

People in each of these segments aren't quite as similar as those in the student segments, which makes them harder to reach with a marketing program or action. Think about (1) whether the needs of all these segments are different and (2) how various advertising media can be used to reach these groups effectively.

Ways to Segment Organizational Markets

There are also a number of variables that might be used to segment organizational markets. For example, a product manager at Xerox responsible for its new line of color printers might use several of these segmentation variables, as follows:

- *Geographic customer characteristic: Statistical area.* Firms located in a metropolitan statistical area might receive a personal sales call, whereas those in a micropolitan statistical area might be contacted by telephone.
- *Demographic customer characteristic: NAICS code.* Firms categorized by the North American Industry Classification System code as manufacturers that deal with customers throughout the world might have different document printing needs than do retailers or lawyers serving local customers.
- *Demographic customer characteristic: Number of employees.* The size of the firm is related to the volume of digital documents produced for a given industry or NAICS, so firms with varying numbers of employees might be specific target markets for different Xerox systems.
- *Benefits sought: Product features.* Similar to this segmentation variable for consumer markets, features are often of major importance in organizational markets. So Xerox can target organizations needing fast printing, copying, and scanning in color—the benefits and features emphasized in the ad for its new Xerox WorkCentre C2424 system.

Concept Check

1. The process of segmenting and targeting markets is a bridge between what two marketing activities?
2. What are two main ways to segment consumer and organizational markets?

Step 2: Group Products to Be Sold into Categories

Finding a means of grouping the products a firm sells into meaningful categories is as important as grouping customers into segments. If the firm has only one product or service, this isn't a problem, but when it has dozens or hundreds, these must be grouped in some way so buyers can relate to them. This is why department stores and supermarkets are organized into product groups, with the departments or aisles containing related merchandise. Likewise, manufacturers have product lines that are the groupings they use in the catalogs sent to customers.

What are the product groupings for your Wendy's restaurant? It could be the item purchased, such as a Frosty, chili, hamburgers, and french fries. This is where judgment—the qualitative aspect of marketing—comes in. Students really buy an eating experience, or a meal that satisfies a need at a particular time of day, so the product grouping can be defined by meal or time of day as breakfast, lunch, between-meal snack, dinner, and after-dinner snack. These groupings are more closely related to the way purchases are actually made and permit you to market the entire meal, not just your french fries or Frosties.

Step 3: Develop a Market-Product Grid and Estimate Size of Markets

Developing a market-product grid means labeling the markets (or horizontal rows) and products (or vertical columns), as shown in Figure 9–5. In addition, the size of the market in each cell (the market-product combination) must be estimated. For your restaurant, this involves estimating the sales of each kind of meal that can reasonably be expected to be sold to each market segment. This is a form of the usage rate analysis discussed earlier in the chapter.

The market sizes in Figure 9–5 may be simple "guesstimates" if you don't have time for formal marketing research (as discussed in Chapter 8). But even such crude estimates of the size of specific markets using a market-product grid are helpful in determining which target market segments to select and which product groupings to offer.

Step 4: Select Target Markets

A firm must take care to choose its target market segments carefully. If it picks too narrow a set of segments, it may fail to reach the volume of sales and profits it needs. If it selects too broad a set of segments, it may spread its marketing efforts so thin that the extra expenses are more than the increased sales and profits.

Criteria to Use in Picking the Target Segments There are two different kinds of criteria in the market segmentation process: (1) those to use in dividing the market into segments (discussed earlier) and (2) those to use in actually picking the target segments. Even experienced marketing executives often confuse these two different sets of criteria. The five criteria to use in actually selecting the target segments apply to your Wendy's restaurant this way:

- *Market size.* The estimated size of the market in the segment is an important factor in deciding whether it's worth going after. There is really no market for breakfasts among dormitory students (Figure 9–5), so why devote any marketing effort toward reaching a small or nonexistent segment?

FIGURE 9–5
Selecting a target market for your Wendy's fast-food restaurant next to an urban university (target market is shaded)

	PRODUCTS: MEALS				
MARKETS	BREAK-FAST	LUNCH	BETWEEN-MEAL SNACK	DINNER	AFTER-DINNER SNACK
Student					
Dormitory	0	1	3	0	3
Apartment	1	3	3	1	1
Day commuter	0	3	2	1	0
Night commuter	0	0	1	3	2
Nonstudent					
Faculty or staff	0	3	1	1	0
Live in area	0	1	2	2	1
Work in area	1	3	0	1	0

Key: 3 = Large market; 2 = Medium market; 1 = Small market; 0 = No market.

- *Expected growth.* Although the size of the market in the segment may be small now, perhaps it is growing significantly or is expected to grow in the future. Between now and 2007, sales of fast-food meals eaten outside the restaurants are projected to grow three times as fast as those eaten inside. And Wendy's is the fast-food leader in average time to serve a drive-thru order—for example, 16.7 seconds faster than McDonald's. This speed and convenience is potentially very important to night commuters in adult education programs.[12]
- *Competitive position.* Is there a lot of competition in the segment now or is there likely to be in the future? The less the competition, the more attractive the segment is. For example, if the college dormitories announce a new policy of "no meals on weekends," this segment is suddenly more promising for your restaurant. With McDonald's recent successful launch of healthful items like premium salads and yogurt parfaits, will Wendy's have to offer similar choices to its customers?[13]
- *Cost of reaching the segment.* A segment that is inaccessible to a firm's marketing actions should not be pursued. For example, the few nonstudents who live in the area may not be reachable with ads in newspapers or other media. As a result, do not waste money trying to advertise to them.
- *Compatibility with the organization's objectives and resources.* If your restaurant doesn't have the cooking equipment to make breakfasts and has a policy against spending more money on restaurant equipment, then don't try to reach the breakfast segment.

As is often the case in marketing decisions, a particular segment may appear attractive according to some criteria and very unattractive according to others.

Choose the Segments Ultimately, a marketing executive has to use these criteria to choose the segments for special marketing efforts. As shown in Figure 9–5, let's assume you've written off the breakfast product grouping for two reasons: too small of a market size and incompatibility with your objectives and resources. In terms of competitive position and cost of reaching the segment, you choose to focus on the four student segments and not the three nonstudent segments (although you're certainly not going to turn away business from the nonstudent segments). This combination of market-product segments—your target market—is shaded in Figure 9–5.

How can Wendy's target different market segments like night customers or commuting college students with different advertising programs? For the answer, see the text and Figure 9–6.

Step 5: Take Marketing Actions to Reach Target Markets

The purpose of developing a market-product grid is to trigger marketing actions to increase sales and profits. This means that someone must develop and execute an action plan.

Your Wendy's Segmentation Strategy With your Wendy's restaurant you've already reached one significant decision: There is a limited market for breakfast, so you won't open for business until 10:30 A.M. In fact, Wendy's first attempt at a breakfast menu was a disaster and was discontinued in 1986. Wendy's evaluates possible new menu items continuously, not only to compete with McDonald's and Burger King but with a complex array of supermarkets, convenience stores, and gas stations that sell reheatable packaged foods as well as new "easy-lunch" products.

Another essential decision is where and what meals to advertise to reach specific market segments. An ad in the student newspaper could reach all the student segments, but you might consider this approach too expensive and want a more focused effort to reach smaller segments. If you choose three segments for special actions (Figure 9–6 on the next page), advertising actions to reach them might include:

- *Day commuters* (an entire market segment). Run ads inside commuter buses and put flyers under the windshield wipers of cars in parking lots

FIGURE 9–6
Advertising actions to reach specific student segments

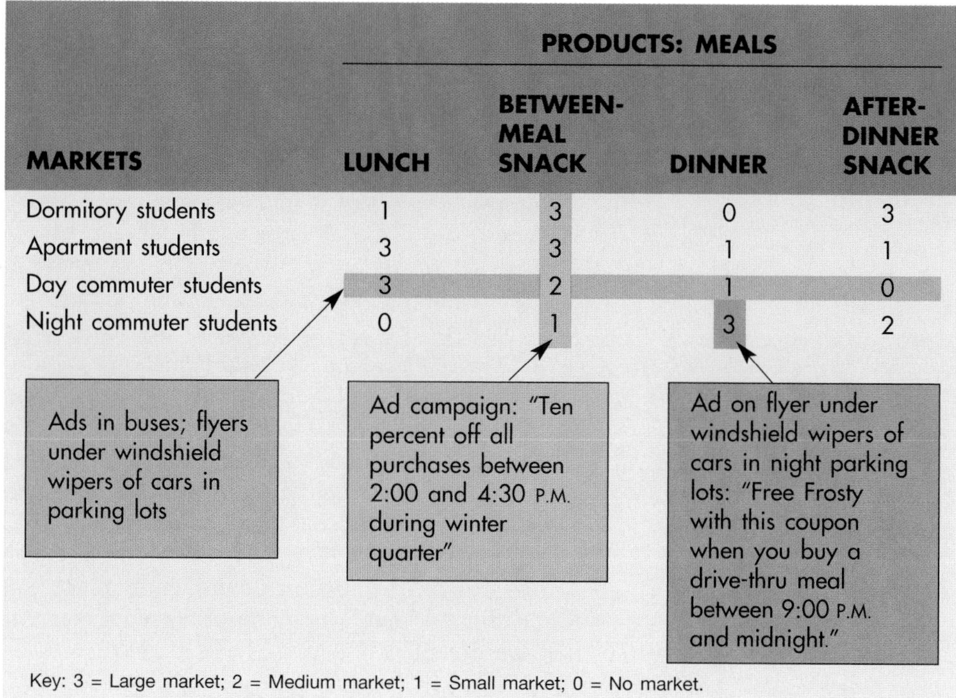

MARKETS	PRODUCTS: MEALS LUNCH	BETWEEN-MEAL SNACK	DINNER	AFTER-DINNER SNACK
Dormitory students	1	3	0	3
Apartment students	3	3	1	1
Day commuter students	3	2	1	0
Night commuter students	0	1	3	2

Ads in buses; flyers under windshield wipers of cars in parking lots
Ad campaign: "Ten percent off all purchases between 2:00 and 4:30 P.M. during winter quarter"
Ad on flyer under windshield wipers of cars in night parking lots: "Free Frosty with this coupon when you buy a drive-thru meal between 9:00 P.M. and midnight."

Key: 3 = Large market; 2 = Medium market; 1 = Small market; 0 = No market.

How has Apple moved from its 1977 Apple II to today's Power Macintosh G5? The Marketing NewsNet and text discussion provide insights into Apple's current market segmentation strategy.

used by day commuters. These ads and flyers promote all the meals at your restaurant to a single segment of students, a horizontal cut through the market-product grid.

- *Between-meal snacks* (directed to all four student markets). To promote eating during this downtime for your restaurant, offer "Ten percent off all purchases between 2:00 and 4:30 P.M. during winter quarter." This ad promotes a single meal to all four student segments, a vertical cut through the market-product grid.
- *Dinners to night commuters.* The most focused of all three campaigns, this ad promotes a single meal to the single segment of night commuter students. The campaign might consist of a windshield flyer offering a free Frosty with the coupon when the person buys a drive-thru meal between 9:00 P.M. and midnight.

Depending on how your advertising actions work, you can repeat, modify, or drop them and design new campaigns for other segments you feel are worth the effort.

This example of advertising your Wendy's restaurant is just a small piece of a complete marketing program using all the elements of the marketing mix. For example, in 2004 Wendy's introduced new menu items to appeal to segments in the various nutritional concerns, from Homestyle Chicken Strips to Garden Sensations Salads. In 2005 its Frescata cold sandwiches with focaccia bread appeared. And a special success is Wendy's new focus on the after-dinner snack column in Figure 9–6: As shown in Wendy's ad on the previous page, its late-night pickup window is open until midnight or later, even though most of its restaurants close their doors to customers at 10:00 P.M.

Apple's Ever-Changing Segmentation Strategy Steve Jobs and Steve Wozniak didn't realize they were developing today's multibillion-dollar PC industry when they invented the Apple I in a garage on April Fool's Day, 1976. Hobbyists, the initial target market, were not interested in the product. However, when the Apple II was displayed at a computer trade show in 1977, consumers loved it and Apple Computer was born. Typical of young companies, Apple focused on its products and had little concern for its markets. When IBM—"Big Blue"—entered the PC market in 1981, Apple was forced to become a "real company," much to the disappointment of its creative young engineers who were likened to "Boy Scouts without adult supervision."[14]

MARKETING NEWSNET

Apple's Segmentation Strategy—Camp Runamok No Longer

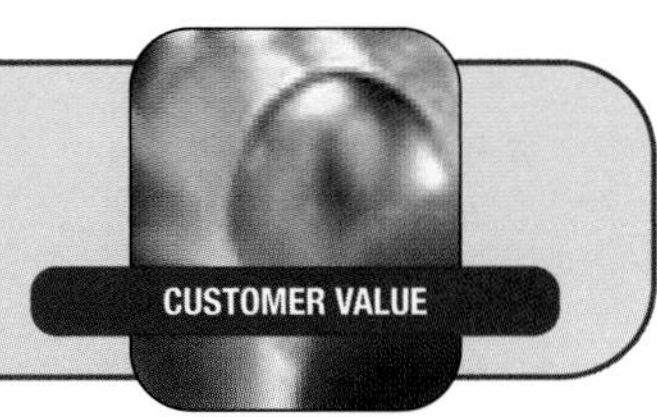

Camp Runamok was the nickname given to Apple Computer in the early 1980s because the innovative company had no coherent series of product lines directed at identifiable market segments.

Today, Apple has targeted its various lines of Macintosh computers at specific market segments, as shown in the market-product grid below. Because the market-product grid shifts as a firm's strategy changes, the one below is based on Apple's product lines in late 2005. This market-product grid is a simplification because each product grouping consists of a line of Apple hardware products. Nevertheless, the grid suggests the market segmentation strategy Steve Jobs is using to compete in what he sees as the Age of the Digital Lifestyle, as described in the text.

MARKETS		HARDWARE PRODUCTS					
SECTOR	SEGMENT	Power Macintosh G5	PowerBook G4	iMac G5	iBook	eMac	iPod
CONSUMER	Individuals	✓	✓	✓	✓	✓	✓
	Small/home office	✓	✓	✓	✓	✓	
	Students			✓	✓	✓	✓
	Teachers	✓	✓	✓		✓	
PROFESSIONAL	Medium/large business	✓	✓	✓			
	Creative	✓	✓	✓			✓
	College faculty	✓	✓	✓			✓
	College staff			✓	✓	✓	

With the introduction of the IBM PC, Big Blue quickly dominated the fledgling market, having licensed the DOS operating system from Bill Gates of Microsoft. Apple lost significant market share, and sales fell off dramatically, eventually leading to the departure of Steve Jobs from Apple in 1985. Unfortunately, Apple continued to languish under new, changing leadership as it constantly altered its market-product strategies.

When Steve Jobs returned in 1997, he detailed his vision for a reincarnated Apple by describing a new market segmentation strategy that he called the "Apple Product Matrix." This strategy consisted of developing two general types of computers (desktops and portables) targeted at two general kinds of market segments—the consumer and professional sectors shown in the accompanying Marketing NewsNet. He also announced the controversial "Think Different" advertising campaign. In 1998, Apple retargeted the consumer and educational markets by introducing the revolutionary new iMac, the greatest PC product launch in history.

Fast-forward to the twenty-first century. Jobs believes that the personal computer entered the Age of the Digital Lifestyle in 2001. In a keynote address, Jobs said that "the proliferation of digital devices—CD players, MP3 players, cell phones, handheld organizers, digital cameras, digital camcorders, and more—will never have enough processing power and memory to stand alone." Jobs enthusiastically proclaimed, "the Mac can become the digital hub of this new digital lifestyle." By repositioning Apple as the "digital hub" with "killer apps," such as iTunes, iMovie, iDVD, iPhoto, iPod nano, and iPod video—Jobs believes consumers can exploit the new digital lifestyle era.[15]

In most segmentation situations, a single product does not fit into an exclusive market niche. Rather, there is overlap among products in the product line and also among the markets to which they are directed. But a market segmentation strategy enables Apple to offer different products to meet the needs of different market segments, as shown in the Marketing NewsNet. Stay tuned to see if Steve Jobs and these market-product strategies for his vision of the digital lifestyle era are on target. He's betting the company on it![16]

Market-Product Synergies: A Balancing Act

Recognizing opportunities for key synergies—that is, efficiencies—is vital to success in selecting target market segments and making marketing decisions. Market-product grids illustrate where such synergies can be found. How? Let's consider Apple's market-product grid in the accompanying Marketing NewsNet and examine the difference between marketing synergies and product synergies shown there.

- *Marketing synergies*. Running horizontally across the grid, each row represents an opportunity for efficiency in terms of a market segment. Were Apple to focus on just one group of consumers, such as the medium/large business segment, its marketing efforts could be streamlined. Time would not have to be spent learning about the buying habits of students or college faculty. So it could probably do a single ad piece to reach the medium/large business target segment (the yellow row), highlighting the only products they'd need to worry about developing: Power Mac G5, the PowerBook G4, and the iMac G5. Although clearly this is not Apple's strategy today, focusing on a single customer segment is a common marketing strategy for new companies.
- *Product synergies*. Running vertically down the market-product grid, each column represents an opportunity for efficiency in research and development (R&D) and production. If Apple wanted to simplify its product line, reduce R&D and production expenses, and manufacture only one computer, which might it choose? Based on the market-product grid, Apple might do well to focus on the iMac G5 (the brown column), since the iMac G5 is purchased by the most consumer segments—in this case, every segment.

A choice to take advantage of marketing synergies can often come at the expense of production ones because a single customer segment will likely require a variety of products, each of which will have to be designed and manufactured. The company saves money on marketing but spends more in production. Conversely, if product synergies are emphasized, marketing will have to address the concerns of a wide variety of consumers, which costs more time and money. Marketing managers responsible for developing a company's product line must balance both product and marketing synergies as they try to increase the company's profits.

Concept Check

1. What are some criteria used to decide which segments to choose for targets?
2. In a market-product grid, what factor is estimated or measured for each of the cells?
3. What is the difference between marketing synergies and product synergies in a market-product grid?

POSITIONING THE PRODUCT

product positioning
The space a product occupies in consumers' minds on important features relative to competing products

When a company offers a product for sale, a decision critical to its long-term success is how to position it in the market upon introduction. **Product positioning** refers to the place an offering occupies in consumers' minds on important attributes relative to competitive offerings. By understanding where consumers see a company's product or brand today, a marketing manager can seek to change its future position in their minds.

Chocolate Milk . . . for Adults?

Finding the right way to position a product or service in the minds of potential customers is hard, creative work for a marketing manager.

Good nutrition is an increasing concern of Americans. It gets highlighted in comparing recent U.S. annual capita consumption of soft drinks versus milk: 52 gallons of soft drinks versus 25 gallons of milk, even with all milk's benefits of calcium and vitamins.[17]

Several years ago dairies got the idea to target chocolate milk sales at a new market—adults. Note on the perceptual map where adults positioned chocolate milk then and suggest (*a*) in which lettered location dairies might reposition chocolate milk targeted at adults and (*b*) what kind of packaging might appeal to them.

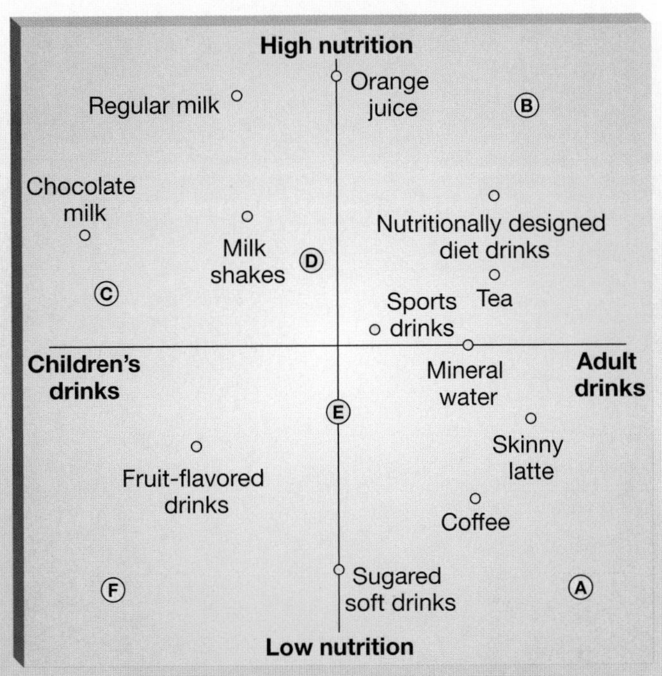

FIGURE 9–7
Your challenge as a marketing manager: Try to position chocolate milk to make it more appealing to adults

Product Positioning Using Perceptual Maps

A key to positioning a product or brand effectively is the perceptions of customers. In determining its position and the preferences of customers, companies obtain three types of data from consumers:

perceptual map
Means of displaying the position of products or brands in the consumers' minds

1. Identification of the important attributes for a product class.
2. Judgments of existing products or brands with respect to these attributes.
3. Ratings of an "ideal" product's or brand's attributes.

The firm can then develop market strategies to move its product or brand to any ideal position.

From these data, it is possible to develop a **perceptual map**, a means of displaying or graphing in two dimensions the location of products or brands in the minds of consumers to enable a manager to see how consumers perceive competing products or brands and then take marketing actions. Look at Figure 9–7 and develop a positioning strategy to make chocolate milk more appealing to adults.

More "zip" for chocolate milk? The text and Figure 9–8 describe a successful positioning strategy.

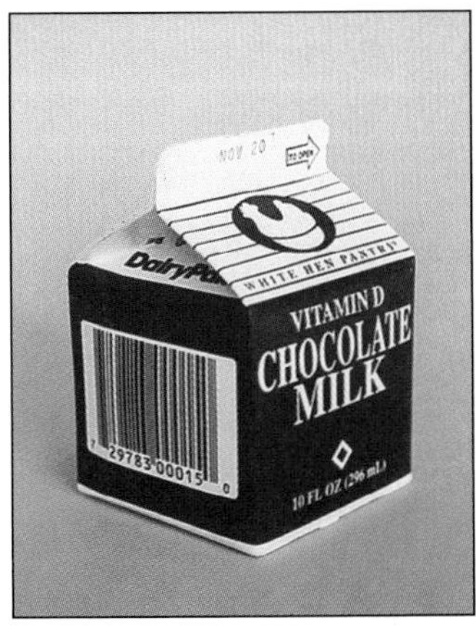

Positioning Chocolate Milk for Adults

Figure 9–8 shows the positions that consumer beverages might occupy in the minds of American adults. Note that even these positions vary from one consumer to another. But for simplicity, let's assume these are the typical positions on the beverage perceptual map of adult Americans.

U.S. dairies, struggling to increase milk sales, hit on a wild idea: Try to target adults by repositioning chocolate milk to the location of the star shown in the perceptual map in Figure 9–8—location B in Figure 9–7. Their arguments are nutritionally powerful. For women chocolate milk provides calcium, critically important in female diets. And dieters can get a more filling, nutritious beverage than with a soft drink for about the same calories. The result: Chocolate milk sales increased dramatically, much of it because of adult consumption.[18] Part is due to

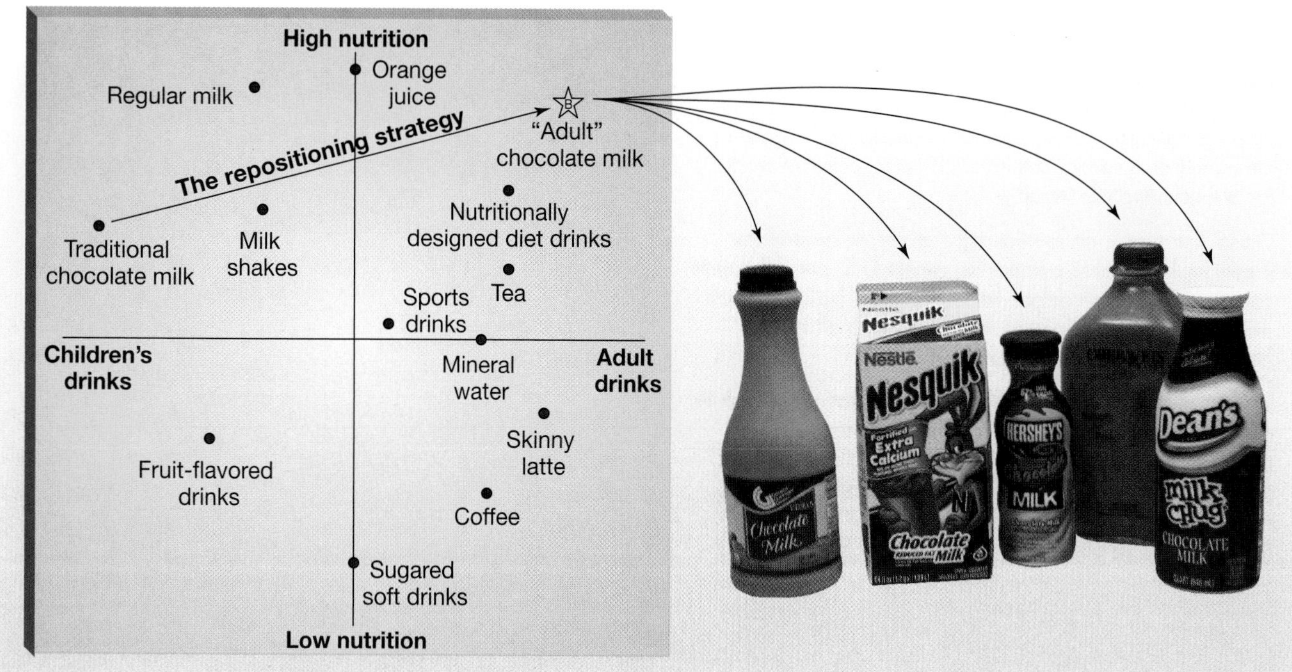

FIGURE 9-8
A perceptual map to suggest a strategy for positioning chocolate milk to reach adults

giving chocolate milk "nutritional respectability" for adults, but another part is due to the innovative packaging that enables many containers to fit in a car's cup holders.

Concept Check

1. What is product positioning?
2. Why do marketers use perceptual maps in product positioning decisions?

CHAPTER IN REVIEW

1 *Explain what market segmentation is and when to use it.*
Market segmentation involves aggregating prospective buyers into groups that (*a*) have common needs and (*b*) will respond similarly to a marketing action. Organizations go to the trouble and expense of segmenting their markets when it increases their sales, profits, and ability to serve customers better.

2 *Identify the five steps involved in segmenting and targeting markets.*
Step 1 is to group potential buyers into segments. Buyers within a segment should have similar characteristics to each other and respond similarly to marketing actions like a new product or a lower price. Step 2 involves putting related products to be sold into groups. In step 3, organizations develop a market-product grid with estimated size of markets in each of the market-product cells of the resulting table. Step 4 involves selecting the target market segments on which the organization should focus. Step 5 involves taking marketing mix actions—often in the form of a marketing program—to reach the target market segments.

3 *Recognize the different factors used to segment consumer and organizational markets.*
Factors used to segment consumer markets include customer characteristics (geographic, demographic, and psychographic variables) and buying situations. Organizational markets use related variables except for psychographic ones.

4 *Know how to develop a market-product grid to identify a target market and recommend resulting actions.*
Organizations use five key criteria to segment markets, whose groupings appear in the rows of the market-product grid. Groups of related products appear in the columns. After estimating the size of market in each cell in the grid, they select the target market segments on which to focus. They then identify marketing mix actions—often in a marketing program—to reach the target market most efficiently.

5 *Explain how marketing managers position products in the marketplace.*
Marketing managers often locate competing products on two-dimensional perceptual maps to visualize the products in the minds of consumers. They then try to position products in this space to attain the maximum sales and profits.

FOCUSING ON KEY TERMS

80/20 rule p. 195
market-product grid p. 190
market segmentation p. 189
market segments p. 189
perceptual map p. 203
product differentiation p. 189
product positioning p. 202
synergy p. 192
usage rate p. 195

DISCUSSION AND APPLICATION QUESTIONS

1 What variables might be used to segment these consumer markets? (*a*) lawnmowers, (*b*) frozen dinners, (*c*) dry breakfast cereals, and (*d*) soft drinks.

2 What variables might be used to segment these industrial markets? (*a*) industrial sweepers, (*b*) photocopiers, (*c*) computerized production control systems, and (*d*) car rental agencies.

3 In Figure 9–5, the dormitory market segment includes students living in college-owned residence halls, sororities, and fraternities. What market needs are common to these students that justify combining them into a single segment in studying the market for your Wendy's restaurant?

4 You may disagree with the estimates of market size given for the rows in the market-product grid in Figure 9–5. Estimate the market size, and give a brief justification for these market segments: (*a*) dormitory students, (*b*) day commuters, and (*c*) people who work in the area.

5 Suppose you want to increase revenues for your fast-food restaurant even further. Referring to Figure 9–6, what advertising actions might you take to increase revenues from (*a*) dormitory students, (*b*) dinners, and (*c*) after-dinner snacks from night commuters?

6 In 1999, entrepreneurs Mary Ann and George Clark founded MacFarms, Inc., to introduce milk beverages with enough appeal to wean children from soft drinks and athlete-oriented drinks. Their patented invention: carbonated milk beverages in various flavors.[19] Look again at Figure 9–7 and (*a*) select one of the lettered positions on the perceptual map and (*b*) suggest packaging for these drinks.

GOING ONLINE Apple's Latest Market-Product Strategies

In its 25-year history, Apple Computer has initiated a series of creative market segmentation strategies, with new product lines targeted at specific market segments. For the latest updates of Apple's market-product strategies, go to www.apple-history.com and click on the "Intro" and "History" menu options. As you read the narrative, identify the new and remaining markets Apple has targeted with new and existing products compared to those described in the text and the Marketing NewsNet. Do you think Apple will succeed in its quest to lead us into the digital lifestyle age? Can Apple survive as a niche PC marketer like BMW has with autos? Why or why not?

BUILDING YOUR MARKETING PLAN

Your marketing plan needs (*a*) a market-product grid to focus your marketing efforts and also (*b*) leads to a forecast of sales for the company. Use these steps:

1 Define the market segments (the rows in your grid) using the segmentation factors discussed in the chapter.

2 Define the groupings of related products (the columns in your grid).

3 Form your grid and estimate the size of market in each market-product cell.

4 Select the target market segments on which to focus your efforts with your marketing program.

VIDEO CASE 9 Nokia: A Phone for Every Segment

"While practically everybody today is a potential mobile phone customer, everybody is simultaneously different in terms of usage, needs, lifestyles, and individual preferences," explains Keith Nowak, Nokia's media relations manager. Understanding those differences requires that Nokia conduct ongoing research among different consumer groups throughout the world. The approach is reflected in the company's business strategy:

> We intend to exploit our leadership role by continuing to target and enter segments of the communications market that we believe will experience rapid growth or grow faster than the industry as a whole and that cater to the diverse needs, lifestyles, and preferences of our customers.

In fact, Nowak believes that "to be successful in the mobile phone business of today and tomorrow, Nokia has to fully understand the fundamental nature and rationale of segmentation."

THE COMPANY

Nokia started in 1865, when a mining engineer built a wood-pulp mill in southern Finland to manufacture paper. Over the next century, the company diversified into industries ranging from paper to chemicals and rubber. In the 1960s, Nokia ventured into telecommunications by developing a digital telephone exchange switch. In the 1980s, Nokia developed its first "transportable" car mobile phone and the first "handportable" one. During the early 1990s, Nokia divested all of its nontelecommunications operations to focus on its telecommunications and mobile handset businesses.

Today, Nokia is the world leader in mobile communications. Globally, the company generates sales of about $40 billion in more than 130 countries and employs more than 51,000 people. Its Mobile Phones, Enterprise Solutions, and Multimedia business groups account for more than 75 percent of sales. Nokia's mission is simple: "Connecting People," which is accomplished by understanding consumer needs and providing offerings that meet or exceed those needs. Nokia believes that designing state-of-the-art mobile phones for its global customers is critical to its continued success in the rapidly changing mobile phone market.

THE MOBILE PHONE MARKET

In the 1980s, first generation (1G) mobile phones consisted of voice-only analog devices with limited roaming and features that were sold mainly in North America. In the 1990s, second generation (2G and 2.5G) devices consisted of voice/data digital mobile phones with higher data transfer rates, expanded range, and more features. Sales of these devices grew initially in Europe and Asia. In the twenty-first century, Nokia and other companies are combining digital audio, video, and data technologies into third generation (3G) communication devices that reach consumers globally. The convergence of the mobile phone (audio), digital camera (video), personal digital assistant (PDA), Internet and e-mail services (data), and other multimedia technologies will usher in the fourth generation (4G) of global communication devices.

The annual global demand for mobile phones has increased significantly over the years—from more than 400 million units in 2000 to about 650 million units shipped in 2004. In 2008, mobile phone shipments could exceed 950 million units. Marketers of 1G and 2G mobile phones used a geographic segmentation strategy as wireless communication networks were developed. Most started with the United States and then proceeded to Europe and Asia. However, each market grew at different rates. In 2004, Asia was the largest mobile phone market with 240 million, or 37 percent of all handsets sold that year. Europe was second with 240 million shipments (19 percent), followed by North America at 110 million shipments (17 percent).

Nokia led all marketers with a 29 percent market share in mid-2004, followed by Motorola (16 percent), Samsung (14 percent), Siemens (7 percent), and Sony Ericsson (6 percent). The total number of worldwide wireless subscribers reached 1.5 billion in 2004 and is expected to increase to 2.0 billion by 2008. The increase is due to the growing demand by teens for high-speed handsets that will provide digital audio, video, and data applications. According to Cellular Telecommunications & Internet Association (CTIA), U.S. wireless subscribers reached 170 million by 2004 and spent an average of $50 per month on calls.

HOW NOKIA SEGMENTS ITS MARKETS

According to Keith Nowak,

> Different people have different usage needs. Some people want and need all of the latest and most advanced data-related features and functions, while others are happy with basic voice connectivity. Even people with similar usage needs often have differing lifestyles representing various value sets. For example, some people have an active lifestyle in which sports and fitness play an important role, while for others arts, fashion, and trends may be very important.

Based on its information about consumer usage, lifestyles, price sensitivity, and individual preferences,

Nokia currently defines and markets mobile phone handsets to the following six segments: "Basic" consumers, first-time buyers who are very price driven and only need voice connectivity; "Expression" consumers, younger buyers who want to customize and personalize features; "Active" consumers, who are looking for a rugged product to stand up to an active lifestyle; "Classic" consumers, who prefer a more traditional mobile phone with some features at a modest price; "Fashion" consumers, who want a very small phone as a fashion item; and "Premium" consumers, who are interested in all the high-end technological and service features. Nokia also markets a number of very focused products, including the "Communicator" line, for business users who want more sophisticated convergent devices that contain telephone, pager, PDA, Internet, streaming multimedia, and other functions, and the "N-Gage" line of mobile game decks, designed to provide a mobile, connected video game platform.

NOKIA'S PRODUCT LINES

Nokia has recently introduced several innovative products to meet the needs of these segments. To target the Basic segment, Nokia provides very easy-to-use, low-priced phones, such as the 1000 and 2000 series. "The idea behind a product like this is to bring voice communication to emerging markets and help people take life mobile," explains Nowak.

Products designed for the Expression segment are still in the lower price range but allow young adults to have fun while communicating with friends. These products often feature changeable covers, color displays, embedded lights or game controls, and a wide selection of high-fidelity ring tones and downloadable games. Examples include the 3000 series of mobile phones, which offers all of these features, plus the unique option for owners to design their own custom cover inserts.

For the sports enthusiast segment, Nokia designs products in the Active segment. The 5000 series of mobile phones offer a youthful and vibrant style with improved durability. Features include a removable shell, built-in timers and stopwatch, a digital compass, a digital camera, a "Fitness Monitor" that monitors activity level and calorie consumption, and "Fitness Coach" personal trainer software.

Nokia's 6000 series of mobile phones allow Classic consumers to roam between various global networks. Some models have Bluetooth technology, voice dialing, voice recording, and Internet access while others have a camera, a document viewer to read e-mails, a browser, and a wireless keyboard for entering data into a personal information manager (phone book and calendar).

Nokia also designs phones for the Fashion segment—people who want a phone to "show off." The Nokia 7000 series of mobile phones are in this category. They allow these consumers to have a device with unique styling and materials that allow the owner to communicate their individual sense of style. In addition, Nokia offers phones for the Premium segment—people who also want a distinctive and elegant design, but as a functional phone to use rather than to show off. The Nokia 8000 series features titanium or stainless steel construction and a color screen.

THE FUTURE FOR NOKIA AND THE MOBILE PHONE INDUSTRY

By the end of 2010, the total number of mobile phone users worldwide could approach 3 billion due to the growth in emerging markets like China, India, and Latin America. This will spur the development of mobile phones that will work in all geographic markets. Nokia, Motorola, and Samsung have recently introduced phones, initially targeted at business users, which will work regardless of the location of the user.

3G mobile phone products and services continue to be rolled out in the United States. Wireless services providers, such as AT&T Wireless and Verizon Wireless, have introduced 3G services in selected U.S. cities in 2004. The convergence of digital devices may accelerate as key features from mobile phones, higher-resolution digital cameras, TV-quality video streaming, PDAs, the Internet, music players, games, and so forth become standard in the offerings of mobile phone marketers. What's on the horizon? The development of 4G! A forum of the top 15 mobile phone marketers recently gathered to plan for the offering of high-speed wireless technology that will allow for mobile shopping and video streaming at reasonable prices.

Finally, a fast-growing segment for mobile phones is the automobile. Many automobile manufacturers, in partnership with mobile phone marketers like Nokia, have recently introduced products that integrate "hands-free, voice-activated" technology to reduce mobile phone-related automobile accidents. The CTIA has recently developed public service announcements (PSAs) to promote more responsible behavior and forestall federal and state legislation designed to eliminate mobile phone use in the car.

Questions

1 Why has segmentation been a successful marketing strategy for Nokia?

2 What customer characteristics were used by mobile phone marketers during the industry's early stages of growth? Which customer characteristics and segmentation variables does Nokia use?

3 Create a market-product grid for Nokia today. What potential new markets could you add to the grid?

PART

PART 1
Initiating the Marketing Process

PART 2
Understanding Buyers and Markets

PART 3
Targeting Marketing Opportunities

PART 4
Satisfying Marketing Opportunities

4 SATISFYING MARKETING OPPORTUNITIES

HOW PART 4 FITS INTO THE BOOK

The chapters in Part 4 cover the marketing mix—the four Ps that are the key product, price, place, and promotion actions marketing managers use to implement their marketing program.

GREPTILE™ GRIP

Get a Better Grip on Glove Sales

Increase Club Head Speed and Distance

3M's proprietary Greptile™ micro-replication technology gives golfers a tighter grip with less effort. Using thousands of micro-replication fingers, the glove creates optimal gripping friction to reduce slip and increase swing control.

• 3M Greptile™ Golf Glove 252.8 yards

• Leading Competitor 244.5 yards

0 50 100 150 200 250 300

*Leading competitor glove compared to a 3M Greptile™ glove in dry conditions. Tested by 3M Performance Laboratories. Individual results may vary.

3M GREPTILE™ GOLF GLOVES GRIP TIGHTLY – EVEN IF YOU DON'T!

- Maximum gripping power with minimal gripping pressure
- Exceptional grip and dexterity – in wet or dry conditions
- 100% Cabretta leather for the balance of the glove gives a natural, comfortable fit
- One of the greatest innovations in golf glove design in the last 25 years!

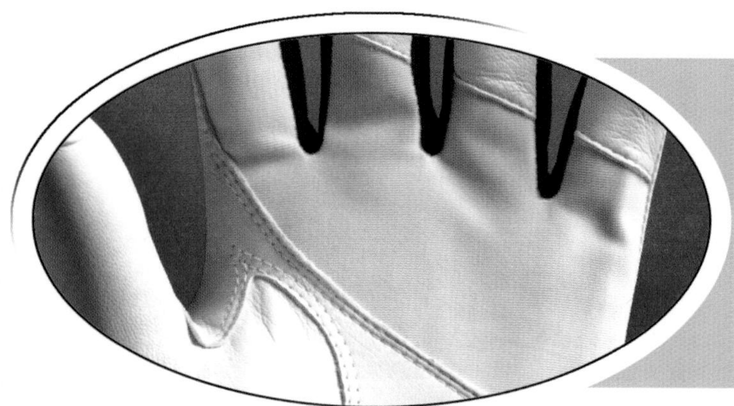

THERE'S NEVER BEEN A GRIP LIKE GREPTILE™

Greptile™ micro-replication technology forms a sea of gripping fingers that maintain their grip even immersed in water.

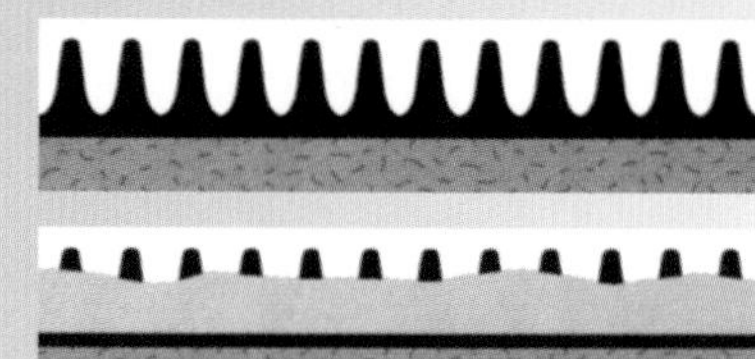

Revolutionary Gripping Technology, another 3M Innovation!

CHAPTER 10

DEVELOPING NEW PRODUCTS AND SERVICES

LEARNING OBJECTIVES

After reading this chapter you should be able to:

1 Recognize the various terms that pertain to products and services.

2 Identify the ways in which consumer and business goods and services can be classified.

3 Explain the significance of "newness" in new products and services as it relates to the degree of consumer learning involved.

4 Describe the factors contributing to a new product's or service's success or failure.

5 Explain the purposes of each step of the new-product process.

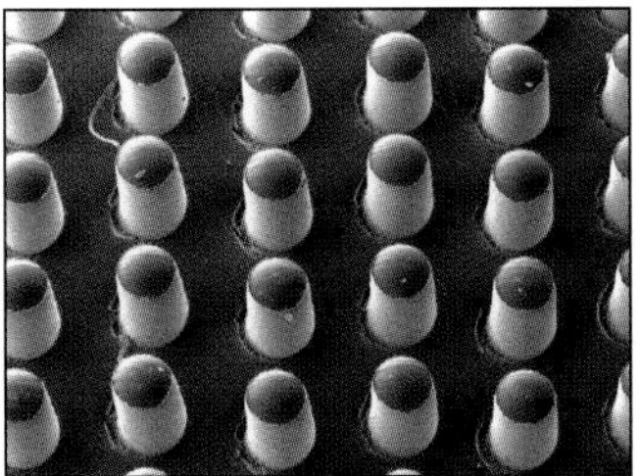

3M'S NEW GREPTILE GRIP GOLF GLOVE: HOW TO GET TO THE TOP OF THE LEADER BOARD

"We look around the company for underutilized technologies that can result in exciting new products for niche markets," says Dr. George Dierberger, marketing and international manager for Sports and Leisure Products at 3M. Turning 3M's microreplication technology into a golf glove is a prime example.

3M's innovative Greptile™ Grip golf glove helps golfers wearing the glove to hit longer drives and more accurate shots. This should give lower scores through improved control of the golf club swing under both wet and dry conditions. Here's a quick take on the marketing issues Dierberger faced when introducing this new product in 2004:[1]

- *The product?* A golf glove that integrates 3M's revolutionary Greptile urethane gripping material, a technology that consists of thousands of "microscopic fingers," (shown at left) into a golf glove. The material is sewn in the "gripping channel" of the lower fingers and upper palm of the glove to reduce the slip of a golfer's grip when swinging the club.
- *The target market?* Golfers who want to improve their scores—only, say, 100 percent of the market. But then the market segments get more specific: golfers playing in hot or humid conditions, or those needing a stronger grip due to their skill level, age, or arthritis.
- *The special marketing task?* Leverage 3M's strong brand reputation for using its world-class technologies to introduce innovative, high-quality products in other markets as a means of entering the intensely competitive golf equipment market.

Dierberger and his marketing and engineering team created the ad for distributors and retailers shown on page 210. The team's continuing challenge is to communicate the product's benefits in its packaging and promotions to its targeted retailers and customers to overcome the lack of 3M brand recognition in a market dominated by FootJoy, Titleist, Nike, and other golf glove marketers.

3M's new-product research has enabled the company to become a global leader in adhesive technology. This has led to dozens of 3M adhesive products, such as Nexcare™ Tattoo™ Waterproof Bandages for kids and Post-it® Notes.

product
Good, service, or idea consisting of tangible and intangible features that satisfies consumers and is received in exchange for money or some other unit of value

The essence of marketing is in developing products such as a new, technologically advanced adhesive to meet buyer needs. A **product** is a good, service, or idea consisting of a bundle of tangible and intangible attributes that satisfies consumers and is received in exchange for money or some other unit of value. Tangible attributes include physical characteristics such as color or sweetness, and intangible attributes include becoming healthier or wealthier. Hence, a product includes the breakfast cereal you eat, the accountant who fills out your tax return, or your local art museum.

The life of a company often depends on how it conceives, produces, and markets new products. This is the exact reason that 3M spends $1.1 billion on research annually and has over 5,000 engineers and scientists around the globe looking for what *BusinessWeek* calls the Next Big Thing for 3M.[2] Later we describe how 3M strives to "delight its customers" using cross-functional teams and "Six Sigma" initiatives.

This chapter covers decisions involved in developing and marketing new products and services. Chapter 11 discusses the process of managing existing products, services, and brands.

THE VARIATIONS OF PRODUCTS

A product varies in terms of whether it is a consumer or business good. For most organizations the product decision is not made in isolation because companies often offer a range of products. To better appreciate the product decision, let's first define some terms pertaining to products.

Product Line and Product Mix

product line
Group of products that are closely related because they satisfy a class of needs, are used together, are sold to the same customer group, are distributed through the same outlets, or fall within a given price range

A **product line** is a group of products that are closely related because they satisfy a class of needs, are used together, are sold to the same customer group, are distributed through the same type of outlets, or fall within a given price range. Nike's product lines are shoes and clothing, whereas the Mayo Clinic's product lines consist of inpatient hospital care, outpatient physician services, and medical research. Each product line has its own marketing strategy.

The product line for the Little Remedies® Products consists of more than a dozen nonprescription medicines for infants and children six years old and younger. An important benefit of having a broad product line like that for Little Remedies is it enables both consumers and retailers to simplify their buying decisions. For example, a family that has a good experience with one Little Remedies product might buy another one. Also its extensive product line enables it to obtain distribution in retail chains like Babies "Я" Us and Wal-Mart.[3]

Within each product line is the *product item,* a specific product as noted by a unique brand, size, or price. For example, Downy softener for clothes comes in 20-ounce and 40-ounce sizes; each size is considered a separate item or *stock keeping unit* (SKU), which is a unique identification number that defines an item for ordering or inventory purposes.

product mix
All the product lines offered by a company

The third way to look at products is by the **product mix**, or the number of product lines offered by a company. Cray, Inc., has a single product line consisting of supercomputers, which are sold mostly to governments and large businesses. Fortune

An extensive product line can benefit both consumers and retailers. To discover how Little Remedies' product line helps achieve this, see the text.

Brands, however, has many product lines such as sporting equipment (Titleist golf balls) and office products (Swingline staplers).

Classifying Products

Both the federal government and companies classify products, but for different purposes. The government's classification method helps it collect information on industrial activity. Companies classify products to help develop similar marketing strategies for the wide range of products offered. Two major ways to classify products are by type of user and degree of product tangibility.

Type of User The first major type of product classification is according to the user. **Consumer goods** are products purchased by the ultimate consumer, whereas **business goods** (also called *B2B goods, industrial goods,* or *organizational goods*) are products that assist directly or indirectly in providing products for resale.

There are difficulties, however, with this classification because some products can be considered both consumer and business items. An Apple computer can be sold to consumers as a final product or to business firms for office use. Each classification results in different marketing actions. Viewed as a consumer product, the Apple computer would be sold through computer stores or directly from the company's website. As a business product, the Apple computer might be sold by a salesperson offering discounts for multiple purchases.

consumer goods
Products purchased by the ultimate consumer

business goods
Products that assist directly or indirectly in providing products for resale

services
Intangible activities or benefits that an organization provides to consumers in exchange for money or something else of value.

Degree of Tangibility Classification by degree of tangibility divides products into one of three categories. First is a *nondurable* good, an item consumed in one or a few uses, such as food products and fuel. A *durable* good is one that usually lasts over an extended number of uses, such as appliances, automobiles, and stereo equipment. **Services** are defined as intangible activities or benefits that an organization provides to consumers in exchange for money or something else of value.

This classification method also provides direction for marketing actions. For nondurable products like Wrigley's gum, inexpensive and purchased frequently, consumer advertising and wide distribution in retail outlets is essential. Durable products like cars, however, generally cost more than nondurable goods and last longer, so personal selling is an important marketing activity in answering consumer questions and concerns. Because services are intangible, special marketing effort is usually needed to communicate their benefits to potential buyers.

The Uniqueness of Services

Services have become one of the most important components of the U.S. economy. As shown in Figure 10–1 on the next page, services account for approximately 40 percent of the gross domestic product (GDP). There are four unique elements to services: intangibility, inconsistency, inseparability, and inventory. These four elements are referred to as the *four I's of services.*

Intangibility Services are intangible; that is, they can't be held, touched, or seen before the purchase decision. In contrast, before purchasing a traditional product, a consumer can touch a box of laundry detergent, kick the tire of an automobile, or sample a new breakfast cereal. Because services tend to be a performance rather than an object, they are much more difficult for consumers to evaluate. To help consumers assess and compare services marketers try to make them tangible or show the benefits of using the service.

Inconsistency Developing, pricing, promoting, and delivering services is challenging because the quality of a service is often inconsistent. Because services depend on the

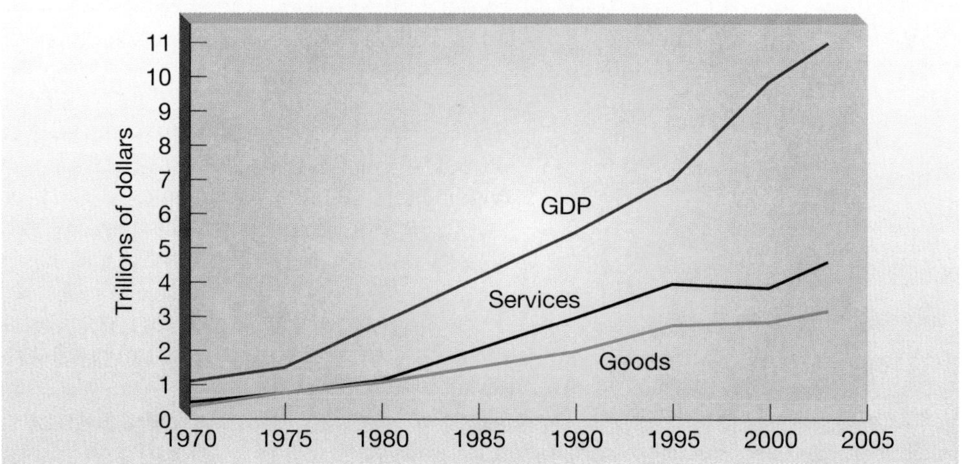

FIGURE 10–1
Importance of services in the U.S. gross domestic product (GDP)

people who provide them, their quality varies with each person's capabilities and day-to-day job performance. Inconsistency is much more of a problem in services than it is with tangible goods. One day the Philadelphia Phillies baseball team may have great hitting and pitching and look like a pennant winner and the next day lose by 10 runs.

Inseparability Inseparability means that consumers often cannot distinguish the deliverer of the service from the service itself. For example, at a university the quality of lectures may be excellent, but if students can't get questions answered, find counseling and placement services poor, or do not receive adequate library or computer assistance, they may not be satisfied with their university experience. So these students don't separate their perception of their "university experience"—the service itself—from all the people involved with delivering the educational services.

Inventory Inventory of services is different from that of goods. Inventory problems exist with goods because many items are perishable and because there are "carrying costs" associated with handling and storing inventory. With services, inventory carrying costs are more subjective and are related to **idle production capacity**, which is when the service provider is available but there is no demand. The inventory cost of a service is the cost of paying the people used to provide the service along with any needed equipment. If a physician is paid to see patients but no one schedules an appointment, the idle physician's salary is an example of idle production capacity. In service businesses involving a commission (the Merrill Lynch stockbroker) or a part-time employee (a clerk at Sears) the idle production capacity can be lowered because of the commission compensation system (the stockbroker) or reducing the hours worked (the clerk at Sears).

idle production capacity
When the supply of the service exceeds demand for it

CLASSIFYING GOODS AND SERVICES

Because marketing focuses on the buyer—that is, the product user—let's look a bit more closely at the two types of users and how goods and services are classified as consumer or business products.

Classifying Consumer Goods

Convenience, shopping, specialty, and unsought products are the four types of consumer goods. They differ in terms of (1) effort the consumer spends on the decision, (2) attributes used in purchase, and (3) frequency of purchase.

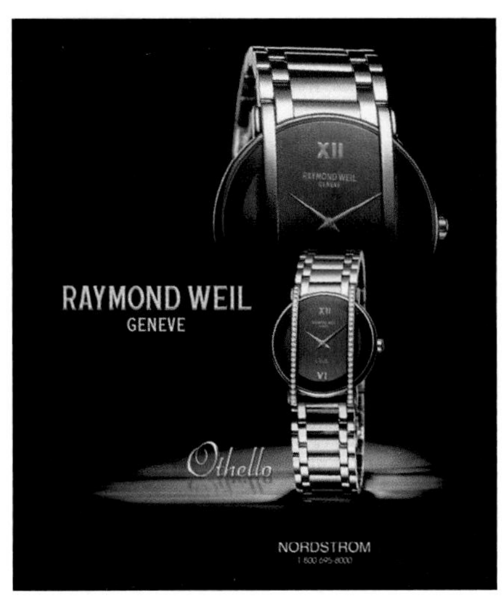

Specialty goods like Raymond Weil watches require distinct marketing programs to reach narrow target markets.

Convenience goods are items, such as toothpaste, that the consumer purchases frequently and with a minimum of shopping effort. *Shopping goods,* such as everyday clothing, are items for which the consumer compares several alternatives on criteria, such as price, quality, or style. *Specialty goods* are items, such as Raymond Weil watches, that a consumer makes a special effort to search out and buy. *Unsought goods* are items that the consumer either does not know about or knows about but does not initially want. Figure 10–2 shows how the classification of a consumer product into one of these four types results in different aspects of the marketing mix being stressed. Consumers display different degrees of brand loyalty and amounts of shopping effort for products in each of the four classes.

The manner in which a consumer good is classified depends on the individual. One person may view a camera as a shopping good and visit several stores before deciding on a brand, whereas a friend may view cameras as a specialty good and will only buy a Nikon.

Classifying Business Goods

A major characteristic of business goods is that their sales are often the result of *derived demand;* that is, sales of industrial products frequently result, or are derived, from the sale of consumer goods. For example, if consumer demand for Ford cars (a consumer product) increases, the company may increase its demand for paint spraying equipment (a business product). Business goods may be classified as production or support goods.

FIGURE 10–2
Classification of consumer goods

BASIS OF COMPARISON	TYPE OF CONSUMER GOOD: CONVENIENCE	SHOPPING	SPECIALTY	UNSOUGHT
Product	Toothpaste, cake mix, handsoap, laundry detergent	Cameras, TVs, briefcases, clothing	Rolls-Royce cars, Rolex watches	Burial insurance, thesaurus
Price	Relatively inexpensive	Fairly expensive	Usually very expensive	Varies
Place (distribution)	Widespread; many outlets	Large number of selective outlets	Very limited	Often limited
Promotion	Price, availability, and awareness stressed	Differentiation from competitors stressed	Uniqueness of brand and status stressed	Awareness is essential
Brand loyalty of consumers	Aware of brand but will accept substitutes	Prefer specific brands but will accept substitutes	Very brand loyal; will not accept substitutes	Will accept substitutes
Purchase behavior of consumers	Frequent purchases; little time and effort spent shopping	Infrequent purchases; needs much comparison shopping time	Infrequent purchases; needs extensive search and decision time	Very infrequent purchases; some comparison shopping

Production Goods Items used in the manufacturing process that become part of the final product are *production goods*. These include raw materials, such as grain or lumber, or component parts, such as door hinges used by Ford in its car doors.

Support Goods The second class of business goods is *support goods,* which are items used to assist in producing other goods and services. Support goods include installations, accessory equipment, supplies, and services.

- *Installations* consist of buildings and fixed equipment. Industrial buyers purchase these through sales representatives, who often submit competitive bids.
- *Accessory equipment* includes tools and office equipment and is usually purchased in small-order sizes by buyers. So sellers of industrial accessories often use distributors to reach directly a large number of buyers.
- *Supplies* are similar to consumer convenience goods and consist of products such as stationery, paper clips, and brooms. These are purchased with little effort, using the straight rebuy decision sequence discussed in Chapter 6.
- *Services* are intangible activities to assist the industrial buyer. This category can include maintenance and repair services and advisory services such as tax or legal counsel, where the seller's reputation is critical.

Classifying Services

Services can be classified in several ways, according to whether (1) they are delivered by people or equipment, (2) they are profit or nonprofit, or (3) they are government sponsored.

Delivery by People or Equipment In today's marketplace, services delivered by people include professional services like those offered by physicians or attorneys. Skilled labor is required to offer services such as Sears appliance repair. Unskilled labor such as that used by Brinks store-security forces is also a service provided by people.

Equipment-based services do not have the marketing concerns of inconsistency because people are not involved directly in providing the service. People can receive electricity from utilities or use Schwab's online stock trading service without interacting directly with any service employees.[4]

Profit or Nonprofit Organizations Many organizations involved in services also distinguish themselves by their tax status as profit or nonprofit organizations. In contrast to *profit organizations, nonprofit organizations'* excesses in revenue over expenses are not taxed or distributed to shareholders but go back into the organization's treasury to allow continuation of the service.

The American Red Cross, United Way, Outward Bound, and the University of Florida are nonprofit organizations. Historically, misconceptions have limited the use of marketing practices by such organizations.[5] This is now changing for many nonprofit organizations such as hospitals, universities, and museums. For example, the Girl Scouts of America adopted a marketing orientation that reversed its declining membership trend and attracted more than 2.7 million young girls to become Girl Scouts.[6] The 1.1 million nonprofit organizations in the United States now generate 7 percent of the gross domestic product.[7]

Government Sponsored A third way to classify services is based on whether they are government sponsored. Although there is no direct ownership and they are nonprofit organizations, governments at the federal, state, and local levels provide a broad range of services. The United States Postal Service, for example, has adopted many marketing activities. Its "Easy Come. Easy Go" campaign is designed to change its image of a huge bureaucracy, to focus its efforts on customer satisfaction, and to allow it to compete with UPS, FedEx, foreign postal services, and electronic communication technologies.

Concept Check

1. Explain the difference between product mix and product line.
2. What are the four main types of consumer goods?
3. What are three ways to classify services?

NEW PRODUCTS AND WHY THEY SUCCEED OR FAIL

New products are the lifeblood of a company and keep it growing, but the financial risks can be large. Before discussing how new products reach the market, we'll begin by looking at *what* a new product is.

What Is a New Product?

The term *new* is difficult to define. Was Sony's PlayStation 2 *new* when there was a PlayStation 1? Was Microsoft's Xbox *new* when Microsoft wasn't previously a video console manufacturer? What does *new* mean for new-product marketing?

The answer is, it depends. *New* can refer to a product being *functionally* different than existing products. However, the U.S. Federal Trade Commission advises that the term *new* be limited to use with a product only up to six months after it enters regular distribution (whatever *that* is). Overlapping with these views is the company idea that a new product is simply anything different. That difference could be as little as shrinking Apple's iPod to result in its "iPod nano" or as significant as introducing a truly revolutionary product like the first Apple computer in 1976.

Once again, marketing's focus is on the customer: Newness from the point of view of consumers is what counts most. Marketers often classify new products according to the degree of learning required by a consumer in order to use the product properly. Figure 10–3 on the next page summarizes the three categories.

With *continuous innovation,* no new behaviors must be learned to use these products. In marketing its Greptile Grip golf glove, 3M communicates the message that the glove can help users improve their game. Clearly, 3M is marketing a continuous innovation *not* requiring new learned behaviors. So effective marketing here depends

As you read the discussion about what *new* means in new-product development, think about how it affects the marketing strategies of Sony and Microsoft in their *new* video-game launches.

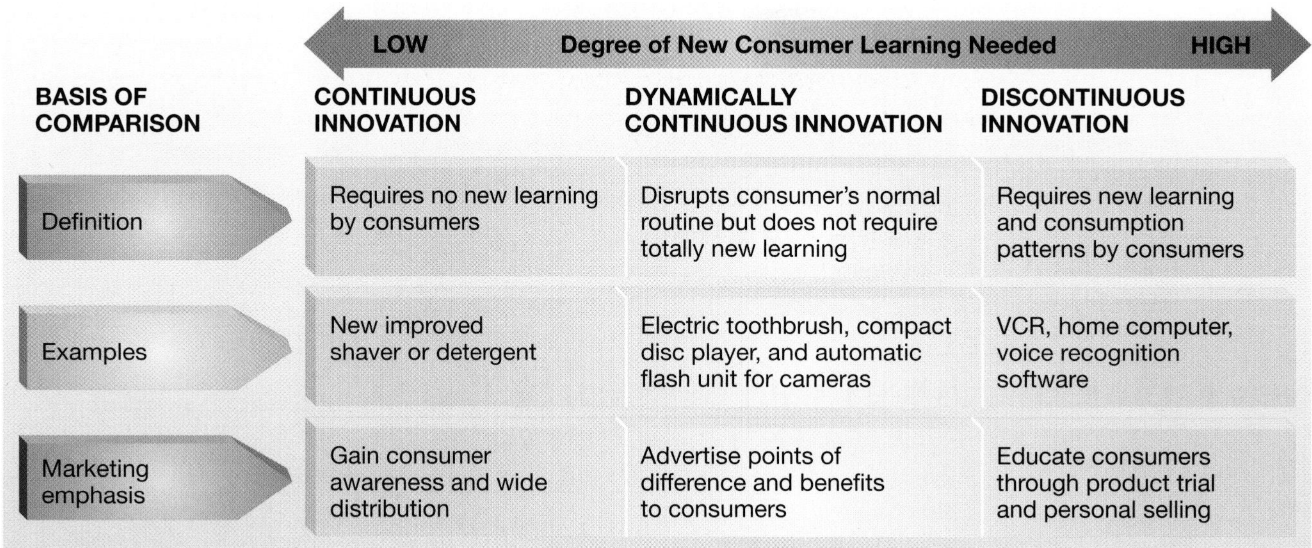

BASIS OF COMPARISON	CONTINUOUS INNOVATION	DYNAMICALLY CONTINUOUS INNOVATION	DISCONTINUOUS INNOVATION
	LOW ← Degree of New Consumer Learning Needed		→ HIGH
Definition	Requires no new learning by consumers	Disrupts consumer's normal routine but does not require totally new learning	Requires new learning and consumption patterns by consumers
Examples	New improved shaver or detergent	Electric toothbrush, compact disc player, and automatic flash unit for cameras	VCR, home computer, voice recognition software
Marketing emphasis	Gain consumer awareness and wide distribution	Advertise points of difference and benefits to consumers	Educate consumers through product trial and personal selling

FIGURE 10–3
Product "newness," as defined by the degree of consumer learning needed to use the product

on generating awareness and having strong distribution in appropriate outlets, not completely reeducating customers.

With *dynamically continuous innovation,* only minor changes in behavior are required to use these new products. An example is built-in, fold-down child seats such as those available in Chrysler minivans. Built-in car seats for children require only minor education and changes in behavior, so the marketing strategy is to educate prospective buyers on their benefits, advantages, and proper use.

A *discontinuous innovation* involves making the consumer learn entirely new consumption patterns in order to use the product. After decades of research, IBM introduced its ViaVoice speech recognition software for which you speak into a microphone connected to your computer and watch your words appear on the screen. IBM's risk in introducing this discontinuous innovation is that consumers must learn new behaviors in producing their word-processed memos and reports. Marketing discontinuous innovations involves heavy expenses in gaining initial consumer awareness and then educating consumers on the proper use of the new product.

Why Products Succeed or Fail

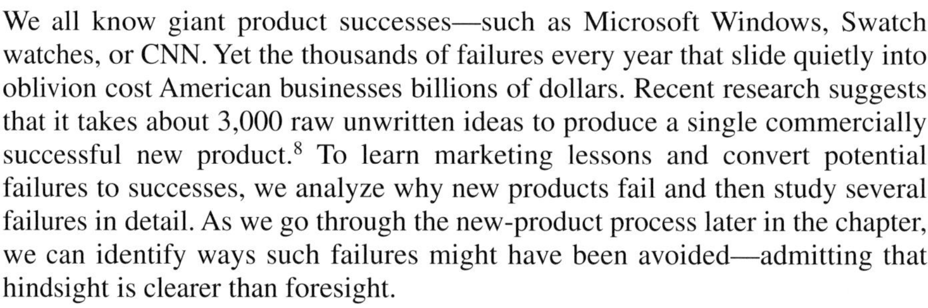

We all know giant product successes—such as Microsoft Windows, Swatch watches, or CNN. Yet the thousands of failures every year that slide quietly into oblivion cost American businesses billions of dollars. Recent research suggests that it takes about 3,000 raw unwritten ideas to produce a single commercially successful new product.[8] To learn marketing lessons and convert potential failures to successes, we analyze why new products fail and then study several failures in detail. As we go through the new-product process later in the chapter, we can identify ways such failures might have been avoided—admitting that hindsight is clearer than foresight.

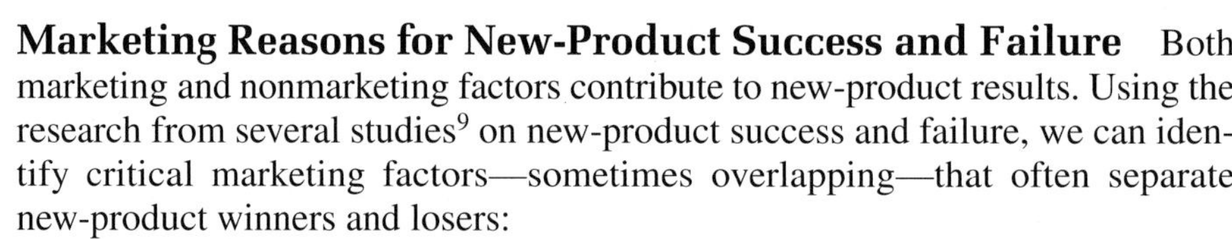

Marketing Reasons for New-Product Success and Failure Both marketing and nonmarketing factors contribute to new-product results. Using the research from several studies[9] on new-product success and failure, we can identify critical marketing factors—sometimes overlapping—that often separate new-product winners and losers:

1. *Insignificant point of difference.* A distinctive point of difference is essential for a new product to defeat competitive ones—through having superior characteristics that deliver unique benefits to the user. In the mid-1990s, General Mills introduced Fingos, a sweetened cereal flake about the size

MARKETING NEWSNET

When Less Is More—How Reducing the Number of Features Can Open Up Huge Markets

New products! To invent them the natural thing is to add more features, new technologies, more glitz. Many new-product successes described in the chapter do just that.

But huge new markets can open up if firms move the opposite direction by taking features away and simplifying the product. Here are some less-is-more new-product breakthroughs that revolutionized national or global markets:

1. *Canon's tabletop copiers.* Canon found it couldn't sell its little copiers to big companies, which were happy with their large Xerox machines. So Canon sold its little machines to little companies with limited copying needs by the zillions.
2. *Palm Computing's PalmPilot PDA.* Apple Computer's Newton personal digital assistant (PDA) was a great idea but was too complicated for users. Enter: PalmPilot inventors Donna Dubinsky and Jeff Hawkins, who deleted features to achieve the market breakthrough.
3. *Intuit's QuickBooks accounting software.* Competitors offered complex accounting software containing every feature professional accountants might possibly want. Intuit then introduced QuickBooks, a smaller, cheaper program with less functionality that won 70 percent of the huge market for small-business accounting software within two years.
4. *Swatch watches.* In 1983, a slim plastic watch with only 51 components appeared on the global market. That simplicity—plus top quality, affordable price, and creative designs—is the reason that more than 250 million Swatch watches have been sold.

Sometimes much less is much, much more!

One surprise: Innovation research shows that firms using disruptive innovation and creating newness by simplifying the product are often *not* the industry leaders selling the more sophisticated high-end products with more features.

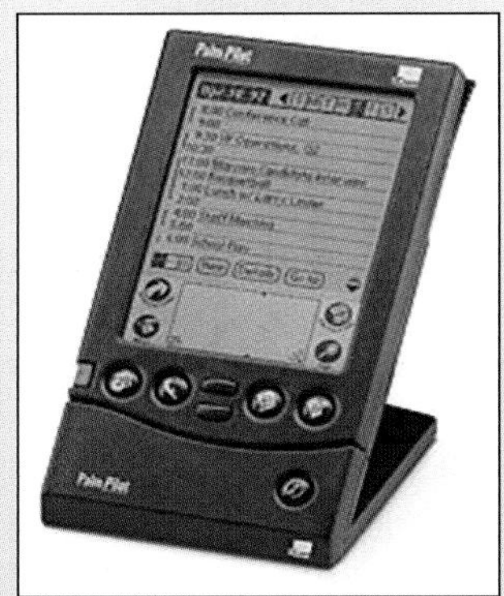

of a corn chip. Consumers were supposed to snack on them dry, but they didn't.[10] The point of difference was not important enough to get consumers to give up eating competing snacks such as popcorn, potato chips, or Cheerios from the box late at night.

2. *Incomplete market and product definition before product development starts.* Ideally, a new product needs a precise *protocol,* a statement that, before product development begins, identifies: (1) a well-defined target market; (2) specific customers' needs, wants, and preferences; and (3) what the product will be and do. Without this precision, loads of money disappear as research and development (R&D) tries to design a vague product for a phantom market. Apple Computer's hand-sized Newton personal digital assistant (PDA) fizzled badly because no clear protocol existed and the device became too complicated.
3. *Too little market attractiveness.* Market attractiveness refers to the ideal situation every new-product manager looks for: a large target market with high growth and real buyer need. But often, when looking for ideal market niches, the target market is too small and competitive to warrant the R&D, production, and marketing expenses necessary to reach it. In the early 1990s, Kodak discontinued its Ultralife lithium battery with its 10-year shelf life, although the battery was touted as

lasting twice as long as an alkaline battery. Yet the product was only available in the 9-volt size, which accounted for less than 10 percent of the U.S. battery market.

4. *Poor execution of the marketing mix: name, package, price, promotion, distribution.* Coca-Cola thought its Minute Maid Squeeze-Fresh frozen orange juice concentrate in a squeeze bottle was a hit. The idea was that consumers could make one glass of juice at a time, and the concentrate stayed fresh in the refrigerator for over a month. After two test markets, the product was finished. Consumers loved the idea, but the product was messy to use, and the advertising and packaging didn't educate them effectively on how much concentrate to mix.
5. *Poor product quality or sensitivity to customer needs on critical factors.* Overlapping somewhat with point 1, this factor stresses that problems on one or two critical factors can kill the product, even though the general quality is high. For example, the Japanese, like the British, drive on the left side of the road. Until 1996, U.S. carmakers sent Japan few right-drive cars—unlike German carmakers that exported right-drive models in a number of their brands.[11] As described in the Marketing NewsNet "When Less Is More," sometimes large markets can be served by taking features *out* of a product and actually making it simpler.[12]
6. *Bad timing.* The product is introduced too soon, too late, or at a time when consumer tastes are shifting dramatically. Bad timing gives new-product managers nightmares. IBM, for example, killed several laptop computer prototypes because competitors introduced better, more advanced machines to the marketplace before IBM could get there.
7. *No economical access to buyers.* Grocery products provide an example. Today's mega-supermarkets carry more than 30,000 different SKUs. With more than 33,000 new packaged goods products (food, beverage, health and beauty aids, household, and pet items) introduced in 2003, the fight for exposure is tremendous in terms of costs for advertising, distribution, and shelf space.[13] Because shelf space is judged in terms of sales per square foot, Thirsty Dog! (a zesty beef-flavored, vitamin-enriched, mineral-loaded, lightly carbonated bottled water for your dog) must displace an existing product on the supermarket shelves, a difficult task with the precise measures of revenues per square foot these stores use.

A Look at Some Failures Before reading the next two paragraphs, study the product failures described in Figure 10–4. Then think for several minutes to try to identify which of the seven reasons listed in the text is the most likely explanation for their failure. The two examples are discussed in greater detail below.

FIGURE 10–4
Why did these products fail?

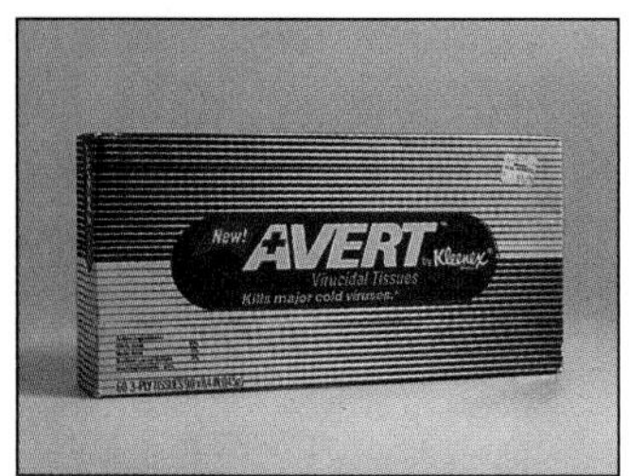

As explained in detail in the text, new products often fail because of one or a combination of seven reasons. Look at the two products described below, and try to identify which reason explains why they failed in the marketplace.

- Kimberly Clark's Avert Virucidal tissues that contained vitamin C derivatives scientifically designed to kill cold and flu germs when users sneezed, coughed, or blew their nose into them.
- OUT! International's Hey! There's A Monster In My Room spray that was designed to rid scary creatures from kids' rooms and had a bubble-gum fragrance.

Compare your insights with those in the text.

Kimberly Clark's Avert Virucidal tissues lasted 10 months in a test market in upstate New York before being pulled from the shelves. People didn't believe the claims and were frightened by the "-cidal" in the name, which they connected to terms like *suicidal*. So the tissue probably failed because of not having a clear point of difference and a bad name, and, hence, bad marketing mix execution—probably reasons 1 and 4 in the list in the text.

OUT! International's Hey! There's A Monster In My Room spray was creative and cute when introduced in 1993. But the name probably kept the kids awake at night more than their fear of the monsters because it suggested the monster was still hiding in the room. Question: Wouldn't calling it the Monster-Buster Spray—the secondary name shown at the bottom of the package—have licked the name problem? It looks like the spray was never really defined well in a protocol (reason 2) and definitely had poor name execution (reason 4).[14]

Simple marketing research on consumers should have revealed the problems. The likelihood of success is improved by paying attention to the early steps of the new-product process described in the next section of the text.

Concept Check

1. From a consumer's viewpoint, what kind of innovation would an improved electric toothbrush be?
2. What does "insignificant point of difference" mean as a reason for new-product failure?

THE NEW-PRODUCT PROCESS

new-product process
Sequence of activities a firm uses to identify business opportunities and convert them into salable goods or services

Companies such as General Electric, Sony, and 3M take a specific sequence of steps before their products are ready for market. Figure 10–5 shows the seven stages of the **new-product process**, the stages a firm goes through to identify business opportunities and convert them to a salable good or service. This sequence begins with new-product strategy development and ends with commercialization.

New-Product Strategy Development

For companies, *new-product strategy development* is the stage of the new-product process that defines the role for a new product in terms of the firm's overall corporate objectives. This step in the new-product process has been added by many companies recently to provide a needed focus for ideas and concepts developed in later stages.

FIGURE 10–5
Stages in the new-product process

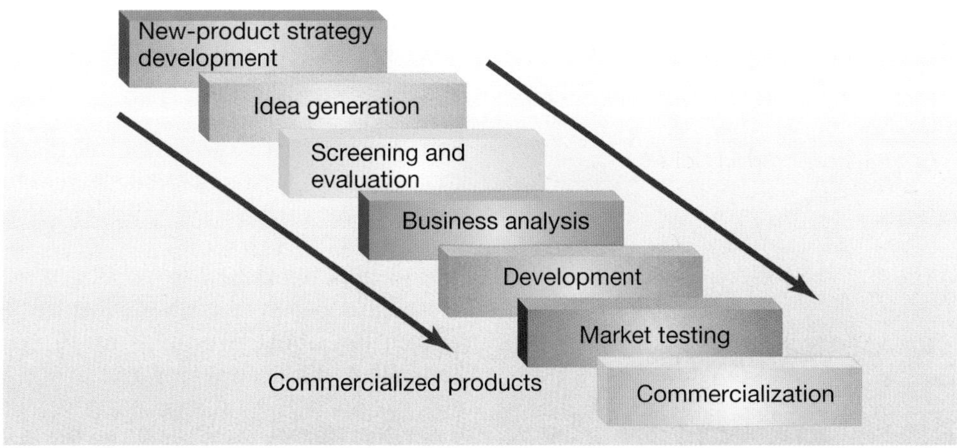

Objectives of the Stage: Identify Markets and Strategic Roles During this new-product strategy development stage the company uses the environmental scanning process described in Chapter 3 to identify trends that pose either opportunities or threats. Relevant company strengths and weaknesses are also identified. The outcome of new-product strategy development is not only new-product ideas but also identifying markets for which new products will be developed and strategic roles new products might serve.

3M: Cross-Functional Teams and Six Sigma When James McNerney left General Electric to become chairman and CEO of 3M in 2001, he soon made a major discovery: 3M's legendary success using its vaunted labs and scientists to turn out commercial hits had bogged down. His immediate actions were to refocus 3M's research and development efforts on technologies that would result in commercially successful products and getting 3M scientists to communicate earlier in the new-product sequence with its marketing and manufacturing people to focus 3M's lab work better.

One key to success in new-product development is 3M's use of *cross-functional teams,* a small number of people from different departments in an organization who are mutually accountable to a common set of performance goals. Today in 3M, these teams are especially important so that individuals from R&D, marketing, sales, and manufacturing can simultaneously work together to focus on new product and market opportunities. Important today in 3M's cross-functional teams is *Six Sigma,* a means to "delight the customer" by achieving quality through a highly disciplined process to focus on developing and delivering near-perfect products and services.[15]

Idea Generation

The stage of the new-product process that involves developing a pool of concepts as candidates for new products, or *idea generation,* must build on the previous stage's results. New-product ideas are generated by customers, suppliers, employees, basic R&D, and competitors.

Customer and Supplier Suggestions Companies often talk to customers and suppliers to discover new-product opportunities. Whirlpool, trying to reduce costs by cutting the number of different product platforms in half, got ideas from customers on ways to standardize components.[16] Business researchers now emphasize that firms must actively involve customers and suppliers in the product development process.[17] This often means focusing on what the new product will actually *do* for them rather than simply *what they want.*[18]

A. G. Lafley, the chief executive officer of Procter & Gamble (P&G), gives his executives a *revolutionary* thought: "Look outside the company for solutions to problems, rather than insisting P&G knows best." An example from his days running P&G's laundry detergent business: While consumers said P&G's laundry boxes were "easy to open," cameras they agreed to have installed in their laundry rooms showed they were opening the boxes with *screwdrivers.* His fix: Redesign the laundry boxes so they are easy to open![19]

Would women *really* help design this car? For how Volvo said yes, see the text.

Employee and Co-Worker Suggestions Employees may be encouraged to suggest new-product ideas through suggestion boxes or contests. The idea for Nature Valley Granola Bars from General Mills came when one of its marketing managers observed co-workers bringing granola to work in plastic bags.

As described at the start of Chapter 5, auto industry studies show that women buy about two-thirds of all vehicles and also influence about 85 percent of all sales. However, many auto manufacturers get ideas on new-car features by doing marketing research on gear-head guys who love cars. That's *exactly opposite* to what Volvo did recently in trying to bridge the gender gap. Volvo first obtained ideas on new-car features from all-female focus groups drawn from its Swedish workforce. It then named a five-woman team of Volvo managers to design a "concept car"—what the auto industry uses to test new designs, technical innovations, and consumer reactions. One innovative feature is automatically opening doors so that the driver presses a button on the car key and the gull-wing doors pop open, the chassis rises a few inches, and the steering wheel pulls in to make sliding into the driver's seat easier.[20]

Research and Development Breakthroughs Another source of new products is a firm's basic research, but the costs can be huge. Sony is a world leader in new-product development in electronics. Sony's technical breakthroughs have made it a legend in the electronics industry, popularizing VCRs, the Walkman, and—coming into your future?—flat-panel Organic Electroluminescence (OEL) monitors the thickness of a credit card providing brighter images on 30-inch screens.

Not all R&D labs have Sony's genius for moving electronic breakthroughs into the marketplace. Take Xerox Corporation's Palo Alto Research Center (PARC). In maybe the greatest electronic fumble of all time, by 1979 PARC had what's in your computer system now: graphical user interfaces, mice, windows and pull-down menus, laser printers, and distributed computing. Concerned with aggressive competition from Japan in its core photocopier business, Xerox didn't even bother to patent these breakthroughs. Apple Computer's Steven Jobs visited PARC in 1979, adapted many of the ideas for the Macintosh, and the rest is history.

Professional R&D laboratories also provide new-product ideas. Labs at Arthur D. Little helped put the crunch in Cap'n Crunch cereal and the flavor in Carnation Instant Breakfast.

Competitive Products New-product ideas can also be found by analyzing the competition. In 2000, your cell phone was a pretty simple electronic device—it was a wireless means of making telephone calls easily. In what some call the "convergence of digital devices," your cell phone today probably has many more uses. Like being a handheld organizer, or a digital camera, or a computer with keyboard and screen for Internet access, or an MP3 or videogame player, or all of the above. The result is that electronic device manufacturers that used to offer just one of these features in their products are now looking at these from competitors in completely different electronic industries to develop their own next generation of products.[21]

Screening and Evaluation

Screening and evaluation is the stage of the new-product process that involves internal and external evaluations of the new-product ideas to eliminate those that warrant no further effort.

Snacks with no trans fats? To see how Frito-Lay uses consumer ideas, read the text.

Internal Approach Internally, the firm evaluates the technical difficulty of the proposal and whether the idea meets the objectives defined in the new-product strategy development step. In the 1990s, Penn Racquet Sports, the largest U.S. producer of tennis balls, faced flat sales because of a decade-long lull in recreational tennis. What to do? Penn Racquet employees observed that many used tennis balls were given as a toy to the family dog. So the company designed and introduced R. P. Fetchem—a dye-free "natural felt fetch toy" that looks remarkably like . . . a tennis ball![22]

External Approach Concept tests are external evaluations that consist of preliminary testing of the new-product idea (rather than the actual product) with consumers. Generally, these tests are more useful with minor modifications of existing products than with really new, innovative products not familiar to consumers.[23] Concept tests usually rely on written descriptions of the product but may be augmented with sketches, mockups, or promotional literature. Several key questions are asked during concept testing: How does the customer perceive the product? Who would use it? How would it be used?

Frito-Lay spent a year interviewing 10,000 consumers about the concept of a multigrain snack chip before introducing its highly successful Sun Chips.

But the consumers are now changing, concerned about healthy snacks, low-carb foods, Atkin's diets, trans fats, and so on—topics few Americans even thought about a couple of years ago. Frito-Lay is now focusing efforts on a critical research issue: healthy snacks that taste good. Frito-Lay's big challenge is that healthy snacks taste distinctly . . . uh . . . healthy because they lack the salt, fats, and sugars that give the taste that is the reason most Americans eat them.

So Frito-Lay in 2003 launched a line of natural snacks, including such consumer favorites as Ruffles, Tostitos, and Cheetos. In fall 2003, Frito-Lay announced that it cooks these snacks in oils without trans fat, a big benefit for health because research shows trans fats raise the level of LDL, what doctors call the "bad cholesterol." The company was one of the first to put nutrition labels on the front of its snacks that included fat content. Purchase decisions by consumers like you will determine the success of this new line of Frito-Lay healthier snacks.[24]

Concept Check

1. What are the seven stages in the new-product process?
2. What are the main sources of new-product ideas?

Business Analysis

Business analysis involves specifying the features of the product and the marketing strategy needed to commercialize it—that is, bring it to market—and making necessary financial projections. This is the last checkpoint before significant resources are invested in creating a *prototype*—usually, a full-scale operating model of the product.

Assessing the "Business Fit" of the New Product The business analysis stage of new product development really involves assessing the total "business fit" of the proposed new product with the company's mission and objectives—from whether the product can be developed and manufactured economically to the marketing strategy needed to have it succeed in the marketplace.

This process requires not only detailed financial analyses and projections but also assessments of the marketing and product synergies related to the company's existing operations and products. Will the product require a lot of new machinery to produce it or can we utilize unused capacity of existing machines? Will adding the new product cannibalize sales of our existing products or increase revenues by reaching new market segments? Can the new product be protected with a patent or copyright? Financial projections of expected profits require estimates of units to be sold and expected prices per unit, as well as detailed estimates of the costs of R&D, production, and marketing.

Can this biscuit dough be "wrapped around something" to provide a new product from General Mills? For some possible answers, see the text and the Marketing NewsNet.

Big G plus Pillsbury: Finding Synergies, Segments, and Partners Combining General Mills and Pillsbury operations resulted in a firm with more than $10 billion in annual sales. Steve Sanger, CEO of the merged firm, gets excited when he talks about carrying his consumer convenience and "one-handedness" synergies into the Pillsbury product line. So on the drawing boards may be a Pillsbury biscuit or cookie dough "wrapped around something," a new product you might be able to buy soon.

MARKETING NEWSNET Keeping Planning Simple at Big G: "One-Handed" Convenience plus Cover All the Bases

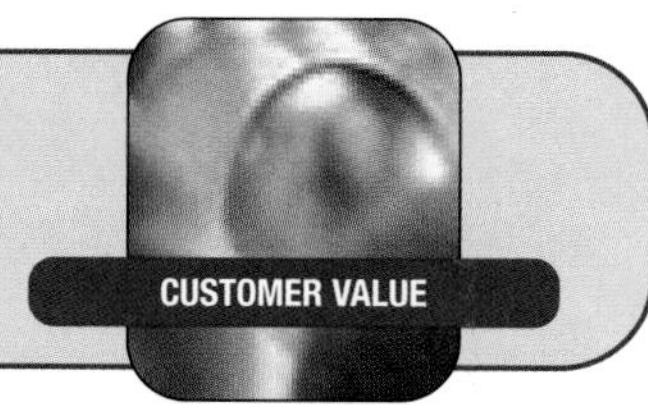

What do you do if you are the chief executive officer of a firm in the low-growth food industry? This is the problem facing Steve Sanger, CEO of General Mills. His remarkable answers: one-handedness and covering all the bases, both built on a focus on today's consumers.

One-Handedness

When Steve Sanger gets proposals for a new food product, he asks one question, "Can we make it 'one-handed'?" This doesn't mean *build* it one-handed but being able to *eat* it one-handed! This lets consumers have a free hand while eating and typing or driving. A Yoplait Nouriche Light yogurt smoothie, and Big G Milk 'n Cereal Bars are examples of Sanger's one-handed strategy.

Cover All the Bases

Big G covers all bases using market and product strategies like those with the brands shown below. This also involves joint ventures with other firms with special expertise, like Nestlé to reach Polish consumers.

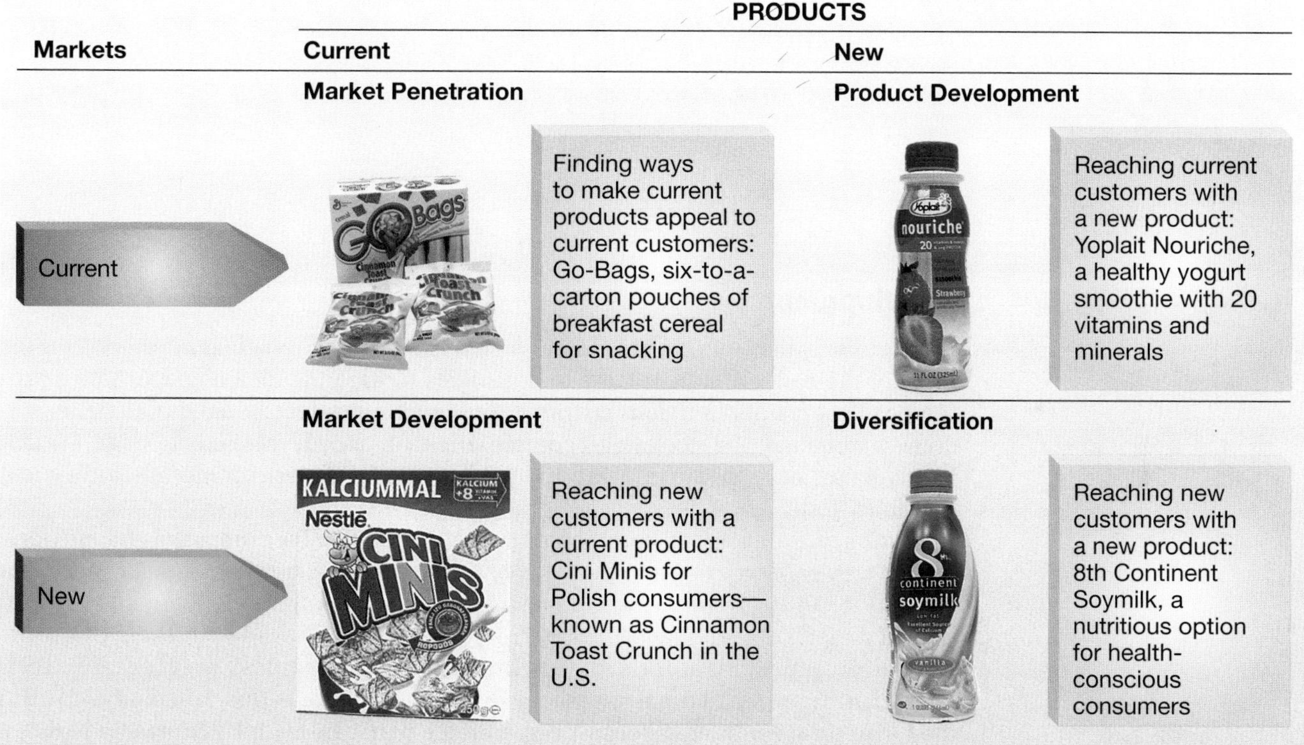

PRODUCTS
Markets
Current
New
Market Penetration
Product Development
Current
Finding ways to make current products appeal to current customers: Go-Bags, six-to-a-carton pouches of breakfast cereal for snacking
Reaching current customers with a new product: Yoplait Nouriche, a healthy yogurt smoothie with 20 vitamins and minerals
Market Development
Diversification
New
Reaching new customers with a current product: Cini Minis for Polish consumers—known as Cinnamon Toast Crunch in the U.S.
Reaching new customers with a new product: 8th Continent Soymilk, a nutritious option for health-conscious consumers
Go Bags
nouriche
KALCIUMMAL
Nestlé
CINI MINIS
continent
soymilk

As shown in the Marketing NewsNet, General Mills—or "Big G," from its cereal logo—has new products and brands targeted at many segments, some large and others only niche segments. With Big G's Go-Bags, Yoplait Nouriche, and Milk 'n Cereal Bars, commuters on the way to work can try "dashboard dining"—eating breakfast with only one hand and without a bowl or spoon.[25]

General Mills is increasing its presence in global and domestic markets through joint ventures and partnering. Its Cereal Partners Worldwide (CPW), a joint venture with Nestlé, now holds 22 percent market share across 75 countries, enabling General Mills food products to reach new segments of international consumers. To exploit innovative new technology, General Mills has a soy joint venture with Du Pont to develop and introduce 8th Continent™ Soymilk in both regular and light versions, giving nutritious new options for breakfast.

ETHICS AND SOCIAL RESPONSIBILITY ALERT

SUVs and Pickups versus Cars—Godzilla Meets a Chimp?

Make car collisions safe. Sound silly? But . . . the problem is death! The high-bumper pickups and sport utility vehicles (SUVs)—termed *light trucks* in the industry—are now involved in about 20 percent of all U.S. highway deaths.

When one of these light trucks, which is often a ton heavier than a car, collides with a car, the car comes off second best. A special problem is that the bumper of the pickup truck or SUV is as much as nine inches higher than the car's bumper, a problem referred to as *compatibility* in the auto industry.

How serious is the problem? Highway data from 2003 show that in a head-on collision between a car and a light truck, the car occupants were 3.3 times more likely to die than those in the light truck. Occupants in a car struck in the side by a light truck are 21 times as likely to be killed than the truck occupants.

What to do? In late 2003, 15 automakers from four countries voluntarily agreed to redesign their light trucks to make their bumper height more compatible with cars. They are also likely to protect car passengers from side impacts from light trucks by making side air bags standard equipment in cars sold in the United States. The new designs will start appearing in 2007, with all vehicles meeting the standards for the 2010 model year. The design changes are expected to save thousands of lives annually.

Are the voluntary agreements from automakers good enough? Or should federal laws be passed? Or insurance companies lobby Congress?

To see how your vehicle measures up on various crash tests, go to the website of the Insurance Institute of Highway Safety (www.hwysafety.org) and click on "Vehicle Ratings."

Development

Product ideas that survive the business analysis proceed to actual *development,* the stage of the new-product process that involves turning the idea on paper into a prototype. This results in a demonstrable, producible product in hand. Outsiders seldom understand the technical complexities of the development stage, which involves not only manufacturing the product but also performing laboratory and consumer tests.

Some new products can be so important and costly that the company is literally betting its very existence on success. In the pharmaceutical industry, no more than one out of every 5,000 to 10,000 new compounds developed in the labs emerges as an approved drug.[26]

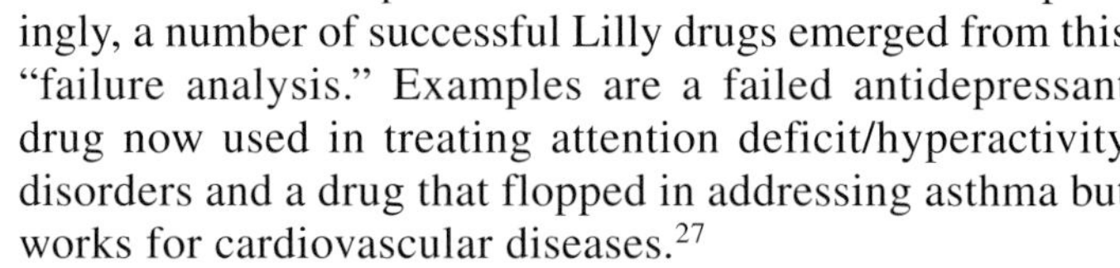

Pharmaceutical giant Eli Lilly has initiated "failure parties" to recognize excellent scientific work that unfortunately resulted in products that failed anyway. But the failed drug compound doesn't end with the party. Instead, Lilly usually names a team of doctors and scientists to learn the specific reasons for the failure. Surprisingly, a number of successful Lilly drugs emerged from this "failure analysis." Examples are a failed antidepressant drug now used in treating attention deficit/hyperactivity disorders and a drug that flopped in addressing asthma but works for cardiovascular diseases.[27]

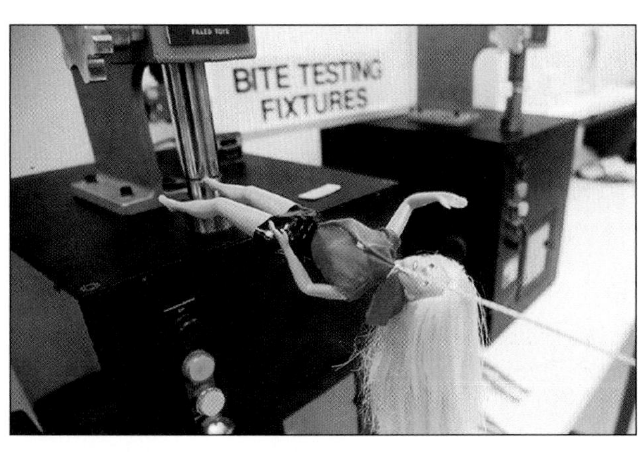

Safety tests are especially critical for when the product isn't used as planned. To make sure seven-year-olds can't bite Barbie's head off and choke, Mattel clamps her foot in steel jaws in a test stand and then pulls on her head with a wire. Similarly, car manufacturers have done extensive safety tests by crashing their cars into concrete walls. As mentioned in the Ethics and Social Responsibility Alert, consumer groups are increasingly concerned about what happens when a pickup truck or sport utility vehicle hits a small car when their bumpers don't line up.[28] Auto industry tests are identifying some feasible, but costly, solutions.

Market Testing

Market testing is the stage of the new-product process that involves exposing actual products to prospective consumers under realistic purchase conditions to see if they will buy. Often a product is developed, tested, refined, and then tested again to get consumer reactions through either test marketing or simulated test markets.

Test Marketing *Test marketing* involves offering a product for sale on a limited basis in a defined area. This test is done to determine whether consumers will actually buy the product and to try different ways of marketing it. Only about a third of the products test marketed do well enough to go on to the next phase. These market tests are usually conducted in cities that are viewed as being representative of U.S. consumers like the six shown in Figure 10–6. Of these cities, Wichita Falls, Texas, most closely matches the U.S. average found in the 2000 Census. Other criteria used in selecting test market cities are brand purchase patterns resembling the U.S. average, small towns far enough from big markets to allow low-cost advertising purchases, cable systems to deliver different ads to different homes, and tracking systems like those of AC Nielsen to measure sales resulting from different advertising campaigns.[29]

This gives the company an indication of potential sales volume and market share in the test area. Market tests are also used to check other elements of the marketing mix besides the product itself such as price, level of advertising support, and distribution. These market tests also are time consuming and expensive because production lines as well as promotion and sales programs must be set up. A concern: Costs can run several million dollars and also reveal plans to competitors.

When Test Markets Don't Work Test marketing is a valuable step in the new-product process, but not all products can use it. Testing a service beyond the concept level is very difficult because the service is intangible and consumers often can't see what they are buying. For example, how could Google easily have test marketed the mid-2004 launch of its Gmail, an e-mail service users get free in exchange for accepting ads with its Gmail?[30]

Similarly, test markets for expensive consumer products such as cars or VCRs or costly industrial products such as jet engines or computers are impractical. For these products consumer reactions to mockup designs or one-of-a-kind prototypes are all that is feasible.

FIGURE 10–6
Six important U.S. test markets and the "demographics winner": Wichita Falls, Texas, metropolitan statistical area

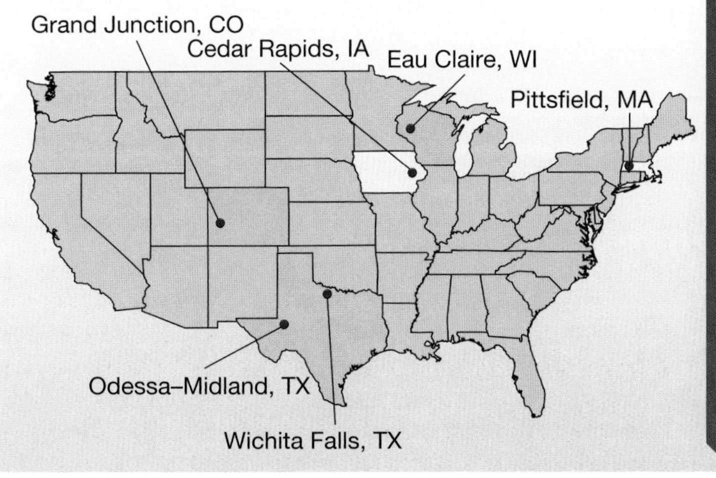

Demographic Characteristic	USA	Wichita Falls, TX
2000 population	281.4 mil.	140,518
Median age (years)	35.3	33.6
% of family households with children under 18	32.8%	33.8%
% Hispanic or Latino of any race	12.5%	11.8%
% African American	12.3%	9.6%
% Asian American	3.6%	1.7%
% Native American	1.5%	1.7%

Commercialization

Finally, the product is brought to the point of *commercialization*—the stage of the new-product process that involves positioning and launching a new product in full-scale production and sales. Companies proceed very carefully at the commercialization stage because this is the most expensive stage for most new products, especially consumer products. If competitors introduce a product that leapfrogs the firm's own new product or if cannibalization of its own existing products look significant, the firm may halt the new-product launch permanently.[31] Large companies use *regional rollouts,* introducing the product sequentially into geographical areas of the United States to allow production levels and marketing activities to build up gradually to minimize the risk of new-product failure. Grocery product manufacturers and some telephone service providers are two examples of firms that use this strategy.

Figure 10–7 identifies the purpose of each stage of the new-product process and the kinds of marketing information and methods used. The third column of the figure also suggests information that might help avoid some new-product failures. Although using the new-product process does not guarantee successful products, it does increase a firm's success rate.

Burger King's French Fries: The Complexities of Commercialization Burger King's "improved french fries" are an example of what can go wrong at the commercialization stage. In the fast-food industry, McDonald's french

FIGURE 10–7
Marketing information and methods used in the new-product process

STAGE OF PROCESS	PURPOSE OF STAGE	MARKETING INFORMATION AND METHODS USED
New-product strategy development	Identify new-product niches to reach in light of company objectives	Company objectives; assessment of firm's current strengths and weaknesses in terms of market and product
Idea generation	Develop concepts for possible products	Ideas from employees and co-workers, consumers, R&D, and competitors; methods of brainstorming and focus groups
Screening and evaluation	Separate good product ideas from bad ones inexpensively	Screening criteria, concept tests, and weighted point systems
Business analysis	Identify the product's features and its marketing strategy, and make financial projections	Product's key features, anticipated marketing mix strategy; economic, marketing, production, legal, and profitability analyses
Development	Create the prototype product, and test it in the laboratory and on consumers	Laboratory and consumer tests on product prototypes
Market testing	Test product and marketing strategy in the marketplace on a limited scale	Test markets, simulated test markets (STMs)
Commercialization	Position and offer product in the marketplace	Perceptual maps, product positioning, regional rollouts

Commercializing a new french fry: To learn how Burger King's improved french fries confronted McDonald's fries, see the text.

fries are the gold standard against which all other fries are measured. In 1996, Burger King decided to take on McDonald's fries and spent millions of R&D dollars developing a starch-coated fry designed to retain heat longer and add crunch.

A 100-person team set to work and developed the starch-coated fry that beat McDonald's fries in taste tests, 57 percent to 35 percent, with 8 percent no opinion. After "certifrying" 300,000 managers and employees on the new frying procedures, the fries were launched in early 1998 with a $70 million marketing budget. The launch turned to disaster. The reason: The new fry proved too complicated to get right day after day in Burger King restaurants, except under ideal conditions.[32]

By summer 2000, Burger King realized something had to be done. Solution: Launch a "new," coated fry in early 2001 that is easier for its kitchens to prepare. A commercialization stage success? You be the judge.

Winning Strategies in Commercializing Services The very intangibility of services means that a marketing strategy that simplifies and clarifies the key points of difference and benefits to consumers can result in huge success. Two examples:

- Airline passengers on JetBlue know they will get no meals, no round-trip fares, and no first-class seating but that they are paying the same cheap ticket price as everyone else—no one having a special "deal."
- Customers at Commerce Bank in the Middle Atlantic states are offered only four kinds of checking accounts, but they don't care because the bank positions itself as "the most convenient bank in America." It's open seven days a week, including evenings, and offers free coffee and newspapers.

Effective cross-functional teams at Hewlett-Packard have reduced new-product development times significantly.

How have these strategies worked out? By early 2005, JetBlue had 16 profitable quarters in a row and Commerce Bank's deposits had quintupled in five years.[33]

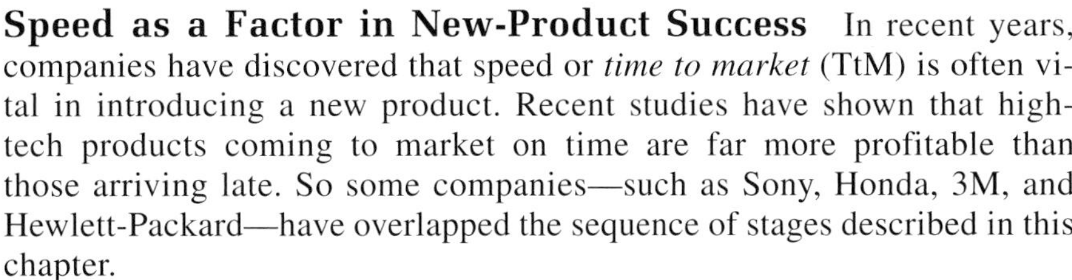

Speed as a Factor in New-Product Success In recent years, companies have discovered that speed or *time to market* (TtM) is often vital in introducing a new product. Recent studies have shown that high-tech products coming to market on time are far more profitable than those arriving late. So some companies—such as Sony, Honda, 3M, and Hewlett-Packard—have overlapped the sequence of stages described in this chapter.

With this approach, termed *parallel development,* cross-functional team members who conduct the simultaneous development of both the product and the production process stay with the product from conception to production. This has enabled Hewlett-Packard to reduce the development time for computer printers from 54 months to 22. In software development, *fast prototyping* uses a "do it, try it, fix it" approach—encouraging continuing improvements even after the initial design. One result: HP introduced 100 new printer products in late 2003.[34]

Concept Check

1. How does the development stage of the new-product process involve testing the product inside and outside the firm?
2. What is a test market?
3. What is commercialization of a new product?

CHAPTER IN REVIEW

1 *Recognize the various terms that pertain to products and services.*
A product is a good, service, or idea consisting of a bundle of tangible and intangible attributes that satisfies consumers and is received in exchange for money or some other unit of value. Firms can offer a range of products, which involve decisions regarding the product item, product line, and product mix.

2 *Identify the ways in which consumer and business goods and services can be classified.*
Products can be classified by type of user and tangibility. By user, the major distinctions are consumer goods, which are products purchased by the ultimate consumer, and business goods, which are products that assist in providing other products for resale. By degree of tangibility, products may be classified as (*a*) nondurable goods, which are consumed in one or a few uses, (*b*) durable goods, which are items that usually last over an extended number of uses, or (*c*) services, which are activities, benefits, or satisfactions offered for sale.

Consumer goods can further be broken down based on the effort involved in the purchase decision process, marketing mix attributes used in the purchase, and the frequency of purchase: (*a*) convenience goods are items that consumers purchase frequently and with a minimum of shopping effort, (*b*) shopping goods are items for which consumers compare several alternatives on selected criteria, (*c*) specialty goods are items that consumers make special efforts to seek out and buy, and (*d*) unsought goods are items that consumers do not either know about or initially want.

Business goods can further be broken down into (*a*) production goods, which are items used in the manufacturing process that become part of the final product, such as raw materials or component parts, and (*b*) support goods, which are items used to assist in producing other goods and services and include installations, accessory equipment, supplies, and services.

Services can be classified according to whether they are provided by people or equipment, in terms of tax status (profit versus not-for-profit), or whether the service is provided by a government agency.

3 *Explain the significance of "newness" in new products and services as it relates to the degree of consumer learning involved.*
From the important perspective of the consumer, "newness" is often seen as the degree of learning that a consumer must engage in to use the product. With a continuous innovation, no new behaviors must be learned. With a dynamically continuous innovation, only minor behavioral changes are needed. With a discontinuous innovation, consumers must learn entirely new consumption patterns.

4 *Describe the factors contributing to a new product's or service's success or failure.*
A new product often succeeds or fails for these marketing reasons: (*a*) insignificant points of difference, (*b*) incomplete market and product definition before product development begins, (*c*) too little market attractiveness, (*d*) poor execution of the marketing mix, (*e*) poor product quality on critical factors, (*f*) bad timing, and (*g*) no economical access to buyers.

5 *Explain the purposes of each step of the new-product process.*
The new-product process consists of seven stages a firm uses to develop a salable good or service: (1) New-product strategy development involves defining the role for the new product within the firm's overall objectives. (2) Idea generation involves developing a pool of concepts from consumers, employees, basic R&D, and competitors to serve as candidates for new products. (3) Screening and evaluation involves evaluating new product ideas to eliminate those that are not feasible from a technical or consumer perspective. (4) Business analysis involves defining the features of the new product, developing the marketing strategy and marketing program to introduce it, and making a financial forecast. (5) Development involves not only producing a prototype product but also testing it in the lab and on consumers to see that it meets the standards set for it. (6) Market testing involves exposing actual products to prospective consumers under realistic purchasing conditions to see if they will buy the product. (7) Commercialization involves positioning and launching a product in full-scale production and sales with a specific marketing program.

FOCUSING ON KEY TERMS

business goods p. 213
consumer goods p. 213
idle production capacity p. 214
new-product process p. 221
product p. 212
product line p. 212
product mix p. 212
services p. 213

DISCUSSION AND APPLICATION QUESTIONS

1 Products can be classified as either consumer or business goods. How would you classify the following products? (*a*) Johnson's baby shampoo, (*b*) a Black & Decker two-speed drill, and (*c*) an arc welder.

2 Are products such as Nature Valley Granola bars and Eddie Bauer hiking boots convenience, shopping, specialty, or unsought goods?

3 Based on your answer to question 2, how would the marketing actions differ for each product and the classification to which you assigned it?

4 In terms of the behavioral effect on consumers, how would a PC, such as an Apple PowerBook, be classified? In light of this classification, what actions would you suggest to the manufacturers of these products to increase their sales in the market?

5 What methods would you suggest to assess the potential commercial success for the following new products? (*a*) a new, improved ketchup, (*b*) a three-dimensional television system that took the company 10 years to develop, and (*c*) a new children's toy on which the company holds a patent.

6 Concept testing is an important step in the new-product process. Outline the concept tests for (*a*) an electrically powered car and (*b*) a new loan payment system for automobiles that is based on a variable interest rate. What are the differences in developing concept tests for products as opposed to services?

GOING ONLINE Jalapeño Soda, Anyone?

Jalapeño soda? Aerosol mustard? Fingos? These are just three of the more than 70,000 products (both successes and failures) on the shelves of the NewProductWorks Showcase in Ann Arbor, Michigan. Visit its new website (www.newproductworks.com). Study the "Hits & Misses" categories such as "We Expect Them to Be Successes," which are those that probably will be commercial successes; "Jury Is Out," products whose future is in doubt; "Failures," which are recent products that have failed miserably; and "Favorite Failures," which are those that cause people to ask "What *were* they thinking?" Pick two of the failed products and try to identify the reasons discussed earlier in the chapter that may have led to their failure. Contrast these failed products with those that are deemed successes to learn why they became "sure-fire winners."

BUILDING YOUR MARKETING PLAN

In fine-tuning the product strategy for your marketing plan, do these two things:

1 Develop a simple two-column table in which (*a*) market segments of potential customers are in the first column and (*b*) the one or two key points of differences of the product to satisfy the segment's needs are in the second column.

2 Look back at Figure 2–3, which describes four alternative market-product strategies to expand sales revenues. Write specific ideas for market and product opportunities for your business in each of the four cells in the figure.

VIDEO CASE 10 3M Greptile Grip Golf Glove: Great Gripping!

"Marketing is not brain surgery," says Dr. George Dierberger, marketing and international manager of 3M's Sports and Leisure Products Project. "We tend to make it a lot more difficult than it is. 3M wins with its technology. We're not in the 'me-too' business and in marketing we've got to remember that."

3M'S MICROREPLICATION TECHNOLOGY AND ITS GREPTILE GOLF GLOVE

3M is a $20 billion global, diversified technology company. Among its well-known brands are Post-it Notes, Scotch tape, Scotch Brite scouring pads, and Nexcare bandages. The key to 3M's marketing successes is its commitment to innovation. For more than a century, 3M's management has given its employees the freedom to try new ideas. This "culture of creativity" has led to the commercialization of more than 50,000 products.

The Sports and Leisure Products Project is a business unit managed by Dierberger and his marketing staff. Recently, Dierberger and his staff changed the conventional thinking about golfing. Using 3M's proprietary "microreplication" technology, and applying it to a golf glove, the new Greptile gripping material consists of thousands of tiny "gripping fingers" sewn into the upper palm and lower fingers of a golf glove. According to Dierberger, "It is the only glove on the market that actively improves a golfer's hold on the club by allowing a more relaxed grip, leading to greater driving distance with less grip pressure, even under wet conditions." Laboratory tests found that the Greptile material offers 610 percent greater gripping power than leather and 340 percent greater than tackified (sticky) grips. The result: On drives, the golf ball travels an average 10.5 feet farther!

Introduced in 2004, the new 3M Greptile Grip golf glove is made primarily of high-quality Cabretta sheep leather to give it a soft feel. Initially, 3M sold the Greptile Grip golf glove through Wal-Mart and other mass merchandisers for a suggested retail price of $11.95 to $15.95. And now it's also being stocked by golf retailers across the country like Golfsmith, Austad's, Golf Galaxy, and Target. The golf glove is available in both men's and women's left hand versions and in small, medium, medium/large, large, and extra-large hand sizes. A right hand version for both genders appeared in 2005. 3M projected first year sales of $1 million in the United States.

THE GOLF MARKET

Several socioeconomic and demographic trends impact the golf glove market favorably. First, the huge baby boomer population (those born between 1946 and 1964) has matured, reaching its prime earning potential. This allows for greater discretionary spending on leisure activities, such as golf. According to the National Golf Foundation (NGF), most spending on golf equipment (clubs, bags, balls, shoes, gloves, etc.) is by consumers 50 and older—today's baby boomers. Second, according to the U.S. Census, the U.S. population has shifted regionally from the East and North to the South and West, where golfing is popular year around due to the temperate weather. Third, the number of U.S. golf courses has been growing, totaling about 16,000 at the end of 2005.

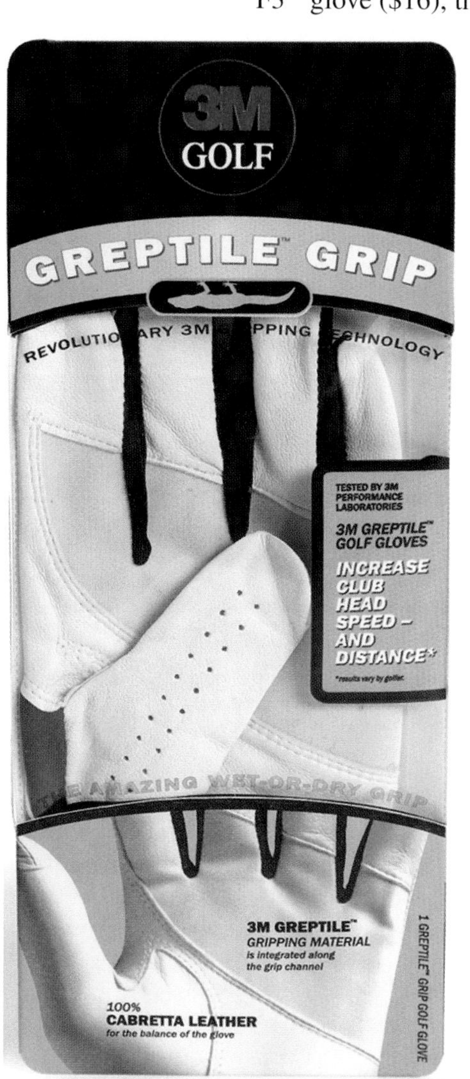

Finally, golf is becoming an increasingly popular leisure activity for all age groups and ethnic backgrounds. According to the NGF, golf participants in the United States totaled 30.3 million in 2004. Female golfers now account for about 25 percent of all golfers while minority participation has increased to over 10 percent. According to the National Sporting Goods Association, sales of golf equipment was $3.2 billion in 2005, an increase of 3 percent from 2004.

THE GOLF GLOVE MARKET

The global market for golf gloves is estimated at $300 million, with the United States at $180 million or 60 percent of worldwide sales. Historically, about 80 percent of golf gloves are sold through public and private on- and off-course golf pro specialty shops, golf superstores, and sporting good superstores. However, mass merchandisers have recently increased their shares due to the typically lower prices offered by these retailers. FootJoy and Titleist, both owned by Acushnet, are the top two golf glove market share leaders. Nike, which recently entered the golf equipment market with Tiger Woods as its spokesperson, has a measurable share of the golf glove market. These golf glove marketers focus on technology and comfort to create points of difference from its competitors, such as the recently introduced FootJoy F3™ glove ($16), the Titleist Players-Tech™ glove ($22), and the Custom Crested Tech Xtreme glove ($22).

3M'S NEW PRODUCT PROCESS

Since about half of 3M's products are less than five years old, the process used by 3M to develop new product innovations is critical to its success and continued growth. Every innovation must meet 3M's new product criteria: (1) be a patentable or trademarked technology; (2) offer a superior value proposition to consumers; and (3) change the basis of competition by achieving a significant point of difference.

When developing a new product innovation such as the 3M Greptile Grip golf glove, 3M uses a rigorous seven-step process: (1) ideas, (2) concept, (3) feasibility, (4) development, (5) scale-up, (6) launch, and (7) post-launch. "But innovation is not a linear path—not just A, then B, then C," says Dierberger. "It's the adjustments you make after you've developed the product that determines your success. And it's learning lessons from testing on real customers to make the final 'tweaks'—changing the price points, improving the benefits statement on the packaging, and sharpening the advertising appeals."

In the case of the 3M Greptile Grip golf glove, countless other examples of these adjustments appeared. Mike Kuhl, marketing coordinator at 3M, points out, "Consumer testing labs said the information on the back of our package was incomplete so we had dozens of golfers hit drives using our glove and competitive gloves to compare driving distance." And says 3M packaging engineer Travis Strom, "Our first glove package 'pillowed'—bulked up—on the shelf, had hard-to-read text, and wasn't appealing to golfers, so we had to redesign it. After all, you only have a few seconds to capture the customer's attention with the package and make a sale."

THE FUTURE OF 3M GOLF AND GREPTILE

In 2005, 3M Golf launched a premium golf glove consisting of the highest quality Cabretta leather and selling for a suggested retail price of $16.95 to $19.95. On the drawing board are some 3M Greptile Grip products that may be in retail stores when you read this: baseball and softball batting gloves and work gloves for the home-improvement market. In 2006, 3M launched versions of its Greptile Grip golf gloves in Japan and Europe, the second and third largest golf markets behind the United States.

Questions

1 What are the characteristics of the target market for the 3M Greptile Grip golf glove?

2 What are the key points of difference of the 3M Greptile Grip golf glove when compared to competitors' products, such as FootJoy and Nike? Substitute products, such as golf grips?

3 How does the Greptile Grip golf glove meet 3M's three criteria for new products?

4 Since 3M has no prior products for the golf market, what special promotion and distribution problems might 3M have?

5 How would you rate the 3M Greptile Grip golf glove on the following reasons for success and failure? (*a*) significant points of difference; (*b*) size and growth of the golf market; (*c*) product quality; (*d*) market timing; (*e*) execution of the marketing mix; (*f*) synergy or fit with 3M's R&D, manufacturing, or marketing capabilities; and (*g*) access to consumers.

PROPER HYDRATION
ISN'T ROCKET SCIENCE.
IT'S CHEMISTRY.

Athletes perform at their best when they replace the essential elements they sweat out.
Water doesn't have them. Gatorade does. Nothing rehydrates, replenishes, and refuels athletes better.

is it in you?

gatorade.com

CHAPTER

11

MANAGING PRODUCTS, SERVICES, AND BRANDS

LEARNING OBJECTIVES

After reading this chapter you should be able to:

1. Explain the product life-cycle concept.
2. Identify ways that marketing executives manage a product's life cycle.
3. Recognize the importance of branding and alternative branding strategies.
4. Describe the role of packaging and labeling in the marketing of a product.
5. Recognize how the four Ps framework applies to services.

GATORADE: AN UNQUENCHABLE THIRST FOR COMPETITION

The thirst for Gatorade is unquenchable. This brand powerhouse has posted yearly sales gains over four decades and commands more than 80 percent of the sports beverage market in the United States.

Like Kleenex in the tissue market and Jello among gelatin desserts, Gatorade has become synonymous with sports beverages. Concocted in 1965 at the University of Florida as a rehydration beverage for the school's football team, the drink was coined "Gatorade" by an opposing team's coach after watching his team lose to the Florida Gators in the Orange Bowl. The name stuck, and a new beverage product class was born.

Stokely–Van Camp Inc. made a deal for the Gatorade formula in 1967 and commercialized the product. The original Gatorade was a liquid with a lemon-lime flavor. An orange flavor was introduced in 1971 and a fruit punch flavor in 1983. Instant Gatorade was launched in 1979. The Quaker Oats Company purchased Stokely–Van Camp in 1983, and Quaker Oats executives quickly grew sales through a variety of means. More flavors were added and multiple package sizes were offered using different containers—glass and plastic bottles and aluminum cans. Regional distribution expanded first including new distribution in convenience stores and supermarkets, followed by vending machines and fountain service. Consistent advertising and promotion effectively conveyed the product's unique benefits and links to athletic competition using popular athletes such as Michael Jordan and Mia Hamm as spokespersons. International opportunities

Gatorade's success is a direct result of masterful product and brand management.

were vigorously pursued. Today, Gatorade is sold in 94 countries in North America, Europe, Latin America, the Middle East, Africa, and Australasia and has become a global brand.

Brand development has been a key factor in Gatorade's success. Gatorade Frost was introduced in 1997, with a "lighter, crisper," taste aimed at expanding the brand's reach beyond participants in organized sports to other usage occasions. Gatorade Fierce with a "bolder" taste was launched in 1999. In the same year, Gatorade entered the bottled-water category with Propel Fitness Water, a lightly flavored water fortified with vitamins. In 2001, the Gatorade Performance Series was introduced, featuring the Gatorade Energy Bar, Gatorade Energy Drink, and Gatorade Nutritional Shake. Brand development continued after PepsiCo, Inc., purchased Quaker Oats and the Gatorade brand in 2001. Gatorade All Stars, specifically designed for teens, and Gatorade Xtremo, developed for Latino consumers with an exotic blend of flavors and a bilingual label, were introduced in 2002. Gatorade X-Factor, with three unique flavors of its own, followed in 2003, bringing the total number of Gatorade flavors to 30. Gatorade Endurance Formula, a specialized sports drink designed to meet the needs of athletes, was launched in 2005. Today, more than 40 years after its creation, Gatorade is a two-plus-billion-dollar growth brand with seemingly unlimited potential.[1]

The marketing of Gatorade illustrates effective product and brand management in a dynamic marketplace. This chapter shows how the actions taken by Gatorade executives are typical of those made by successful marketers.

THE PRODUCT LIFE CYCLE

product life cycle
Stages a new product goes through in the market place: introduction, growth, maturity, and decline

Products, like people, have been viewed as having a life cycle. The concept of the **product life cycle** describes the stages a new product goes through in the marketplace: introduction, growth, maturity, and decline (Figure 11–1). There are two curves shown in this figure, total industry sales dollars (revenue) and total industry profit. The reasons for the changes in each curve and the marketing decisions involved are discussed in the following pages.

Introduction Stage

The introduction stage of the product life cycle occurs when a product is first introduced to its intended target market. During this period, sales grow slowly, and profit is minimal. The lack of profit is often the result of large investment costs in product development, such as the $1 billion spent by Gillette to develop and launch the MACH3 razor shaving system.[2] The marketing objective for the company at this stage is to create consumer awareness and stimulate trial—that first purchase of a product by a consumer.

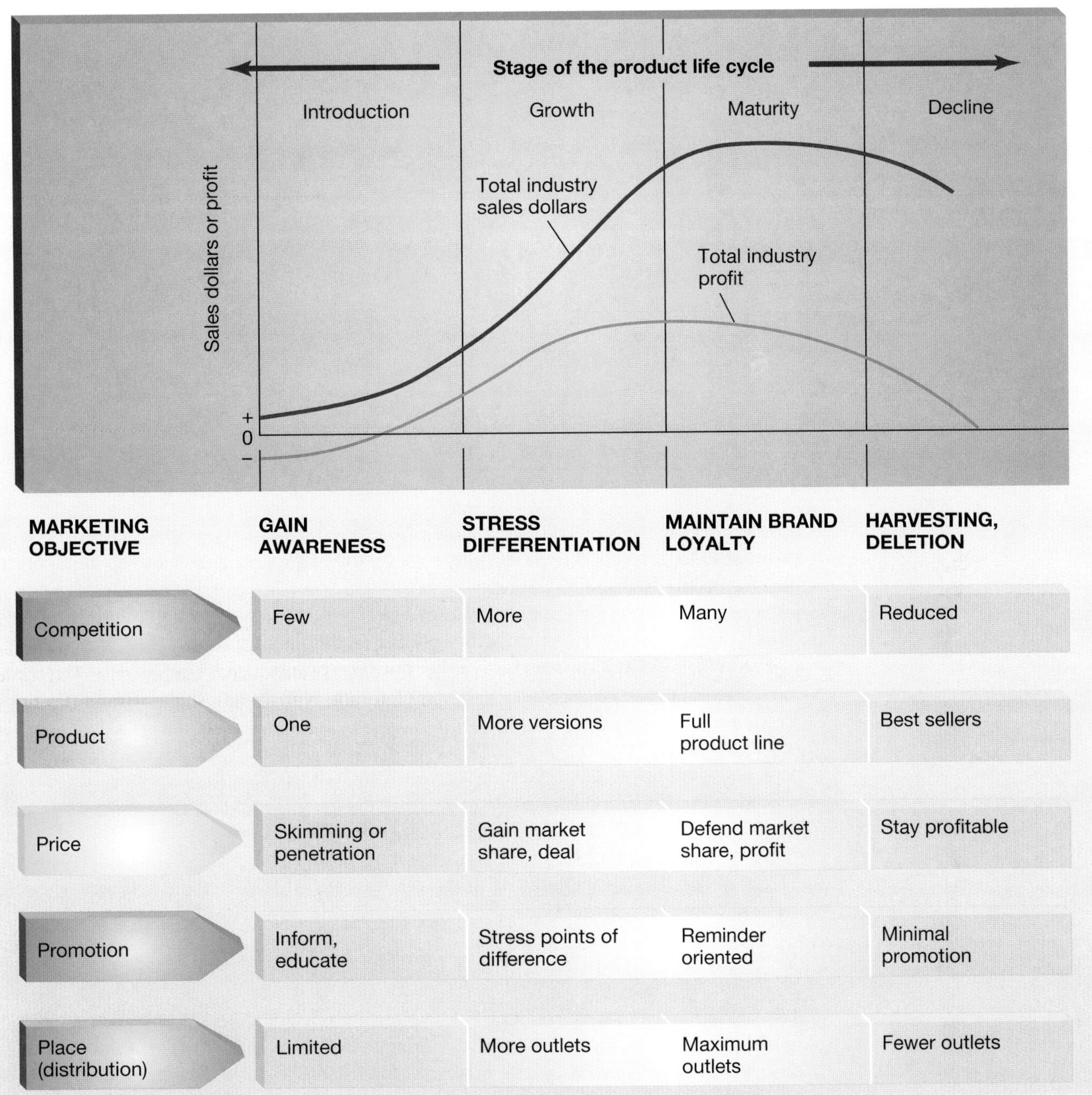

Stage of the product life cycle
Introduction
Growth
Maturity
Decline
Sales dollars or profit
Total industry sales dollars
Total industry profit
+
0
−
MARKETING OBJECTIVE
GAIN AWARENESS
STRESS DIFFERENTIATION
MAINTAIN BRAND LOYALTY
HARVESTING, DELETION
Competition
Few
More
Many
Reduced
Product
One
More versions
Full product line
Best sellers
Price
Skimming or penetration
Gain market share, deal
Defend market share, profit
Stay profitable
Promotion
Inform, educate
Stress points of difference
Reminder oriented
Minimal promotion
Place (distribution)
Limited
More outlets
Maximum outlets
Fewer outlets

FIGURE 11–1
How stages of the product life cycle relate to a firm's marketing objectives and marketing mix actions

Companies often spend heavily on advertising and other promotion tools to build awareness among consumers in the introduction stage. These expenditures are often made to stimulate *primary demand,* or desire for the product class rather than for a specific brand since there are few competitors with the same product. As more competitors introduce their own products and the product progresses along its life cycle, company attention is focused on creating *selective demand,* or demand for a specific brand.

Other marketing mix variables also are important at this stage. Gaining distribution can be a challenge because channel members may be hesitant to carry a new product. Moreover, in this stage a company often restricts the number of variations of the product to ensure control of product quality. For example, Gatorade came in only one flavor. Gillette offered only a single version of the MACH3 razor.

During introduction, pricing can be either high or low. A high initial price may be used as part of a *skimming* strategy to help the company recover the costs of

FIGURE 11–2
Product life cycle for the stand-alone fax machine for business use: 1970–2008

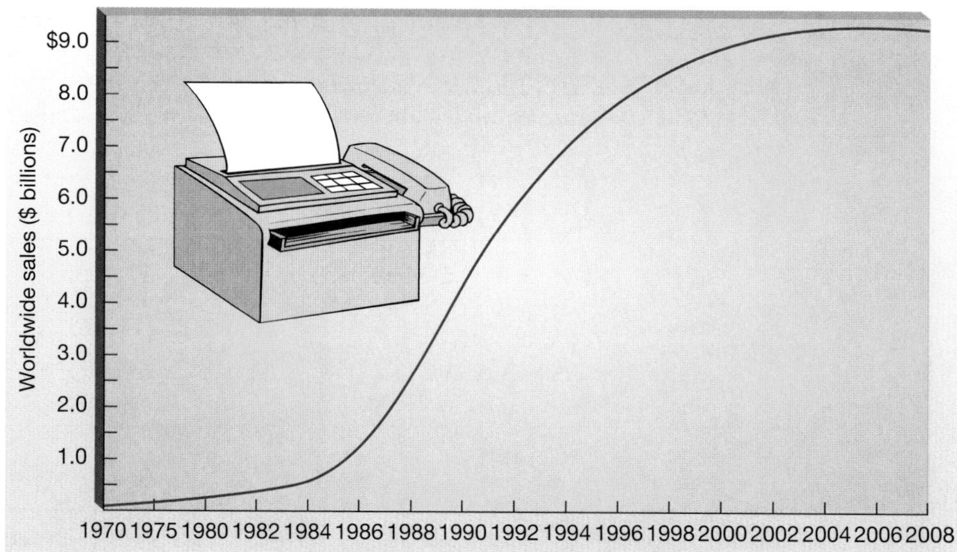

development as well as take advantage of the price insensitivity of early buyers. High prices tend to attract competitors eager to enter the market because they see the opportunity for profit. To discourage competitive entry, a company can price low, referred to as *penetration pricing.* This pricing strategy helps build unit volume, but a company must closely monitor costs. These and other pricing techniques are covered in Chapter 12.

Figure 11–2 charts the stand-alone fax machine product life cycle for business use in the United States from the early 1970s through 2008.[3] As shown, sales grew slowly in the 1970s and early 1980s after Xerox pioneered the first portable fax machine that sent and received documents. Fax machines were originally sold direct to businesses through company salespeople and were premium priced. The average price for a fax machine in 1980 was $12,700. By today's standards, those fax machines were primitive. They contained mechanical parts, not electronic circuitry, and offered few features seen in today's models.

Several product classes are now in the introductory stage of the product life cycle. These include flat-panel high-definition televisions (HDTV) and hybrid (gasoline- and electric-powered) automobiles.

Growth Stage

The second stage of the product life cycle, growth, is characterized by rapid increases in sales. It is in this stage that competitors appear. For example, Figure 11–2 shows the dramatic increase in sales of fax machines from 1986 to 1992. The number of companies selling fax machines was also increasing, from one in the early 1970s to seven manufacturers in 1983, which sold nine brands. By 1992 there were some 25 manufacturers and 60 brands from which to choose.

The result of more competitors and more aggressive pricing is that profit usually peaks during the growth stage. For instance, the average price for a fax machine declined from $3,300 in 1985 to $1,500 in 1992. At this point the emphasis of advertising shifts to stimulating selective demand, in which product benefits are compared with those of competitors' offerings.

Product sales in the growth stage grow at an increasing rate because of new people trying or using the product and a growing proportion of *repeat purchasers*—people who tried the product, were satisfied, and bought again. As a product moves through the life cycle, the ratio of repeat to trial purchasers grows. Failure to obtain repeat purchasers usually means an early death for a product. Durable fax machines meant that replacement purchases were rare; however, it was common for more than one machine to populate a business as their use became more widespread. In 1995, there was one fax machine for every eight people in a business in the United States.

Changes start to appear in the product during the growth stage. To help differentiate a company's brand from its competitors, an improved version or new features are added to the original design, and product proliferation occurs. Changes in fax machines included (1) models with built-in telephones; (2) models that used plain, rather than thermal, paper for copies; (3) models that integrated telex for electronic mail purposes; and (4) models that allowed for secure (confidential) transmissions. For Gatorade, new flavors and package sizes were added during the growth stage.

In the growth stage it is important to gain as much distribution for the product as possible. Early in the fax machine growth stage, only 11 percent of office machine dealers carried this equipment. By the mid-1990s, over 70 percent of these dealers carried fax equipment and distribution was expanded to other stores selling electronic equipment.

Numerous product classes or industries are in the growth stage of the product life cycle. Examples include DVD players and digital cameras.

Maturity Stage

The third stage, maturity, is characterized by a slowing of total industry sales for the product class. Also, weaker competitors begin to leave the market. Most consumers who would buy the product are either repeat purchasers of the item or have tried and abandoned it. Sales increase at a decreasing rate in the maturity stage as fewer new buyers enter the market. Profit declines because there is fierce price competition among many sellers. By 2007, the average price for a fax machine had dropped below $100.

Marketing attention in the maturity stage is often directed toward holding market share through further product differentiation and finding new buyers. Gillette, for example, differentiated its MACH3 razor through new product features specifically designed for women and then launched the Gillette Venus Razor for Women just as the MACH3 razor entered its maturity stage. Fax machine manufacturers developed

Hybrid automobiles made by Honda are in the introductory stage of the product life cycle. Digital cameras are in the growth stage. Each product and company faces unique challenges based on its product life cycle stage.

MARKETING NEWSNET

Will E-Mail Spell Doom for the Familiar Fax?

Technological substitution often causes the decline stage in the product life cycle. Will the Internet and e-mail replace fax machines?

This question has caused heated debates. Even though sales of computers with Internet access are in the growth stage of the product life cycle, fax machine sales continue to grow as well. Industry analysts estimate that there are 1.5 billion e-mail mailboxes worldwide. However, the growth of e-mail has not affected faxing because the two technologies do not directly compete for the same messaging applications.

E-mail is used for text messages and faxing is predominately used for communicating formatted documents by business users. Fax usage is expected to increase through 2007, even though unit sales of fax machines has plateaued on a worldwide basis. Internet technology may eventually replace facsimile technology, but not in the immediate future.

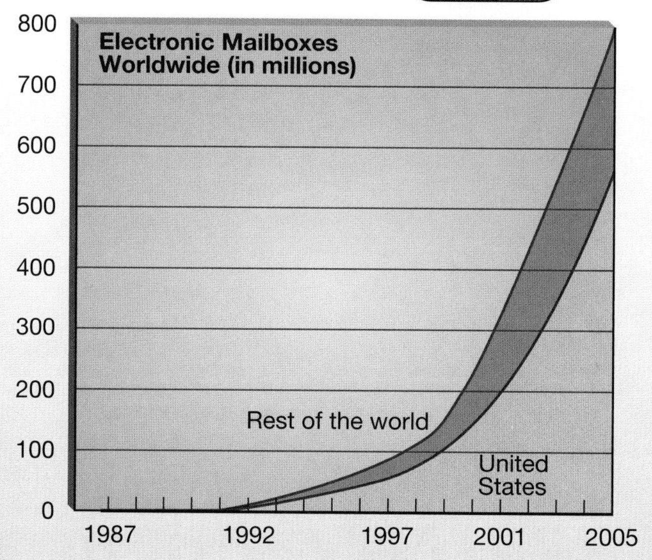

Internet-enabled models and introduced product features suitable for small and home businesses, which today represent a significant portion of industry sales.

Stand-alone fax machines for business use entered the maturity stage in the late 1990s. By 2007, 90 percent of industry sales were captured by five producers (Hewlett-Packard, Matsushita, Lexmark, Brother, and Sharp), reflecting the departure of weak competitors. By late 2007, 100 million stand-alone fax machines for business use were installed throughout the world.

Many product classes and industries are in the maturity stage of their product life cycle. These include soft drinks, automobiles, and conventional TVs.

Decline Stage

The decline stage occurs when sales begin to drop. Frequently, a product enters this stage not because of any wrong strategy on the part of the company but because of environmental changes. Technological innovation often comes before the decline stage as newer technologies replace older ones. The word-processing capability of personal computers pushed typewriters into decline. Compact discs did the same to cassette tapes in the prerecorded music industry. Will Internet technology and e-mail spell doom for fax machines? The accompanying Marketing NewsNet offers one perspective on this question.[4]

A company will follow one of two strategies to handle a declining product: deletion or harvesting.

Deletion Product *deletion,* or dropping the product from the company's product line, is the most drastic strategy. Because a residual core of consumers still consume or use a product even in the decline stage, product elimination decisions are not taken lightly. For example, Gillette still sells its Liquid Paper correction fluid for use with typewriters in the era of word-processing equipment.

Harvesting A second strategy, *harvesting,* is when a company keeps the product but reduces marketing costs. The product continues to be offered to meet customer requests. Coca-Cola, for instance, still offers Tab, its first diet cola, to a small group of die-hard fans. According to Coke's CEO, "It shows you care. We want to make sure those who want Tab, get Tab."[5]

Some Dimensions of the Product Life Cycle

Two important aspects of product life cycles are (1) their length and (2) the shape of their curves.

Length of the Product Life Cycle There is no exact time that a product takes to move through its life cycle. As a rule, consumer products have shorter life cycles than business products. For example, many new consumer food products such as Frito-Lay's Stax potato crisps move from the introduction stage to maturity in 18 months. The availability of mass communication vehicles—such as television and the Internet—informs consumers faster and shortens life cycles. Also, technological change tends to shorten product life cycles as new product innovation replaces existing products. Video game consoles move from the introduction stage to the maturity stage in five years and are then replaced by advanced models. Sony's PlayStation 3, Microsoft's Xbox 360, and Nintendo's Revolution arrived in 2006—on schedule.

Shape of the Product Life Cycle The product life-cycle curve shown in Figure 11–1 is the *generalized life cycle,* but not all products have the same shape to their curve. In fact, there are different life-cycle curves, each type suggesting different marketing strategies. Figure 11–3 shows the shape of life-cycle curves for four different product types: high-learning, low-learning, fashion, and fad products.

A *high-learning product* is one for which significant education of the customer is required and there is an extended introductory period (Figure11–3A). Convection ovens, for example, required a consumer to learn a new way of cooking and alter familiar recipes.

In contrast, for a *low-learning product* sales begin immediately because little learning is required by the consumer, and the benefits of purchase are readily understood (Figure 11–3B). This product often can be easily imitated by competitors, so the marketing strategy is to broaden distribution quickly. In this way, as competitors rapidly enter, most retail outlets already have the first product. It is also important to have the manufacturing

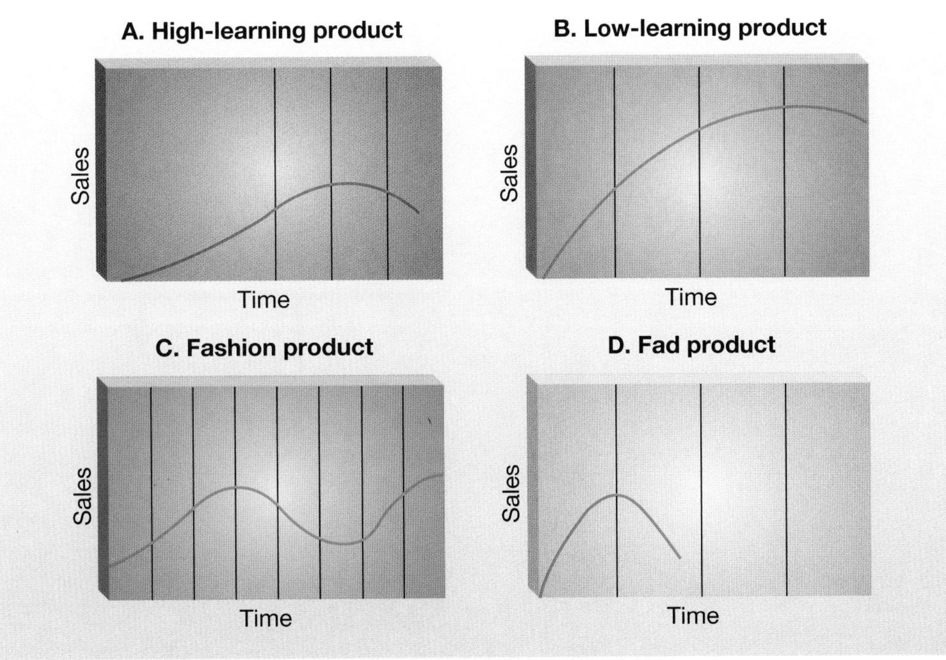

FIGURE 11–3
Alternative product life cycles

capacity to meet demand. An example of a successful low-learning product is Gillette's MACH3 razor. MACH3 recorded $9 billion in worldwide sales in the brief span of five years.[6]

A *fashion product* (Figure 11–3C), such as hemline lengths on skirts or lapel widths on jackets, is introduced, declines, and then seems to return. Life cycles for fashion products most often appear in women's and men's clothing styles. The length of the cycles may be years or decades.

A *fad* experiences rapid sales on introduction and then an equally rapid decline (Figure 11–3D). These products are novelties and have a short life cycle. They include car tattoos sold in southern California and described as the first removable and reusable graphics for automobiles, vinyl dresses, fleece bikinis, and an AstroTurf miniskirt made by Thump, Inc., a Minnesota clothing company.[7]

The Life Cycle and Consumers The life cycle of a product depends on sales to consumers. Not all consumers rush to buy a product in the introductory stage, and the shapes of the life-cycle curves indicate that most sales occur after the product has been on the market for some time. In essence, a product diffuses, or spreads, through the population, a concept called the *diffusion of innovation.*[8]

Some people are attracted to a product early, but others buy it only after they see their friends with the item. Figure 11–4 shows the consumer population divided into five categories of product adopters based on when they adopt, or choose to buy, a new product. Brief profiles accompany each category. For any product to be successful, it must be purchased by innovators and early adopters. This is why manufacturers of new pharmaceuticals try to gain adoption by leading hospitals, clinics, and physicians that are widely respected in the medical field. Once accepted by innovators and early adopters, the adoption of new products moves on to the early majority, late majority, and laggard categories.

Several factors affect whether a consumer will adopt a new product or not. Common reasons for resisting a product in the introduction stage are usage barriers (the product is not compatible with existing habits), value barriers (the product provides no incentive to change), risk barriers (physical, economic, or social), and psychological barriers (cultural differences or image).[9]

Companies attempt to overcome these barriers in numerous ways. They provide warranties, money-back guarantees, extensive usage instructions, demonstrations, and

FIGURE 11–4
Five categories and profiles of product adopters

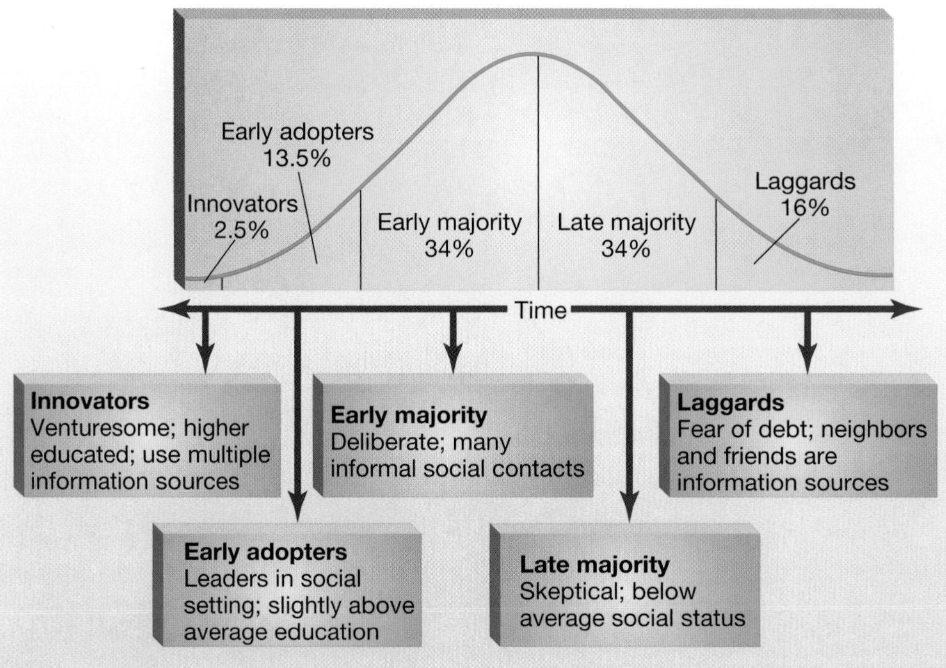

free samples to stimulate initial trial of new products. For example, software developers offer demonstrations downloaded from the Internet. Maybelline allows consumers to browse through the Cover Girl Color Match system on its website to find out how certain makeup products will look. Free samples are one of the most popular means to gain consumer trial. In fact, 71 percent of consumers consider a sample to be the best way to evaluate a new product.[10]

Concept Check

1. Advertising plays a major role in the ____________ stage of the product life cycle, and ____________ plays a major role in maturity.
2. How do high-learning and low-learning products differ?

MANAGING THE PRODUCT LIFE CYCLE

An important task for a firm is to manage its products through the successive stages of their life cycles. Marketers rely on three ways to manage a product through its life cycle: modifying the product, modifying the market, and repositioning the product.

Modifying the Product

Product modification involves altering a product's characteristic, such as its quality, performance, or appearance, to try to increase and extend the product's sales. Harley-Davidson modified its entry-level Sportster line of motorcycles by including smaller hand grips, a lower seat, and an easier-to-pull clutch lever to create a more comfortable ride for first-time motorcycle buyers.[11]

New features, packages, or scents can be used to change a product's characteristics and give the sense of a revised product. Procter & Gamble revamped Pantene shampoo and conditioner with a new vitamin formula and relaunched the brand with a multimillion-dollar advertising and promotion campaign. The result? Pantene, a brand first introduced in the 1940s, became the top-selling shampoo and conditioner in the United States in an industry with more than 1,000 competitors.[12]

Modifying the Market

With *market modification* strategies, a company tries to find new customers, increase a product's use among existing customers, or create new use situations.

Finding New Users Produce companies have begun marketing and packaging prunes as dried plums for the purpose of attracting younger buyers. Sony has expanded its user base by developing PlayStation video games for children under 13 years old.

Increasing Use Promoting more frequent usage has been a strategy of Campbell Soup Company. Because soup consumption rises in the winter and declines during the summer, the company now advertises more heavily in warm months to encourage consumers to think of soup as more than a cold-weather food. Similarly, the Florida Orange Growers Association advocates drinking orange juice throughout the day rather than for breakfast only.

Creating New Use Situations Finding new uses for an existing product has been the strategy behind Woolite, a laundry soap. Originally intended for the hand washing of woolen material, Woolite now promotes itself for use with all fine clothing items. The Milk Processor Education Program suggests a new use situation by substituting milk for water or other ingredients in preparing food.

The Milk Processor Education Program (MilkPEP) promotes the use of milk rather than water or other ingredients in preparing food. According to a MilkPEP executive, "If every household one day a week added milk rather than water to instant coffee and made a caffe latte, it would add [up to] $100 million to the bottom line of the milk industry."

Repositioning the Product

Often a company decides to reposition its product or product line in an attempt to increase sales. *Product repositioning* is changing the place a product occupies in a consumer's mind relative to competitive products. A firm can reposition a product by changing one or more of the four marketing mix elements. Four factors that trigger a repositioning action are discussed next.

Reacting to a Competitor's Position One reason to reposition a product is because a competitor's entrenched position is adversely affecting sales and market share. New Balance, Inc., successfully repositioned its athletic shoes to focus on fit and comfort rather than competing head-on against Nike and Reebok on fashion and sport. The company offers an expansive range of shoe widths with the message, "N is for fit," and it networks with podiatrists, not sport celebrities.[13]

Reaching a New Market When Unilever introduced iced tea in Britain in the mid-1990s, sales were disappointing. British consumers viewed it as leftover hot tea, not suitable for drinking. The company made its tea carbonated and repositioned it as a cold soft drink to compete as a carbonated beverage and sales improved. Johnson & Johnson effectively repositioned St. Joseph Aspirin from one for infants to an adult low-strength aspirin to reduce the risk of heart problems or strokes.[14]

Catching a Rising Trend Changing consumer trends can also lead to repositioning. Growing consumer interest in foods that offer health and dietary benefits is an example. Many products have been repositioned to capitalize on this trend. Quaker Oats now makes the FDA-approved claim that oatmeal, as part of a low saturated fat, low cholesterol diet, may reduce the risk of heart disease. Calcium-enriched products, such as Nutri-Grain bars and Uncle Ben's Calcium Plus rice, emphasize healthy bone structure for children and adults. Marketers of juices, such as V8 and Tropicana, focus on the natural health benefits of their products.

Changing the Value Offered In repositioning a product, a company can decide to change the value it offers buyers and trade up or down. *Trading up* involves adding value to the product (or line) through additional features or higher-quality materials. Michelin and Goodyear have done this with a "run-flat" tire that can travel up to 50 miles at 55 miles-per-hour after suffering total air loss.

ETHICS AND SOCIAL RESPONSIBILITY ALERT

Consumer Economics of Downsizing—Get Less, Pay More

For more than 30 years, Starkist put 6.5 ounces of tuna into its regular-sized can. Today, Starkist puts 6.125 ounces of tuna into its can, but charges the same price. Frito-Lay (Doritos and Lay's snack chips), Procter & Gamble (Pampers and Luvs disposable diapers), Nestlé (Poland Spring and Calistoga bottled waters) have whittled away at package contents 5 to 10 percent while maintaining their products' package size, dimensions, and prices. Kimberly-Clark cut its retail price on its jumbo pack of Huggies diapers from $13.50 to $12.50, but reduced the number of diapers per pack from 48 to 42. Georgia-Pacific reduced the content of its Brawny paper towel six-roll pack by 20 percent without lowering the price.

Consumer advocates charge that downsizing the content of packages while maintaining prices is a subtle and unannounced way of taking advantage of consumer buying habits. They also say downsizing is a price increase in disguise and deceptive, but legal. Manufacturers argue that this practice is a way of keeping prices from rising beyond psychological barriers for their products.

Is downsizing an unethical practice if manufacturers do not inform consumers that the package contents are less than they were previously?

Trading down involves reducing the number of features, quality, or price. For example, airlines have added more seats, thus reducing leg room, and eliminated extras, such as food service. Trading down often exists when companies engage in *downsizing*—reducing the content of packages without changing package size and maintaining or increasing the package price. Firms have been criticized for this practice, as described in the accompanying Ethics and Social Responsibility Alert.[15]

Concept Check

1. What does "creating new use situations" mean in managing a product's life cycle?
2. Explain the difference between trading up and trading down in repositioning.

BRANDING AND BRAND MANAGEMENT

branding
Organization's use of a name, phrase, design, symbol, or combination of these to identify and distinguish its products

brand name
Any word, device (design, shape, sound, or color), or combination of these used to distinguish a seller's goods or services

A basic decision in marketing products is **branding**, in which an organization uses a name, phrase, design, symbol, or combination of these to identify its products and distinguish them from those of competitors. A **brand name** is any word, device (design, sound, shape, or color), or combination of these used to distinguish a seller's goods or services. Some brand names can be spoken, such as a Gatorade or Rollerblade. Other brand names cannot be spoken, such as the rainbow-colored apple (the *logotype* or *logo*) used by Apple Computer.

Consumers may benefit most from branding. Recognizing competing products by brand names allows them to be more efficient shoppers. Consumers can recognize and avoid products with which they are dissatisfied, while becoming loyal to other, more satisfying brands. As discussed in Chapter 5, brand loyalty often eases consumers' decision making by eliminating the need for an external search.

Brand Personality and Brand Equity

brand personality
Set of human characteristics associated with a brand name

Product managers recognize that brands offer more than product identification and a means to distinguish their products from competitors. Successful and established brands take on a **brand personality**, a set of human characteristics associated with a brand name.[16] Research shows that consumers often assign personality traits to products—traditional, romantic, rugged, sophisticated, rebellious—and choose brands that are consistent with their own or desired self-image. Marketers can and do provide a brand with a personality through advertising that depicts a certain user or usage situation and conveys certain emotions or feelings to be associated with the brand. For example, the personality traits associated with Coca-Cola are all-American, real, and cool; with Pepsi, young, exciting, and hip; and with Dr Pepper, nonconforming, unique, and fun.

brand equity
Added value a given brand name gives to a product beyond the functional benefits provided

Brand name importance to a company has led to a concept called **brand equity**, the added value a given brand name gives to a product beyond the functional benefits provided.[17] This value has two distinct advantages. First, brand equity provides a competitive advantage, such as the Sunkist label that implies quality fruit and the Disney name that defines children's entertainment. A second advantage is that consumers are often willing to pay a higher price for a product with brand equity. Brand equity, in this instance, is represented by the premium a consumer will pay for one brand over another when the functional benefits provided are identical. Intel microchips, Bose audio systems, Duracell batteries, Microsoft computer software, and Louis Vuitton luggage all enjoy a price premium arising from brand equity.

Creating Brand Equity Brand equity doesn't just happen. It is carefully crafted and nurtured by marketing programs that forge strong, favorable, and unique

Can you describe the brand personality traits for these two brands?

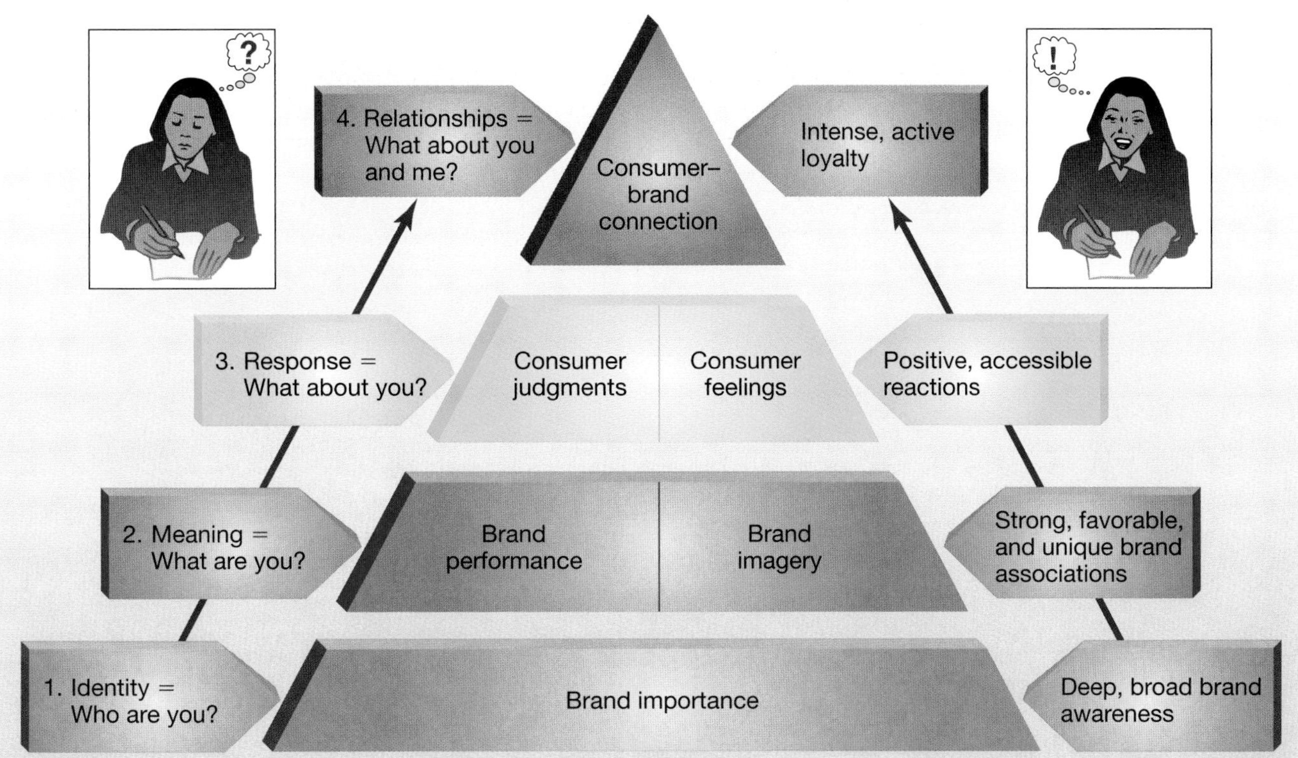

FIGURE 11–5
Customer-based brand equity pyramid

consumer associations and experiences with a brand. Brand equity resides in the minds of consumers. It results from what they have learned, felt, seen, and heard about a brand over time. Marketers recognize that brand equity is not easily or quickly achieved. Rather, it arises from a sequential building process consisting of four steps (Figure 11–5).[18]

- The first step is to develop positive brand awareness and an association of the brand in consumers' minds with a product class or need to give the brand an identity. Gatorade and Kleenex have done this in the sports drink and facial tissue product classes, respectively.
- Next, a marketer must establish a brand's meaning in the minds of consumers. Meaning arises from what a brand stands for and has two dimensions—a functional, performance-related dimension and an abstract, imagery-related dimension. Nike has done this through continuous product development and improvement and its links to peak athletic performance in its integrated marketing communications program.
- The third step is to elicit the proper consumer responses to a brand's identity and meaning. Here attention is placed on how consumers think and feel about a brand. Thinking focuses on a brand's perceived quality, credibility, and superiority relative to other brands. Feeling relates to the consumer's emotional reaction to a brand. Michelin elicits both responses for its tires. Not only is Michelin thought of as a credible and superior-quality brand, but consumers also acknowledge a warm and secure feeling of safety, comfort, and self-assurance without worry or concern about the brand.
- The final, and most difficult, step is to create a consumer–brand resonance evident in an intense, active loyalty relationship between consumers and the brand. A deep psychological bond characterizes a consumer–brand connection and the personal identification consumers have with the brand. Examples of brands that have achieved this status include Harley-Davidson, Apple, and eBay.

General Motors is the worldwide leader in licensed product sales among automakers. A recent licensing arrangement is for Hummer Footwear made by Roper Footwear & Apparel.

Valuing Brand Equity Brand equity also provides a financial advantage for the brand owner.[19] Successful, established brand names, such as Gillette, Nike, Gatorade, and Nokia, have an economic value. They are intangible assets. The recognition that brands are assets is apparent in the decision to buy and sell brands. For example, Triarc Companies bought the Snapple brand from Quaker Oats in 1997 for $300 million and sold it to Cadbury Schweppes in 2000 for $900 million. This example illustrates that brands, unlike physical assets that depreciate with time and use, can appreciate in value when effectively marketed. However, brands can lose value when they are not managed properly. Consider the purchase and sale of Lender's Bagels. Kellogg bought the brand for $466 million only to sell it to Aurora Foods for $275 million three years later following deteriorating sales and profits.

Financially lucrative brand licensing opportunities arise from brand equity. *Brand licensing* is a contractual agreement whereby one company (licensor) allows its brand name(s) or trademark(s) to be used with products or services offered by another company (licensee) for a royalty or fee. For example, Disney makes billions of dollars each year licensing its characters for children's toys, apparel, and games. Licensing fees for Winnie the Pooh alone exceed $3 billion annually. General Motors sells more than $2 billion in licensed products each year.[20]

Successful brand licensing requires careful marketing analysis to assure a proper match between the licensor's brand and the licensee's products. World-renowned designer Ralph Lauren has built a $5 billion business licensing his Ralph Lauren, Polo, and Chaps brands for dozens of products, including paint by Sherwin-Williams, furniture by Hendredon, footwear by Rockport, and fragrances by Cosmair. Mistakes, such as Kleenex diapers, Bic perfume, and Domino's fruit-favored bubble gum, are just a few examples of poor matches and licensing failures.

Picking a Good Brand Name

We take brand names such as iPod, Sanyo, Porsche, and Adidas for granted, but it is often a difficult and expensive process to pick a good name. Companies will spend between $25,000 and $100,000 to identify and test a new brand name.[21] For instance, Intel spent $45,000 for the Pentium name given its family of microchips. There are five criteria mentioned most often when selecting a good brand name:[22]

- The name should suggest the product benefits. For example, Accutron (watches), Easy Off (oven cleaner), Glass Plus (glass cleaner), Cling-Free (antistatic cloth for drying clothes), Powerbook (laptop computer), and Tidy Bowl (toilet bowl cleaner) all clearly describe the benefits of purchasing the product.
- The name should be memorable, distinctive, and positive. In the auto industry, when a competitor has a memorable name, others quickly imitate. When Ford named a car the Mustang, Pintos, Colts, and Broncos soon followed. The Thunderbird name led to the Phoenix, Eagle, Sunbird, and Firebird.
- The name should fit the company or product image. Sharp is a name that can apply to audio and video equipment. Excedrin, Bufferin, Anacin, and Nuprin are scientific-sounding names, good for an analgesic.
- The name should have no legal or regulatory restrictions. Companies that attempt to use others' trademarked material may face lawsuits. Regulatory restrictions arise through improper use of words. For example, the U.S. Food and Drug Administration discourages the use of the word *heart* in food brand names. This restriction led to changing the name of Kellogg's Heartwise cereal to Fiberwise, and Clorox's Hidden Valley Ranch Take Heart Salad Dressing had to be modified to Hidden Valley Ranch Low-Fat Salad Dressing. Increasingly, brand names need a corresponding address on the Internet. This further complicates name selection because millions of domain names are already registered.
- Finally, the name should be simple (such as Bold laundry detergent, Sure deodorant, and Bic pens) and should be emotional (such as Joy and Obsession perfumes). In the development of names for international use, having a nonmeaningful brand name has been considered a benefit. A name such as Exxon does not have any prior impressions or undesirable images among a diverse world population of different languages and cultures. The 7Up name is another matter. In Shanghai, China, the phrase means "death through drinking" in the local dialect, and sales have suffered as a result.

multiproduct branding *Manufacturer's branding strategy that uses one name for all products*

Branding Strategies

Companies can employ several different branding strategies, including multiproduct branding, multibranding, private branding, or mixed branding (Figure 11–6).

Multiproduct Branding With **multiproduct branding**, a company uses one name for all its products in a product class. This approach is sometimes called

FIGURE 11–6
Alternative branding strategies

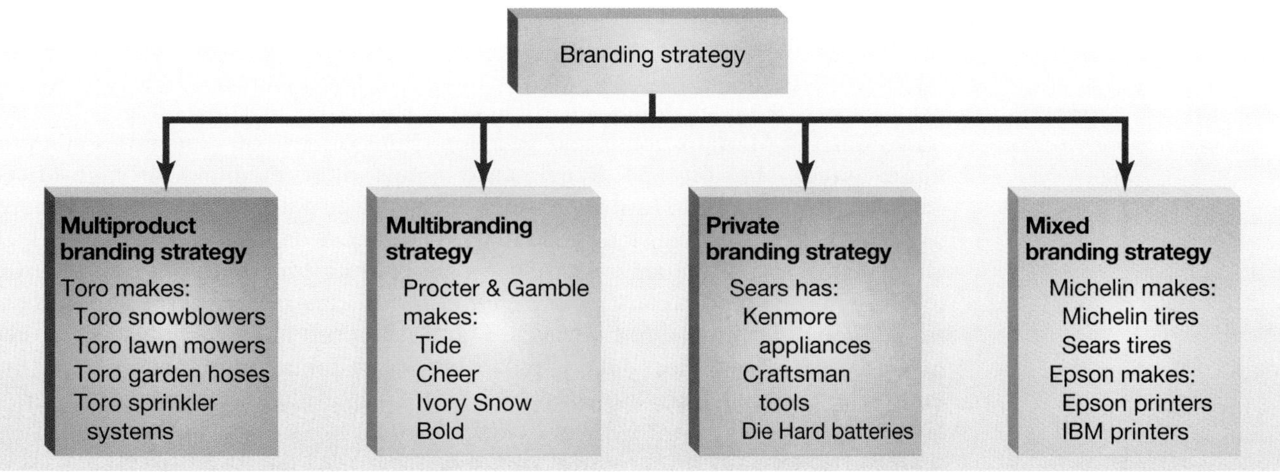

family branding, or *corporate branding* when the company's name is used. For example, General Electric, Gerber, and Sony engage in corporate branding—the company's name and brand name are identical. Church & Dwight employs the Arm & Hammer family brand name for all its products featuring baking soda as the primary ingredient.

There are several advantages to multiproduct branding. Capitalizing again on brand equity, consumers who have a good experience with the product will transfer this favorable attitude to other items in the product class with the same name. Therefore, this brand strategy makes possible *line extensions,* the practice of using a current brand name to enter a new market segment in its product class. Campbell Soup Company effectively employs a multiproduct branding strategy with soup line extensions. It offers regular Campbell soup, home-cooking style, and chunky varieties and more than 100 soup flavors. This strategy can also result in lower advertising and promotion costs because the same name is used on all products, thus raising the level of brand awareness. A risk with line extension is that sales of an extension may come at the expense of other items in the company's product line. Therefore, line extensions work best when they provide incremental company revenue by taking sales away from competing brands or attracting new buyers.

Some companies employ *subbranding,* which combines a corporate or family brand with a new brand. Gatorade has successfully used subbranding with the introduction of Gatorade Frost, Gatorade Fierce, and Gatorade X-Factor, with unique flavors developed for each.

A strong brand equity also allows for *brand extension,* the practice of using a current brand name to enter a completely different product class. For instance, the equity in the Tylenol name as a trusted pain reliever allowed Johnson & Johnson to successfully extend this name to Tylenol Cold & Flu and Tylenol PM, a sleep aid. Honda's established name for motor vehicles has extended easily to snowblowers, lawn mowers, marine engines, and snowmobiles.

However, there is a risk with brand extensions. Too many uses for one brand name can dilute the meaning of a brand for consumers. Marketing experts claim this has happened to the Arm & Hammer brand given its use for toothpaste, laundry detergent, gum, cat litter, air freshener, carpet deodorizer, and antiperspirant.[23]

multibranding
Manufacturer's branding strategy that gives each product a distinct name

Multibranding Alternately, a company can engage in **multibranding**, which involves giving each product a distinct name. Multibranding is a useful strategy when each brand is intended for a different market segment. P&G makes Camay soap for those concerned with soft skin and Safeguard for those who want deodorant protection. Black & Decker markets its line of tools for the household do-it-yourselfer segment with the Black & Decker name but uses the DeWalt name for its professional tool line. Disney uses the Miramax and Touchstone Pictures names for films directed at adults and its Disney name for children's films.

Multibranding is applied in a variety of ways. Some companies array their brands on the basis of price-quality segments.[24] Marriott International offers 14 hotel and resort brands, each suited for a particular traveler experience and budget. To illustrate, Marriott Marquis hotels and Vacation Clubs offer luxury amenities at a premium price. Marriott and Renaissance hotels offer medium- to high-priced accommodations. Courtyard hotels and Town Place Suites appeal to economy-minded travelers, whereas the Fairfield Inn is for those on a very low travel budget. Other multibrand companies introduce new product brands as defensive moves to counteract competition. Called *fighting brands,* their chief purpose is to confront competitor brands. For instance, Mattel launched its Flava brand of hip-hop fashion dolls in response to the popularity of Bratz brand dolls sold by MGA Entertainment, which were attracting the 8-to-12-year-old girl segment of Barbie brand sales.

Black & Decker's multibranding strategy allows it to reach do-it-yourselfers with the Black & Decker name and professionals with the DeWalt name.

Compared with the multiproduct approach, promotional costs tend to be higher with multibranding. The company must generate awareness among consumers and retailers for each new brand name without the benefit of any previous impressions. The advantages of this approach are that each brand is unique to each market segment and there is no risk that a product failure will affect other products in the line. Nevertheless, some large multibrand firms have found that the complexity and expense of implementing this strategy can outweigh the benefits. For example, Unilever recently pruned its brands from some 1,600 to 400 through product deletion and sales to other companies.

Private Branding A company uses *private branding,* often called *private labeling* or *reseller branding,* when it manufactures products but sells them under the brand name of a wholesaler or retailer. Rayovac, Paragon Trade Brands, and Ralcorp Holding are major suppliers of private label alkaline batteries, diapers, and grocery products, respectively. Radio Shack, Sears, Kmart, and Kroger are large retailers that have their own brand names. Private branding is popular because it typically produces high profits for manufacturers and resellers. Consumers also buy them. It is estimated that one of every five items purchased at U.S. supermarkets, drugstores, and mass merchandisers such as Wal-Mart bears a private brand.[25]

Mixed Branding A compromise between manufacturer and private branding is *mixed branding,* where a firm markets products under its own name and that of a reseller because the segment attracted to the reseller is different from their own market. Elizabeth Arden is a case in point. The company sells its Elizabeth Arden brand through department stores and a line of skin care products at Wal-Mart with the "skin-simple" brand name.

MARKETING NEWSNET

Creating Customer Value through Packaging—Pez Heads Dispense More than Candy

CUSTOMER VALUE

Customer value can assume numerous forms. For Pez Candy, Inc. (www.pez.com), customer value manifests itself in some 300 Pez character candy dispensers. Each 99 cent refillable dispenser ejects tasty candy tablets in a variety of flavors that delight preteen and teens alike.

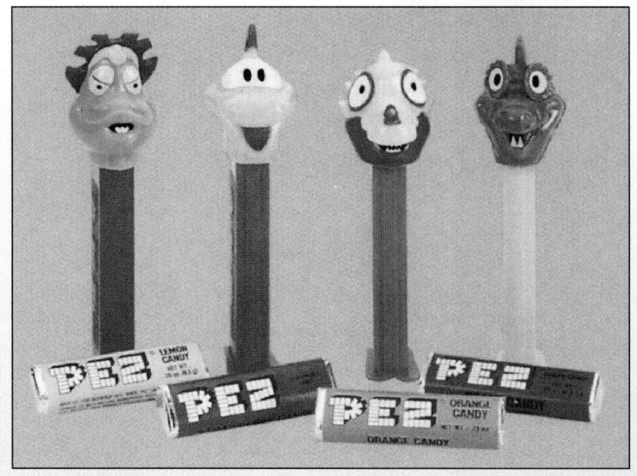

Pez was formulated in 1927 by Austrian food mogul Edward Haas III and successfully sold in Europe as an adult breath mint. Pez, which comes from the German word for peppermint, *pfefferminz,* was originally packaged in a hygienic, headless plastic dispenser. Pez first appeared in the United States in 1953 with a headless dispenser, marketed to adults. After conducting extensive marketing research, Pez was repositioned with fruit flavors, repackaged with licensed character heads on top of the dispenser, and remarketed as a children's product in the mid-1950s. Since then, most top-level licensed characters and hundreds of other characters have become Pez heads. Consumers in 60 countries eat more than 3 billion Pez tablets annually, and company sales growth exceeds that of the candy industry as a whole.

The unique Pez package dispenses a "use experience" for its customers beyond the candy itself, namely, fun. And fun translates into a 98 percent awareness level for Pez among teenagers and 89 percent among mothers with children. Pez has not advertised its product for years. With that kind of awareness, who needs advertising?

CREATING CUSTOMER VALUE THROUGH PACKAGING AND LABELING

packaging
Part of a product that refers to any container in which it is offered for sale and on which label information is displayed

The **packaging** component of a product refers to any container in which it is offered for sale and on which label information is conveyed. A *label* is an integral part of the package and typically identifies the product or brand, who made it, where and when it was made, how it is to be used, and product contents and ingredients. To a great extent, the customer's first exposure to a product is the package and label and both are an expensive and important part of marketing strategy. For Pez Candy, Inc., the character head-on-a-stick plastic container that dispenses a miniature brick candy is the central element of its marketing strategy as described in the accompanying Marketing NewsNet.[26]

Packaging and labeling cost companies more than $100 billion annually and account for about 15 cents of every dollar spent by consumers for products.[27] Despite the cost, packaging and labeling are essential because both provide important benefits for the manufacturer, retailer, and ultimate consumer.

Communication Benefits

A major benefit of packaging is the label information on it conveyed to the consumer, such as directions on how to use the product and what the product is made of, which is needed to satisfy legal requirements of product disclosure. For example, the labeling system for packaged and processed foods, which created a uniform format for nutritional and dietary information, became effective in the mid-1990s at a cost of $2 billion to food companies. Other information consists of seals and symbols, either government required or commercial seals of approval (such as the Good Housekeeping seal).

Which chip stacks up better? Frito-Lay's recent introduction of Lay's Stax potato crisps to compete against Procter & Gamble's Pringles illustrates the role of packaging in product and brand management.

Packaging also can have brand equity benefits for a company. According to the director of marketing for L'eggs hosiery, "Packaging is important to the equity of the L'eggs brand." Why? Packaging has been shown to enhance brand recognition and facilitate the formation of strong, favorable, and unique brand associations.[28]

Functional Benefits

Packaging often plays an important functional role, such as storage, convenience, protection, or product quality.[29] Storing food containers is one example, and beverage companies have developed lighter and easier ways to stack products on shelves and in refrigerators. Examples include Coca-Cola beverage packs designed to fit neatly onto refrigerator shelves and Ocean Spray Cranberries' rectangular juice bottles that allow 10 units per package versus 8 of its former round bottles.

The convenience dimension of packaging is also important. Kraft Miracle Whip salad dressing, Heinz ketchup, and Skippy Squeez'It peanut butter are sold in squeeze bottles; microwave popcorn has been a major market success; and Chicken of the Sea tuna and Folgers coffee are packaged in single-serving portions.

Consumer protection has become an important function of packaging, including the development of tamper-resistant containers. Today, companies commonly use safety seals or pop-tops that reveal previous opening. Consumer protection through labeling exists in "open dating," which states the expected shelf life of the product.

Functional features of packaging also can affect product quality. Procter & Gamble's Pringles, with its cylindrical packaging, offers uniform chips, minimal breakage, and for some consumers, better value for the money than flex-bag packages for chips. Not to be outdone, Frito-Lay, the world's leading producer of snack chips recently decided to "stand up" to Pringles with its new line of Lay's Stax potato crisps. Consumers will be the final judge of which chip stacks up better.

Perceptual Benefits

A third component of packaging and labeling is the perception created in the consumer's mind. Just Born Inc., a candy manufacturer of such brands as Jolly Joes and Mike and Ike Treats, discovered the importance of this component of packaging. For many years the brands were sold in old-fashioned black and white packages, but when the packaging was changed to four color, with animated grape and cherry characters, sales increased 25 percent. Celestial Seasonings' packaging and labeling uses delicate illustrations, soft and warm colors, and quotations about life to reinforce the brand's positioning as a New Age, natural herbal tea.

The distinctive design of Celestial Seasonings' tea boxes reinforces the brand's positioning as a New Age, natural herbal tea.

Because labels list a product's source, brands competing in the global marketplace can benefit from "country of origin or manufacture" perceptions as described in Chapter 7. Consumers tend to have stereotypes about country-product pairings that they judge "best"—English tea, French perfume, Italian leather, and Japanese electronics—which can affect a brand's image. Increasingly today, Chinese firms are adopting the English language and Roman letters for their brand labels. This is being done because of the perception in many Asian countries that "things Western are good," even if consumers cannot understand the meaning of the English words.

MANAGING THE MARKETING OF SERVICES

Let's use the four Ps framework of the text for discussing the marketing mix for services.[30]

Product (Service)

To a large extent, the concepts of the product component of the marketing mix apply equally well to Cheerios (a good) and to American Express (a service). Yet there are three aspects of the product/service element of the mix that warrant special attention when dealing with services: exclusivity, brand name, and capacity management.

Exclusivity Chapter 10 pointed out that one favorable dimension in a new product is its ability to be patented. Remember that a patent gives the manufacturer of a product exclusive rights to its production for 17 years. A major difference between products and services is that services cannot be patented. Hence the creator of a successful fast-food hamburger chain could quickly discover the concept being copied by others. Domino's Pizza, for example, has seen competitors copy the quick delivery advantage that propelled the company to success. Many businesses today try to distinguish their core product with new or improved supplementary services through outsourcing: hotels outsource concierge services, airlines outsource maintenance, and banks outsource the mailing of monthly statements.

McDonald's familiar Golden Arches logo is an important part of the company's branding.

Branding An important aspect in marketing goods is the branding strategy used. However, because services are intangible and, therefore, more difficult to describe, the brand name or identifying logo of the service organization is particularly important in consumer decisions. Brand names help make the abstract nature of services more concrete. Service marketers apply branding concepts in the same way as product marketers. Consider American Express. It has applied subbranding with its American Express Green, Gold, Platinum, Optima, and Blue credit cards, with unique service offerings for each.

Capacity Management Most services have a limited capacity due to the inseparability of the service from the service provider and the perishable nature of the service. For example, a patient must be in the hospital at the same time as the surgeon to "buy" an appendectomy, and only one patient can be helped at that time. Similarly, no additional surgery can be conducted tomorrow because of an unused operating room or an available surgeon today—the service capacity is lost if it is not used. So the service component of the mix must be integrated with efforts to influence consumer demand. This is referred to as **capacity management**.

capacity management
Integrating the service component of the marketing mix with efforts to influence consumer demand

Price

In the service industries, *price* is referred to in various ways. Hospitals refer to charges; consultants, lawyers, physicians, and accountants to fees; airlines to fares; and hotels to rates. Regardless of the term used, price plays two essential roles: (1) to affect consumer perceptions and (2) to be used in capacity management. Because of the intangible nature of services, price can indicate the quality of the service. Would you wonder about the quality of a $100 surgery? Studies have shown that when there are few well-known cues by which to judge a product or service quality, consumers use price.[31]

The capacity management role of price is also important to movie theaters, airlines, restaurants, and hotels. Many service businesses use **off-peak pricing**, which consists of charging different prices during different times of the day or days of the week to reflect variations in demand for the service. Airlines offer discounts for weekend travel, and movie theaters offer matinee prices. The New York State Thruway Authority has been testing different toll amounts for different times of the day to try to reduce traffic during rush hour.

off-peak pricing
Charging different prices during different times of the day or days of the week to reflect variations in demand for the service

Easy come. Easy go.
Order pre-paid, flat-rate Priority Mail® envelopes you can fill up and then just hand to your Letter Carrier.
These convenient Priority Mail* envelopes are as easy to order as they are to use. Simply call to order a pack of 10 to keep in your drawer. The next time you need a document sent 2-3 day delivery — just fill one up and hand it to your Letter Carrier. No meters. No hassles. Just pre-paid and easy!
Order a Priority Mail® 10-pack today — only $38.50!
Call 1-800-THE-USPS, ext. 000000 or return the attached form.
* Weight restrictions may apply. See envelope for details.
** One calculator per customer.
Order NOW and we'll send you a calculator!**
UNITED STATES POSTAL SERVICE
© 2004 United States Postal Service. Eagle symbol is a registered trademark of the United States Postal Service.
usps.com

The United States Postal Service uses advertising to stress the convenience of its service.

Place (Distribution)

Place or distribution is a major factor in developing a service marketing strategy because of the inseparability of services from the producer. Historically in services marketing, little attention has been paid to distribution. But as competition grows, the value of convenient distribution is being recognized. Hairstyling chains such as Cost Cutters Family Hair Care, tax preparation offices such as H&R Block, and accounting firms such as PricewaterhouseCoopers all use multiple locations for the distribution of services. In the banking industry, customers of participating banks using the Cirrus system can access any one of thousands of automatic teller systems throughout the United States. The availability of electronic distribution through the Internet now provides global coverage for travel services, banking, entertainment, and many other information-based services.

Promotion

The value of promotion, specifically advertising, for many services is to show the benefits of purchasing the service. It is valuable to stress availability, location, consistent quality, and efficient, courteous service. In addition, services must be concerned with their image. Promotional efforts, such as Merrill Lynch's use of the bull in its ads, contribute to image and positioning strategies. In most cases promotional concerns of services are similar to those of products.

In the past, advertising has been viewed negatively by many nonprofit and professional service organizations. In fact, professional groups such as law, dentistry, and medicine had previously used their respective professional codes of conduct to prevent their members from advertising. A Supreme Court case in 1976, however, struck down this constraint on professional services advertising. Although opposition to advertising remains strong in some professional groups, the barriers to promotion are gradually disappearing. In recent years, advertising has been used by religious groups; legal, medical, and dental services; educational institutions; and many other service organizations.[32]

Another form of promotion, publicity, has played a major role in the promotional strategy of nonprofit services and some professional organizations. Nonprofit organizations such as public school districts, the Chicago Symphony Orchestra, religious organizations, and hospitals have used publicity to disseminate their messages. Because of the heavy reliance on publicity, many services use public service announcements (PSAs), and because PSAs are free, nonprofit groups have tended to rely on them as the foundation of their media plan. However, the timing and location of a PSA are under the control of the medium, not the organization. So the nonprofit service group cannot control who sees the message or when the message is given.

Concept Check

1. What is the difference between a line extension and a brand extension?
2. Explain the role of packaging in terms of perception.
3. How do service businesses use off-peak pricing?

CHAPTER IN REVIEW

1 *Explain the product life-cycle concept.*
The product life cycle describes the stages a new product goes through in the marketplace: introduction, growth, maturity, and decline. Product sales growth and profitability differ at each stage, and marketing managers have marketing objectives and marketing mix strategies unique to each stage based on consumer behavior and competitive factors. In the introductory stage, the need is to establish primary demand, whereas the growth stage requires selective demand strategies. In the maturity stage, the need is to maintain market share; the decline stage necessitates a deletion or harvesting strategy. Some important aspects of product life cycles are their length, the shape of the sales curve, and the rate at which consumers adopt products.

2 *Identify ways that marketing executives manage a product's life cycle.*
Marketing executives manage a product's life cycle three ways. First, they can modify the product itself by altering its characteristics, such as product quality, performance, or appearance. Second, they can modify the market by finding new customers for the product, increasing a product's use among existing customers, or creating new use situations for the product. Finally, they can reposition the product using any one or a combination of marketing mix elements. Four factors trigger a repositioning action. They include reacting to a competitor's position, reaching a new market, catching a rising trend, and changing the value offered to consumers.

3 *Recognize the importance of branding and alternative branding strategies.*
A basic decision in marketing products is branding, in which an organization uses a name, phrase, design, symbols, or a combination of these to identify its products and distinguish them from those of its competitors. Product managers recognize that brands offer more than product identification and a means to distinguish their products from competitors. Successful and established brands take on a brand personality and acquire brand equity—the added value a given brand name gives to a product beyond the functional benefits provided—that is crafted and nurtured by marketing programs that forge strong, favorable, and unique consumer associations with a brand. A good brand name should suggest the product benefits, be memorable, fit the company or product image, be free of legal restrictions, and be simple and emotional. Companies can and do employ several different branding strategies. With multiproduct branding, a company uses one name for all its products in a product class. A multibranding strategy involves giving each product a distinct name. A company uses private branding when it manufactures products but sells them under the brand name of a wholesaler or retailer. Finally, a company can employ mixed branding, where it markets products under its own name(s) and that of a reseller.

4 *Describe the role of packaging and labeling in the marketing of a product.*
Packaging and labeling play numerous roles in the marketing of a product. The packaging component of a product refers to any container in which it is offered for sale and on which label information is conveyed. Manufacturers, retailers, and consumers acknowledge that packaging and labeling provide communication, functional, and perceptual benefits.

5 *Recognize how the four Ps framework applies to services.*
The four Ps framework also applies to services with some adaptations. Because services cannot be patented, unique offerings are difficult to protect. In addition, because services are intangible, brands and logos (which can be protected) are particularly important. The inseparability of production and consumption of services means that capacity management is important to services. The intangible nature of services makes price an important indication of service quality. Distribution has become an important marketing tool for services, and electronic distribution allows some services to provide global coverage. In recent years, service organizations have increased their promotional activities.

FOCUSING ON KEY TERMS

brand equity p. 246
brand name p. 245
brand personality p. 246
branding p. 245
capacity management p. 254
multibranding p. 250
multiproduct branding p. 249
off-peak pricing p. 254
packaging p. 252
product life cycle p. 236

DISCUSSION AND APPLICATION QUESTIONS

1 Listed here are three different products in various stages of the product life cycle. What marketing strategies would you suggest to these companies? (*a*) Canon digital cameras—growth stage, (*b*) Panasonic high-definition television—introductory stage, and (*c*) handheld manual can openers—decline stage.

2 It has often been suggested that products are intentionally made to break down or wear out. Is this strategy a planned product modification approach?

3 The product manager of GE is reviewing the penetration of trash compactors in American homes. After more than two decades in existence, this product is in relatively few homes. What problems can account for this poor acceptance? What is the shape of the trash compactor life cycle?

4 For years, Ferrari has been known as the manufacturer of expensive luxury automobiles. The company plans to attract the major segment of the car-buying market who purchase medium-priced automobiles. As Ferrari considers this trading-down strategy, what branding strategy would you recommend? What are the tradeoffs to consider with your strategy?

GOING ONLINE Brand News You Can Use

Branding and brand management is a challenging task. Brandchannel.com seeks to inform its readers on the important issues facing brands now and in the future from a global perspective. Of particular interest are (1) "features," which discuss the success and failure of particular brands, and (2) "debate," which presents a point/counterpoint discussion related to a brand's strategy.

Visit brandchannel.com (www.brandchannel.com) to complete the following assignment:

1 Pick a brand appearing in Chapter 11 and find a feature or debate pertaining to it either in the archives or from the current page. Summarize the views expressed in brandchannel.com.

2 Click the "papers" icon and read a paper on a topic covered in Chapter 11. Compare and contrast the views in this paper with the coverage found in the chapter.

BUILDING YOUR MARKETING PLAN

For the product offering in your marketing plan,

1 Identify (*a*) its stage in the product life cycle and (*b*) key marketing mix actions that might be appropriate, as shown in Figure 11–1.

2 Develop (*a*) branding and (*b*) packaging strategies, if appropriate for your offering.

VIDEO CASE 11 Philadelphia Phillies, Inc.: Sports Marketing 101

"Bring everyone in closer. Have fans feel 'I'm not alone here; lots of others are in the seats. This is a *happening*!' " chuckles David Montgomery, president and chief executive officer of the Philadelphia Phillies, Inc.

He continues, "Old Veterans Stadium had too big an inventory of seats for baseball. The new facility and the fact that it's a game played in summer out in the open air really takes you to a much broader audience. Our challenge is to appeal to all the segments in that audience." What Montgomery is referring to is the Phillies' new world-class Citizens Bank Park baseball stadium that opened in 2004. It is a baseball-only ballpark, seating 43,500 fans, where every seat is angled toward home plate to give fans the best view of the action. This contrasts the 62,000-seat Veterans Stadium that both the Phillies and the Philadelphia Eagles football team shared from 1971 to 2003 where sightlines were always a compromise for the two sports.

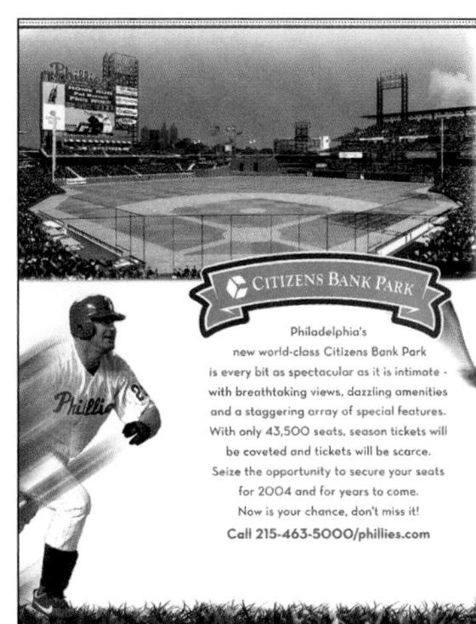

The new fan-friendly Phillies stadium is just one element in today's complex strategy to market the Philadelphia Phillies effectively to many different segments of fans—a far different challenge than in the past. A century ago major-league baseball was pretty simple. You built a stadium. You hired the ballplayers. You printed tickets—hoping and praying a winning team would bring in fans and sell those tickets. And your advertising consisted of printing the team's home schedule in the local paper.

THE PHILLIES TODAY: APPEALS, SEGMENTS, AND ACTIVITIES

Marketing a major-league baseball team is far different today.

"How do you market a product that is all over the board?" asks David Buck, the Phillies' vice president of marketing. He first gives a general answer to his question: "The ballpark experience is the key. As long as you project an image of a fun ballpark experience in everything you do, you're going to be in good shape. Our best advertising is word-of-mouth from happy fans."

Next come the specifics. Marketing the appeal of a fun ballpark experience to all segments of fans is critical because the Phillies can't promise a winning baseball team. Every team, even the New York Yankees, has its ups and downs. The Phillies are no different.

Reaching the different segments of fans is a special challenge because each segment is often looking for different things. Segments often break down by why the fan is there, many tied to special promotions:

- The die-hards. Intense baseball fans that are there to watch the strategy and see the Phillies win.
- Kids 14 years and under. At the game with the family, also to get bat or bobble-head doll premiums and have a "run-the-bases" day.
- Women and men 15 years and older. Special "days out," such as for Mother's Day or Father's Day.
- Seniors, 60 years and over. A "stroll-the-bases" day.
- 20-somethings and 30-somethings. Meet some friends at the ballpark for a fun night out.
- Corporate and community groups. At the game to have fun but also to get to know members of their organization better.

It's clear that not all fans are there for exactly the same "fun ballpark experience."

The segments don't stop there. Marisol Lezeano, the Phillies' community outreach coordinator, says, "In the Philadelphia area we've got a lot of different ethnic groups and we want to make all of them Phillies fans." So she plans special nights for these groups—Latino Family Celebration night with a Latino Legends poster of Phillies Hispanic players; Asia Pacific night with a giant cloth dragon dancing its way across the outfield; and The Sound of Philadelphia night honoring Black Music Month featuring various African-American music groups. "We want all communities to come to the ballpark. We're all fans. It's great. Please be with us," she emphasizes.

The "fun ballpark experience" today also goes beyond simply watching the Phillies play a baseball game. Fans at Citizens Bank Park can also:

- Buy souvenirs at the Phillies store—the "Phanatic Attic."
- Romp in the largest soft-play area for kids in Major League Baseball and scale a giant, inflatable baseball rock-climbing wall.
- Test their skills in a pitching game.
- Play a giant pinball game.
- Stroll through Ashburn Alley (named for a famous Phillie), an outdoor food and entertainment area to see the All-Star Walk and the Wall of Fame.
- Eat at McFadden's Restaurant and Saloon or Harry the K's Bar & Grill.

PROMOTIONAL ACTIVITIES

The range of the Phillies' promotional activities today is mind numbing. They start with "special promotion days," which typically increase fan attendance by 30 to 35 percent for a game, according to David Buck. These days often generate first-time visits by people who have never seen a major league baseball game. They generally fall into two categories: (1) event days and (2) premium gift days.

Event days can involve camera days where fans can take players' photos—three FUJIFILM Fridays each season for the Phillies. Or they can involve fireworks, an old-timers' game, or running or strolling the bases. Some events are especially memorable. Phillies fans still talk about the ostrich race in which a terrified Phillies' broadcaster wound up in the first row of stands when the ostrich pulling him and his cart panicked due to crowd noise.

"Our premiums or giveaways are directed at specific groups," says Scott Brandreth, the Phillies' merchandising manager. "During the year, we probably have 2 or 3 for all fans, 6 or 7 for children 14 years or younger, and maybe 1 for women over 15, and 1 for men over 15—often for Mother's Day and Father's Day." These giveaways range from bobble-head dolls and nesting dolls to baseball caps, rally towels, and Louisville Slugger bats. "A special premium we had that was very successful was a DVD celebrating the tenth anniversary of the Phillies 1993 National League pennant," he says. To control expenses, the Phillies try to keep the cost of the premiums in the range of $1 to $3.

Other promotional activities fall in both the traditional and nontraditional categories. Personal appearances at public and charity events by Phillies' players and their wives, radio and TV ads, and special events paid for by sponsors have been used by baseball teams for decades. But newer, more nontraditional promotions include naming rights (Citizens Bank Park) for the stadium, Phillies Phantasy Camp, luxury suite and special "infield club seats," and Phillies youth baseball clubs and leagues. And getting Phillies updates and ordering tickets on its website (phillies.com) are only a few years old.

Probably the best-known mascot in professional sports, the Phillie Phanatic is almost a Philadelphia legend. This oversized, green furry mascot has been around for over 25 years. Not only does he appear in the ballpark at all Phillies' home games, but he also makes appearances at charity and public events year round. Or rather the *three* Phanatics do so, because the demand is too great for a single Phanatic. "The Phanatic is a great character because he doesn't carry wins or losses," says David Montgomery. "Fans young and old can relate to him . . . He makes you smile, makes you laugh, and adds to the enjoyment of the game."

BOTTOM LINE: REVENUES AND EXPENSES

"We're a private business that serves the public," David Montgomery points out. "And we've got to make sure our revenues more than cover our expenses." He identifies these key sources of revenues and gives the approximate annual percentages of each:

SOURCES OF REVENUE	APPROX. %
1. Ticket sales (home and away games)	52%
2. National media (network TV and radio)	13
3. Local media (over-the-air TV, pay TV, radio)	13
4. Advertising (publications, co-sponsorship promotions)	12
5. Concessions (food, souvenirs, restaurants)	10
Total	100%

Balanced against these revenues are some major expenses that include players' salaries (exceeding $93 million in 2004) and salaries of more than 150 full-time employees. Other expenses are those for scouting and drafting 40 to 60 new players per year, operating six minor-league farm clubs, and operating (with a labor force of 400 persons per game) Citizens Bank Park for the Phillies' 81 home games.

David Montgomery never gets bored. "When I finished business school, I had to choose between a marketing research job at a large paper products company or marketing the Philadelphia Phillies," explains Montgomery, who started with the Phillies by selling season and group tickets. "And it was no real decision because there never has been one day on this job that wasn't different and exciting," he says.

Questions

1 (*a*) What is the "product" that the Phillies market? (*b*) What "products" are the Phillies careful not to market?

2 How does the "quality" dimension in marketing the Philadelphia Phillies differ from that in marketing a consumer product such as a breakfast cereal or cake mix?

3 When David Montgomery talks about reducing the "inventory of seats" in the new versus old stadium, what does he recognize as (*a*) advantages and (*b*) disadvantages?

4 Considering all five elements of the promotional mix (advertising, personal selling, public relations, sales promotion, and direct marketing), what specific promotional activities should the Phillies use? Which should be used off-season? On-season?

5 What kind of special promotion gift days (with premiums) and event days (no premiums) can the Phillies use to increase attendance by targeting these segments: (*a*) 14 and under, (*b*) 15 and over, (*c*) other special fan segments, and (*d*) all fans?

priceline.com

Sign-In • My Profile • My Trips • Check Your Request  Help

 Flights

 Hotels $100 Off

 Rental Cars On Sale

 Vacation Packages

 Cruises

NEW Flights Shop. Compare. Save.

Flights | Hotels | Cars On Sale | Vacation Packages | Cruises

Book together, save up to $200 more: ○ Air+Hotel ○ Air+Hotel+Car

From: (City or Airport)

To: (City or Airport)

Departure Date: 1/15/2006

Return Date: 1/22/2006

Number of Tickets: 1 ticket

Flights On Sale

- One-Way
- Multi-Destination
- Advanced Search

>>> NEXT >>>

More Ways to Search:

- First / Business Class
- Flight Times
- Search By Airline
- Unrestricted Fares
- Non-Stop Only

New to priceline? Find out more.

Rental Car Super Sale

Get Weekend and Weekly Rental Car rates from $12/day Sale ends September 4th!

Top Package Deals

Get our best deals to Florida, Las Vegas, New York, The Caribbean and San Francisco.

Up to $100 off Hotels

Save up to $100 a night on 3 and 4 Star Hotels over leading travel sites.

Home Financing

Great deals on mortgages, and online bank accounts. Save on rates right now!

Browse Our Top Deals

- United on Sale from $85 Round-trip
- Mexico Flights Under $500 Round-trip
- United Fall Sale to Asia

CHAPTER 12

PRICING PRODUCTS AND SERVICES

LEARNING OBJECTIVES

After reading this chapter you should be able to:

1 Identify the elements that make up a price.

2 Describe how to establish the initial approximate price level using demand-oriented, cost-oriented, profit-oriented, and competition-oriented approaches.

3 Explain what a demand curve is and the role of revenues in pricing decisions.

4 Explain the role of costs in pricing decisions.

5 Describe how various combinations of price, fixed cost, and unit variable cost affect a firm's break-even point.

6 Recognize the objectives a firm has in setting prices and the constraints that restrict the range of prices a firm can charge.

7 Describe the steps taken in setting a final price.

WHERE DOT-COMS STILL THRIVE: HELPING YOU GET A $100-A-NIGHT HOTEL ROOM OVERLOOKING NEW YORK'S CENTRAL PARK

"When I travel, I always go through Internet sites," Utah State student Catherine C. Woolley tells *BusinessWeek* magazine.[1] She used this strategy with Priceline.com to reserve a $100-a-night hotel room overlooking Central Park, a glitzy area in New York City. Despite the effects of the September 11, 2001, attacks had on the travel industry, online bookings are expected to rise to $75 billion in 2005, according to Internet travel research firm PhoCusWright. These online websites book airline tickets, hotel rooms, rental cars, and special travel and cruise packages for leisure and business travelers. In terms of market share, the top four online travel websites are Orbitz, Travelocity, Expedia, and Priceline, Catherine Woolley's hotel reservation supplier.

Why Travel Dot-Coms Haven't Tanked "There are a bunch of businesses that don't make sense at all on the Internet," says Mitchell J. Rubin, a money manager who has a lot of his fund invested in Internet travel companies. "Travel is the quintessential one that does," he continues.[2] Travel companies have beaten the dot-com odds by providing two key benefits to customers:

1. *Saving time*. User friendliness makes getting Internet travel reservations easy, often saving much time and misunderstanding.
2. *Saving money.* Customers can achieve substantial price savings using the travel dot-coms instead of using conventional booking services, such as travel agents.

Travel Dot-Com Prices: A Win–Win for Buyers and Sellers But what are the benefits for airlines and hotels? The easy answer: The extra money United Airlines or Marriott Hotels receives when Orbitz or Expedia books their services more than offsets the expenses United or Marriott incurs if their tickets or rooms are sold through travel agencies or its own agent or website channels.

Among all marketing and operations factors in a business firm, price is unique. It is the place where all other business decisions come together. The price must be "right"—in the sense that customers must be willing to pay it and it must generate enough sales dollars to pay for the cost of offering it *and* earn a profit for the company. Small changes in price can have big effects on the number of units sold, as well as on company profit. In fact, among large U.S. companies, research shows that a 1 percent price increase translates to a 8 to 12 percent increase in profitability, other factors remaining the same.[3]

Welcome to the fascinating, and intense, world of pricing, where many forces come together in the price potential buyers are asked to pay. This chapter covers important factors used in setting prices.

NATURE AND IMPORTANCE OF PRICE

The price paid for goods and services goes by many names. You pay *tuition* for your education, *rent* for an apartment, *interest* on a bank credit card, and a *premium* for car insurance. Your dentist or physician charges you a *fee,* a professional or social organization charges *dues,* and airlines charge a *fare*. And what you pay for clothes or a haircut is termed a *price.*

What Is a Price?

price
Money or other considerations exchanged for the ownership or use of a good or service

These examples highlight the many varied ways that price plays a part in our daily lives. From a marketing viewpoint, **price** is the money or other considerations (including other goods and services) exchanged for the ownership or use of a good or service. Recently, Wilkinson Sword exchanged some of its knives for advertising used to promote its razor blades. This practice of exchanging goods and services for other goods and services rather than for money is called *barter.* These transactions account for billions of dollars annually in domestic and international trade.

For most products, money is exchanged. However, the amount paid is not always the same as the list, or quoted, price because of discounts, allowances, and extra fees. While discounts, allowances, and rebates make the effective price lower, other marketing tactics raise the real price. One new twenty-first century pricing tactic is to use *special fees* and *surcharges.* This practice is driven by consumers' zeal for low prices combined with the ease of making price comparisons on the Internet. Buyers are more willing to pay extra fees than a higher list price, so sellers use add-on charges as a way of having the consumer pay more without raising the list price.[4] Examples of such special fees include a Green Bay Packer "user fee" that can add $1,400 to the price of a season ticket or a 5 percent "environmental surcharge" by dry cleaners around the country.

All these different factors that increase or decrease the price are put together in a *price equation,* which is shown for several different products in Figure 12–1.

Suppose you decide you want to buy the newly introduced 2006 Bugatti Veyron, the world's fastest production car, because its 8.0 litre, 1,001-horsepower V-16 engine moves you from 0 to 62 mph in 2.9 seconds at a

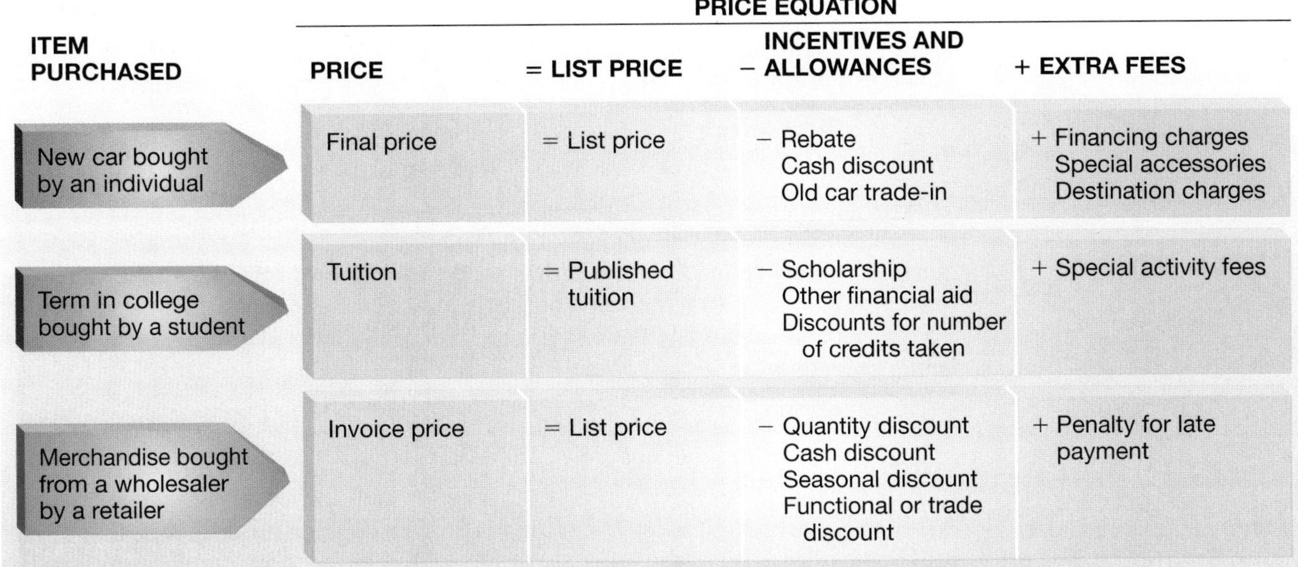

PRICE EQUATION
ITEM PURCHASED
PRICE
= LIST PRICE
INCENTIVES AND − ALLOWANCES
+ EXTRA FEES
New car bought by an individual
Final price
= List price
− Rebate
Cash discount
Old car trade-in
+ Financing charges
Special accessories
Destination charges
Term in college bought by a student
Tuition
= Published tuition
− Scholarship
Other financial aid
Discounts for number of credits taken
+ Special activity fees
Merchandise bought from a wholesaler by a retailer
Invoice price
= List price
− Quantity discount
Cash discount
Seasonal discount
Functional or trade discount
+ Penalty for late payment

FIGURE 12–1
The price of three different purchases

top speed of 250 mph. The Veyron has a list price of $1.2 million, and only 300 are expected to be crafted. However, if you put $500,000 down now and finance the balance over the next year, you will receive a rebate of $100,000 off the list price and pay a finance charge of $26,317. To ship the car from France, you will pay a $5,000 destination charge. For your 2000 Honda Civic DX four-door sedan that has 60,000 miles and is in fair condition, you are given a trade-in allowance of $5,395, which is the *Kelley Blue Book* (www.kbb.com) trade-in value of your car.

Applying the price equation (as shown in Figure 12–1) to your purchase, your final price is:

$$\begin{aligned}\text{Final price} &= \text{List price} - (\text{Incentives} + \text{Allowances}) + \text{Extra fees}\\ &= \$1{,}200{,}000 - (\$100{,}000 + \$5{,}395) + (\$26{,}317 + \$5{,}000)\\ &= \$1{,}135{,}922\end{aligned}$$

Your monthly payment for the one-year loan of $600,000 is $52,193.06.[5] Are you still interested?

Price as an Indicator of Value

For some products, price influences consumers' perception of overall quality and ultimately its value to consumers.[6] In a survey of home furnishing buyers, 84 percent agreed with the statement: "The higher the price, the higher the quality."[7] For example, Kohler introduced a walk-in bathtub that is safer for children and the elderly. Although priced higher than conventional step-in bathtubs, it has proven very successful because buyers are willing to pay more for what they perceive as the value of the extra safety.

From a consumers' standpoint, price is often used to indicate value when price is compared with benefits of the product. At a given price, as perceived benefits increase, value increases. If you're used to paying $10.99 for a medium pizza, wouldn't a large pizza at the same price be more valuable?

Creative marketers, aware that consumers' value assessments are often comparative, engage in *value pricing*. Value pricing is the practice of increasing product and service benefits while maintaining or decreasing price. "Supersizing" at fast-food restaurants is one example. Here value comes from getting "more bang for your buck."

Price in the Marketing Mix

profit equation
Profit = Total revenue − Total cost

Pricing is a critical decision made by a marketing executive because price has a direct effect on a firm's profits. This is apparent from a firm's **profit equation**:

Profit = Total revenue − Total cost
= (Unit price × Quantity sold) − Total cost

What makes this relationship even more complicated is that price affects the quantity sold, as illustrated with demand curves later in this chapter. Furthermore, since the quantity sold sometimes affects a firm's costs because of efficiency of production, price also indirectly affects costs. Thus, pricing decisions influence both total revenue (sales) and total cost, which makes pricing one of the most important decisions marketing executives face.

GENERAL PRICING APPROACHES

A key to a marketing manager's setting a final price for a product is to find an approximate price level to use as a reasonable starting point. Four common approaches to helping find this approximate price level are (1) demand-oriented, (2) cost-oriented, (3) profit-oriented, and (4) competition-oriented approaches (Figure 12–2). Although these approaches are discussed separately below, some of them overlap, and an effective marketing manager will consider several in searching for an approximate price level.

Demand-Oriented Approaches

Demand-oriented approaches emphasize factors underlying expected customer tastes and preferences more than such factors as cost, profit, and competition when selecting a price level.

Skimming Pricing A firm introducing a new product can use *skimming pricing,* setting the highest initial price that customers really desiring the product are willing to pay. These customers are not very price sensitive because they weigh the new product's price, quality, and ability to satisfy their needs against the same characteristics of substitutes. As the demand of these customers is satisfied, the firm lowers the price to attract another, more price-sensitive segment. Thus, skimming pricing gets its name from skimming successive layers of "cream," or customer segments, as prices are lowered in a series of steps.

In early 2003, many manufacturers of flatscreen TVs were pricing them about \$3,000 and using skimming pricing because many prospective customers were willing to buy the product immediately at the high price. But by the time you read this, flatscreen TVs will probably be far less expensive.

FIGURE 12–2
Four approaches for selecting an approximate price level

Demand-oriented approaches
- Skimming
- Penetration
- Prestige
- Odd-even
- Target
- Bundle
- Yield management

Cost-oriented approaches
- Standard markup
- Cost-plus

Profit-oriented approaches
- Target profit
- Target return on sales
- Target return on investment

Competition-oriented approaches
- Customary
- Above, at, or below market
- Loss leader

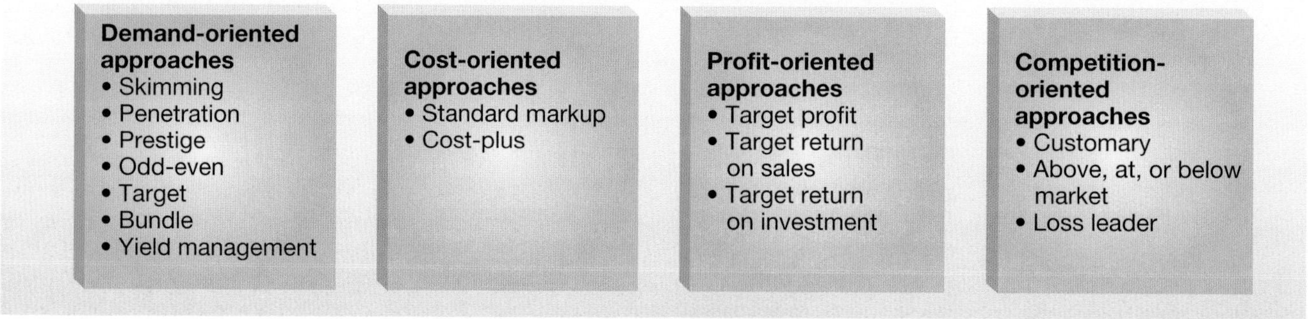

MARKETING NEWSNET

Energizer's Lesson in Price Perception—Value Lies in the Eye of the Beholder

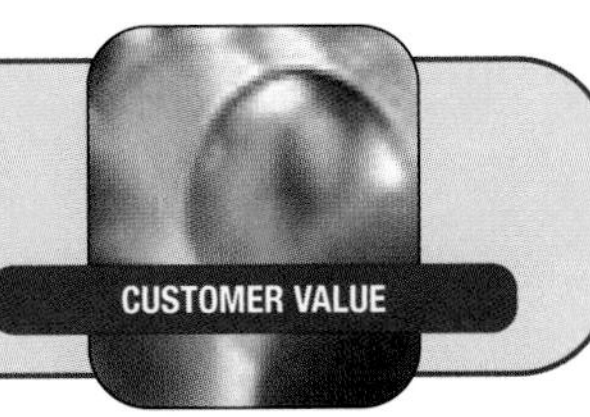

Battery manufacturers are as tireless as a certain drum-thumping bunny in their efforts to create products that perform better, last longer, and not incidentally, outsell the competition. The commercialization of new alkaline battery technology at a price that creates value for consumers is not always obvious or easy. Just ask the marketing executives at Energizer about their experience with pricing Energizer Advanced Formula and Energizer e[2] AA alkaline batteries.

When Duracell launched its high-performance Ultra brand AA alkaline battery with a 25 percent price premium over standard Duracell batteries, Energizer quickly countered with its own high-performance battery—Energizer Advanced Formula. Believing that consumers would not pay the premium price, Energizer priced its Advanced Formula brand at the same price as its standard AA alkaline battery, expecting to gain market share from Duracell. It did not happen. Why? According to industry analysts, consumers associated Energizer's low price with inferior quality in the high-performance segment. Instead of gaining market share, Energizer lost market share to Duracell and Rayovac, the number three battery manufacturer.

Having learned its lesson, Energizer subsequently released its e[2] high-performance battery, this time priced 4 percent higher than Duracell Ultra and about 50 percent higher than Advanced Formula. The result? Energizer recovered lost sales and market share. The lesson learned? Value lies in the eye of the beholder.

Penetration Pricing Setting a low initial price on a new product to appeal immediately to the mass market is *penetration pricing,* the exact opposite of skimming pricing. Nintendo consciously chose a penetration strategy when it introduced its GameCube video game console first in Japan and later in the United States in 2001. GameCube was launched with an introductory price of $199.95—$100.00 less than the list price for Microsoft's Xbox and Sony's PlayStation 2 consoles because many buyers were price sensitive.[8]

Why would Nintendo enter the video game market with a price for its GameCube that was $100 less than its competitors Xbox and PlayStation 2? The text gives the curious answer.

In some situations, penetration pricing may follow skimming pricing. A company might price a product high at first to attract price-insensitive consumers. Once the company has earned back the money spent on research and development and introductory promotions, it uses penetration pricing to appeal to a broader segment of the population and increase market share.[9]

Prestige Pricing Although consumers tend to buy more of a product when the price is lower, sometimes the reverse is true. If consumers are using price as a measure of the quality of an item, a company runs the risk of appearing to offer a low-quality product if it sets the price below a certain point. *Prestige pricing* involves setting a high price so that quality- or status-conscious consumers will be attracted to the product and buy it. Rolls-Royce cars, Chanel perfume, and Cartier jewelry have an element of prestige pricing in them and may sell worse at lower prices than at higher ones. As described in the Marketing NewsNet, this is the pricing strategy Energizer used with its very successful e[2] high-performance AA batteries.[10]

Odd-Even Pricing Sears offers a Craftsman radial saw for $599.99, the suggested retail price for a MACH3 razor set (razor and two blades) is $6.99, and Kmart sells Windex glass cleaner on sale for 99 cents. Why not simply price these items at $600, $7, and $1, respectively? These firms are using *odd-even pricing,* which involves setting prices a few dollars or cents under an even number. The presumption is that consumers see the Sears radial saw as priced at "something over $500" rather than

A price for a Sears Craftsman radial saw of $599.99, not $600? Hmmm??

"about $600." The effect this strategy has is psychological: $599.99 *feels* significantly lower than $600—even though there is only one cent difference. There is some evidence to suggest this does work. However, research suggests that overuse of odd-ending prices tends to mute its effect on demand.[11]

Target Pricing Manufacturers will sometimes estimate the price that the ultimate consumer would be willing to pay for a product. They then work backward through markups taken by retailers and wholesalers to determine what price they can charge wholesalers for the product. This practice, called *target pricing,* results in the manufacturer deliberately adjusting the composition and features of a product to achieve the target price to consumers. Canon uses this practice for pricing its cameras, as does Heinz for its complete line of pet foods.[12]

Bundle Pricing A frequently used demand-oriented pricing practice is *bundle pricing*—the marketing of two or more products in a single package price. For example, Delta Air Lines offers vacation packages that include airfare, car rental, and lodging. Bundle pricing is based on the idea that consumers value the package more than the individual items. This is due to benefits received from not having to make separate purchases as well as increased satisfaction from one item in the presence of another. Bundle pricing often provides a lower total cost to buyers and lower marketing costs to sellers.[13]

Yield Management Pricing Have you ever been on an airplane and discovered the person next to you paid a lower price for her ticket than you paid? Annoying, isn't it? But what you observed is *yield management pricing*—the charging of different prices to maximize revenue for a set amount of capacity at any given time.[14] Airlines, hotels, and car rental firms engage in capacity management by varying prices based on time, day, week, or season to match demand and supply. American Airlines estimates that yield management pricing produces an annual revenue that exceeds $500 million.[15]

Concept Check

1. What is the profit equation?
2. What is the difference between skimming and penetration pricing?
3. What is odd-even pricing?

Cost-Oriented Approaches

With cost-oriented approaches a price setter stresses the cost side of the pricing problem, not the demand side. Price is set by looking at the production and marketing costs and then adding enough to cover direct expenses, overhead, and profit.

Standard Markup Pricing Managers of supermarkets and other retail stores have such a large number of products that estimating the demand for each product as a means of setting price is impossible. Therefore, they use *standard markup pricing,* which involves adding a fixed percentage to the cost of all items in a specific product class. This percentage markup varies depending on the type of retail store (such as furniture, clothing, or grocery) and on the product involved. High-volume products usually have smaller markups than do low-volume products. Supermarkets such as Kroger and Safeway mark up staple items like sugar, flour, and dairy products 10 to 23 percent, whereas they mark up discretionary items like snack foods and candy 27 to 47 percent. These markups must cover all expenses of the store, pay for overhead costs, and contribute something to profits. For supermarkets these markups, which may appear very large, usually result in only a 1 percent profit on sales revenue.

Cost-Plus Pricing Many manufacturing, professional services, and construction firms use a variation of standard markup pricing. *Cost-plus pricing* involves summing

the total unit cost of providing a product or service and adding a specific amount to the cost to arrive at a price. Cost-plus pricing is the most commonly used method to set prices for business products.[16] Increasingly, however, this method is finding favor among business-to-business marketers in the service sector. For example, the rising cost of legal fees has prompted some law firms to adopt a cost-plus pricing approach. Rather than billing business clients on an hourly basis, lawyers and their clients agree on a fixed fee based on expected costs plus a profit for the law firm. Many advertising agencies now use this approach. Here, the client agrees to pay the agency a fee based on the cost of its work plus some agreed-on profit, which is often a percentage of total cost.[17]

Profit-Oriented Approaches

A price setter may choose to balance both revenues and costs to set price using profit-oriented approaches. These might either involve setting a target of a specific dollar volume of profit or expressing this target profit as a percentage of sales or investment.

Target Profit Pricing When a firm sets an annual target of a specific dollar volume of profit, this is called *target profit pricing*. For example, if you owned a picture frame store and wanted to achieve a target profit of \$7,000, how much would you need to charge for each frame? Since profit depends on revenues and costs, you would have to know your costs and then estimate how many frames you would sell. Let's assume, based on sales in previous years, you expect to frame 1,000 pictures next year. The cost of your time and materials to frame an average picture is \$22, while your overhead expenses (rent, manager salaries, etc.) are \$26,000. Finally, your goal is to achieve a profit of \$7,000. How do you calculate your price per picture?

$$\begin{aligned}\text{Profit} &= \text{Total revenue} - \text{Total costs}\\ &= (\text{Pictures sold} \times \text{Price/picture}) - \\ &\quad [(\text{Cost/picture} \times \text{Pictures sold}) + \text{overhead cost}]\end{aligned}$$

Solving for Price/picture, the equation becomes,

$$\begin{aligned}\text{Price/picture} &= \frac{\text{Profit} + [(\text{Cost/picture} \times \text{Pictures sold}) + \text{overhead cost}]}{\text{Pictures sold}}\\ &= \frac{\$7{,}000 + [(\$22 \times 1{,}000) + \$26{,}000]}{1{,}000}\\ &= \frac{\$7{,}000 + \$48{,}000}{1{,}000}\\ &= \$55 \text{ per picture}\end{aligned}$$

Clearly, this pricing method depends on an accurate estimate of demand. Because demand is often difficult to predict, this method has the potential for disaster if the estimate is too high. Generally, a target profit pricing strategy is best for firms offering new or unique products, without a lot of competition. What if other frame stores in your area were charging \$40 per framed picture? As a marketing manager, you'd have to offer increased customer value with your more expensive frames, lower your costs, or settle for less profit.

Target Return-on-Sales Pricing Firms such as supermarkets often use *target return-on-sales pricing* to set prices that will give them a profit that is a specified percentage—say, 1 percent—of the sales volume. This price method is often used because of the difficulty in establishing a benchmark of sales or investment to show how much of a firm's effort is needed to achieve the target.

Target Return-on-Investment Pricing Firms such as General Motors and many public utilities use *target return-on-investment pricing* to set prices to achieve a return-on-investment (ROI) target such as a percentage that is mandated by its board of directors or regulators. For example, an electric utility may decide to seek 10 percent ROI. If its investment in plant and equipment is $50 billion, it would need to set the price of electricity to its customers at a level that results in $5 billion a year in profits.

Competition-Oriented Approaches

Rather than emphasize demand, cost, or profit factors, a price setter can stress what competitors or "the market" is doing.

Customary Pricing For some products where tradition, a standardized channel of distribution, or other competitive factors dictate the price, *customary pricing* is used. Candy bars offered through standard vending machines have a customary price of 75 cents, and a significant departure from this price may result in a loss of sales for the manufacturer. Hershey typically has changed the amount of chocolate in its candy bars depending on the price of raw chocolate rather than vary its customary retail price so that it can continue selling through vending machines.

Above-, At-, or Below-Market Pricing The "market price" of a product is what customers are generally willing to pay, not necessarily the price that the firm sets. For most products it is difficult to identify a specific market price for a product or product class. Still, marketing managers often have a subjective feel for the competitors' price or the market price. Using this benchmark, they then may deliberately choose a strategy of *above-, at-,* or *below-market pricing.*

Among watch manufacturers, Rolex takes pride in emphasizing that it makes one of the most expensive watches you can buy—a clear example of above-market pricing. Manufacturers of national brands of clothing such as Christian Dior and retailers such as Neiman-Marcus deliberately set higher prices for their products than those seen at Sears.

Large mass-merchandise chains such as Sears and JCPenney generally use at-market pricing. These chains often establish the going market price in the minds of their competitors. They also provide a reference price for competitors that use above- and below-market pricing.

In contrast, a number of firms use below-market pricing. Manufacturers of generic products and retailers that offer their own private brands of products ranging from peanut butter to shampoo deliberately set prices for these products about 8 percent to 10 percent below the prices of nationally branded competitive products such as Skippy peanut butter or Vidal Sassoon shampoo.

Loss-Leader Pricing For a special promotion, retail stores deliberately sell a product below its customary price to attract attention to it. The purpose of this *loss-leader pricing* is not to increase sales but to attract customers in hopes they will buy other products as well, particularly the discretionary items with large markups. Mass merchandisers such as Target, Best Buy, and Wal-Mart sell CDs at about half their suggested retail price to attract customers to their stores.[18]

ESTIMATING DEMAND AND REVENUE

Basic to setting a product's price is the extent of customer demand for it. Marketing executives must also translate this estimate of customer demand into estimates of revenues the firm expects to receive.

Fundamentals of Estimating Demand

How much money would you pay for your favorite magazine? If the price kept going up, at some point you would probably quit buying it. Conversely, if the price kept

going down, you might eventually decide not only to keep buying your magazine but also to get your friend a subscription, too. The lower the price, the higher the demand. The publisher wants to sell more magazines, but will it sell enough additional copies to make up for the lower price per copy? That is an important question for marketing managers. Here's how one firm decided to find out.

Newsweek conducted a pricing experiment at newsstands in 11 cities throughout the United States. At that time, Houston newsstand buyers paid \$2.25, while in Fort Worth, New York, Los Angeles, and Atlanta they paid the regular \$2.00 price. In San Diego, the price was \$1.50, while in Minneapolis–St. Paul, New Orleans, and Detroit it was only \$1.00. By comparison, the regular newsstand price for *Time* and *U.S. News & World Report*, *Newsweek*'s competitors, was \$1.95. Why did *Newsweek* conduct the experiment? According to a *Newsweek* executive, "We want to figure out what the demand curve for our magazine at the newsstand is."[19]

The Demand Curve A **demand curve** is a graph relating the quantity sold and price, which shows the maximum number of units that will be sold at a given price. Demand curve D_1 in Figure 12–3A shows the newsstand demand for *Newsweek* under the existing conditions. Note that as price falls, more people decide to buy and unit sales increase. But price is not the complete story in estimating demand. Economists emphasize three other key factors:

demand curve
Graph relating quantity sold and price, which shows how many units will be sold at a given price

1. *Consumer tastes.* As we saw in Chapter 3, these depend on many factors such as demographics, culture, and technology. Because consumer tastes can change quickly, up-to-date marketing research is essential.
2. *Price and availability of similar products.* The laws of demand work for one's competitors, too. If the price of *Time* magazine falls, more people will buy it. That then means fewer people will buy *Newsweek*. *Time* is considered by economists to be a substitute for *Newsweek*. Online magazines are also a substitute—one whose availability has increased tremendously in recent years. The point to remember is, as the price of substitutes falls or their availability increases, the demand for a product (*Newsweek*, in this case) will fall.[20]
3. *Consumer income.* In general, as real consumer income (allowing for inflation) increases, demand for a product also increases.

FIGURE 12–3
Illustrative demand curves for *Newsweek*

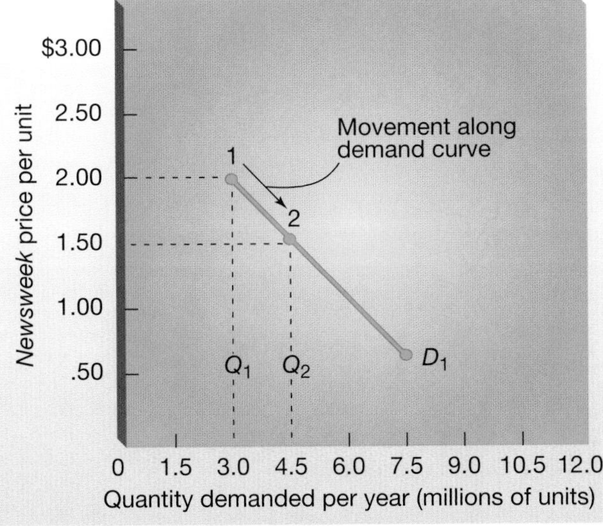

A Demand curve under initial conditions

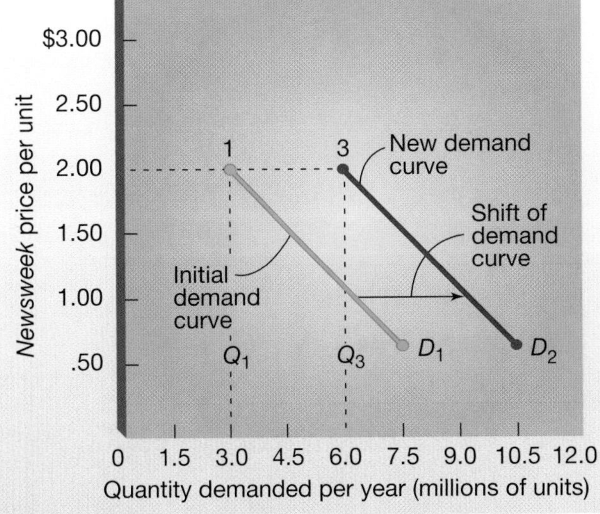

B Shift in the demand curve with more favorable conditions

The first of these two factors influences what consumers *want* to buy, and the third affects what they *can* buy. Along with price, these are often called *demand factors,* or factors that determine consumers' willingness and ability to pay for goods and services. As discussed earlier in Chapters 8 and 10, it is often very difficult to estimate demand for new products, especially because consumer likes and dislikes are often so difficult to read clearly.

Movement Along versus Shift of a Demand Curve Demand curve D_1 in Figure 12–3A shows that as the price is lowered from $2.00 to $1.50, the quantity demanded increases from 3 million (Q_1) to 4.5 million (Q_2) units per year. This is an example of a *movement along a demand curve* and assumes that other factors (consumer tastes, price and availability of substitutes, and consumer income) remain unchanged.

What if some of these factors change? For example, if advertising causes more people to want *Newsweek,* newsstand distribution is increased, or if consumer incomes rise, then the demand increases. Now the original curve, D_1 (the blue line in Figure 12–3B), no longer represents the demand; a new curve must be drawn (D_2). Economists call this a *shift in the demand curve*—in this case, a shift to the right, from D_1 to D_2. This increased demand means that more *Newsweek* magazines are wanted for a given price: At a price of $2, the demand is 6 million units per year (Q_3) on D_2 rather than 3 million units per year (Q_1) on D_1.

What price did *Newsweek* select after conducting its experiment? It kept the price at $2.00. However, through expanded newsstand distribution and more aggressive advertising, *Newsweek* was later able to shift its demand curve to the right and charge a price of $2.50 without affecting its newsstand volume.

Price Elasticity of Demand Marketing managers are especially interested in *price elasticity of demand*—a key consideration related to the product's demand curve. Price elasticity of demand is the percentage change in quantity demanded relative to a percentage change in price. So it measures how sensitive consumer demand and the firm's revenues are to changes in the product's price.

A product with *elastic demand* is one in which a slight decrease in price results in a relatively large increase in demand, or units sold. The reverse is also true: With elastic demand, a slight increase in price results in a relatively large decrease in demand. Marketing experiments on cola, coffee, and snack foods show them often to have elastic demand. So marketing managers may cut price to increase the demand, the units sold, and total revenue for one of these products, depending on what competitors' prices are. Recent research studies show that price elasticity in consumer purchases is increasing, probably because consumers are more often trying to take advantage of temporary price promotions and deals.[21]

In contrast, a product with *inelastic demand* means that slight increases or decreases in price will not significantly affect the demand, or units sold, for the product. Products and services considered as necessities, such as open heart surgery, usually have inelastic demand. What about gasoline for your car or SUV? Will an increase of a few cents per gallon cause you to drive fewer miles and buy less gasoline? No? Then you're like millions of other Americans, which is why gasoline has inelastic demand.[22] This means that an increase of a few cents per gallon may have a relatively minor impact on the number of gallons sold, and may actually increase the total revenue of the gasoline producer.

Concept Check

1. What is loss-leader pricing?
2. What are the three demand factors besides the product's price that determine consumers' willingness and ability to buy the product?
3. What is the difference between movement along a demand curve and a shift in a demand curve?

FIGURE 12–4
Fundamental revenue concept

Total revenue (TR) is the total money received from the sale of a product. If

TR = Total revenue
P = Unit price of the product
Q = Quantity of the product sold

Then

TR = P × Q

Fundamentals of Estimating Revenue

total revenue
Total money received from the sale of a product

While economists may talk about "demand curves," marketing executives are more likely to speak in terms of "revenues generated." Demand curves lead directly to an essential revenue concept critical to pricing decisions: **total revenue**. As summarized in Figure 12–4, total revenue (TR) equals the unit price (P) times the quantity sold (Q). Using this equation, let's recall our picture frame shop and assume our annual demand has improved so we can set a price of $100 per picture and sell 400 pictures per year. So,

$$
\begin{aligned}
TR &= P \times Q \\
&= \$100 \times 400 \\
&= \$40{,}000
\end{aligned}
$$

This combination of price and quantity sold annually will give us a total revenue of $40,000 per year. Is that good? Are you making money, making a profit? Alas, total revenue is only part of the profit equation that we saw earlier:

Total profit = Total revenue − Total cost

The next section covers the other part of the profit equation: cost.

DETERMINING COST, VOLUME, AND PROFIT RELATIONSHIPS

total cost
Total expenses incurred by a firm in producing and marketing a product; total cost is the sum of fixed cost and variable costs

fixed cost
Firm's expenses that are stable and do not change with the quantity of product that is produced and sold

variable cost
Sum of the expenses of the firm that vary directly with the quantity of products that is produced and sold

unit variable cost
Variable cost expressed on a per unit basis

While revenues are the moneys received by the firm from selling its products or services to customers, costs or expenses are the moneys the firm pays out to its employees and suppliers. Marketing managers often use break-even analysis to relate revenues and costs, topics covered in this section.

The Importance of Controlling Costs

Understanding the role and behavior of costs is critical for all marketing decisions, particularly pricing decisions. Four cost concepts are important in pricing decisions: **total cost**, **fixed cost**, **variable cost**, and **unit variable cost** (Figure 12–5 on the next page).

Many firms go bankrupt because their costs get out of control, causing their total costs to exceed their total revenues over an extended period of time. So firms are increasingly trying to control their fixed costs like insurance and executive salaries[23] and reduce the variable costs in their manufactured items by having production done outside the United States.[24] This is why sophisticated marketing managers make pricing decisions that balance both their revenues and costs. As described in the Marketing NewsNet, travel dot-com firms have been more successful than brick-and-mortar dot-coms at least partly because of far lower fixed costs.[25]

FIGURE 12–5
Fundamental cost concepts

Total cost (TC) is the total expense incurred by a firm in producing and marketing a product. Total cost is the sum of fixed cost and variable cost.

Fixed cost (FC) is the sum of the expenses of the firm that are stable and do not change with the quantity of a product that is produced and sold. Examples of fixed costs are rent on the building, executive salaries, and insurance.

Variable cost (VC) is the sum of the expenses of the firm that vary directly with the quantity of a product that is produced and sold. For example, as the quantity sold doubles, the variable cost doubles. Examples are the direct labor and direct materials used in producing the product and the sales commissions that are tied directly to the quantity sold. As mentioned above,

$$TC = FC + VC$$

Variable cost expressed on a per unit basis is called **unit variable cost (UVC)**, or

$$UVC = \frac{VC}{Q}$$

Break-Even Analysis

break-even analysis
Examines the relationship between total revenue and total cost to determine profitability at different levels of output

Marketing managers often employ an approach that considers cost, volume, and profit relationships, based on the profit equation. **Break-even analysis** is a technique that analyzes the relationship between total revenue and total cost to determine profitability at various levels of output. The *break-even point* (BEP) is the quantity at which total revenue and total cost are equal. Profit comes from any units sold beyond the BEP. In terms of the definitions in Figure 12–5,

$$BEP_{Quantity} = \frac{\text{Fixed cost}}{\text{Unit price} - \text{Unit variable cost}}$$

Calculating a Break-Even Point Consider again your picture frame store. Suppose you wish to identify how many pictures you must sell to cover your fixed cost at a given price. Let's assume demand for your framed pictures has increased so the average price customers are willing to pay for each picture is $100. Also, suppose your fixed cost (FC) has grown to $28,000 (for real estate taxes, interest on a bank loan, and other fixed expenses) and unit variable cost (UVC) for a picture is now $30 (for labor, glass, frame, and matting). The row shaded in brown in Figure 12–6 shows that your break-even quantity at a price of $100 per picture is 400 pictures.

FIGURE 12–6
Calculating a break-even point for a picture frame store

QUANTITY OF PICTURES SOLD (Q)	PRICE PER PICTURE (P)	TOTAL REVENUE (TR) = (P × Q)	UNIT VARIABLE COST (UVC)	TOTAL VARIABLE COST (TVC) = (UVC × Q)	FIXED COST (FC)	TOTAL COST (TC) = (FC + TVC)	PROFIT = (TR − TC)
0	$100	$ 0	$30	$ 0	$28,000	$28,000	−$28,000
200	100	20,000	30	6,000	28,000	34,000	−14,000
400	100	40,000	30	12,000	28,000	40,000	0
600	100	60,000	30	18,000	28,000	46,000	14,000
800	100	80,000	30	24,000	28,000	52,000	28,000
1,000	100	100,000	30	30,000	28,000	58,000	42,000
1,200	100	120,000	30	36,000	28,000	64,000	56,000

TECHNOLOGY & E-COMMERCE

MARKETING NEWSNET

Pricing Lessons from the Dot-Coms—Understand Revenues and Expenses

Price, revenue, fixed cost, variable cost. Boring topics from finance or economics? But they are also critical to marketing success, as shown by lessons learned by the successful travel dot-coms so far.

Brick-and-Mortar Dot-Com Failures

During the past decade, hundreds of dot-coms have failed, many of them brick-and-mortar businesses like Pets.com (pet products) and Webvan (online groceries). Here are some reasons for these failures:

- Setting prices too low to cover the huge brick-and-mortar fixed costs of inventory, warehouses, and order fulfillment, especially on low-margin goods like groceries (Webvan).
- Spending too much on promotion, such as Pets.com's $2.2 million on Super Bowl XXXV ads.
- Believing people would forgo shopping at traditional stores, a problem, for example, with Pets.com competing with Petsmart.

Everyone Deserves
a Second Chance, BarNone

As a result, Pets.com was liquidated. However, the Pets.com sock puppet, because of its visibility, was bought by and serves as the "spokespuppet" for BarNone, a firm that helps consumers with poor credit obtain automobiles.

Travel Dot-Com Successes (So Far)

Besides time and money savings for customers, the travel dot-coms have special strategies for success:

- Reaching key customer segments that will actually pay *higher* prices for hotel rooms or airline tickets.
- Reaching customer segments (students, senior citizens) whose last-minute or last-week flexibility enables them to reserve hotel rooms or airline seats that would otherwise go unsold.
- Being able to conduct almost all operations electronically, without the warehousing and order fulfillment problems of their brick-and-mortar dot-com cousins.

Still, travel dot-coms face major uncertainties. One is the appearance of Orbitz.com, an online travel agency owned by five major U.S. airlines.

Your break-even quantity ($BEP_{Quantity}$) is 400 pictures, calculated as follows:

$$
\begin{aligned}
BEP_{Quantity} &= \frac{\text{Fixed cost}}{\text{Unit price} - \text{Unit variable cost}} \\
&= \frac{\$28{,}000}{\$100 - \$30} \\
&= 400 \text{ pictures}
\end{aligned}
$$

At less than 400 pictures your picture frame store incurs a loss, and at more than 400 pictures it makes a profit. Figure 12–6 also shows that if you could double your annual picture sales to 800, your store would make a profit of $28,000—the row shaded in green in the figure.

Figure 12–7 on the next page shows a graphic presentation of the break-even analysis, called a *break-even chart.* It shows that total revenue and total cost intersect and are equal at a quantity of 400 pictures sold, which is the break-even point at which profit is exactly $0. You want to do better? If your frame store could double the quantity sold annually to 800 pictures, the graph in Figure 12–7 shows you can earn an annual profit of $28,000, just as shown by the row shaded in green in Figure 12–6.

Applications of Break-Even Analysis Because of its simplicity, break-even analysis is used extensively in marketing, most frequently to study the impact on profit of changes in price, fixed cost, and variable cost. The mechanics of break-even analysis are the basis of the widely used electronic spreadsheets offered by computer programs such as Microsoft Excel that permit managers to answer hypothetical "what if" questions about the effect of changes in price and cost on their profit.

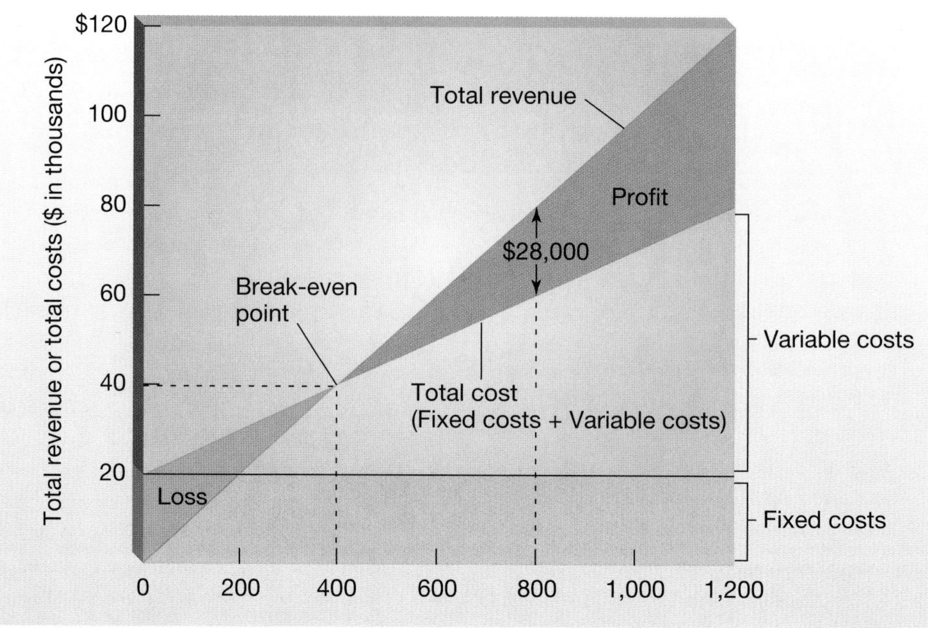

FIGURE 12–7
Break-even chart for a picture frame store

Concept Check

1. What is the difference between fixed costs and variable costs?
2. What is a break-even point?

PRICING OBJECTIVES AND CONSTRAINTS

With such a variety of alternative pricing strategies available, a marketing manager must consider the pricing objectives and constraints that will narrow the range of choices. While pricing objectives frequently reflect corporate goals, pricing constraints often relate to conditions existing in the marketplace.

Identifying Pricing Objectives

pricing objectives
Expectations that specify the role of price in an organization's marketing and strategic plans

Pricing objectives specify the role of price in an organization's marketing and strategic plans. To the extent possible, these pricing objectives are carried to lower levels in the organization, such as in setting objectives for marketing managers responsible for an individual brand. These objectives may change depending on the financial position of the company as a whole, the success of its products, or the segments in which it is doing business. H. J. Heinz, for example, has specific pricing objectives for its Heinz ketchup brand that vary by country.

Profit Three different objectives relate to a firm's profit, which is often measured in terms of return on investment (ROI). These objectives have different implications for pricing strategy. One objective is *managing for long-run profits,* in which a company—such as many Japanese car or TV set manufacturers—gives up immediate profit in exchange for achieving a higher market share. Products are priced relatively low compared to their cost to develop, but the firm expects to make greater profits later because of its high market share.

A *maximizing current profit* objective, such as for a quarter or year, is common in many firms because the targets can be set and performance measured quickly. American firms are sometimes criticized for this short-run orientation. As noted earlier, a *target return* objective occurs when a firm sets a profit goal (such as 20 percent for return on investment), usually determined by its board of directors. These three profit objectives have different implications for a firm's pricing objectives.

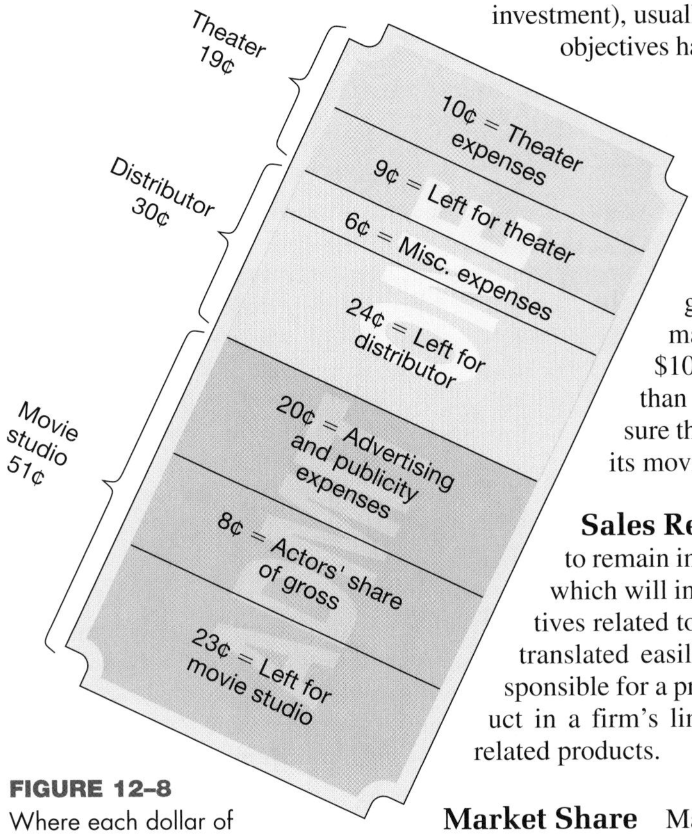

Another profit consideration for firms such as movie studios and manufacturers is to ensure that those firms in their channels of distribution make adequate profits. Without profits for these channel members, the movie studio or manufacturer is cut off from its customers. For example, Figure 12–8 shows where each dollar of your movie ticket goes. The 51 cents the movie studio gets must cover its profit plus the cost of making and marketing the movie, which averaged an all-time high of $103 million in 2004. Although the studio would like more than 51 cents of your dollar, it settles for this amount to make sure theaters and distributors are satisfied and willing to handle its movies.

Theater 19¢
10¢ = Theater expenses
9¢ = Left for theater
Distributor 30¢
6¢ = Misc. expenses
24¢ = Left for distributor
Movie studio 51¢
20¢ = Advertising and publicity expenses
8¢ = Actors' share of gross
23¢ = Left for movie studio

FIGURE 12–8
Where each dollar of your movie ticket goes

Sales Revenue Given that a firm's profit is high enough for it to remain in business, an objective may be to increase sales revenue, which will in turn lead to increases in market share and profit. Objectives related to sales revenue or unit sales have the advantage of being translated easily into meaningful targets for marketing managers responsible for a product line or brand. However, cutting price on one product in a firm's line may increase its sales revenue but reduce those of related products.

Market Share Market share is the ratio of the firm's sales revenues or unit sales to those of the industry (competitors plus the firm itself). Companies often pursue a market share objective when industry sales are relatively flat or declining. In the late 1990s, Boeing cut prices drastically to try to maintain its 60 percent market share and encountered huge losses. Although increased market share is a primary goal of some firms, others see it as a means to other ends: increasing sales and profits.

Unit Volume Many firms use unit volume, the quantity produced or sold, as a pricing objective. These firms often sell multiple products at very different prices and need to match the unit volume demanded by customers with price and production capacity. Using unit volume as an objective can be counterproductive if a volume objective is achieved, say, by drastic price cutting that drives down profit.

Survival In some instances, profits, sales, and market share are less important objectives of the firm than mere survival. Continental Airlines has struggled to attract passengers with low fares and aggressive promotions to improve the firm's cash flow. This pricing objective has helped Continental to stay alive in the competitive airline industry.

Social Responsibility A firm may forgo higher profit on sales and follow a pricing objective that recognizes its obligations to customers and society in general. Medtronics followed this pricing policy when it introduced the world's first heart pacemaker. Gerber supplies a specially formulated product free of charge to children who cannot tolerate foods based on cow's milk.

Identifying Pricing Constraints

pricing constraints
Factors that limit the range of price a firm may set

Factors that limit the range of price a firm may set are **pricing constraints**. Consumer demand for the product clearly affects the price that can be charged. Other constraints on price vary from factors within the organization to competitive factors outside it.

MARKETING NEWSNET — Pricing 101—$4,205 for a 1969 Used Hotwheels Volkswagen Van, or $121,000 for a Mint-Condition 1952 Mickey Mantle Topps Baseball Card?

Prices of collectibles, such as toys or old sneakers, are set by demand and supply forces discussed in this chapter. And for fads, the prices can fluctuate wildly. Here are some 2005 collectibles prices, besides those wild 1998 prices mentioned above:

- Zip the Cat Beanie Baby: $56 (if it has black paws).
- 1985 Nike Dunks, high-top, blue-and-black basketball shoes: $375.
- 2001 Ichiro Suzuki bobble-head doll: $35.

To get a feel for prices of some of these collectibles, visit www.ebay.com.

Marathon runner Malcolm East now wishes he had done a little more research on sneaker prices. At his wife's insistence he threw out six pairs of old shoes—that he now thinks would have fetched $15,000.

Want in on the collectibles business? Think twice. Zip the Cat Beanie Baby sold for $2,250 in 1998, over $2,000 more than in 2005.

Demand for the Product Class, Product, and Brand The number of potential buyers for a product class (cars), product (sports cars), and brand (Bugatti Veyron) clearly affects the price a seller can charge. So does whether the item is a luxury, like a Bugatti, or a necessity, like bread and a roof over your head. Generally speaking, the higher the demand for a product, the higher the price can be set.

Newness of the Product: Stage in the Product Life Cycle The newer the product and the earlier it is in its life cycle, the higher the price that can usually be charged. The high initial price is possible because of patents and limited competition in the early stage.

Sometimes—when nostalgia or fad factors come into play—prices may rise later in the product's life cycle. As described in the Marketing NewsNet, collectibles such as a 1952 Mickey Mantle baseball card or old sneakers can experience skyrocketing prices.[26] But they can take a nosedive, too: The Zip the Cat Beanie Baby sold for $2,250 in 1998, over $2,000 more than in 2005. Publishing competitive prices on the Internet has revolutionized access to price comparisons for both collectors and buyers of more traditional products.[27]

Are these real "collectibles" or "trashables"? The text describes factors that affect a product's price. And you can check the Marketing NewsNet to see if those old Beanie Babies or Nikes in your attic or a recent Ichiro Suzuki bobble-head doll have value.

Cost of Producing and Marketing the Product In the long run, a firm's price must cover all the costs of producing and marketing a product. If the price doesn't cover these costs, the firm will fail; so in the long run, a firm's costs set a floor under its price.

Competitors' Prices A firm must know or anticipate what specific price its present and potential competitors are charging now or will charge. And the firm must assess the possibility of dangerous, costly price wars.[28]

Legal and Ethical Considerations Setting a final price is clearly a complex process. The task is further complicated by legal and ethical issues. Four pricing practices have received special scrutiny over these issues and are described below:

- *Price fixing.* A conspiracy among firms to set prices for a product is termed price fixing. Price fixing is illegal under the Sherman Act. When two or more competitors collude to explicitly or implicitly set prices, this practice is called *horizontal price fixing.* For example, six foreign vitamin companies recently pled guilty to price fixing in the human and animal vitamin industry and paid the largest fine in U.S. history: $335 million. *Vertical price fixing* involves controlling agreements between independent buyers and sellers (a manufacturer and a retailer) whereby sellers are required to not sell products below a minimum retail price. This practice, called *resale price maintenance,* was declared illegal in 1975 under provisions of the Consumer Goods Pricing Act.

- *Price discrimination.* The Clayton Act as amended by the Robinson-Patman Act prohibits price discrimination—the practice of charging different prices to different buyers for goods of like grade and quality. However, not all price differences are illegal; only those that substantially lessen competition or create a monopoly are deemed unlawful.
- *Deceptive pricing.* Price deals that mislead consumers fall into the category of deceptive pricing. Deceptive pricing is outlawed by the Federal Trade Commission. *Bait and switch* is an example of deceptive pricing. This occurs when a firm offers a very low price on a product (the bait) to attract customers to a store. Once in the store, the customer is persuaded to purchase a higher-priced item (the switch) using a variety of tricks, including (1) degrading the promoted item and (2) not having the promised item in stock or refusing to take orders for it.
- *Predatory pricing.* Predatory pricing is charging a very low price for a product with the intent of driving competitors out of business. Once competitors have been driven out, the firm raises its prices. Proving the presence of this practice has been difficult and expensive because it must be shown that the predator explicitly attempted to destroy a competitor and the predatory price was below the defendant's average cost.

It should be clear that laws cannot be passed and enforced to protect consumers and competitors against all of these practices, so it is essential to rely on the ethical standards of those setting prices.

Concept Check

1. What is the difference between pricing objectives and pricing constraints?
2. Explain what bait and switch is and why it is an example of deceptive pricing.

SETTING A FINAL PRICE

The final price set by the marketing manager serves many functions. It must be high enough to cover the cost of providing the product *and* meet the objectives of the company. Yet it must be low enough that customers are willing to pay it. But not too low, or customers may think they're purchasing an inferior product. Dizzy yet? Setting price is one of the most difficult tasks the marketing manager faces, but three generalized steps are useful to follow.

Step 1: Select an Approximate Price Level

Before setting a final price, the marketing manager must understand the market environment, the features and customer benefits of the particular product, and the goals of the firm. A balance must be struck between factors that might drive a price higher (such as a profit-oriented approach) and other forces (such as increased competition from substitutes) that may drive a price down.

Marketing managers consider pricing objectives and constraints first, then choose among the general pricing approaches—demand-, cost-, profit-, or competition-oriented—to arrive at an approximate price level. This price is then analyzed in terms of cost, volume, and profit relationships. Break-even analyses may be run at this point, and finally if this approximate price level "works," it is time to take the next step: setting a specific list or quoted price.

Step 2: Set the List or Quoted Price

A seller must decide whether to follow a one-price or flexible-price policy.

One-Price Policy A *one-price policy* involves setting one price for all buyers of a product or service. For example, Saturn Corporation uses this approach in its stores and features a "no haggle, one price" price for its cars. As mentioned earlier, this one-and-the-same price for all its airline passengers has contributed to JetBlue's success. Some retailers such as Dollar Valley have married this policy with a below-market approach and sell everything in their stores for $1 or less!

Flexible-Price Policy In contrast, a *flexible-price policy* involves setting different prices for products and services depending on individual buyers and purchase situation in light of demand, cost, and competitive factors. Dell Computer recently adopted flexible pricing as it continually adjusts prices in response to changes in its own costs, competitive pressures, and demand from its various personal computer segments (home, small business, corporate, etc.). "Our flexibility allows us to be [priced] different even within a day," says a Dell spokesperson.[29]

Chain apparel stores use the beginning of the week to discover what isn't selling well to make plans for the high-traffic weekends. So the best deals in their flexible-price policy come Wednesdays through Fridays, right before the weekend. Some apparel chains have specific days for nationwide price markdowns: Wednesdays for The Gap and Thursdays for J. Crew and Eddie Bauer.[30]

Step 3: Make Special Adjustments to the List or Quoted Price

When you pay 75 cents for a bag of M&Ms in a vending machine or receive a quoted price of $10,000 from a contractor to renovate a kitchen, the pricing sequence ends with the last step just described: setting the list or quoted price. But when you are a manufacturer of M&M candies and sell your product to dozens or hundreds of wholesalers and retailers in your channel of distribution, you may need to make a variety of special adjustments to the list or quoted price. Wholesalers also must adjust list or quoted prices they set for retailers. Three special adjustments to the list or quoted price are (1) discounts, (2) allowances, and (3) geographical adjustments.

Discounts *Discounts* are reductions from list price that a seller gives a buyer as a reward for some activity of the buyer that is favorable to the seller. Four kinds of discounts are especially important in marketing strategy: (1) quantity, (2) seasonal, (3) trade (functional), and (4) cash.[31]

- *Quantity discounts.* To encourage customers to buy larger quantities of a product, firms at all levels in the channel of distribution offer quantity discounts, which are reductions in unit costs for a larger order. For example, an instant photocopying service might set a price of 10 cents a copy for 1 to 24 copies, 9 cents a copy for 25 to 99, and 8 cents a copy for 100 or more. Because the photocopying service gets more of the buyer's business and has longer production runs that reduce its order-handling costs, it is willing to pass on some of the cost savings in the form of quantity discounts to the buyer.
- *Seasonal discounts.* To encourage buyers to stock inventory earlier than their normal demand would require, manufacturers often use seasonal discounts. A firm such as Toro that manufactures lawn mowers and snow throwers offers seasonal discounts to encourage wholesalers

What is the best day of the week to shop at Eddie Bauer, The Gap, and J. Crew with their flexible-pricing approach? For the answers, see the text.

Manufacturers provide a variety of discounts to assist channel members such as for Payless, a retailer promoting its early summer sandals sale.

and retailers to stock up on lawn mowers in January and February and on snow throwers in July and August—five or six months before the seasonal demand by ultimate consumers. This enables Toro to smooth out seasonal manufacturing peaks and troughs, thereby contributing to more efficient production. It also rewards wholesalers and retailers for the risk they accept in assuming increased inventory carrying costs and having supplies in stock at the time they are wanted by customers.

- *Trade (functional) discounts.* To reward wholesalers and retailers for marketing functions they will perform in the future, a manufacturer often gives trade, or functional, discounts. These reductions off the list or base price are offered to resellers in the channel of distribution on the basis of (1) where they are in the channel and (2) the marketing activities they are expected to perform in the future.

  Traditional trade discounts have been established in various product lines such as hardware, food, and pharmaceutical items. Although the manufacturer may suggest the trade discounts shown in the example just cited, the sellers are free to alter the discount schedule depending on their competitive situation.
- *Cash discounts.* To encourage retailers to pay their bills quickly, manufacturers offer them cash discounts. Suppose a retailer receives a bill quoted at $1,000, 2/10 net 30. This means that the bill for the product is $1,000, but the retailer can take a 2 percent discount ($\$1,000 \times 0.02 = \$20$) if payment is made within 10 days and send a check for $980. If the payment cannot be made within 10 days, the total amount of $1,000 is due within 30 days. It is usually understood by the buyer that an interest charge will be added after the first 30 days of free credit.

  A retailer like Payless that plans an early summer sale on sandals often tries to take advantage of several of these discounts to increase its revenues and profits.

Allowances Allowances—like discounts—are reductions from list or quoted prices to buyers for performing some activity.

- *Trade-in allowances.* A new-car dealer can offer a substantial reduction in the list price of that new Toyota Camry by offering you a trade-in allowance of $500 for your Chevrolet. A trade-in allowance is a price reduction given when a used product is part of the payment on a new product. Trade-ins are an effective way to lower the price a buyer has to pay without formally reducing the list price.
- *Promotional allowances.* Sellers in the channel of distribution can qualify for promotional allowances for undertaking certain advertising or selling activities to promote a product. Various types of allowances include an actual cash payment or an extra amount of "free goods" (as with a free case of pizzas to a retailer for every dozen cases purchased). Frequently, a portion of these savings is passed on to the consumer by retailers.

Some companies, such as Procter & Gamble, have chosen to reduce promotional allowances for retailers by using everyday low pricing. *Everyday low pricing* (EDLP) is the practice of replacing promotional allowances with lower manufacturer list prices. EDLP promises to reduce the average price to consumers while minimizing promotional allowances that cost manufacturers billions of dollars every year.[32]

Geographical Adjustments Geographical adjustments are made by manufacturers or even wholesalers to list or quoted prices to reflect the cost of transportation of the products from seller to buyer. The two general methods for quoting prices related to transportation costs are (1) FOB origin pricing and (2) uniform delivered pricing.

- *FOB origin pricing.* FOB means "free on board" some vehicle at some location, which means the seller pays the cost of loading the product onto the vehicle that is used (such as a barge, railroad car, or truck). FOB origin pricing usually involves the seller's naming the location of this loading as the seller's factory or warehouse (such as "FOB Detroit" or "FOB factory"). The title to the goods passes to the buyer at the point of loading, so the buyer becomes responsible for picking the specific mode of transportation, for all the transportation costs, and for subsequent handling of the product. Buyers farthest from the seller face the big disadvantage of paying the higher transportation costs.

- *Uniform delivered pricing.* When a uniform delivered pricing method is used, the price the seller quotes includes all transportation costs. It is quoted in a contract as "FOB buyer's location," and the seller selects the mode of transportation, pays the freight charges, and is responsible for any damage that may occur because the seller retains title to the goods until delivered to the buyer.

Concept Check

1. What are the three steps in setting a final price?
2. What is the purpose of (*a*) quantity discounts and (*b*) promotional allowances?

CHAPTER IN REVIEW

1 *Identify the elements that make up a price.*
Price is the money or other considerations (such as barter) exchanged for the ownership or use of a good or service. Although price typically involves money, the amount exchanged is often different from the list or quoted price because of incentives (rebates, discounts, etc.), allowances (trade), and extra fees (finance charges, surcharges, etc.).

2 *Describe how to establish the initial approximate price level using demand-oriented, cost-oriented, profit-oriented, and competition-oriented approaches.*
Demand, cost, profit, and competition influence the initial consideration of the approximate price level for a product or service. Demand-oriented pricing approaches stress consumer demand and revenue implications of pricing and include seven types: skimming, penetration, prestige, odd-even, target, bundle, and yield management. Cost-oriented pricing approaches emphasize the cost aspects of pricing and include two types: standard markup and cost-plus pricing. Profit-oriented pricing approaches focus on a balance between revenues and costs to set a price and include three types: target profit, target return-on-sales, and target return-on-investment pricing. And finally, competition-oriented pricing approaches stress what competitors or the marketplace are doing and include three types: customary; above-, at-, or below-market; and loss-leader pricing.

3 *Explain what a demand curve is and the role of revenues in pricing decisions.*
A demand curve is a graph relating the quantity sold and price, which shows the maximum number of units that will be sold at a given price. Three demand factors affect price: (*a*) consumer tastes, (*b*) price and availability of substitute products, and (*c*) consumer income. These demand factors determine consumers' willingness and ability to pay for goods and services. Assuming these demand factors remain unchanged, if the price of a product is lowered or raised, then the quantity demanded for it will increase or decrease, respectively. The demand curve relates to a firm's total revenue, which is the total money received from sale of a product, or the price of one unit times the quantity of units sold.

4 *Explain the role of costs in pricing decisions.*
Four important costs impact a firm's pricing decisions: (*a*) total cost, or total expenses, the sum of fixed cost and variable cost incurred by a firm in producing and marketing a product; (*b*) fixed cost, the sum of expenses of the firm that are stable and do not change with the quantity of a product that is produced and sold; (*c*) variable cost, the sum of expenses of the firm that vary directly with the quantity of a product that is produced and sold; and (*d*) unit variable cost, variable cost expressed on a per unit basis.

5 *Describe how various combinations of price, fixed cost, and unit variable cost affect a firm's break-even point.*
Break-even analysis is a technique that analyzes the relationship between total revenue and total cost to determine profitability at various levels of output. The break-even point is the quantity at which total revenue and total cost are equal. Assuming no change in price, if the costs of a firm's product increase due to higher fixed costs (manufacturing or advertising) or variable costs (direct labor or materials), then its break-even point will be higher. And if total cost is unchanged, an increase in price will reduce the break-even point.

6 *Recognize the objectives a firm has in setting prices and the constraints that restrict the range of prices a firm can charge.*
Pricing objectives specify the role of price in a firm's marketing strategy and may include profit, sales revenue, market share, unit volume, survival, or some socially responsible price level. Pricing constraints that restrict a firm's pricing flexibility include demand, product newness, production and marketing costs, prices of competitive substitutes, and legal and ethical considerations.

7 *Describe the steps taken in setting a final price.*
Three common steps marketing managers often use are: first, select an approximate price level as a starting point; second, set the list or quoted price, choosing between a one-price policy or a flexible-price policy; and third, modify the list or quoted price by considering discounts, allowances, and geographical adjustments.

FOCUSING ON KEY TERMS

break-even analysis p. 272
demand curve p. 269
fixed cost p. 271
price p. 262
pricing constraints p. 275
pricing objectives p. 274
profit equation p. 264
total cost p. 271
total revenue p. 271
unit variable cost p. 271
variable cost p. 271

DISCUSSION AND APPLICATION QUESTIONS

1 How would the price equation apply to the purchase price of (*a*) gasoline, (*b*) an airline ticket, and (*c*) a checking account?

2 What would be your response to the statement, "Profit maximization is the only legitimate pricing objective for the firm"?

3 Touché Toiletries, Inc., has developed an addition to its Lizardman Cologne line tentatively branded Ode d'Toade Cologne. Unit variable costs are 45 cents for a 3-ounce bottle, and heavy advertising expenditures in the first year would result in total fixed costs of $900,000. Ode d'Toade Cologne is priced at $7.50 for a 3-ounce bottle. How many bottles of Ode d'Toade must be sold to break even?

4 Suppose that marketing executives for Touché Toiletries reduced the price to $6.50 for a 3-ounce bottle of Ode d'Toade and the fixed costs were $1,100,000. Suppose further that the unit variable cost remained at 45 cents for a 3-ounce bottle. (*a*) How many bottles must be sold to break even? (*b*) What dollar profit level would Ode d'Toade achieve if 200,000 bottles were sold?

5 Under what conditions would a camera manufacturer adopt a skimming price approach for a new product? A penetration approach?

6 What are some similarities and differences between skimming pricing, prestige pricing, and above-market pricing?

7 The Hesper Corporation is a leading manufacturer of high-quality upholstered sofas. Current plans call for an increase of $600,000 in the advertising budget. If the firm sells its sofas for an average price of $850 and the unit variable costs are $550, then what dollar sales increase will be necessary to cover the additional advertising?

GOING ONLINE Finding the Best Airline Ticket Price

It's Wednesday and you just completed your midterm exams. As a reward for your hard work, a friend has sent you a pair of free tickets to a popular Broadway show in New York City for 7:00 P.M. Saturday night. Check out the following online travel services to book a nonstop, round-trip ticket, leaving from Chicago's O'Hare (ORD) airport around 4:00 P.M. on Friday to New York City's La Guardia (LGA) airport. On Sunday, you'll leave La Guardia around 5:00 P.M. and return to O'Hare.

Which of the following online travel services provides the cheapest fare and is easiest to use? Check out our search and see if you can beat the prices we obtained in late 2005:

- Expedia (www.expedia.com)—Lowest price: $201.00 from United Airlines.
- Orbitz (www.orbitz.com), the online travel service owned by the major airlines—Lowest price: $248.00 from United Airlines.
- Priceline (www.priceline.com)—Lowest price: $199.00 from United Airlines.
- Travelocity (www.travelocity.com)—Lowest price: $201.00 from United Airlines.

(*Note:* Be careful that you do not accidentally purchase an actual ticket because some services require you to make a purchase before receiving information.)

BUILDING YOUR MARKETING PLAN

1 In starting to set a final price, think about your customers and competitors and set three possible prices.

2 Assume a fixed cost and unit variable cost and (*a*) calculate the break-even points and (*b*) plot a break-even chart for the three prices specified in step 2.

3 Using your best judgment, select one of these prices as your final price.

VIDEO CASE 12 Stuart Cellars: Price Is a Matter of Taste

Stuart Cellars is a family-owned winery located in Temecula, California. The winery marked its first harvest in 1999. Forty acres are available for cultivation, giving Stuart Cellars a capacity of some 150 tons of grapes and yielding about 16,000 cases of wine per year. Stuart Cellars offers its Chardonnay, Merlot, Cabernet Sauvignon, Cabernet Franc, Zinfandel, Viognier, and other wines for sale through its tasting room, its website (www.stuartcellars.com), and retailers in California.

Retail prices for Stuart Cellars products range from $13 per bottle for a Chardonnay, Viognier, Sauvignon Blanc, and White Merlot blend, to $46 per bottle for a 2002 Zinfandel Vintage Port. The average retail price for a Stuart Cellars wine is about $28 per bottle. Stuart Cellars Wine Club members enjoy a 20 percent discount and receive additional benefits such as complimentary tasting at the winery, special "member only" wines, additional discounts for reorders of the monthly wine selection, and quantity discounts.

PRICING WINE: CONSIDERING COSTS AND PROFITS

How does Stuart Cellars arrive at its pricing? What factors enter into the pricing decision?

The price floor is usually set by costs. Costs vary widely depending on winery location and number of years in business. There are tremendous economies of scale for larger producers versus smaller boutique wineries such as Stuart Cellars. Grapes, including labor to grow and harvest, can represent up to 60 percent of production expenses. One rule of thumb is that a bottle of wine should be priced at 1/1000 the cost of a ton of grapes. Paying $40,000 for a ton of Cabernet grapes would yield a bottle price of $40. Napa Valley growers' costs range from $2,800 per ton to $10,000 per ton.

Buying land adds to winery costs but provides more operational control. Even wineries that do grow grapes may need to buy grapes on the market to meet their production needs. The impact of land ownership depends on the size of the mortgage and the interest rate to finance the property. Planting costs can be as much as $30,000 per acre, depending on such factors as density of plantings, trellising, and irrigation methods. Winery facilities and equipment—grape press, tanks, barrel racks—can be significant. Winemaking barrels are the second-highest production cost for many wineries. American oak barrels ($300 per barrel) or French oak ($700 per barrel) may have a useful life of two to three years. On the other hand, a stainless tank may last 20 years. And of course, repair and maintenance costs for equipment and facilities can add up.

Because it can be a three-year wait to harvest grapes from new plantings, followed by barrel and bottle aging, wineries can easily have five and a half years of capital and cash flow for red wines—less for white wines that require less aging. Packaging is also important and a reflection of the wine's image. Will the winery use flat-bottomed, Burgundy-style bottles at $.50 each, or thick-glass, thick-neck, deep-punt bottles at $3? Corks can range in price from pennies to dollars a piece.

Advertising, public relations, point-of-sale materials, promotions, salesforce, wine tastings, samples for the wine press, warehousing, shipping, distribution, and excise taxes all mount up and can be about 15 percent of the retail price. Warehousing and shipping are significant because wine is a heavy product.

Many states have regulated distribution systems such as California's three-tier system of wineries, wholesalers, and retailers. Wholesaler markups range from 20–35 percent of what the distributor pays for the wine, with high-volume wines having lower margins as this means less inventory. Retailer markups can vary from 10–50 percent, depending on the type of outlet. Some states have mandated minimum markup to prevent predatory pricing.

The wine business is not known as a highly profitable business. Success comes over the long term as initial investments and expenses are spread out over a number of years and over increasing unit volume.

CONSUMER DEMAND AND COMPETITION

Costs and profit objectives are only part of the pricing formula. Wineries also have to consider buyer characteristics—retailers and consumers. According to Steven Bombola, consulting general manager, Stuart Cellars is targeting the "upper end of wine connoisseurs, people who can afford a premium product at a premium price" and represents perhaps "the top 10–15 percent of the wine purchasing public." These are savvy consumers; they read and follow wine reviews. Wineries also need to consider and compare pricing from competitive wineries. Wine buyers certainly will make these comparisons. And while price is often a cue for quality, there are many great-tasting wines at reasonable prices.

If a wine is priced too low, it will affect consumers' perceptions of quality. However, charging a price significantly higher than competitor prices can drive consumers away to lower-priced competitor products.

"People's perceptions are driven by wine pricing," states Robert Mondavi's senior vice president, Gayle Dargan. "If all consumer decisions were driven by blind-tasting, it would be a very different world. That's not reality. Price is a signal to people of our commitment and the efforts we are taking through out vineyards and our winemaking to put out the best wines."

The average bottle price for wine has been dropping, in large part due to the popularity of Australian and New Zealand wines. Most popular wine brands retail for less than $10 per bottle.

Image is very important in wine marketing. Fancy bottles, elegant and artistic labels, advertising, celebrity endorsements, and wine reviews can all impact consumers' perceptions of the value of a wine. There is often greater prestige from small-production, boutique wineries than larger-volume operations. Scarcity, the real or perceived rarity of a wine, can drive up prices. Demand can be influenced by global supply, those all-important ratings from publications such as the *Wine Spectator*, and the quality of the vintage. All the marketing efforts in the world can't make a poor wine taste good.

Questions

1 What factors related to (*a*) demand, (*b*) cost, (*c*) profit, and (*d*) competition are used by Stuart Cellars to arrive at an approximate price level?

2 Assume that Stuart Cellars annual fixed costs are $1,000,000. With an average retail price of $28 per bottle and assuming estimated unit variable costs of $11.50, calculate break-even volume. If there are 12 bottles per case, how does the break-even unit volume compare to Stuart Cellars' capacity?

3 You are a Stuart Cellars Wine Club member. You want to order Cabernet Sauvignon that normally retails for $45 per bottle. The following discount structure applies: 20 percent discount for purchases of 11 bottles or less; 30 percent discount for purchase of 12 bottles or more. Add 7.75 percent sales tax for California residents.

What price, before shipping and handling, would you pay if (*a*) you order 10 bottles? (*b*) you order 12 bottles? (*c*) What are the implications of this discounting structure?

4 What pricing strategy(ies) does Stuart Cellars appear to be following? What will be the key factors in making these strategies a success?

pro
home

CHAPTER

13

MANAGING MARKETING CHANNELS AND SUPPLY CHAINS

LEARNING OBJECTIVES

After reading this chapter you should be able to:

1 Explain what is meant by a marketing channel of distribution and why intermediaries are needed.

2 Distinguish among traditional marketing channels, electronic marketing channels, and different types of vertical marketing systems.

3 Describe factors that marketing executives consider when selecting and managing a marketing channel.

4 Explain what supply chain and logistics management are and how they relate to marketing strategy.

APPLE STORES: ADDING HIGH-TOUCH TO HIGH-TECH MARKETING CHANNELS

Apple Computer thrives on innovation. Apple ignited the personal computer revolution in the 1970s with the Apple II, reinvented the personal computer in the 1980s with the Macintosh, and captured the imagination of personal computer buyers worldwide in the 1990s with the introduction of the iMac, a design and technological breakthrough. Today, Apple's hot-selling iPod digital music players and popular online music store, iTunes, plus ongoing development projects have revolutionalized digital entertainment.

But there's more. Apple Computer is changing the way consumer electronics are marketed with its company-owned Apple Stores. The thinking behind Apple Stores was to create an atmosphere where consumers can experience the thrill of owning and using Apple's complete line of Macintosh computers and an amazing array of digital cameras, camcorders, the entire iPod family, and more with the assistance of knowledgeable Apple personnel. Apple operates more than 125 stores, mostly in upscale shopping malls in the United States. In 2007, about half of the U.S. population resided within 15 miles of an Apple Store. Success with Apple Stores in Japan and England suggests future growth opportunities outside the United States as well.

Was Apple's decision to open its own stores a wise move? So far, yes. Apple Stores achieved $1 billion in sales faster than any retail business in history, taking just three years to reach that mark. About 40 percent of the people purchasing items at Apple Stores are new customers. Equally important, Apple Stores are profitable.[1]

This chapter focuses on marketing channels of distribution and supply chains. Each is an important component in the marketing mix.

NATURE AND IMPORTANCE OF MARKETING CHANNELS

Reaching potential buyers, either directly or indirectly, is a necessary first step for successful marketing. At the same time, buyers benefit from distribution systems.

What Is a Marketing Channel of Distribution?

marketing channel
Individuals and firms involved in the process of making a product or service available for use or consumption by consumers or industrial users.

You see the results of distribution every day. You may have purchased Lay's Potato Chips at the 7-Eleven store, a book through Amazon.com, and Levi's jeans at Sears. Each of these items was brought to you by a marketing channel of distribution, or simply a **marketing channel**, which consists of individuals and firms involved in the process of making a product or service available for use or consumption by consumers or industrial users.

Marketing channels can be compared with a pipeline through which water flows from a source to an endpoint. Marketing channels make possible the flow of goods from a producer, through intermediaries, to a buyer. Intermediaries go by various names (Figure 13–1) and perform various functions.[2] Some intermediaries actually purchase items from the producer, store them, and resell them to buyers. For example, Sunshine Biscuits produces cookies and sells them to food wholesalers. The wholesalers then sell the cookies to supermarkets and grocery stores, which, in turn, sell them to consumers. Other intermediaries such as brokers and agents represent sellers but do not actually ever own the products—their role is to bring a seller and buyer together. Real estate agents are examples of this type of intermediary.

Value Created by Intermediaries

The importance of intermediaries is made clear when we consider the functions they perform and the value they create for buyers.

FIGURE 13–1
Terms used for marketing intermediaries

TERM	DESCRIPTION
Middleman	Any intermediary between manufacturer and end-user markets
Agent or broker	Any intermediary with legal authority to act on behalf of the manufacturer
Wholesaler	An intermediary who sells to other intermediaries, usually to retailers; term usually applies to consumer markets
Retailer	An intermediary who sells to consumers
Distributor	An imprecise term, usually used to describe intermediaries who perform a variety of distribution functions, including selling, maintaining inventories, extending credit, and so on; a more common term in business markets but may also be used to refer to wholesalers
Dealer	A more imprecise term than *distributor* that can mean the same as distributor, retailer, wholesaler, and so forth

TYPE OF FUNCTION	ACTIVITIES RELATED TO FUNCTION
Transactional function	• *Buying*: Purchasing products for resale or as an agent for supply of a product • *Selling*: Contacting potential customers, promoting products, and seeking orders • *Risk taking*: Assuming business risks in the ownership of inventory that can become obsolete or deteriorate
Logistical function	• *Assorting*: Creating product assortments from several sources to serve customers • *Storing*: Assembling and protecting products at a convenient location to offer better customer service • *Sorting*: Purchasing in large quantities and breaking into smaller amounts desired by customers • *Transporting*: Physically moving a product to customers
Facilitating function	• *Financing*: Extending credit to customers • *Grading*: Inspecting, testing, or judging products, and assigning them quality grades • *Marketing information and research*: Providing information to customers and suppliers, including competitive conditions and trends

FIGURE 13–2
Marketing channel functions performed by intermediaries

Functions Performed by Intermediaries Intermediaries make possible the flow of products from producers to ultimate consumers by performing three basic functions (Figure 13–2). Intermediaries perform a transactional function when they buy and sell goods or services. But an intermediary such as a wholesaler also performs the function of sharing risk with the producer when it stocks merchandise in anticipation of sales. If the stock is unsold for any reason, the intermediary—not the producer—suffers the loss.

The logistics of a transaction (described at length later in this chapter) involve the details of preparing and getting a product to buyers. Gathering, sorting, and dispersing products are some of the logistical functions of the intermediary—imagine the several books required for a literature course sitting together on one shelf at your college bookstore! Finally, intermediaries perform facilitating functions that, by definition, make a transaction *easier* for buyers. For example, Sears issues credit cards to consumers so they can buy now and pay later.

All three groups of functions must be performed in a marketing channel, even though each channel member may not participate in all three. Channel members often negotiate about which specific functions they will perform. Sometimes disagreements result, and a breakdown in relationships among channel members occurs. This happened when PepsiCo's bottler in Venezuela switched to Coca-Cola. Given the intermediary's logistical role—storing and transporting Pepsi to Venezuelan customers in this case—PepsiCo either had to set up its own bottling operation to perform these marketing channel functions, or find another bottler, which it did.[3]

Consumer Benefits from Intermediaries Consumers also benefit from intermediaries. Having the goods and services you want, when you want them, where you want them, and in the form you want them is the ideal result of marketing channels. In more specific terms, marketing channels help create value for consumers through the four utilities described in Chapter 1: time, place, form, and possession. Time utility refers to having a product or service when you want it. For example, FedEx provides next-morning delivery. Place utility means having a product or service available where consumers want it, such as having a Texaco gas station located on a long stretch of lonely highway. Form utility involves enhancing a product or service to make it more appealing to buyers. For example, some computer manufacturers deliver unfinished PCs to dealers, which then add memory, chips, modems, and other parts, based on consumer specifications. Possession utility involves efforts by intermediaries to help buyers take possession of a product or service, such as having airline tickets delivered by a travel agency.

Concept Check

1. What is meant by a marketing channel?
2. What are the three basic functions performed by intermediaries?

CHANNEL STRUCTURE AND ORGANIZATION

A product can take many routes on its journey from a producer to buyers, and marketers search for the most efficient route from the many alternatives available. As you'll see, there are some important differences between the marketing channels for consumer goods and those for business goods.

Marketing Channels for Consumer Goods and Services

Figure 13–3 shows the four most common marketing channels for consumer goods and services. It also shows the number of levels in each marketing channel, as seen by the number of intermediaries between a producer and ultimate buyers. As the number of intermediaries between a producer and buyer increases, the channel is viewed as increasing in length. The producer → wholesaler → retailer → consumer channel is longer than the producer → consumer channel.

Channel A in Figure 13–3 represents a *direct channel* because a producer and ultimate consumers deal directly with each other. Many products and services are distributed this way. A number of insurance companies sell their financial services using a direct channel and branch sales offices. Schwan's Sales Enterprises of Marshall, Minnesota, markets a full line of frozen foods in 48 states using door-to-door salespeople who sell from refrigerated trucks. Because there are no intermediaries with a direct channel, the producer must perform all channel functions.

FIGURE 13–3
Common marketing channels for consumer goods and services

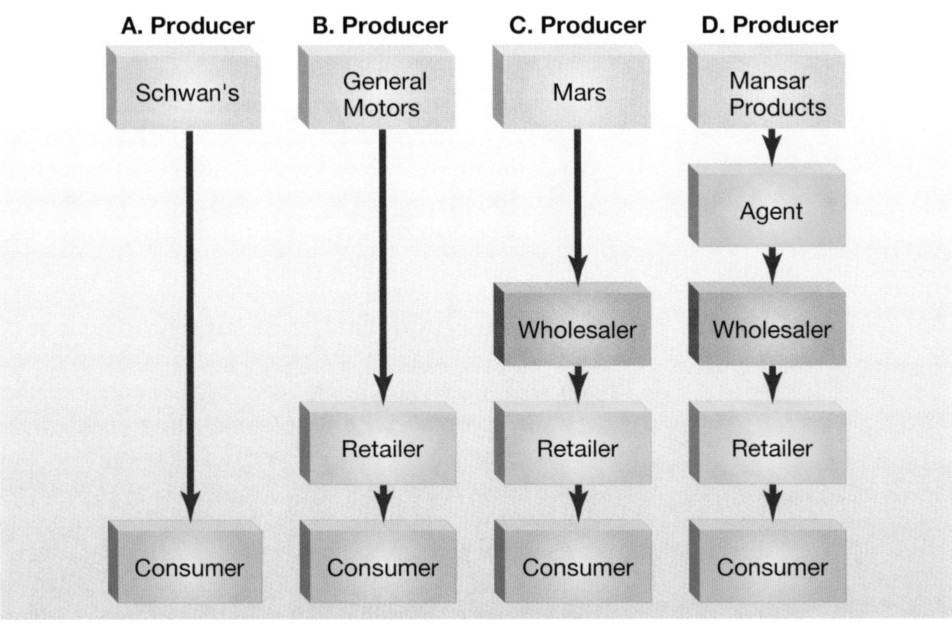

The remaining three channel forms are *indirect channels* because intermediaries are inserted between the producer and consumers and perform numerous channel functions. Channel B, with a retailer added, is most common when the retailer is large and can buy in large quantities from a producer or when the cost of inventory makes it too expensive to use a wholesaler. Automobile manufacturers use this channel, with a local car dealer acting as a retailer. Why is there no wholesaler? So many variations exist in the product that it would be impossible for a wholesaler to stock all the models required to satisfy buyers; in addition, the cost of maintaining an inventory would be too high. However, large retailers such as Target, 7-Eleven, and Safeway buy in sufficient quantities to make it cost effective for a producer to deal with only a retail intermediary.

Adding a wholesaler in channel C is most common for low-cost, low-unit value items that are frequently purchased by consumers, such as candy, confectionary items, and magazines. For example, Mars sells its line of candies to wholesalers in case quantities; then they can break down (sort) the cases so that individual retailers can order in boxes or much smaller quantities.

Channel D, the most indirect channel, is employed when there are many small manufacturers and many small retailers and an agent is used to help coordinate a large supply of the product. Mansar Products, Ltd., is a Belgian producer of specialty jewelry that uses agents to sell to wholesalers in the United States, which then sell to many small retailers.

Marketing Channels for Business Goods and Services

The four most common channels for business goods and services are shown in Figure 13–4. In contrast with channels for consumer products, business channels typically are shorter and rely on one intermediary or none at all because business users are fewer in number, tend to be more concentrated geographically, and buy in larger quantities.

Channel A, represented by IBM's large, mainframe computer business, is a direct channel. Firms using this kind of channel maintain their own sales force and perform all channel functions. This channel is employed when buyers are large and well defined, the sales effort requires extensive negotiations, and the products are of high unit value and require hands-on expertise in terms of installation or use. Lockheed Martin and Airbus would be other examples.

Channels B, C, and D are indirect channels with one or more intermediaries to reach industrial users. In channel B an *industrial distributor* performs a variety of marketing

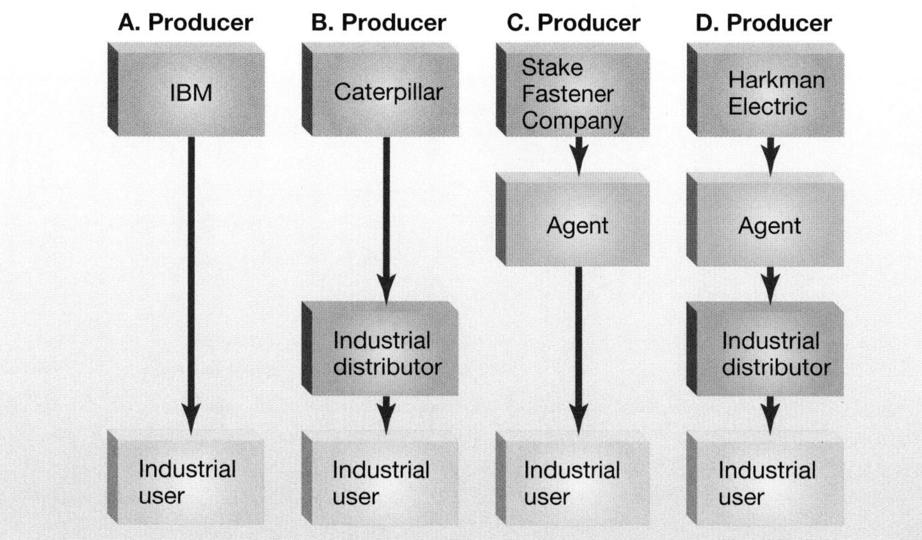

FIGURE 13–4
Common marketing channels for business goods and services

channel functions, including selling, stocking, and delivering a full product assortment and financing. In many ways, industrial distributors are like wholesalers in consumer channels. Caterpillar relies on industrial distributors to sell and service its construction and mining equipment in almost 200 countries.

Channel C introduces a different intermediary, an *agent,* who serves primarily as the independent selling arm of producers and represents a producer to industrial users. For example, Stake Fastener Company, a producer of industrial fasteners, has an agent call on industrial users rather than employing its own salesforce. Such agents often sell many different items, representing numerous companies, to the same industrial buyer.

Channel D is the longest channel and includes both agents and distributors. For instance, Harkman Electric, a small producer of electric products, uses agents to call on distributors who sell to industrial users.

Electronic Marketing Channels

These common marketing channels for consumer and business goods and services are not the only routes to the marketplace. Advances in electronic commerce have opened new avenues for reaching buyers and creating customer value.

Interactive electronic technology has made possible *electronic marketing channels,* which employ the Internet to make goods and services available to consumers or business buyers. A unique feature of these channels is that they combine electronic and traditional intermediaries to create time, place, form, and possession utility for buyers.[4]

Figure 13–5 shows the electronic marketing channels for books (Amazon.com), automobiles (Auto-By-Tel.com), reservation services (Orbitz.com), and personal computers (Dell.com). Are you surprised that they look a lot like common marketing channels? An important reason for the similarity resides in channel functions detailed in Figure 13–2. Electronic intermediaries can and do perform transactional and facilitating functions effectively and at a relatively lower cost than traditional intermediaries because of efficiencies made possible by information technology. However, electronic intermediaries are incapable of performing elements of the logistical function, particularly for products such as books and automobiles. This function remains with traditional intermediaries or with the producer, as seen with Dell, Inc., with its direct channel.

Many services are distributed through electronic marketing channels, such as travel reservations marketed by Travelocity.com, financial securities by Schwab.com, and insurance by MetLife.com. Software too can be marketed this way. However,

FIGURE 13–5
Representative consumer electronic marketing channels

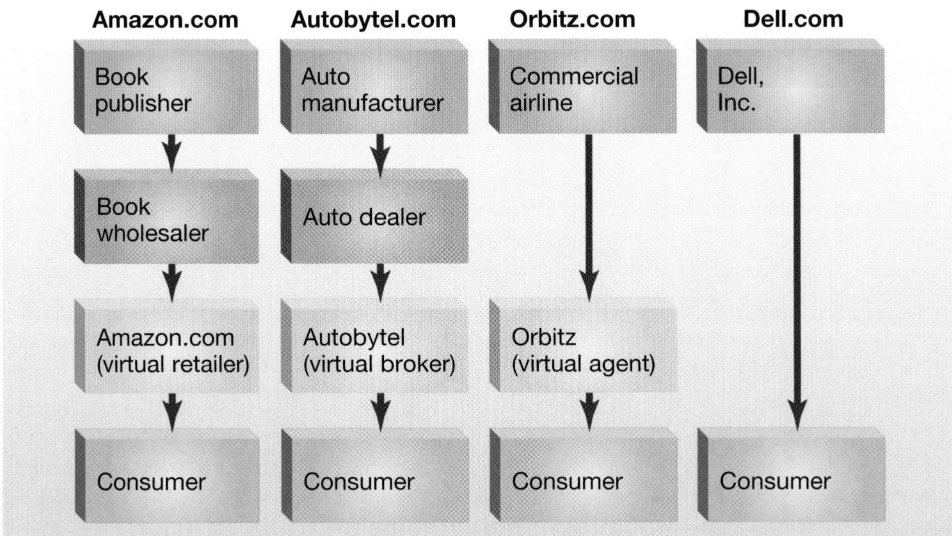

MARKETING NEWSNET

Nestlé and General Mills—Cereal Partners Worldwide

Can you say Nestlé Cheerios *miel amandes?* Millions of French start their day with this European equivalent of General Mills' Honey Nut Cheerios, made possible by Cereal Partners Worldwide (CPW). CPW is the food industry's first strategic alliance designed to be a global business; it joined the cereal manufacturing and marketing capability of U.S.-based General Mills with the worldwide distribution clout of Swiss-based Nestlé.

From its headquarters near Lake Geneva, Switzerland, CPW first launched General Mills cereals under the Nestlé label in France, the United Kingdom, Spain, and Portugal in 1991. Today, CPW competes in 75 international markets.

The General Mills–Nestlé strategic channel alliance is also likely to increase the ready-to-eat cereal worldwide market share of these companies, which are already rated as the two best-managed firms in the world. CPW is on track to reach its goal of a 20 percent worldwide share.

many other services such as health care and auto repair still involve traditional intermediaries.

Multiple Channels and Strategic Alliances

dual distribution
Arrangement whereby a firm reaches buyers by using two or more different types of channels for the same basic product

In some situations producers use **dual distribution**, an arrangement whereby a firm reaches different buyers by employing two or more different types of channels for the same basic product. For instance, GE sells its large appliances directly to home and apartment builders but uses retail stores, including Wal-Mart, to sell to consumers. In some instances, firms pair multiple channels with a multibrand strategy. This is done to minimize cannibalization of the firm's family brand and to differentiate the channels. For example, Hallmark sells its Hallmark greeting cards through Hallmark stores and select department stores, and its Ambassador brand of cards through discount and drugstore chains.

A recent development in marketing channels is the use of *strategic channel alliances,* whereby one firm's marketing channel is used to sell another firm's products. An alliance between Kraft Foods and Starbucks is a case in point. Kraft distributes Starbucks coffee in U.S. supermarkets and internationally. Strategic alliances are popular in global marketing, where the creation of marketing channel relationships is expensive and time consuming. For example, General Mills and Nestlé have an extensive alliance that spans 75 international markets from Brazil to Poland to Thailand. Read the accompanying Marketing NewsNet so you won't be surprised when you are served Nestlé (not General Mills) Cheerios in Europe, South America, and parts of Asia.[5]

Vertical Marketing Systems

vertical marketing systems
Professionally managed and centrally coordinated marketing channels designed to achieve channel economies and maximum marketing impact

The traditional marketing channels described so far represent a loosely knit network of independent producers and intermediaries brought together to distribute goods and services. However, channel arrangements have emerged for the purpose of improving efficiency in performing channel functions and achieving greater marketing effectiveness. These arrangements are called vertical marketing systems. **Vertical marketing systems** are professionally managed and centrally coordinated marketing channels

Sherwin-Williams and H&R Block represent two different types of vertical marketing systems. Read the text to find out how they differ.

designed to achieve channel economies and maximum marketing impact.[6] Figure 13–6 depicts the major types of vertical marketing systems: corporate, contractual, and administered.

Corporate Systems The combination of successive stages of production and distribution under a single ownership is a *corporate vertical marketing system.* For example, a producer might own the intermediary at the next level down in the channel. This practice, called *forward integration,* is exemplified by Polo/Ralph Lauren, which manufactures clothing and also owns apparel shops. Other examples of forward integration include Goodyear and Sherwin-Williams. Alternatively, a retailer might own a manufacturing operation, a practice called *backward integration.* For example, Kroger supermarkets operate manufacturing facilities that produce everything from aspirin to cottage cheese, for sale under the Kroger label.

Companies seeking to reduce distribution costs and gain greater control over supply sources or resale of their products pursue forward and backward integration. However, both types of integration increase a company's costs. For this reason, many companies favor contractual vertical marketing systems to achieve channel efficiencies and marketing effectiveness.

Contractual Systems Under a *contractual vertical marketing system,* independent production and distribution firms combine their efforts on a contractual basis to obtain greater functional economies and marketing impact than they could achieve alone. Contractual systems are the most popular among the three types of vertical marketing systems. They account for about 40 percent of all retail sales.

Three variations of contractual systems exist. *Wholesaler-sponsored voluntary chains* involve a wholesaler that develops a contractual relationship with small, independent retailers to standardize and coordinate buying practices, merchandising programs, and inventory management efforts. With the organization of a large number of independent retailers, economies of scale and volume discounts can be achieved to compete with chain stores. IGA and Ben Franklin variety and craft stores represent wholesaler-sponsored voluntary chains.

Retailer-sponsored cooperatives exist when small, independent retailers form an organization that operates a wholesale facility cooperatively. Member retailers then concentrate their buying power through the wholesaler and plan collaborative promotional and pricing activities. Examples of retailer-sponsored cooperatives include Associated Grocers and Ace Hardware.

The most visible variation of contractual systems is **franchising**, a contractual arrangement between a parent company (a franchiser) and an individual or firm

franchising
Contractual arrangement in which a parent company (the franchiser) allows an individual or firm (the franchisee) to operate a certain type of business under an established name and according to specific rules

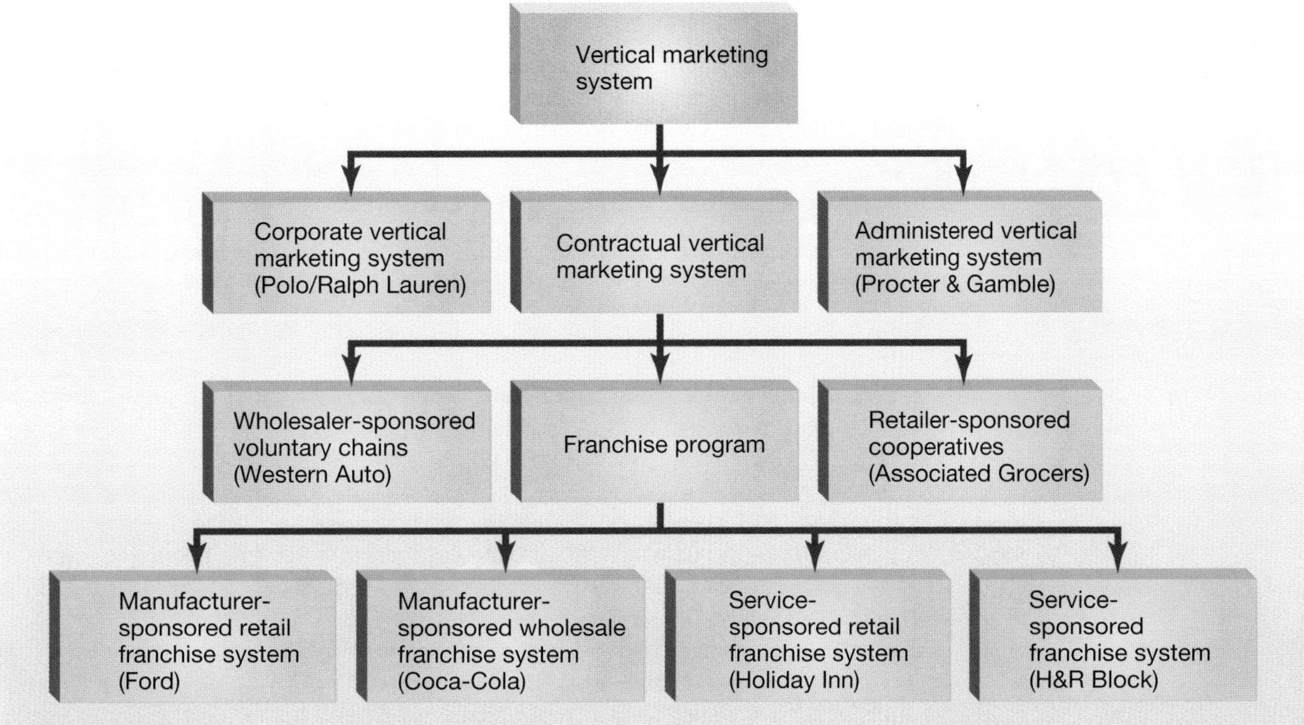

FIGURE 13–6
Types of vertical marketing systems

(a franchisee) that allows the franchise to operate a certain type of business under an established name and according to specific rules.

Four types of franchise arrangements are most popular. *Manufacturer-sponsored retail franchise systems* are prominent in the automobile industry, where a manufacturer such as Ford licenses dealers to sell its cars subject to various sales and service conditions. *Manufacturer-sponsored wholesale franchise systems* appear in the soft-drink industry, where Pepsi-Cola licenses wholesalers (bottlers) that purchase concentrate from Pepsi-Cola and then carbonate, bottle, promote, and distribute its products to supermarkets and restaurants. *Service-sponsored retail franchise systems* are provided by firms that have designed a unique approach for performing a service and wish to profit by selling the franchise to others. Holiday Inn, Avis, and McDonald's represent this franchising approach. *Service-sponsored franchise systems* exist when franchisers license individuals or firms to dispense a service under a trade name and specific guidelines. Examples include Snelling and Snelling, Inc., employment services and H&R Block tax services. Service-sponsored franchise arrangements are the fastest-growing type of franchise.

Administered Systems In comparison, *administered vertical marketing systems* achieve coordination at successive stages of production and distribution by the size and influence of one channel member rather than through ownership. Procter & Gamble, given its broad product assortment ranging from disposable diapers to detergents, is able to obtain cooperation from supermarkets in displaying, promoting, and pricing its products. Wal-Mart can obtain cooperation from manufacturers in terms of product specifications, price levels, and promotional support, given its position as the world's largest retailer.

Concept Check

1. What is the difference between a direct and an indirect channel?
2. What is the major distinction between a corporate vertical marketing system and an administered vertical marketing system?

CHANNEL CHOICE AND MANAGEMENT

Marketing channels not only link a producer to its buyers but also provide the means through which a firm executes various elements of its marketing strategy. Therefore, choosing a marketing channel is a critical decision.

Factors in Choosing a Marketing Channel

Marketing executives consider three questions when choosing a marketing channel and intermediaries:

1. Which channel and intermediaries will provide the best coverage of the target market?
2. Which channel and intermediaries will best satisfy the buying requirements of the target market?
3. Which channel and intermediaries will be the most profitable?

Target Market Coverage Achieving the best coverage of the target market requires attention to the density—that is, the number of stores in a given geographical area—and type of intermediaries to be used at the retail level of distribution. Three degrees of distribution density exist: intensive, exclusive, and selective.

intensive distribution
A firm tries to place its products or services in as many outlets as possible

exclusive distribution
Only one retail outlet in a specific geographical area carries the firm's products

Intensive distribution means that a firm tries to place its products and services in as many outlets as possible. Intensive distribution is usually chosen for convenience products or services, such as candy, newspapers, ATMs, and soft drinks. For example, Coca-Cola's retail distribution objective is to place its products "within an arm's reach of desire."

Exclusive distribution is the extreme opposite of intensive distribution because only one retail outlet in a specified geographical area carries the firm's products. Exclusive distribution is typically chosen for specialty products or services such as automobiles, some women's fragrances, men's and women's apparel and accessories, and yachts. Gucci, one of the world's leading luxury goods companies, uses exclusive distribution in the marketing of its Yves Saint Laurent, Sergio Rossi, Boucheron, Opium, and Gucci brands. Sometimes retailers sign exclusive distribution agreements with manufacturers and suppliers. For instance, Radio Shack sells only Compaq and Hewlett-Packard personal computers and Thomson SA's RCA brand of audio and video products in its 7,000 stores.

selective distribution
A firm selects a few retail outlets in a specific geographical area to carry its products

Selective distribution lies between these two extremes and means that a firm selects a few retail outlets in a specific geographical area to carry its products. Selective distribution combines some of the market coverage benefits of intensive distribution with the control over resale possible with exclusive distribution. For this reason, selective distribution is the most common form of distribution density. It is usually associated with shopping goods or services such as Rolex watches, Wilson tennis racquets, and LensCrafters vision care.

Satisfying Buyer Requirements A second objective in channel design is gaining access to channels and intermediaries that satisfy at least some of the interests buyers might have when they purchase a firm's products or services. These requirements fall into four categories: (1) information, (2) convenience, (3) variety, and (4) pre- or postsale services.

Information is an important requirement when buyers have limited knowledge or desire specific data about a product or service. Properly chosen intermediaries communicate with buyers through in-store displays, demonstrations, and personal selling. Consumer electronics manufacturers such as Sony, Palm, and Apple Computer have opened their own retail outlets staffed with highly trained personnel, to inform buyers how their products can better meet each customer's needs.

Convenience has multiple meanings for buyers, such as proximity or driving time to a retail outlet or hours of operation. For example, 7-Eleven stores with more than

Read the text to learn which buying requirements are satisfied by Jiffy Lube and Petco.

27,500 outlets worldwide, many of which are open 24 hours a day, satisfy this interest for buyers. Candy, beverage, and snack-food firms benefit by gaining display space in these stores. For other consumers, convenience means a minimum of time and hassle. Jiffy Lube and Q-Lube, which promise to change engine oil and filters quickly, appeal to this aspect of convenience.

Variety reflects buyers' interest in having numerous competing and complementary items from which to choose. Variety is seen in both the breadth and depth of products carried by intermediaries, which enhances their attractiveness to buyers. Thus, manufacturers of pet food and supplies seek distribution through pet superstores such as Petco and PetsMart, which offer a wide array of pet products.

Pre- or postsale services provided by intermediaries are an important buying requirement for products such as large household appliances that require delivery, installation, and credit. Therefore, Whirlpool seeks dealers that provide such services.

Profitability The third consideration in designing a channel is profitability, which is determined by the revenues earned minus cost for each channel member and for the channel as a whole. Cost is the critical factor of channel profitability. These costs include distribution, advertising, and selling expenses. The extent to which channel members share these costs determines the profitability of each member and of the channel as a whole.

Channel Relationships: Conflict and Cooperation

Unfortunately, because channels consist of independent individuals and firms, there is always potential for disagreements concerning who performs which channel functions, how profits are distributed, which products and services will be provided by whom, and who makes critical channel-related decisions. These channel conflicts necessitate measures for dealing with them.

channel conflict
Arises when one channel member believes another channel member is engaged in behavior that prevents it from achieving its goals

Conflict in Marketing Channels **Channel conflict** arises when one channel member believes another channel member is engaged in behavior that prevents it from achieving its goals. Two types of conflict occur in marketing channels: vertical conflict and horizontal conflict.[7]

Vertical conflict occurs between different levels in a marketing channel; for example, between a manufacturer and a wholesaler or between a wholesaler and a retailer. Three sources of vertical conflict are most common. First, conflict arises when a

disintermediation
Channel conflict that arises when a channel member bypasses another member and sells or buys products direct

channel member bypasses another member and sells or buys products direct, a practice called **disintermediation**. Such a conflict emerged when Jenn-Air, a producer of kitchen appliances, decided to terminate its distributors and sell direct to retailers. Second, disagreements over how profits are distributed among channel members produce conflict. This happened when the world's biggest music company, Universal Music Group, adopted a pricing policy for CDs that squeezed the profit margins for music retailers, such as Tower Records. A third conflict situation arises when manufacturers believe wholesalers or retailers are not giving their products adequate attention. For example, Nike stopped shipping popular sneakers such as Nike Shox NZ to Foot Locker in retaliation for the retailer's decision to give more shelf space to shoes costing under \$120.[8]

Horizontal conflict occurs between intermediaries at the same level in a marketing channel, such as between two or more retailers (Target and Kmart) or two or more wholesalers that handle the same manufacturer's brands. For instance, the launch of Elizabeth Taylor's Black Pearls fragrance by Elizabeth Arden was put on hold when department store chains such as May and Dillard refused to stock the item once they learned that mass merchants Sears and JCPenney would also carry the brand. Elizabeth Arden subsequently introduced the brand only through department stores.[9]

Cooperation in Marketing Channels Conflict can have destructive effects on the workings of a marketing channel, so it is necessary to secure cooperation among channel members. One means is through a *channel captain,* a channel member that coordinates, directs, and supports other channel members. Channel captains can be producers, wholesalers, or retailers. Procter & Gamble assumes this role because it has a strong consumer following in brands such as Crest, Tide, and Pampers. Therefore, it can set policies or terms that supermarkets will follow. McKesson, a pharmaceutical drug wholesaler, is a channel captain because it coordinates and supports the product flow from numerous small drug manufacturers to thousands of drugstores and hospitals nationwide. Wal-Mart is a retail channel captain because of its strong consumer image, number of outlets, and purchasing volume.

A firm becomes a channel captain because it is the channel member with the ability to influence the behavior of other members.[10] Influence can take four forms. First, economic influence arises from the ability of a firm to reward other members because of its strong financial position. Microsoft Corporation and Wal-Mart have such influence. Expertise is a second source of influence. For example, American Hospital Supply helps its customers (hospitals) manage inventory and streamline order processing for hundreds of medical supplies. Third, identification with a particular channel member creates influence for that channel member. For instance, retailers may compete to carry the Ralph Lauren line, or clothing manufacturers may compete to be carried by Neiman-Marcus or Nordstrom. In both instances the desire to be associated with a channel member gives that firm influence over others. Finally, influence can arise from the legitimate right of one channel member to direct the behavior of other members. This situation occurs under contractual vertical marketing systems where a franchiser can legitimately direct how a franchisee behaves.

Concept Check

1. What are the three degrees of distribution density?
2. What are the three questions marketing executives consider when choosing a marketing channel and intermediaries?

LOGISTICS AND SUPPLY CHAIN MANAGEMENT

logistics
Activities that focus on getting the right amount of the right products to the right place at the right time at the lowest possible cost

A marketing channel relies on logistics to make products available to consumers and industrial users. **Logistics** involves those activities that focus on getting the right amount of the right products to the right place at the right time at the lowest possible cost. The performance of these activities is *logistics management,* the practice of organizing the cost-effective flow of raw materials, in-process inventory, finished goods, and related information from point of origin to point of consumption to satisfy *customer requirements.*

Three elements of this definition deserve emphasis. First, logistics deals with decisions needed to move a product from the source of raw materials to consumption—that is, the *flow* of the product. Second, those decisions have to be *cost effective.* While it is important to drive down logistics costs, there is a limit: a firm needs to drive down logistics costs as long as it can deliver expected *customer service,* which means satisfying customer requirements. The role of management is to see that customer needs are satisfied in the most cost-effective manner. When properly done, the results can be spectacular. Procter & Gamble is a case in point. Beginning in the 1990s, the company set out to meet the needs of consumers more effectively by collaborating and partnering with its suppliers and retailers to ensure that the right products reached store shelves at the right time and at a lower cost. The effort was judged a success when, during an 18-month period, P&G's retail customers recorded a $65 million savings in logistics costs while customer service increased.[11]

The Procter & Gamble experience is not an isolated incident. Today, logistics management is embedded in a broader view of physical distribution. Companies now recognize that getting the right items needed for consumption or production to the right place at the right time in the right condition at the right cost is often beyond their individual capabilities and control. Instead, collaboration, coordination, and information sharing among manufacturers, suppliers, and distributors are necessary to create a seamless flow of goods and services to customers. This perspective is represented in the concept of a supply chain and the practice of supply chain management.

Supply Chains versus Marketing Channels

supply chain
Sequence of firms that perform activities required to create and deliver a product to consumers or industrial users

A **supply chain** is a sequence of firms that perform activities required to create and deliver a good or service to consumers or industrial users. It differs from a marketing channel in terms of the firms involved. A supply chain includes suppliers that provide raw material inputs to a manufacturer as well as the wholesalers and retailers that deliver finished goods to consumers. The management process is also different. *Supply chain management* is the integration and organization of information and logistics activities *across firms* in a supply chain for the purpose of creating and delivering goods and services that provide value to consumers. The relation among marketing channels, logistics management, and supply chain management is shown in Figure 13–7 on the next page. An important feature of supply chain management is its application of sophisticated information technology that allows companies to share and operate systems for order processing, transportation scheduling, and inventory and facility management.

Sourcing, Assembling, and Delivering a New Car: The Automotive Supply Chain

All companies are members of one or more supply chains. A supply chain is essentially a series of linked suppliers and customers in which every customer is, in turn, a supplier to another customer until a finished product reaches the ultimate consumer. Even

FIGURE 13–7
Relating marketing channels, logistics management, and supply chain management

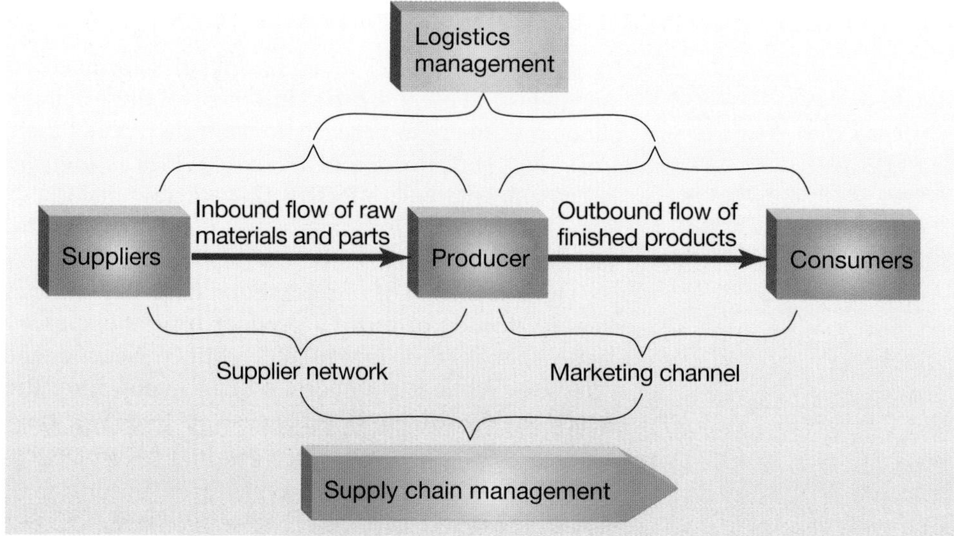

a simplified supply chain diagram for carmakers shown in Figure 13–8 illustrates how complex a supply chain can be.[12] A carmaker's supplier network includes thousands of firms that provide the 5,000 or so parts in a typical automobile. They provide items ranging from raw materials such as steel and rubber to components, including transmissions, tires, brakes, and seats, to complex subassemblies and assemblies such as in chassis and suspension systems that make for a smooth, stable ride. Coordinating and scheduling material and component flows for their assembly into actual automobiles by carmakers is heavily dependent on logistical activities, including transportation, order processing, inventory control, materials handling, and information technology. A central link is the carmaker supply chain manager, who is responsible for translating customer requirements into actual orders and arranging for delivery dates and financial arrangements for automobile dealers.

Logistical aspects of the automobile marketing channel are also an important part of the supply chain. Major responsibilities include transportation (which involves the selection and oversight of external carriers—trucking, airline, railroad, and shipping companies—for cars and parts to dealers), the operation of distribution centers, the management of finished goods inventories, and order processing for sales. Supply chain managers also play an important role in the marketing channel. They work with extensive car dealer networks to ensure that the right mix of automobiles is delivered to each location. In addition, they make sure that spare and service parts are available so that dealers can meet the car maintenance and repair needs of consumers. All of this is done with the help of information technology that links the entire automotive supply chain. What does all of this cost? It is estimated that logistics costs represent 25 to 30 percent of the retail price of a typical new car.

FIGURE 13–8
The automotive supply chain

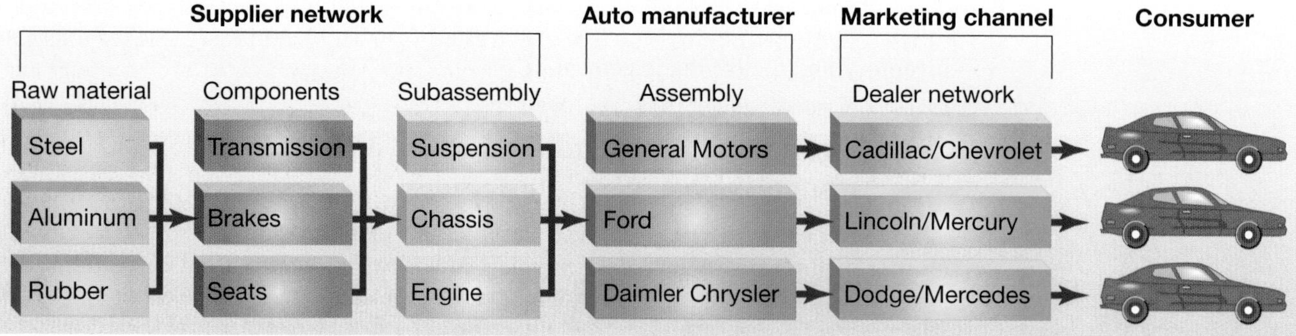

World-class marketers Dell Computer and Wal-Mart emphasize responsiveness and efficiency in their supply chains, respectively.

Supply Chain Management and Marketing Strategy

The automotive supply chain illustration shows how logistics activities are interrelated and organized across firms to create and deliver a car for you. What's missing from this illustration is the linkage between a specific company's supply chain and its marketing strategy. Just as companies have different marketing strategies, they also manage supply chains differently. The goals to be achieved by a firm's marketing strategy determine whether its supply chain needs to be more responsive or more efficient in meeting customer requirements.

Aligning a Supply Chain with Marketing Strategy There are a variety of supply chain configurations, each of which is designed to perform different tasks well. Marketers today recognize that the choice of a supply chain follows from a clearly defined marketing strategy and involves three steps:[13]

1. *Understand the customer.* To understand the customer, a company must identify the needs of the customer segment being served. These needs, such as a desire for a low price or convenience of purchase, help a company define the relative importance of efficiency and responsiveness in meeting customer requirements.
2. *Understand the supply chain.* Second, a company must understand what a supply chain is designed to do well. Supply chains range from those that emphasize being responsive to customer requirements and demand to those that emphasize efficiency with a goal of supplying products at the lowest possible delivered cost.
3. *Harmonize the supply chain with the marketing strategy.* Finally, a company needs to ensure that what the supply chain is capable of doing well is consistent with the targeted customer's needs and its marketing strategy. If a mismatch exists between what the supply chain does particularly well and a company's marketing strategy, the company will either need to redesign the supply chain to support the marketing strategy or change the marketing strategy. Read the Marketing NewsNet on the next page to learn how IBM overhauled its complete supply chain to support its new "On-Demand Business" marketing strategy.[14]

How are these steps applied and how are efficiency and responsive considerations built into a supply chain? Let's look at how two market leaders—Dell and Wal-Mart—have harmonized their supply chain and marketing strategy.[15]

Dell: A Responsive Supply Chain The Dell marketing strategy targets customers who desire having the most up-to-date personal computer equipment customized to their needs. These customers are also willing to (1) wait to have their customized personal computer delivered in a few days, rather than picking out a model at a retail store; and (2) pay a reasonable, though not the lowest, price in the marketplace. Given Dell's customer segment, the company has the option of choosing either an efficient or a responsive supply chain. An efficient supply chain may use inexpensive but slower modes of transportation, emphasize economies of scale in its production process by reducing the variety of PC configurations offered, and limit its assembly and inventory storage facilities to a single location, say Austin, Texas, where the company

MARKETING NEWSNET IBM—Creating an On-Demand Supply Chain

Have you seen IBM's "On-Demand Business" advertising campaign? This campaign features IBM's commitment to being responsive and flexible to changes in customer requirements and the marketplace. The campaign reflects IBM's companywide marketing initiative to be the world's premier on-demand business.

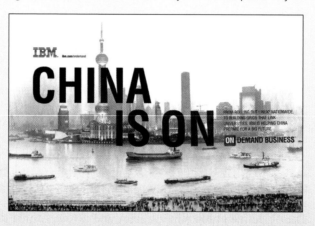

What you probably haven't seen is IBM's transformed supply chain that makes on-demand business possible. Beginning in 2001, IBM set about to build a single integrated supply chain that would handle raw material procurement, manufacturing, logistics, customer support, order entry, and customer fulfillment across all of IBM—something that had never been done before. Why would IBM undertake this task? According to IBM's CEO, Samuel J. Paimisano, "You cannot hope to thrive in the IT industry if you are a high-cost, slow-moving company. Supply chain is one of the new competitive battlegrounds. We are committed to being the most efficient and productive player in our industry."

The task wasn't easy. With factories in 10 countries, IBM buys 2 billion parts a year from 33,000 suppliers, offers 78,000 products available in 3 million possible variations, processes 1.7 million customer orders annually, and operates in 150 countries. Yet with surprising efficiency, IBM overhauled its supply chain end-to-end from raw material sourcing to post-sales support by 2004. Along the way, IBM posted cost savings of $5.6 billion in 2002 and $7 billion in 2003.

Today, IBM is uniquely poised to configure and deliver a tailored mix of hardware, software, and service to customers on demand. This would have been impossible without the changes made in IBM's supply chain.

is headquartered. If Dell opted only for efficiency in its supply chain, it would be difficult if not impossible to satisfy its target customer's desire for rapid delivery and a wide variety of customizable products. Dell instead has opted for a responsive supply chain. It relies on more expensive express transportation for receipt of components from suppliers and delivery of finished products to customers. The company achieves product variety and manufacturing efficiency by designing common platforms across several products and using common components. Dell operates manufacturing facilities in Texas, Tennessee, Brazil, Ireland, Malaysia, and China to assure rapid delivery. Dell also has invested heavily in information technology to link itself with suppliers and customers.

Wal-Mart: An Efficient Supply Chain Now let's consider Wal-Mart. Wal-Mart's marketing strategy is to be a reliable, lower-price retailer for a wide variety of mass consumption consumer goods. This strategy favors an efficient supply chain designed to deliver products to consumers at the lowest possible cost. Efficiency is achieved in a variety of ways. For instance, Wal-Mart keeps relatively low inventory levels, and most is stocked in stores available for sale, not in warehouses gathering dust. The low inventory arises from Wal-Mart's use of *cross-docking*—a practice that involves unloading products from suppliers, sorting products for individual stores, and quickly reloading products onto its trucks for a particular store. No warehousing or storing of products occurs, except for a few hours or, at most, a day. Cross-docking allows Wal-Mart to operate only a small number of distribution centers to service its vast network of Wal-Mart Stores, Supercenters, Neighborhood Markets, and Sam's Clubs, which contributes to efficiency. On the other hand, the company runs its own fleet of trucks to service its stores. This does increase cost and investment, but the benefits in terms of responsiveness justify the cost in Wal-Mart's case. Wal-Mart has invested significantly more than its competitors in information technology to operate its supply chain. The company feeds information about customer requirements and demand from its stores back to its suppliers, which manufacture only what is being demanded. This large investment has improved the efficiency of Wal-Mart's supply chain and made it responsive to customer needs.

Three lessons can be learned from these two examples. First, there is no one best supply chain for every company. Second, the best supply chain is the one that is consistent with the needs of the customer segment being served and complements a company's marketing strategy. And finally, supply chain managers are often called upon to make trade-offs between efficiency and responsiveness on various elements of a company's supply chain.

Concept Check

1. What is the principal difference between a marketing channel and a supply chain?
2. The choice of a supply chain involves what three steps?

TWO CONCEPTS OF LOGISTICS MANAGEMENT IN A SUPPLY CHAIN

The objective of logistics management in a supply chain is to minimize total logistics costs while delivering the appropriate level of customer service.

Total Logistics Cost Concept

total logistics cost
Expenses associated with transportation, materials handling and warehousing, inventory, stockouts, order processing, and return goods handling

For our purposes **total logistics cost** includes expenses associated with transportation, materials handling and warehousing, inventory, stockouts (being out of inventory), order processing, and return goods handling.[16] Note that many of these costs are interrelated so that changes in one will impact the others. For example, as the firm attempts to minimize its transportation costs by shipping in larger quantities, it will also experience an increase in inventory levels. Larger inventory levels will not only increase inventory costs but should also reduce stockouts. It is important, therefore, to study the impact on all of the logistics decision areas when considering a change.

Customer Service Concept

customer service
Ability of logistics management to satisfy users in terms of time, dependability, communication, and convenience

Because a supply chain is a *flow,* the end of it—or *output*—is the service delivered to customers. Within the context of a supply chain, **customer service** is the ability of logistics management to satisfy users in terms of time, dependability, communication, and convenience. As suggested by Figure 13–9 on the next page, a supply chain manager's key task is to balance these four customer service factors against total logistics cost factors.

Time In a supply chain setting, time refers to *order cycle* or *replenishment* time for an item, which means the time between the ordering of an item and when it is received and ready for use or sale. The various elements that make up the typical order cycle include recognition of the need to order, order transmittal, order processing, documentation, and transportation. A current emphasis in supply chain management is to reduce order cycle time so that the inventory levels of customers may be minimized. Another emphasis is to make the process of reordering and receiving products as simple as possible, often through inventory systems called *quick response* and *efficient consumer response* delivery systems. For example, at Saks Fifth Avenue, point-of-sale scanner technology records each day's sales. When

FIGURE 13–9
Supply chain managers balance total logistics cost factors against customer service factors

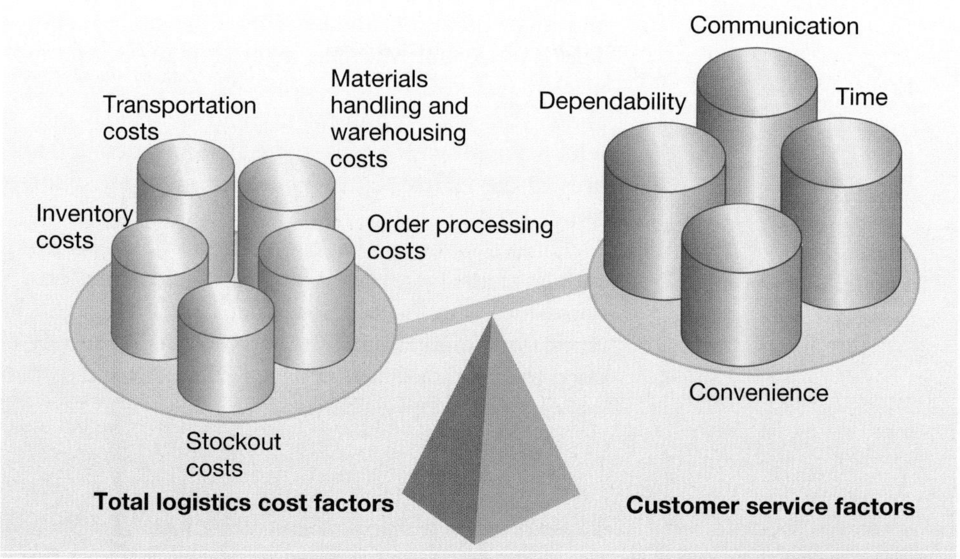

stock falls below a minimum level, a replenishment order is automatically produced. Vendors such as Donna Karan (DKNY) receive the order, which is processed and delivered within 48 hours.[17]

Dependability Dependability is the consistency of replenishment. This is important to all firms in a supply chain—and to consumers. How often do you return to a store if it fails to have in stock the item you want to purchase? Dependability can be broken into three elements: consistent lead time, safe delivery, and complete delivery. Consistent service allows planning (such as appropriate inventory levels), whereas inconsistencies create surprises. Intermediaries may be willing to accept longer lead times if they know about them in advance and can thus make plans.

Communication Communication is a two-way link between buyer and seller that helps in monitoring service and anticipating future needs. Status reports on orders are a typical example of communication between buyer and seller.

Convenience The concept of convenience for a supply chain manager means that there should be a minimum of effort on the part of the buyer in doing business with the seller. Is it easy for the customer to order? Are the products available from many outlets? Will the seller arrange all necessary details, such as transportation? This customer service factor has promoted the use of **vendor-managed inventory** (VMI), whereby the *supplier* determines the product amount and assortment a customer (such as a retailer) needs and automatically delivers the appropriate items.

vendor-managed inventory
Inventory management system whereby the supplier determines the product amount and assortment a customer (such as a retailer) needs and automatically delivers the appropriate items

Campbell Soup's system illustrates how VMI works.[18] Every morning, retailers electronically inform the company of their demand for all Campbell products and the inventory levels in their distribution centers. Campbell uses that information to forecast future demand and determine which products need replenishment based on upper and lower inventory limits established with each retailer. Trucks leave the Campbell shipping plant that afternoon and arrive at the retailer's distribution centers with the required replenishments the same day.

Concept Check

1. What is the logistics management objective in a supply chain?
2. A manager's key task is to balance which four customer service factors against which five logistics cost factors?

CHAPTER IN REVIEW

1 *Explain what is meant by a marketing channel of distribution and why intermediaries are needed.*
A marketing channel of distribution, or simply a marketing channel, consists of individuals and firms involved in the process of making a product or service available for use or consumption by consumers or industrial users. Intermediaries make possible the flow of products from producers to buyers by performing three basic functions. The transactional function involves buying, selling, and risk taking because intermediaries stock merchandise in anticipation of sales. The logistical function involves the gathering, storing, and dispensing of products. The facilitating function assists producers in making goods and services more attractive to buyers. The performance of these functions by intermediaries creates time, place, form, and possession utility for consumers.

2 *Distinguish among traditional marketing channels, electronic marketing channels, and different types of vertical marketing systems.*
Traditional marketing channels describe the route taken by products and services from producers to buyers. This route can range from a direct channel with no intermediaries, because a producer and ultimate consumers deal directly with each other, to indirect channels where intermediaries (agents, wholesalers, distributors, or retailers) are inserted between a producer and consumer and perform numerous channel functions. Electronic marketing channels employ the Internet to make goods and services available for consumption or use by consumer or business buyers. Vertical marketing systems are professionally managed and centrally coordinated marketing channels designed to achieve channel economics and maximum marketing impact. There are three major types of vertical marketing systems (VMS). A corporate VMS combines successive stages of production and distribution under a single ownership. A contractual VMS exists when independent production and distribution firms integrate their efforts on a contractual basis to obtain greater functional economies and marketing impact than they could achieve alone. An administered VMS achieves coordination at successive stages of production and distribution by the size and influence of one channel member rather than through ownership.

3 *Describe factors that marketing executives consider when selecting and managing a marketing channel.*
Marketing executives consider three questions when selecting and managing a marketing channel and intermediaries. First, which channel and intermediaries will provide the best coverage of the target market? Marketers typically choose one of three levels of market coverage: intensive, selective, or exclusive distribution. Second, which channel and intermediaries will best satisfy the buying requirements of the target market? These buying requirements fall into four categories: information, convenience, variety, and attendant services. Finally, which channel and intermediaries will be the most profitable? Here marketers look at the margins earned (revenues minus cost) for each channel member and for the channel as a whole.

4 *Explain what supply chain and logistics management are and how they relate to marketing strategy.*
A supply chain is a sequence of firms that perform activities required to create and deliver a good or service to consumers or industrial users. Supply chain management is the integration and organization of information and logistics across firms for the purpose of creating value for consumers. Logistics involves those activities that focus on getting the right amount of the right products to the right place at the right time at the lowest possible cost. Logistics management includes the coordination of the flows of both inbound and outbound goods, an emphasis on making these flows cost effective, and customer service. A company's supply chain follows from a clearly defined marketing strategy. The alignment of a company's supply chain with its marketing strategy involves three steps. First, a supply chain must reflect the needs of the customer segment being served. Second, a company must understand what a supply chain is designed to do well. Supply chains range from those that emphasize being responsive to customer requirements and demands to those that emphasize efficiency with the goal of supplying products at the lowest possible delivered cost. Finally, a supply chain must be consistent with the targeted customer's needs and the company's marketing strategy. The Dell and Wal-Mart examples in the chapter illustrate how this alignment is achieved by two market leaders.

FOCUSING ON KEY TERMS

channel conflict p. 295
customer service p. 301
disintermediation p. 296
dual distribution p. 291
exclusive distribution p. 294
franchising p. 292
intensive distribution p. 294
logistics p. 297
marketing channel p. 286
selective distribution p. 294
supply chain p. 297
total logistics cost p. 301
vendor-managed inventory p. 302
vertical marketing systems p. 291

DISCUSSION AND APPLICATION QUESTIONS

1 A distributor for Celanese Chemical Company stores large quantities of chemicals, blends these chemicals to satisfy requests of customers, and delivers the blends to a customer's warehouse within 24 hours of receiving an order. What utilities does this distributor provide?

2 Suppose the president of a carpet manufacturing firm has asked you to look into the possibility of bypassing the firm's wholesalers (who sell to carpet, department, and furniture stores) and selling direct to these stores. What caution would you voice on this matter, and what type of information would you gather before making this decision?

3 What type of channel conflict is likely to be caused by dual distribution, and what type of conflict can be reduced by direct distribution? Why?

4 How does the channel captain idea differ among corporate, administered, and contractual vertical marketing systems with particular reference to the use of the different forms of influence available to firms?

5 List the customer service factors that would be vital to buyers in the following types of companies: (*a*) manufacturing, (*b*) retailing, (*c*) hospitals, and (*d*) construction.

GOING ONLINE Finding a Franchise for You

Franchising is a large and growing industry both inside and outside the United States. For many individuals, franchising offers an opportunity to operate one's own business.

The Internet provides a number of websites that feature franchising opportunities. The International Franchise Association (www.franchise.org) features an extensive array of information, including answers to questions about franchising. Franchise.com (www.franchise.com) shows franchise opportunities for the aspiring franchisee.

1 Visit the Franchise.com website, and click on the "Franchise Buyer" link. Which franchise opportunities fit you?

2 Visit the International Franchise Association website, and click on the "Resource Center" link. Then, click on the "News" link. What are the current trends in franchising?

BUILDING YOUR MARKETING PLAN

Does your marketing plan involve selecting channels and intermediaries? If the answer is no, read no further and do not include this element in your plan. If the answer is yes,

1 Identify which channel and intermediaries will provide the best coverage of the target market for your product or service.

2 Specify which channel and intermediaries will best satisfy the important buying requirements of the target market.

3 Determine which channel and intermediaries will be the most profitable.

4 Select your channel(s) and intermediary(ies).

VIDEO CASE 13 Golden Valley Microwave Foods: The Surprising Channel

"We developed the technology that launched the microwave popcorn business and helped make ACT II the number one brand in the world," says Jack McKeon, president of Golden Valley Microwave Foods, a division of ConAgra Foods, Inc. "But we were also lucky along the way, as we backed into what has become one of the biggest distribution channels in the industry today, one that no one ever saw coming."

Founded in 1978, today Golden Valley is the global leader in producing and marketing microwave popcorn. Its ACT II brand is no. 1 in the industry. But it hasn't always been easy.

THE LAUNCH: THE IDEA AND THE TECHNOLOGY

In 1978 only about 15 percent of U.S. households had microwave ovens, so launching a microwave foods business was risky. Golden Valley's initial marketing research turned up two key points of difference or benefits that people wanted in their microwave popcorn: (1) fewer unpopped kernels and (2) good popping results in all types of microwave ovens, even low-powered ovens—the kind that many households with microwaves had at the time. Golden Valley's research and development (R&D) staff successfully addressed these wants by developing a microwave popcorn bag utilizing a thin strip of material laminated between layers of paper, which focused the microwave energy to produce high-quality popped corn, regardless of an oven's power. This breakthrough significantly increased the size of the microwave popcorn market (and is still used in all microwave popcorn bags today). Using its revolutionary package, Golden Valley introduced ACT II in 1984.

THE LUCKY DAY: BOTH CAPITAL AND MASS MERCHANDISERS

From its founding in 1978 until a public offering of its stock in September 1986, Golden Valley was privately owned and, like most startups, was severely undercapitalized. Due to the cost of developing and introducing ACT II, Golden Valley needed a partner to help develop the business. Its solution was to enter into a licensing agreement to share its technology for packaging microwave popcorn with one of the largest food manufacturers in the industry. The licensing partner would sell the popcorn under its own brand name in grocery stores and supermarkets. In turn, Golden Valley agreed it would not distribute its ACT II brand in U.S. grocery stores or supermarkets for ten years. This meant that Golden Valley had to find other channels of distribution in which to sell its microwave popcorn.

For the next 10 years the company developed many new channels. ACT II products were sold through vending machines, video stores (e.g., Blockbuster), institutions (e.g., movie theaters, colleges, military bases), drug stores (e.g., Walgreen's, Rite-Aid, Eckerd Drugs), club stores (e.g., Sam's, Costco, and BJ's), and convenience stores. "But the huge opportunity we discovered and developed was the mass-merchandiser channel through chains like Wal-Mart and Target," says McKeon.

> ACT II microwave popcorn was the first item of any kind to sell a million units in a week for Target, and that happened in 1987. Wal-Mart, too, was on the front end of this market and today is the top seller of microwave popcorn in any channel, selling far more popcorn than the leading grocery chains. Mass merchandisers now account for over a third of all the microwave popcorn sold in the United States. They created the ACT II business as we know it today, and it was accomplished without a dime of conventional consumer promotions. That's one of the really unique parts of the ACT II story.

THE SITUATION TODAY

In the United States today, over 90 percent of households own microwave ovens, and more than 60 percent of households are microwave popcorn consumers who spend more than $688 million on the product each year. "Our marketing research shows ACT II is especially strong in young families with kids," says Frank Lynch, vice president of marketing at Golden Valley. This conjures up an image of mom and dad watching a movie on TV with the kids and eating ACT II popcorn, a picture close to reality. "ACT II has good market penetration in almost all age, income, urban versus rural, and ethnic segments," he continues.

"From the beginning, Golden Valley has been the leader in the microwave popcorn industry," says McKeon, "and we plan to continue that record." As evidence, he cites a number of Golden Valley's "firsts":

- First mass-marketed microwave popcorn.
- First flavored microwave popcorn.
- First microwave popcorn tub.
- First fat-free microwave popcorn.
- First extra-butter microwave popcorn.
- First one-step sweetened microwave popcorn.

This list highlights a curious market segmentation phenomenon that has emerged in the last five years: the no-butter versus plenty-of-butter consumers. Originally popcorn was seen as junk food. Later studies by nutritionists pointed out its health benefits: low calories and high fiber. This caused Golden Valley to introduce its low-fat popcorn in the late 1990s to appeal to the health-conscious segment of consumers. When it comes to eating popcorn while watching a movie at home on TV, however, the more butter on their popcorn, the better. Recently, much of the growth in popcorn sales has been in the spoil-yourself-with-a lot-of-butter-on-your-popcorn segment.

Because of these diverse consumer tastes in popcorn, Golden Valley has developed a variety of popcorn products around its ACT II brand. Besides the low-fat and extra butter versions, these include the original flavors (natural and butter), sweet glazed products, popcorn in tubs, and Kettle Corn. In 2004, ACT II Big Boy was introduced to appeal to the economy segment. It also has a line of ACT II non-popcorn snacks such as soft pretzels and snack mixes.

Golden Valley positions ACT II as unpretentious, fun, and youthful—a great product at a reasonable price. By stressing the value aspect of ACT II, Golden Valley has positioned the brand to appeal to today's growing value consciousness of consumers seeking quality products at reasonable prices. In terms of market share, these strategies have enabled ACT II to become the leader in the microwave popcorn market.

OPPORTUNITIES FOR FUTURE GROWTH

For many years the growth of the microwave popcorn industry closely followed the growth of household ownership of microwave ovens—from under 20 percent to over 90 percent. But now, with a microwave oven in virtually every U.S. home, Golden Valley is trying to identify new market segments, new products, and innovative ways to appeal to all the major marketing channels.

In the United States, Golden Valley's strategy must include finding creative ways to continue to work with existing channels where it has special strength, such as the mass merchandiser channel. It also needs to further develop opportunities in the grocery store and supermarket channel. Now that the 10-year restriction on sales in grocery stores and supermarkets has expired, distribution through wholesalers which reach grocery stores and supermarkets is possible.

Global markets, too, present opportunities. Golden Valley has followed the penetration of microwave ovens in countries around the world, and used brokers to help gain distribution in those markets. Currently, Golden Valley has sales in more than 32 countries and the leading share in most of those markets. However, foreign markets represent foreign tastes, something that does not always lend itself to standardized products. United Kingdom consumers, for example, think of popcorn as a candy or child's food rather than the salty snack it is in the United States. Even in the Disney Park in Paris,

American-style popcorn is absent, as French consumers sprinkle sugar on their popcorn. Swedes like theirs very buttery, whereas many Mexicans like jalapeño-flavored popcorn.

Questions

1 Visit ACT II's website at www.actii.com and examine the assortment of products offered today. Are (*a*) the assortment or (*b*) the packaging related to Golden Valley's distribution channels or the segments they serve?

2 Use Figure 13–3 to create a description of the channels of distribution being used by Golden Valley today.

3 Compared to selling through the nongrocery channels, what kind of product, price, and promotion strategies might Golden Valley use to reach the grocery channel more effectively?

4 What special marketing issues does Golden Valley face as it pursues growth in global markets?

The lamp shade you need. 14.99

CHAPTER 14

RETAILING AND WHOLESALING

LEARNING OBJECTIVES

After reading this chapter you should be able to:

1. Identify retailers in terms of the utilities they provide.
2. Explain the alternative ways to classify retail outlets.
3. Describe the many methods of nonstore retailing.
4. Develop retailing mix strategies over the life cycle of a retail store.
5. Describe the types and functions of firms that perform wholesaling activities.

TRADING UP . . . AT TARGET

Are you one of the millions of consumers who selectively trade up to better products in some categories? Have you noticed the growing preference for brands that provide higher quality and emotional value? Consultants Michael Silverstein and Neil Fiske noticed, and they wrote about it in their book *Trading Up: The New American Luxury,* in which they describe the success of businesses that offer "new luxury" items, which can include clothing, appliances, and even personal care products. Target Stores noticed too and has repositioned the store as an "upscale discounter."

The first step in the strategy was to establish the red Target logo as a recognizable symbol of quality and value. The first campaign, called "Bulls-Eye World," featured the Target logo on everything in print and television ads—clothing, wallpaper, dogs—everything! Other promotions emphasized the high-quality brands available in Target stores. Then, Target added exclusive lines by well-known designers such as Thomas O'Brien "Vintage Modern" home furnishings, Michael Graves housewares, Swell bed and bath products, Amy Coe infant bedding, Mossimo clothing, and Sonia Kashuk makeup. You may remember the familiar "Everything You Want, You've Got It" campaign that showed the broad range of products available in the stores.

Target recently began opening stores with a new design that includes a Starbucks café at the front of the store; a larger food area, which includes the Target food brand, Archer Farms; destination areas for categories such as baby merchandise; and more convenient locations of related categories such as movies, books, and music. Other marketing activities include Target's bridal registry, Club Wedd, and the Target Baby registry for new parents. Its website, Target.com, provides access to its brands for consumers in locales where no stores exist. Target has also developed partnerships with FTD, Yahoo!, and The Knot (wedding planning service).

Target's most recent campaign builds on the trading-up theme by encouraging customers to "Expect More, Pay Less." One industry expert observed that Target has "been able to carve out the ultimate retail positioning with both a perception of having the highest-quality products and, at the same time, a perception of being a "low-price leader." Of course, Target is facing direct competition from Wal-Mart, but to attract and keep upscale consumers who like high-quality bargains, it also faces competition from traditional department stores. In what may be the most dramatic statement of its repositioning strategy, watch for Target to try new locations in suburban malls.[1]

Target is just one example of many dynamic and exciting retailers you may encounter today. This chapter examines the critical role of retailing in the marketplace and the challenging decisions retailers face as they strive to create value for customers.

What types of products will consumers buy through catalogs, television, the Web, or by telephone? In what type of store will consumers look for products they don't buy directly? How important is the location of the store? Will customers expect services such as alterations, delivery, installation, or repair? What price should be charged for each product? These are difficult and important questions that are an integral part of retailing. In the channel of distribution, retailing is where the customer meets the product. It is through retailing that exchange (a central aspect of marketing) occurs. **Retailing** includes all activities involved in selling, renting, and providing goods and services to ultimate consumers for personal, family, or household use.

retailing
All activities involved in selling, renting, and providing goods and services to ultimate consumers for personal, family, or household use

THE VALUE OF RETAILING

Retailing is an important marketing activity. Not only do producers and consumers meet through retailing actions, but retailing also creates customer value and has a significant impact on the economy. To consumers, the value of retailing is in the form of utilities provided (Figure 14–1). Retailing's economic value is represented by the

FIGURE 14–1
Which company best represents which utilities?

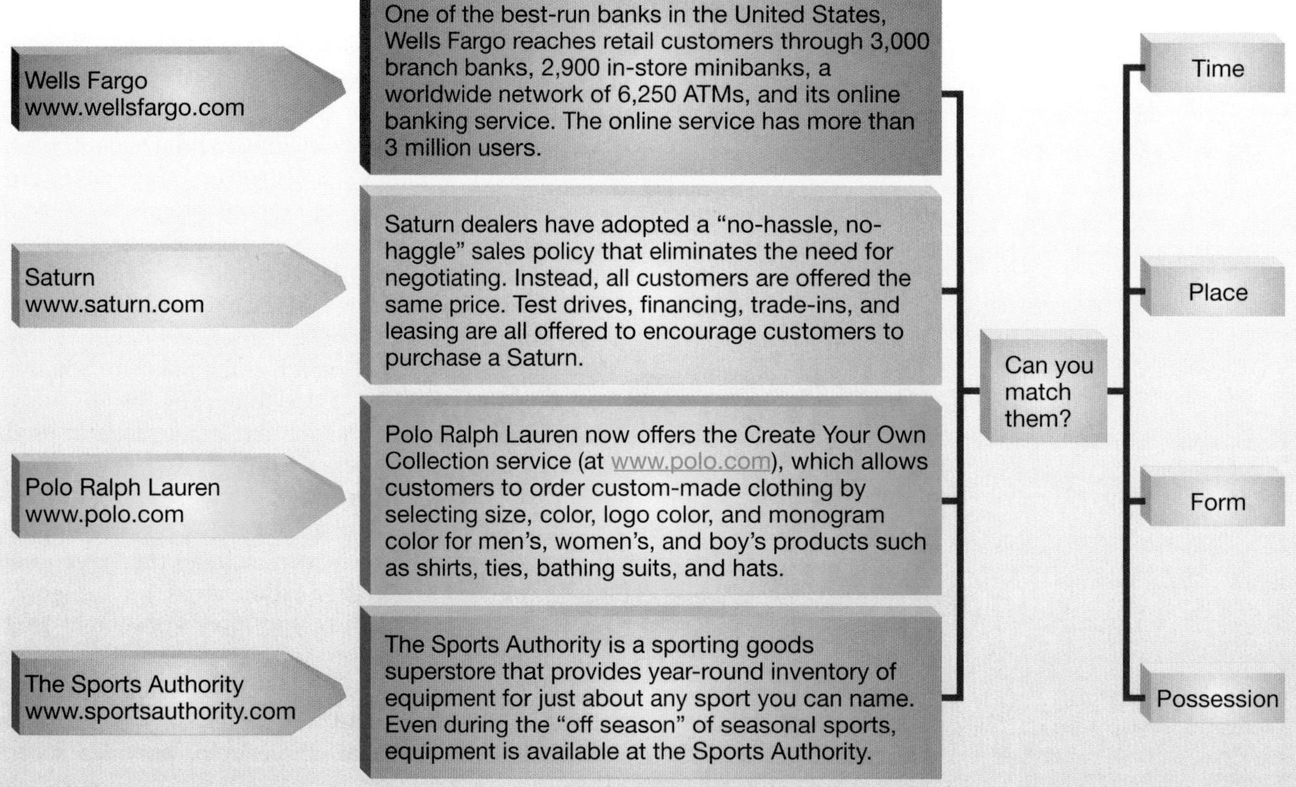

people employed in retailing as well as by the total amount of money exchanged in retail sales.

Consumer Utilities Offered by Retailing

The utilities provided by retailers create value for consumers. Time, place, form, and possession utilities are offered by most retailers in varying degrees, but one utility is often emphasized more than others. Look at Figure 14–1 to see how well you can match the retailer with the utility being emphasized in the description.

Providing minibanks in supermarkets, as Wells Fargo does, puts the bank's products and services close to the consumer, providing place utility. By providing financing or leasing and taking used cars as trade-ins, Saturn makes the purchase easier and provides possession utility. Form utility—production or alteration of a product—is offered by Polo Ralph Lauren through its online Create Your Own Collection service, which offers products that meet each customer's specifications. Finding the right sporting equipment during the off-season is the time utility provided by the Sports Authority. Many retailers offer a combination of the four basic utilities. Some supermarkets, for example, offer convenient locations (place utility) and are open 24 hours (time utility). In addition, consumers may seek additional utilities such as entertainment, recreation, or information.[2]

The Global Economic Impact of Retailing

Retailing is also important to the U.S. and global economies. Four of the 30 largest businesses in the United States are retailers (Wal-Mart, Home Depot, Target, and Costco).[3] Wal-Mart's $288 billion of sales in 2004 surpassed the gross domestic product of Sweden for that same year. Wal-Mart, Home Depot, and Target together have more than 2.3 million employees—more than the number of people who live in Austin, Texas, Spokane, Washington, and Norwich, Connecticut, combined. Many other retailers, including food stores, automobile dealers, and general merchandise outlets, are also significant contributors to the U.S. economy.[4]

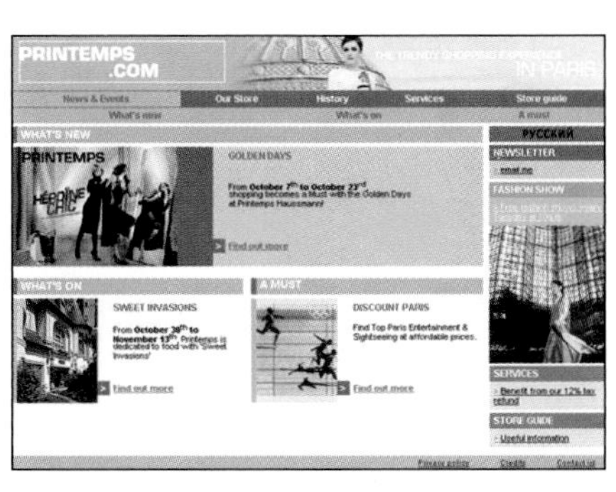

Outside the United States, large retailers include Daiei in Japan, Pinault-Printemps in France, Karstadtquelle in Germany, and Marks & Spencer in Britain.[5] In emerging economies such as China and Mexico, a combination of local and global retailers is evolving. Wal-Mart, for example, has 1,570 stores outside the United States, including stores in Mexico, Puerto Rico, Canada, Argentina, Brazil, China, Korea, Germany, and the United Kingdom.

Concept Check

1. When Polo makes clothing cut to a customer's exact preferences, what utility is provided?
2. Two measures of the impact of retailing in the global economy are ______________ and ______________.

CLASSIFYING RETAIL OUTLETS

For manufacturers, consumers, and the economy, retailing is an important component of marketing that has several variations. Because of the large number of alternative forms of retailing, it is easier to understand the differences among retail institutions by recognizing that outlets can be classified in several ways. First, *form of ownership* distinguishes retail outlets based on whether individuals, corporate chains, or contractual

MARKETING NEWSNET Say Good-Bye to Bar Codes

New technologies are continually changing the marketing and retailing environment. The next big thing, however, may be tiny microchips known as radio frequency identification (RFID) tags, which are so small and inexpensive that they can be attached to pallets, cases, cartons, or even individual items. The new technology allows manufacturers, distributors, and retailers to collect detailed information about a product's origin, distribution path, and price, eliminating the need for the current bar codes used to track goods. Wal-Mart and Target have already

mandated that their top vendors begin using RFID tags, and manufacturers such as Gillette, Procter & Gamble, Nestlé,

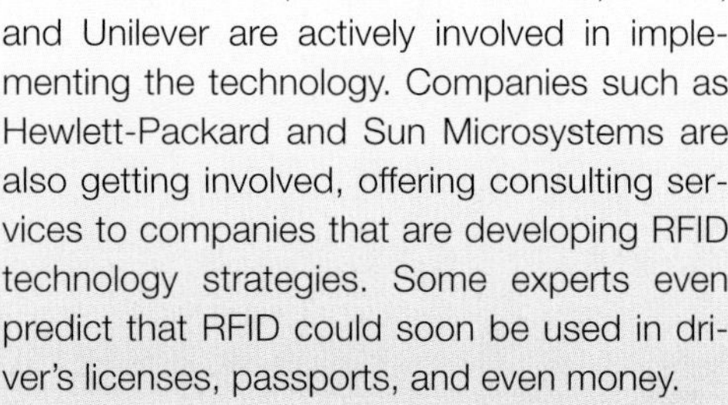

and Unilever are actively involved in implementing the technology. Companies such as Hewlett-Packard and Sun Microsystems are also getting involved, offering consulting services to companies that are developing RFID technology strategies. Some experts even predict that RFID could soon be used in driver's licenses, passports, and even money.

systems own the outlet. Second, *level of service* is used to describe the degree of service provided to the customer. Three levels of service are provided by self-, limited-, and full-service retailers. Finally, the type of *merchandise line* describes how many different types of products a store carries and in what assortment. The alternative types of outlets are discussed in greater detail in the following pages.

Form of Ownership

Independent Retailer One of the most common forms of retail ownership is the independent business, owned by an individual. Small retailers account for most of the 1.5 million retail establishments in the United States and include hardware stores, bakeries, clothing stores, and restaurants. In addition, there are 29,000 jewelry stores, 26,000 florists, and 43,000 sporting good and hobby stores. The advantage of this form of ownership for the owner is that he or she can be his or her own boss. For customers, the independent store can offer convenience, quality personal service, and lifestyle compatibility.[6]

Corporate Chain A second form of ownership, the corporate chain, involves multiple outlets under common ownership. If you've ever shopped at Bloomingdale's or Macy's, you've shopped at a chain outlet owned by Federated Department Stores Inc. In a chain operation, centralization in decision making and purchasing is common. Chain stores have advantages in dealing with manufacturers, particularly as the size of the chain grows. A large chain can bargain with a manufacturer to obtain good service or volume discounts on orders. Consumers also benefit in dealing with chains because there are multiple outlets with similar merchandise and consistent management policies.

Retailing has become a high-tech business for many large chains. Wal-Mart, for example, has developed a sophisticated inventory management and cost control system that allows rapid price changes for each product in every store. In addition, stores such as Wal-Mart and Target are implementing pioneering new technologies such as radio frequency identification (RFID) tags to improve the quality of information available about products. The accompanying Marketing NewsNet describes the trend.[7]

Contractual Systems Contractual systems involve independently owned stores that band together to act like a chain. The three kinds described in Chapter 13

are retailer-sponsored cooperatives, wholesaler-sponsored voluntary chains, and franchises. One retailer-sponsored cooperative is the Associated Grocers, which consists of neighborhood grocers that all agree with several other independent grocers to buy their meat from the same wholesaler. In this way, members can take advantage of volume discounts commonly available to chains and also give the impression of being a large chain, which may be viewed more favorably by some consumers. Wholesaler-sponsored voluntary chains such as Ace Hardware and Independent Grocers' Alliance (IGA) try to achieve similar benefits.

As noted in Chapter 13, in a franchise system an individual or firm (the franchisee) contracts with a parent company (the franchisor) to set up a business or retail outlet. The franchisor usually assists in selecting the location, setting up the store or facility, advertising, and training personnel. The franchisee usually pays a onetime franchise fee and an annual royalty, usually tied to franchise's sales. There are two general types of franchises: *business-format franchises,* such as McDonald's, Radio Shack, and Blockbuster, and *product-distribution franchises,* such as a Ford dealership or a Coca-Cola distributor. In business-format franchising, the franchisor provides step-by-step procedures for most aspects of the business and guidelines for the most likely decisions a franchisee will face.

Franchise fees paid to the franchisor can range from $10,000 for a Subway franchise to $45,000 for a McDonald's restaurant franchise. When the fees are combined with other costs such as real estate and equipment, however, the total investment can be much higher. By selling franchises, an organization reduces the cost of expansion but loses some control. A good franchisor, however, will maintain strong control of the outlets in terms of delivery and presentation of merchandise and try to enhance recognition of the franchise name.[8] What is the fastest-growing franchise? For the past year it has been Subway, which now has 21,000 locations, including 4,000 stores outside of the United States.[9]

Level of Service

Even though most customers perceive little variation in retail outlets by form of ownership, differences among retailers are more obvious in terms of level of service. In some department stores, such as Loehman's, very few services are provided. Some grocery stores, such as the Cub chain, allow customers to bag the food themselves. Other outlets, such as Neiman Marcus, provide a wide range of customer services from gift wrapping to wardrobe consultation.

Self-Service Self-service requires that the customer performs many functions and little is provided by the outlet. Warehouse stores, for example, are usually self-service, with all nonessential customer services eliminated. Similarly, most gas stations today are self-service. New forms of self-service are being developed in grocery stores, airlines, camera/photo stores, and hotels. Delta Airlines has installed more than 600 self-service kiosks in all 81 of its U.S. terminals to allow passengers to find a seat and print out a boarding pass without the help of an attendant. Hilton is currently testing self-service kiosks in its Chicago and New York hotels. Customers swipe a credit card, select from room availability options, and then receive an encoded key card.[10]

Limited Service Limited-service outlets provide some services, such as credit and merchandise return, but not others, such as clothing alterations. General merchandise stores such as Wal-Mart, Kmart, and Target are usually considered limited service outlets. Customers are responsible for most shopping activities, although salespeople are available in departments such as consumer electronics, jewelry, and lawn and garden.

Full-Service Full-service retailers, which include most specialty stores and department stores, provide many services to their customers. Neiman Marcus, Nordstrom, and Saks Fifth Avenue, for example, all rely on better service to sell more distinctive, higher-margin goods. Nordstrom offers a wide variety of services, including free exchanges, easy returns, credit cards, Nordstrom bank, a live help line, an online gift finder, catalogs, and a beauty hotline. Some Nordstrom stores also offer a "Personal Touch" department, which provides shopping assistants for consumers who need help with style, color, and size selection, and a concierge service for assistance with anything else. Nordstrom stores typically have 50 percent more salespeople on the floor than similarly sized stores, and the salespeople are renowned for their professional and personalized attention to customers.[11]

Type of Merchandise Line

Retail outlets also vary by their merchandise lines, the key distinction being the breadth and depth of the items offered to customers (Figure 14–2). *Depth of product line* means that the store carries a large assortment of each item, such as a shoe store that offers running shoes, dress shoes, and children's shoes. *Breadth of product line* refers to the variety of different items a store carries, such as appliances and CDs.

Depth of Line Stores that carry a considerable assortment (depth) of a related line of items are limited-line stores. Oshman's sporting goods stores carry considerable depth in sports equipment ranging from weight-lifting accessories to running shoes. Stores that carry tremendous depth in one primary line of merchandise are single-line stores. Victoria's Secret, a nationwide chain, carries great depth in women's lingerie. Both limited- and single-line stores are often referred to as *specialty outlets.*

Specialty discount outlets focus on one type of product, such as electronics (Circuit City), office supplies (Staples), or books (Barnes and Noble) at very competitive prices. These outlets are referred to in the trade as *category killers* because they often dominate the market. Staples, for example, controls 37 percent of the office supply market.[12]

FIGURE 14–2
Breadth versus depth of merchandise lines

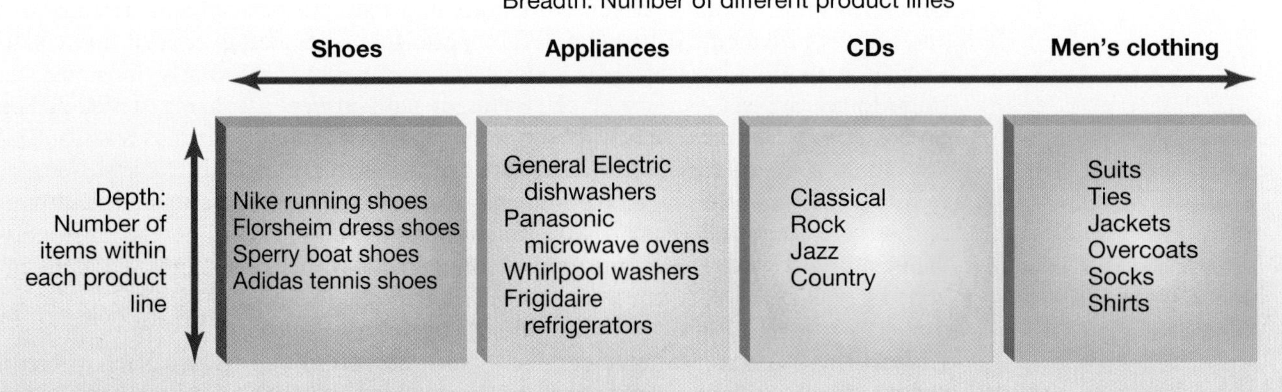

Breadth of Line Stores that carry a broad product line, with limited depth, are referred to as *general merchandise stores*. For example, large department stores such as Dillard's, Macy's, Marshall Field's, and Neiman Marcus carry a wide range of different types of products but not unusual sizes. The breadth and depth of merchandise lines are important decisions for a retailer. Traditionally, outlets carried related lines of goods. Today, however, **scrambled merchandising**, offering several unrelated product lines in a single store, is common. The modern drugstore carries food, camera equipment, magazines, paper products, toys, small hardware items, and pharmaceuticals. Supermarkets rent DVDs, print photos, and sell flowers.

scrambled merchandising
Offering several unrelated product lines in a single retail store

Concept Check

1. Centralized decision making and purchasing are an advantage of ____________ ownership.
2. What are some examples of new forms of self-service retailers?
3. Would a shop for big men's clothes carrying pants in sizes 40 to 60 have a broad or deep product line?

NONSTORE RETAILING

Most of the retailing examples discussed earlier in the chapter, such as corporate chains, department stores, and limited- and single-line specialty stores, involve store retailing. Many retailing activities today, however, are not limited to sales in a store. Nonstore retailing occurs outside a retail outlet through activities that involve varying levels of customer and retailer involvement. Six forms of nonstore retailing include automatic vending, direct mail and catalogs, television home shopping, online retailing, telemarketing, and direct selling.

Automatic Vending

Nonstore retailing includes vending machines, which make it possible to serve customers when and where stores cannot. Machine maintenance, operating costs, and location leases can add to the cost of the products, so prices in vending machines tend to be higher than those in stores. About 29 percent of the products sold from vending machines are cold beverages, another 26 percent are candy and snacks, and another 29 percent is food. Other products are likely to be available in vending machines soon, however. Staples recently installed vending machines with office supplies in Boston's Logan International Airport and on several college campuses. Similarly, Flickstation Media is placing DVD vending machines in high-rise office complexes. The 5.6 million vending machines currently in use in the United States generated more than \$21 billion in sales last year.[13]

Improved technology is making vending machines easier to use by reducing the need for cash. Many machines already accept credit cards, and cashless purchases using cell phones are likely in the near future. Japan's largest mobile phone company, DoCoMo, is working with Sony to introduce cell phones equipped with an electronic cash system called Edy (*e*uro, *d*ollar, *y*en), which will allow consumers to charge vending machine purchases to their cell phone accounts. Another improvement in vending machines is the use of wireless technology to notify vendors when their machines are empty. Nestlé, for example, is installing hundreds of ice cream vending machines in France and England that send wireless messages to supply truck drivers. Finally, one of the biggest developments in vending is being tested by Vision Inc.—it is

experimenting with huge vending machines for parking lots that will be fully automated convenience stores.[14]

Direct Mail and Catalogs

Direct-mail and catalog retailing are attractive because they eliminate the cost of a store and clerks. For example, it costs a traditional retail store $34 to acquire a new customer, whereas catalog customers are acquired for approximately $14. In addition, catalogs improve marketing efficiency through segmentation and targeting, and they create customer value by providing a fast and convenient means of making a purchase. The Direct Marketing Association predicts that catalog sales will reach $175 billion by 2008. Catalogs are popular outside of the United States also. Furniture retailer IKEA delivered 130 million copies of its catalog to 36 countries in 28 languages. Five million copies went to Canada, 11 million to the United States, 14 million to Britain, and every household in Sweden received a copy.[15]

One reason for the growth in catalog sales is that traditional retailers such as Crate and Barrel, OfficeMax, and Sears are adding catalog operations. As consumer's direct-mail purchases have increased, the number of catalogs and the number of products sold through catalogs have increased. A typical household now receives more than 50 of the 16 billion catalogs mailed each year. The competition, combined with increases in postal rates, however, have caused catalog retailers to focus on proven customers rather than prospective customers. Another successful approach used by many catalog retailers is to send specialty catalogs to market niches identified in their databases. L. L. Bean, a long-standing catalog retailer, has developed an individual catalog for fishing enthusiasts. Similarly, Lillian Vernon Corporation sends a specialty catalog called "Lilly's Kids" to customers with children or grandchildren, and Sears sends a catalog called "Big and Tall" to customers who have purchased large-size clothing.[16]

Television Home Shopping

Television home shopping is possible when consumers watch a shopping channel on which products are displayed; orders are then placed over the telephone or the Internet. Currently, the three largest programs are QVC, HSN, and ShopNBC. QVC ("quality, value, convenience") broadcasts live 24 hours each day, 364 days a year and reaches 145 million households in the United States, United Kingdom, Germany, and Japan. The company generates sales of more than $4.8 billion from its 29 million customers by offering 250 new products each week and shipping more than 120 million packages each year. Because television home shopping programs typically attract women over age 35, other programs such as MTV's *House of Style* with host Molly Sims, and the complementary website, MTV Shop, are designed to attract a younger audience. The television shopping programs are using other forms of retailing also. QVC now has three types of retail stores: a studio store at its headquarters, QVC @ the Mall in the Mall of America, and six outlet stores. Similarly, the Home Shopping Network has added catalogs to its online and television offerings. Finally, several television shopping programs are testing interactive television technology that allows viewers to place orders with their remote control rather than the telephone.[17]

Online Retailing

Online retailing allows consumers to search for, evaluate, and order products through the Internet. For many consumers the advantages of this form of retailing are the 24-hour access, the ability to comparison shop, in-home privacy, and variety. Studies of online shoppers indicated that men were initially more likely than women to buy something online. As the number of online households increased, however, the profile of online shoppers changed to include all shoppers. In addition, the number of online retailers grew rapidly for several years and then declined as many stand-alone, Internet-only businesses failed or consolidated. Today, there has been a melding of traditional and online retailers—"bricks and clicks"—that are using experiences from both approaches to create better value and experiences for customers. At Walmart.com, for example, CEO Jeanne Jackson has advocated a streamlined and intuitive website layout and new services such as real-time inventories in individual stores that allow customers to decide whether to go to the store or to buy online. Experts predict that online sales will reach $255 billion by 2007.[18]

Online retail purchases can be the result of several very different approaches. First, consumers can pay dues to become a member of an online discount service such as www.netMarket.com. The service offers more than 800,000 items at very low prices to its 25 million subscribers. Another approach to online retailing is to use a shopping "bot" such as www.mysimon.com. This site searches the Web for a product specified by the consumer and provides a report on the locations of the best prices available. A final approach to online retailing is the online auction, such as www.ebay.com, where consumers bid on more than 1,000 categories of products.[19]

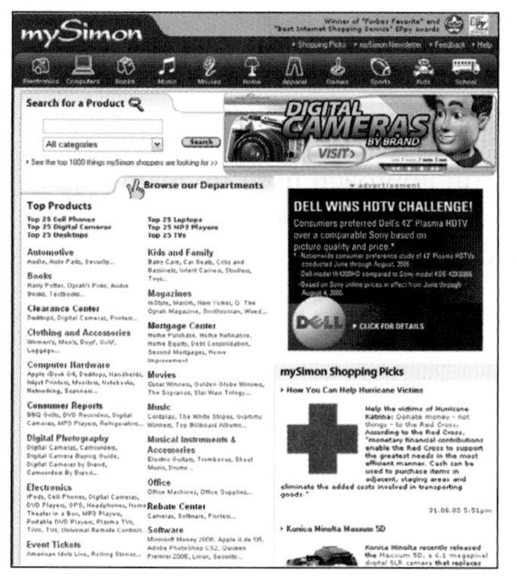

One of the biggest problems online retailers face is that nearly two-thirds of online shoppers make it to "checkout" and then leave the website to compare shipping costs and prices on other sites. Of the shoppers who leave, 70 percent do not return. One way online retailers are addressing this issue is to offer consumers a comparison of competitors' offerings. At booksamillion.com, for example, consumers can use a "comparison engine" to compare prices with Amazon.com, Barnesandnoble.com, and Borders.com.[20] Online retailers are also trying to improve the online retailing experience by adding experiential or interactive activities to their websites. Car manufacturers like BMW, Mercedes, and Jaguar, for example, encourage website visitors to "build" a vehicle by selecting interior and exterior colors, packages, and options and then view the customized virtual car. Other changes on the horizon include the merger of television home shopping and online retailing which will be possible through TV-based Internet platforms such as Microsoft's MSN TV.

Telemarketing

telemarketing
Using the telephone to interact with and sell directly to consumers

Another form of nonstore retailing, called **telemarketing**, involves using the telephone to interact with and sell directly to consumers. Compared with direct mail, telemarketing is often viewed as a more efficient means of targeting consumers. Insurance companies, brokerage firms, and newspapers have often used this form of retailing as a way to cut costs but still maintain access to their customers. According to the Direct Marketing Association, annual telemarketing sales exceed $500 billion.[21]

The telemarketing industry has recently gone through dramatic changes as a result of new legislation related to telephone solicitations. Issues such as consumer privacy, industry standards, and ethical guidelines have encouraged discussion among consumers, Congress, the Federal Trade Commission, and businesses. The result was legislation that created the National Do-Not-Call registry (www.donotcall.gov) for consumers who do not want to receive telephone calls related to company sales efforts. The American Teleservices Association asked the Supreme Court to review the implications of the legislation in terms of its restrictions on free speech. Although the Supreme Court decided not to review the case, companies that use telemarketing have already adapted by adding compliance software to ensure that numbers on the list are not called. In addition, some firms are considering shifting their telemarketing budgets to direct-mail and door-to-door techniques.[22]

Direct Selling

Direct selling, sometimes called door-to-door retailing, involves direct sales of goods and services to consumers through personal interactions and demonstrations in their home or office. A variety of companies, including familiar names such as Fuller Brush, Avon, World Book, and Mary Kay Cosmetics, have created an industry with more than $16 billion in sales by providing consumers with personalized service and convenience. In the United States, however, sales have been declining as retail chains such as Wal-Mart begin to carry similar products at discount prices and as the increasing number of dual-career households reduces the number of potential buyers at home.

In response to the changes in the United States, many direct selling retailers are expanding into other markets. Avon, for example, already has 4 million sales representatives in 137 countries including Mexico, Poland, Argentina, and China.[23] Similarly, other retailers such as Amway, Herbalife, and Electrolux are rapidly expanding. More than 70 percent of Amway's $7 billion in sales now comes from outside the United States, and sales in Japan alone exceed sales in North America.[24] Direct selling is likely to continue to grow in markets where the lack of effective distribution channels increases the importance of door-to-door convenience and where the lack of consumer knowledge about products and brands will increase the need for a person-to-person approach.[25]

Concept Check

1. Successful catalog retailers often send _____________ catalogs to _____________ markets identified in their databases.
2. How are retailers increasing consumer interest and involvement in online retailing?
3. Where are direct selling retail sales growing? Why?

RETAILING STRATEGY

retailing mix
The goods and services, physical distribution, and communications tactics chosen by a store

This section describes specific actions a retail store can take to develop a retailing strategy. In developing retailing strategy, managers work with the **retailing mix**, which includes activities related to managing the store and the merchandise in the store. The retailing mix, shown in Figure 14–3, is similar to the marketing mix and includes retail pricing, store location, retail communication, and merchandise.

Retail Pricing

In setting prices for merchandise, retailers must decide on the markup, markdown, and timing for markdowns. The *markup* refers to how much should be added to the cost the retailer paid for a product to reach the final selling price. Retailers decide on the *original markup,* but by the time the product is sold, they end up with a *maintained markup.* The original markup is the difference between retailer cost and initial selling price. When products do not sell as quickly as anticipated, their price is reduced. The

FIGURE 14–3
Elements of a retailing strategy

difference between the final selling price and retailer cost is the maintained markup, which is also called the *gross margin.*

Discounting a product, or taking a *markdown,* occurs when the product does not sell at the original price and an adjustment is necessary. Often new models or styles force the price of existing models to be marked down. Discounts may also be used to increase demand for complementary products.[26] For example, retailers might take a markdown on CD players to increase sales of CDs or reduce the price of cake mix to generate frosting purchases. The *timing* of a markdown can be important. Many retailers take a markdown as soon as sales fall off to free up valuable selling space and cash. However, other stores delay markdowns to discourage bargain hunters and maintain an image of quality. There is no clear answer, but retailers must consider how the timing might affect future sales. Recent research indicates that frequent promotions increase consumers' ability to remember regular prices.[27]

Although most retailers plan markdowns, many retailers use price discounts as a part of their regular merchandising policy. Wal-Mart and Home Depot, for example, emphasize consistently low prices and eliminate most markdowns with a strategy often called *everyday low pricing.*[28] Because consumers often use price as an indicator of product quality, however, the brand name of the product and the image of the store become important decision factors in these situations.[29] Another strategy, *everyday fair pricing,* is advocated by retailers which may not offer the lowest price but try to create value for customers through its service and the total buying experience.[30] Consumers often use the prices of *benchmark* or *signpost* items, such as a can of Coke, to form an overall impression of the store's prices.[31] In addition, price is the most likely to influence consumers' assessment of merchandise value.[32]

shrinkage
Breakage and theft of merchandise by customers and employees

A special issue for retailers trying to keep prices low is **shrinkage**, or breakage and theft of merchandise by customers and employees. Who do you think steals more? For the answer see the Ethics and Social Responsibility Alert on the next page.[33]

Off-price retailing is a retail pricing practice that is used by retailers such as T.J. Maxx, Burlington Coat Factory, and Ross Stores. *Off-price retailing* involves selling brand-name merchandise at lower than regular prices. The difference between the off-price retailer and a discount store is that off-price merchandise is bought by the retailer from manufacturers with excess inventory at prices below wholesale prices, while the discounter buys at full wholesale price (but takes less of a markup than do traditional department stores). Because of this difference in the way merchandise is purchased by the retailer, selection at an off-price retailer

ETHICS AND SOCIAL RESPONSIBILITY ALERT

Who Takes the Five-Finger Discount? You'll Be Surprised!

Retailers lose almost 2 percent of their sales to theft each year. To combat the problem many stores attempt to discourage consumers from shoplifting with magnetic detectors, locked cases, and other deterrents. What you may find surprising, though, is that more than 50 percent of the thefts are not made by consumers but by employees. The most popular items to steal are candy from convenience stores, shirts from department stores, batteries from discount stores, and cigarettes from drugstores. When does this happen? The most popular time is between 3 and 6 P.M. Why do you think shoplifting is such a large problem? What recommendations would you make to retailers?

is unpredictable, and searching for bargains has become a popular activity for many consumers. "It's more like a sport than it is like ordinary shopping," says Christopher Boring of Columbus, Ohio's Retail Planning Associates.[34] Savings to the consumer at off-price retailers are reported as high as 70 percent off the prices of a traditional department store.

Store Location

A second aspect of the retailing mix involves deciding where to locate the store and how many stores to have. Department stores, which started downtown in most cities, have followed customers to the suburbs, and in recent years more stores have been opened in large regional malls. Most stores today are near several others in one of five settings: the central business district, the regional center, the community shopping center, the strip, or the power center.

The *central business district* is the oldest retail setting, the community's downtown area. Until the regional outflow to suburbs, it was the major shopping area, but the suburban population has grown at the expense of the downtown shopping area. Consumers often view central business district shopping as less convenient because of lack of parking, higher crime rates, and exposure to the weather. Many cities such as Cincinnati, Denver, and San Antonio have implemented plans to revitalize shopping in central business districts by attracting new offices, entertainment, and residents to downtown locations.

Regional shopping centers consist of 50 to 150 stores that typically attract customers who live or work within a 5- to 10-mile range. These large shopping areas often contain two or three *anchor stores,* which are well-known national or regional stores such as Sears, Saks Fifth Avenue, and Bloomingdale's. The largest variation of a regional center is the West Edmonton Mall in Alberta, Canada. The shopping center is a conglomerate of 800 stores, seven amusement centers, 110 restaurants, and a 355-room Fantasyland hotel.[35]

Not every suburban store is located in a shopping mall. Many neighborhoods have clusters of stores, referred to as a *strip location,* to serve people who are within a 5- to 10-minute drive. Gas station, hardware, laundry, grocery, and pharmacy outlets are commonly found in a strip location. Unlike the larger shopping centers, the composition of these stores is usually unplanned. A variation of the strip shopping location is called the *power center,* which is a huge shopping strip with multiple anchor (or national) stores. Power centers are seen as having the convenient location found in many strip centers and the additional power of national stores. These large strips often have two to five anchor stores and often contain a supermarket, which brings the shopper to the power center on a weekly basis.[36]

The many forms of retail distribution described in this section and previously in this chapter represent an exciting menu of choices for creating customer value in the marketplace. Each format allows retailers to offer unique benefits and meet particular needs of various customer groups. Today, retailers combine many of the forms of distribution to offer a broader spectrum of benefits and experiences.[37] These **multichannel retailers** utilize and integrate a combination of traditional store formats and nonstore formats such as catalogs, television, and online retailing.[38] Barnes and Noble, for example, created Barnesandnoble.com to compete with Amazon.com. Similarly, Office Depot integrated its store, catalog, and Internet channels to make shopping simpler and more convenient.

multichannel retailers
Use a combination of traditional store formats and nonstore formats such as catalogs, television, and online retailing

Retail Communication

As the chapter's opening example about Target illustrates, a retailer's communication activities can play an important role in positioning a store and creating its image. While the traditional elements of communication and promotion are discussed in Chapter 16 on advertising and Chapter 17 on personal selling, the message communicated by the many other elements of the retailing mix are also important.

Deciding on the image of a retail outlet is an important retailing mix factor that has been widely recognized and studied since the late 1950s. Pierre Martineau described image as "the way in which the store is defined in the shopper's mind," partly by its functional qualities and partly by an aura of psychological attributes.[39] In this definition, *functional* refers to mix elements such as price ranges, store layouts, and breadth and depth of merchandise lines. The psychological attributes are the intangibles such as a sense of belonging, excitement, style, or warmth. Image has been found to include impressions of the corporation that operates the store, the category or type of store, the product categories in the store, the brands in each category, merchandise and service quality, and the marketing activities of the store.[40]

Closely related to the concept of image is the store's atmosphere or ambiance. Many retailers believe that sales are affected by layout, color, lighting, and music in the store as well as by how crowded it is. In addition, the physical surroundings that influence customers may affect the store's employees.[41] In creating the right image and atmosphere, a retail store tries to attract its target audience with what those consumers seek from the buying experience, so the store will fortify the beliefs and the emotional reactions buyers are seeking.[42] Sears, for example, is attempting to shift from its appliance and tool image with advertising that speaks to all members of a family. The new "Good Life. Great Price." campaign emphasizes a broad range of brand-name merchandise and one-stop shopping.[43]

Merchandise

A final element of the retailing mix is the merchandise offering. Managing the breadth and depth of the product line requires retail buyers who are familiar with the needs of the target market and the alternative products available from the many manufacturers that might be interested in having a product available in the store. A popular approach to managing the assortment of merchandise today is called **category management**. This approach assigns a manager with the responsibility for selecting all products that consumers in a market segment might view as substitutes for each other, with the objective of maximizing sales and profits in the category. For example, a category manager might be responsible for shoes in a department store or paper products in a grocery store.

category management
An approach to managing the assortment of merchandise which maximizes sales and profits

Many retailers are developing an advanced form of category management called *consumer marketing at retail* (CMAR). Recent surveys show that, as part of their CMAR programs, retailers are conducting research, analyzing the data to identify shopper problems, translating the data into retailing mix actions, executing shopper-friendly in-store programs, and monitoring the performance of the merchandise. Wal-Mart, for example, has used the approach to test baby-product and dollar-product categories. Grocery stores such as Safeway and Kroger use the approach to determine the appropriate mix of brand name and private label products. Specialty retailer Barnes &

Noble recently won a best practice award for its application of the approach to the selection, presentation, and promotion of magazines.[44]

Concept Check

1. How does original markup differ from maintained markup?
2. A huge shopping strip with multiple anchor stores is a __________ center.
3. What is a popular approach to managing the assortment of merchandise in a store?

THE CHANGING NATURE OF RETAILING

Retailing is the most dynamic aspect of a channel of distribution. Stores such as factory outlets show that new retailers are always entering the market, searching for a new position that will attract customers. The reason for this continual change is explained by two concepts: the wheel of retailing and the retail life cycle.

The Wheel of Retailing

wheel of retailing
A concept that describes how new forms of retail outlets enter the market

The **wheel of retailing** describes how new forms of retail outlets enter the market.[45] Usually they enter as low-status, low-margin stores such as a drive-in hamburger stand with no indoor seating and a limited menu (Figure 14–4, box 1). Gradually these outlets add fixtures and more embellishments to their stores (in-store seating, plants, and chicken sandwiches as well as hamburgers) to increase the attractiveness for customers. With these additions, prices and status rise (box 2). As time passes, these outlets add still more services and their prices and status increase even further (box 3).

FIGURE 14–4
The wheel of retailing

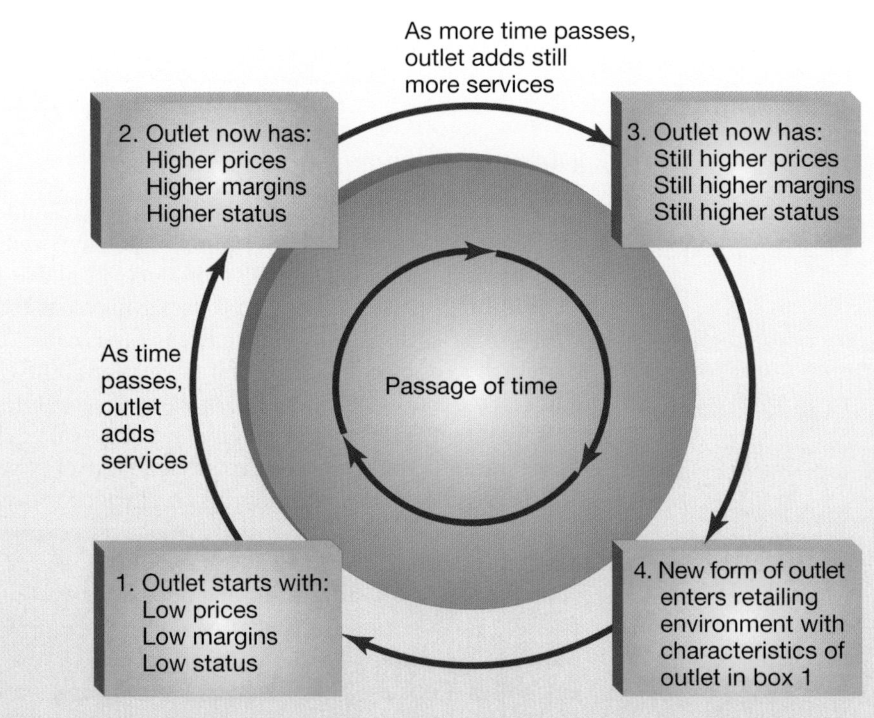

These retail outlets now face some new form of retail outlet that again appears as a low-status, low-margin operator (box 4), and the wheel of retailing turns as the cycle starts to repeat itself.

In the 1950s, McDonald's and Burger King had very limited menus of hamburgers and french fries. Most stores had no inside seating for customers. Over time, the wheel of retailing for fast-food restaurants has turned. These chains have changed by altering their stores and expanding their menus. Today, McDonald's is testing new products such as its all white-meat Chicken McNuggets, chicken breast strips called Big Dippers, and the Go Active Happy Meal for adults; new formats such as its coffee, pastry, and sandwich outlets called McCafe; and new service options such as wireless Internet connections.[46] The changes are leaving room for new forms of outlets such as Checkers Drive-In Restaurants. The chain opened fast-food stores that offered only basics—burgers, fries, and cola, a drive-thru window, and no inside seating—and now has more than 775 stores.[47] The wheel is turning for other outlets too—Boston Market has added sophisticated soups, salads, and desserts to its original menu, is testing home delivery in Washington, D.C., and recently introduced a full-service format called Rotisserie Grill in Tallahassee, Florida. For still others, the wheel has come full circle. Taco Bell is now opening small, limited-offering outlets in gas stations, discount stores, or "wherever a burrito and a mouth might possibly intersect."[48]

The Retail Life Cycle

retail life cycle
The process of growth and decline that retail outlets, like products, experience over time

The process of growth and decline that retail outlets, like products, experience is described by the **retail life cycle**.[49] Figure 14–5 shows the retail life cycle and the position of various current forms of retail outlets on it. Early growth is the stage of emergence of a retail outlet, with a sharp departure from existing competition. Market

FIGURE 14–5
The retail life cycle

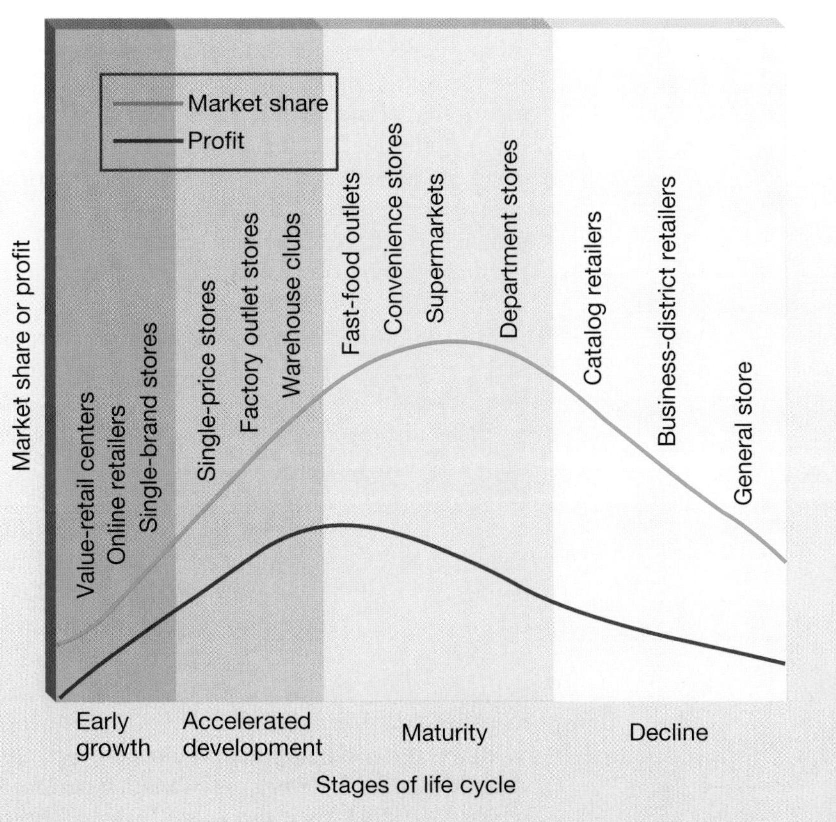

share rises gradually, although profits may be low because of start-up costs. In the next stage, accelerated development, both market share and profit achieve their greatest growth rates. Usually multiple outlets are established as companies focus on the distribution element of the retailing mix. In this stage, some later competitors may enter. Wendy's, for example, appeared on the hamburger chain scene almost 20 years after McDonald's had begun operation. The key goal for the retailer in this stage is to establish a dominant position in the fight for market share.

The battle for market share is usually fought before the maturity stage, and some competitors drop out of the market. In the wars among hamburger chains, Jack in the Box, Gino Marchetti's, and Burger Chef used to be more dominant outlets. New retail forms enter in the maturity stage, stores try to maintain their market share, and price discounting occurs. For example, when McDonald's introduced its Extra Value Meal, a discounted package of burger, fries, and drink, Wendy's followed with a kid's Value Menu.

WHOLESALING

Many retailers depend on intermediaries that engage in wholesaling activities—selling products and services for the purposes of resale or business use. There are several types of intermediaries, including wholesalers and agents (described briefly in Chapter 13), as well as manufacturers' sales offices, which are important to understand as part of the retailing process.

Merchant Wholesalers

merchant wholesalers
Independently owned firms that take title to the merchandise they handle

Merchant wholesalers are independently owned firms that take title to—that is, they own—the merchandise they handle. They go by various names described in detail below. About 83 percent of the firms engaged in wholesaling activities are merchant wholesalers.

Merchant wholesalers are classified as either full-service or limited-service wholesalers, depending on the number of functions performed. Two major types of full-service wholesalers exist. *General merchandise* (or *full-line*) *wholesalers* carry a broad assortment of merchandise and perform all channel functions. This type of wholesaler is most prevalent in the hardware, drug, and clothing industries. However, these wholesalers do not maintain much depth of assortment within specific product lines. *Specialty merchandise* (or *limited-line*) *wholesalers* offer a relatively narrow range of products but have an extensive assortment within the product lines carried. They perform all channel functions and are found in the health foods, automotive parts, and seafood industries.

Four major types of limited-service wholesalers exist. *Rack jobbers* furnish the racks or shelves that display merchandise in retail stores, perform all channel functions, and sell on consignment to retailers, which means they retain the title to the products displayed and bill retailers only for the merchandise sold. Familiar products such as hosiery, toys, housewares, and health and beauty items are sold by rack jobbers. *Cash and carry wholesalers* take title to merchandise but sell only to buyers who call on them, pay cash for merchandise, and furnish their own transportation for merchandise. They carry a limited product assortment and do not make deliveries, extend credit, or supply market information. This wholesaler is common in electric supplies, office supplies, hardware products, and groceries. *Drop shippers,* or *desk jobbers,* are wholesalers that own the merchandise they sell but do not physically handle, stock, or deliver it. They simply solicit orders from retailers and other wholesalers and have the merchandise shipped directly from a producer to a buyer. Drop shippers are used for bulky products such as coal, lumber, and chemicals, which are sold in extremely large quantities. *Truck jobbers* are small wholesalers that have a small warehouse from which they stock their trucks for distribution to retailers. They usually handle limited assortments of fast-moving or perishable items that are sold for cash directly from trucks in their original packages. Truck jobbers handle products such as bakery items, dairy products, and meat.

Agents and Brokers

Unlike merchant wholesalers, agents and brokers do not take title to merchandise and typically provide fewer channel functions. They make their profit from commissions or fees paid for their services, whereas merchant wholesalers make their profit from the sale of the merchandise they own.

manufacturer's agents
Work for several producers and carry noncompetitive, complementary merchandise in an exclusive territory

Manufacturer's agents and selling agents are the two major types of agents used by producers. **Manufacturer's agents**, or *manufacturer's representatives,* work for several producers and carry noncompetitive, complementary merchandise in an exclusive territory. Manufacturer's agents act as a producer's sales arm in a territory and are principally responsible for the transactional channel functions, primarily selling. They are used extensively in the automotive supply, footwear, and fabricated steel industries. However, Swank Jewelry and Japanese computer firms have used manufacturer's agents as well. By comparison, *selling agents* represent a single producer and are responsible for the entire marketing function of that producer. They design promotional plans, set prices, determine distribution policies, and make recommendations on product strategy. Selling agents are used by small producers in the textile, apparel, food, and home furnishing industries.

brokers
Independent firms or individuals whose main function is to bring buyers and sellers together to make sales

Brokers are independent firms or individuals whose principal function is to bring buyers and sellers together to make sales. Brokers, unlike agents, usually have no continuous relationship with the buyer or seller but negotiate a contract between two parties and then move on to another task. Brokers are used extensively by producers of seasonal products (such as fruits and vegetables) and in the real estate industry.

A unique broker that acts in many ways like a manufacturer's agent is a food broker, representing buyers and sellers in the grocery industry. Food brokers differ from conventional brokers because they act on behalf of producers on a permanent basis and receive a commission for their services. For example, Nabisco uses food brokers to sell its candies, margarine, and Planters peanuts, but it sells its line of cookies and crackers directly to retail stores.

Manufacturer's Branches and Offices

Unlike merchant wholesalers, agents, and brokers, manufacturer's branches and sales offices are wholly owned extensions of the producer that perform wholesaling activities. Producers assume wholesaling functions when there are no intermediaries to perform these activities, customers are few in number and geographically concentrated, or orders are large or require significant attention. A *manufacturer's branch office* carries a producer's inventory and performs the functions of a full-service wholesaler. A *manufacturer's sales office* does not carry inventory, typically performs only a sales function, and serves as an alternative to agents and brokers.

Concept Check

1. According to the wheel of retailing, when a new retail form appears, how would you characterize its image?
2. Market share is usually fought out before the ____________ stage of the retail life cycle.
3. What is the difference between merchant wholesalers and agents?

CHAPTER IN REVIEW

1 *Identify retailers in terms of the utilities they provide.*
Retailers provide time, place, form, and possession utilities. Time utility is provided by stores with convenient time-of-day (e.g., open 24 hours) or time-of-year (e.g., seasonal sports equipment available all year) availability. Place utility is provided by the number and location of the stores. Possession utility is provided by making a purchase possible (e.g., financing) or easier (e.g., delivery). Form utility is provided by producing or altering a product to meet the customer's specifications (e.g., custom-made shirts).

2 *Explain the alternative ways to classify retail outlets.*
Retail outlets can be classified by their form of ownership, level of service, and type of merchandise line. The forms of ownership include independent retailers, corporate chains, and contractual systems that include retailer-sponsored cooperatives, wholesaler-sponsored voluntary chains, and franchises. The levels of service include self-service, limited-service, and full-service outlets. Stores classified by their merchandise line include stores with depth, such as sporting good specialty stores, and stores with breadth, such as large department stores.

3 *Describe the many methods of nonstore retailing.*
Nonstore retailing includes automatic vending, direct mail and catalogs, television home shopping, online retailing, telemarketing, and direct selling. The methods of nonstore retailing vary by the level of involvement of the retailer and the level of involvement of the customer. Vending, for example, has low involvement, whereas both the consumer and the retailer have high involvement in direct selling.

4 *Develop retailing mix strategies over the life cycle of a retail store.*
The retail life cycle describes the process of growth and decline for retail outlets through four stages: early growth, accelerated development, maturity, and decline. The retail mix—pricing, store location, communication, and merchandise—can be managed to match the retail strategy with the stage of the life cycle. The challenge facing retailers is to delay entering the decline stage, where market share and profit fall rapidly.

5 *Describe the types and functions of firms that perform wholesaling activities.*
There are three types of firms that perform wholesaling functions. First, merchant wholesalers are independently owned and take title to merchandise. They include general merchandise wholesalers, specialty merchandise wholesalers, rack jobber, cash and carry wholesalers, drop shipper, and truck jobbers and can perform a variety of channel functions. Second, agents and brokers do not take title to merchandise and primarily perform marketing functions. Finally, manufacturer's branches, which may carry inventory, and sales offices, which perform sales functions, are wholly owned by the producer.

FOCUSING ON KEY TERMS

brokers p. 325
category management p. 321
manufacturer's agents p. 325
merchant wholesalers p. 324
multichannel retailers p. 321
retailing p. 310
retailing mix p. 318
retail life cycle p. 323
scrambled merchandising p. 315
shrinkage p. 319
telemarketing p. 317
wheel of retailing p. 322

DISCUSSION AND APPLICATION QUESTIONS

1 Discuss the impact of the growing number of dual-income households on (*a*) nonstore retailing and (*b*) the retailing mix.

2 In retail pricing, retailers often have a maintained markup. Explain how this maintained markup differs from original markup and why it is so important.

3 What are the similarities and differences between the product and retail life cycles?

4 How would you classify Wal-Mart in terms of its position on the wheel of retailing versus that of an off-price retailer?

5 Develop a chart to highlight the role of each of the four main elements of the retailing mix across the four stages of the retail life cycle.

6 Breadth and depth are two important components in distinguishing among types of retailers. Discuss the breadth and depth implications of the following retailers discussed in this chapter: (*a*) Levi Strauss, (*b*) Wal-Mart, (*c*) L. L. Bean, and (*d*) Circuit City.

7 According to the wheel of retailing and the retail life cycle, what will happen to factory outlet stores?

8 The text discusses the development of online retailing in the United States. How does the development of this retailing form agree with the implications of the retail life cycle?

9 Comment on this statement: The only distinction among merchant wholesalers and agents and brokers is that merchant wholesalers take title to the products they sell.

GOING ONLINE Consumers Can Now "Shop with Their Bot"

For many consumers, comparison shopping is not appealing because of the inconvenience of traveling to multiple locations. Even on the Internet, finding and searching multiple websites can be tedious. One solution is a form of software called an *intelligent agent,* or *bot* (derived from robot), which automatically searches for the best price. Try each of the following shopping bots—www.mysimon.com and www.shopping.com—to find the best price for one of the following products:

1 Wilson tennis racket
2 Sony TV
3 Guess jeans

How did the two bots differ? What range of prices did you obtain? What shipping and handling charges would apply to each purchase? Why are different recommendation made by the agents?

BUILDING YOUR MARKETING PLAN

Does your marketing plan involve using retailers? If the answer is no, read no further and do not include a retailing element in your plan. If the answer is yes,

1 Use Figure 14–3 to develop your retailing strategy by specifying an appropriate combination of retail pricing, store location, retail communication, and merchandise assortment.

2 Develop a multichannel approach to meet the needs of several customer groups.

VIDEO CASE 14 Mall of America: Shopping and a Whole Lot More

"Build it and they will come" not only worked in the movie *Field of Dreams* but applies—big time—to Mall of America.

Located in a suburb of Minneapolis, Mall of America (www.mallofamerica.com) is the largest completely enclosed retail and family-entertainment complex in the United States. "We're more than a mall, we're a destination," explains Maureen Cahill, an executive at Mall of America. More than 100,000 people each day—40 million visitors each year—visit the one-stop complex offering retail shopping, guest services, convenience, a huge variety of entertainment, and fun for all. "Guest services" include everything from high school and college classrooms to a doctor's office and wedding chapel.

THE CONCEPT AND CHALLENGE

The idea for the Mall of America came from the West Edmonton Mall in Alberta, Canada. The Ghermezian Brothers, who developed that mall, sought to create a unique mall that would attract not only local families but tourists from the Upper Midwest, nation, and even abroad.

The two challenges for Mall of America: How can it (1) attract and keep the large number of retail establishments needed to (2) continue to attract even more millions of visitors than today? A big part of the answer is in Mall of America's positioning—"There is a place for fun in your life!"

THE STAGGERING SIZE AND OFFERINGS

Opened August 1992 amid tremendous worldwide publicity, Mall of America faced skeptics who had their doubts because of its size, its unique retail-entertainment mix, and the nationwide recession. Despite these concerns, it opened with more than 80 percent of its space leased and attracted more than one million visitors its first week.

Mall of America is 4.2 million square feet, the equivalent of 88 football fields. This makes it three to four times the size of most other regional malls. It includes four anchor department stores: Nordstrom, Macy's, Bloomingdale's, and Sears. It also includes more than 520 specialty stores, from Brooks Brothers and Sharper Image to Marshall's and DSW Shoe Warehouse. Approximately 36 percent of Mall of America's space is devoted to anchors and 64 percent to specialty stores. This makes the space allocation the reverse of most regional malls.

The retail-entertainment mix of Mall of America is incredibly diverse. For example, there are more than 100 apparel and accessory stores, 17 jewelry stores, and 24 shoe stores. Two food courts with 27 restaurants plus more than 30 other restaurants scattered throughout the building meet most food preferences of visitors. Another surprise: Mall of America is home to many "concept stores," where retailers introduce a new type of store or design. Because of its incredible size, the mall has 194 stores not found at competing regional malls. In addition, it has an entrepreneurial program for people with an innovative retail idea and limited resources. They can open up a kiosk, wall unit, or small store for a specified time period or as a temporary seasonal tenant.

Unique features of Mall of America include:

- Camp Snoopy, a seven-acre theme park with more than 50 attractions and rides, including a roller coaster, Ferris wheel, and games in a glass-enclosed, skylighted area with more than 400 trees.
- Underwater Adventures, where visitors are surrounded by tropical sharks, stingrays, and sea turtles; can adventure among fish native to the north woods; and can discover what lurks at the bottom of the Mississippi River.
- The Upper East Side, on the fourth floor, with its bars, nightclubs, game rooms, 14-screen theater, comedy club, and state-of-the-art bowling alley.
- The LEGO Land Imagination Center, a 6,000 square foot showplace with more than 30 full-sized models that include dinosaurs and astronauts.

As a host to corporate events and private parties, Mall of America has a rotunda that opens to all four floors that facilitates presentations, demonstrations, and exhibits. Organizations like Pepsi, Visa-USA, and the U.S. Postal Service have used the facilities to gain shopper awareness. Mall of America is a rectangle with the anchor department stores at the corners and Camp Snoopy in the skylighted central area, making it easy for shoppers to understand and navigate. It has 12,750 free parking ramp spaces on site and another 7,000 spaces nearby during peak times.

THE MARKET

The Minneapolis–St. Paul metropolitan area is a market with 3 million people. A total of 28 million people live within 400 miles or a day's drive of Mall of America. A survey of its shoppers showed that 43 percent of the shoppers come from outside Minnesota and account for 56 percent of the sales revenues. Located three miles from the thirteenth busiest international airport in the world, Mall of America provides a shuttle bus from the airport every half hour. Light-rail service from the airport and downtown Minneapolis begins in late 2004.

About 6 percent of visitors come from outside the United States. Some come just to see and experience Mall of America, while others take advantage of the cost savings available on goods (Japan) or taxes (Canada and states with sales taxes on clothing).

THE FUTURE: FACING THE CHALLENGES

Where does Mall of America head in the future?

"We just did a brand study and found that Mall of America is one of the most recognized brands in the world," says Maureen Cahill. "They might not know where we are sometimes, but they've heard of Mall of America and they know they want to come.

"What we've learned since 1992 is to keep the Mall of America fresh and exciting," she explains. "We're constantly looking at what attracts people and adding to that. We're adding new stores, new attractions, and new events. We hold more than 350 events a year and with everyone from Garth Brooks to Sara Ferguson to N Sync."

Mall of America recently announced a plan for a 5.7 million square foot expansion, the area of another 117 football fields, connected by pedestrian skyway to the present building. "The second phase will not be a duplicate of what we have," says Cahill. "We have plans for at least three hotels, a performing arts center, a business office complex, an art or history museum, and possibly even a television broadcast facility."

IKEA just opened a 336,000 square foot furniture store in the expansion phase, and Caesar's is exploring adding a casino, hotel, and entertainment complex. Both reinforce that Mall of America is a destination for shopping and a whole lot more. In addition, the mall has taken out a $100 million terrorist insurance policy and moved the transit hub outside the mall in the wake of 9/11.

Questions

1 Why has Mall of America been such a marketing success so far?

2 What (*a*) retail and (*b*) consumer trends have occurred since Mall of America was opened in 1992 that it should consider when making future plans?

3 (*a*) What criteria should Mall of America use in adding new facilities to its complex? (*b*) Evaluate (*i*) retail stores, (*ii*) entertainment offerings, and (*iii*) hotels on these criteria.

4 What specific marketing actions would you propose that Mall of America managers take to ensure its continuing success in attracting visitors (*a*) from the local metropolitan area and (*b*) from outside of it?

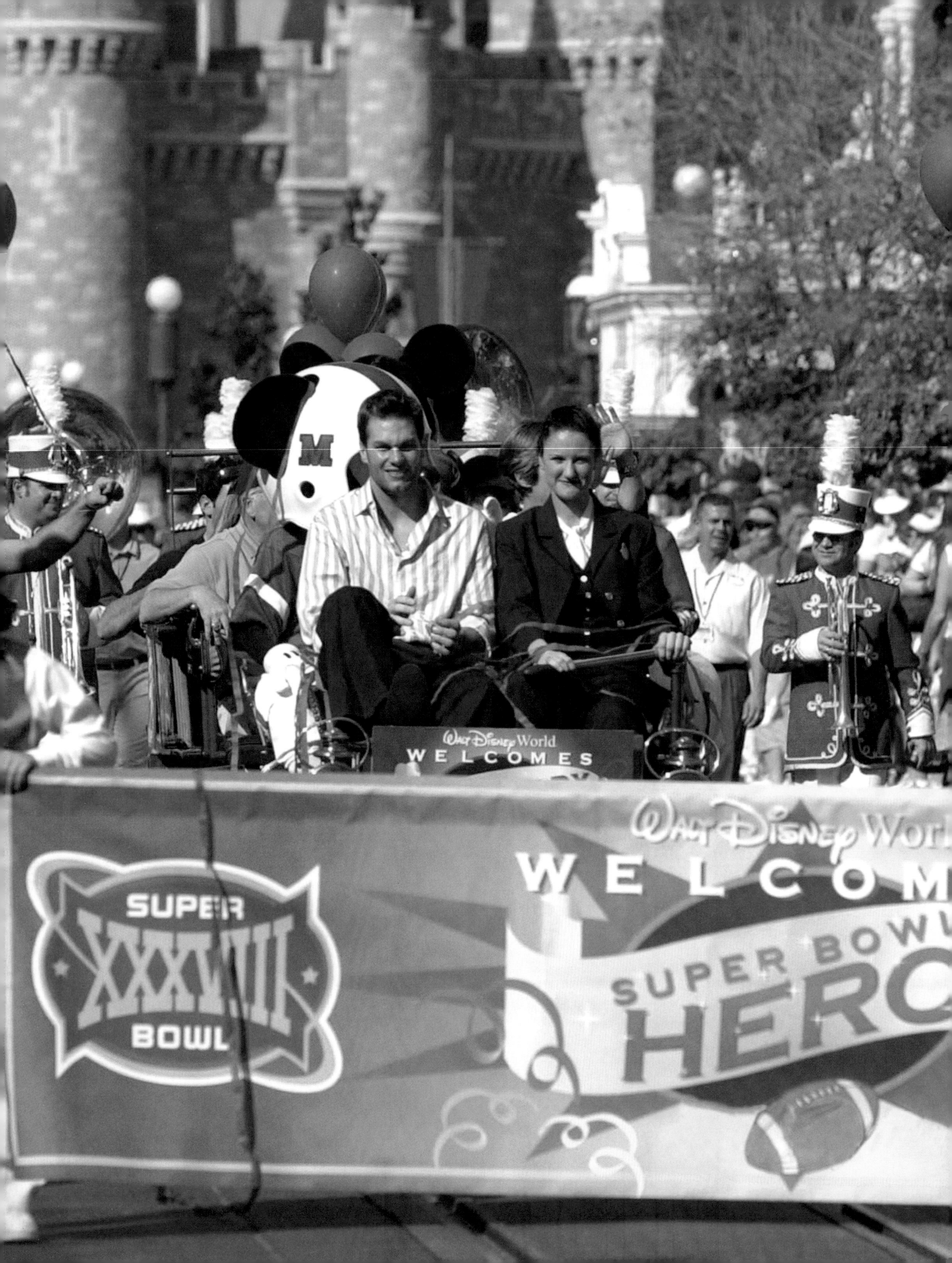

SUPER
XXXVII
BOWL

CHAPTER

15

INTEGRATED MARKETING COMMUNICATIONS AND DIRECT MARKETING

LEARNING OBJECTIVES

After reading this chapter you should be able to:

1 Discuss integrated marketing communication and the communication process.

2 Describe the promotional mix and the uniqueness of each component.

3 Select the promotional approach appropriate to a product's life-cycle stage.

4 Discuss the characteristics of push and pull strategies.

5 Describe the elements of the promotion decision process.

6 Explain the value of direct marketing for consumers and sellers.

WHO IS GOING TO DISNEY WORLD NEXT?

Since 1987 there have been more than 34 episodes of Disney's "What's Next?" campaign—you know, the commercials where a successful athlete is asked "What are you going to do next?" and they shout, "I'm going to Disney World!" The first to go was New York Giants' quarterback Phil Simms, and since then athletes such as Michael Jordan, Barry Bonds, John Elway, Mark McGwire, and Tom Brady have been featured in the campaign. Ken Potrock, senior vice president of Walt Disney World Alliance Marketing, explains that "we select players based on success on the field and a Cinderella-type story." While many players have been selected from Super Bowl games, standouts from Major League Baseball, the NBA, the NHL, the Olympics, and World Cup events have also been in the commercials.

The What's Next? campaign is just one of many forms of communication Disney uses to get its message to Disney fans. Other forms of communication include partnerships with other companies, direct marketing, Internet promotions, online games, and additional advertising. Disney uses its marketing expertise to integrate the plan and provide a consistent message and image to its many consumers.

The most recent plan calls for an 18-month global campaign called the "Happiest Celebration on Earth" to commemorate the 50th anniversary of the opening of Disney's first theme park. The campaign includes television advertising that shows Disney's signature characters arriving for a gigantic party, newspaper inserts, and streaming video on Yahoo!, MSN, About.com, Excite.com, and Google. Partnerships include agreements with Chase to offer a Disney Visa card with special 50th anniversary benefits, McDonald's to offer a tie-in with its Happy Meals, and Kodak to offer an on-pack sweepstakes with a grand prize trip to the original Disneyland. Direct marketing includes special offers to the millions of households in Disney's database. The website Disneyland.com provides information and special offers on the Web. To help develop relationships with children, Disney recently launched a multiplayer online game called Virtual Magic Kingdom. All of these communications are designed and integrated to increase attendance at all of Disney's theme parks.

Disney applies a similar, integrated approach to the marketing of all its products, services, and events. Other promotional activities include advertising on Radio Disney, sponsorship of documentaries on the ABC television network, Internet-linked kiosks to allow potential customers to check for location and availability of products at its stores, and contests and giveaways. In addition, Disney stores use in-store promotion that complements the online offerings (at disneystore.com) and the Disney catalogs.[1]

promotional mix
Combination of one or more of the communication tools used to inform, persuade, or remind prospective buyers

The many types of promotion used by Disney demonstrate the opportunity for creativity in communicating with potential customers and the importance of integrating the various elements of a communication program. Promotion represents the fourth element in the marketing mix. The promotional element consists of communication tools, including advertising, personal selling, sales promotion, public relations, and direct marketing. The combination of one or more of these communication tools is called the **promotional mix**. All of these tools can be used to (1) inform prospective buyers about the benefits of the product, (2) persuade them to try it, and (3) remind them later about the benefits they enjoyed by using the product. In the past, marketers often viewed the communication tools as separate and independent. The advertising department, for example, often designed and managed its activities without consulting departments or agencies that had responsibility for sales promotion or public relations. The result was often an overall communication effort that was uncoordinated and, in some cases, inconsistent. Today, the concept of designing marketing communications programs that coordinate all promotional activities—advertising, personal selling, sales promotion, public relations, and direct marketing—to provide a consistent message across all audiences is referred to as **integrated marketing communications** (IMC).

integrated marketing communications
Concept of designing marketing communications programs that coordinate all promotional activities to provide a consistent message across all audiences

This chapter provides an overview of the communication process, a description of the promotional mix elements, several tools for integrating the promotional mix, and a process for developing a comprehensive promotion program. One of the promotional mix elements, direct marketing, is also discussed in this chapter. Chapter 16 covers advertising, sales promotion, and public relations, and Chapter 17 discusses personal selling.

THE COMMUNICATION PROCESS

communication
Process of conveying a message to others

Communication is the process of conveying a message to others and requires six elements: a source, a message, a channel of communication, a receiver, and the processes of encoding and decoding[2] (Figure 15–1). The *source* may be a company or person who has information to convey. The information sent by a source, such as a description of a new cellular telephone, forms the *message*. The message is conveyed by means of a *channel of communication* such as a salesperson, advertising media, or public relations tools. Consumers who read, hear, or see the message are the *receivers*.

FIGURE 15–1
The communication process

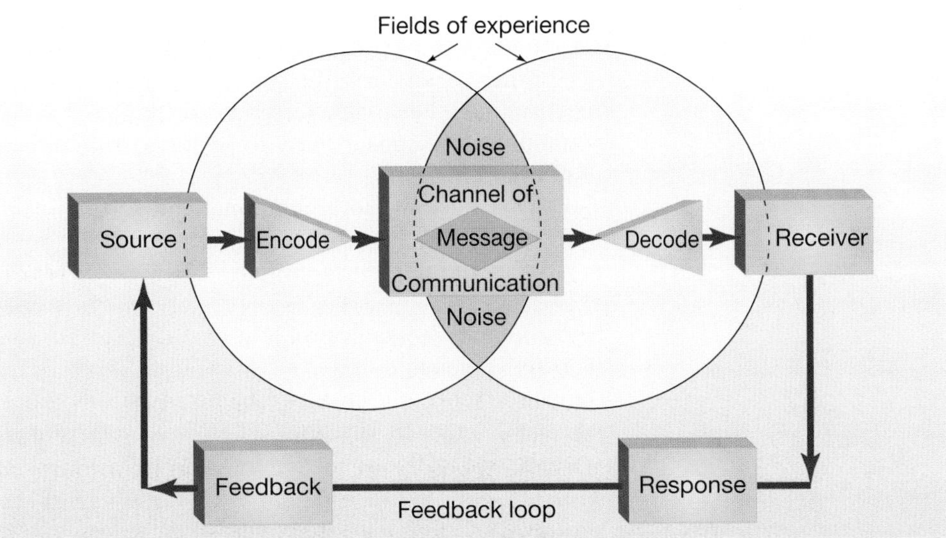

Encoding and Decoding

Encoding and decoding are essential to communication. *Encoding* is the process of having the sender transform an idea into a set of symbols. *Decoding* is the reverse, or the process of having the receiver take a set of symbols, the message, and transform them back to an idea. Look at the accompanying automobile advertisement: Who is the source, and what is the message?

Decoding is performed by the receivers according to their own frame of reference: their attitudes, values, and beliefs.[3] In the ad shown here, Hummer is the source and the advertisement is the message: The ad appeared in *Wired* magazine (the channel). How would you interpret (decode) this advertisement? The picture and text in the advertisement show that the source's intention is to generate interest in a new vehicle, the H3, that is "Like Nothing Else"—a statement the source believes will appeal to the readers of the magazine.

The process of communication is not always a successful one. Errors in communication can happen in several ways. The source may not adequately transform the

abstract idea into an effective set of symbols, a properly encoded message may be sent through the wrong channel and never make it to the receiver, the receiver may not properly transform the set of symbols into the correct abstract idea, or finally, feedback may be so delayed or distorted that it is of no use to the sender. Although communication appears easy to perform, truly effective communication can be very difficult.

For the message to be communicated effectively, the sender and receiver must have a mutually shared *field of experience*—a similar understanding and knowledge they apply to the message. Figure 15–1 shows two circles representing the fields of experience of the sender and receiver, which overlap in the message. Some of the better-known message problems have occurred when U.S. companies have taken their messages to cultures with different fields of experience. Many misinterpretations are merely the result of bad translations. For example, KFC made a mistake when its "finger-lickin' good" slogan was translated into Mandarin Chinese as "eat your fingers off!"[4]

Feedback

Figure 15–1 shows a line labeled *feedback loop,* which consists of a response and feedback. A *response* is the impact the message had on the receiver's knowledge, attitudes, or behaviors. *Feedback* is the sender's interpretation of the response and indicates whether the message was decoded and understood as intended. Chapter 16 reviews approaches called *pretesting* that ensure that messages are decoded properly.

Noise

Noise includes extraneous factors that can work against effective communication by distorting a message or the feedback received (Figure 15–1). Noise can be a simple error, such as a printing mistake that affects the meaning of a newspaper advertisement, or using words or pictures that fail to communicate the message clearly. Noise can also occur when a salesperson's message is misunderstood by a prospective buyer, such as when a salesperson's accent, use of slang terms, or communication style make hearing and understanding the message difficult.

Concept Check

1. What are the six elements required for communication to occur?
2. A difficulty for U.S. companies advertising in international markets is that the audience does not share the same ________________.
3. A misprint in a newspaper ad is an example of ________________.

THE PROMOTIONAL ELEMENTS

To communicate with consumers, a company can use one or more of five promotional alternatives: advertising, personal selling, public relations, sales promotion, and direct marketing. Figure 15–2 summarizes the distinctions among these five elements. Three of these elements—advertising, sales promotion, and public relations—are often said to use *mass selling* because they are used with groups of prospective buyers. In contrast, personal selling uses *customized interaction* between a seller and a prospective buyer. Personal selling activities include face-to-face, telephone, and interactive electronic communication. Direct marketing also uses messages customized for specific customers.

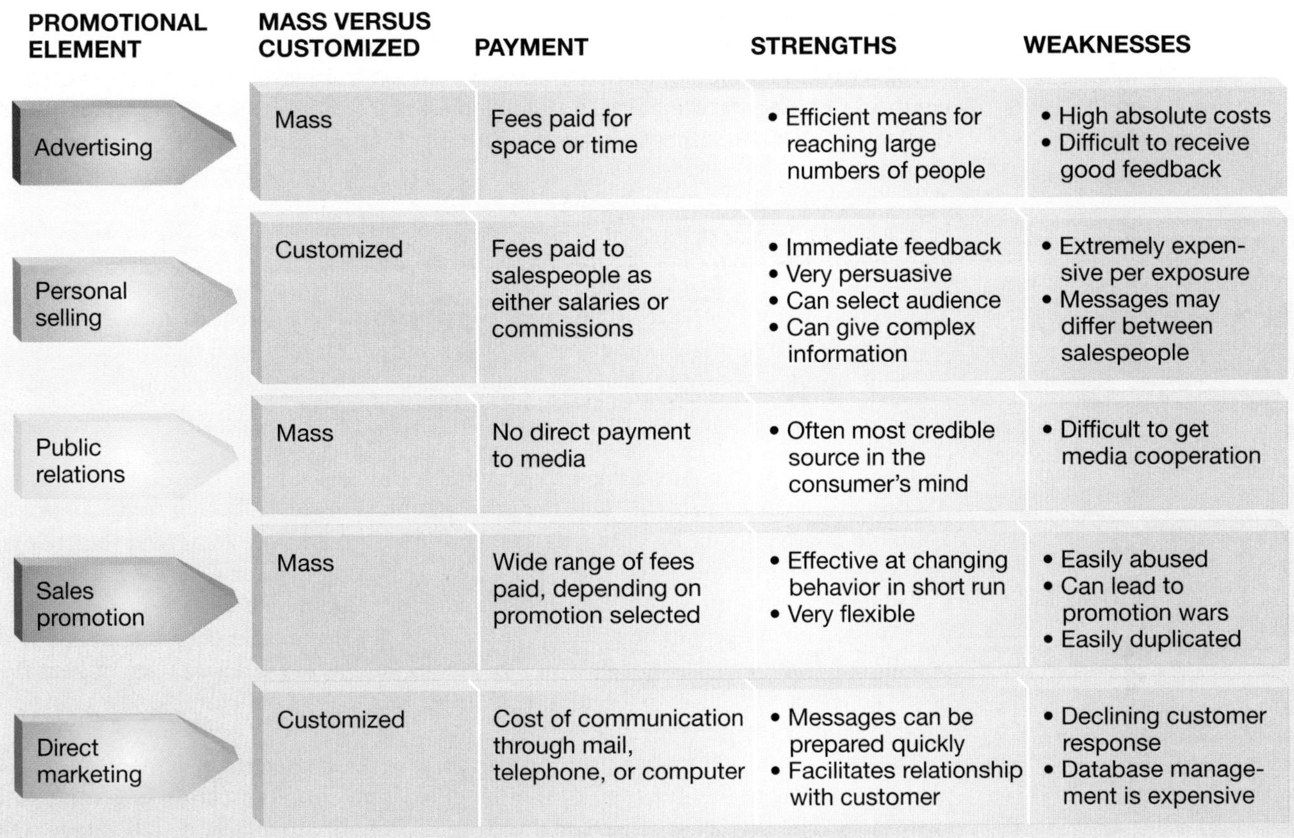

PROMOTIONAL ELEMENT	MASS VERSUS CUSTOMIZED	PAYMENT	STRENGTHS	WEAKNESSES
Advertising	Mass	Fees paid for space or time	• Efficient means for reaching large numbers of people	• High absolute costs • Difficult to receive good feedback
Personal selling	Customized	Fees paid to salespeople as either salaries or commissions	• Immediate feedback • Very persuasive • Can select audience • Can give complex information	• Extremely expensive per exposure • Messages may differ between salespeople
Public relations	Mass	No direct payment to media	• Often most credible source in the consumer's mind	• Difficult to get media cooperation
Sales promotion	Mass	Wide range of fees paid, depending on promotion selected	• Effective at changing behavior in short run • Very flexible	• Easily abused • Can lead to promotion wars • Easily duplicated
Direct marketing	Customized	Cost of communication through mail, telephone, or computer	• Messages can be prepared quickly • Facilitates relationship with customer	• Declining customer response • Database management is expensive

FIGURE 15–2
The promotional mix

advertising
Any paid form of nonpersonal communication about an organization, good, service, or idea by an identified sponsor

Advertising

Advertising is any paid form of nonpersonal communication about an organization, good, service, or idea by an identified sponsor. The *paid* aspect of this definition is important because the space for the advertising message normally must be bought. An occasional exception is the public service announcement, where the advertising time or space is donated. A full-page, four-color ad in *Time* magazine, for example, costs $234,000. The *nonpersonal* component of advertising is also important. Advertising involves mass media (such as TV, radio, and magazines), which are nonpersonal and do not have an immediate feedback loop as does personal selling. So before the message is sent, marketing research plays a valuable role; for example, it determines that the target market will actually see the medium chosen, and that the message will be understood.

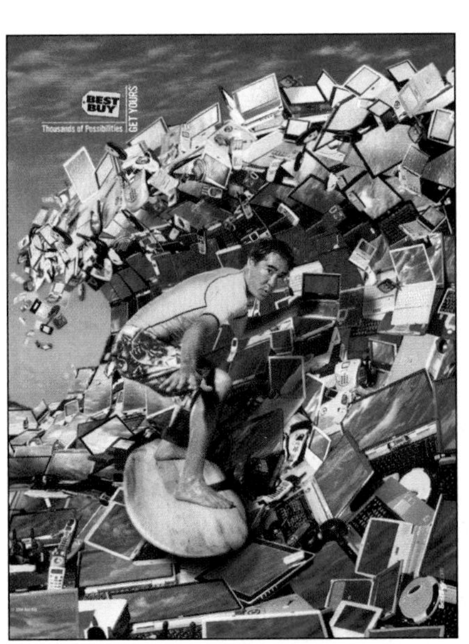

There are several advantages to a firm using advertising in its promotional mix. It can be attention-getting—as with this Best Buy ad—and also can communicate specific product benefits to prospective buyers. By paying for the advertising space, a company can control *what* it wants to say and, to some extent, to *whom* the message is sent. If an electronics company wants college students to receive its message about CD players, advertising space is purchased in a college campus newspaper. Advertising also allows the company to decide *when* to send its message (which includes how often). The nonpersonal aspect of advertising also has its advantages. Once the message is created, the same message is sent to all receivers in a market segment. If the pictorial, text, and brand elements of an advertisement are properly pretested, an advertiser can ensure the ad's ability to capture consumers' attention[5] and trust that the same message will be decoded by all receivers in the market segment.

Advertising has some disadvantages. As shown in Figure 15–2 and discussed in depth in Chapter 16, the costs to produce and place a message are significant, and the lack of direct feedback makes it difficult to know how well the message was received.

Personal Selling

personal selling
Two-way flow of communication between a buyer and seller, often in a face-to-face encounter, designed to influence a person's or group's purchase decision

The second major promotional alternative is **personal selling**, defined as the two-way flow of communication between a buyer and seller, designed to influence a person's or group's purchase decision. Unlike advertising, personal selling is usually face-to-face communication between the sender and receiver. Why do companies use personal selling?

There are important advantages to personal selling, as summarized in Figure 15–2. A salesperson can control to *whom* the presentation is made. Although some control is available in advertising by choosing the medium, some people may read the college newspaper, for example, who are not in the target audience for CD players. For the CD-player manufacturer, those readers outside the target audience are *wasted coverage.* Wasted coverage can be reduced with personal selling. The personal component of selling has another advantage over advertising in that the seller can see or hear the potential buyer's reaction to the message. If the feedback is unfavorable, the salesperson can modify the message.

The flexibility of personal selling can also be a disadvantage. Different salespeople can change the message so that no consistent communication is given to all customers. The high cost of personal selling is probably its major disadvantage. On a cost-per-contact basis, it is generally the most expensive of the five promotional elements.

Public Relations

public relations
Form of communication management that seeks to influence the feelings, opinions, or beliefs held by customers, potential customers, stockholders, suppliers, employees, and others about a company and its products or services

publicity
Nonpersonal, indirectly paid presentation of an organization, good, or service

Public relations is a form of communication management that seeks to influence the feelings, opinions, or beliefs held by customers, prospective customers, stockholders, suppliers, employees, and other publics about a company and its products or services.[6] Many tools such as special events, lobbying efforts, annual reports, press conferences,[7] and image management may be used by a public relations department, although publicity often plays the most important role. **Publicity** is a nonpersonal, indirectly paid presentation of an organization, good, or service. It can take the form of a news story, editorial, or product announcement. A difference between publicity and both advertising and personal selling is the "indirectly paid" dimension. With publicity a company does not pay for space in a mass medium (such as television or radio) but attempts to get the medium to run a favorable story on the company. In this sense, there is an indirect payment for publicity in that a company must support a public relations staff.

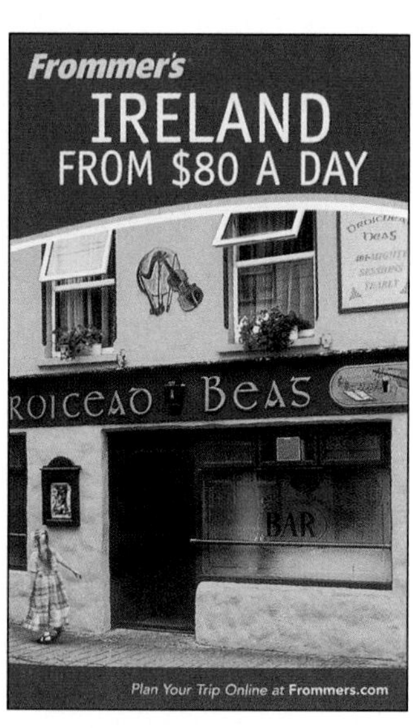

An advantage of publicity is credibility. When you read a favorable story about a company's product (such as a glowing restaurant review), there is a tendency to believe it. Travelers throughout the world have relied on Arthur Frommer's guides such as *Ireland from $80 a Day.* These books outline out-of-the-way, inexpensive restaurants, hotels, inns, and bed-and-breakfast rooms, giving invaluable publicity to these establishments. Such businesses do not (nor can they) buy a mention in the guide, which in recent years has sold millions of copies.

The disadvantage of publicity relates to the lack of the user's control over it. A company can invite a news team to preview its innovative exercise equipment and hope for a favorable mention on the 6 P.M. newscasts. But without buying advertising time, there is no guarantee of any mention of the new equipment or that it will be aired when the target audience is watching. The company representative who calls the station and asks for a replay of the story may be told, "Sorry, it's only news once." With publicity there is little control over what is said, to whom, or when. As a result, publicity is rarely the main component of a promotional campaign.

Sales Promotion

sales promotion
A short-term offer designed to arouse interest in buying a good or service

A fourth promotional element is **sales promotion**, a short-term inducement of value offered to arouse interest in buying a good or service. Used in conjunction with advertising or personal selling, sales promotions are offered to intermediaries as well as to ultimate consumers. Coupons, rebates, samples, and sweepstakes are just a few examples of sales promotions discussed later in this chapter.

The advantage of sales promotion is that the short-term nature of these programs (such as a coupon or sweepstakes with an expiration date) often stimulates sales for their duration. Offering value to the consumer in terms of a cents-off coupon or rebate may increase store traffic from consumers who are not store-loyal.[8] However, sales promotions cannot be the sole basis for a campaign because gains are often temporary and sales drop off when the deal ends.[9] Advertising support is needed to convert the customer who tried the product because of a sales promotion into a long-term buyer.[10] If sales promotions are conducted continuously, they lose their effectiveness. Customers begin to delay purchase until a coupon is offered, or they question the product's value. Some aspects of sales promotions also are regulated by the federal government. These issues are reviewed in detail later in Chapter 16.

Direct Marketing

direct marketing
Promotional element that uses direct communication with consumers to generate a response in the form of an order, a request for further information, or a visit to a retail outlet

Another promotional alternative, **direct marketing**, uses direct communication with consumers to generate a response in the form of an order, a request for further information, or a visit to a retail outlet.[11] The communication can take many forms including face-to-face selling, direct mail, catalogs, telephone solicitations, direct response advertising (on television and radio and in print), and online marketing. Like personal selling, direct marketing often consists of interactive communication. It also has the advantage of being customized to match the needs of specific target markets. Messages can be developed and adapted quickly to facilitate one-to-one relationships with customers.

While direct marketing has been one of the fastest-growing forms of promotion, it has several disadvantages. First, most forms of direct marketing require a comprehensive and up-to-date database with information about the target market. Developing and maintaining the database can be expensive and time consuming. In addition, growing concern about privacy has led to a decline in response rates among some customer groups. Companies with successful direct marketing programs are sensitive to these issues and often use a combination of direct marketing alternatives together, or direct marketing combined with other promotional tools, to increase value for customers.

Concept Check

1. Explain the difference between advertising and publicity when both appear on television.
2. Which promotional element should be offered only on a short-term basis?
3. Cost per contact is high with the __________________ element of the promotional mix.

INTEGRATED MARKETING COMMUNICATIONS—DEVELOPING THE PROMOTIONAL MIX

A firm's promotional mix is the combination of one or more of the promotional tools it chooses to use. In putting together the promotional mix, a marketer must consider two issues. First, the balance of the elements must be determined. Should advertising be emphasized more than personal selling? Should a promotional rebate be offered? Would public relations activities be effective? Several factors affect such decisions: the target audience for the promotion,[12] the stage of the product's life cycle, characteristics of the product, decision stage of the buyer, and even the channel of distribution. Second, because the various promotional elements are often the responsibility of different departments, coordinating a consistent promotional effort is necessary. A promotional planning process designed to ensure integrated marketing communications can facilitate this goal.

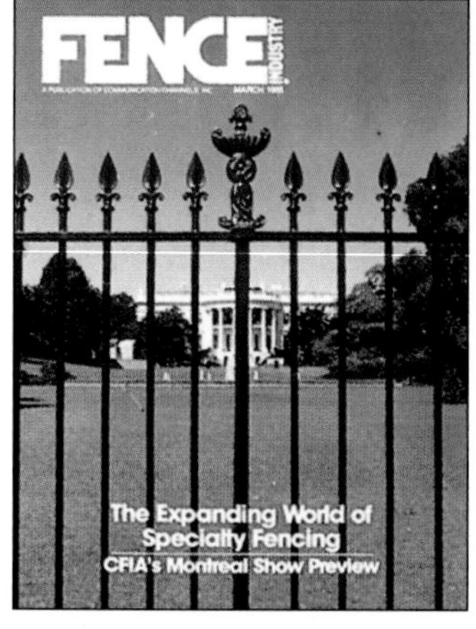

The Target Audience

Promotional programs are directed to the ultimate consumer, to an intermediary (retailer, wholesaler, or industrial distributor), or to both. Promotional programs directed to buyers of consumer products often use mass media because the number of potential buyers is large. Personal selling is used at the place of purchase, generally the retail store. Direct marketing may be used to encourage first-time or repeat purchases. Combinations of many media alternatives are a necessity for some target audiences today. The Marketing NewsNet describes how Generation Y consumers give media only partial attention but can be reached through integrated programs.[13]

MARKETING NEWSNET

Gen Y Applies Multitasking to Media Consumption—29 Hours per Day!

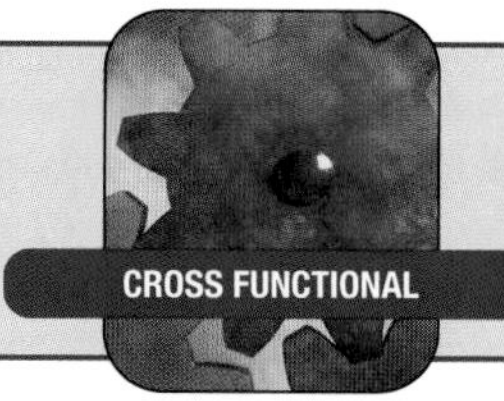

Consumers are increasingly multitasking, or doing many things at the same time. The concept of multitasking applied to communication—watching TV while surfing the Internet, or reading a magazine while listening to the radio—has led to the term *simultaneous media usage* (SIMM). Generation Y seems to be particularly adept at SIMM as recent research found that 75 percent of the age group does something else while watching TV. In fact, SIMM has created 29.8 hour "media days" for this group. One reason is that media are pervasive—the average student may be exposed to 5,000 messages each day—but other reasons are the desires to be informed and to keep in touch. As a result, consumers in this group probably don't give full attention to any single message. Instead, they use continuous partial attention to scan the media.

Marketers can still communicate with Gen Y by utilizing a variety of promotional tools—from advertising to packaging to word-of-mouth communication—with an integrated message. Which media work particularly well with Gen Y? The most popular television channel is MTV. The most popular magazines are *Sports Illustrated* and *Seventeen.* Favorite websites include anything with content related to their interests: celebrities, music, sports, and games. Another approach growing in popularity is viral, or "buzz," marketing. When BMW dealers started selling the new MINI convertible, for example, they held contests to see how long drivers could go before putting the top up. The drivers and potential buyers started talking about the contests and the new car, for at least part of the 29.8 hour day.

Advertising directed to business buyers is used selectively in trade publications, such as *Fence* magazine for buyers of fencing material. Because business buyers often have specialized needs or technical questions, personal selling is particularly important. The salesperson can provide information and the necessary support after sales.

Intermediaries are often the focus of promotional efforts. As with business buyers, personal selling is the major promotional ingredient. The salespeople assist intermediaries in making a profit by coordinating promotional campaigns sponsored by the manufacturer and by providing marketing advice and expertise. Intermediaries' questions often pertain to the allowed markup, merchandising support, and return policies.

The Product Life Cycle

Purina Dog Chow: in the maturity stage of its product life cycle.

All products have a product life cycle (see Chapter 11), and the composition of the promotional mix changes over the four life-cycle stages:

- *Introduction stage.* Informing consumers in an effort to increase their level of awareness is the primary promotional objective in the introduction stage of the product life cycle. In general, all the promotional mix elements are used at this time.
- *Growth stage.* The primary promotional objective of the growth stage is to persuade the consumer to buy the product. Advertising is used to communicate brand differences, and personal selling is used to solidify the channel of distribution.
- *Maturity stage.* In the maturity stage the need is to maintain existing buyers. Advertising's role is to remind buyers of the product's existence. Sales promotion, in the form of discounts and coupons, is important in maintaining loyal buyers.
- *Decline stage.* The decline stage of the product life cycle is usually a period of phase-out for the product, and little money is spent in the promotional mix.

Figure 15–3 shows how the promotional mix for Purina Dog Chow might change through the product life cycle.

FIGURE 15–3
Promotional tools used over the product life cycle of Purina Dog Chow

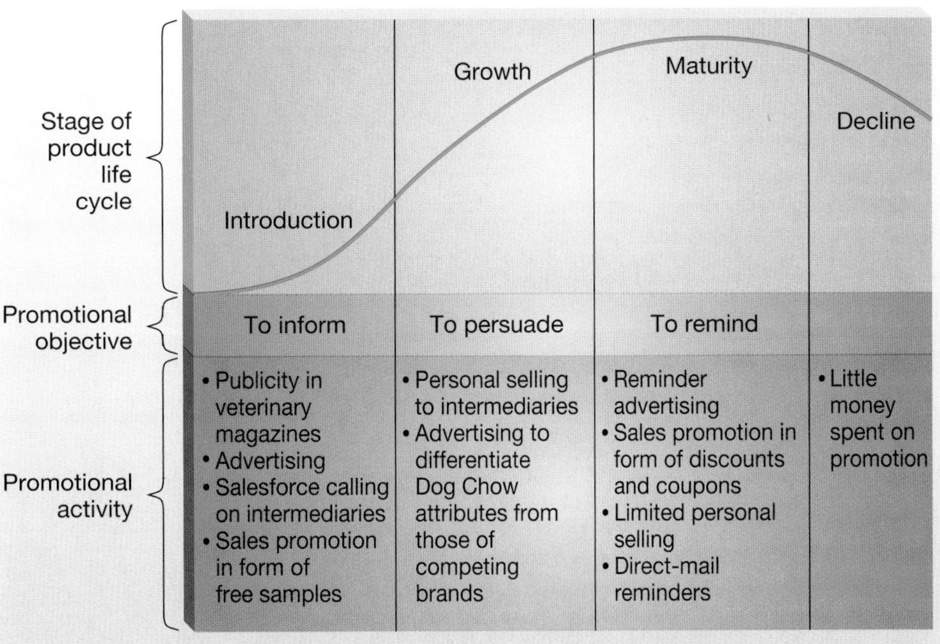

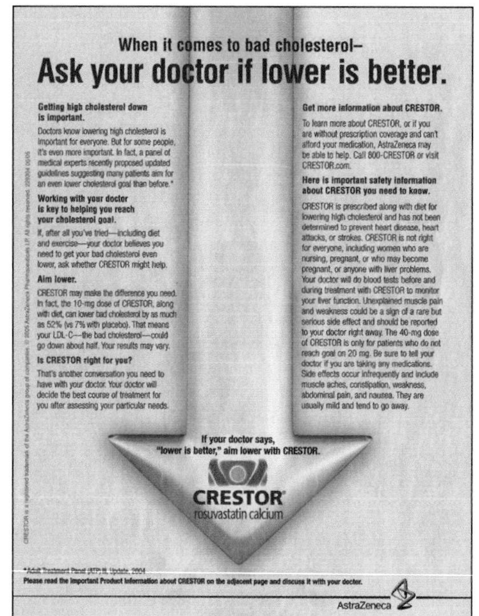

Channel Strategies

Chapter 13 discussed the channel flow from a producer to intermediaries to consumers. Achieving control of the channel is often difficult for the manufacturer, and promotional strategies can assist in moving a product through the channel of distribution. This is where a manufacturer has to make an important decision about whether to use a push strategy, pull strategy, or both in its channel of distribution.[14]

Push Strategy Figure 15–4A shows how a manufacturer uses a **push strategy**, directing the promotional mix to channel members to gain their cooperation in ordering and stocking the product. In this approach, personal selling and sales promotions play major roles. Salespeople call on wholesalers to encourage orders and provide sales assistance. Sales promotions, such as case discount allowances (20 percent off the regular case price), are offered to stimulate demand. By pushing the product through the channel, the goal is to get channel members to push it to their customers.

push strategy
Directing the promotional mix to channel members to encourage them to order and stock a product

pull strategy
Directing the promotional mix at ultimate consumers to encourage them to ask the retailer for the product

Pull Strategy In some instances, manufacturers face resistance from channel members who do not want to order a new product or increase inventory levels of an existing brand. As shown in Figure 15–4B, a manufacturer may then elect to implement a **pull strategy** by directing its promotional mix at ultimate consumers to encourage them to ask the retailer for a product. Seeing demand from ultimate consumers, retailers order the product from wholesalers and thus the item is pulled through the intermediaries. Pharmaceutical companies, for example, now spend more than $1.2 billion annually on *direct-to-consumer* prescription drug advertising, to complement traditional personal selling and free samples directed only at doctors.[15] The strategy is designed to encourage consumers to ask their doctor for a specific drug by name—pulling it through the channel. Successful campaigns such as the print ad for Crestor, which says "Ask your doctor if lower is better," can have dramatic effects on the sales of a product.

FIGURE 15–4
A comparison of push and pull promotional strategies

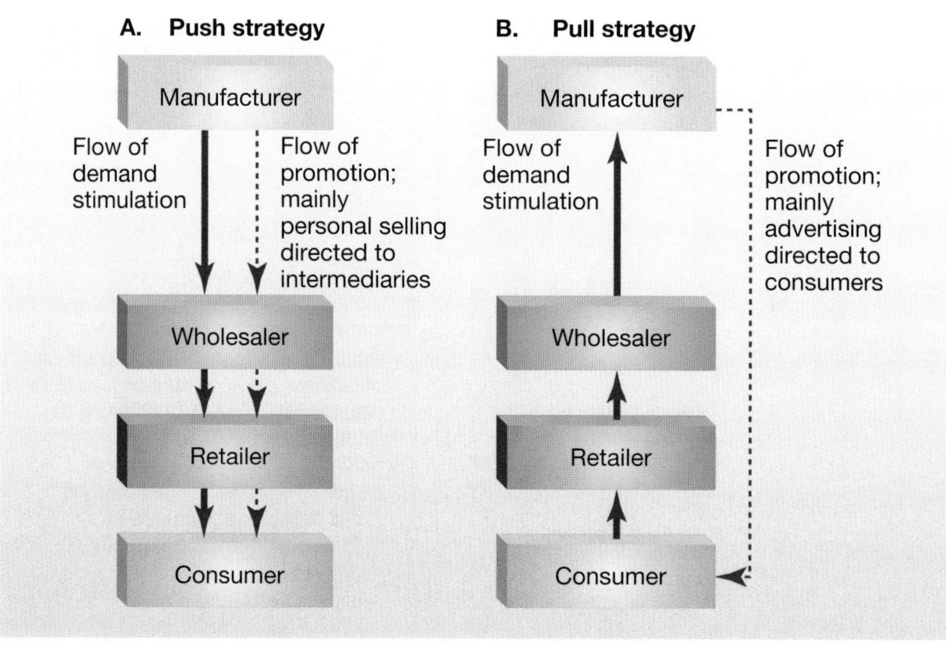

Concept Check

1. Promotional programs can be directed to ____________, to ____________, or to both.
2. Describe the promotional objective for each stage of the product life cycle.
3. Explain the differences between a push strategy and a pull strategy.

DEVELOPING AN IMC PROGRAM

Because media costs are high, promotion decisions must be made carefully, using a systematic approach. Paralleling the planning, implementation, and control steps described in the strategic marketing process (Chapter 2), the promotion decision process is divided into (1) developing, (2) executing, and (3) evaluating the promotion program (Figure 15–5).

Identifying the Target Audience

The first decision in developing the promotion program is identifying the *target audience,* the group of prospective buyers toward which a promotion program is directed. To the extent that time and money permit, the target audience for the promotion program is the target market for the firm's product, which is identified from marketing research and market segmentation studies. The more a firm knows about its target audiences—including their lifestyle, attitudes, and values—the easier it is to develop a promotion program. If a firm wanted to reach you with television and magazine ads, for example, it would need to know what TV shows you watch and what magazines you read.

Specifying Promotion Objectives

hierarchy of effects
Sequence of stages a prospective buyer goes through: awareness, interest, evaluation, trial, and adoption

After the target audience is identified, a decision must be reached on what the promotion should accomplish. Consumers can be said to respond in terms of a **hierarchy of effects**, which is the sequence of stages a prospective buyer goes through from initial awareness of a product to eventual action (either trial or adoption of the product).[16] The five stages are

- *Awareness.* The consumer's ability to recognize and remember the product or brand name.
- *Interest.* An increase in the consumer's desire to learn about some of the features of the product or brand.

FIGURE 15–5
The promotion decision process

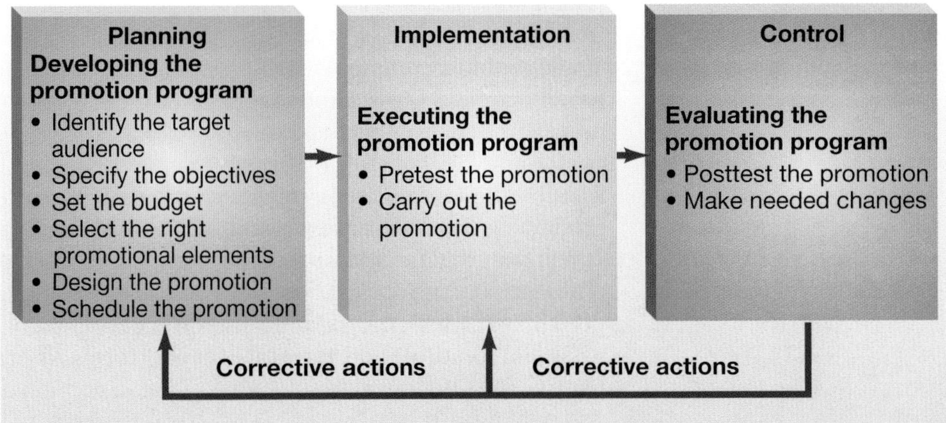

- *Evaluation.* The consumer's appraisal of the product or brand on important attributes.
- *Trial.* The consumer's actual first purchase and use of the product or brand.
- *Adoption.* Through a favorable experience on the first trial, the consumer's repeated purchase and use of the product or brand.

For a totally new product, the sequence applies to the entire product category, but for a new brand competing in an established product category it applies to the brand itself. These steps can serve as guidelines for developing promotion objectives.

Setting the Promotion Budget

After setting the promotion objectives, a company must decide on how much to spend. The promotion expenditures needed to reach U.S. households are enormous. Seven companies—General Motors, Procter & Gamble, Time Warner, Pfizer, DaimlerChrysler, Ford, and Disney—each spend a total of more than $2 billion annually on promotion.[17] Determining the ideal amount for the budget is difficult because there is no precise way to measure the exact results of spending promotion dollars. However, there are several methods used to set the promotion budget:[18]

- *Percentage of sales.* In the percentage of sales budgeting approach, the amount of money spent on promotion is a percentage of past or anticipated sales. A common budgeting method,[19] this approach is often stated in terms such as "our promotion budget for this year is 3 percent of last year's gross sales."
- *Competitive parity.* Competitive parity budgeting matches the competitor's absolute level of spending or the proportion per point of market share.[20]
- *All you can afford.* Common to many businesses, the all-you-can-afford budgeting method allows money to be spent on promotion only after all other budget items—such as manufacturing costs—are covered.
- *Objective and task.* The best approach to budgeting is objective and task budgeting, whereby the company (1) determines its promotion objectives, (2) outlines the tasks to accomplish these objectives, and (3) determines the promotion cost of performing these tasks.[21]

Of the various methods, only the objective and task method takes into account what the company wants to accomplish and requires that the objectives be specified.[22]

Selecting the Right Promotional Tools

Once a budget has been determined, the combination of the five basic IMC tools—advertising, personal selling, sales promotion, public relations, and direct marketing—can be specified. While many factors provide direction for selection of the appropriate mix, the large number of possible combinations of the promotional tools means that many combinations can achieve the same objective. Therefore, an analytical approach and experience are particularly important in this step of the promotion decision process. The specific mix can vary from a simple program using a single tool to a comprehensive program using all forms of promotion. The Olympics have become a very visible example of a comprehensive integrated communication program. Because the Games are repeated every two years, the promotion is almost continuous. Included in the program are advertising campaigns, personal selling efforts by the Olympic committee and organizers, sales promotion activities such as product tie-ins and sponsorships, public relations programs managed by the host cities, and direct marketing efforts targeted at a variety of audiences including governments, organizations, firms, athletes, and individuals.[23] At this stage, it is also important to assess the relative importance of the various tools. While it may be desirable to utilize and integrate several forms of promotion, one may deserve emphasis. The Olympics, for example, place exceptional importance on public relations and publicity.

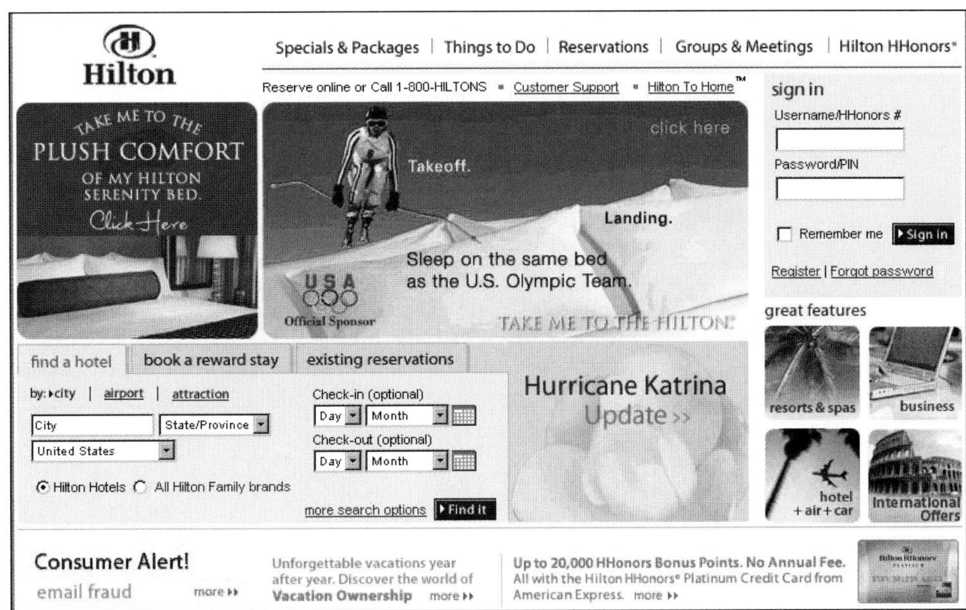

Hilton is one of the official sponsors of the U.S. Olympic Team.

Designing the Promotion

The central element of a promotion program is the promotion itself. Advertising consists of advertising copy and the artwork that the target audience is intended to see or hear. Personal selling efforts depend on the characteristics and skills of the salesperson. Sales promotion activities consist of the specific details of inducements such as coupons, samples, and sweepstakes. Public relations efforts are readily seen in tangible elements such as news releases, and direct marketing actions depend on written, verbal, and electronic forms of delivery. The design of the promotion will play a primary role in determining the message that is communicated to the audience. This design activity is frequently viewed as the step requiring the most creativity. In addition, successful designs are often the result of insight regarding consumer's interests and purchasing behavior. All of the promotion tools have many design alternatives. Advertising, for example, can utilize fear, humor, attractiveness, or other themes in its appeal.[24] Similarly, direct marketing can be designed for varying levels of personal or customized appeals. One of the challenges of IMC is to design each promotional activity to communicate the same message.

Scheduling the Promotion

Once the design of each of the promotional program elements is complete, it is important to determine the most effective timing of their use. The promotion schedule describes the order in which each promotional tool is introduced and the frequency of its use during the campaign. New Line Cinema, for example, developed one of the longest promotion schedules on record for its *Lord of the Rings* movie trilogy. To generate interest in each movie before its release, a movie "trailer" was shown on television and in theaters. Then movie-related products were released, followed by special promotions by Burger King, General Mills, and the NBA. After all three movies had been released, New Line ran a 30-second ad with high-definition footage to promote DVD sales.[25] Overall, the scheduling of the various promotions was designed to generate interest, bring consumers into theaters, and then encourage additional purchases after seeing the movie.

Several factors such as seasonality and competitive promotion activity can also influence the promotion schedule. Businesses such as ski resorts, airlines, and professional sports teams are likely to reduce their promotional activity during the "off" season. Similarly, restaurants, retail stores, and health clubs are likely to increase their promotional activity when new competitors enter the market.

EXECUTING AND EVALUATING THE PROMOTION PROGRAM

As shown earlier in Figure 15–5, the ideal execution of a promotion program involves pretesting each design before it is actually used to allow for changes and modifications which improve its effectiveness. Similarly, posttests are recommended to evaluate the impact of each promotion and the contribution of the promotion toward achieving the program objectives. The most sophisticated pretest and posttest procedures have been developed for advertising and are discussed in Chapter 16. Testing procedures for sales promotion and direct marketing efforts currently focus on comparisons of different designs or responses of different segments. To fully benefit from IMC programs, companies must create and maintain a test-result database that allows comparisons of the relative impact of the promotional tools and their execution options in varying situations. Information from the database will allow informed design and execution decisions and provide support for IMC activities during internal reviews by financial or administrative personnel. The San Diego Padres baseball team, for example, developed a database of information relating attendance to its integrated campaign using a new logo, special events, merchandise sales, and a loyalty program.

Carrying out the promotion program can be expensive and time consuming. One researcher estimates that "an organization with sales less than $10 million can successfully implement an IMC program in one year, one with sales between $200 million and $500 million will need about three years, and one with sales between $2 billion and $5 billion will need five years." To facilitate the transition, there are approximately 200 integrated marketing communications agencies in operation. In addition, some of the largest agencies are adopting approaches that embrace "total communications solutions." Starcom MediaVest, which recently won *Advertising Age* magazine's Media Agency of the Year award, for example, has created an integrated network of 3,800 employees who specialize in media management, Internet and digital communications, direct response media, entertainment marketing, sports sponsorships, event marketing, and multicultural marketing. One of their integrated campaigns for Coca-Cola Venezuela created a partnership with the *Who Wants to Be a Millionaire* television program that led to increased awareness and preference for Coca-Cola in the teen market.[26] While many agencies still have departments dedicated to promotion, direct marketing, and other specialties, the trend today is clearly toward a long-term perspective in which all forms of promotion are integrated.[27]

Concept Check

1. What are the stages of the hierarchy of effects?
2. What are four approaches to setting the promotion budget?
3. How have advertising agencies changed to help companies develop IMC programs?

DIRECT MARKETING

Direct marketing is a promotional element that uses direct communication with consumers to encourage them to place an order, request more information, or visit a store. Direct marketing has many forms and utilizes a variety of media. Several forms of direct marketing—direct mail and catalogs, television, telemarketing, and direct selling—were discussed as methods of nonstore retailing in Chapter 14. In addition, although advertising is discussed in Chapter 16, a form of advertising—direct response advertising—is an important form of direct marketing. Finally, interactive or online marketing is discussed in detail in Chapter 18. In this section, the growth of direct marketing, its value for consumers and sellers, and key global, technological, and ethical issues are discussed.

The Growth of Direct Marketing

The increasing interest in customer relationship management is reflected in the dramatic growth of direct marketing. The ability to customize communication efforts and create one-to-one interactions is appealing to most marketers, particularly those with IMC programs. While direct marketing methods are not new, the ability to design and use them has increased with the availability of databases. In recent years, direct marketing growth—in terms of spending, revenue generated, and employment—has outpaced total economic growth. Direct marketing expenditures of $217 billion in 2004 are expected to grow to $255 billion by 2007. Similarly, 2004 revenues of $2.3 trillion are expected to grow to $3 trillion by 2007. Employment has also grown and now numbers more than 17 million employees.[28]

The Value of Direct Marketing

One of the most visible indicators of the value of direct marketing for consumers is the level of use of various forms of direct marketing. For example, 68 percent of the U.S. population has ordered merchandise or services by phone or mail; more than 12 million adults have purchased items from a television offer; the average adult spends more than 30 hours per year accessing online services; and more than 21 percent of all adults make three to five purchases from a catalog each year. Consumers report many benefits, including the following: They don't have to go to a store; they can usually shop 24 hours a day; buying direct saves time; they avoid hassles with salespeople; they can save money; it's fun and entertaining; and direct marketing offers more privacy than in-store shopping. Many consumers also believe that direct marketing provides excellent customer service.[29] Toll-free telephone numbers, customer service representatives with access to information regarding purchasing preferences, overnight delivery services, and unconditional guarantees all help create value for direct marketing customers. At Landsend.com, when customers need assistance they can click a "help" icon and a sales rep will take control of their browser until the correct product is found. "It's like we were walking down the aisle in a store," says one Lands' End customer.[30]

The value of direct marketing for sellers can be described in terms of the responses it generates.[31] **Direct orders** are the result of offers that contain all the information necessary for a prospective buyer to make a decision to purchase and complete the transaction. Club Med, for example, uses direct e-mail offers to sell "last-minute specials" to people in its database. The messages, which are sent midweek, describe rooms and air transportation available at a 30 to 40 percent discount if the customer can make the decision to travel on such short notice.[32] **Lead generation** is the result of an offer designed to generate interest in a product or service and a request for additional information. America Online announced a contest with direct advertising and used a direct-mail trial offer to generate interest in its latest release.[33] Finally, **traffic generation** is the outcome of an offer designed to motivate people to visit a business. Mitsubishi recently mailed a sweepstakes offer to 1 million prospective buyers to encourage them to visit a Mitsubishi dealer and test drive the new Galant. The names of prospects who took test drives were entered in the sweepstakes, which included a Galant, a trip to Hawaii, and large-screen TVs as prizes.[34]

direct orders
The result of direct marketing offers that contain all the information necessary for a potential buyer to make a decision to purchase and complete the transaction

lead generation
Result of direct marketing offer designed to generate interest in a product or a service and a request for additional information

traffic generation
Outcome of direct marketing offer designed to motivate people to visit a business

Technological, Global, and Ethical Issues in Direct Marketing

The information technology and databases described in Chapter 8 are key elements in any direct marketing program. Databases are the result of organizations' efforts to collect demographic, media, and consumption profiles of customers so that direct marketing tools, such as catalogs, can be directed at specific customers. For example, Lillian Vernon started her very successful mail-order company four decades ago at her kitchen table by putting all her merchandise in a single catalog: Laundry baskets and men's slippers on one page might be followed by toys on the next. But in the last few years Lillian Vernon has shifted to a database approach with the 150 million catalogs she mails annually. There are now home-oriented, children's, and Christmas-ornament catalogs targeted at customers who have purchased these kinds of merchandise from her main catalog in the past.[35]

Technology may also prove to be important in the global growth of direct marketing. Compared with the United States, other countries' direct marketing systems are undeveloped. The mail and telephone systems in many countries are likely to improve, however, creating many new direct marketing opportunities. Developments in international marketing research and database management will also facilitate global growth. In Argentina, for example, mail service is very slow, telephone service is poor, and response to some forms of direct marketing such as coupons is negligible. The country is the first, however, to fully deregulate its postal service and expects rapid improvement from the private company, Correo Argentino. In Mexico, direct marketing activities are more advanced. Pond's recently mailed 20,000 direct-mail offers within Mexico and was surprised by a 33 percent response.[36] Another issue for global direct marketers is payment. Because fewer consumers have credit cards, alternatives such as C.O.D. and bank deposits are needed.

Global and domestic direct marketers both face challenging ethical issues today. Of course there has been considerable attention given to some annoying direct marketing activities such as telephone solicitations during dinner and evening hours. Concerns about privacy, however, have led to various attempts to provide guidelines that balance consumer and business interests. The European Union recently passed a consumer privacy law, called the Data Protection Directive, after several years of discussion with the Federation of European Direct Marketing and the U.K.'s Direct Marketing Association. In the United States, the Federal Trade Commission and many state legislatures have also been concerned about privacy.[37] Another issue, the proliferation of e-mail advertising, has received increasing attention from consumers and marketers recently. The accompanying Ethics and Social Responsibility Alert offers some of the details of the debate.[38]

Global marketer Porsche uses direct marketing to facilitate growth.

ETHICS AND SOCIAL RESPONSIBILITY ALERT

How Do You Like Your E-Mail? "Opt-out" or "Opt-in" Are Your Choices

More than 1 billion e-mail messages are sent each day in the United States. You've probably noticed that many of them are direct marketing messages—personalized offers from companies such as Pepsi, Victoria's Secret, Toyota, and Hertz. In fact, e-mail advertisers spend more than $2 billion on their campaigns each year. One reason is that e-mail offers one-to-one conversations with each prospective consumer. Another reason is that the average cost per e-mail message is less than $.01 compared to $0.75 to $2.00 for direct mail and $1 to $3 for telemarketing.

WHERE ARE YOU @?
Tell us at hertzgold.com and earn double miles.
#1Club

Two general approaches to managing e-mail are being discussed. The "opt-out" system allows recipients to decline future messages after the first contact. The "opt-in" system requires advertisers to obtain e-mail addresses from registration questions on websites, business-reply cards, and even entry forms for contests or sweepstakes. Surveys indicate that about 77 percent of the unsolicited e-mails are deleted without being read, while only 2 percent of the e-mails received with the consumer's permission are deleted.

In January 2004, the Controlling the Assault of Non-Solicited Pornography and Marketing Act (CAN-SPAM) went into effect. The law does not prohibit spam but requires it to be truthful and to provide an opt-out return e-mail address. Some companies, however, have adopted opt-in policies. Hertz, for example, uses ads to ask customers to contact the company. What is your opinion? Why?

Concept Check

1. The ability to design and use direct marketing programs has increased with the availability of ________________ and ________________.
2. What are the three types of responses generated by direct marketing activities?

CHAPTER IN REVIEW

1 *Discuss integrated marketing communication and the communication process.*
Integrated marketing communication is the concept of designing marketing communications programs that coordinate all promotional activities—advertising, personal selling, sales promotion, public relations, and direct marketing—to provide a consistent message across all audiences. The communication process conveys messages with six elements: a source, a message, a channel of communication, a receiver, and encoding and decoding. The communication process also includes a feedback loop and can be distorted by noise.

2 *Describe the promotional mix and the uniqueness of each component.*
There are five promotional alternatives. Advertising, sales promotion, and public relations are mass selling approaches, whereas personal selling and direct marketing use customized messages. Advertising can have high absolute costs but reaches large numbers of people. Personal selling has a high cost per contact but provides immediate feedback. Public relations is often difficult to obtain but is very credible. Sales promotion influences short-term consumer behavior. Direct marketing can help develop customer relationships although maintaining a database can be very expensive.

3 *Select the promotional approach appropriate to a product's life-cycle stage.*
The promotional mix changes over the four product life-cycle stages. During the introduction stage, all the promotional mix elements are used. In the growth stage, the primary promotional element is advertising. The maturity stage utilizes sales promotion and direct marketing. During the decline stage, little money is spent on the promotional mix.

4 *Discuss the characteristics of push and pull strategies.*
A push strategy directs the promotional mix to channel members to gain their cooperation in ordering and stocking the product. Personal selling and sales promotion are commonly used in push strategies. A pull strategy directs the promotional mix at ultimate customers to encourage them to ask the retailer for the product. Direct-to-consumer advertising is typically used in pull strategies.

5 *Describe the elements of the promotion decision process.*
The promotional decision process consists of three steps: planning, implementation, and control. The planning step consists of six elements: identify the target audience, specify the objectives, set the budget, select the right promotional elements, design the

promotion, and schedule the promotion. The implementation step includes pretesting. The control step includes posttesting.

6 *Explain the value of direct marketing for consumers and sellers.*
The value of direct marketing for consumers is indicated by its level of use. For example, 68 percent of them made a purchase by phone or mail, and 12 million people have purchased items from a television offer. The value of direct marketing for sellers can be measured in terms of three types of responses: direct orders, lead generation, and traffic generation.

FOCUSING ON KEY TERMS

advertising p. 335
communication p. 332
direct marketing p. 337
direct orders p. 345
hierarchy of effects p. 341
integrated marketing communications p. 332
lead generation p. 345
personal selling p. 336
promotional mix p. 332
publicity p. 336
public relations p. 336
pull strategy p. 340
push strategy p. 340
sales promotion p. 337
traffic generation p. 345

DISCUSSION AND APPLICATION QUESTIONS

1 After listening to a recent sales presentation, Mary Smith signed up for membership at the local health club. On arriving at the facility, she learned there was an additional fee for racquetball court rentals. "I don't remember that in the sales talk; I thought they said all facilities were included with the membership fee," complained Mary. Describe the problem in terms of the communication process.

2 Develop a matrix to compare the five elements of the promotional mix on three criteria—to *whom* you deliver the message, *what* you say, and *when* you say it.

3 Explain how the promotional tools used by an airline would differ if the target audience were (*a*) consumers who travel for pleasure and (*b*) corporate travel departments that select the airlines to be used by company employees.

4 Suppose you introduced a new consumer food product and invested heavily both in national advertising (pull strategy) and in training and motivating your field salesforce to sell the product to food stores (push strategy). What kinds of feedback would you receive from both the advertising and your salesforce? How could you increase both the quality and quantity of each?

5 Fisher-Price Company, long known as a manufacturer of children's toys, has introduced a line of clothing for children. Outline a promotional plan to get this product introduced in the marketplace.

6 Many insurance companies sell health insurance plans to companies. In these companies the employees pick the plan, but the set of offered plans is determined by the company. Recently Blue Cross–Blue Shield, a health insurance company, ran a television ad stating, "If your employer doesn't offer you Blue Cross–Blue Shield coverage, ask why." Explain the promotional strategy behind the advertisement.

7 Identify the sales promotion tools that might be useful for (*a*) Tastee Yogurt, a new brand introduction, (*b*) 3M self-sticking Post-it notes, and (*c*) Wrigley's Spearmint Gum.

8 Design an integrated marketing communications program—using each of the five promotional elements—for Music Boulevard, the online music store.

9 BMW recently introduced its first sport utility vehicle, the X5, to compete with other popular 4 × 4 vehicles such as the Mercedes-Benz M-class and Jeep Grand Cherokee. Design a direct marketing program to generate (*a*) leads, (*b*) traffic in dealerships, and (*c*) direct orders.

10 Develop a privacy policy for database managers that provides a balance of consumer and seller perspectives. How would you encourage voluntary compliance with your policy? What methods of enforcement would you recommend?

GOING ONLINE Agencies Adopt IMC Approaches

Several large advertising agencies have described shifts in their philosophies to include IMC approaches to communication. In many cases, the outcome has been campaigns that utilize a combination of the five promotional elements. Go to Digitas' website at www.digitas.com and review the promotions for several Digitas clients (click on "Results," then "Customer Experience").

1 Describe the promotional elements of one of the campaigns. Why were these elements selected? How are they integrated?

2 How would you evaluate the effectiveness of each of the promotional elements used? How would you evaluate the effectiveness of the entire campaign?

BUILDING YOUR MARKETING PLAN

To develop the promotion strategy for your marketing plan, follow the steps suggested in the planning phase of the promotion decision process described in Figure 15–5.

1 You should (*a*) identify the target audience, (*b*) specify the promotion objectives, (*c*) set the promotion budget, (*d*) select the right promotion tools, (*e*) design the promotion, and (*f*) schedule the promotion.

2 Also specify the pretesting and posttesting procedures needed in the implementation and control phases.

3 Finally, describe how each of your promotion tools are integrated to provide a consistent message.

VIDEO CASE 15 UPS: Repositioning a Business with IMC

"As a business we have, for decades, been primarily in the business of small package transportation and delivery," observes Paul Meyer, group manager of UPS Brand Communications, "which is how the vast majority of our customers and the population at large know us today." Now UPS is undertaking the challenge of expanding into new businesses and it must change the perceptions of the services it provides. As Meyers explains, the question he faces is "How do we position UPS as an enterprise . . . into a new space that we can define?"

THE COMPANY

UPS was founded in Seattle by 19-year-old James Casey in 1907 as a messenger service called the American Messenger Company. As the use of telephones and automobiles increased, the demand for message delivery declined, and Casey began to focus his business on package delivery for retail stores. In 1919 the company expanded into California and adopted its present name, United Parcel Service. The expansion continued to the East coast and Canada, necessitating the development of air and ground delivery routes. As retail stores moved to large suburban shopping centers with large parking lots, however, the demand for retail package delivery began to decline and UPS decided to expand its delivery service to include all possible customers, both private and commercial.

The decision to become a "common carrier" put UPS in direct competition with the U.S. Postal Service and in conflict with regulations of the Interstate Commerce Commission. Federal authority was needed to cross state borders and each state had to authorize the movement of packages within its borders. Over 30 years UPS made hundreds of applications to regulatory commissions and the courts for shipping rights. Finally, in 1975, UPS became the first package delivery company with federal and state authorization to serve every address in the 48 contiguous United States.

Today, UPS has grown into a $33 billion corporation and the world's largest package delivery service. The company consists of 357,000 employees, 88,000 package cars, vans, and motorcycles, and 269 airplanes which operate in 200 countries and territories worldwide. UPS now ships more than 13.6 million packages and documents each day to more than 7.9 million customers.

REPOSITIONING UPS

During the late 1990s UPS began to evaluate its core business—the distribution and delivery of goods—and the possibility of expanding into new services. Managers at UPS realized that commerce consisted of more than the flow of goods; it also included the flow of information and capital, so they began to build a network of services to help UPS customers with all three components. UPS began a series of acquisitions which created UPS Supply Chain Solutions, UPS Capital, UPS Mail Innovations, and UPS Consulting. In addition, it acquired the Mail Boxes Etc. franchise. UPS hoped that these new offerings would reposition UPS into a marketspace the company called "synchronized commerce."

Through its acquisitions UPS had the potential to be a comprehensive enabler of global commerce. It hoped to offer customized supply chain, information, and financial product solutions for each individual customer. Despite its new services, however, the company was challenged by the perception that it only provided package delivery. "We found that we needed to help our customers, and the different decision makers that we engage," explains Meyers. "We had to find a way to build a bridge for them from what they knew us to be as a small package transportation company into something larger than that. We do more than just deliver packages was the basic proposition," he says.

THE UPS IMC CAMPAIGN

UPS needed to convey its new capabilities, and its transformation to the "synchronized" commerce positioning, to current and potential customers. An integrated marketing communications campaign was needed. UPS started by conducting two years of strategic research and planning to guide the new communication activities. The result was a comprehensive campaign that included advertising, public relations, personal selling and promotional efforts.

The first announcement was the new logo. UPS had utilized four logos in its history. The first logo was adopted in 1916 and featured an eagle carrying a package on a shield with the words "Safe, Swift, Sure." The second logo retained the shield, added the letters "UPS" and the phrase "The Delivery System for Stores of Quality." The third logo simplified UPS's identity by adding a bow-tied package above the shield and the letters UPS, and eliminating all words and phrases. This logo was used without change for 42 years. Finally, the new logo removed the bow-tied package to underscore the company's expanded services, and simply retained the shield and the letters "UPS." The new logo now appears on all UPS vehicles and aircraft, and its 45,000 drop-off boxes and 1 million uniform pieces.

Another element of the communication campaign was to rename 3,300 U.S. locations of Mail Boxes Etc. as *The UPS Store*—with the new logo prominent in the new store signage. The retail presence gave UPS the world's largest and fastest-growing shipping and business services outlet, and access to a variety of small businesses, sales personnel, and retail consumers. In response, competitor FedEx purchased Kinko's 1,200 retail outlets for $2.4 billion in the hope that it would add new locations to pick up packages.

Advertising also supports the changes at UPS. The company's largest national campaign "What Can Brown Do for You?" emphasizes the color that was selected by one of the company's founders because it reflected class, elegance, and professionalism. The color is viewed as a creative platform that ties all pieces of the campaign together. It is part of the presentation of all vehicles, planes, uniforms, and packaging. In addition, although brown will remain the primary color representing UPS, other new complementary colors will become part of new designs of company assets. The advertising also emphasizes the theme of "synchronizing the world of commerce."

UPS has identified five segments it tries to reach with its advertising. They are shipping decision makers, front office decision makers, small business owners, senior level managers, and retail consumers. Each campaign has a specific context and emphasizes benefits important to that segment. All campaigns, however, utilize the color brown theme as a means of integration.

The color brown is such an important part of the UPS image that UPS registered two trademarks on the color brown which prevent other delivery companies from using the color for vehicles or clothing if it creates confusion in the marketplace. It takes more than 142,000 gallons of brown paint to keep UPS's fleet of vehicles brown, and 1,673,000 yards of brown cloth to make the 188,000 hats, 459,000 shirts, 303,000 pants, and 192,000 pairs of shorts needed to keep all UPS drivers in uniform.

Another element of the integrated program is the web page (www.ups.com) which now receives 115 million hits per day, including 9.1 million online tracking requests. UPS's new CampusShip service allows consumers to operate a virtual post office online. From any location, customers can build an online address list, print labels, track a package, and e-mail shipping notifications. UPS even uses its online capabilities to manage online orders for companies such as Jockey International. Apparel bought on the Jockey website is boxed by UPS

employees managing the Jockey warehouse, and delivered by UPS drivers.

Other elements of the campaign include promotions, personal selling activities, and public relations efforts which influence executives' public appearances and copy in popular business press such as *The Wall Street Journal* and *Fortune.*

FUTURE STRATEGY

How can UPS managers assess the success of their campaign? There are several measures that give an indication of the impact of the various message activities. First, there have been a variety of awards. For example, the "What Can Brown Do for You?" advertising was selected for an American Marketing Association EFFIE award, and *BtoB Magazine* cited the campaign as one of the best integrated advertising campaigns. Meyer explains, "people across all of our target audiences have such a powerful association of the color brown with the company UPS, and the brand UPS, that we can use the color to personify the brand without even mentioning the brand and still get nearly 100 percent recall on all of our messaging."

Another measure of success is the new revenue being generated by logistics customers—a market growing at a rate of about 20 percent. In addition, some experts estimate that the new logistics business generates an additional $2 billion in shipping volume. Finally, a growing number of businesses such as Ford and Birkenstock Footprint Sandals have given UPS complete responsibility for their distribution networks. At Ford, UPS cut the time it takes a car to move from product to the dealer by 40 percent, 14 to 10 days, and at Birkenstock, UPS cut the time it takes shoes to get to stores by 50 percent.

For UPS it's all about helping customers effectively operate their supply chains by simultaneously managing the flow of goods, information, and money. In the future UPS will need to continue to evolve by developing new capabilities and by continuing to ask "What Can Brown Do for You?"

Questions

1 What information about consumer perceptions of UPS led the company to pursue an integrated marketing communications campaign? What was UPS's promotional objective as it repositioned itself in the "synchronized commerce" marketspace?

2 Which of the promotional elements described in Figure 15–2 were used by UPS in its integrated campaign? Describe how UPS might use different media or promotional elements to reach each of the five segments.

3 Why does the color brown provide a useful "creative platform" for UPS's IMC campaign? What is your first reaction to the advertising theme "What Can Brown Do for You?"

4 As UPS has expanded throughout the world it has chosen to use a global marketing strategy, as defined in Chapter 7. What are the advantages and disadvantages of this strategy for UPS?

250
08:07
x 43
OAKLEY
250
08:18
x 42
OAKLEY

CHAPTER

16

ADVERTISING, SALES PROMOTION, AND PUBLIC RELATIONS

LEARNING OBJECTIVES

After reading this chapter you should be able to:

1 Explain the differences between product advertising and institutional advertising and the variations within each type.

2 Describe the steps used to develop, execute, and evaluate an advertising program.

3 Explain the advantages and disadvantages of alternative advertising media.

4 Discuss the strengths and weaknesses of consumer-oriented and trade-oriented sales promotions.

5 Recognize public relations as an important form of communication.

WELCOME TO THE NEW WORLD OF ADVERTISING

Consumers like you are changing the way they use media, and those changes are creating an entirely new world of advertising. Recent studies show that many consumers often use more than one potential source of advertising at the same time. While watching television, 67 percent of young consumers also use the Internet, 66 percent sometimes read a magazine, 56 percent are instant-messaging, and 34 percent are listening to the radio. While this means consumers may be exposed to many more ads, it also suggests that consumers may not be paying close attention to them. As a result, advertisers are adding attention-getting media such as Internet promotions, direct mail, and events to their campaigns, using technology to integrate their ads with the media.

Technology is also allowing advertisers to match messages with consumers' personal interests. By 2007, 50 percent of the nation's households are expected to have personal video recorders like TiVo, which enable viewers to specify the type of programs that should be recorded. Personalization software will enable an advertiser to insert ads that are specific to the viewer of that television. So if parents typically watch a different television than their children, the ads on the two TVs are likely to be different even if the same program is tuned in.

The popularity of video games and the growing interest in massive multiplayer games (MMPs) has led to a new form of advertising called *advergaming,* or the integration of advertising messages in the virtual world of the games. Currently, advertisers spend more than $100 million to be included in game settings. Nike and Levi's, for example, are included in a popular game called *There,* which allows players to use Therebucks to purchase in-game products. Online game publisher WildTangent recently released *Snowboard SuperJam* with advertising billboards by Jeep and Oakley embedded in the game. According to one expert, advergaming will become much more sophisticated than signs. Chad Stoller, director of communications solutions at Arnell Group in New York, suggests that games such as Tony Hawk Underground might be designed so that "a skateboarder has to do a trick off the Jeep Liberty to accomplish a goal" in the game.[1]

advertising
Any paid form of nonpersonal communication about an organization, good, service, or idea by an identified sponsor

Personalization, advergaming, and the use of new media are just a few of the many exciting changes taking place in the field of advertising today. Chapter 15 described **advertising** as any paid form of nonpersonal communication about an organization, a good, a service, or an idea by an identified sponsor. This chapter describes three of the promotional mix elements—advertising, sales promotion, and public relations.

TYPES OF ADVERTISEMENTS

As you look through any magazine, watch television, listen to the radio, or browse the Internet, the variety of advertisements you see or hear may give you the impression that they have few similarities. Advertisements are prepared for different purposes, but they basically consist of two types: product advertisements and institutional advertisements.

Product Advertisements

product advertisements
Advertisements that focus on selling a good or service; forms include pioneering (informational), competitive (persuasive), and reminder

Focused on selling a good or service, **product advertisements** take three forms: (1) pioneering (or informational), (2) competitive (or persuasive), and (3) reminder. Look at the ads by AOL, Tums, and 1-800-flowers.com to determine the type and objective of each ad.

Used in the introductory stage of the product life cycle, *pioneering* advertisements tell people what a product is, what it can do, and where it can be found. The key objective of a pioneering advertisement (such as the ad for the new AOL) is to inform the target market. Informative ads have been found to be interesting, convincing, and effective.[2]

Advertising that promotes a specific brand's features and benefits is *competitive.* The objective of these messages is to persuade the target market to select the firm's brand rather than that of a competitor. An increasingly common form of competitive advertising is *comparative* advertising, which shows one brand's strengths relative to

Advertisements serve varying purposes. Which ad would be considered a (1) pioneering, (2) competitive, and (3) reminder ad?

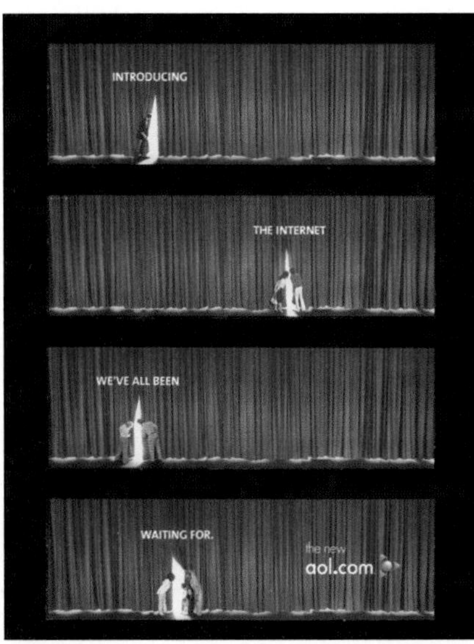

those of competitors.[3] The Tums ad, for example, highlights the competitive advantage of Tums over its primary competitor Prilosec. Studies indicate that comparative ads attract more attention and increase the perceived quality of the advertiser's brand.[4] Firms that use comparative advertising need market research to provide legal support for their claims.[5]

Reminder advertising is used to reinforce previous knowledge of a product. The 1-800-flowers.com ad shown reminds consumers about the association between its product and a special event, in this case, Valentine's Day. Reminder advertising is good for products that have achieved a well-recognized position and are in the mature phase of their product life cycle. Another type of reminder ad, *reinforcement,* is used to assure current users they made the right choice. One example: "Aren't you glad you use Dial. Don't you wish everybody did?"

Institutional Advertisements

institutional advertisements
Advertisements designed to build goodwill or an image for an organization, rather than promote a specific good or service

The objective of **institutional advertisements** is to build goodwill or an image for an organization rather than promote a specific good or service. Institutional advertising has been used by companies such as Texaco, Pfizer, and IBM to build confidence in the company name.[6] Often this form of advertising is used to support the public relations plan or counter adverse publicity. Four alternative forms of institutional advertisements are often used:

1. *Advocacy* advertisements state the position of a company on an issue. Lorillard Tobacco Company places ads discouraging teenagers from smoking. Another form of advocacy advertisement is used when organizations make a request related to a particular action or behavior, such as a request by American Red Cross for blood donations.
2. *Pioneering institutional* advertisements, like the pioneering ads for products discussed earlier, are used for announcements about what a company is, what it can do, or where it is located. Recent Bayer ads stating "We cure more headaches than you think" are intended to inform consumers that the company produces many products in addition to aspirin. When Philip Morris changed its name to Altria, it ran pioneering institutional ads to inform consumers.
3. *Competitive institutional* advertisements promote the advantages of one product class over another and are used in markets where different product classes compete for the same buyers. America's milk processors and dairy farmers use their "Got Milk?" campaign to increase demand for milk as it competes against other beverages.
4. *Reminder institutional* advertisements, like the product form, simply bring the company's name to the attention of the target market again. The four branches of the U.S. military sponsor the "Today's Military" campaign to remind potential recruits of the opportunities in the active military, the National Guard, and the reserves.

Concept Check

1. What is the difference between pioneering and competitive ads?
2. What is the purpose of an institutional advertisement?

DEVELOPING THE ADVERTISING PROGRAM

The promotion decision process described in Chapter 15 can be applied to each of the promotional elements. Advertising, for example, can be managed by following the three steps (developing, executing, and evaluating) of the process.

Identifying the Target Audience

To develop an effective advertising program advertisers must identify the target audience. All aspects of an advertising program are likely to be influenced by the characteristics of the prospective consumer. Understanding the lifestyles, attitudes, and demographics of the target market is essential. When Hummer, the biggest and most expensive sport utility vehicle in the market, began its $3 million campaign targeted at "rugged individualists" with incomes above $200,000, it selected *Wired, Spin, Red Herring, BusinessWeek, Skiing,* and *Cigar Aficionado* to carry the ads.[7] Even scheduling can depend on the audience. Claritin, a popular allergy medication, schedules its use of brochures, in-store displays, coupons, and advertising to correspond to the allergy season, which varies by geographic region.[8] To eliminate possible bias that might result from subjective judgments about some population segments, the Federal Communications Commission suggests that advertising program decisions be based on market research about the target audience.[9]

Specifying Advertising Objectives

The guidelines for setting promotion objectives described in Chapter 15 also apply to setting advertising objectives. This step helps advertisers with other choices in the promotion decision process such as selecting media and evaluating a campaign. Advertising with an objective of creating awareness, for example, would be better matched with a magazine than a directory such as the Yellow Pages.[10] The Magazine Publishers of America believe objectives are so important that they offer a $100,000 prize each year to the campaign that best meets its objectives. A recent winner, Apple, won with its "Silhouettes" campaign, which helped achieve the objective of making the iPod the number one MP3 player.[11] Similarly, the Advertising Research Foundation is collecting information about the effectiveness of advertising, particularly new forms such as online advertising.[12]

Setting the Advertising Budget

Do you remember this Pepsi ad from the Super Bowl?

You might not remember who advertised during the 1990 Super Bowl, but it cost the companies $700,000 to place a 30-second ad. By 2005, the cost of placing a 30-second ad during Super Bowl XXXIX was $2.4 million. The reason for the escalating cost is the growing number of viewers: 41.1 million homes and 86.1 million people tune in. While not all advertising options are as expensive as the Super Bowl, most alternatives still represent substantial financial commitments and require a formal budgeting process. In the luxury car market, for example, the BMW 7 series and the Jaguar S-type have market shares of 5.0 and 3.6 percent and advertising budgets of $38.9 and $27.0 million, respectively. Using a competitive parity budgeting approach, each company spends between $7 and $8 million for each percent of market share. Using an objective and task approach, Chrysler allocated $60 million to reintroduce its Dodge Charger, which has not been sold since 1988.[13]

Designing the Advertisement

An advertising message usually focuses on the key benefits of the product that are important to a prospective buyer in making trial and adoption decisions. The message depends on the general form or appeal used in the ad and the actual words included in the ad.

Message Appeal Most advertising messages are made up of both informational and persuasional elements. Information and persuasive content can be combined in the

ETHICS AND SOCIAL RESPONSIBILITY ALERT

Who Decides What Is "Appropriate" Advertising?

The controversy created by Janet Jackson's halftime performance in Super Bowl XXXVIII has sparked a complicated debate about what is appropriate content for media and advertising and who should decide what is appropriate. The Federal Communications Commission is legally responsible for policing the airwaves. Congress can also influence the industry with laws such as the recently proposed Clean Airwaves Act. Large media and retailing companies are also weighing in: Wal-Mart banned some magazines such as *Maxim* and *Stuff* from its stores, and six Clear Channel radio stations dropped Howard Stern from their programming. Finally, companies have made changes in their marketing activities: Anheuser-Busch decided to stop using several popular ads, Victoria's Secret canceled its TV fashion show, and Abercrombie & Fitch is dropping its suggestive quarterly catalog.

For each group, the difficulty is in trying to match content with consumer preferences, because preferences vary from segment to segment. The FCC, Congress, and large and small companies have all received complaints about advertising content from conservative segments of the population. At the same time, a recent survey reported that 74 percent of consumers ages 12–20 think that many people have overreacted to the issue. Some experts are anticipating that the result will be a continuum of media and content options from children's programming, to network television, to cable TV and satellite radio, to pay-per-view and Internet options. What is your opinion?

form of an appeal to provide a basic reason for the consumer to act. Although the marketer can use many different types of appeals, common advertising appeals include fear appeals,[14] sex appeals, and humorous appeals.

Fear appeals suggest to the consumer that he or she can avoid some negative experience through the purchase and use of a product or service, or through a change in behavior. Examples with which you may be familiar include fire or smoke detector ads that depict a home burning and social cause ads warning of the serious consequences of drug and alcohol use or AIDS. When using fear appeals, the advertiser must be sure that the appeal is strong enough to get the audience's attention and concern but not so strong that it will lead them to tune out the message. In fact, recent research on antismoking ads indicates that stressing the severity of long-term health risks may actually enhance smoking's allure among youth.[15]

In contrast, *sex appeals* suggest to the audience that the product will increase the attractiveness of the user. Sex appeals can be found in almost any product category, from automobiles to toothpaste. The contemporary women's clothing store bebe, for example, designs its advertising to "attract customers who are intrigued by the playfully sensual and evocative imagery of the bebe lifestyle." Unfortunately, many commercials that use sex appeals are only successful at gaining the attention of the audience; they have little impact on how consumers think, feel, or act. Some advertising experts even argue that such appeals get in the way of successful communication by distracting the audience from the purpose of the ad. Public response to a performance by Janet Jackson during a Super Bowl halftime show has led many advertisers to modify the content of their promotions.[16] See the Ethics and Social Responsibility Alert for a discussion of the complexity of the issues involved.[17]

Humorous appeals imply either directly or subtly that the product is more fun or exciting than competitors' offerings. As with fear and sex appeals, the use of humor is widespread in advertising and can be found in many product categories. The Cannes Advertising Festival, held in June each year, recognized Burger King for its use of humor in websites designed to support messages also promoted in TV ads. For example, the "Have it your way" message is the theme of a site (www.subserviantchicken.com) where millions of visitors have commanded a chicken to do stunts. You may have a favorite humorous ad character, such as the Energizer battery bunny, the AFLAC duck, or the Geico gecko. Unfortunately for the advertiser, humor tends to wear out quickly,

eventually boring the consumer. Another problem with humorous appeals is that their effectiveness may vary across cultures if used in a global campaign.[18]

Creating the Actual Message Copywriters are responsible for creating the text portion of the messages in advertisements. Translating the copywriter's ideas into an actual advertisement is a complex process. Designing quality artwork, layout, and production for the advertisements is costly and time consuming. High-quality TV commercials typically cost about $372,000 to produce a 30-second ad, a task done by about 2,000 small commercial production companies across the United States. One reason for the high costs is that as companies have developed global campaigns, the need to shoot commercials in exotic locations has increased. Audi recently filmed commercials in Germany, Australia, and Morocco. Actors are expensive also. The Screen Actors Guild reports that an actor in a typical network TV car ad would earn between $12,000 and $15,000.[19]

Advertising agency Crispin was recently designated as *Advertising Age* magazine's Agency of the Year for creating campaign ideas that "translate across major media as well as . . . other marketing disciplines." For example, its campaign for Mini Cooper included magazine advertising, billboards, and public relations events. Other clients include Burger King (the Subserviant Chicken campaign), Molson, Maxim, Victoria's Secret, EarthLink, The Gap, and Virgin Atlantic.[20]

Concept Check

1. The Federal Communications Commission suggests that advertising program decisions be based on ______________.
2. Describe three common forms of advertising appeals.

Selecting the Right Media

Every advertiser must select the *advertising media* in which to place its ads. Examples of media options include newspapers, magazines, radio, and TV. This media selection decision is related to the target audience, type of product, nature of the message, campaign objectives, available budget, and the costs of the alternative media. Figure 16–1 shows the distribution of the $263 billion spent on advertising among the many media alternatives.[21]

In deciding where to place advertisements, a company has several media to choose from and a number of alternatives, or vehicles, within each medium. Often advertisers use a mix of media forms and vehicles to maximize the exposure of the message to the target audience while at the same time minimizing costs. These two conflicting goals of (1) maximizing exposure and (2) minimizing costs are of central importance to media planning.

Because advertisers try to maximize the number of individuals in the target market exposed to the message, they must be concerned with reach. *Reach* is the number of different people or households exposed to an advertisement. The exact definition of reach sometimes varies among alternative media. Newspapers often use reach to describe their total circulation or the number of different households that buy the paper. Television and radio stations, in contrast, describe their reach using the term *rating*—the percentage of households in a market that are tuned to a particular TV show or radio station. In general, advertisers try to maximize reach in their target market at the lowest cost.

Although reach is important, advertisers are also interested in exposing their target audience to a message more than once. This is because consumers often do not pay

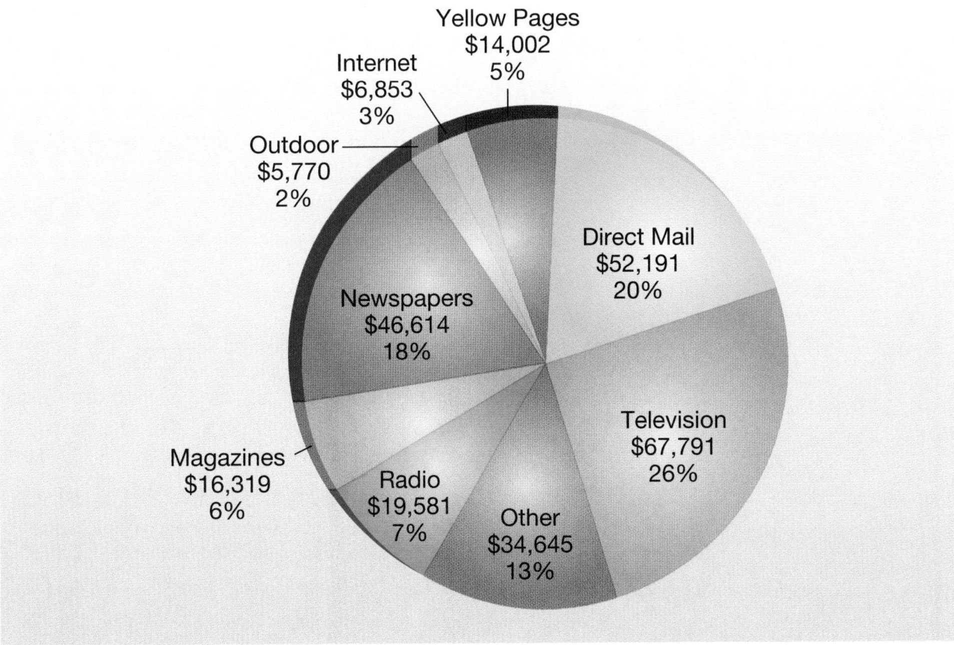

FIGURE 16–1
U.S. advertising expenditures, by category (in millions of dollars)

close attention to advertising messages, some of which contain large amounts of relatively complex information. When advertisers want to reach the same audience more than once, they are concerned with *frequency,* the average number of times a person in the target audience is exposed to a message or advertisement. Like reach, greater frequency is generally viewed as desirable.[22] Studies indicate that with repeated exposure to advertisements consumers respond more favorably to brand extensions.[23]

When reach (expressed as a percentage of the total market) is multiplied by frequency, an advertiser will obtain a commonly used reference number called *gross rating points* (GRPs). To obtain the appropriate number of GRPs to achieve an advertising campaign's objectives, the media planner must balance reach and frequency. The balance will also be influenced by cost. *Cost per thousand* (CPM) refers to the cost of reaching 1,000 individuals or households with the advertising message in a given medium (*M* is the Roman numeral for 1,000).

Different Media Alternatives

Figure 16–2 (on the next page) summarizes the advantages and disadvantages of the major advertising media, which are described in more detail below. Direct mail was discussed in Chapter 15.

Television Television is a valuable medium because it communicates with sight, sound, and motion. Print advertisements alone could never give you the sense of a sports car accelerating from a stop or cornering at high speed. In addition, network television is the only medium that can reach 95 percent of the homes in the United States.[24] Recent studies have shown that *out-of-home TV* reaches another 20 million viewers in bars, hotels, offices, and college campuses each week.[25] In addition, cable channels such as ESPN, MTV, We, the Speed Channel, the History Channel, and the Outdoor Life Network reach very narrowly defined audiences.

Television's major disadvantage is cost: The price of a prime-time, 30-second ad run on *American Idol* is $518,466, and the average price for all prime-time programs is approximately $150,000.[26] Because of these high charges, many advertisers choose less expensive "spot" ads, which run between programs in 10-, 15-, 30-, or 60-second lengths. Shorter ads reduce costs but severely restrict the amount of information and emotion that can be conveyed. Research indicates, however, that two different versions of a 15-second commercial, run back-to-back, will increase recall over long intervals.[27]

MEDIUM	ADVANTAGES	DISADVANTAGES
Television	Reaches extremely large audience; uses picture, print, sound, and motion for effect; can target specific audiences	High cost to prepare and run ads; short exposure time and perishable message; difficult to convey complex information
Radio	Low cost; can target specific local audiences; ads can be placed quickly; can use sound, humor, and intimacy effectively	No visual element; short exposure time and perishable message; difficult to convey complex information
Magazines	Can target specific audiences; high-quality color; long life of ad; ads can be clipped and saved; can convey complex information	Long time needed to place ad; relatively high cost; competes for attention with other magazine features
Newspapers	Excellent coverage of local markets; ads can be placed and changed quickly; ads can be saved; quick consumer response; low cost	Ads compete for attention with other newspaper features; short life span; poor color
Yellow pages	Excellent coverage of geographic segments; long use period; available 24 hours/365 days	Proliferation of competitive directories in many markets; difficult to keep up-to-date
Internet	Video and audio capabilities; animation can capture attention; ads can be interactive and link to advertiser	Animation and interactivity require large files and more time to load; effectiveness is still uncertain
Outdoor	Low cost; local market focus; high visibility; opportunity for repeat exposures	Message must be short and simple; low selectivity of audience; criticized as a traffic hazard
Direct mail	High selectivity of audience; can contain complex information and personalized messages; high-quality graphics	High cost per contact; poor image (junk mail)

SOURCES: William F. Arens, *Contemporary Advertising,* 9th ed. (New York: McGraw-Hill/Irwin, 2004), pp. 268, R20; and William G. Nickels, James M. McHugh, and Susan M. McHugh, *Understanding Business,* 7th ed. (Burr Ridge, IL: McGraw-Hill/Irwin, 2005), p. 493.

FIGURE 16–2
Advantages and disadvantages of major advertising media

Another popular form of television advertising is the infomercial. **Infomercials** are program-length (30-minute) advertisements that take an educational approach to communication with potential customers. Today, more than 90 percent of all TV stations air infomercials, and more than 25 percent of all consumers have purchased a product as a result of seeing an infomercial.

infomercials
Program-length (30-minute) advertisements that take an educational approach to communication with potential customers

Radio There are seven times as many radio stations as television stations in the United States. The major advantage of radio is that it is a segmented medium. There are the Farm Radio Network, the Physicians' Network, all-talk shows, and hard rock stations, all listened to by different market segments. The average college student is a surprisingly heavy radio listener and spends more time during the day listening to radio than watching network television—2.2 hours versus 1.6 hours. Thus, advertisers with college students as their target market must consider radio.

The disadvantage of radio is that it has limited use for products that must be seen. Another problem is the ease with which consumers can tune out a commercial by switching stations. A new form of radio available through satellite services offers up to

100 digital-quality coast-to-coast radio channels to consumers for a monthly subscription fee. Sirius Satellite Radio and XM Satellite Radio offer commercial-free channels and channels with only about 6 minutes of advertising per hour compared with 15 to 20 minutes heard on "free" channels.[28] Radio is also a medium that competes for people's attention as they do other activities such as driving, working, or relaxing. Peak radio listening time is during the drive times (6 to 10 A.M. and 4 to 7 P.M.).

Magazines Magazines have become a very specialized medium, primarily because there are currently more than 6,200 magazines. New magazines are introduced each year, such as *Budget Living,* a personal finance magazine for women; and *American Thunder,* a magazine about NASCAR racing for men. The marketing advantage of this medium is the great number of special-interest publications that appeal to narrowly defined segments. Runners read *Runner's World,* sailors buy *Yachting,* gardeners subscribe to *Garden Design,* and teenagers peruse *Teen People.* More than 675 publications focus on computers and technology, 669 are dedicated to travel, and 500 magazine titles are related to music.[29] Each magazine's readers often represent a unique profile. Take the *Rolling Stone* reader, who tends to listen to music more than most people—so Sony knows an ad for its E500 Network Walkman (which includes an MP3 player and an FM tuner) in *Rolling Stone* is reaching the desired target audience. In addition to the distinct audience profiles of magazines, good color production is an advantage that allows magazines to create strong images.[30]

The cost of advertising in national magazines is a disadvantage, but many national publications publish regional and even metro editions, which reduce the absolute cost and wasted coverage. *Time* publishes well over 400 different editions, including Latin American, Canadian, Asian, South Pacific, European, and U.S. editions. The U.S. editions include national, demographic, regional, state, and city options.

Newspapers Newspapers are an important local medium with excellent reach potential. Because of the daily publication of most papers, they allow advertisements to focus on specific current events, such as a 24-hour sale. Local retailers often use newspapers as their sole advertising medium. Newspapers are rarely saved by the purchaser, however, so companies are generally limited to ads that call for an immediate customer response (although customers can clip and save ads they select). Companies also cannot depend on newspapers for color reproduction as good as that in most magazines.

National advertising campaigns rarely include this medium except in conjunction with local distributors of their products. In these instances, both parties often share the advertising costs using a cooperative advertising program, which is described later in this chapter. Another exception is the use of newspapers such as *The Wall Street Journal* and *USA Today,* each of which have national distribution of more than 2 million readers.

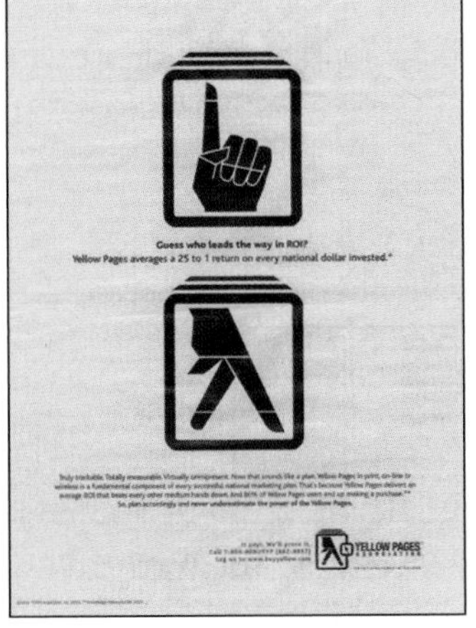

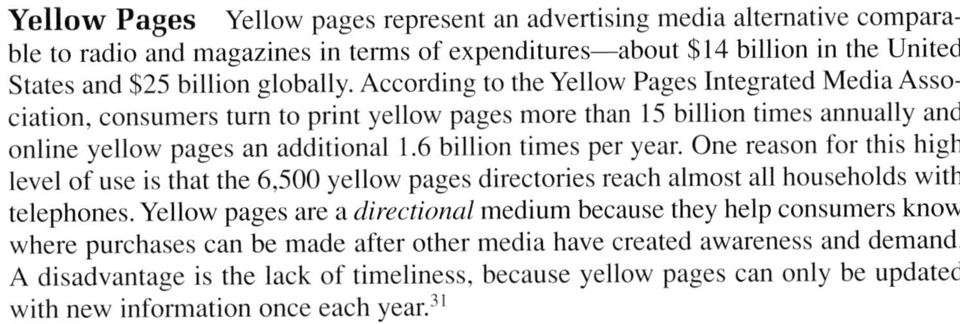

Yellow Pages Yellow pages represent an advertising media alternative comparable to radio and magazines in terms of expenditures—about $14 billion in the United States and $25 billion globally. According to the Yellow Pages Integrated Media Association, consumers turn to print yellow pages more than 15 billion times annually and online yellow pages an additional 1.6 billion times per year. One reason for this high level of use is that the 6,500 yellow pages directories reach almost all households with telephones. Yellow pages are a *directional* medium because they help consumers know where purchases can be made after other media have created awareness and demand. A disadvantage is the lack of timeliness, because yellow pages can only be updated with new information once each year.[31]

Internet The Internet represents a relatively new medium for advertisers although it has already attracted a wide variety of industries. Online advertising is similar to print advertising in that it offers a visual message. It has additional advantages, however, because it can also use the audio and video capabilities of the Internet. Sound and movement may simply attract more attention from viewers, or they may

provide an element of entertainment to the message. Online advertising also has the unique feature of being interactive. Called *rich media,* these interactive ads have drop-down menus, built-in games, or search engines to engage viewers.[32] Although online advertising is relatively small compared to other traditional media, it offers an opportunity to reach younger consumers who have developed a preference for online communication.[33]

A disadvantage to online advertising is the difficulty of measuring impact. Online advertising lags behind radio, TV, and print in offering advertisers proof of effectiveness. To address this issue several companies are testing methods of tracking where viewers go on their computer in the days and weeks after seeing an ad. Nielsen's rating service, for example, measures actual click-by-click behavior through meters installed on the computers of 225,000 individuals in 26 countries both at home and at work (see www.nielsen-netratings.com for recent ratings).

Outdoor A very effective medium for reminding consumers about your product is outdoor advertising, such as the *billboards* used by Calvin Klein. This most common form of outdoor advertising often results in good reach and frequency and has been shown to increase purchase rates.[34] The visibility of this medium is good supplemental reinforcement for well-known products, and it is a relatively low-cost, flexible alternative. A company can buy space just in the desired geographical market. A disadvantage to billboards, however, is that no opportunity exists for lengthy advertising copy. Also, a good billboard site depends on traffic patterns and sight lines. In many areas, environmental laws have limited the use of this medium.

If you have ever lived in a metropolitan area, chances are you might have seen another form of outdoor advertising, *transit advertising.* This medium includes messages on the interior and exterior of buses, subway cars, and taxis. As use of mass transit grows, transit advertising may become increasingly important. Selectivity is available to advertisers, who can buy space by neighborhood or bus route. One disadvantage to this medium is that the heavy travel times, when the audiences are the largest, are not conducive to reading advertising copy. People are standing shoulder to shoulder on the subway, hoping not to miss their stop, and little attention is paid to the advertising.

Other Media As traditional media have become more expensive and cluttered, advertisers have been attracted to a variety of nontraditional advertising options, called *place-based media.* Messages are placed in locations that attract a specific target audience such as airports, doctors' offices, health clubs, theaters (where ads are played on the screen before the movies are shown), even bathrooms of bars, restaurants, and nightclubs.[35] Soon there will be advertising on video screens on gas pumps, ATMs, and in elevators. New York's La Guardia airport has started putting ads on baggage conveyors, and Beach 'n Billboard will even imprint ads in the sand on a beach.[36]

Scheduling the Advertising

There is no correct schedule to advertise a product, but three factors must be considered. First is the issue of *buyer turnover,* which is how often new buyers enter the market to buy the product. The higher the buyer turnover, the greater is the amount of advertising required. A second issue in scheduling is the *purchase frequency;* the more frequently the product is purchased, the less repetition is required. Finally, companies must consider the *forgetting rate,* the speed with which buyers forget the brand if advertising is not seen.

Setting schedules requires an understanding of how the market behaves. Most companies tend to follow one of three basic approaches:

1. *Continuous (steady) schedule.* When seasonal factors are unimportant, advertising is run at a continuous or steady schedule throughout the year.
2. *Flighting (intermittent) schedule.* Periods of advertising are scheduled between periods of no advertising to reflect seasonal demand.
3. *Pulse (burst) schedule.* A flighting schedule is combined with a continuous schedule because of increases in demand, heavy periods of promotion, or introduction of a new product.

For example, products such as dry breakfast cereals have a stable demand throughout the year and would typically use a continuous schedule of advertising. In contrast, products such as snow skis and suntan lotions have seasonal demands and receive flighting-schedule advertising during the seasonal demand period. Some products such as toys or automobiles require pulse-schedule advertising to facilitate sales throughout the year and during special periods of increased demand (such as holidays or new car introductions).

Concept Check

1. You see the same ad in *Time* and *Fortune* magazines and on billboards and TV. Is this an example of reach or frequency?
2. Why has the Internet become a popular advertising medium?
3. Describe three approaches to scheduling advertising.

EXECUTING THE ADVERTISING PROGRAM

Executing the advertising program involves pretesting the advertising copy and actually carrying out the advertising program. John Wanamaker, the founder of Wanamaker's Department Store in Philadelphia, remarked, "I know half my advertising is wasted, but I don't know what half." By evaluating advertising efforts, marketers can try to ensure that their advertising expenditures are not wasted.[37] Evaluation is done usually at two separate times: before and after the advertisements are run in the actual campaign. Several methods used in the evaluation process at the stages of idea formulation and copy development are discussed below. Posttesting methods are reviewed in the section on evaluation.

Pretesting the Advertising

pretests
Tests conducted before an advertisement is placed to determine whether it communicates the intended message or to select among alternative versions of an advertisement

To determine whether the advertisement communicates the intended message or to select among alternative versions of the advertisement, **pretests** are conducted before the advertisements are placed in any medium.

Portfolio Tests Portfolio tests are used to test copy alternatives. The test ad is placed in a portfolio with several other ads and stories, and consumers are asked to read through the portfolio. Afterward, subjects are asked for their impressions of the ads on several evaluative scales, such as from "very informative" to "not very informative."

Jury Tests Jury tests involve showing the ad copy to a panel of consumers and having them rate how they liked it, how much it drew their attention, and how attractive they thought it was. This approach is similar to the portfolio test in that consumer reactions are obtained. However, unlike the portfolio test, a test advertisement is not hidden within other ads.

Theater Tests Theater testing is the most sophisticated form of pretesting. Consumers are invited to view new television shows or movies in which test commercials are also shown. Viewers register their feelings about the advertisements either on handheld electronic recording devices used during the viewing or on questionnaires afterward.

Carrying Out the Advertising Program

The responsibility for actually carrying out the advertising program can be handled by one of three types of agencies. The *full-service agency* provides the most complete range of services, including market research, media selection, copy development, artwork, and production. Agencies that assist a client by both developing and placing advertisements have traditionally charged a commission of 15 percent of media costs. As corporations have introduced integrated marketing approaches, however, most (70 percent) advertisers have switched from paying commissions to incentives or fees based on performance. The most common performance criteria used are sales, brand and ad awareness, market share, and copy test results. *Limited-service agencies* specialize in one aspect of the advertising process such as providing creative services to develop the advertising copy or buying previously unpurchased media space. Limited-service agencies that deal in creative work are compensated by a contractual agreement for the services performed. Finally, *in-house agencies* made up of the company's own advertising staff may provide full services or a limited range of services.

EVALUATING THE ADVERTISING PROGRAM

The advertising decision process does not stop with executing the advertising program. The advertisements must be posttested to determine whether they are achieving their intended objectives, and results may indicate that changes must be made in the advertising program.

Posttesting the Advertising

posttests
Tests conducted after an advertisement has been shown to the target audience to determine whether it has accomplished its intended purpose

An advertisement may go through **posttests** after it has been shown to the target audience to determine whether it accomplished its intended purpose. Five approaches common in posttesting are discussed here.[38]

Aided Recall (Recognition-Readership) After being shown an ad, respondents are asked whether their previous exposure to it was through reading, viewing, or listening. The Starch test shown in the accompanying photo uses aided recall to determine the percentage of those (1) who remember seeing a specific magazine ad (*noted*), (2) who saw or read any part of the ad identifying the product or brand (*seen-associated*), and (3) who read at least half of the ad (*read most*). Elements of the ad are then tagged with the results, as shown in the picture.

Starch scores an advertisement.

Unaided Recall A question such as "What ads do you remember seeing yesterday?" is asked of respondents without any prompting to determine whether they saw or heard advertising messages.

Attitude Tests Respondents are asked questions to measure changes in their attitudes after an advertising campaign, such as whether they have a more favorable attitude toward the product advertised.[39]

Inquiry Tests Additional product information, product samples, or premiums are offered to an ad's readers or viewers. Ads generating the most inquiries are presumed to be the most effective.

Sales Tests Sales tests involve studies such as controlled experiments (e.g., using radio ads in one market and newspaper ads in another and comparing the results) and consumer purchase tests (measuring retail sales that result from a given advertising campaign). The most sophisticated experimental methods today allow a manufacturer, a distributor, or an advertising agency to manipulate an advertising variable (such as schedule or copy) through cable systems and observe subsequent sales effects by monitoring data collected from checkout scanners in supermarkets.[40]

Concept Check

1. Explain the difference between pretesting and posttesting advertising copy.
2. What is the difference between aided and unaided recall posttests?

SALES PROMOTION

Sales promotion has become a key element of the promotional mix, which now accounts for more than $288 billion in annual expenditures. In a recent survey by the Promotion Marketing Association, marketing professionals reported that approximately 23 percent of their budgets were allocated to advertising, 15 percent to consumer promotion, 19 percent to trade promotion, and 7 percent to public relations and customer service.[41] The allocation of marketing expenditures reflects the trend toward integrated promotion programs which include a variety of promotion elements. Selection and integration of the many promotion techniques require a good understanding of the advantages and disadvantages of each kind of promotion.[42]

Consumer-Oriented Sales Promotions

consumer-oriented sales promotions
Sales tools, such as coupons, sweepstakes, and samples, used to support a company's advertising and personal selling efforts directed to ultimate consumers

Directed to ultimate consumers, **consumer-oriented sales promotions**, or simply *consumer promotions,* are sales tools used to support a company's advertising and personal selling. The alternative consumer-oriented sales promotion tools include coupons, deals, premiums, contests, sweepstakes, samples, loyalty programs, point-of-purchase displays, rebates, and product placement.

Coupons Coupons are sales promotions that usually offer a discounted price to the consumer, which encourages trial. Approximately 258 billion coupons are distributed in the United States each year. The redemption rate is typically about 2 percent, and the average face value of redeemed coupons is about $.80. In recent years the average face value of coupons, the number of coupons with multiple-purchase requirements, and the time until expiration have all been increasing.[43]

Coupons are often far more expensive than the face value of the coupon; a 25 cent coupon can cost three times that after paying for the advertisement to deliver it, dealer handling, clearinghouse costs, and redemption. In addition, misredemption, or paying the face value of the coupon even though the product was not purchased, should be added to the cost of the coupon. The Coupon Information Corporation estimates that companies pay out refunds of more than $500 million each year as a result of coupon fraud.[44]

Deals Deals are short-term price reductions, commonly used to increase trial among potential customers or to retaliate against a competitor's actions. For example, if a rival manufacturer introduces a new cake mix, the company responds with a "two packages for the price of one" deal. This short-term price reduction builds up the stock on the kitchen shelves of cake mix buyers and makes the competitor's introduction more difficult. However, a deal may also reduce the perceived value of the product.

Premiums A promotional tool often used with consumers is the premium, which consists of either merchandise offered free or merchandise offered at a significant savings over its retail price. This latter type of premium is called *self-liquidating* because the cost charged to the consumer covers the cost of the item. Milk-Bone dog biscuits used a self-liquidating premium when it offered a ball toy for $8.99 and two proofs of purchase.[45] By offering a premium, companies encourage customers to return frequently or to use more of the product, although they may buy only for the premium rather than the product.

Contests A fourth sales promotion is the contest, where consumers apply their skill or analytical or creative thinking to try to win a prize. For example, Brawny paper towel brand sponsored the "Do You Know a Brawny Man?" contest, which asked participants to send photos and a 150-word description explaining why the nominee was as rugged as the product. The winning nominee got a Dodge Durango and his photo on the Brawny packages. The contest increased the number of households using the product by 10 percent and increased sales by 12 percent.[46] If you like contests, you can even enter online now at websites such as www.playhere.com.

Sweepstakes *Readers Digest* and Publisher's Clearing House are two well-known sweepstakes. These sales promotions require participants to submit some kind of entry but are purely games of chance requiring no analytical or creative effort by the consumer.[47] Two variations of sweepstakes are popular now. First is the instant-win game such as Nestlé's music download promotion. The second is the sweepstakes that offers an "experience" as the prize. For example, AT&T's "Live Like an Idol" sweepstakes offers viewers of *American Idol* a trip to New York City or Los Angeles if they win. Federal laws, the Federal Trade Commission, and state legislatures have issued rules

Consumer-oriented promotions use sweepstakes to attract prospective customers and loyalty programs to reward repeat customers.

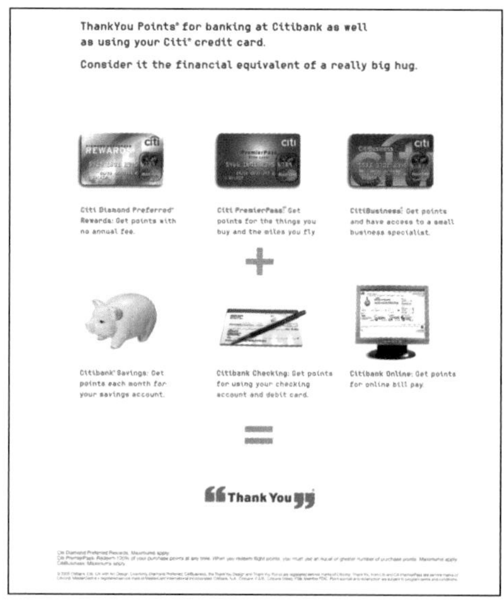

covering sweepstakes, contests, and games to regulate fairness, ensure that the chance for winning is represented honestly, and guarantee that the prizes are actually awarded.[48]

Samples Another common consumer sales promotion is sampling, which is offering the product free or at a greatly reduced price. Often used for new products, sampling puts the product in the consumer's hands. A trial size is generally offered that is smaller than the regular package size. If consumers like the sample, it is hoped they will remember and buy the product. When Mars changed its Milky Way Dark to Milky Way Midnight, it gave away more than 1 million samples to college students at night clubs, several hundred campuses, and popular spring break locations. Awareness of the candy bar rose to 60 percent, trial rose 166 percent, and sales rose 25 percent. Overall, companies invest more than $1.5 billion in sampling programs each year.[49]

Loyalty Programs Loyalty programs are a sales promotion tool used to encourage and reward repeat purchases by acknowledging each purchase made by a consumer and offering a premium as purchases accumulate. The most popular loyalty programs today are the frequent-flier and frequent-traveler programs used by airlines, hotels, and car rental services to reward loyal customers. American Airlines customers, for example, earn points for each mile they fly and can then redeem the accumulated points for free tickets or upgrades on the airline. Loyalty programs are also becoming popular in other product categories. Citibank, for example, offers "ThankYou Points" to its banking and credit card customers. How many people participate in loyalty programs? There are now more than 4 billion memberships, for an average of four for each adult in the United States.[50]

Point-of-Purchase Displays In a store aisle, you often encounter a sales promotion called a *point-of-purchase display.* These product displays take the form of advertising signs, which sometimes actually hold or display the product, and are often located in high-traffic areas near the cash register or the end of an aisle. The accompanying picture shows a point-of-purchase display for Nabisco's annual back-to-school program. The display is designed to maximize the consumer's attention to lunch box and after-school snacks, and to provide storage for the products. A recent survey of retailers found that 87 percent plan to use more point-of-purchase materials in the future, particularly for products that can be purchased on impulse,[51] although aisle space is limited.

Rebates Another consumer sales promotion, the cash rebate, offers the return of money based on proof of purchase. This tool has been used heavily by car manufacturers facing increased competition. For example, Ford offers recent college graduates a $400 rebate on many of its vehicles, as part of its College Graduate Purchase Program.[52] When a rebate is offered on lower-priced items, the time and trouble of mailing in a proof of purchase to get the rebate check often means that many buyers never take advantage of it. However, this "slippage" is less likely to occur with frequent users of rebate promotions.[53] In addition, online consumers are more likely to take advantage of rebates.

product placement
Using a brand-name product in a movie, television show, video, or commercial for another product

Product Placement A final consumer promotion, **product placement**, involves the use of a brand-name product in a movie, television show, video, or commercial for another product. It was Steven Spielberg's placement of Hershey's Reese's Pieces in *E.T.* that first brought a lot of interest to the candy. Similarly, when Tom Cruise wore Bausch and Lomb's Ray-Ban sunglasses in *Risky Business* and its Aviator glasses in *Top Gun,* sales skyrocketed from 100,000 pairs to 7,000,000 pairs in five years. More recently, you might remember seeing participants in the television show *Survivor* eating Doritos and drinking Mountain Dew, actors in the *Matrix* movies using Samsung cellular telephones, and women in the cast of *All My Children* using

Can you identify these product placements?

Revlon products. The James Bond movie *Die Another Day* features Jaguars, Aston Martins, and Thunderbirds, all Ford products. Similarly, Cameron Diaz and Shirley MacLaine drive Jaguars in *In Her Shoes*. Another form of product placement uses new digital technology that can make virtual placements in an existing program. Reruns of *Seinfeld,* for example, could insert a Pepsi on a desktop, a Lexus parked on the street, or a box of Tide on the countertop.[54]

Trade-Oriented Sales Promotions

trade-oriented sales promotions
Sales tools used to support a company's advertising and personal selling efforts directed to wholesalers, distributors, or retailers

Trade-oriented sales promotions, or simply *trade promotions,* are sales tools used to support a company's advertising and personal selling directed to wholesalers, retailers, or distributors. Some of the sales promotions just reviewed are used for this purpose, but there are three other common approaches targeted uniquely to these intermediaries: (1) allowances and discounts, (2) cooperative advertising, and (3) training of distributors' salesforces.

Allowances and Discounts Trade promotions often focus on maintaining or increasing inventory levels in the channel of distribution. An effective method for encouraging such increased purchases by intermediaries is the use of allowances and discounts. However, overuse of these price reductions can lead to retailers changing their ordering patterns in the expectation of such offerings. Although there are many variations that manufacturers can use with discounts and allowances, three common approaches are the merchandise allowance, the case allowance, and the finance allowance.[55]

Reimbursing a retailer for extra in-store support or special featuring of the brand is a *merchandise allowance.* Performance contracts between the manufacturer and trade member usually specify the activity to be performed, such as a picture of the product in a newspaper with a coupon good at only one store. The merchandise allowance then consists of a percentage deduction from the list case price ordered during the promotional period. Allowances are not paid by the manufacturer until it sees proof of performance (such as a copy of the ad placed by the retailer in the local newspaper).

A second common trade promotion, a *case allowance,* is a discount on each case ordered during a specific time period. These allowances are usually deducted from the invoice. A variation of the case allowance is the "free goods" approach, whereby retailers receive some amount of the product free based on the amount ordered, such as 1 case free for every 10 cases ordered.[56]

A final trade promotion, the *finance allowance,* involves paying retailers for financing costs or financial losses associated with consumer sales promotions. This trade promotion is regularly used and has several variations. One type is the floor stock protection program—manufacturers give retailers a case allowance price for products in their warehouse, which prevents shelf stock from running down during the promotional period. Also common are freight allowances, which compensate retailers that transport orders from the manufacturer's warehouse.

cooperative advertising
Advertising programs by which a manufacturer pays a percentage of the retailer's local advertising expense for advertising the manufacturer's products

Cooperative Advertising Resellers often perform the important function of promoting the manufacturer's products at the local level. One common sales promotional activity is to encourage both better quality and greater quantity in the local advertising efforts of resellers through **cooperative advertising**. These are programs by which a manufacturer pays a percentage of the retailer's local advertising expense for advertising the manufacturer's products.

Usually the manufacturer pays a percentage, often 50 percent, of the cost of advertising up to a certain dollar limit, which is based on the amount of the purchases the retailer makes of the manufacturer's products. In addition to paying for the advertising, the manufacturer often furnishes the retailer with a selection of different ad executions, sometimes suited for several different media. A manufacturer may provide, for example, several different print layouts as well as a few broadcast ads for the retailer to adapt and use.[57]

Training of Distributors' Salesforces One of the many functions the intermediaries perform is customer contact and selling for the producers they represent. Both retailers and wholesalers employ and manage their own sales personnel. A manufacturer's success often rests on the ability of the reseller's salesforce to represent its products.

Thus, it is in the best interest of the manufacturer to help train the reseller's salesforce. Because the reseller's salesforce is often less sophisticated and knowledgeable about the products than the manufacturer might like, training can increase their sales performance. Training activities include producing manuals and brochures to educate the reseller's salesforce. The salesforce then uses these aids in selling situations.

PUBLIC RELATIONS

publicity tools
Methods of obtaining nonpersonal presentation of an organization, good, or service without direct cost

As noted in Chapter 15, public relations is a form of communication management that seeks to influence the image of an organization and its products and services. In developing a public relations campaign, several methods of obtaining nonpersonal presentation of an organization, good, or service without direct cost—**publicity tools**—are available to the public relations director. Many companies frequently use the *news release,* consisting of an announcement regarding changes in the company or the product line. The objective of a news release is to inform a newspaper, radio station, or other medium of an idea for a story. A recent study found that more than 40 percent of all free mentions of a brand name occur during news programs.[58]

A second common publicity tool is the *news conference.* Representatives of the media are all invited to an informational meeting, and advance materials regarding the content are sent. This tool is often used when negative publicity—as in the cases of the Ford Explorer rollover problem, the NASCAR Daytona 500 accident that killed Dale Earnhardt, and the *Exxon Valdez* oil spill—requires a company response.[59]

Nonprofit organizations rely heavily on *public service announcements* (PSAs), which are free space or time donated by the media. For example, the charter of the American Red Cross prohibits any local chapter from advertising, so to solicit blood donations local chapters often depend on PSAs on radio or television to announce their needs.

Concept Check

1. Which sales promotional tool is most common for new products?
2. Which trade promotion is used to encourage local advertising efforts of resellers?
3. What is a news release?

CHAPTER IN REVIEW

1 *Explain the differences between product advertising and institutional advertising and the variations within each type.*
Product advertisements focus on selling a good or service and take three forms: Pioneering advertisements tell people what a product is, what it can do, and where it can be found; competitive advertisements persuade the target market to select the firm's brand rather than a competitor's; and reminder advertisements reinforce previous knowledge of a product. Institutional advertisements are used to build goodwill or an image for an organization. They include advocacy advertisements, which state the position of a company on an issue, and pioneering, competitive, and reminder advertisements, which are similar to the product ads but focused on the institution.

2 *Describe the steps used to develop, execute, and evaluate an advertising program.*
The promotion decision process can be applied to each of the promotional elements. The steps to develop an advertising program include identify the target audience, specify the advertising objectives, set the advertising budget, design the advertisement, create the message, select the media, and schedule the advertising. Executing the program requires pretesting, and evaluating the program requires posttesting.

3 *Explain the advantages and disadvantages of alternative advertising media.*
Television advertising reaches large audiences and uses picture, print, sound, and motion; its disadvantages, however, are that it is expensive and perishable. Radio advertising is inexpensive and can be placed quickly, but it has no visual element and is perishable. Magazine advertising can target specific audiences and can convey complex information, but it takes a long time to place the ad and is relatively expensive. Newspapers provide excellent coverage of local markets and can be changed quickly, but they have a short life span and poor color. Yellow pages advertising has a long use period and is available 24 hours per day; a disadvantage, however, is that they cannot be updated frequently. Internet advertising can be interactive, but its effectiveness is difficult to measure. Outdoor advertising provides repeat exposures, but its message must be very short and simple. Direct mail can be targeted at very selective audiences, but its cost per contact is high.

4 *Discuss the strengths and weaknesses of consumer-oriented and trade-oriented sales promotions.*
Coupons encourage consumer trial but are more expensive than face value. Deals respond to competitor actions but reduce perceived value. Premiums offer consumers additional merchandise they want, but they may be purchasing only for the premium. Contests create involvement but require creative thinking. Sweepstakes are popular and substantially regulated. Samples put the product in consumers' hands but are expensive. Loyalty programs encourage repeat purchases but are expensive to run. Displays provide visibility but are difficult to place in retail space. Rebates stimulate demand but are easily copied. Product placement provides a positive message in a noncommercial setting but is difficult to control. Trade-oriented sales promotions include (*a*) allowances and discounts, which increase purchases but may change retailer ordering patterns, (*b*) cooperative advertising, which encourages local advertising, and (*c*) salesforce training, which helps increase sales by providing the salespeople with product information and selling skills.

5 *Recognize public relations as an important form of communication.*
Public relations activities usually focus on communicating positive aspects of the business. A frequently used public relations tool is publicity. Publicity tools include news releases and news conferences. Nonprofit organization often use public service announcements.

FOCUSING ON KEY TERMS

advertising p. 354
consumer-oriented sales promotions p. 365
cooperative advertising p. 368
infomercials p. 360
institutional advertisements p. 355
posttests p. 364
pretests p. 363
product advertisements p. 354
product placement p. 367
publicity tools p. 369
trade-oriented sales promotions p. 368

DISCUSSION AND APPLICATION QUESTIONS

1 How does competitive product advertising differ from competitive institutional advertising?

2 Suppose you are the advertising manager for a new line of children's fragrances. Which form of media would you use for this new product?

3 You have recently been promoted to be director of advertising for the Timkin Tool Company. In your first meeting with Mr. Timkin, he says, "Advertising is a waste! We've been advertising for six months now and sales haven't increased. Tell me why we should continue." Give your answer to Mr. Timkin.

4 A large life insurance company has decided to switch from using a strong fear appeal to a humorous approach. What are the strengths and weaknesses of such a change in message strategy?

5 Which medium has the lowest cost per thousand?

MEDIUM	COST	AUDIENCE
TV show	$5,000	25,000
Magazine	2,200	6,000
Newspaper	4,800	7,200
FM radio	420	1,600

6 Some national advertisers have found that they can have more impact with their advertising by running a large number of ads for a period and then running no ads at all for a period. Why might such a flighting schedule be more effective than a continuous schedule?

7 Each year managers at Bausch and Lomb evaluate the many advertising media alternatives available to them as they develop their advertising program for contact lenses. What advantages and disadvantages of each alternative should they consider? Which media would you recommend to them?

8 What are two advantages and two disadvantages of the advertising posttests described in the chapter?

9 Federated Banks is interested in consumer-oriented sales promotions that would encourage senior citizens to direct deposit their Social Security checks with the bank. Evaluate the sales promotion options, and recommend two of them to the bank.

10 How can public relations be used by Firestone and Ford following investigations into complaints about tire failures?

GOING ONLINE Advertising on the Internet

Most websites accept some form of advertising. If you were to advise your college or university to advertise on the Internet, what three sites would you recommend? Visit the Interactive Advertising Bureau website (www.iab.com) and review the "Standards and Guidelines" section to determine what type of online ad you would recommend.

1 How many types of (*a*) rectangles and pop-ups, (*b*) banners and buttons, and (*c*) skyscrapers does the IAB specify?

2 Describe the profile of the audience for each of the websites.

3 What does the IAB suggest you include in your online advertising privacy policy?

BUILDING YOUR MARKETING PLAN

To augment your promotion strategy from Chapter 15,

1 Use Figure 16–2 to select the advertising media you will include in your plan by analyzing how combinations of media (e.g., television and Internet advertising, radio and yellow pages advertising) can complement each other.

2 Select your consumer-oriented sales promotion activities.

3 Specify which trade-oriented sales promotions and public relations activities you will use.

VIDEO CASE 16 Fallon Worldwide: In the *Creativity* Business

"Most people think of Fallon as being in the advertising business, but we don't really think of ourselves that way," says Rob White, president of Fallon Worldwide. "We believe that we are a creativity company that happens to do some advertising," he continues. As an example, he points out that Fallon starts upstream of a firm's communication issues to identify the key business problem and uses creativity to help solve it. Sometimes this involves a heavy dose of advertising and other times almost none. But it always takes a very creative flair.

Founded in 1981, Fallon Worldwide—or simply Fallon—has won dozens of advertising awards. This includes two Agency of the Year awards given by *Advertising Age* magazine. "I think Fallon's success is due to two important things," says White. "One is the people and the other one is the culture that bonds the people together. When you create a special kind of culture with collaboration and teamwork from a very high level and people with different backgrounds, amazing things can happen," he explains.

Bruce Bildsten, Fallon creative group director, echoes this focus on creativity: "It's always a challenge as creative director to try to stay at the forefront and come up with something that people haven't seen. I desperately try not to look at other advertising for ideas. I always challenge our people to look at work from other parts of the world—film, novels, music—for inspiration."

A look at two promotional campaigns developed at Fallon show how creativity, teamwork, and not looking at traditional ads from other agencies come together to build award-winning campaigns. Both campaigns discussed below have been recognized for their creativity and their success at achieving the clients' objectives.

CITIBANK: ATTRACTING BALANCE SEEKERS

Citibank approached Fallon because it knew it had a problem. Citi had been successful in the past by being a low cost provider, having great service, and by focusing on direct marketing. Suddenly that wasn't enough. Competition had increased significantly and customer perceptions of banks and credit card companies had changed. Laurel Flatt, Fallon account director on the Citibank account, describes the challenge: "New banks were springing up all over the place. There were new credit card companies. Consumers looked at financial services as simply a commodity. Your relationship with your bank, your credit card company was once a very, very special relationship." Now, however, consumers viewed one bank as being no different than another.

When Citibank came to Fallon, it said that it really wanted to be "un-banklike," it wanted to be different. Fallon asked the question, "What is the right way to be un-banklike in a way that will generate results for the Citi brand?" Qualitative and quantitative research identified a segment of consumers that Fallon labeled "balance seekers." This group amounted to about 50 percent of the market for financial services. Balance seekers viewed financial services and money as a means to an end, something that helps them lead the life they live. This segment also shared an attitude that was receptive to the idea of an un-banklike message, though they had different income levels, assets, ages, and other demographic characteristics.

Fallon translated un-banklike to mean very friendly, human, and a little bit quirky—very different from the serious tone of traditional bank and financial services companies. In addition, Fallon wanted the Citi brand to represent a healthy approach to money. Finally, Fallon wanted to communicate that the credit card protects consumers and their purchases.

Fallon's ad executions were funny, and engaging. One ad shows a middle aged woman from Minnesota getting a tattoo. The tag line is "It didn't seem right to us, either" and talks about Citi's Fraud Early Warning system to identify unusual spending behavior. Another ad shows a truck driver from Iowa asleep under a hair dryer at La Petite Lily Day Spa with the same tag line and message about how Citi's identity theft solutions can help make things right. The Citi campaign utilized billboards and wall advertising, bus shelter kiosks, magazines, and television.

Fallon used brand-tracking to chart the degree of differentiation of the Citi brand. Over time, the differentiation climbed as more and more people perceived Citi as different from other banks yet relevant in their lives. Sales results were also positive. Card acquisition and card usage increased dramatically.

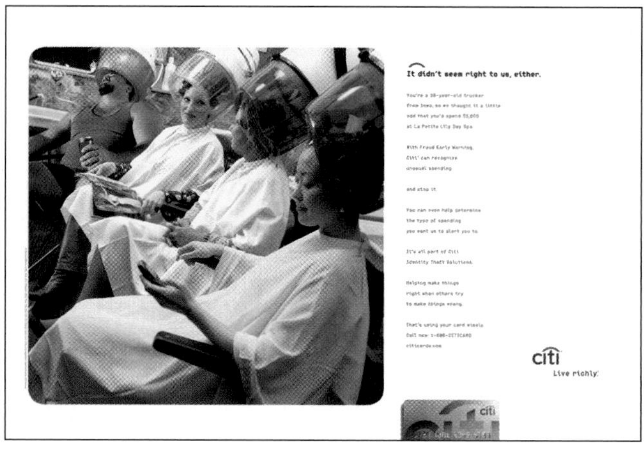

BMW: GRABBING ATTENTION WITH "THE HIRE"

Working closely together in the late 1990s, BMW and Fallon brainstormed, talked to consumers, and agonized over what the positioning of BMW should be. Their answer: "Responsiveness"—which means a performance vehicle that includes not only acceleration and braking but also its cornering, its safety.

The only problem with this was that soon major competitors like Mitsubishi and Ford were trying to adopt this "responsiveness" positioning for themselves. "So our first promotional objective was to separate BMW from its competitors as the only true, cool, legitimate, ultimate driving machine," says Ginny Grossman, Fallon group director. "We wanted the ownership of the 'responsiveness' position. We wanted people to associate that with BMW and only BMW."

"The target audience for 'The Hire' was BMW's future customer," says Erin Tait, Fallon senior account planner. "Today the average age of a BMW driver is 42. So what we wanted to do was make sure that the future audience, the 20- and 30-year-olds felt as good about the BMW brand as the 40- and 50-year-olds did. So, this campaign 'The Hire' was about making sure that the BMW brand was relevant and attractive to that younger audience."

Overseen by Hollywood directors such as Ang Lee and John Frankenheimer, "The Hire" is the title given to a series of short films launched on the Internet. They feature Clive Owen as the driver and carry provocative titles such as "Ambush," "Chosen," "The Follow," "Star," and "Powder Keg" in the first "season," and "Hostage," "Ticker," and "Beat the Devil" more recently in "The Hire II."

In trying to reach this younger market, a special problem emerged. "When we spoke to 20- and 30-year-olds about the BMW brand and what they thought it meant to them, they talked about things like being really into aggressive driving and risk-taking. That's the kind of person that would choose a BMW. But unfortunately, a lot of those attributes got taken in kind of a negative way," explains Tait.

"So our challenge was to take the positive value of the BMW brand. That's what Clive Owen in 'The Hire' really helped to do because the decisions he makes and the risks he takes are all for the good and for helping the person he's been hired to drive," says Tait. "You learn about this character through these movies which helps shape your perception of the kind of person that would choose a BMW. Plus it gives you a great sense for how the car performs in treacherous, difficult driving situations."

BMW and Fallon's next challenge was how to use these creative films to attract the attention of 20- and 30-year-olds and achieve "water cooler talk" the next day after they saw them on the Internet.

PUSHING THE CREATIVE BARRIERS

How does Fallon keep the creative juices flowing—from developing new promotional campaigns to using new media like the Internet? This involves continuing to develop award-winning commercials like "It's Time to Fly" for United Airlines and "Havana Nights" for Virgin Mobil, as well as the Citi and BMW campaigns.

Concerning new media, Kevin Flatt, Fallon Creative-Interactive, talks about the increasing importance of the Internet: "A number of our clients are recognizing now that they can get more focused connections to meaningful consumers with the Internet and be able to measure whether it's working or not." For people thinking about going into advertising, he tells what his job means to him: "If you love it, it is the most rewarding job because of how wonderful it is to be able to go and tell somebody 'I love what I do!'"

Questions

1 Fallon Worldwide stresses its creativity, as shown by comments from the Fallon people in the case. In what ways do the Citi and BMW campaigns reflect their creativity? Compare the sources of the ideas in the two campaigns.

2 In the Citi and BMW campaigns how were (*a*) the target markets and (*b*) each brand's positioning changed from the situation prior to the campaign?

3 Compare the media used for the Citi and BMW campaigns. Why were these media chosen? Do you expect the use of these or other media to change in the future?

4 How might Fallon and its clients measure the success of (*a*) the Citi and (*b*) the BMW campaigns?

CHAPTER 17

PERSONAL SELLING AND SALES MANAGEMENT

LEARNING OBJECTIVES

After reading this chapter you should be able to:

1. Discuss the nature and scope of personal selling and sales management in marketing.
2. Identify the different types of personal selling.
3. Explain the stages in the personal selling process.
4. Describe the major functions of sales management.

SELLING THE WAY CUSTOMERS WANT TO BUY

Anne Mulcahy has a challenging assignment. As the chairman of the board and chief executive officer at Xerox Corporation, she is in the midst of successfully implementing one of the greatest feats in the annals of business history: restoring Xerox's legendary marketing and financial vitality. Her success can be attributed to staying in sync with Xerox customers and employees. "I believe strongly that my success as a leader is driven by my commitment to understanding and meeting customers' requirements, as well as developing and nurturing a motivated and proud workforce," says Mulcahy (shown on the opposite page). "With the right amount of focus, the two have the potential to drive exceptional results."

Mulcahy is ideally suited to the task. She began her 30-year Xerox career as a field sales representative and assumed increasingly responsible management and executive positions. These included chief staff officer, president of Xerox's General Markets Operations, and president and chief operating officer of Xerox. As chairman and CEO, Mulcahy has to muster the knowledge and experience gained from this varied background. Not surprisingly, her sales background has played a pivotal role.

"We will win back market share one customer at a time, one sale at a time," Mulcahy says. "We'll do that by providing greater value than our competitors—and that means selling the way customers want to buy." She adds that Xerox must offer a broad range of products and services at competitive prices through direct, indirect, Internet, and telephone sales, and customer support. Her approach to sales, coupled with her considerable management experience, has already borne fruit as Xerox positions itself for future sales and profit growth.[1]

This chapter describes the scope and significance of personal selling and sales management in marketing. It first highlights the many forms of personal selling and outlines the selling process. Salesforce management functions are then described, including recent advances in salesforce automation and customer relationship management.

SCOPE AND SIGNIFICANCE OF PERSONAL SELLING AND SALES MANAGEMENT

Chapter 15 described personal selling and management of the sales effort as being part of the firm's promotional mix. Although it is important to recognize that personal selling is a useful means of communicating with present and potential buyers, it is much more.

Nature of Personal Selling and Sales Management

personal selling
The two-way flow of communication between a buyer and seller, often in a face-to-face encounter, designed to influence a person's or group's purchase decision

sales management
Planning the selling program and implementing the personal selling effort of the firm

Personal selling involves the two-way flow of communication between a buyer and seller, often in a face-to-face encounter, designed to influence a person's or group's purchase decision. However, with advances in telecommunications, personal selling also takes place over the telephone, through video teleconferencing and Internet-enabled links between buyers and sellers.

Personal selling remains a highly human-intensive activity despite the use of technology. Accordingly, the people involved must be managed. **Sales management** involves planning the selling program and implementing and controlling the personal selling effort of the firm. The tasks involved in managing personal selling include (1) setting objectives; (2) organizing the salesforce; (3) recruiting, selecting, training, and compensating salespeople; and (4) evaluating the performance of individual salespeople.

Selling Happens Almost Everywhere

"Everyone lives by selling something," wrote author Robert Louis Stevenson a century ago. His observation still holds true today. The Bureau of Labor Statistics reports that

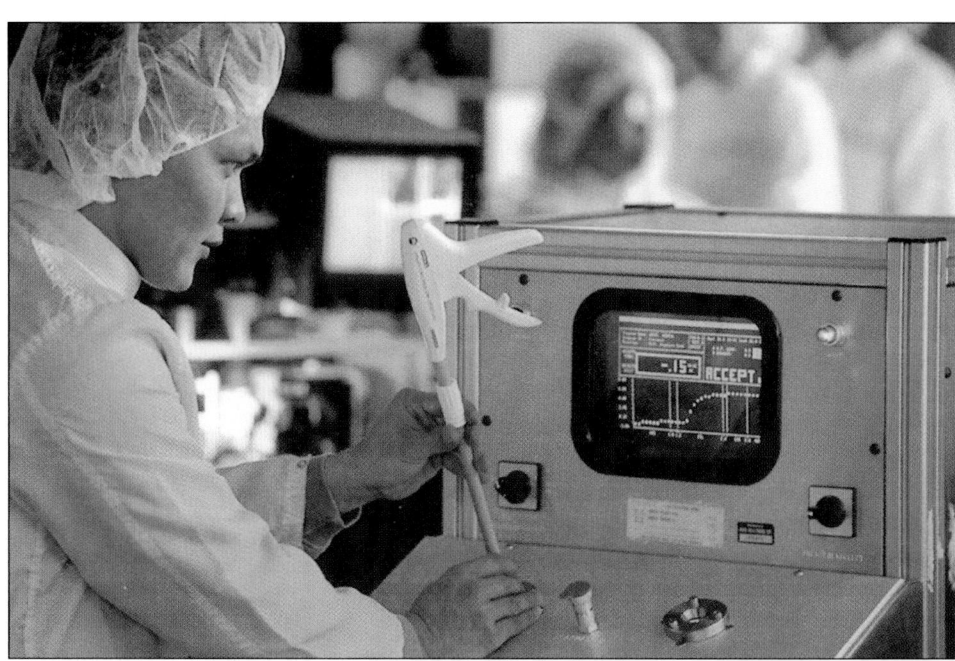

Could this be a salesperson in the operating room? Read the text to find why Medtronic salespeople visit hospital operating rooms.

almost 16 million people are employed in sales positions in the United States. Included in this number are manufacturing sales personnel, real estate brokers, stockbrokers, and salesclerks who work in retail stores. In reality, virtually every occupation that involves customer contact has an element of personal selling. For example, attorneys, accountants, bankers, and company personnel recruiters perform sales-related activities, whether or not they acknowledge it. About 20 percent of the chief executive officers in the largest U.S. corporations have significant sales and marketing experience in their work history like Anne Mulcahy at Xerox.[2] Thus, selling can serve as a stepping-stone to top management, as well as being a career path in itself.

Personal Selling in Marketing

Personal selling serves three major roles in a firm's overall marketing effort. First, salespeople are the critical link between the firm and its customers. This role requires that salespeople match company interests with customer needs to satisfy both parties in the exchange process. Second, salespeople *are* the company in a consumer's eyes. They represent what a company is or attempts to be and are often the only personal contact a customer has with the company. For example, the "look" projected by Gucci salespeople is an important factor in communicating the style of the company's apparel line. Third, personal selling may play a dominant role in a firm's marketing program. Avon, for example, pays almost 40 percent of its total sales dollars for selling expenses.

Creating Customer Value through Salespeople: Relationship Selling

As the critical link between the firm and its customers, salespeople can create customer value in many ways. For instance, by being close to the customer, salespeople can identify creative solutions to customer problems. Salespeople at Medtronic, Inc., the world leader in the heart pacemaker market, are in the operating room for more than 90 percent of the procedures performed with their product and are on call, wearing pagers, 24 hours a day. "It reflects the willingness to be there in every situation, just in case a problem arises—even though nine times out of ten the procedure goes just fine," notes a satisfied customer.[3] Salespeople can create value by easing the customer buying process. This happened at AMP, Inc., a producer of electrical products. Salespeople and customers had a difficult time getting product specifications and performance data on AMP's 70,000 products quickly and accurately. The company now records all information on CD-ROM disks that can be scanned instantly by salespeople and customers. Customer value is also created by salespeople who follow through after the sale. At Jefferson Smurfit Corporation, a multibillion-dollar supplier of packaging products, one of its salespeople juggled production from three of the company's plants to satisfy an unexpected demand for boxes from General Electric. This person's action led to the company being given GE's Distinguished Supplier Award.

relationship selling
Practice of building ties to customers based on a salesperson's attention and commitment to customer needs over time

Customer value creation is made possible by **relationship selling**, the practice of building ties to customers based on a salesperson's attention and commitment to customer needs over time. Relationship selling involves mutual respect and trust among buyers and sellers. It focuses on creating long-term customers, not a onetime sale. A recent survey of 300 senior sales executives revealed that 96 percent consider "building long-term relationships with customers" to be the most important activity affecting sales performance. Companies such as American Express, Electronic Data Systems, Motorola, and Owens-Corning have made relationship building a core focus of their sales effort.[4]

Relationship selling represents another dimension of customer relationship management. It emphasizes the importance of learning about customer needs and wants and tailoring solutions to customer problems as a means to customer value creation.

Concept Check

1. What is personal selling?
2. What is involved in sales management?

THE MANY FORMS OF PERSONAL SELLING

Personal selling assumes many forms based on the amount of selling done and the amount of creativity required to perform the sales task. Broadly speaking, two types of personal selling exist: order taking and order getting. While some firms use only one of these types of personal selling, others use a combination of both.

Order Taking

order taker
Processes routine orders or reorders for products that were already sold by the company

Typically, an **order taker** processes routine orders or reorders for products that were already sold by the company. The primary responsibility of order takers is to preserve an ongoing relationship with existing customers and maintain sales.

Two types of order takers exist. *Outside order takers* visit customers, arrange displays, and replace inventory stocks of resellers, such as retailers or wholesalers. For example, Frito-Lay salespeople call on supermarkets, neighborhood grocery stores, and other establishments to ensure that the company's line of snack products (such as Doritos and Tostitos tortilla chips) is in adequate supply. *Inside order takers,* also called *order clerks* or *salesclerks,* typically answer simple questions, take orders, and complete transactions with customers. Many retail clerks are inside order takers. Inside order takers are often employed by companies that use *inbound telemarketing,* the use of toll-free telephone numbers that customers can call to obtain information about products or services and make purchases.

Order takers generally do little selling in a conventional sense and engage in only modest problem solving with customers. They often represent products that have few options, such as confectionary items, magazine subscriptions, and highly standardized

A Frito-Lay salesperson takes inventory of snacks for the store manager to sign. In this situation, the manager will make a straight rebuy decision.

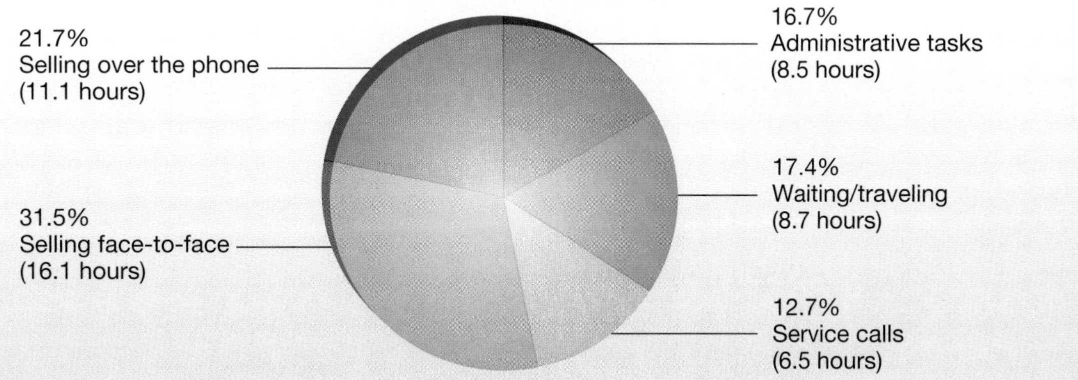

FIGURE 17–1
How outside order-getting salespeople spend their time each week

industrial products. Inbound telemarketing is also an essential selling activity for more customer-service–driven firms, such as Dell. At these companies, order takers undergo extensive training so that they can better assist callers with their purchase decisions.

Order Getting

order getter
Salesperson who sells in a conventional sense and identifies prospective customers, provides customers with information, persuades customers to buy, closes sales, and follows up on customers' use of a product or service

An **order getter** sells in a conventional sense and identifies prospective customers, provides customers with information, persuades customers to buy, closes sales, and follows up on customers' use of a product or service. Like order takers, order getters can be inside (an automobile salesperson) or outside (a Xerox salesperson). Order getting involves a high degree of creativity and customer empathy. This type of personal selling is typically required for complex or technical products with many options, so much product knowledge and sales training are necessary. An order getter acts as a problem solver who identifies how a particular product may satisfy a customer's need. Similarly, in the purchase of a service, such as insurance, a Metropolitan Life insurance agent can provide a mix of plans to satisfy a buyer's needs depending on income, stage of the family's life cycle, and investment objectives.

Order getting is not a 40-hour-per-week job. Industry research indicates that outside order getters, or field service representatives, work about 51 hours per week. As shown in Figure 17–1, 53 percent of their time is spent selling and another 13 percent is devoted to customer service calls. The remainder of their work is occupied by getting to customers and performing numerous administrative tasks.[5]

Order getting by outside salespeople is also expensive. It is estimated that the average cost of a single field sales call on a business customer is about $350, factoring in salespeople compensation, benefits, and travel-and-entertainment expenses.[6] This cost illustrates why outbound telemarketing is so popular today. *Outbound telemarketing* is the practice of using the telephone rather than personal visits to contact customers. A significantly lower cost per sales call (in the range of $20 to $25) and little or no field expense are the reasons for its widespread appeal. Some 40 million outbound telemarketing calls are made each year in the United States.[7]

Concept Check

1. What is the main difference between an order taker and an order getter?
2. What percentage of an order-getting salesperson's time is spent selling?

THE PERSONAL SELLING PROCESS: BUILDING RELATIONSHIPS

personal selling process
Sales activities occurring before and after the sale itself, consisting of six stages: (1) prospecting, (2) preapproach, (3) approach, (4) presentation, (5) close, and (6) follow-up

Selling, and particularly order getting, is a complicated activity that involves building buyer–seller relationships. Although the salesperson–customer interaction is essential to personal selling, much of a salesperson's work occurs before this meeting and continues after the sale itself. The **personal selling process** consists of six stages: (1) prospecting, (2) preapproach, (3) approach, (4) presentation, (5) close, and (6) follow-up (Figure 17–2).

Prospecting

Personal selling begins with *prospecting*—the search for and qualification of potential customers. For infrequently purchased products such as vacuum cleaners, continual prospecting is necessary to maintain sales. There are three types of prospects. A *lead* is the name of a person who may be a possible customer. A *prospect* is a customer who wants or needs the product. If an individual wants the product, can afford to buy it, and is the decision maker, this individual is a *qualified prospect.*

FIGURE 17–2
Stages and objectives of the personal selling process

STAGE	OBJECTIVE	COMMENTS
1. Prospecting	Search for and qualify prospects	Start of the selling process; prospects produced through advertising, referrals, and cold canvassing
2. Preapproach	Gather information and decide how to approach the prospect	Information sources include personal observation, other customers, and own salespeople
3. Approach	Gain prospect's attention, stimulate interest, and make transition to the presentation	First impression is critical; gain attention and interest through reference to common acquaintances, a referral, or product demonstration
4. Presentation	Begin converting a prospect into a customer by creating a desire for the product or service	Different presentation formats are possible; however, involving the customer in the product or service through attention to particular needs is critical; important to deal professionally and ethically with prospect skepticism, indifference, or objections
5. Close	Obtain a purchase commitment from the prospect and create a customer	Salesperson asks for the purchase; different approaches include the trial close and assumptive close
6. Follow-up	Ensure that the customer is satisfied with the product or service	Resolve any problems faced by the customer to ensure customer satisfaction and future sales possibilities

Trade shows are a popular source for leads and prospects. Companies like TSCentral provide comprehensive trade show information.

Leads and prospects are generated using several sources. For example, advertising may contain a coupon or a toll-free number to generate leads. Some companies use exhibits at trade shows, professional meetings, and conferences to generate leads or prospects. Staffed by salespeople, these exhibits are used to attract the attention of prospective buyers and to give out information. Others use lists and directories. Another approach for generating leads is through *cold canvassing* in person or by telephone. This approach simply means that a salesperson may open a directory, pick a name, and visit or call that individual or business. Although the refusal rate is high with cold canvassing, this approach can be successful. For example, 41 brokers at Lehman Brothers recently identified 18,004 prospects, qualified 1,208 of them, made 659 sales presentations, and opened 40 new accounts in four working days.[8]

Cold canvassing is often criticized by U.S. consumers and is now regulated. A recent survey reported that 75 percent of U.S. consumers consider this practice an intrusion on their privacy, and 72 percent find it distasteful.[9] The *Telephone Consumer Protection Act* (1991) contains provisions to curb abuses such as early morning or late night calling. Additional federal regulations require more complete disclosure regarding solicitations, include provisions that allow consumers to avoid being called at any time through the Do Not Call Registry, and impose fines up to $11,000 for violations.

Preapproach

Once a salesperson has identified a qualified prospect, preparation for the sale begins with the preapproach. The *preapproach* stage involves obtaining further information on the prospect and deciding on the best method of approach. Knowing how the prospect prefers to be approached and what the prospect is looking for in a product or service is essential. For example, a Merrill Lynch stockbroker will need information on a prospect's discretionary income, investment objectives, and preference for discussing brokerage services over the telephone or in person. Identifying the best time to contact a prospect is also important. For instance, Northwestern Mutual Life Insurance Company suggests the best times to call on people in different occupations: dentists before

9:30 A.M., lawyers between 11:00 A.M. and 2:00 P.M., and college professors between 7:00 and 8:00 P.M.

Successful salespeople recognize that the preapproach stage should never be shortchanged. Their experience coupled with research on customer complaints indicates that failure to learn as much as possible about the prospect is unprofessional and can be the ruin of a sales call.

Approach

The *approach* stage involves the first meeting between the salesperson and prospect, where the objectives are to gain the prospect's attention, stimulate interest, and build the foundation for the sales presentation itself and the basis for a working relationship. The first impression is critical at this stage, and it is common for salespeople to begin the conversation with a reference to common acquaintances, a referral, or even the product or service itself. Which tactic is taken will depend on the information obtained in the prospecting and preapproach stages.

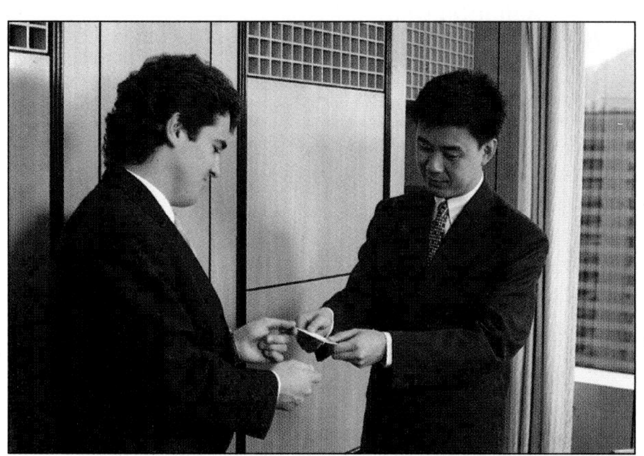

The approach stage is very important in international settings.[10] In many societies outside the United States, much time is devoted to nonbusiness talk designed to establish a friendly basis for developing a relationship between buyers and sellers. In the Middle East and Asia, it is common for two or three meetings to occur before business matters are discussed. Gestures are also very important. The first meeting between a salesperson and a prospect in the United States customarily begins with a firm handshake. Handshakes also apply in France, but they are gentle, not firm. Forget the handshake in Japan. A bow is appropriate. What about business cards? Business cards should be printed in English on one side and the language of the prospective customer on the other. Knowledgeable U.S. salespeople know that their business cards should be handed to Asian customers using both hands, with the name facing the receiver. In Asia, anything involving names demands respect.

Presentation

The *presentation* is at the core of the order-getting selling process, and its objective is to convert a prospect into a customer by creating a desire for the product or service. Three major presentation formats exist: (1) stimulus-response format, (2) formula selling format, and (3) need-satisfaction format.

Stimulus-Response Format The *stimulus-response presentation* format assumes that given the appropriate stimulus by a salesperson, the prospect will buy. With this format the salesperson tries one appeal after another, hoping to hit the right button. A counter clerk at McDonald's is using this approach when he or she asks whether you'd like an order of french fries or a dessert with your meal. The counter clerk is engaging in what is called *suggestive selling.* Although useful in this setting, the stimulus-response format is not always appropriate, and for many products a more formalized format is necessary.

Formula Selling Format A more formalized presentation, the *formula selling presentation* format, is based on the view that a presentation consists of information that must be provided in an accurate, thorough, and step-by-step manner to inform the prospect. A popular version of this format is the *canned sales presentation,* which is a memorized, standardized message conveyed to every prospect. Used frequently by firms in telephone and door-to-door selling of consumer products (for example,

Kirby vacuum cleaners), this approach treats every prospect the same, regardless of differences in needs or preference for certain kinds of information.

Canned sales presentations can be advantageous when the differences between prospects are unknown or with novice salespeople who are less knowledgeable about the product, service, or selling process than experienced salespeople. Although it guarantees a thorough presentation, it often lacks flexibility and spontaneity and, more important, does not provide for feedback from the prospective buyer—a critical component in the communication process and the start of a relationship.

Need-Satisfaction Format The stimulus-response and formula selling formats share a common characteristic: The salesperson dominates the conversation. By comparison, the *need-satisfaction presentation* format emphasizes probing and listening by the salesperson to identify needs and interests of prospective buyers. Once these are identified, the salesperson tailors the presentation to the prospect and highlights product benefits that may be valued by the prospect. The need-satisfaction format, which emphasizes problem solving, is the most consistent with the marketing concept and relationship building.

adaptive selling
A need-satisfaction sales presentation that involves adjusting the presentation to fit the selling situation

consultative selling
Focuses on problem definition, where the salesperson serves as an expert on problem recognition and resolution

Two selling styles are associated with the need-satisfaction format.[11] **Adaptive selling** involves adjusting the presentation to fit the selling situation, such as knowing when to offer solutions and when to ask for more information. Sales research and practice show that knowledge of the customer and sales situation are key ingredients for adaptive selling. Many consumer service firms, such as insurance companies, and consumer product firms like Gillette effectively apply this selling style. **Consultative selling** focuses on problem identification, where the salesperson serves as an expert on problem recognition and resolution. With consultative selling, problem solution options are not simply a matter of choosing from an array of existing products or services. Rather, novel solutions often arise, thereby creating unique value for the customer. Consultative selling is prominent in business-to-business marketing. IBM's Global Services, DHL Worldwide Express, and Xerox are known for their consultative selling style. According to a Xerox sales executive, "Our business is no longer about selling boxes. It's about selling digital, networked-based information management solutions, and this requires a highly customized and consultative selling process."[12]

Handling Objections A critical concern in the presentation stage is handling objections. *Objections* are excuses for not making a purchase commitment or decision. Some objections are valid and are based on the characteristics of the product or service or price. However, many objections reflect prospect skepticism or indifference. Whether valid or not, experienced salespeople know that objections do not put an end to the presentation. Rather, techniques can be used to deal with objections in a courteous, ethical, and professional manner. The following six techniques are the most common:[13]

1. *Acknowledge and convert the objection.* This technique involves using the objection as a reason for buying. For example, a prospect might say, "The price is too high." The reply: "Yes, the price is high because we use the finest materials. Let me show you. . . ."
2. *Postpone.* The postpone technique is used when the objection will be dealt with later in the presentation: "I'm going to address that point shortly. I think my answer would make better sense then."
3. *Agree and neutralize.* Here a salesperson agrees with the objection, then shows that it is unimportant. A salesperson would say, "That's true and others have said the same. However, they concluded that issue was outweighed by the other benefits."
4. *Accept the objection.* Sometimes the objection is valid. Let the prospect express such views, probe for the reason behind it, and attempt to stimulate further discussion on the objection.

5. *Denial.* When a prospect's objection is based on misinformation and clearly untrue, it is wise to meet the objection head on with a firm denial.
6. *Ignore the objection.* This technique is used when it appears that the objection is a stalling mechanism or is clearly not important to the prospect.

Each of these techniques requires a calm, professional interaction with the prospect and is most effective when objections are anticipated in the preapproach stage. Handling objections is a skill requiring a sense of timing, appreciation for the prospect's state of mind, and good communication. Objections also should be handled ethically. Lying or misrepresenting product or service features is an extremely unethical practice.

Close

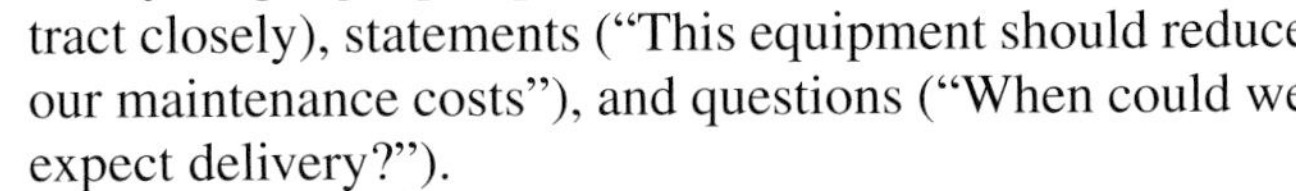

The *closing* stage in the selling process involves obtaining a purchase commitment from the prospect. This stage is the most important and the most difficult because the salesperson must determine when the prospect is ready to buy. Telltale signals indicating a readiness to buy include body language (prospect reexamines the product or contract closely), statements ("This equipment should reduce our maintenance costs"), and questions ("When could we expect delivery?").

The close itself can take several forms. Three closing techniques are used when a salesperson believes a buyer is about ready to make a purchase: (1) trial close, (2) assumptive close, and (3) urgency close. A *trial close* involves asking the prospect to make a decision on some aspect of the purchase: "Would you prefer the blue or gray model?" An *assumptive close* involves asking the prospect to consider choices concerning delivery, warranty, or financing terms under the assumption that a sale has been finalized. An *urgency close* is used to commit the prospect quickly by making reference to the timeliness of the purchase: "The low-interest financing ends next week," or "That is the last model we have in stock." Of course, these statements should be used only if they accurately reflect the situation; otherwise, such claims would be unethical. When a prospect is clearly ready to buy, the *final close* is used, and a salesperson asks for the order.

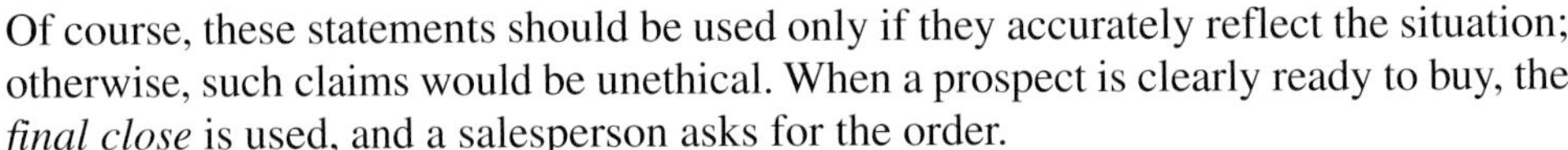

Follow-Up

The selling process does not end with the closing of a sale. Rather, professional selling requires customer follow-up. One marketing authority equated the follow-up with courtship and marriage by observing, "the sale merely consummates the courtship. Then the marriage begins. How good the marriage is depends on how well the relationship is managed."[14] The *follow-up* stage includes making certain the customer's purchase has been properly delivered and installed. Any difficulties experienced with the use of the item are addressed. Attention to this stage of the selling process solidifies the buyer–seller relationship. Moreover, the cost and effort to obtain repeat sales from a satisfied customer is roughly half of that necessary to gain a sale from a new customer. In short, today's satisfied customers become tomorrow's qualified prospects or referrals.

Concept Check

1. What are the six stages in the personal selling process?
2. Which presentation format is most consistent with the marketing concept? Why?

THE SALES MANAGEMENT PROCESS

Selling must be managed if it is going to contribute to a firm's overall objectives. Although firms differ in the specifics of how salespeople and the selling effort are managed, the sales management process is similar across firms. Sales management consists of three interrelated functions: (1) sales plan formulation, (2) sales plan implementation, and (3) evaluation of the salesforce (Figure 17–3).

Sales Plan Formulation: Setting Direction

sales plan
Statement describing what is to be achieved and where and how the selling effort of salespeople is to be directed

Formulating the sales plan is the most basic of the three sales management functions. According to the vice president of the Harris Corporation, a global communications company, "If a company hopes to implement its marketing strategy, it really needs a detailed sales planning process."[15] The **sales plan** is a statement describing what is to be achieved and where and how the selling effort of salespeople is to be directed. Formulating the sales plan involves three tasks: (1) setting objectives, (2) organizing the salesforce, and (3) developing account management policies.

Setting Objectives Setting objectives is central to sales management because this task specifies what is to be achieved. In practice, objectives are set for the total sales force and for each salesperson. Selling objectives can be output related and focused on dollar or unit sales volume, number of new customers added, and profit. Or they can be input related and emphasize the number of sales calls and selling expenses. Output- and input-related objectives are used for the salesforce as a whole and for each salesperson. A third type of objective is behaviorally related and is typically specific for each salesperson: his or her product knowledge, customer service, and selling and communication skills.

Organizing the Salesforce Establishing a selling organization is the second task in formulating the sales plan. Companies organize their salesforce on the basis of (1) geography, (2) customer, or (3) product or service. A geographical structure is the simplest organization, where the United States, or indeed the globe, is first divided into regions and each region is divided into districts or territories. Salespeople are assigned to each district with defined geographical boundaries and call on all customers and represent all products sold by the company. The main advantage of this structure is that it can minimize travel time, expenses, and duplication of selling effort. However, if a firm's products or customers require specialized knowledge, then a geographical structure is not suitable.

A customer sales organizational structure is used when different types of buyers have different needs. In practice this means that a different salesforce calls on each separate type of buyer or marketing channel. For example, Kodak recently switched from a geographical to a marketing channel structure with different sales teams serving specific retail channels: mass merchandisers, photo specialty outlets, and food and drug stores. The rationale for this approach is that more effective, specialized customer support and knowledge are provided to buyers. However, this structure often leads to

FIGURE 17–3
The sales management process

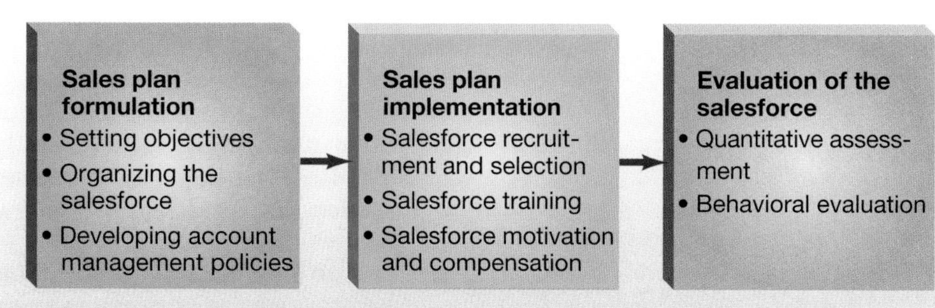

MARKETING NEWSNET

Creating and Sustaining Customer Value through Cross-Functional Team Selling

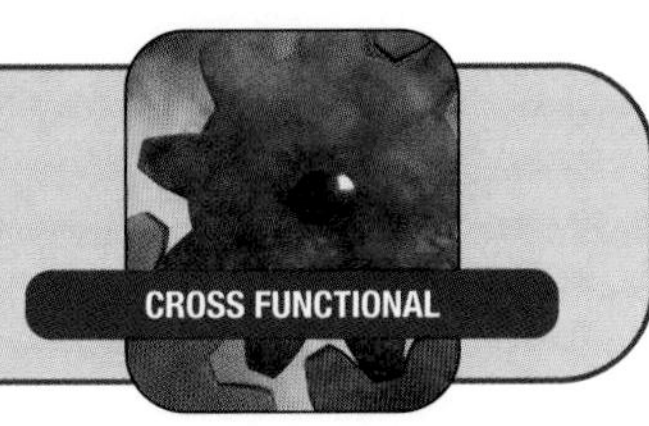

The day of the lone salesperson calling on a customer is becoming history. Many companies today use cross-functional teams of professionals to work with customers to improve relationships, find better ways of doing things, and, of course, create and sustain customer value.

Xerox and IBM pioneered cross-functional team selling, but other firms were quick to follow as they spotted the potential to generate value for their customers. Recognizing that corn growers needed a herbicide they could apply less often, a Du Pont team of chemists, sales and marketing executives, and regulatory specialists created just the right product that recorded sales of $57 million in its first year. Pitney Bowes, Inc., which produces sophisticated computer systems that weigh, rate, and track packages for firms such as UPS and FedEx, also uses sales teams to meet customer needs. These teams consist of sales personnel, "carrier management specialists," and engineering and administrative executives who continually find ways to improve the technology of shipping goods across town and around the world.

Efforts to create and sustain customer value through cross-functional team selling have become a necessity as customers seek greater value for their money. According to the vice president for procurement of a Fortune 500 company, "Today, it's not just getting the best price but getting the best value—and there are a lot of pieces to value."

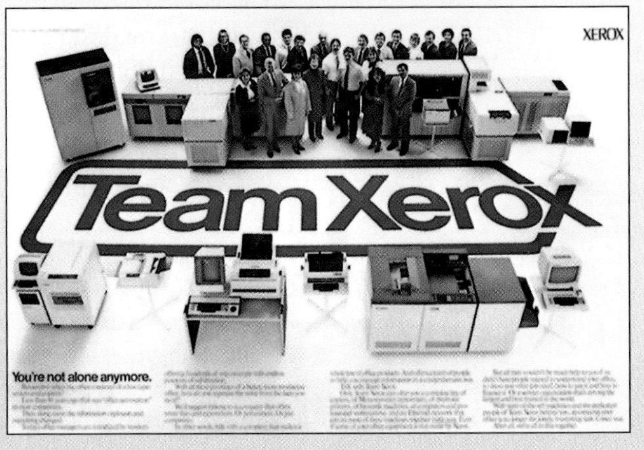

higher administrative costs and some duplication of selling effort, because two separate salesforces are used to represent the same products.

major account management
Practice of using team selling to focus on important customers so as to build mutually beneficial, long-term, cooperative relationships; also called key account management

A variation of the customer organizational structure is **major account management**, or *key account management,* the practice of using team selling to focus on important customers so as to build mutually beneficial, long-term, cooperative relationships. Major account management involves teams of sales, service, and often technical personnel who work with purchasing, manufacturing, engineering, logistics, and financial executives in customer organizations. This approach, which often assigns company personnel to a customer account, results in "customer specialists" who can provide exceptional service. Procter & Gamble uses this approach with Wal-Mart as does Black & Decker with Home Depot. Other companies have embraced this practice as described in the accompanying Marketing NewsNet.[16]

A product sales organization is used when specific knowledge is required to sell a product. For example, Lone Star Steel has a salesforce that sells drilling pipe to oil companies and another that sells specialty steel products to manufacturers. The primary advantage of this structure is that salespeople can develop expertise with technical characteristics, applications, and selling methods associated with a particular product or family of products. However, this structure also produces high administrative costs and duplication of selling effort because two company salespeople may call on the same customer.

In short, there is no one best sales organization for all companies in all situations. Rather, the organization of the salesforce should reflect the marketing strategy of the firm. Each year about 10 percent of U.S. firms change their sales organizations to implement new marketing strategies.

account management policies
Policies that specify whom salespeople should contact, what kinds of selling and customer service activities should be engaged in, and how these activities should be carried out

Developing Account Management Policies The third task in formulating a sales plan involves developing **account management policies** specifying whom salespeople should contact, what kinds of selling and customer service activities should be engaged in, and how these activities should be carried out. These policies might state which individuals in a buying organization should be contacted, the amount of sales and service effort that different customers should receive, and the kinds of information salespeople should collect before or during a sales call.

An example of an account management policy in Figure 17–4 shows how different accounts or customers can be grouped by level of opportunity and the firm's competitive sales position.[17] When specific account names are placed in each cell, salespeople clearly see which accounts should be contacted, with what level of selling and service activity, and how to deal with them. Accounts in cells 1 and 2 might have high frequencies of personal sales calls and increased time spent on a call. Cell 3 accounts will have lower call frequencies. Cell 4 accounts might be contacted through telemarketing or direct mail rather than in person. For example, Union Pacific Railroad recently put its 20,000 smallest accounts on a telemarketing program. A subsequent survey of these accounts indicated that 84 percent rated Union Pacific's sales effort "very effective" compared with 67 percent before the switch.

Sales Plan Implementation: Putting the Plan into Action

The sales plan is put into practice through the tasks associated with sales plan implementation. Whereas sales plan formulation focuses on "doing the right things," implementation emphasizes "doing things right." The three major tasks involved in implementing a sales plan are (1) salesforce recruitment and selection, (2) salesforce training, and (3) salesforce motivation and compensation.

Salesforce Recruitment and Selection Effective recruitment and selection of salespeople is one of the most crucial tasks of sales management. It involves finding people who match the type of sales position required by a firm. Recruitment and selection practices would differ greatly between order-taking and order-getting sales positions, given the differences in the demands of these two jobs. Therefore, recruitment and selection begin with a carefully crafted job analysis and job description, followed by a statement of job qualifications.[18]

FIGURE 17–4
Account management policy grid

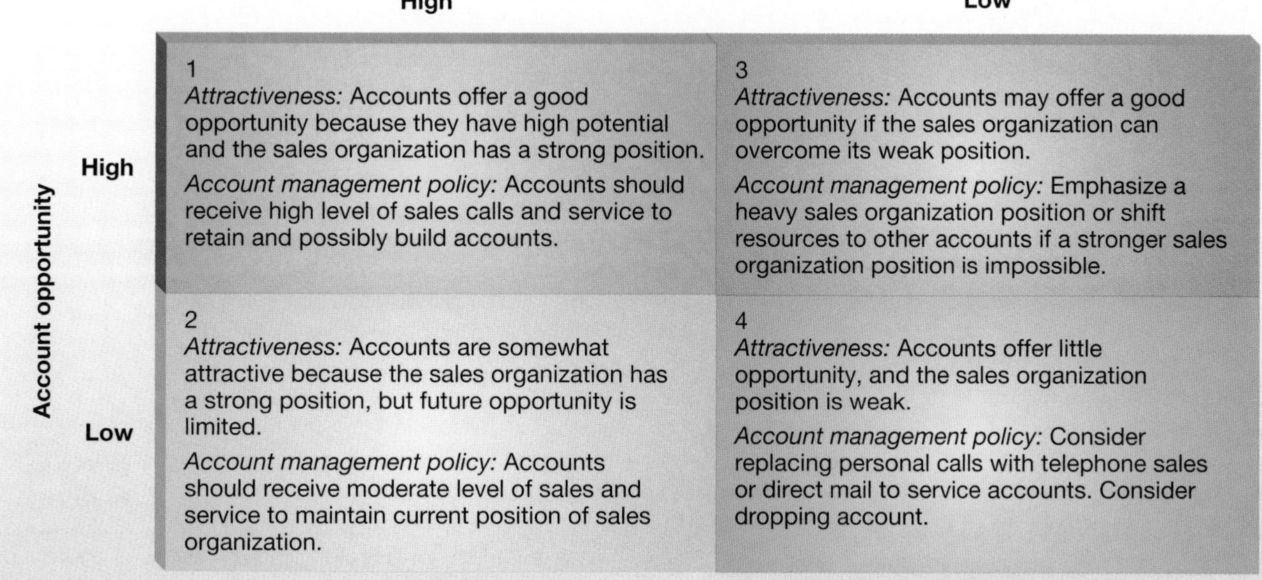

Competitive position of sales organization
High
Low
Account opportunity
High
Low
1
Attractiveness: Accounts offer a good opportunity because they have high potential and the sales organization has a strong position.
Account management policy: Accounts should receive high level of sales calls and service to retain and possibly build accounts.
3
Attractiveness: Accounts may offer a good opportunity if the sales organization can overcome its weak position.
Account management policy: Emphasize a heavy sales organization position or shift resources to other accounts if a stronger sales organization position is impossible.
2
Attractiveness: Accounts are somewhat attractive because the sales organization has a strong position, but future opportunity is limited.
Account management policy: Accounts should receive moderate level of sales and service to maintain current position of sales organization.
4
Attractiveness: Accounts offer little opportunity, and the sales organization position is weak.
Account management policy: Consider replacing personal calls with telephone sales or direct mail to service accounts. Consider dropping account.

A *job analysis* is a study of a particular sales position, including how the job is to be performed and the tasks that make up the job. Information from a job analysis is used to write a *job description,* a written document that describes job relationships and requirements that characterize each sales position. It explains (1) to whom a salesperson reports, (2) how a salesperson interacts with other company personnel, (3) the customers to be called on, (4) the specific activities to be carried out, (5) the physical and mental demands of the job, and (6) the types of products and services to be sold. The job description is then translated into a statement of job qualifications, including the aptitudes, knowledge, skills, and a variety of behavioral characteristics considered necessary to perform the job successfully. Qualifications for order-getting sales positions often mirror the expectations of buyers: (1) imagination and problem-solving ability, (2) honesty, (3) intimate product knowledge, and (4) attentiveness reflected in responsiveness to buyer needs, customer loyalty, and follow-up. Firms use a variety of methods for evaluating prospective salespeople. Personal interviews, reference checks, and background information provided on application forms are the most frequently used methods.

The search for qualified salespeople has produced an increasingly diverse salesforce in the United States. Women now represent half of all professional salespeople, and minority representation is growing. The fastest growth rate is among salespeople of Asian and Hispanic descent (see Figure 17–5).[19]

Salesforce Training Whereas recruitment and selection of salespeople is a one-time event, salesforce training is an ongoing process that affects both new and seasoned salespeople. Sales training covers much more than selling practices. For example, IBM Global Services salespeople, who sell consulting and various information technology services, take at least two weeks of in-class and Web-based training on both consultative selling and the technical aspects of business. On-the-job training is the most popular type of training, followed by individual instruction taught by experienced salespeople. Formal classes and seminars taught by sales trainers are also popular.

Salesforce Motivation and Compensation A sales plan cannot be successfully put in place without motivated salespeople. Research on salesperson motivation suggests that (1) a clear job description, (2) effective sales management practices, (3) a personal need for achievement, and (4) proper compensation, incentives, or rewards will produce a motivated salesperson.[20]

FIGURE 17–5
U.S. salesforce composition and change

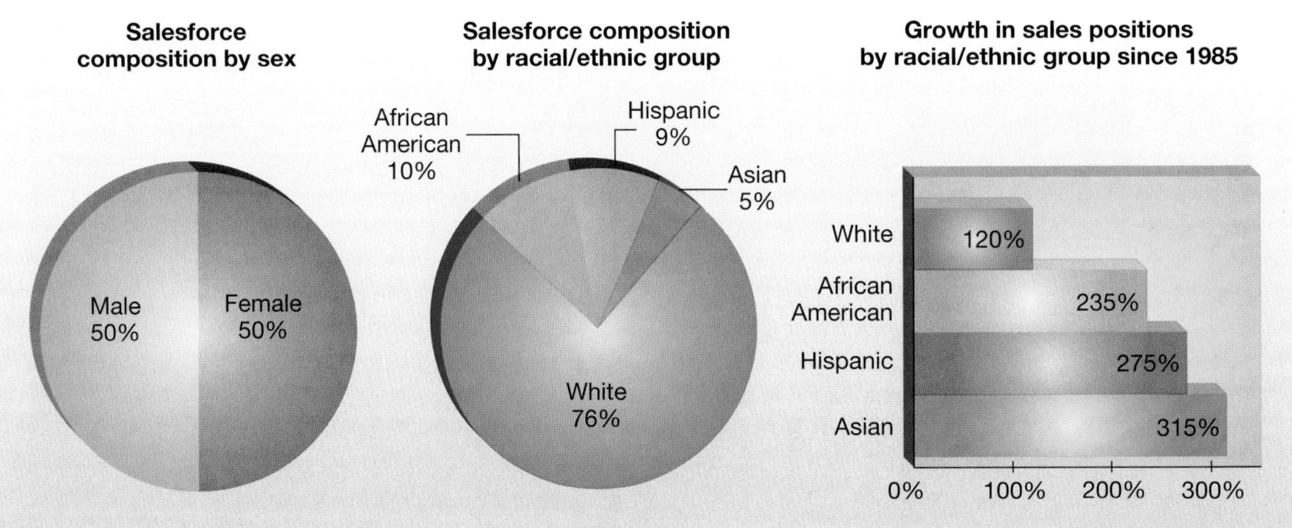

The importance of compensation as a motivating factor means that close attention must be given to how salespeople are financially rewarded for their efforts. Salespeople are paid using one of three plans: (1) straight salary, (2) straight commission, or (3) a combination of salary and commission. Under a *straight salary compensation plan* a salesperson is paid a fixed fee per week, month, or year. With a *straight commission compensation plan* a salesperson's earnings are directly tied to the sales or profit generated. For example, an insurance agent might receive a 2 percent commission of $2,000 for selling a $100,000 life insurance policy. A *combination compensation plan* contains a specified salary plus a commission on sales or profit generated.

Each compensation plan has its advantages and disadvantages. A straight salary plan is easy to administer and gives management a large measure of control over how salespeople spend their time. However, it provides little incentive to expand sales volume. This plan is used when salespeople engage in many nonselling activities, such as account servicing. A straight commission plan provides the maximum amount of selling incentive but can detract salespeople from providing customer service. This plan is common when nonselling activities are minimal. Combination plans are most preferred by salespeople and attempt to build on the advantages of salary and commission plans while reducing potential shortcomings of each.

Mary Kay Cosmetics recognizes a top salesperson at its annual sales meeting.

Nonmonetary rewards are also given to salespeople for meeting or exceeding objectives. These rewards include trips, honor societies, distinguished salesperson awards, and letters of commendation. Some unconventional rewards include the new pink Cadillacs and Pontiacs, fur coats, and jewelry given by Mary Kay Cosmetics to outstanding salespeople. Mary Kay, with 10,000 cars, has the largest fleet of General Motors cars in the world![21]

Salesforce Evaluation and Control: Measuring Results

The final function in the sales management process involves evaluating the salesforce. It is at this point that salespeople are assessed as to whether sales objectives were met and account management policies were followed. In order to evaluate different selling dimensions, both quantitative and behavioral measures are used.

Quantitative Assessments Quantitative assessments, called *quotas,* are based on input- and output-related objectives set forth in the sales plan. Input-related measures focus on the actual activities performed by salespeople, such as those involving sales calls, selling expenses, and account management policies. The number of sales calls made, selling expense related to sales made, and the number of reports submitted to superiors are frequently used input measures.

sales quota
Specific goals assigned to a salesperson, sales team, branch sales office, or sales district for a stated period

Output measures often appear in a sales quota. A **sales quota** contains specific goals assigned to a salesperson, sales team, branch sales office, or sales district for a stated period. Dollar or unit sales volume, last year/current sales ratio, sales of specific products, new accounts generated, and profit achieved are typical goals. The time period can range from one month to one year.

Behavioral Evaluation Behavioral measures are also used to evaluate salespeople. These include assessments of a salesperson's attitude, attention to customers, product knowledge, selling and communication skills, appearance, and professional demeanor.

About 60 percent of U.S. companies now include customer satisfaction as a behavioral measure of salesperson performance.[22] Indianapolis Power & Light, for example, asks major customers to grade its salespeople from A to F. IBM Siebel Systems has been the most aggressive in using this behavioral measure. Forty percent of an IBM

Siebel salesperson's evaluation is linked to customer satisfaction; the remaining 60 percent is linked to profits achieved.

Salesforce Automation and Customer Relationship Management

salesforce automation
Use of technology to make the sales function more effective and efficient

Personal selling and sales management are undergoing a technological revolution with the integration of salesforce automation into customer relationship management processes. In fact, the convergence of computer, information, communication, and Internet technologies has transformed the sales function in many companies and made the promise of customer relationship management a reality. **Salesforce automation** (SFA) is the use of these technologies to make the sales function more effective and efficient. SFA applies to a wide range of activities, including each stage in the personal selling process and management of the salesforce itself.

Salesforce Computerization Computer technology has become an integral part of field selling. For example, salespeople for Godiva Chocolates use their laptop computers to process orders, plan time usage, forecast sales, and communicate with Godiva personnel and customers. In a department store candy buyer's office, such as Neiman Marcus, a salesperson can calculate the order cost (and discount), transmit the order, and obtain a delivery date within minutes from Godiva's order processing department.[23]

Toshiba America Medical System salespeople now use laptop computers with built-in CD-ROM capabilities to provide interactive presentations for their computerized tomography (CT) and magnetic resonance imaging (MRI) scanners. In it the customer sees elaborate three-dimensional animations, high-resolution scans, and video clips of the company's products in operation as well as narrated testimonials from satisfied customers. Toshiba has found this application to be effective both for sales presentations and for training its salespeople.[24]

Salesforce Communication Technology also has changed the way salespeople communicate with customers, other salespeople and sales support personnel, and management. Facsimile, electronic mail, and voice mail are three common communication technologies used by salespeople today. Cellular (phone) technology, which now allows salespeople to exchange data as well as voice transmissions, is equally popular. Whether traveling or in a customer's office, these technologies provide information at the salesperson's fingertips to answer customer questions and solve problems.

Advances in communication and computer technologies have made possible the mobile and home sales office. Some salespeople now equip minivans with a fully functional desk, swivel chair, light, computer, printer, fax machine, cellular phone, and a satellite dish. Jeff Brown, an agent manager with U.S. Cellular, uses such a mobile office. He says, "If I arrive at a prospect's office and they can't see me right away, then I can go outside to work in my office until they're ready to see me." Home offices are

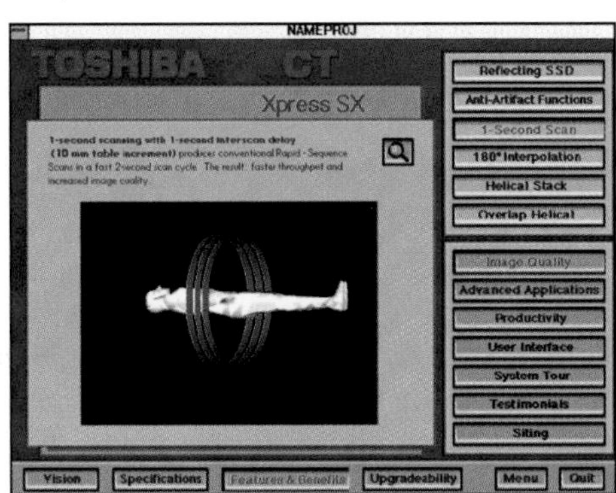

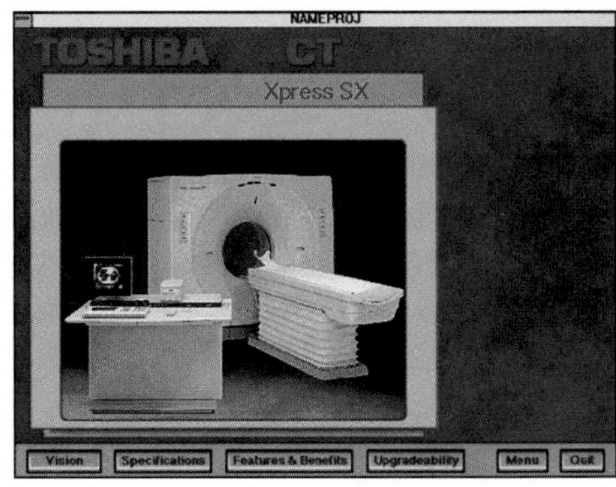

Toshiba America Medical System salespeople have found computer technology to be an effective sales tool and training device.

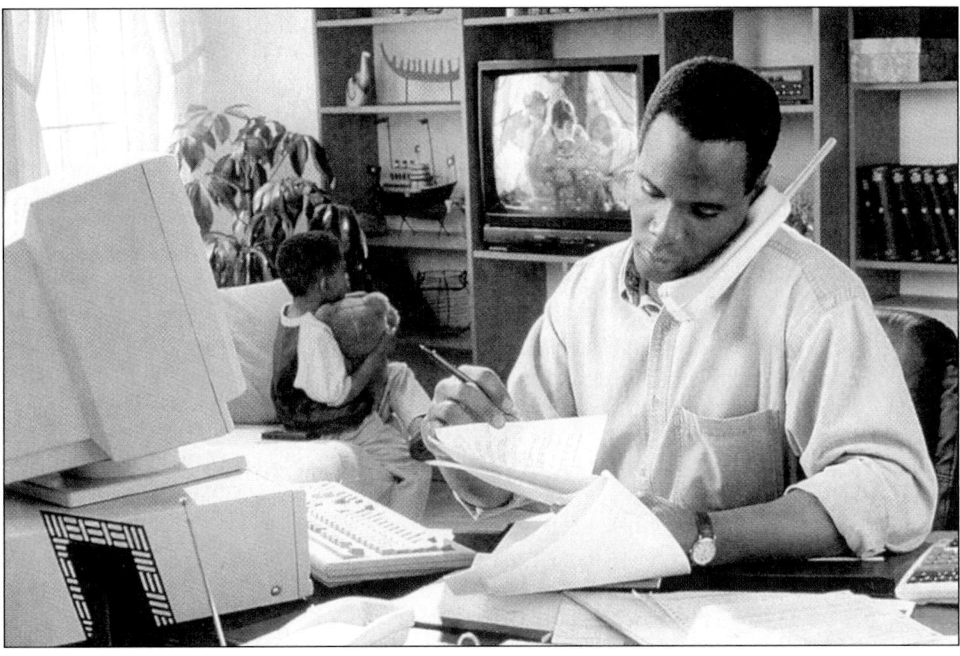

Computer and communication technologies have made it possible for Hewlett-Packard salespeople to work out of their homes.

now common. Hewlett-Packard is a case in point. The company recently shifted its entire 224-person U.S. salesforce into home offices, closed three regional sales offices, and saved $10 million in staff salaries and office rent. A fully equipped home office for each salesperson costs the company about $8,000 and includes a notebook computer, fax/copier, cellular phone, two phone lines, and office furniture.[25]

Perhaps the greatest impact on salesforce communication is the application of Internet technology. Today, salespeople are using their company's intranet for a variety of purposes. At EDS, a professional services firm, salespeople access its intranet to download client material, marketing content, account information, technical papers, and competitive profiles. In addition, EDS offers 7,000 training classes that salespeople can take anytime, anywhere.[26]

Salesforce automation is clearly changing how selling is done and how salespeople are managed. As applications increase, SFA has the potential to transform selling and sales management.

Concept Check

1. What are the three types of selling objectives?
2. What three factors are used to structure sales organizations?

CHAPTER IN REVIEW

1 *Discuss the nature and scope of personal selling and sales management in marketing.*

Personal selling involves the two-way flow of communication between a buyer and seller, often in a face-to-face encounter, designed to influence a person's or group's purchase decision. Sales management involves planning the selling program and implementing and controlling the personal selling effort of the firm. The scope of selling and sales management is apparent in three ways. First, virtually every occupation that involves customer contact has an element of personal selling. Second, selling plays a significant role in a company's overall marketing effort. Salespeople occupy a boundary position between buyers and sellers; they *are* the company to many buyers and account for a major cost of marketing in a variety of industries; and they can create value for customers. Finally, through relationship selling, salespeople play a central role in tailoring solutions to customer problems as a means to customer value creation.

2 *Identify the different types of personal selling.*

Two major types of personal selling exist: order taking and order getting. Each type differs from the other in terms of actual selling done and the amount of creativity required to perform the sales task. Order takers process routine orders or reorders for products that were already sold by the company. They generally do little selling in a conventional sense and engage in only modest problem solving with customers. Order getters sell in a conventional sense and identify prospective customers, provide customers with information, persuade customers to buy, close sales, and follow up on customers' use of a product or service. Order getting involves a high degree of creativity and customer empathy and is typically required for selling complex or technical products with many options.

3 *Explain the stages in the personal selling process.*
The personal selling process consists of six stages: (*a*) prospecting, (*b*) preapproach, (*c*) approach, (*d*) presentation, (*e*) close, and (*f*) follow-up. Prospecting involves the search for and qualification of potential customers. The preapproach stage involves obtaining further information on the prospect and deciding on the best method of approach. The approach stage involves the initial meeting between the salesperson and prospect. The presentation stage involves converting a prospect into a customer by creating a desire for the product or service. The close involves obtaining a purchase commitment from the prospect. The follow-up stage involves making certain that the customer's purchase has been properly delivered and installed and difficulties experienced with the use of the item are addressed.

4 *Describe the major functions of sales management.*
Sales management consists of three interrelated functions: (*a*) sales plan formulation, (*b*) sales plan implementation, and (*c*) evaluation and control of the salesforce. Sales plan formulation involves setting objectives, organizing the salesforce, and developing account management policies. Sales plan implementation involves salesforce recruitment, selection, training, motivation, and compensation. Finally, evaluation and control of the salesforce focuses on quantitative assessments of sales performance and behavioral measures such as customer satisfaction that are linked to selling objectives and account management policies.

FOCUSING ON KEY TERMS

account management policies p. 386
adaptive selling p. 383
consultative selling p. 383
major account management p. 386
order getter p. 379
order taker p. 378
personal selling p. 376
personal selling process p. 380
relationship selling p. 377
salesforce automation p. 390
sales management p. 376
sales plan p. 385
sales quota p. 389

DISCUSSION AND APPLICATION QUESTIONS

1 Jane Dawson is a new sales representative for the Charles Schwab brokerage firm. In searching for clients, Jane purchased a mailing list of subscribers to *The Wall Street Journal* and called them all regarding their interest in discount brokerage services. She asked if they have any stocks and if they have a regular broker. Those people without a regular broker were asked their investment needs. Two days later Jane called back with investment advice and asked if they would like to open an account. Identify each of Jane Dawson's actions in terms of the steps of selling.

2 For the first 50 years of business the Johnson Carpet Company produced carpets for residential use. The salesforce was structured geographically. In the past five years, a large percentage of carpet sales has been to industrial users, hospitals, schools, and architects. The company also has broadened its product line to include area rugs, Oriental carpets, and wall-to-wall carpeting. Is the present salesforce structure appropriate, or would you recommend an alternative?

3 Where would you place each of the following sales jobs on the order-taker/order-getter continuum shown below? (*a*) Burger King counter clerk, (*b*) automobile insurance salesperson, (*c*) IBM computer salesperson, (*d*) life insurance salesperson, and (*e*) shoe salesperson.

Order taker —————————— **Order getter**

4 Listed below are two different firms. Which compensation plan would you recommend for each firm, and what reasons would you give for your recommendations? (*a*) A newly formed company that sells lawn care equipment on a door-to-door basis directly to consumers; and (*b*) the Nabisco Company, which sells heavily advertised products in supermarkets by having the salesforce call on these stores and arrange shelves, set up displays, and make presentations to store buying committees.

5 Suppose someone said to you, "The only real measure of a salesperson is the amount of sales produced." How might you respond?

GOING ONLINE Getting the Scoop on Selling

A unique resource for the latest developments in personal selling and sales management is the Sales Marketing Network (SMN) at www.info-now.com. SMN provides highly readable reports on a variety of topics including many discussed in this chapter, such as telemarketing, motivation, sales training, and sales management. These reports contain concise overviews, definitions, statistics, and reviews of critical issues. They also include references to additional information and links to related material elsewhere on the SMN site. Registration (at no cost) is required to view some of the reports.

Visit the SMN site and do the following:

1 Select a chapter topic, and update the statistics for, say, sales training costs or the popularity of different salesforce incentives.

2 Select a topic covered in the chapter such as telemarketing, and summarize the critical issues identified for this practice.

BUILDING YOUR MARKETING PLAN

Does your marketing plan involve a personal selling activity? If the answer is no, read no further and do not include a personal selling element in your plan. If the answer is yes:

1 Identify the likely prospects for your product or service.

2 Determine what information you should obtain about the prospect.

3 Describe how you would approach the prospect.

4 Outline the presentation you would make to the prospect for your product or service.

5 Develop a sales plan, focusing on the organizational structure you would use for your salesforce (geography, product, or customer).

VIDEO CASE 17 Reebok: Relationship Selling and Customer Value

"I think face-to-face selling is the most important and exciting part of this whole job. It's not writing the sales reports. It's not analyzing trends and forecasting. It's the two hours that you have to try to sell the buyer your products in a way that's profitable for both you and the retailer," relates Robert McMahon, key account sales representative for Reebok Northeast. As the person in charge of Reebok's largest accounts in New England—including MVP Sports, recently acquired by Decathlon Sports, Modell's, and City Sports—McMahon's job encompasses a myriad of activities, from supervising other sales representatives to attending companywide computer training sessions to monitoring competitors' activities. But it's the actual selling that is most appealing to McMahon. "That's the challenging, stimulating part of the job. Selling to the buyer is a different challenge every day. Every sales call, as well as you may have preplanned it, can change based on shifts and trends in the market. So you need to be able to react to those changes and really think on your feet in front of the buyer."

REEBOK—HOT ON NIKE'S HEELS IN THE ATHLETIC SHOE AND APPAREL MARKET

Reebok is the second-largest athletic shoe manufacturer behind the market leader, Nike. In addition to its athletic shoes, Reebok also sells Rockport, Greg Norman Collection, and Ralph Lauren Footwear shoes. The Reebok sporting goods line remains the flagship brand, though, and distinguishes itself on the market through the DMX cushioning technology in its footwear. Reebok concentrates its resources on getting its footwear and sporting goods gear into a diversified mix of distribution channels such as athletic footwear specialty stores, department stores, and large sporting goods stores. Reebok is unique in that it emphasizes relationships with the retailers as an integral part of its marketing strategy. As an employee at MVP Sports, one of Reebok's major retailers, puts it, "Reebok is the only company that comes in on a regular basis and gives us information. Nike comes in once in a great while. New Balance comes in every six months. Saucony has come in twice. That's been it. Reebok comes in every month to update us on new information and new products. They tell us about the technology so we can tell the customers." Says Laurie Sipples, "vector" representative for Reebok, "There's a partnership that exists between Reebok and an account like MVP Sports that sets us apart. That relationship is a great asset that Reebok has because the retailer feels more in touch with us than other brands."

THE SELLING PROCESS AT REEBOK

Selling at Reebok includes three elements—building trust between the salesperson and the retailer, providing enough information to the retailer for them to be successful selling Reebok products, and finally supporting the retailer after the sale. Sean Neville, senior vice president and general manager of Reebok North America, explains, "Our goal is not to sell to the retailer; our goal is ultimately to sell to the consumer, and so we use the retailer as a partner. The salespeople are always keeping their eyes open and thinking like the retailer and selling to the consumer."

Reebok sells in teams that consist of the account representatives, who do the actual selling to the retailer, and the vector representatives, who spend their time in the stores training the store salespeople and reporting trends back to the account manager. The selling teams are organized geographically so that the salespeople live and work in the area they are selling. This allows the sales team to understand the consumer intuitively. Neville explains, "If you have someone from New York City fly to L.A. and try to tell someone on the streets of Los Angeles what's happening from a trends standpoint and what products to purchase, it's very difficult."

On average, Reebok salespeople spend 70 percent of their time preparing for a sale and 30 percent of their time actually selling. The sales process at Reebok typically follows the six steps of the personal selling process identified in Figure 17–2: (1) Reebok identifies the outlets it would like to carry its athletic gear; (2) the salesforce prepares for the a presentation by familiarizing themselves with the store and its customers; (3) a Reebok representative approaches the prospect and suggests a meeting and presentation; (4) as the presentation begins, the salesperson summarizes relevant market conditions and consumer trends to demonstrate Reebok's commitment to a partnership with the retailer, states what he or she hopes to get out of the sales meeting, explains how the products work, and reinforces the benefits of Reebok products; (5) the salesperson engages in an action close (gets a signed document or a firm confirmation of the sale); and (6) later, various members of the salesforce frequently visit the retailer to provide assistance and monitor consumer preferences.

THE SALES MANAGEMENT PROCESS AT REEBOK

The sales teams at Reebok are organized based on Reebok's three major distribution channels: athletic specialty stores, sporting goods stores, and department stores. The smaller stores have sales teams assigned to them based on geographical location within the United States (west coast, central, southeast, and northeast). The salesforce is then further broken down into footwear and apparel teams. The salesforce is primarily organized by distribution channel because this is most responsive to customer needs and wants. The salesforce is compensated on both a short-term and long-term basis. In the short term, salespeople are paid based on sales results and profits for the current quarter as well as forecasting. In the long term, salespeople are compensated based on

their teamwork and teambuilding efforts. As Neville explains, "Money is typically fourth or fifth on the list of pure motivation. Number one is recognition for a job well done. And that drives people to succeed." Management at Reebok is constantly providing feedback to the salesforce acknowledging their success, not just during annual reviews, and Neville feels this is the key to the high level of motivation, energy, and excitement that exists in the salesforce at Reebok.

WHAT'S NEW ON THE HORIZON FOR THE SALESFORCE AT REEBOK?

Reebok has recently issued laptop computers to its entire salesforce that enable the salespeople to check inventories in the warehouses, make sure orders are being shipped on time, and even enter orders while they're out in the field. Reebok is also focusing more on relationship selling. McMahon describes his relationship with a major buyer as "one of trust and respect. It's gotten to the point now where we're good friends. We go to a lot of sporting events together, which I think really helps." Another recent innovation is for the salesforce to incentivize the stores' sales clerks. For instance, whoever sells the most pairs of Reebok shoes in a month will get tickets to a concert or a football game.

Questions

1 How does Reebok create customer value for its major accounts through relationship selling?

2 How does Reebok utilize team selling to provide the highest level of customer value possible to its major accounts?

3 Is Reebok's salesforce organized based on geography, customer, or product?

4 What are some ways Reebok's selling processes are changing due to technical advancements?

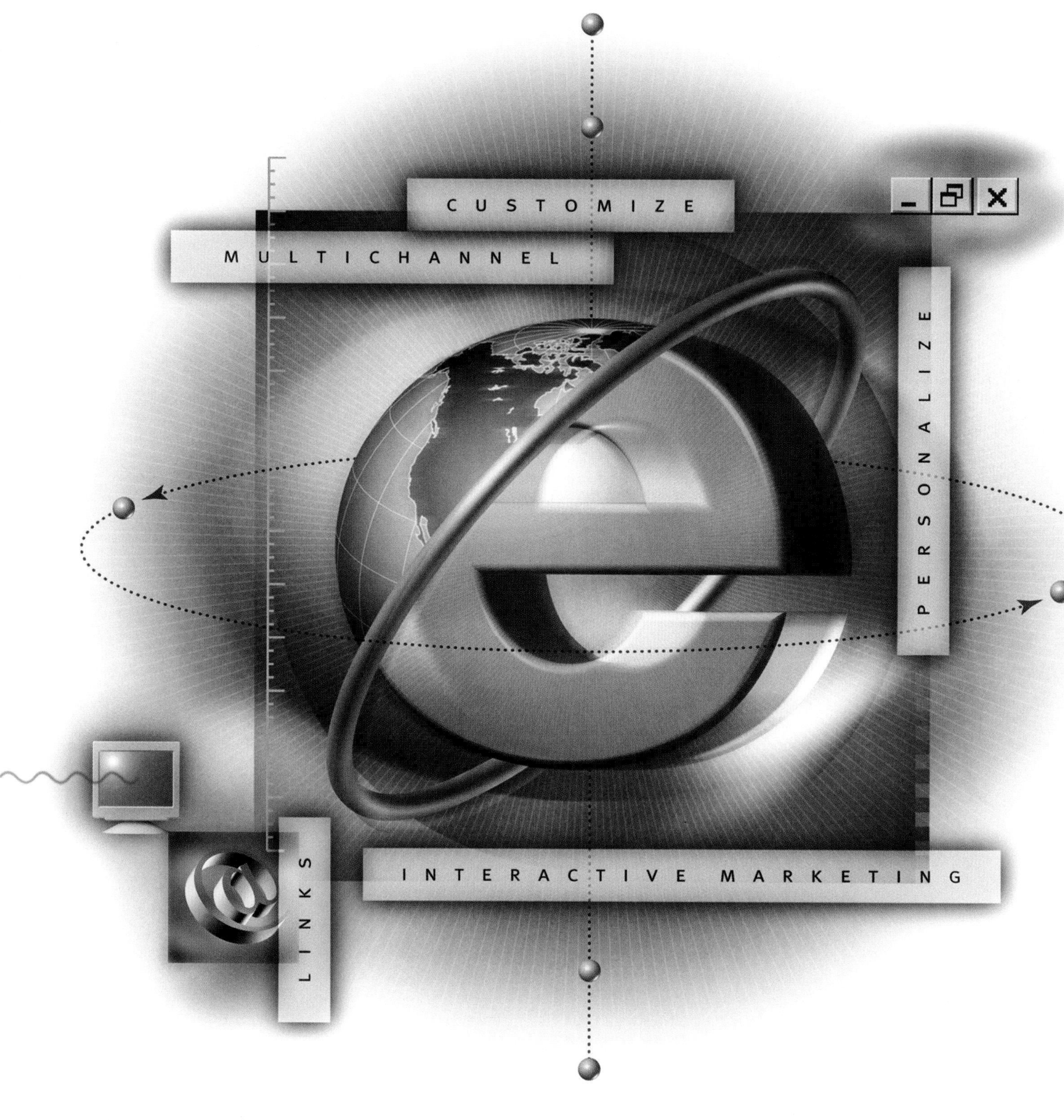
CUSTOMIZE
MULTICHANNEL
PERSONALIZE
LINKS
INTERACTIVE MARKETING

CHAPTER 18

IMPLEMENTING INTERACTIVE AND MULTICHANNEL MARKETING

LEARNING OBJECTIVES

After reading this chapter you should be able to:

1 Describe what interactive marketing is and how it creates customer value, customer relationships, and customer experiences.

2 Explain why certain types of products and services are particularly suited for interactive marketing.

3 Describe why consumers shop and buy online and how marketers influence online purchasing behavior.

4 Define multichannel marketing and the role of transactional and promotional websites in reaching online consumers.

ONE BIKE: YOURS

"One bike: Yours" is the company motto for Seven Cycles, Inc., for a good reason. Seven Cycles is the largest custom bicycle frame builder in the world. The company produces a huge range of road, mountain, cyclo-cross, triathlon, single-speed, and tandem bikes annually, and no two are alike. At Seven Cycles, attention is focused on each customer's cycling experience through the optimum fit, function, performance, and comfort of his or her very own bike.

The marketing success of Seven Cycles is due certainly to its state-of-the-art bicycle frames. But as company founder and president Ron Vandermark, says, "Part of our success is that we are tied to a business model that includes the Internet." Seven Cycles uses its website (www.sevencycles.com) to let customers get deeply involved in the frame-building process and the selection of hubs, spokes, and handlebars to complete the bike. It enables customers to design their own bike frames using the company's Custom Kit™ fitting system that considers the rider's size and riding habits. Then, customers can track their custom frame all the way through the development and production process by clicking "Where's My Frame?" on the Seven Cycles website.

This chapter describes how companies design and implement marketing programs that capitalize on the unique value-creation capabilities of Internet technology. We begin by explaining how this technology can create customer value, build customer relationships, and produce customer experiences in novel ways. Next, we describe how Internet technology affects consumer behavior and marketing practice. Finally, we show how marketers integrate and leverage their communication and delivery channels using Internet technology.[1]

CREATING CUSTOMER VALUE, RELATIONSHIPS, AND EXPERIENCES IN MARKETSPACE

Consumers and companies populate two market environments today. One is the traditional marketplace. Here buyers and sellers engage in face-to-face exchange relationships in a material environment characterized by physical facilities (stores and offices) and mostly tangible objects. The other is the marketspace, an Internet-enabled digital environment characterized by "face-to-screen" exchange relationships and electronic images and offerings.

The existence of two market environments has been a boon for consumers. Today, consumers can shop for and purchase a wide variety of products and services in either market environment. Actually, many consumers now browse and buy in both market environments, and more are expected to do so in the future as access to and familiarity with Internet technology grows. As an illustration, Figure 18–1 shows the growth trend in estimated online shoppers and online retail sales in the United States.[2]

Customer Value Creation in Marketspace

Despite the widespread interest in marketspace, its economic significance remains small compared with the traditional marketplace. Electronic commerce is expected to represent less than 20 percent of total U.S. consumer and business goods and services expenditures in 2008, and less than 10 percent of global expenditures.[3] Why then has the marketspace captured the eye and imagination of marketers?

Marketers believe that the possibilities for customer value creation are greater in marketspace than in the traditional marketplace. Recall from Chapter 1 that marketing creates time, place, form, and possession utilities for customers, thereby providing value. In marketspace, the provision of direct, on-demand information is possible from marketers *anywhere* to customers *anywhere at any time.* Why? Operating hours and geographical constraints do not exist in marketspace. For example, Recreational Equipment (www.rei.com), an outdoor gear marketer, reports that 35 percent of its orders are placed between 10:00 P.M. and 7:00 A.M., long after and before retail stores are open for business. This isn't surprising. About 58 percent of Internet users prefer to shop and buy in their night clothes or pajamas![4] Similarly, a U.S. consumer from Chicago can access Marks & Spencer (www.marks-and-spencer.co.uk), the

FIGURE 18–1
Trend in online shoppers and online retail sales revenue in the United States

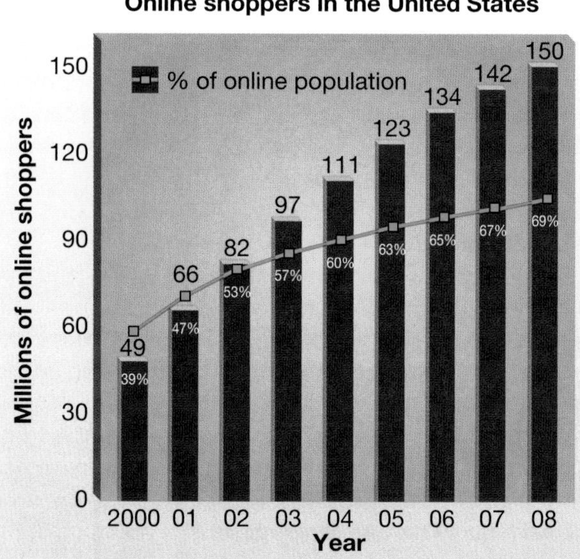

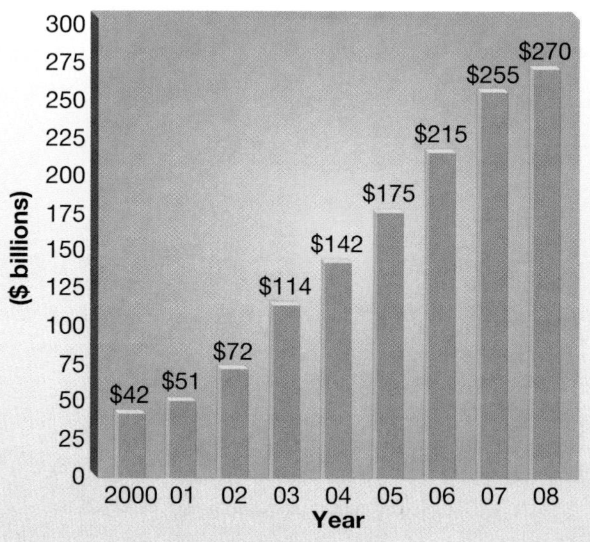

well-known British department store, to shop for clothing as easily as a person living near London's Piccadilly Square. Possession utility—getting a product or service to consumers so they can own or use it—is accelerated. Airline, car rental, and lodging electronic reservation systems such as Orbitz (www.orbitz.com) allow comparison shopping for the lowest fares, rents, and rates and almost immediate access to and confirmation of travel arrangements and accommodations.

The greatest marketspace opportunity for marketers, however, lies in its potential for creating form utility. Interactive two-way Internet-enabled communication capabilities in marketspace invite consumers to tell marketers specifically what their requirements are, making customization of a product or service to fit the buyer's exact needs possible. For instance, at Godiva.com, customers can choose an assortment of their favorite chocolates from an online catalog for a gift or a delectable self-indulgent treat.

Interactivity, Individuality, and Customer Relationships in Marketspace

Marketers also benefit from two unique capabilities of Internet technology that promote and sustain customer relationships. One is *interactivity;* the other is *individuality.*[5] Both capabilities are important building blocks for buyer–seller relationships. For these relationships to occur, companies need to interact with their customers by listening and responding to their needs. Marketers must also treat customers as individuals and empower them to (1) influence the timing and extent of the buyer–seller interaction and (2) have a say in the kind of products and services they buy, the information they receive, and in some cases, the prices they pay.

interactive marketing
Two-way buyer–seller electronic communications in a computer-mediated environment in which the buyer controls the kind and amount of information received from the seller

Internet technology allows for interaction, individualization, and customer relationship building to be carried out on a scale never before available and makes interactive marketing possible. **Interactive marketing** involves two-way buyer–seller electronic communication in a computer-mediated environment in which the buyer controls the kind and amount of information received from the seller. Interactive marketing is characterized by sophisticated choiceboard and personalization systems that transform information supplied by customers into customized responses to their individual needs.

Godiva creates form utility in the creation of personal assortments for its customers.

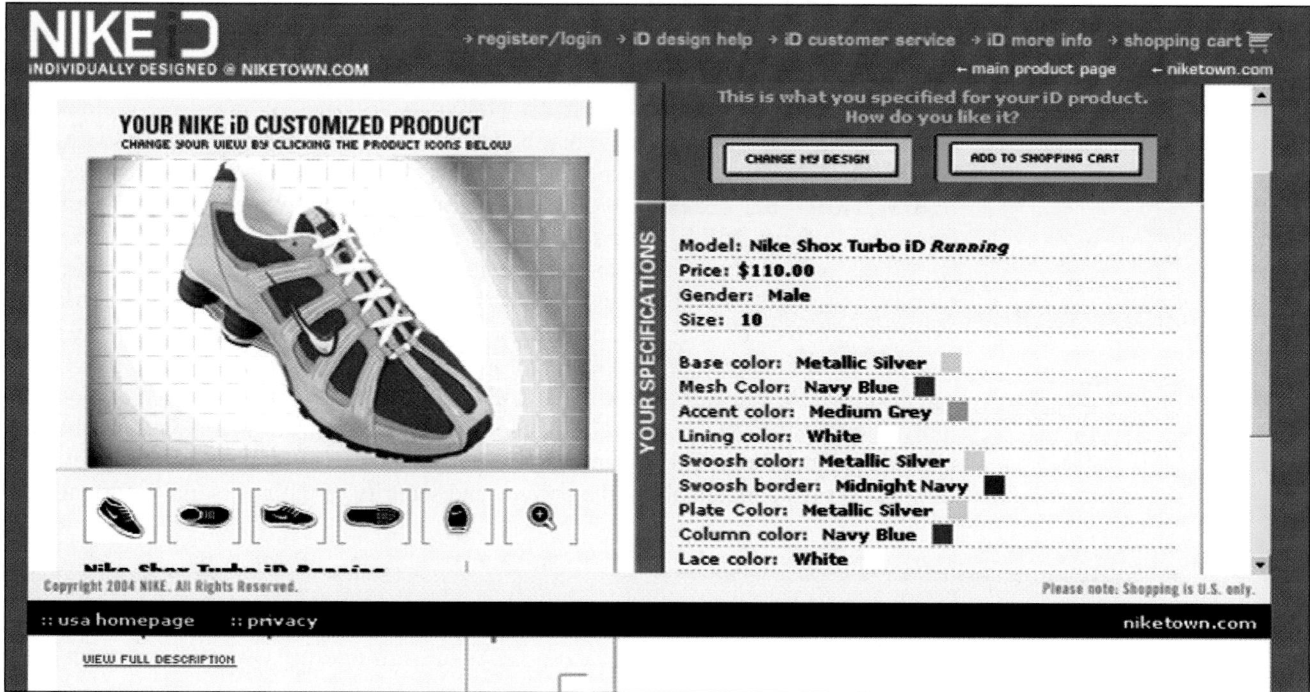

Nike has effectively used choiceboard technology for customizing athletic shoes.

choiceboard
Interactive, Internet-enabled system that allows individual customers to design their own products and services

Choiceboards A **choiceboard** is an interactive, Internet-enabled system that allows individual customers to design their own products and services by answering a few questions and choosing from a menu of product or service attributes (or components), prices, and delivery options.[6] Customers today can design their own computers with Dell's online configurator, style their own athletic shoe at Niketown.com, assemble their own investment portfolios with Schwab's mutual fund evaluator, build their own bicycle at SevenCycles.com, and create a diet and fitness program at eDiets.com that fits their lifestyle. Because choiceboards collect precise information about preferences and behavior of individual buyers, a company becomes more knowledgeable about a customer and better able to anticipate and fulfill that customer's needs.

collaborative filtering
Process that automatically groups people with similar buying intentions, preferences, and behaviors and predicts future purchases

Most choiceboards are essentially transaction devices. However, companies such as Dell have expanded the functionality of choiceboards using collaborative filtering technology. **Collaborative filtering** is a process that automatically groups people with similar buying intentions, preferences, and behaviors and predicts future purchases.[7] For example, say two people who have never met buy a few of the same CDs over time. Collaborative filtering software is programmed to reason that these two buyers might have similar musical tastes: If one buyer likes a particular CD, then the other will like it as well. The outcome? Collaborative filtering gives marketers the ability to make a dead-on sales recommendation to a buyer in *real time.* You see collaborative filtering applied each time you view a selection at Amazon.com and see "Customers who bought this (item) also bought. . . ."

Choiceboards and collaborative filtering represent two important capabilities of Internet technology and have changed the way companies operate today. According to an electronic commerce manager at IBM, "The business model of the past was make and sell. Now instead of make and sell, it's sense and respond."[8]

personalization
Consumer-initiated practice of generating content on a marketer's website that is tailored to an individual's specific needs and preferences

Personalization Choiceboards and collaborative filtering are marketer-initiated efforts to provide customized responses to the needs of individual buyers. Personalization systems are typically buyer-initiated efforts. **Personalization** is the consumer-initiated practice of generating content on a marketer's website that is custom tailored to an individual's specific needs and preferences. For example, Yahoo! (www.yahoo.com) allows users to create personalized My Yahoo pages. Users can add or delete a variety of types of information from their personal pages, including specific stock quotes, weather conditions in any city in the world, and local television schedules. In turn, Yahoo! can use the buyer profile data entered when users register at the site to tailor e-mail messages, advertising, and content to the individual—and even post a happy birthday greeting on the user's special day.

permission marketing
Asking for a consumer's consent (called opt-in*) to receive e-mail and advertising based on personal data supplied by the consumer*

An aspect of personalization is a buyer's willingness to have tailored communications brought to his or her attention. Obtaining this approval is called **permission marketing**—the solicitation of a consumer's consent (called *opt-in*) to receive e-mail and advertising based on personal data supplied by the consumer. Permission marketing is a proven vehicle for building and maintaining customer relationships, provided it is properly used. Companies that successfully employ permission marketing adhere to three rules. First, they make sure opt-in customers only receive information that is relevant and meaningful to them. Second, their customers are given the option of *opting out,* or changing the kind, amount, or timing of information sent to them. Finally, their customers are assured that their name or buyer profile data will not be sold or shared with others. This assurance is important because 70 percent of Internet users have expressed concern about the privacy and security of their personal information.[9]

Creating an Online Customer Experience

A continuing challenge for companies is the design and execution of marketing programs that capitalize on the unique and evolving customer value-creation capabilities of Internet technology. Companies realize that simply applying Internet technology to create time, place, form, and possession utility is not enough to claim a meaningful marketspace presence. The quality of the customer experience produced by a company is the standard by which a meaningful marketspace presence is measured.

customer experience
The sum total of interactions that a customer has with a company's website

From an interactive marketing perspective, **customer experience** is defined as the sum total of the interactions that a customer has with a company's website, from the initial look at a homepage through the entire purchase decision process.[10] Companies produce a customer experience through seven website design elements. These elements are context, content, community, customization, communication, connection, and commerce, each of which is summarized in Figure 18–2. A closer look at these elements illustrates how each contributes to customer experience.

FIGURE 18–2
Website design elements that drive customer experience

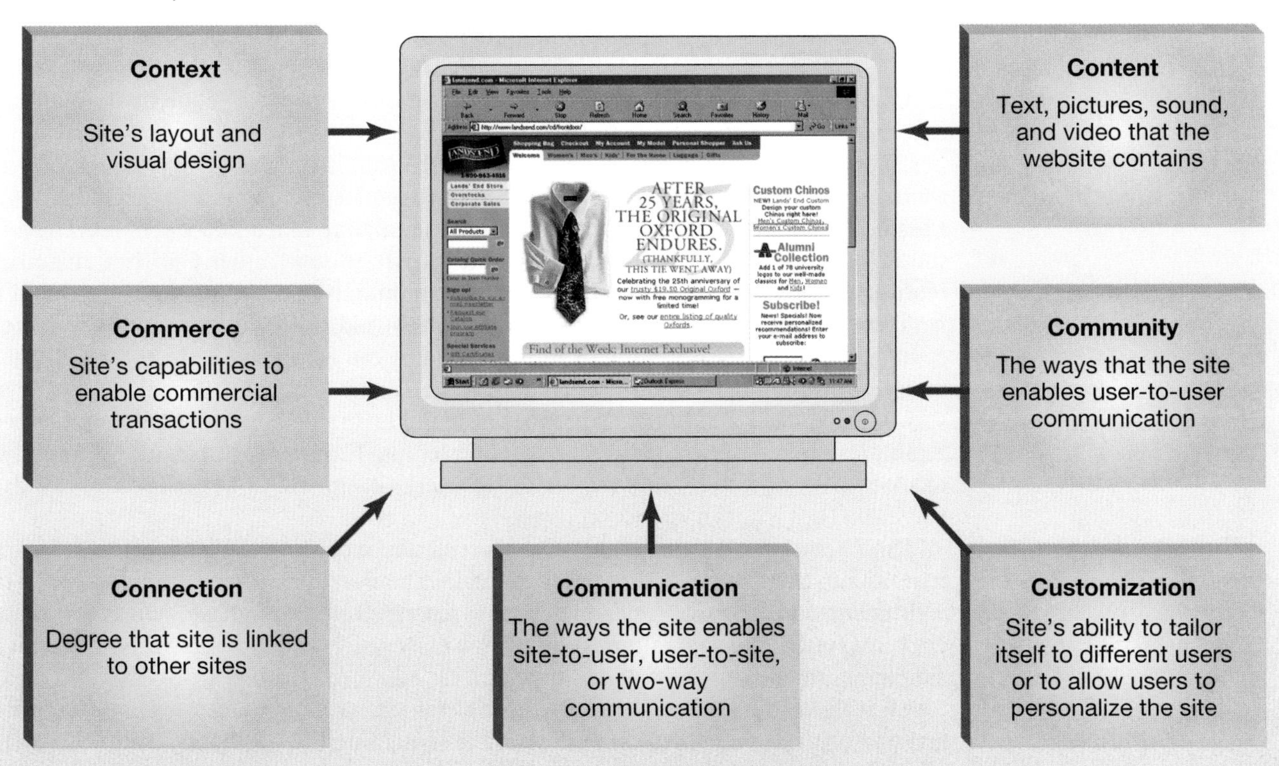

Context
Site's layout and visual design
Content
Text, pictures, sound, and video that the website contains
Commerce
Site's capabilities to enable commercial transactions
Community
The ways that the site enables user-to-user communication
Connection
Degree that site is linked to other sites
Communication
The ways the site enables site-to-user, user-to-site, or two-way communication
Customization
Site's ability to tailor itself to different users or to allow users to personalize the site
AFTER 25 YEARS, THE ORIGINAL OXFORD ENDURES.
(THANKFULLY, THIS TIE WENT AWAY)
Custom Chinos
Alumni Collection
Subscribe!
Find of the Week: Internet Exclusive!

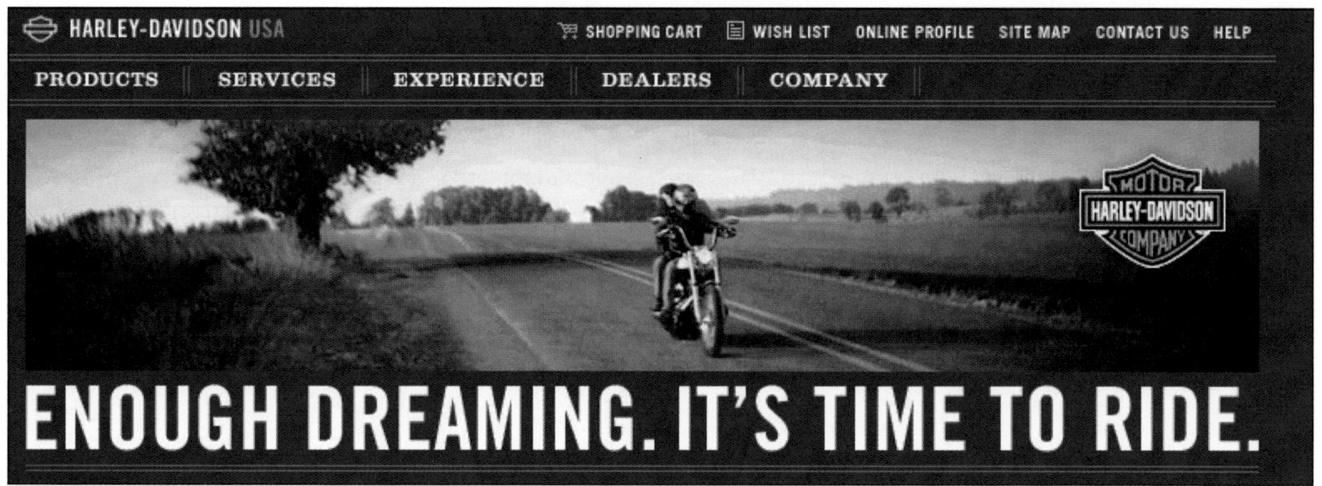

Harley-Davidson pays close attention to creating a favorable customer experience at its website.

Context refers to a website's aesthetic appeal and functional look and feel reflected in site layout and visual design. A functionally oriented website focuses largely on the company's offering, be it products, services, or information. For instance, travel websites tend to be functionally oriented with an emphasis on destinations, scheduling, and prices. In contrast, beauty websites, such as Covergirl.com, are more aesthetically oriented. As these examples suggest, context attempts to convey the core consumer benefit provided by the company's offerings. *Content* applies to all digital information on a website, including the presentation form—text, video, audio, and graphics. Content quality and presentation along with context dimensions combine to engage a website visitor and provide a platform for the five remaining design elements.

Website *customization* is the ability of a site to modify itself to, or be modified by, each individual user. This design element is prominent in websites that offer personalized content, such as My eBay and MyYahoo. The *connection* element in website design is the network of formal linkages between a company's site and other sites. These links are embedded in the website; appear as highlighted words, a picture, or graphic; and allow a user to effortlessly visit other sites with a mouse click. Connection is a major design element for informational websites such as *The New York Times*. For example, users of NYTimes.com can access the book review section and link to Barnes & Noble to order a book or browse related titles without ever visiting a store.

Communication refers to the dialogue that unfolds between the website and its users. Consumers—particularly those who have registered at a site—expect that communication be interactive and individualized in real time much like a personal conversation. In fact, some websites now enable a user to talk directly with a customer representative while shopping the site. For example, two-thirds of the sales through Dell.com involve human sales representatives. In addition, many company websites encourage user-to-user communications hosted by the company to create virtual communities, or simply, *community*. This design element is popular because it has been shown to enhance customer experience and build favorable buyer–seller relationships. Examples of communities range from the Parenting Community hosted by Kimberly-Clark (www.huggies.com) to the Harley Owners Group (HOG) sponsored by Harley-Davidson (www.harley-davidson.com).

The seventh design element is *commerce*—the website's ability to conduct sales transactions for products and services. Online transactions are quick and simple in well-designed websites. Amazon.com has mastered this design element with "one-click shopping," a patented feature that allows users to place and order products with a single mouse click.

All websites do not include every design element. Although every website has context and content, they differ in the use of the remaining five elements. Why? Websites have different purposes. For example, only websites that emphasize the actual sale of products and services include the commerce element. Websites that are used primarily for advertising and promotion purposes emphasize the communication element. The difference between these two types of websites is discussed later in the chapter.

Concept Check

1. The greatest marketspace opportunity for marketers lies in the creation of what kind of utility?
2. Companies produce a customer experience through what seven website design elements?

ONLINE CONSUMER BEHAVIOR AND MARKETING PRACTICE IN MARKETSPACE

Who are online consumers, and what do they buy? Why and when do they choose to shop and purchase products and services in the marketspace rather than or in addition to the traditional marketplace? Answers to these questions have a direct bearing on marketspace marketing practices.

Who Is the Online Consumer?

Many labels are given to online consumers—cybershoppers, Netizens, and e-shoppers—suggesting they are all alike. They are not, but as a group, they do differ demographically from the general population. Online consumers differ from the general population in one important respect. They own or have access to a computer or an Internet-enabled device, such as a wireless cellular telephone or personal digital assistant.

Online consumers are the subsegment of all Internet users who use this technology to research products and services and make purchases. About 85 percent of all adult Internet users have sought online product or service information at one time or another.[11] For example, 75 percent of prospective travelers have researched travel information online, even though fewer than 25 percent have actually made online travel reservations. Over 70 percent have researched cell phones before making a purchase, but only 5 percent of users actually bought a cell phone online. About 70 percent of Internet users have actually purchased a product or service online.

As a group, online consumers, like all Internet users, are evenly split between men and women and tend to be better educated, younger, and more affluent than the general U.S. population, which makes them an attractive market. Even though online shopping and buying is growing in popularity, a small percentage of online consumers still account for a disproportionate share of online retail sales in the United States. It is estimated that 20 percent of online consumers who spend $1,000-plus per year online account for 87 percent of total consumer online retail sales.[12] Also, women tend to purchase more goods and services online than men.

Numerous marketing research firms have studied the lifestyles and shopping habits of online consumers. A recurrent insight is that online consumers are diverse and represent different kinds of people seeking different kinds of online experiences. As an illustration, the Marketing NewsNet on the next page provides an in-depth look at life styles and shopping habits of today's "Internet mom."[13]

What Online Consumers Buy

Much still needs to be learned about online consumer purchase behavior. Although research has documented the most frequently purchased products and services bought online, marketers also need to know why these items are popular in the marketspace.

MARKETING NEWSNET

Meet Today's Internet Mom—All 31 Million!

TECHNOLOGY & E-COMMERCE

Do you have fond childhood memories of surfing the Internet with your mother? Today's children between the ages of 6 and 14 probably will.

Recent research indicates that 31 million mothers are online regularly. They're typically 38 years old and tend to be married, college educated, and working outside the home. A study conducted by C&R Research on behalf of Disney Online has identified four segments of mothers based on their Internet usage. The *Yes Mom* segment represents 14 percent of online moms. They work outside the home, go online 8 hours per week, and value the convenience of obtaining information about products and services. The *Mrs. Net Skeptic* segment accounts for 31 percent of online moms. They tend to be stay-at-home moms, are extremely family-oriented, and go online 6 hours per week for parenting and children's education information and food and cooking tips. The *Tech Nester* mom (32 percent of online moms) believes the Internet brings their family closer together. They average 10 hours per week online and prefer online shopping to in-store shopping. The fourth segment—*Passive under Pressure* moms—tend to be Internet newbies and go online, but infrequently.

The first three segments, which account for 77 percent of online moms, agree that the Internet has simplified their lives. They also say that the Internet has been in invaluable information source for vacation travel, financial products, and automobiles and providing useful ideas and suggestions on family-related topics. Online moms ranked weather, food and cooking, entertainment, news, health, and parenting as the most popular websites to visit.

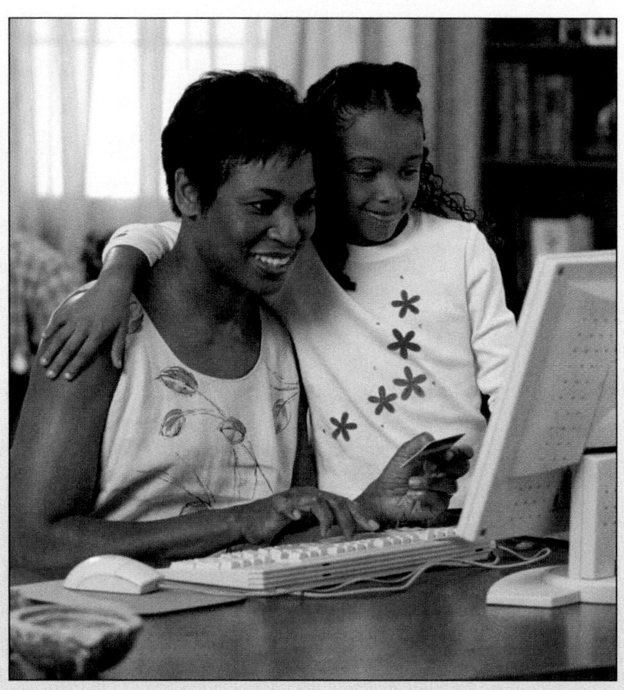

There are six general product and service categories that dominate online consumer buying today and for the foreseeable future. One category consists of items for which product information is an important part of the purchase decision, but prepurchase trial is not necessarily critical. Items such as computers, computer accessories, and consumer electronics sold by Dell.com fall into this category. So do books sold by Amazon.com and Barnes & Noble (www.barnesandnoble.com). Both booksellers publish short reviews of new books that visitors to their websites can read before making a purchase decision. According to an authority on electronic commerce, "You've read the reviews, you want it, you don't need to try it on."[14] A second category includes items for which audio or video demonstration is important. This category consists of CDs, videos, and DVDs sold by columbiahouse.com and cdnow.com. The third category contains items that can be delivered digitally, including computer software, travel and lodging reservations and confirmations, financial brokerage services, and electronic ticketing. Popular websites for these items include travelocity.com, ticketmaster.com, and schwab.com.

Unique items, such as collectibles, specialty goods, and foods and gifts, represent a fourth category. Collectible auction houses (www.sothebys.com and www.butterfields.com), gourmet foods (www.gourmetfoodmall.com), and flower and gift marketer 1-800-Flowers (www.1800flowers.com) sell these products. A fifth category includes items that are regularly purchased and where convenience is very important. Many consumer-packaged goods, such as grocery products, fall into this category. A final

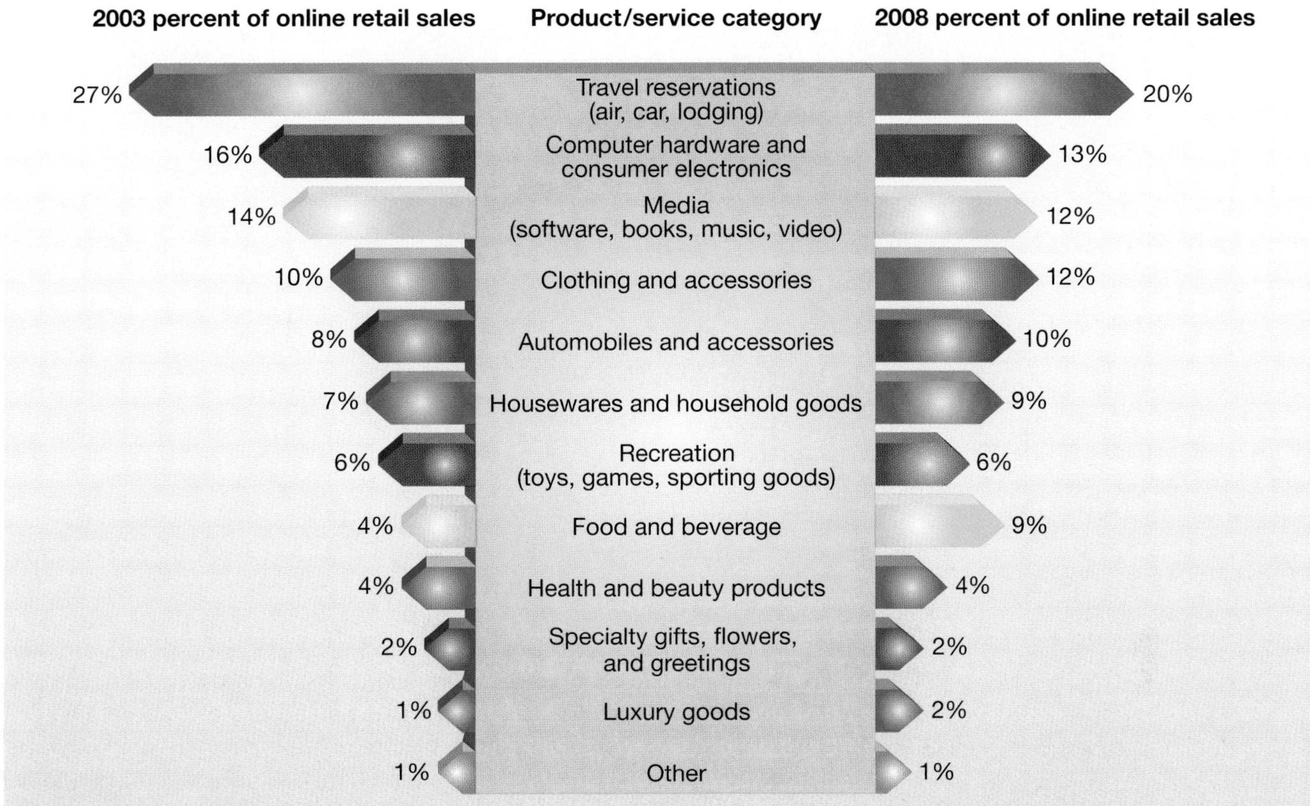

FIGURE 18–3
Estimated online retail sales by product/service category: 2003 and 2008

category of items consists of highly standardized products and services for which information about price is important. Certain kinds of insurance (auto and homeowners), home improvement products, casual apparel, and toys make up this category. Figure 18–3 shows the breakdown of estimated online retail sales by product and service category for 2003 and 2008.[15]

Why Consumers Shop and Buy Online

Marketers emphasize the customer value-creation possibilities, the importance of interactivity, individuality and relationship building, and producing customer experience in the marketspace. However, consumers typically refer to six reasons why they shop and buy online: convenience, choice, customization, communication, cost, and control (Figure 18–4 on the next page).

bots
Electronic shopping agents or robots that comb websites to compare prices and product or service features

Convenience Online shopping and buying is *convenient.* Consumers can visit Wal-Mart at www.walmart.com to scan and order from among thousands of displayed products without fighting traffic, finding a parking space, walking through long aisles, and standing in store checkout lines. Alternatively, online consumers can use **bots**, electronic shopping agents or robots that comb websites to compare prices and product or service features. In either instance, an online consumer has never ventured from his or her computer monitor. But, for convenience to remain a source of customer value creation, websites must be easy to locate and navigate, and image downloads must be fast.

Choice *Choice,* the second reason consumers shop and buy online, has two dimensions. First, choice exists in the product or service selection offered to consumers. Buyers desiring selection can avail themselves of numerous websites for almost anything they want. For instance, online buyers of consumer electronics can shop individual

FIGURE 18–4
Why consumers shop and buy online

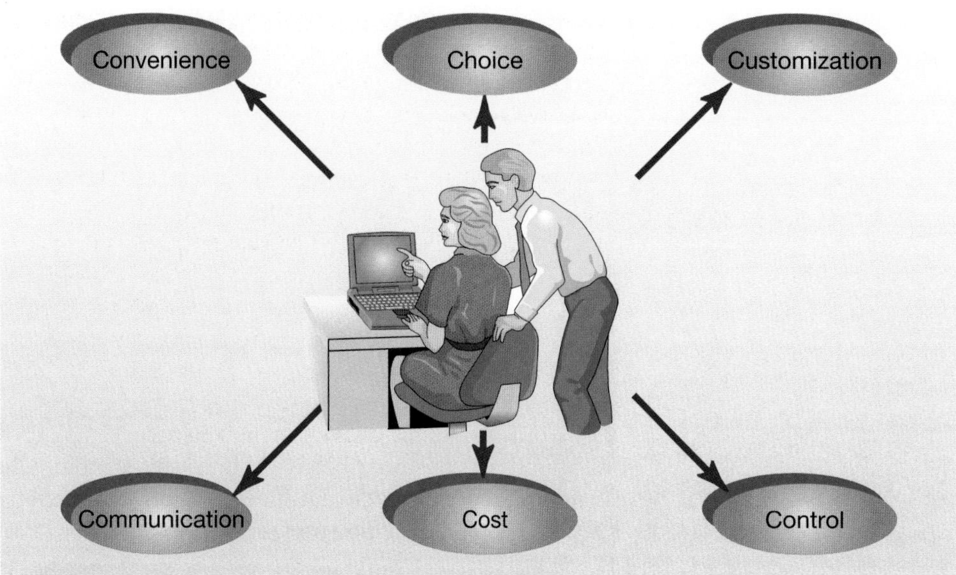

manufacturers such as Bose (www.bose.com) or Sony (www.sony.com), or visit QVC.com, a general merchant, that offers more than 100,000 products. Choice assistance is the second dimension. Here, the interactive capabilities of Internet-enabled technologies invite customers to engage in an electronic dialogue with marketers for the purpose of making informed choices. Lands' End (www.landsend.com) provides choice assistance with its "My Virtual Model" apparel service. Men and women submit their body shape, skin color, hair style, height, weight, and other attributes. The model then "tries on" outfits identified by the customer. Like any good salesperson, the service recommends flattering outfits for purchase.

Customization Even with a broad selection and choice assistance, some customers prefer one-of-a-kind items that fit their specific needs. *Customization* arises from Internet-enabled capabilities that make possible a highly interactive and individualized information and exchange environment for shoppers and buyers. Remember the earlier Nike, Schwab, Dell, and Seven Cycles examples? To varying degrees, online consumers also benefit from **customerization**—the practice of not only customizing a product or service but also personalizing the marketing and overall shopping and buying interaction for each customer.[16] Customerization seeks to do more than offer consumers the right product, at the right time, at the right price. It combines choiceboard and personalization systems to expand the exchange environment beyond a transaction and makes shopping and buying an enjoyable, personal experience.

customerization
The practice of customizing not only a product or service but also personalizing the marketing and overall shopping and buying interaction for each customer

Communication Online consumers particularly welcome the *communication* capabilities of Internet-enabled technologies. This communication can take three forms: (1) marketer-to-consumer e-mail notification, (2) consumer-to-marketer buying and service requests, and (3) consumer-to-consumer chat rooms and instant messaging. This communication capability is evidenced in the fact that over 20 trillion e-mail messages are sent annually worldwide and about 800 million instant messages are sent daily on America Online.[17]

Communication has proven to be a double-edged sword for online consumers.[18] On the one hand, the interactive communication capabilities of Internet-enabled technologies increase consumer convenience, reduce information search costs, and make choice assistance and customization possible. Communication also promotes the development of company-hosted and independent **web communities**—websites that allow people to congregate online and exchange views on topics of common interest. For instance, iVillage.com is a web community for women and includes topics such as

web communities
Websites that allow people to meet online and exchange views on topics of common interest

career management, personal finances, parenting, relationships, beauty, and health. A recent development is the creation of web logs, or blogs. A *blog* is a webpage that serves as a publicly accessible personal journal for an individual. Blogs have grown in popularity because they provide online forums on a wide variety of subjects ranging from politics to car repair.

spam
Electronic junk mail or unsolicited e-mail

On the other hand, communications can take the form of electronic junk mail or unsolicited e-mail, called **spam**. The prevalence of spam has prompted some online services such as Hotmail to institute policies and procedures to prevent spammers from spamming their subscribers, and several states have antispamming laws. In 2004, the CAN-SPAM (*Controlling the Assault of Non-Solicited Pornography and Marketing*) Act became effective and restricts information collection and unsolicited e-mail promotions on the Internet.

Internet-enabled communication capabilities also make possible *buzz,* a popular term for word-of-mouth behavior in marketspace. Chapter 5 described the importance of word of mouth in consumer behavior. Internet technology has magnified its significance. In marketspace, the scope and speed of word of mouth has increased fourfold on average because of consumer chat rooms, blogs, instant messaging, and product and service review websites such as epinions.com and consumerreview.com.[19] Buzz is particularly influential for toys, cars, sporting goods, motion pictures, apparel, consumer electronics, pharmaceuticals, health and beauty products, and health care services. Some marketers have capitalized on this phenomenon by creating buzz through viral marketing.

viral marketing
Internet-enabled promotional strategy that encourages users to forward market-initiated messages to others via e-mail

Viral marketing is an Internet-enabled promotional strategy that encourages individuals to forward marketer-initiated messages to others via e-mail. There are three approaches to viral marketing. First, marketers can embed a message in the product or service so that customers hardly realize they are passing it along. The classic example is Hotmail, which was one of the first companies to provide free, Internet-based e-mail. Each outgoing e-mail message has the tagline: Get Your Private, Free Email from MSN Hotmail. Today, Hotmail has more than 100 million users. Second, marketers can make the website content so compelling that viewers want to share it with others. De Beers has done this at www.adiamondisforever.com, where users can design their own rings and show them to others. One out of five website visitors e-mail their ring design to friends and relatives who visit the site. Similarly, eBay reports that more than half its visitors are referred by other visitors. Finally, marketers can offer incentives (discounts, sweepstakes, or free merchandise) for referrals. Procter & Gamble did this for its Physique shampoo. People who referred 10 friends to the shampoo's website (www.physique.com) received a free, travel-sized styling spray and were entered in a sweepstakes to win a year's supply of the shampoo. The response? The promotion generated 2 million referrals and made Physique the most successful new shampoo ever launched in the United States.

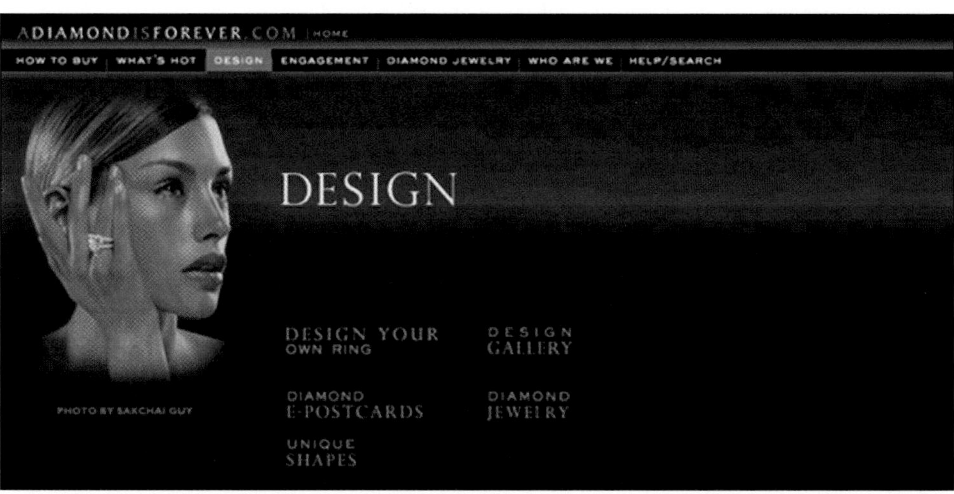

De Beers effectively applied viral marketing in the launch of its custom ring website.

How did Procter & Gamble use viral marketing techniques to make Physique shampoo the most successful new shampoo ever launched in the United States? Read the text to find the answer.

Cost Consumer *cost* is a fifth reason for online shopping and buying. Research indicates that many popular items bought online can be purchased at the same price or cheaper than in retail stores.[20] Lower prices also result from Internet-enabled software that permits **dynamic pricing**, the practice of changing prices for products and services in real time in response to supply and demand conditions. Dynamic pricing is a form of flexible pricing and can often result in lower prices. It is typically used for pricing time-sensitive items like airline seats, scarce items found at art or collectible auctions, and out-of-date items such as last year's models of computer equipment and accessories. A consumer's cost of external information search, including time spent and often the hassle of shopping, is also reduced. Greater shopping convenience and lower external search costs are two major reasons for the popularity of online shopping and buying among women, and particularly for those who work outside the home.

dynamic pricing
Practice of changing prices for products and services in real time in response to supply and demand conditions

Control The sixth reason consumers prefer to buy online is the *control* it gives them over their shopping and purchase decision process. Online shoppers and buyers are empowered consumers. They deftly use Internet technology to seek information, evaluate alternatives, and make purchase decisions on their own time, terms, and conditions. Nearly 80 percent of online consumers regularly engage **portals** and search engines, which are electronic gateways to the Internet that supply a broad array of news and entertainment, information resources, and shopping services. Yahoo!, America Online, and MSN.com are well-known portals. Google is a popular search engine. To evaluate alternatives, consumers visit comparison shopping websites such as comparenet.com and price.com or employ bots such as Yahoo! Shopping, which provide product descriptions and prices for a wide variety of brands and models. The result of these activities is a more informed consumer and discerning shopper. In the words of one marketing consultant, "In the marketspace, the customer is in charge."[21]

portals
Electronic gateways to the Internet that supply a broad array of news and entertainment, information resources, and shopping services

Even though consumers have many reasons for shopping and buying online, a segment of Internet users refrain from making purchases for privacy and security reasons as described in the accompanying Ethics and Social Responsibility Alert.[22] These consumers are concerned about a rarely mentioned seventh C—cookies. **Cookies** are computer files that a marketer can download onto the computer of an online shopper who visits the marketer's website. Cookies allow the marketer's website to record a user's visit, track visits to other websites, and store and retrieve this information in the future. Cookies also contain information provided by visitors, such as expressed product preferences, personal data, passwords, and financial information, including credit card numbers. Clearly, cookies make possible customized and personalized content for online shoppers. The controversy surrounding cookies is summed up by an authority on the technology: "At best a cookie makes for a user-friendly Web world: like a doorman or salesclerk who knows who you are. At worst, cookies represent a potential loss of privacy."[23]

cookies
Computer files that a marketer can download onto the computer of an online shopper who visits the marketer's website

ETHICS AND SOCIAL RESPONSIBILITY ALERT

Sweet and Sour Cookies in the Marketspace

Privacy and security are two key reasons consumers are leery of online shopping and buying. A recent Jupiter Research poll reported that 70 percent of online consumers are concerned about threats to their personal privacy on the Internet. Even more telling, 53 percent have stopped shopping a website or forgone an online purchase because of privacy and security concerns. Industry analysts estimate that low consumer confidence in privacy and security will result in lost sales of $27 billion by 2008.

The privacy and security concerns of online consumers are related to the cookies described in the text and how those cookies can be used or misused. A percolating issue is whether the U.S. government should pass more stringent Internet privacy and security laws. About 70 percent of online consumers favor such action. Companies have adopted initiatives to develop their own privacy standards without government action. The Online Privacy Alliance (www.privacyalliance.org) is a consortium of businesses and associations that aims to promote electronic commerce through online privacy and security policies and self-regulation. TRUSTe (www.truste.com) awards its trademark to websites that comply with standards of privacy protection and disclosure.

Do you think that governmental or self-regulation is the best way to deal with issues of privacy and security in the marketspace?

When and Where Online Consumers Shop and Buy

Shopping and buying also happen at different times in marketspace than in the traditional marketplace.[24] About 80 percent of online retail sales occur Monday through Friday. The busiest shopping day is Wednesday. By comparison, 35 percent of retail store sales are registered on the weekend. Saturday is the most popular shopping day. Monday through Friday online shopping and buying often occurs during normal work hours—some 40 percent of online consumers say they visit websites from their place of work, which partially accounts for the sales level during the workweek. Favorite websites for workday shopping and buying include those featuring event tickets, auctions, online periodical subscriptions, flowers and gifts, consumer electronics, and travel. Websites offering health and beauty items, apparel and accessories, and music and video tend to be browsed and bought from a consumer's home.

Consumers are more likely to browse than buy online. Although 9 in 10 online consumers regularly browse in the marketspace of websites, more than half (51 percent) confine most of their purchases to the traditional retail store marketplace.[25] Consumer marketspace browsing and buying in the traditional marketplace has popularized multichannel marketing, which is described next.

Concept Check

1. What is viral marketing?
2. What are the six reasons consumers prefer to shop and buy online?

MULTICHANNEL MARKETING TO THE ONLINE CONSUMER

The fact that a large number of consumers browse and buy in two market environments means that few companies limit their marketing programs exclusively to the traditional marketplace or marketspace. Today, it is commonplace for companies to maintain a presence in both market environments of some kind and measure. This dual presence is made possible by multichannel marketing.

Integrating and Leveraging Multiple Channels with Multichannel Marketing

Companies often employ multiple marketing channels for their products and services as described in Chapter 13. *Dual distribution* is the term used to describe this practice, which focuses on reaching different consumers through different marketing channels. For example, Avon markets its health and beauty products directly through Avon sales representatives, a brochure, kiosks in shopping malls, and an Avon website. The various communication (representatives and brochures) and delivery (kiosks) channels allow Avon to reach different consumers, feature different brands, and provide different shopping and buying experiences.

Multichannel marketing bears some resemblance to dual distribution. For example, different communication and delivery channels are used such as catalogs, kiosks, retail stores, personal selling, and websites. In fact, retailers that employ two or more of these channels are labeled *multichannel retailers* as described in Chapter 14. However, the resemblance ends at this point. **Multichannel marketing** is the *blending* of different communication and delivery channels that are *mutually reinforcing* in attracting, retaining, and building relationships with consumers who shop and buy in the traditional marketplace and marketspace. Multichannel marketing seeks to integrate a firm's communication and delivery channels, not differentiate them. In doing so, consumers can browse and buy "anytime, anywhere, anyway," expecting that the experience will be similar regardless of channel. At Eddie Bauer, for example, every effort is made to make the apparel shopping and purchase process for its customers the same in its retail stores, with its catalog, and at its website. According to an Eddie Bauer marketing manager, "We don't distinguish between channels because it's all Eddie Bauer to our customers."[26]

multichannel marketing
Blending of different communication and delivery channels that are mutually reinforcing in attracting, retaining, and building relationship with consumers

Multichannel marketing also can leverage the value-adding capabilities of different channels.[27] For example, retail stores can leverage their physical presence by allowing customers to pick up their online orders at a nearby store or return or exchange nonstore purchases if they wish. Catalogs can serve as shopping tools for online purchasing, as they do for store purchasing. Websites can help consumers do their homework before visiting a store. Office Depot has leveraged its store, catalog, and website channels with impressive results. The company, which is the world's largest office supply retail chain, is the second-largest Internet retailer in the world (behind Amazon.com), doing more than $2 billion in online retail sales annually.

Implementing Multichannel Marketing

Not all companies employ websites for multichannel marketing the same way. This should not be surprising. Different companies apply the value-creation capabilities of Internet technology differently depending on their overall marketing program.

Websites play a multifaceted role in multichannel marketing because they can serve as either a communication or delivery channel. Two general applications of websites exist based on their intended purpose: (1) transactional websites and (2) promotional websites.

Multichannel Marketing with Transactional Websites *Transactional websites* are essentially electronic storefronts. They focus principally on converting an online browser into an online, catalog, or in-store buyer using the website design elements described earlier. Transactional websites are most common among store and catalog retailers and direct selling companies, such as Tupperware. The Gap, for instance, generates more sales volume from its website (www.gap.com) than any one of its stores, save one.[28] Retailers and direct selling firms have found that their websites, while cannibalizing sales volume from stores, catalogs, and sales representatives, attract new customers and influence sales.[29] Consider Victoria's Secret, the well-known specialty retailer of intimate apparel for women age 18 to 45. It reports that almost 60 percent of its website customers are men, most of whom generate new sales volume for the company. Likewise, Sears.com is estimated to account for more than $600 million worth of Sears, Roebuck & Co. merchandise sales. Why? Sears customers first research merchandise online before visiting a store.

Transactional websites are used less often by manufacturers of consumer products. A recurring issue for manufacturers is the threat of *channel conflict,* described in Chapter 13, and the potential harm to trade relationships with their retailing intermediaries. Still, manufacturers do use transactional websites, often cooperating with retailers. For example, Ethan Allen, the furniture manufacturer, markets its product line at www.ethanallen.com. Whenever feasible, Ethan Allen retailers fill online orders and receive 25 percent of the sales price. For items shipped directly from the Ethan Allen factory, the store nearest the customer receives 10 percent of the sales price.[30] In addition, Ethan Allen, like other manufacturers, typically lists stores on their website where their merchandise can be shopped and bought. More frequently, however, manufacturers engage multichannel channels, using websites as advertising and promotion vehicles.

Multichannel Marketing with Promotional Websites *Promotional websites* have a very different purpose than transactional sites. They advertise and promote a company's products and services and provide information on how items can be used and where they can be purchased. They often engage the visitor in an interactive experience involving games, contests, and quizzes with electronic coupons and other gifts as prizes. Procter & Gamble maintains separate websites for its leading brands, including Pringles potato chips (www.pringles.com), Vidal Sassoon hair products (www.vidalsassoon.com), Scope mouthwash (www.scope-mouthwash.com), and Pampers diapers (www.pampers.com). Promotional sites can be effective in generating interest in and trial of a company's products and services (see Figure 18–5).[31] General Motors reports that 80 percent of the people visiting a Saturn store first visited the brand's website (www.saturn.com) and 70 percent of Saturn leads come from its website.

Promotional websites also can be used to support a company's traditional marketing channel and build customer relationships. This is the objective of the Clinique Division

FIGURE 18–5
Implementing multichannel marketing with promotional websites

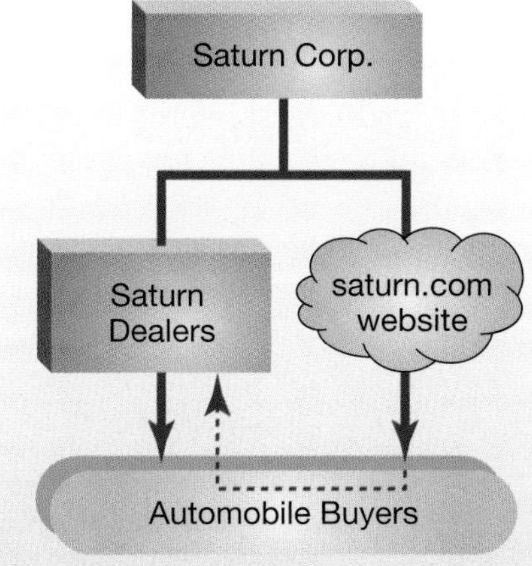

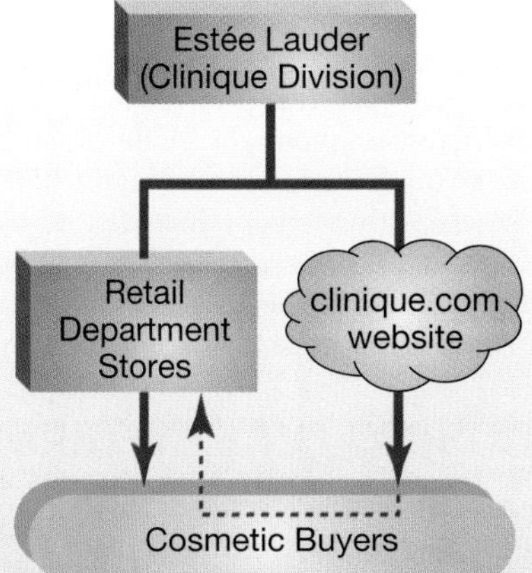

- 70% of Saturn leads come from its website.
- 80% of people visiting a Saturn dealer first visited its website.

- 80% of current Clinique buyers who visit its website later purchase a Clinique product at a store.
- 37% of non-Clinique buyers make a Clinique purchase after visiting its website.

of Estée Lauder, Inc., which markets cosmetics through department stores. Clinique reports that 80 percent of current customers who visit its website (www.clinique.com) later purchase a Clinique product at a department store; 37 percent of non-Clinique buyers make a Clinique purchase after visiting the company's website.

The popularity of multichannel marketing is apparent in its growing impact on online retail sales.[32] Fully 65 percent of U.S. online retail sales in 2005 were made by companies that practiced multichannel marketing. Multichannel marketers are expected to register about 85 percent of U.S. online retail sales in 2010.

Concept Check

1. Multichannel marketing is ________________.
2. Channel conflict between manufacturers and retailers is likely to arise when manufacturers use ________________ websites.

CHAPTER IN REVIEW

1 *Describe what interactive marketing is and how it creates customer value, customer relationships, and customer experiences.*

Interactive marketing involves two-way buyer–seller electronic communication in a computer-mediated environment in which the buyer controls the kind and amount of information received from the seller. It creates customer value by providing time, place, form, and possession utility for consumers. Customer relationships are created and sustained through two unique capabilities of Internet technology: interactivity and individuality. From an interactive marketing perspective, customer experience represents the sum total of the interactions that a customer has with a company's website, from the initial look at a homepage through the entire purchase decision process. Companies produce a customer experience through seven website design elements. These elements are context, content, community, customization, communication, connection, and commerce.

2 *Explain why certain types of products and services are particularly suited for interactive marketing.*

Certain types of products and services seem to be particularly suited for interactive marketing. One category consists of items for which product information is an important part of the purchase decision, but prepurchase trial is not necessarily critical. A second category involves items for which audio or video demonstration is important. A third category contains items that can be digitally delivered. Unique items represent a fourth category. A fifth category includes items that are regularly purchased and where convenience is very important. A final category consists of highly standardized items for which information about price is important.

3 *Describe why consumers shop and buy online and how marketers influence online purchasing behavior.*

There are six reasons consumers shop and buy online. They are convenience, choice, customization, communication, cost, and control. Marketers have capitalized on these reasons through a variety of means. For example, they provide choice assistance using choiceboard and collaborative filtering technology, which also provides opportunities for customization. Company-hosted web communities and viral marketing practices capitalize on the communications dimensions of Internet-enabled technologies. Dynamic pricing provides real-time responses to supply and demand conditions, often resulting in lower prices to consumers. Permission marketing is popular given consumer interest in control.

4 *Define multichannel marketing and the role of transactional and promotional websites in reaching online consumers.*

Multichannel marketing is the blending of different communication and delivery channels that are mutually reinforcing in attracting, retaining, and building relationships with consumers who shop and buy in the traditional marketplace and marketspace. In practice, this means that companies simultaneously market their products through personal selling, retail stores, websites, catalogs, and kiosks. Websites play a multifaceted role in multichannel marketing because they can serve as either a delivery or communication channel. In this regard, transactional websites are essentially electronic storefronts. They focus principally on converting an online browser into an online, catalog, or in-store buyer using the website design elements described earlier. On the other hand, promotional websites serve to advertise and promote a company's products and services and provide information on how items can be used and where they can be purchased.

FOCUSING ON KEY TERMS

bots p. 405
choiceboard p. 400
collaborative filtering p. 400
cookies p. 408
customer experience p. 401
customerization p. 406
dynamic pricing p. 408
interactive marketing p. 399
multichannel marketing p. 410
permission marketing p. 401
personalization p. 400
portals p. 408
spam p. 407
viral marketing p. 407
web communities p. 406

DISCUSSION AND APPLICATION QUESTIONS

1 About 70 percent of Internet users had actually purchased something online. Have you made an online purchase? If so, why do you think so many people who have access to the Internet are not also online buyers? If not, why are you reluctant to do so? Do you think that the Internet benefits consumers even if they don't make a purchase online?

2 Like the traditional marketplace, marketspace offers marketers opportunities to create greater time, place, form, and possession utility. How do you think Internet-enabled technology rates in terms of creating these values? Take a shopping trip at a virtual retailer of your choice (don't buy anything unless you really want to). Then compare the time, place, form, and possession utility provided by the virtual retailer with what you enjoyed during a nonelectronic experience shopping for the same product category.

3 Visit Amazon.com (www.amazon.com) or Barnes & Noble (www.barnesandnoble.com). As you tour the company's website, think about how shopping for books online compares with a trip to your university bookstore to buy books. Specifically, compare and contrast your shopping experiences with respect to convenience, choice, customization, communication, cost, and control.

4 Suppose you are planning to buy a new car so you decide to visit www.carpoint.com. Based on your experience visiting that site, do you think you would enjoy more or less control in negotiating with the dealer when you actually purchase your vehicle?

5 Visit the website for your university or college. Based on your visit, would you conclude that the site is a transactional site or a promotional site? Why? How would you rate the site in terms of the six website design elements that affect customer experience?

GOING ONLINE Tracking Trends in Interactive Marketing

What are the most recent statistics and trends in interactive and multichannel marketing? Look no further than Clickz.com, an online service that abstracts up-to-date research on Internet usage and applications from around the world. Clickz.com conveniently organizes research by business, social, technical, demographic, and geographical categories for easy inspection.

Visit the Clickz website at www.clickz.com, then click the "Stats" link. Your assignment is as follows:

1 Choose a topic covered in the chapter that interests you, such as the demographics of Internet users. Compare and contrast the most recent research published in Clickz.com with information contained in the chapter. Don't be surprised if you find differences.

2 Choose two regions of the world, such as North America and Europe. How do Internet usage and interactive marketing differ between the two regions based on the most recent research?

BUILDING YOUR MARKETING PLAN

Does your marketing plan involve a marketspace presence for your product or service? If the answer is no, read no further and do not include this element in your plan. If the answer is yes, then attention must be given to developing a website in your marketing plan. A useful starting point is to:

1 Describe how each website element—context, content, community, customization, communication, connection, and commerce—will be used to create a customer experience.

2 Identify a company's website that best reflects your website conceptualization.

VIDEO CASE 18 McFarlane Toys: The Best of Interactive Marketing

"All my life, I've been underwhelmed by the sports action figures sold in the toy aisles," says Todd McFarlane, founder of McFarlane Toys.

This assessment of the marketplace led McFarlane to create his own toy manufacturing company, an entirely new category of toys called "upscale figures," and an extraordinarily sophisticated marketing strategy based on traditional and interactive approaches. McFarlane Toys is now one of the world's largest toy companies. The company's products include action figures of professional athletes, rock stars, NASCAR drivers, and characters from movies such as *The Terminator, The Matrix,* and *Austin Powers.* Its marketing programs have used Internet contests, virtual showrooms, online catalogs, and a variety of other award-winning tools. Overall, McFarlane Toys has transformed a category that used to be just plastic replicas for children into an art collectible for adults. McFarlane explains, "It's about creating a toy that, if you had it on your shelf, somebody wouldn't say, 'Are you collecting toys? How old are you?'"

THE COMPANY

McFarlane started his career as an artist for Marvel/Epic Comics, working on issues of *Incredible Hulk, Amazing Spider-Man, Batman,* and *Coyote.* Eventually he formed Image Comics with six other Marvel artists and began work on his own comic book, *Spawn.* The first issue of *Spawn* sold a record-breaking 1.7 million copies. Since then the series has become a top-selling comic published in 16 languages and sold in more than 120 countries.

The success of *Spawn* soon generated licensing proposals from toy companies, movies studios, and television producers. When Todd met with each of the companies, however, he was concerned about his ability to have creative control over the toy production. As a result, he started his own toy company, McFarlane Toys, in order to guarantee his fans high quality, intricately detailed, and reasonably priced action figures. *Spawn* action figures quickly became one of the most successful toys on the market.

Following the introduction of the Spawn action figures, McFarlane began producing action figures of pop culture icons in film, music, gaming, and sports. The company also signed license agreements with the four major North American sports leagues—football, baseball, basketball, and hockey. In addition, McFarlane Toys produced toys for licensors such as the Beatles, *Shrek,* KISS, *X-Files, Alien,* AC/DC, Jimi Hendrix, and many others. The quality and the collectibility of the figures has given McFarlane Toys a worldwide reputation among retailers and consumers.

When he founded McFarlane Toys, Todd said, "I'm just going to do action figures. I'm going to be the king of Aisle 7." Other opportunities soon appeared, however, and Todd became involved in the production of feature films, music videos, electronic games, and animated television. Some of these projects have included: the live-action film *Spawn* which grossed $50 million in just 19 days; the HBO series *Todd McFarlane's Spawn* which won an Emmy award; and the music video for Korn's *Freak on a Leash* which received a Grammy award. All of these activities have helped expand the growing number of McFarlane Toy fans.

Today, McFarlane Toys is ranked among the top five makers of action figures, with sales estimated between $25 and $125 million. McFarlane manages the company as the "creative force" from its headquarters in Tempe, Arizona. The toy designers work in New Jersey and the toys are manufactured in China. Currently, it takes about 12 months for a product idea on paper to make its way through the rigorous process of becoming a toy on the shelf.

THE TOY INDUSTRY

Toys are big business. Worldwide toy sales exceed $59 billion. The United States is the largest toy market and accounts for 35 percent of worldwide industry sales. A child in the United States receives about $242 worth of toys per year on average. By comparison, the average annual expenditure per child outside the United States is $26. Dolls represent the largest single category of toys, although action figures account for $1.2 billion in sales. Figure 1 shows the dollar sales of individual toy categories in the United States:

CATEGORY	SALES ($ BILLIONS)
Action figures and accessories	$ 1.2
Arts and crafts	2.4
Building sets	0.6
Dolls	2.8
Games/puzzles	2.4
Infant/preschool	2.6
Learning and exploration	0.5
Outdoor and sports toys	2.4
Plush	1.4
Vehicles	2.0
All other toys	2.5
Total	$20.8

FIGURE 1
Toy Category Sales in the United States (listed alphabetically)

U.S. mass merchants are the principal retailers of toys. General merchandise and discounters like Wal-Mart and Target register 51 percent of retail toy sales. Toy chains account for 25 percent of retail sales. Other retailers, such as catalog, toy, hobby and game stores, department stores, and food and drug stores, record 24 percent of sales. Wal-Mart stores are the number one toy retailer in the United States.

The worldwide toy industry is dominated by two U.S. toy makers: Mattel and Hasbro. Japan's Bandai Company and Sanrio, and Denmark's LEGO Company are also major toy makers.

E-COMMERCE AND INTERACTIVE MARKETING AT MCFARLANE TOYS

Shortly after forming McFarlane Toys, Todd set up a booth in the annual industry trade show in New York called Toy Fair. Even though the new company didn't have any toys produced yet, an action figure buyer from a toy chain store saw photos of the proposed toys and agreed to place an order. Other traditional retailing opportunities in large discount stores such as Wal-Mart, entertainment outlets such as Sam Goody and Tower Records, and small, local comic book stores such as Diamonds soon followed. McFarlane Toys also utilized traditional forms of marketing, including media interviews and public relations events, to reach buyers who represented toy stores. McFarland also recently opened its first retail store in Arizona, which showcases current products and prototypes of future releases of the various lines of action figures. Collectors from around the world have visited the store to purchase products, attend artist autograph sessions, and to meet Todd.

Since the target market for McFarlane Toys products is older children and young adults—who make 30 to 40 percent of all action figure purchases—e-commerce and interactive marketing offered another opportunity to reach action figure consumers. The McFarlane Toys website (www.spawn.com) is a good example of the *convenience* online marketing can offer. The site provides a store for purchasing action figures in each of the lines (e.g., movie figures, music figures, baseball figures, comic book figures, etc.). High quality images allow shoppers to view each figure before adding it to a "basket" and then placing the order. The site also offers visitors a *choice* for the location of their purchase. A "Where to Buy" link lists all retailers and other online "e-tailers" such as www.comicsplusonline.com and www.allstarfigures.com.

The website also provides a variety of opportunities for *communication.* Consumer-to-marketer communication is provided through the "Contact Us" link. In addition, marketer-to-consumer information is provided through the McFarlane newsletter, which is sent to visitors who register to receive the update. Finally, consumers can use the spawn.com message board to participate in discussions about action figures, movies, and comics, or to buy, sell, and trade McFarlane products. There are 32,500 registered users of the message board forums, and as many as 690 of them have been online at the same time. A unique way that McFarlane provides *customization* of his offerings for his customers is through the Collector's Club, which offers exclusive, limited-edition action figures to members.

Online consumers are also typically concerned about *cost* and *control.* McFarlane tries to keep the cost of most of his toys between $10 and $15 by keeping production expenses low. Online shoppers also receive special offers when warehouse inventory is being reduced or eliminated. Of course, sales and discounts can often be found by utilizing the links to the many stores and online retailers that carry McFarlane Toys. Online users control their interaction with McFarlane by providing information only through opt-in solicitation for purchases, message board use, and newsletter e-mail delivery.

As McFarlane's focus on interactive marketing increased, the importance of the trade show where the first order came in declined. In fact, McFarlane recently stopped attending the trade show and began announcing its new products on its website with an online event called ToyFest. The event generated close to 200 million hits and 600,000 unique visitors. McFarlane explains, "It's always been strange to me that consumers were not allowed at Toy Fair, but with spawn.com our consumers can view our new lines at the same time as everybody else."

ISSUES FOR THE FUTURE

Of course, McFarlane's success has attracted attention from consumers, retailers, and competitors. New small firms such as Palisades Toys, Art Asylum, Playmates, and Mezco are now turning out action figures. Larger firms are also trying to compete. Hasbro, for example, recently won an award for its *Star Wars* figures. As more companies enter the category, obtaining new licensing agreements is also becoming more difficult.

While McFarlane has been heard to comment, "It's just stuff," he is very committed to continuing to develop and grow the category he created. In the future, expect to see additional action figures, movies, music videos, and video games. McFarlane Toys is also working at maintaining the strong relationship with its loyal customers through online contests, customer polls about potential new products, and a new product idea link to company designers.

Finally, in a move completely unrelated to action figures, McFarlane bought notable home run baseballs, including Mark McGwire's 70th home run ball for $3 million, to create The McFarlane Collection. The collection is touring stadiums and special events to raise money to battle Lou Gehrig's disease. More than 2 million fans have seen the exhibit.

Questions

1 Describe the channels of distribution McFarlane Toys uses to reach its action figure customers.

2 Why have interactive marketing strategies been successful for McFarlane Toys? What unique elements are part of its online experience?

3 How does McFarlane Toys address each of the six Cs consumers consider when shopping and buying online?

APPENDIX

B PLANNING A CAREER IN MARKETING

GETTING A JOB: THE PROCESS OF MARKETING YOURSELF

Getting a job is usually a lengthy process, and it is exactly that—a *process* that involves careful planning, implementation, and control. You may have everything going for you: a respectable grade point average (GPA), relevant work experience, several extracurricular activities, superior communication skills, and demonstrated leadership qualities. Despite these, you still need to market yourself systematically and aggressively; after all, even the best products lie dormant on the retailer's shelves unless marketed effectively.

The process of getting a job involves the same activities marketing managers use to develop and introduce products into the marketplace.[1] The only difference is that you are marketing yourself, not a product. You need to conduct marketing research by analyzing your personal qualities (performing a self-audit) and by identifying job opportunities. Based on your research results, select a target market—those job opportunities that are compatible with your interests, goals, skills, and abilities—and design a marketing mix around that target market. *You* are the "product";[2] you must decide how to "position" yourself in the job market. The price component of the marketing mix is the salary range and job benefits (such as health and life insurance, vacation time, and retirement benefits) that you hope to receive. Promotion involves communicating with prospective employers through written and electronic correspondence (advertising) and job interviews (personal selling). The place element focuses on how to reach prospective employers—at the career services office or job fairs, for example.

This appendix will assist you in career planning by (1) providing information about careers in marketing and (2) outlining a job search process.

CAREERS IN MARKETING

The diversity of marketing opportunities is reflected in the many types of marketing jobs, ranging from product management to marketing research to public relations. The growing interest in marketing by service organizations such as athletic teams, law firms, and banks, and nonprofit organizations such as universities, the performing arts, and government agencies, has added to the numerous opportunities offered by traditional employers such as manufacturers, retailers, and advertising agencies. In addition, e-commerce has created a variety of new opportunities such as product development managers for application service providers, data miners, and permission marketing managers for graduates with marketing skills.[3]

Recent studies of career paths and salaries suggest that marketing careers can also provide excellent opportunities for advancement and substantial pay. For example, about one of every five chief executive officers (CEOs) of the nation's 500 most valuable publicly held companies have a career history that is heaviest in marketing.[4] Similarly, reports of average starting salaries of college graduates indicate that salaries in marketing compare favorably with those in many other fields. The average starting salary of new marketing undergraduates in 2004 was $34,712, compared with $26,758 for journalism majors and $29,543 for advertising majors.[5] The future is likely to be even better. The U.S. Department of Labor reports that marketing and sales will be one of the fastest-growing occupations through 2012.[6]

Figure B–1 describes marketing occupations in six major categories: product management and physical distribution, advertising and promotion, retailing, sales, marketing research, and nonprofit marketing. One of these may be right for you. (Additional sources of marketing career information are provided at the end of this appendix.)

Product Management and Physical Distribution

Many organizations assign one manager the responsibility for a particular product. For example, Procter & Gamble (P&G) has separate managers for Tide, Cheer, Gain, and Bold. Product or brand managers are involved in all aspects of a product's marketing program, such as marketing research, sales, sales promotion, advertising, and pricing, as well as manufacturing. Managers of similar products typically report to a category manager and may be part of a *product management team*.[7]

PRODUCT MANAGEMENT AND PHYSICAL DISTRIBUTION

Product development manager creates a road map for new products by working with customers to determine their needs and with designers to create the product.

Product manager is responsible for integrating all aspects of a product's marketing program including research, sales, sales promotion, advertising, and pricing.

Supply chain manager oversees the part of a company that transports products to consumers and handles customer service.

Operations manager supervises warehousing and other physical distribution functions and often is directly involved in moving goods on the warehouse floor.

Inventory control manager forecasts demand for goods, coordinates production with plant managers, and tracks shipments to keep customers supplied.

Physical distribution specialist is an expert in the transportation and distribution of goods and also evaluates the costs and benefits of different types of transportation.

SALES

Direct or retail salesperson sells directly to consumers in the salesperson's office, the consumer's home, or a retailer's store.

Trade salesperson calls on retailers or wholesalers to sell products for manufacturers.

Industrial or semitechnical salesperson sells supplies and services to businesses.

Professional salesperson sells complicated or custom-designed products to businesses. This requires understanding of the product technology.

Customer service manager maintains good relations with customers by coordinating the sales staff, marketing management, and physical distribution management.

NONPROFIT MARKETING

Marketing manager develops and directs marketing campaigns, fundraising, and public relations.

ADVERTISING AND PROMOTION

Account executive maintains contact with clients while coordinating the creative work among artists and copywriters. Account executives work as partners with the client to develop marketing strategy.

Media buyer deals with media sales representatives in selecting advertising media and analyzes the value of media being purchased.

Copywriter works with art director in conceptualizing advertisements and writes the text of print or radio ads or the storyboards of television ads.

Art director handles the visual component of advertisements.

Sales promotion manager designs promotions for consumer products and works at an ad agency or a sales promotion agency.

Public relations manager develops written or filmed messages for the public and handles contacts with the press.

Internet marketing manager develops and executes the e-business marketing plan and manages all aspects of the advertising, promotion, and content for the online business.

RETAILING

Buyer selects products a store sells, surveys consumer trends, and evaluates the past performance of products and suppliers.

Store manager oversees the staff and services at a store.

MARKETING RESEARCH

Project manager for the supplier coordinates and oversees the market studies for a client.

Account executive for the supplier serves as a liaison between client and market research firm, like an advertising agency account executive.

In-house project director acts as project manager (see above) for the market studies conducted by the firm for which he or she works.

Competitive intelligence researcher uses new information technologies to monitor the competitive environment.

Data miner compiles and analyzes consumer data to identify behavior patterns, preferences, and user profiles for personalized marketing programs.

SOURCE: Adapted from David W. Rosenthal and Michael A. Powell, *Careers in Marketing,* ©1984, pp. 352–54.

FIGURE B–1
Marketing occupations

Several other jobs related to product management deal with physical distribution issues such as storing the manufactured product (inventory), moving the product from the firm to the customers (transportation), and engaging in many other aspects of the manufacture and sale of goods. Prospects for these jobs are likely to increase as wholesalers increase their involvement with selling and distribution activities and begin to take advantage of overseas opportunities.[8]

Advertising and Promotion

Advertising positions are available in three kinds of organizations: advertisers, media companies, and agencies. Advertisers include manufacturers, retail stores, service firms, and many other types of companies. Often they have an advertising department responsible for preparing and placing their own ads. Advertising careers are also possible with the media: television, radio stations, magazines, and newspapers. Finally, advertising agencies offer job opportunities through their use of account management, research, media, and creative services.

Starting positions with advertisers and advertising agencies are often as assistants to employees with several years of experience. An assistant copywriter facilitates the development of the message, or copy, in an advertisement. An assistant art director participates in the design of visual components of advertisements. Entry-level media positions involve buying the media that will carry the ad or selling air time on radio or television or page space in print media. Advancement to supervisory positions requires planning skills, a broad vision, and an affinity for spotting an effective advertising idea. Students interested in advertising should develop good communication skills and try to gain advertising experience through summer employment opportunities or internships.[9]

Retailing

There are two separate career paths in retailing: merchandise management and store management. The key position in merchandising is that of a buyer, who is responsible for selecting merchandise, guiding the promotion of the merchandise, setting prices, bargaining with wholesalers, training the salesforce, and monitoring the competitive environment. The buyer must also be able to organize and coordinate many critical activities under severe time constraints. In contrast, store management involves the supervision of personnel in all departments and the general management of all facilities, equipment, and merchandise displays. In addition, store managers are responsible for the financial performance of each department and for the store as a whole. Typical positions beyond the store manager level include district manager, regional manager, and divisional vice president.[10]

Most starting jobs in retailing are trainee positions. A trainee is usually placed in a management training program and then given a position as an assistant buyer or assistant department manager. Advancement and responsibility can be achieved quickly because there is a shortage of qualified personnel in retailing and because superior performance of an individual is quickly reflected in sales and profits—two visible measures of success. In addition, the growth of multichannel retailing has created new opportunities such as website management and online merchandise procurement.[11]

Sales

College graduates from many disciplines are attracted to sales positions because of the increasingly professional nature of selling jobs and the many opportunities they can provide. A selling career offers benefits that are hard to match in any other field: (1) the opportunity for rapid advancement (into management or to new territories and accounts); (2) the potential for extremely attractive compensation (the average salary of all sales representatives is $111,135);[12] (3) the development of personal satisfaction, feelings of accomplishment, and increased self-confidence; and (4) independence—salespeople often have almost complete control over their time and activities.

Employment opportunities in sales occupations are found in a wide variety of organizations, including insurance agencies, retailers, and financial service firms. In addition, many salespeople work as manufacturer's representatives for organizations that have selling responsibilities for several manufacturers.[13] Activities in sales jobs include *selling duties,* such as prospecting for customers, demonstrating the product, or quoting prices; *sales-support duties,* such as handling complaints and helping solve technical problems; and *nonselling duties,* such as preparing reports, attending sales meetings, and monitoring competitive activities. Salespeople who can deal with these varying activities are critical to a company's success. According to RJR Nabisco, its recruiting priority is "finding quality people who can analyze data from customers, see things from the consumer's

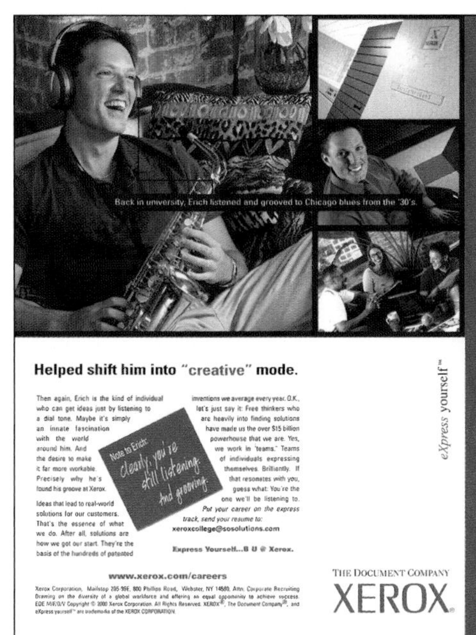

eyes, use available sales tools like laptops and syndicated data, and interface with the marketing people at headquarters."[14]

Marketing Research

Marketing researchers play important roles in many organizations today. They are responsible for obtaining, analyzing, and interpreting data to facilitate making marketing decisions. This means marketing researchers are basically problem solvers. Success in the area requires not only an understanding of statistics, computers, and the Internet but also a broad base of marketing knowledge[15] and an ability to communicate with management. Individuals who are inquisitive, methodical, analytical, and solution oriented find the field particularly rewarding.

The responsibilities of the men and women currently working in the market research industry include defining the marketing problem, designing the questions, selecting the sample, collecting and analyzing the data, and, finally, reporting the results of the research. These jobs are available in three kinds of organizations. *Marketing research consulting firms* contract with large companies to provide research about their products or services.[16] *Advertising agencies* may provide research services to help clients with questions related to advertising and promotional problems. Finally, some companies have an *in-house research staff* to design and execute their research projects. Online marketing research is rapidly requiring understanding of new tools such as dynamic scripting, response validation, intercept sampling, and online consumer panels.[17]

International Careers

Many of the careers just described can be found in international settings—in multinational U.S. corporations, small- to medium-size firms with export business, and franchises. The international public relations firm Burson-Marstellar, for example, has offices in New York, Buenos Aires, Sydney, Copenhagen, and Bangkok. Similarly, franchises such as Blockbuster Entertainment are expanding in many other markets outside of the United States. The changes in the European Union and among Asian countries may provide other opportunities. Variations of the permanent international career are also possible—for example, some companies may alternate periods of work at "headquarters" with "field" assignments in foreign countries.[18] Finally, a domestic international career—working for a foreign-owned company with an office in the United States—may be appealing.[19]

THE JOB SEARCH PROCESS

Activities you should consider during your job search process include assessing yourself, identifying job opportunities, preparing your résumé and related correspondence, and going on job interviews.

Assessing Yourself

You must know your product—you—so that you can market yourself effectively to prospective employers. Consequently, a critical first step in your job search is conducting a self-analysis, which involves critically examining yourself on the following dimensions: interests, abilities, education, experience, personality, desired job environment, and personal goals.[20] The importance of performing this assessment was stressed by a management consultant:[21]

> Many graduates enter the world of work without even understanding the fact that they are specific somebodies, much less knowing the kinds of competencies and motivations with

FIGURE B–2
Hypothetical list of a job candidate's strengths and weaknesses

STRENGTHS	WEAKNESSES
I have good communication skills.	I have minimal work experience.
I work well independently.	I have a mediocre GPA.
I am honest and dependable.	I will not relocate.
I am willing to travel in the job.	I lack a customer orientation.
I am a good problem solver.	I have poor technical skills.

> which they have been endowed. . . . The tragedy of not knowing is awesome. Ignorant of who they are, most graduates are doomed to spend too much of their lives in work for which they are poorly suited. . . . Self-knowledge is critical to effectively managing your career.

A self-analysis, in part, entails identifying your strengths and weaknesses. To do so, draw a vertical line down the middle of a sheet of paper and label one side of the paper "strengths" and the other side "weaknesses." Record your strong and weak points in their respective column. Ideally, this cataloging should be done over a few days to give you adequate time to reflect on your attributes. In addition, you might seek input from others who know you well (such as parents, close relatives, friends, professors, or employers) and can offer more objective views. A hypothetical list of strengths and weaknesses is shown in Figure B–2.

Personality and vocational interest tests, provided by many colleges and universities, can also give you ideas about yourself. After tests have been administered and scored, test takers meet with testing service counselors to discuss the results. Test results generally suggest jobs for which students have an inclination. The most common tests at the college level are the Strong Interest Inventory and the Campbell Interest and Skill Survey. Some counseling centers also administer the Myers-Briggs Type Indicator—a personality measure that helps identify professions you may enjoy.[22] If you have not already done so, you may wish to see whether your school offers such testing services.

Identifying Your Job Opportunities

To identify and analyze the job market, you must conduct some marketing research to determine what industries *and* companies offer promising job opportunities that relate to the results of your self-analysis. Several sources that can help in your search are discussed next.

Career Services Office Your career services office is an excellent source of job information. Personnel in that office can (1) inform you about which companies will be recruiting on campus, (2) alert you to unexpected job openings, (3) advise you about short- and long-term career prospects, (4) offer advice on résumé construction, (5) assess your interviewing strengths and weaknesses, and (6) help you evaluate a job offer. In addition, the office usually contains a variety of written materials focusing on different industries and companies and tips on job hunting.

Online Career and Employment Services Many companies no longer make frequent on-campus visits. Instead, they may use the many online services available to advertise an employment opportunity or to search for candidate information. The National Association of Colleges and Employers, for example, maintains an Internet site called JobWeb (www.jobweb.org). Similarly, monster.com and careerbuilder.com are online databases of employment ads, candidate résumés, and other career-related information. Some of the information resources include career guidance,

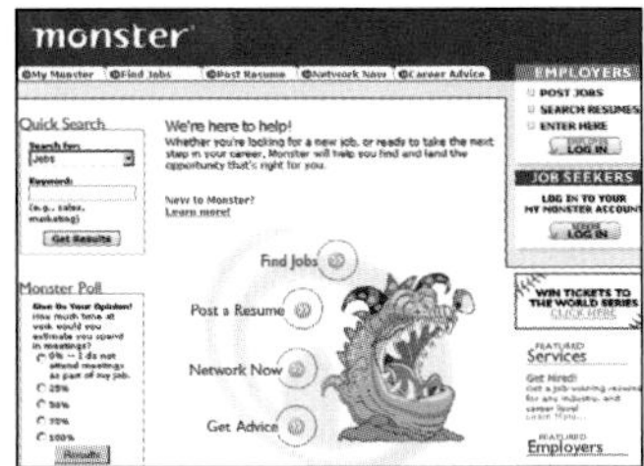

a cover letter library, occupational profiles, résumé templates, and networking services.[23] Employers may contact students directly when the candidate's qualifications meet their specific job requirements.

Library The public or college library can provide you with reference material that, among other things, describes successful firms and their operations, defines the content of various jobs, and forecasts job opportunities. For example, *Fortune* publishes a list of the 1,000 largest U.S. and global companies and their respective sales and profits, and Dun & Bradstreet publishes directories of all companies in the United States with a net worth of at least $500,000. A librarian can indicate reference materials that will be most pertinent to *your* job search.

Advertisements Help-wanted advertisements provide an overview of what is happening in the job market. Local (particularly Sunday editions) and college newspapers, trade press (such as *Marketing News* or *Advertising Age*), and business magazines (such as *Sales & Marketing Management*) contain classified advertisement sections that generally have job opening announcements, often for entry-level positions. Reviewing the want ads can help you identify what kinds of positions are available and their requirements and job titles, which firms offer certain kinds of jobs, and levels of compensation.

Employment Agencies An employment agency can make you aware of several job opportunities very quickly because of its large number of job listings available through computer databases. Many agencies specialize in a particular field (such as sales and marketing). The advantages of using an agency include that it (1) reduces the cost of a job search by bringing applicants and employers together, (2) often has exclusive job listings available only by working through the agency, (3) performs much of the job search for you, and (4) tries to find a job that is compatible with your qualifications and interests.[24]

Personal Contacts and Networking An important source of job information that students often overlook is their personal contacts. People you know often may know of job opportunities, so you should advise them that you're looking for a job. Relatives and friends might aid your job search. Instructors you know well and business contacts can provide a wealth of information about potential jobs and even help arrange an interview with a prospective employer. They may also help arrange *informational interviews* with employers that do not have immediate openings. These interviews allow you to collect information about an industry or an employer and give you an advantage if a position does become available. It is a good idea to leave your résumé with all your personal contacts so they can pass it along to those who might be in need of your services. Creating a network of professional contacts is one of the most important career planning activities you can undertake.[25]

State Employment Office State employment offices have listings of job opportunities in their state and counselors to help arrange a job interview for you. Although state employment offices perform functions similar to employment agencies, they differ in listing only job opportunities in their state and providing their services free.

Direct Contact Another means of obtaining job information is direct contact—personally communicating to prospective employers (either by mail, e-mail, or in person) that you would be interested in pursuing job opportunities with them. Often you may not even know whether jobs are available in these firms. If you correspond with the companies in writing, a letter of introduction and an attached résumé should serve as your initial form of communication. Your major goal in direct contact is ultimately to arrange a job interview.

Writing Your Résumé

A résumé is a document that communicates to prospective employers who you are. An employer reading a résumé focuses on two key questions: (1) What is the candidate like? and (2) What can the candidate do for me?[26] It is imperative that you design a résumé that addresses these two questions and presents you in a favorable light. Personnel in your career services office can provide assistance in designing résumés.

The Résumé Itself A well-constructed résumé generally contains up to nine major sections: (1) identification (name, address, and telephone number), (2) job or career objective, (3) educational background, (4) extracurricular activities, (5) work experience or history, (6) skills or capabilities (that pertain to a particular kind of job for which you may be interviewing), (7) accomplishments or achievements, (8) personal interests, and (9) personal references.[27] If possible, you should include quantitative information about your accomplishments and experience, such as "increased sales revenue by 20 percent" for the year you managed a retail clothing store.

Technology has created a need for a new type of résumé—the electronic résumé. Although traditional versions of résumés may be visually appealing, today most career experts suggest that résumés accommodate delivery through mail, e-mail, and fax machines. In addition, résumés must accommodate employers who use scanning technology to enter résumés into their own databases or who search commercial online databases. To fully utilize online opportunities, an electronic résumé with a popular font (e.g., Times Roman) and relatively large font size (e.g., 10–14 pt.)—and without italic text, graphics, shading, underlining, or vertical lines—must be available. In addition, because online recruiting starts with a keyword search, it is important to include key words, focus on nouns rather than verbs, and avoid abbreviations.[28]

Letter Accompanying a Résumé The letter accompanying a résumé, or cover letter, serves as the job candidate's introduction. As a result, it must gain the attention and interest of the reader or it will fail to give the incentive to examine the résumé carefully. In designing a letter to accompany your résumé, address the following issues:[29]

- Address the letter to a specific person.
- Identify the position for which you are applying and how you heard of it.
- Indicate why you are applying for the position.
- Summarize your most significant credentials and qualifications.
- Refer the reader to the enclosed résumé.
- Request a personal interview, and advise the reader when and where you can be reached.

As a general rule, nothing works better than an impressive cover letter and good academic credentials.[30]

Interviewing for Your Job

The job interview is a conversation between a prospective employer and a job candidate that focuses on determining whether the employer's needs can be satisfied by the candidate's qualifications. The interview is a "make or break" situation: If the interview goes well, you have increased your chances of receiving a job offer; if it goes poorly, you probably will be eliminated from further consideration.

Preparing for a Job Interview To be successful in a job interview, you must prepare for it so you can exhibit professionalism and indicate to a prospective employer that you are serious about the job. When preparing for the interview, several critical activities need to be performed.

FIGURE B–3
Questions frequently asked by interviewers

INTERVIEWER QUESTIONS
1. What do you consider to be your greatest strengths and weaknesses?
2. What do you see yourself doing in 5 years? In 10 years?
3. What are three important leadership qualities? How have you demonstrated these qualities?
4. What jobs have you enjoyed the most? The least? Why?
5. Why do you want to work for our company?

Before the interview, gather facts about the industry, the prospective employer, and the job. Relevant information might include the general description for the occupation; the firm's products or services; the firm's size, number of employees, and financial and competitive position; the requirements of the position; and the name and personality of the interviewer.[31] Obtaining this information will provide you with additional insight into the firm and help you formulate questions to ask the interviewer. This information might be gleaned, for example, from corporate annual reports, *The Wall Street Journal,* Standard & Poor's *Register of Corporations, Directors, and Executives, The Directory of Corporate Affiliations,* selected issues of *BusinessWeek,* or the company's web page. If information is not readily available, you could call the company and indicate that you wish to obtain some information about the firm before your interview.

Preparation for the job interview should also involve role-playing, or pretending that you are in the "hot seat" being interviewed. Before role-playing, anticipate questions interviewers may pose and how you might address them (Figure B–3). Do not memorize your answers, though, because you want to appear spontaneous, yet logical and intelligent. Nonetheless, it is helpful to practice how you might respond to the questions. You should also anticipate a substance abuse screening process, now common among a wide variety of organizations.[32] In addition, develop questions you might ask the interviewer that are important and of concern to you (Figure B–4). "It's an opportunity to show the recruiter how smart you are," comments one recruiter.[33]

Before the job interview you should attend to several details. Know the exact time and place of the interview; write them down—do not rely on your memory. Get the full company name straight. Find out what the interviewer's name is and how to pronounce it. Bring a notepad and pen along on the interview, in case you need to record anything. Make certain that your appearance is clean, neat, professional, and conservative. And be punctual; arriving tardy to a job interview gives you an appearance of being unreliable.

FIGURE B–4
Questions frequently asked by interviewees

INTERVIEWEE QUESTIONS
1. Describe the typical first-year assignment for this job.
2. How is an employee evaluated?
3. What is the company's promotion policy?
4. How much responsibility would I have in this job?
5. Why do you enjoy working for your firm?

Succeeding in Your Job Interview You have done your homework, and at last the moment arrives and it is time for the interview. Although you may experience some apprehension, view the interview as a conversation between the prospective employer and you. Both of you are in the interview to look over the other party, to see whether there might be a good match. You know your subject matter (you); furthermore, because you did not have a job with the firm when you walked into the interview, you really have nothing to lose if you don't get it—so relax.[34]

When you meet the interviewer, greet him or her by name, be cheerful, smile, and maintain good eye contact. Take your lead from the interviewer at the outset. Sit down after the interviewer has offered you a seat. Sit up straight in your chair, and look alert and interested at all times. Appear relaxed, not tense. Be enthusiastic.

During the interview, be yourself. If you try to behave in a manner that is different from the real you, your attempt may be transparent to the interviewer or you may ultimately get the job but discover that you aren't suited for it. In addition to assessing how well your skills match those of the job, the interviewer will probably try to assess your long-term interest in the firm. William Kucker, a recruiter for General Electric, explains, "We're looking for people to make a commitment."[35]

As the interview comes to a close, leave it on a positive note. Thank the interviewer for his or her time and the opportunity to discuss employment opportunities. If you are still interested in the job, express this to the interviewer. The interviewer will normally tell you what the employer's next step is—probably a visit to the company.[36] Rarely will a job offer be made at the end of the initial interview. If it is and you want the job, accept the offer; if there is any doubt in your mind about the job, however, ask for time to consider the offer.

Following Up on Your Job Interview After your interview, send a thank-you note to the interviewer and indicate whether you are still interested in the job. If you want to continue pursuing the job, polite persistence may help you get it. According to one expert, "Many job hunters make the mistake of thinking that their career fate is totally in the hands of the interviewer once the job interview is finished."[37] You *can* have an impact on the interviewer *after* the interview is over.

As you conduct your follow-up, be persistent but polite. If you are too eager, one of two things could happen to prevent you from getting the job: The employer might feel that you are a nuisance and would exhibit such behavior on the job, or the employer may perceive that you are desperate for the job and thus are not a viable candidate.

Handling Rejection You have put your best efforts into your job search. You developed a well-designed résumé and prepared carefully for the job interview. Even the interview appears to have gone well. Nevertheless, a prospective employer

may send you a rejection letter. ("We are sorry that our needs and your superb qualification don't match.") Although you will probably be disappointed, not all interviews lead to a job offer because there normally are more candidates than there are positions available. Try to learn lessons to apply in future interviews. Keep interviewing and gaining interview experience; your persistence will eventually pay off.

SELECTED SOURCES OF MARKETING CAREER INFORMATION

The following is a selected list of marketing information sources that you should find useful during your academic studies and professional career.

BUSINESS AND MARKETING PUBLICATIONS

Jeffrey Heilbrunn, ed., *Marketing Encyclopedia* (Lincolnwood, IL: NTC Business Books, 1995). This book provides a collection of essays by professional and academic marketing experts on issues and trends shaping the future of marketing.

Hoover's Handbook of World Business, 10th ed. (Austin, TX: Hoover's Business Press, 2004). A detailed source of information about companies outside of the United States, including firms from Canada, Europe, Japan, China, India, and Taiwan.

Paige Leavitt, John Prescott, Darcy Lemon, and Farida Hasanali, *Competitive Intelligence: A Guide for Your Journey to Best-Practice Processes* (Houston: American Productivity and Quality Center, 2004). This book provides a five-step model for developing and implementing a competitive intelligence effort; it explains how to collect, coordinate, and interpret actionable information.

Barbara Lewis and Dale Littler, eds., *The Blackwell Encyclopedic Dictionary of Marketing* (Cambridge, MA: Blackwell Publishers, 1999). Part of the 10-volume *Blackwell Encyclopedia of Management,* this book provides clear, concise, up-to-the-minute, and highly informative definitions and explanations of the key concepts and terms in marketing.

Cynthia L. Shamel, *Introduction to Online Market and Industry Research* (Mason, OH: Thomson Learning, 2004). This comprehensive reference provides search strategies and valuable data source information, including rankings of data sources, for industry researchers.

Betsy-Ann Toffler, *Dictionary of Marketing Terms,* 3rd ed. (Hauppauge, NY: Barrons Educational Series, 2000). This dictionary contains definitions of more than 4,000 marketing terms.

CAREER PLANNING PUBLICATIONS

Richard N. Bolles, *The 2006 What Color Is Your Parachute? A Practical Manual for Job-Hunters and Career-Changers* (Berkeley, CA: Ten Speed Press, 2005). A companion workbook is also available. See www.jobhuntersbible.com.

Dennis V. Damp and Samuel Concialdi, *The Book of U.S. Government Jobs: Where They Are, What's Available, and How to Get One,* 9th ed. (Moon Township, PA: Bookhaven Press, 2005).

Diane Darling, *The Networking Survival Guide: Get the Success You Want by Tapping into the People You Know* (New York: McGraw-Hill, 2003).

Margaret Riley Dikel and Frances E. Roehm, *Guide to Internet Job Searching* (New York: McGraw-Hill, 2004).

Jack Evans and Barry Berman, *Careers in Marketing,* 2nd ed. (Englewood Cliffs, NJ: Prentice Hall, 1995).

SELECTED PERIODICALS

Advertising Age, Crain Communications, Inc. (weekly). See www.adage.com. (subscription rate: $149)

BusinessWeek, McGraw-Hill Companies (weekly). See www.businessweek.com. (subscription rate: $45.97)

Journal of Marketing, American Marketing Association (quarterly). See www.marketingpower.com. (subscription rates: $90 nonmembers; $53 members)

Marketing Management, American Marketing Association (six times per year). See www.marketingpower.com. (subscription rates: $59.95 nonmembers; $53 members)

Marketing News, American Marketing Association (biweekly). See www.marketingpower.com. (subscription rates: $100 nonmembers; $39 members)

Marketing Research, American Marketing Association (quarterly). See www.marketingpower.com. (subscription rates: $75 nonmembers; $53 members)

The Wall Street Journal Interactive, Dow Jones & Company, Inc. (weekly). See www.wsj.com. (subscription rates: $198 print; $79 online; $34.95 (15 weeks) for students, both print and online)

PROFESSIONAL AND TRADE ASSOCIATIONS

American Advertising Federation
1101 Vermont Ave. NW., Suite 500
Washington, DC 20005-6306
(202) 898-0089
www.aaf.org

American e-Commerce Association
2346 Camp St.
New Orleans, LA 70130
(504) 495-1748
www.aeaus.com

American Marketing Association
311 S. Wacker Dr., Suite 5800
Chicago, IL 60606
(800) AMA-1150
www.marketingpower.com

Direct Marketing Association
1120 Avenue of the Americas
New York, NY 10036-6700
(212) 768-7277
www.the-dma.org

Marketing Science Institute
1000 Massachusetts Ave.
Cambridge, MA 02138-5396
(617) 491-2060
www.msi.org

Sales and Marketing Executives International
P.O. Box 1390
Sumas, WA 98295-1390
(312) 893-0751
www.smei.org

GLOSSARY

80/20 rule A concept that suggests 80 percent of a firm's sales are obtained from 20 percent of its customers. p. 195

account management policies Specifies whom salespeople should contact, what kinds of selling and customer service activities should be engaged in, and how these activities should be carried out. p. 386

adaptive selling A need-satisfaction presentation format that involves adjusting the presentation to fit the selling situation, such as knowing when to offer solutions and when to ask for more information. p. 383

advertising Any paid form of nonpersonal communication about an organization, good, service, or idea by an identified sponsor. pp. 335, 354

attitude A learned predisposition to respond to an object or class of objects in a consistently favorable or unfavorable way. p. 109

baby boomers The generation of children born between 1946 and 1964. p. 62

back translation A translated word or phrase is retranslated back into the original language by a different interpreter to catch errors. p. 148

beliefs One's perception of how a product or brand performs on different attributes based on personal experience, advertising, and discussions with other people. p. 109

bots Electronic shopping agents or robots that comb websites to compare prices and product or service features. p. 405

brand equity The added value a given brand name gives to a product beyond the functional benefits provided. p. 246

brand loyalty A favorable attitude toward and consistent purchase of a single brand over time. p. 108

brand name Any word, device (design, sound, shape, or color), or combination of these used to distinguish a seller's goods or services. p. 245

brand personality A set of human characteristics associated with a brand name. p. 246

branding A basic decision in marketing products in which an organization uses a name, phrase, design, symbol, or combination of these to identify its products and distinguish them from those of competitors. p. 245

break-even analysis A technique that analyzes the relationship between total revenue and total cost to determine profitability at various levels of output. p. 272

brokers Independent firms or individuals whose principal function is to bring buyers and sellers together to make sales. p. 325

business goods Products that assist directly or indirectly in providing products for resale. Also called *B2B goods, industrial goods,* or *organizational goods*. p. 213

business marketing The marketing of goods and services to companies, governments, or not-for-profit organizations for use in the creation of goods and services that they can produce and market to others. p. 122

business plan A road map for the entire organization for a specified future period of time, such as one year or five years. p. 44

buy classes Consists of three types of organizational buying situations: straight rebuy, new buy, and modified rebuy. p. 130

buying center The group of people in an organization who participate in the buying process and share common goals, risks, and knowledge important to purchase decisions. p. 129

capacity management Integrating the service component of the marketing mix with efforts to influence consumer demand. p. 254

category management An approach to managing the assortment of merchandise in which a manager is assigned the responsibility for selecting all products that consumers in a market segment might view as substitutes for each other, with the objective of maximizing sales and profits in the category. p. 321

cause marketing Occurs when the charitable contributions of a firm are tied directly to the customer revenues produced through the promotion of one of its products. p. 88

channel conflict Arises when one channel member believes another channel member is engaged in behavior that prevents it from achieving its goals. p. 295

choiceboard An interactive, Internet-enabled system that allows individual customers to design their own products and services by answering a few questions and choosing from a menu of product or service attributes (or components), prices, and delivery options. p. 400

code of ethics A formal statement of ethical principles and rules of conduct. p. 84

collaborative filtering A process that automatically groups people with similar buying intentions, preferences, and behaviors and predicts future purchases. p. 400

communication The process of conveying a message to others and requires six elements: a source, a message, a channel of communication, a receiver, and the processes of encoding and decoding. p. 332

competition The alternative firms that could provide a product to satisfy a specific market's needs. p. 69

consultative selling A need-satisfaction presentation format that focuses on problem identification, where the salesperson serves as an expert on problem recognition and resolution. p. 383

consumer behavior The actions a person takes in purchasing and using products and services, including the mental and social processes that come before and after these actions. p. 100

Consumer Bill of Rights (1962) A law that codified the ethics of exchange between buyers and sellers, including the rights to safety, to be informed, to choose, and to be heard. p. 83

consumer goods Products purchased by the ultimate consumer. p. 213

consumerism A grassroots movement started in the 1960s to increase the influence, power, and rights of consumers in dealing with institutions. p. 71

consumer-oriented sales promotions Sales tools used to support a company's advertising and personal selling directed to ultimate consumers. p. 365

cookies Computer files that a marketer can download onto the computer of an online shopper who visits the marketer's website. p. 408

cooperative advertising Advertising programs by which a manufacturer pays a percentage of the retailer's local advertising expense for advertising the manufacturer's products. p. 368
cross-cultural analysis The study of similarities and differences among consumers in two or more nations or societies. p. 146
cultural symbols Things that represent ideas and concepts. p. 147
culture The set of values, ideas, and attitudes that are learned and shared among the members of a group. p. 65
currency exchange rate The price of one country's currency expressed in terms of another country's currency. p. 149
customer experience The sum total of the interactions that a customer has with a company's website, from the initial look at a homepage through the entire purchase decision process. p. 401
customer service The ability of logistics management to satisfy users in terms of time, dependability, communication, and convenience. p. 301
customer value The unique combination of benefits received by targeted buyers that includes quality, price, convenience, on-time delivery, and both before-sale and after-sale service. p. 13
customerization The practice of not only customizing a product or service but also personalizing the marketing and overall shopping and buying interaction for each customer. p. 406
customs What is considered normal and expected about the way people do things in a specific country. p. 146

data The facts and figures related to the problem, divided into two main parts: secondary data and primary data. p. 168
demand curve A graph relating the quantity sold and price, which shows the maximum number of units that will be sold at a given price. p. 269
demographics Describing a population according to selected characteristics such as age, gender, ethnicity, income, and occupation. p. 61
derived demand The demand for industrial products and services is driven by, or derived from, demand for consumer products and services. p. 124
direct investment A global market-entry strategy that entails a domestic firm actually investing in and owning a foreign subsidiary or division. p. 153
direct marketing A promotion alternative that uses direct communication with consumers to generate a response in the form of an order, a request for further information, or a visit to a retail outlet. p. 337
direct orders The result of direct marketing offers that contain all the information necessary for a prospective buyer to make a decision to purchase and complete the transaction. p. 345
disintermediation Channel conflict that arises when a channel member bypasses another member and sells or buys products direct. p. 296
dual distribution An arrangement whereby a firm reaches different buyers by employing two or more different types of channels for the same basic product. p. 291
dumping When a firm sells a product in a foreign country below its domestic price or below its actual cost. p. 156
dynamic pricing The practice of changing prices for products and services in real time in response to supply and demand conditions. p. 408

economy Pertains to the income, expenditures, and resources that affect the cost of running a business and household. p. 65
e-marketplaces Online trading communities that bring together buyers and supplier organizations to make possible the real time exchange of information, money, products, and services. Also called *B2B exchanges* or *e-hubs*. p. 132
environmental forces The uncontrollable factors involving social, economic, technological, competitive, and regulatory forces. p. 12
environmental scanning The process of continually acquiring information on events occurring outside the organization to identify and interpret potential trends. p. 60
ethics The moral principles and values that govern the actions and decisions of an individual or group. p. 80
exchange The trade of things of value between buyer and seller so that each is better off after the trade. p. 8
exclusive distribution A level of distribution density whereby only one retail outlet in a specific geographical area carries the firm's products. p. 294
exporting A global market-entry strategy in which a company produces goods in one country and sells them in another country. p. 150

family life cycle The distinct phases that a family progresses through from formation to retirement, each phase bringing with it identifiable purchasing behaviors. p. 113
fixed cost The sum of the expenses of the firm that are stable and do not change with the quantity of a product that is produced and sold. p. 271
Foreign Corrupt Practices Act (1977) A law that makes it a crime for U.S. corporations to bribe an official of a foreign government or political party to obtain or retain business in a foreign country. p. 147
franchising A contractual arrangement between a parent company (a franchiser) and an individual or a firm (a franchisee) that allows the franchisee to operate a certain type of business under an established name and according to specific rules. p. 292

Generation X The 15 percent of the U.S. population born between 1965 and 1976. Also called *baby bust*. p. 62
Generation Y The 72 million Americans born between 1977 and 1994. Also called *echo boom* or *baby boomlet*. p. 63
global brand A brand marketed under the same name in multiple countries with similar and centrally coordinated marketing programs. p. 144
global competition Exists when firms originate, produce, and market their products and services worldwide. p. 142
global consumers Customer groups living in many different countries who have similar needs or seek similar features and benefits from products or services. p. 144
global marketing strategy Transnational firms that employ the practice of standardizing marketing activities when there are cultural similarities and adapting them when cultures differ. p. 143
goals These convert the mission into targeted levels of performance to be achieved, often by a specific time. Also called *objectives*. p. 27
gray market A situation where products are sold through unauthorized channels of distribution. Also called *parallel importing*. p. 156
green marketing Marketing efforts to produce, promote, and reclaim environmentally sensitive products. p. 88

hierarchy of effects The sequence of stages a prospective buyer goes through from initial awareness of a product to eventual action (either trial or adoption of the product). The stages include awareness, interest, evaluation, trial, and adoption. p. 341

idle production capacity Occurs when the service provider is available but there is no demand. p. 214
infomercials Program-length (30-minute) advertisements that take an educational approach to communication with potential customers. p. 360
institutional advertisements Advertisements designed to build goodwill or an image for an organization rather than promote a specific good or service. p. 355
integrated marketing communications The concept of designing marketing communications programs that coordinate all promotional activities—advertising, personal selling, sales promotion, public relations, and direct marketing—to provide a consistent message across all audiences. p. 332
intensive distribution A level of distribution density whereby a firm tries to place its products and services in as many outlets as possible. p. 294
interactive marketing Two-way buyer–seller electronic communication in a computer-mediated environment in which the buyer controls the kind and amount of information received from the seller. p. 399
involvement The personal, social, and economic consequences of the purchase to the consumer. p. 102

joint venture A global market-entry strategy in which a foreign company and a local firm invest together to create a local business in order to share ownership, control, and profits of the new company. p. 152

laws Society's values and standards that are enforceable in the courts. p. 80
lead generation The result of a direct marketing offer designed to generate interest in a product or a service and a request for additional information. p. 345
learning Those behaviors that result from (1) repeated experience or (2) reasoning. p. 108
logistics Those activities that focus on getting the right amount of the right products to the right place at the right time at the lowest possible cost. p. 297

major account management The practice of using team selling to focus on important customers so as to build mutually beneficial, long-term, cooperative relationships. Also called *key account management*. p. 386
manufacturer's agents Agents who work for several producers and carry noncompetitive, complementary merchandise in an exclusive territory. Also called *manufacturer's representatives*. p. 325
market People with both the desire and the ability to buy a specific product. p. 11
market orientation An organization that focuses its efforts on: (1) continuously collecting information about customers' needs, (2) sharing this information across departments, and (3) using it to create customer value. p. 17
market segmentation Involves aggregating prospective buyers into groups, or segments, that (1) have common needs and (2) will respond similarly to a marketing action. pp. 35, 189
market segments The relatively homogeneous groups of prospective buyers that result from the market segmentation process. p. 189
market share The ratio of sales revenue of the firm to the total sales revenue of all firms in the industry, including the firm itself. p. 27
marketing An organizational function and a set of processes for creating, communicating, and delivering value to customers and for managing customer relationships in ways that benefit the organization and its stakeholders. p. 8
marketing channel Individuals and firms involved in the process of making a product or service available for use or consumption by consumers or industrial users. p. 286
marketing concept The idea that an organization should (1) strive to satisfy the needs of consumers (2) while also trying to achieve the organization's goals. p. 17
marketing mix The marketing manager's controllable factors—product, price, promotion, and place—that can be used to solve a marketing problem. p. 12
marketing plan A road map for the marketing activities of an organization for a specified future period of time, such as one year or five years. p. 33
marketing program A plan that integrates the marketing mix to provide a good, service, or idea to prospective buyers. p. 14
marketing research The process of defining a marketing problem and opportunity, systematically collecting and analyzing information, and recommending actions. p. 164
marketing strategy The means by which a marketing goal is to be achieved, usually characterized by a specified target market and a marketing program to reach it. p. 38
marketing tactics Detailed day-to-day operational decisions essential to the overall success of marketing strategies. p. 39
market-product grid A framework to relate the market segments of potential buyers to products offered or potential marketing actions by the firm. p. 190
marketspace An information- and communication-based electronic exchange environment mostly occupied by sophisticated computer and telecommunication technologies and digitized offerings. p. 68
measures of success Criteria or standards used in evaluating proposed solutions to the problem. p. 166
merchant wholesalers Independently owned firms that take title to the merchandise they handle. p. 324
mission A statement of the organization's scope, often identifying its customers, markets, products, technology, and values. Also called *vision*. p. 25
moral idealism A personal moral philosophy that considers certain individual rights or duties as universal, regardless of the outcome. p. 85
motivation The energizing force that stimulates behavior to satisfy a need. p. 105
multibranding A branding strategy that involves giving each product a distinct name when each brand is intended for a different market segment. p. 250
multichannel marketing The blending of different communication and delivery channels that are mutually reinforcing in attracting, retaining, and building relationships with consumers who shop and buy in the traditional marketplace and marketspace. p. 410
multichannel retailers Retailers that utilize and integrate a combination of traditional store formats and nonstore formats such as catalogs, television, and online retailing. p. 321
multicultural marketing Combinations of the marketing mix that reflect the unique attitudes, ancestry, communication preferences, and lifestyles of different races. p. 65

multidomestic marketing strategy Multinational firms that have as many different product variations, brand names, and advertising programs as countries in which they do business. p. 143

multiproduct branding A branding strategy in which a company uses one name for all its products in a product class. p. 249

new-product process The stages a firm goes through to identify business opportunities and convert them to a salable good or service. p. 221

North American Industry Classification System (NAICS) Provides common industry definitions for Canada, Mexico, and the United States, which makes easier the measurement of economic activity in the three member countries of the North American Free Trade Agreement (NAFTA). p. 123

objectives These convert the mission into targeted levels of performance to be achieved, often by a specific time. Also called *goals*. p. 27

observational data Facts and figures obtained by watching, either mechanically or in person, how people actually behave. p. 170

off-peak pricing Charging different prices during different times of the day or days of the week to reflect variations in demand for the service. p. 254

opinion leaders Individuals who have social influence over others. p. 111

order getter Sells in a conventional sense and identifies prospective customers, provides customers with information, persuades customers to buy, closes sales, and follows up on customers' use of a product or service. p. 379

order taker Processes routine orders or reorders for products that were already sold by the company. p. 378

organizational buyers Those manufacturers, wholesalers, retailers, and government agencies that buy goods and services for their own use or for resale. pp. 18, 122

organizational buying behavior The decision-making process that organizations use to establish the need for products and services and identify, evaluate, and choose among alternative brands and suppliers. p. 128

organizational culture A set of values, ideas, and attitudes that is learned and shared among the members of an organization. p. 26

packaging A component of a product that refers to any container in which it is offered for sale and on which label information is conveyed. p. 252

perceived risk The anxieties felt because the consumer cannot anticipate the outcomes of a purchase but believes that there may be negative consequences. p. 107

perception The process by which an individual selects, organizes, and interprets information to create a meaningful picture of the world. p. 106

perceptual map A means of displaying or graphing in two dimensions the location of products or brands in the minds of consumers to enable a manager to see how consumers perceive competing products or brands and then take marketing actions. p. 203

permission marketing The solicitation of a consumer's consent (called *opt-in*) to receive e-mail and advertising based on personal data supplied by the consumer. p. 401

personal selling Involves the two-way flow of communication between a buyer and seller, often in a face-to-face encounter, designed to influence a person's or group's purchase decision. pp. 336, 376

personal selling process Sales activities occurring before and after the sale itself, consisting of six stages: (1) prospecting, (2) preapproach, (3) approach, (4) presentation, (5) close, and (6) follow-up. p. 380

personality A person's consistent behaviors or responses to recurring situations. p. 105

personalization The consumer-initiated practice of generating content on a marketer's website that is custom tailored to an individual's specific needs and preferences. p. 400

points of difference Those characteristics of a product that make it superior to competitive substitutes. p. 36

portals Electronic gateways to the Internet that supply a broad array of news and entertainment, information resources, and shopping services. p. 408

posttests Tests conducted after an advertisement has been shown to the target audience to determine whether it accomplished its intended purpose. p. 364

pretests Tests conducted before the advertisements are placed in any medium to determine whether it communicates the intended message or to select among alternative versions of the advertisement. p. 363

price The money or other considerations (including other goods and services) exchanged for the ownership or use of a good or service. p. 262

pricing constraints Factors that limit the range of price a firm may set. p. 275

pricing objectives Specifying the role of price in an organization's marketing and strategic plans. p. 274

primary data Facts and figures that are newly collected for the project. p. 168

product A good, service, or idea consisting of a bundle of tangible and intangible attributes that satisfies consumers and is received in exchange for money or some other unit of value. p. 212

product advertisements Advertisements that focus on selling a good or service and which take three forms: (1) pioneering (or informational), (2) competitive (or persuasive), and (3) reminder. p. 354

product differentiation A marketing strategy that involves a firm's using different marketing mix activities, such as product features and advertising, to help consumers perceive the product as being different and better than competing products. p. 189

product life cycle Describes the stages a new product goes through in the marketplace: introduction, growth, maturity, and decline. p. 236

product line A group of products that are closely related because they satisfy a class of needs, are used together, are sold to the same customer group, are distributed through the same type of outlets, or fall within a given price range. p. 212

product mix The number of product lines offered by a company. p. 212

product placement A sales promotion tool that uses a brand-name product in a movie, television show, video, or a commercial for another product. p. 367

product positioning The place an offering occupies in consumers' minds on important attributes relative to competitive products. p. 202

profit The reward to a business firm for the risk it undertakes in offering a product for sale; the money left over after a firm's total expenses are subtracted from its total sales. p. 24

profit equation Profit = Total revenue minus Total cost; or Profit = (Unit price times Quantity sold) minus Total cost. p. 264

promotional mix The combination of one or more of the communication tools used to (1) inform prospective buyers about the benefits of the product, (2) persuade them to try it, and (3) remind them later about the benefits they enjoyed by using the product. p. 332

protectionism The practice of shielding one or more industries within a country's economy from foreign competition, usually through the use of tariffs or quotas. p. 140

public relations A form of communication management that seeks to influence the feelings, opinions, or beliefs held by customers, prospective customers, stockholders, suppliers, employees, and other publics about a company and its products or services. p. 336

publicity A nonpersonal, indirectly paid presentation of an organization, good, or service. p. 336

publicity tools Methods of obtaining nonpersonal presentation of an organization, good, or service without direct cost. Examples include news releases, news conferences, and public service announcements. p. 369

pull strategy Directing the promotional mix at ultimate consumers to encourage them to ask the retailer for a product. p. 340

purchase decision process The stages a buyer passes through in making choices about which products and services to buy. p. 100

push strategy Directing the promotional mix to channel members to gain their cooperation in ordering and stocking the product. p. 340

questionnaire data Facts and figures obtained by asking people about their attitudes, awareness, intentions, and behaviors. p. 173

quota A restriction placed on the amount of a product allowed to enter or leave a country. p. 140

reference groups People to whom an individual looks as a basis for self-appraisal or as a source of personal standards. p. 113

regulation Restrictions state and federal laws place on business with regard to the conduct of its activities. p. 70

relationship marketing Linking the organization to its individual customers, employees, suppliers, and other partners for their mutual long-term benefits. p. 14

relationship selling The practice of building ties to customers based on a salesperson's attention and commitment to customer needs over time. p. 377

retail life cycle The process of growth and decline that retail outlets, like products, experience and which consists of the early growth, accelerated development, maturity, and decline stages. p. 323

retailing All activities involved in selling, renting, and providing goods and services to ultimate consumers for personal, family, or household use. p. 310

retailing mix The activities related to managing the store and the merchandise in the store, which include retail pricing, store location, retail communication, and merchandise. p. 318

reverse auction In an e-marketplace, an online auction in which a buyer communicates a need for a product or service and would-be suppliers are invited to bid in competition with each other. p. 133

sales forecast The total sales of a product that a firm expects to sell during a specified time period under specified environmental conditions and its own marketing efforts. p. 180

sales management Planning the selling program and implementing and controlling the personal selling effort of the firm. p. 376

sales plan A statement describing what is to be achieved and where and how the selling effort of salespeople is to be directed. p. 385

sales promotion A short-term inducement of value offered to arouse interest in buying a good or service. p. 337

sales quota Specific goals assigned to a salesperson, sales team, branch sales office, or sales district for a stated period. p. 389

salesforce automation The use of computer, information, communication, and Internet technologies to make the sales function more effective and efficient. p. 390

scrambled merchandising Offering several unrelated product lines in a single store. p. 315

secondary data Facts and figures that have already been recorded before the project at hand. p. 168

selective distribution A level of distribution density whereby a firm selects a few retail outlets in a specific geographical area to carry its products. p. 294

self-regulation An alternative to government control where an industry attempts to police itself. p. 73

services Intangible activities or benefits that an organization provides to consumers in exchange for money or something else of value. p. 213

shrinkage Breakage and theft of merchandise by customers and employees. p. 319

situation analysis Taking stock of where the firm or product has been recently, where it is now, and where it is headed in terms of the organization's plans and the external factors and trends affecting it. p. 33

social audit A systematic assessment of a firm's objectives, strategies, and performance in terms of social responsibility. p. 88

social forces The demographic characteristics of the population and its values. p. 61

social responsibility The idea that organizations are part of a larger society and are accountable to that society for their actions. p. 86

societal marketing concept The view that organizations should discover and satisfy the needs of its consumers in a way that also provides for society's well-being. p. 17

spam Communications that take the form of electronic junk mail or unsolicited e-mail. p. 407

strategic marketing process The approach whereby an organization allocates its marketing mix resources to reach its target markets. p. 33

subcultures Subgroups within the larger, or national, culture with unique values, ideas, and attitudes. p. 114

supply chain A series of firms that perform activities required to create and deliver a good or service to consumers or industrial users. p. 297

supply partnership A relationship that exists when a buyer and its supplier adopt mutually beneficial objectives, policies, and procedures for the purpose of lowering the cost or increasing the value of products and services delivered to the ultimate consumer. p. 128

SWOT analysis An acronym describing an organization's appraisal of its internal **S**trengths and **W**eaknesses and its external **O**pportunities and **T**hreats. p. 33

synergy The increased customer value achieved through performing organizational functions more efficiently. p. 192

target market One or more specific groups of potential consumers toward which an organization directs its marketing program. p. 12
tariff A government tax on goods or services entering a country to raise the price of an imported product. p. 140
technology Inventions or innovations from applied science or engineering research. p. 67
telemarketing Using the telephone to interact with and sell directly to consumers. p. 317
total cost The total expense incurred by a firm in producing and marketing a product. Total cost is the sum of fixed cost and variable cost. p. 271
total logistics cost Expenses associated with transportation, materials handling and warehousing, inventory, stockouts (being out of inventory), order processing, and return goods handling. p. 301
total revenue The total money received from the sale of a product. p. 271
trade-oriented sales promotions Sales tools used to support a company's advertising and personal selling directed to wholesalers, retailers, or distributors. Also called *trade promotions*. p. 368
traditional auction In an e-marketplace, an online auction in which a seller puts an item up for sale and would-be buyers are invited to bid in competition with each other. p. 132
traffic generation The outcome of a direct marketing offer designed to motivate people to visit a business. p. 345

ultimate consumers The people who use the goods and services purchased for a household. p. 18
unit variable cost Variable cost expressed on a per unit basis. p. 271
usage rate The quantity consumed or patronage (store visits) during a specific period. Also called *frequency marketing*. p. 195
utilitarianism A personal moral philosophy that focuses on "the greatest good for the greatest number" by assessing the costs and benefits of the consequences of ethical behavior. p. 86
utility The benefits or customer value received by users of the product. p. 18

values A society's socially preferable modes of conduct or states of existence that tend to persist over time. p. 146
variable cost The sum of the expenses of the firm that vary directly with the quantity of a product that is produced and sold. p. 271
vendor-managed inventory An inventory management system whereby the supplier determines the product amount and assortment a customer (such as a retailer) needs and automatically delivers the appropriate items. p. 302
vertical marketing systems Professionally managed and centrally coordinated marketing channels designed to achieve channel economies and maximum marketing impact. p. 291
viral marketing An Internet-enabled promotional strategy that encourages individuals to forward marketer-initiated messages to others via e-mail. p. 407

web communities Websites that allow people to congregate online and exchange views on topics of common interest. p. 406
wheel of retailing A concept that describes how new forms of retail outlets enter the market. p. 322
whistle-blowers Employees who report unethical or illegal actions of their employers. p. 85
word of mouth People influencing others during conversations. p. 112
World Trade Organization An institution that sets rules governing trade between its members through panels of trade experts who decide on trade disputes between members and issue binding decisions. p. 140

CHAPTER NOTES

CHAPTER 1

1. The 3M Post-it® Flag Highlighter and Post-it® Flag Pen examples are based on a series of interviews and meeting with David Windorski, 3M, in 2004 and 2005.
2. Bruce Einhorn, "Your Next TV," *BusinessWeek,* April 4, 2005, pp. 33–36.
3. See the website of the American Marketing Association, www.marketingpower.com.
4. "The Rise of the Creative Consumer," *The Economist,* March 12, 2005, pp. 54–60.
5. Productscan® Online database of new products, from Marketing Intelligence Service, December 17, 2003, www.productscan.com.
6. Robert M. McMath and Thom Forbes, *What Were They Thinking?* (New York: Times Business, 1998), pp. 3–22.
7. From the NewProductWorks website, "Favorite Failures," www.newproductworks.com.
8. From the Hot Pockets website, www.chefamerica.com and www.hotpockets.com.
9. From the iRobot website, irobot.com.
10. Chad Terhune, "Coca-Cola's Low-Carb Soda Loses Its Fizz," *The Wall Street Journal,* October 20, 2004, pp. B1, B9.
11. Peter Brownfeld, "Groups, States Target Distracted Drivers," Fox News Channel, January 15, 2004, www.foxnews.com; Debbie Howlett, "Americans Driving to Distraction," *USA Today,* March 3, 2004, www.usatoday.com/news/nation/2004-03-04-distracted-usat_x.htm; "Cingular Teen Distracted Driving Program Reaches 5.6 Million Students," January 28, 2004, www.cell-phone-plans.net; and numerous resources from the Cellular Telecommunications and Internet Association, www.wow-com.com; the ads were created by the Safe Communities of Wright County, Minnesota, and sponsored by the Minnesota Department of Public Safety, Office of Traffic Safety.
12. E. Jerome McCarthy, *Basic Marketing: A Managerial Approach* (Homewood, IL: Richard D. Irwin, 1960); and Walter van Waterschoot and Christophe Van den Bulte, "The 4P Classification of the Marketing Mix Revisited," *Journal of Marketing,* October 1992, pp. 83–93.
13. James Surowiecki, "The Return of Michael Porter," *Fortune,* February 1999, pp. 135–38; and Kathleen M. Eisenhardt and Shona L. Brown, "Time Pacing: Competing in Markets That Won't Stand Still," *Harvard Business Review,* March–April 1998, pp. 59–69.
14. Werner J. Reinartz and V. Kumar, "On the Profitability of Long-Life Customers in a Noncontractual Setting: An Empirical Investigation and Implications for Marketing," *Journal of Marketing,* October 2000, pp. 17–35; and "What's a Loyal Customer Worth?" *Fortune,* December 11, 1995, p. 182.
15. Michael Treacy and Fred D. Wiersema, *The Discipline of Market Leaders* (Reading, MA: Addison-Wesley, 1995); Michael Treacy and Fred Wiersema, "How Market Leaders Keep Their Edge," *Fortune,* February 6, 1995, pp. 88–89; and Michael Treacy, "You Need a Value Discipline—But Which One?" *Fortune,* April 17, 1995, p. 195.
16. *Annual Report* (New York: General Electric Company, 1952), p. 21.
17. John C. Narver, Stanley F. Slater, and Brian Tietje, "Creating a Market Orientation," *Journal of Market Focused Management,* no. 2 (1998), pp. 241–55; Stanley F. Slater and John C. Narver, "Market Orientation and the Learning Organization," *Journal of Marketing,* July 1995, pp. 63–74; and George S. Day, "The Capabilities of Market-Driven Organizations," *Journal of Marketing,* October 1994, pp. 37–52.
18. The definition of customer relationship management is adapted from Rajendra K. Srivastava, Tasadduq A. Shervani, and Liam Fahey, "Marketing, Business Processes, and Shareholder Value: An Embedded View of Marketing Activities and the Discipline of Marketing," *Journal of Marketing,* special issue (1999), pp. 168–79.
19. Michael E. Porter and Claas van der Linde, "Green and Competitive Ending the Stalemate," *Harvard Business Review,* September–October 1995, pp. 120–34; Jacquelyn Ottman, "Edison Winners Show Smart Environmental Marketing," *Marketing News,* July 17, 1995, pp. 16, 19; and Jacquelyn Ottman "Mandate for the '90s: Green Corporate Image," *Marketing News,* September 11, 1995, p. 8.
20. Philip Kotler and Sidney J. Levy, "Broadening the Concept of Marketing," *Journal of Marketing,* January 1969, pp. 10–15.

Rollerblade: This case was written by William Rudelius and Michael J. Vessey and is based on personal interviews with Jeremy Stonier and Nicholas Skally and on "New Rollerblade Crossfire 4D and Activa 4D Skates Have Multiple Personalities," Rollerblade press release, June 1, 2005.

CHAPTER 2

1. www.benjerry.com.
2. Blair S. Walker, "Good-Humored Activist Back to the Fray," *USA Today,* December 8, 1992, pp. 1B–2B.
3. Jim Castelli, "Finding the Right Fit: Are You Weird Enough?" *HR Magazine,* September 1990, pp. 38–39.
4. "Ben & Jerry's Homemade, Inc.," news release, Burlington, VT, January 19, 2005.
5. Roger A. Kerin, Vijay Mahajan, and P. Rajan Varadarajan, *Contemporary Perspectives on Strategic Marketing Planning* (Boston: Allyn & Bacon, 1990), chap. 1; and Orville C. Walker, Jr., Harper W. Boyd, Jr., and Jean-Claude Larreche, *Marketing Strategy* (Burr Ridge, IL: Richard D. Irwin, 1992), chaps. 1 and 2.
6. Theodore Levitt, "Marketing Myopia," *Harvard Business Review,* July–August 1960, pp. 45–56.
7. Kenneth E. Goodpaster and Thomas E. Holloran, "Anatomy of Spiritual and Social Awareness: The Case of Medtronic, Inc.," Third International Symposium on Catholic Social Thought and Management Education, Goa, India, 1999, pp. 9–11.
8. Amy Merrick, "Sears Orders Fashion Makeover from the Lands' End Catalog," *The Wall Street Journal,* January 28, 2004, pp. A1, A8.
9. George Stalk, Phillip Evans, and Lawrence E. Shulman, "Competing on Capabilities. The New Rules of Corporate Strategy," *Harvard Business Review,* March–April 1992, pp. 57–69.
10. Michael Arndt, "High-Tech and Handcrafted," *BusinessWeek,* July 5, 2004, pp. 86–87.
11. Roger A. Kerin and Robert A. Peterson, *Strategic Marketing Problems: Cases and Comments,* 10th ed. (Englewood Cliffs, NJ: Prentice Hall, 2004), pp. 2–3; and Derek F. Abell, *Defining the Business* (Englewood Cliffs, NJ: Prentice Hall, 1980), p. 18.
12. Andy Serwer, "The Education of Michael Dell," *Fortune,* March 7, 2005, pp. 73–82.
13. Adapted from "The Experience Curve Reviewed, IV. The Growth Share Matrix of the Product Portfolio" (Boston: The Boston Consulting Group, 1973).
14. Kerin, Mahajan, and Vardarajan, *Contemporary Perspectives,* p. 52.
15. "Another Kodak Moment," *The Economist,* May 14, 2005, p. 69.
16. "Has Kodak Missed the Moment?" *The Economist,* January 3, 2004, pp. 46–47.
17. Beth Snyder Bulik, "Kodak Scores with Digital Cameras but Film-Biz Losses Cloud Big Picture," *Advertising Age,* April 25, 2005, pp. 4, 51.
18. Faith Keenan and Cathy Schottenstein, "Big Yellow's Digital Dilemma," *BusinessWeek,* March 24, 2003, pp. 80–81.
19. William C. Symonds and Peter Burrows, "A Digital Warrior for Kodak, "*BusinessWeek,* May 23, 2005, p. 42.

20. Ben Dobbin, "Kodak Unveils Photo Kiosk to Develop Film in Minutes," *StarTribune,* February 9, 2004, startribune.com; Pui-Wing Tam, "Digital Snaps in a Snap," *The Wall Street Journal,* August 4, 2005, pp. B1, B5.
21. Strengths and weaknesses of the BCG technique are based on Derek F. Abell and John S. Hammond, *Strategic Market Planning: Problem and Analytic Approaches* (Englewood Cliffs, NJ: Prentice Hall, 1979); Yoram Wind, Vijay Mahajan, and Donald Swire, "An Empirical Comparison of Standardized Portfolio Models," *Journal of Marketing,* Spring 1983, pp. 89–99; and J. Scott Armstrong and Roderick J. Brodie, "Effects of Portfolio Planning Methods on Decision Making: Experimental Results," *International Journal of Research in Marketing,* Winter 1994, pp. 73–84.
22. H. Igor Ansoff, "Strategies for Diversification," *Harvard Business Review,* September–October 1957, pp. 113–24.
23. Linda Swenson and Kenneth E. Goodpaster, *Medtronic in China (A)* (Minneapolis, MN: University of St. Thomas, 1999), pp. 4–5.
24. Joseph Nocera, "Kodak: The CEO vs. the Gadfly," *Fortune,* January 12, 2004, pp. 85–92.
25. James Bandler, "Kodak to Cut Staff Up to 21%, EasyShare up 81% Amid Digital Push," *The Wall Street Journal,* January 23, 2004, pp. A1, A7.
26. Todd Wasserman, "The Mercenary (a.k.a 'Super') CMO," *BrandWeek,* June 21, 2004, pp. S6–S18.
27. "Has Kodak Missed the Moment?" *The Economist,* January 3, 2004, pp. 46–47.
28. Ibid.
29. Steve Alexander, "The Decline of Digital," *StarTribune,* May 27, 2005, pp. D1, D2.

The BP case was prepared by Steven Hartley, William Rudelius, and Michael J. Vessey based on an interview with Luis Sierra, the BP corporate website, and these other sources: William Echikson, "When Oil Gets Connected," *BusinessWeek e.biz,* December 3, 2001, pp. EB28–EB30; Martha Hamilton, "Giving Drivers Their Fill: Service Stations Modernized as BP Consolidates Merged Oil Firms," July 25, 2000, downloaded from *The Washington Post,* and Alexei Barrionuevo and Ann Zimmerman, "Latest Supermarket Special—Gasoline," *The Wall Street Journal,* April 30, 2001, pp. B1, B4.

APPENDIX A

1. Personal interview with Authur R. Kydd, St. Croix Management Group.
2. Examples of guides to writing marketing plans include William A. Cohen, *The Marketing Plan* (New York: Wiley, 1995); Mark Nolan, *The Instant Marketing Plan* (Santa Maria, CA: Puma Publishing Company, 1995); and Roman G. Hiebing, Jr., and Scott W. Cooper, *The Successful Marketing Plan,* 2nd ed. (Lincolnwood, IL: NTC Business Books, 1997).
3. Examples of guides to writing business plans include Rhonda M. Abrahms, *The Successful Business Plan: Secrets & Strategies,* 3rd ed. (Grants Pass, OR: Oasis Press/PSI Research, 2000); Joseph A. Covello and Brian J. Hazelgren, *The Complete Book of Business Plans* (Naperville, IL: Sourcebooks, 1995); Joseph A. Covello and Brian J. Hazelgren, *Your First Business Plan,* 3rd ed. (Naperville, IL: Sourcebooks, 1998); and Angela Shupe, ed., *Business Plans Handbook,* vols. 1–4 (Detroit: Gale Research, 1997).
4. Abrahms, *The Successful Business Plan*, p. 30.
5. Some of these points are adapted from Abrahms, pp. 30–38; others are adapted from William Rudelius, *Guidelines for Technical Report Writing* (Minneapolis: University of Minnesota, undated). See also William Strunk, Jr., and E. B. White, *The Elements of Style* (New York, Macmillan, 1979).
6. Rebecca Zimoch, "The Dawn of the Frozen Age," *Grocery Headquarters,* December 2002; see www.groceryheadquarters.com.
7. ACNielsen Strategic Planner as reported to the National Frozen & Refrigerated Foods Association for the week ending April 17, 2004; see www.nfraweb.org.
8. Chuck Van Hyning, *NPD's National Eating Trends;* see www.npdfoodworld.com.
9. Rebecca Zimoch, "Understanding the Hispanic Consumer," *Grocery Headquarters,* May 2003; see www.groceryheadquarters.com.
10. Interview with Don Montouri, *Packaged Facts;* see www.packagedfacts.com.

The authors are indebted to Randall F. Peters and Leah Peters for being allowed to adapt elements of a business plan for Paradise Kitchens, Inc., for the sample marketing plan and for their help and suggestions.

CHAPTER 3

1. Peter Burrows, "Show Time!" *BusinessWeek,* February 2, 2004, pp. 57–64; and Devine Leonard, "Songs in the Key of Steve," *Fortune,* May 12, 2003, pp. 52–62.
2. Fred Vogelstein, "10 Tech Trends to Bet On," *Fortune,* February 23, 2004, pp. 76–88; Alison Stein Wellner, "The Next 25 Years," *American Demographics,* April 2003, pp. 24–27; Stephen B. Shepard, "You Read It Here First," *BusinessWeek,* March 15, 2004, p. 16; Catherine Arnold, "Anti-Smoking Trend Hits Asia," *Marketing News,* January 15, 2004, p. 4; Arundhati Parmar, "Outlook 2004: Competitive Intelligence," *Marketing News,* January 15, 2004, pp. 16–17; and Steve Jarvis, "Internet Privacy at the Plate, Net Names, Taxes on Deck Too," *Marketing News,* January 1, 2001, pp. 12–14.
3. World Population Clock, www.census.gov/main/www/popclock.html, May 23, 2005; *World Population Prospects: The 2002 Revision* (2003), United Nations, table A4; and Carl Haub, "2003 World Population Data Sheet," Population Reference Bureau.
4. Haub, "2003 World Population Data Sheet"; "World Population at a Glance: 1998 and Beyond," U.S. Department of Commerce, Bureau of the Census, January 1999; "Global Demographics: The Group of Seven's Senior Moment," *BusinessWeek Online,* March 17, 2003; and "New Facts on Globalization, Poverty, and Income Distribution," International Chamber of Commerce, January 15, 2003.
5. U.S. Population Clock, www.census.gov/main/www/popclock.html, August 31, 2005; Alison Stein Wellner, "The Next 25 Years," *American Demographics,* April 2003, pp. 24–27.
6. Pamela Paul, "Meet the Parents," *American Demographics,* January 2002, pp. 42–47; and Toddi Gutner, "Generation X: To Be Young, Thrifty, and in the Black," *BusinessWeek,* July 21, 1997, p. 76.
7. Michael J. Weiss, "To Be about to Be," *American Demographics,* September 2003, pp. 29–36; Peter Francese, "Ahead of the Next Wave," *American Demographics,* September 2003, pp. 42–43; and Don O'Briant, "Millenials: The Next Generation," *Atlanta Journal-Constitution,* August 11, 2003, p. 1D.
8. Pamela Paul, "Global Generation Gap," *American Demographics,* March 2002, pp. 18–19; and Allyson L. Stewart-Allen, "EU's Future Consumers: 3 Groups to Watch," *Marketing News,* June 4, 2001, p. 9.
9. Marc J. Perry and Paul J. Mackun, "Population Change and Distribution," Census 2000 Brief: U.S. Bureau of the Census, April 2001; and Paul Campbell, "Population Projection: States, 1995–2025," Current Population Report, U.S. Department of Commerce, May 1997.
10. Joshua Bolten, "Update of Statistical Area Definitions and Additional Guidance on Their Use," Office of Management and Budget, OMB Bulletin No. 04–03, February 18, 2004; and "About Metropolitan and Micropolitan Statistical Areas," U.S. Census Bureau, www.census.gov/population/www/estimates/aboutmetro.html.
11. Alison Stein Wellner, "Our True Colors," *American Demographics,* November 2002, pp. S2–S20; Eduardo Porter, "Even 126 Sizes Don't Fit All," *The Wall Street Journal,* March 2, 2001, pp. B1, B4; and William H. Frey, "Micro Melting Pots," *American Demographics,* June 2001, pp. 20–23.
12. Brian Grow, "Hispanic Nation," *BusinessWeek,* March 15, 2004, pp. 58–70; Wellner, "Our True Colors"; Deborah L. Vence, "You Talkin' to Me?" *Marketing News,* March 1, 2004, pp. 1, 9–11; and Wellner, "The Next 25 Years."

13. Edward B. Keller and Thomas A. W. Miller, "Re-mapping the World of Consumers," *American Demographics,* October 2000, pp. S1–S20; and Sandra Yin, "Making a Healthy Choice," *American Demographics,* July 2001, pp. 40–41.
14. Mortimer B. Zuckerman, "A Truly Cruel College Squeeze," *U.S. News & World Report,* March 8, 2004, p. 80.
15. Michael J. Mandel, "Inventing the Clinton Recession," *BusinessWeek,* February 23, 2004, p. 48; and James Cooper, Kathleen Madigan, and James Mehring, "Welcome to the Growth Recession," *BusinessWeek,* July 2, 2001, pp. 87–90.
16. Carmen DeNavas-Walt, Bernadette D. Proctor, and Robert J. Mills, "Income, Poverty and Health Insurance Coverage in the United States: 2003"; "Income in the United States," *Current Population Reports,* U.S. Census Bureau, August 2004, p. 27.
17. Don Carlson, "The Old Economy in the New Economy," *BusinessWeek,* November 13, 2000, p. 42H; Owen Ullmann, "Forget Saving, America. Your Job Is to Spend," *BusinessWeek,* December 28, 1998, p. 54; Gene Koretz, "Savings' Death Is Exaggerated," *BusinessWeek,* September 14, 1998, p. 26; and Marcia Mogelonsky, "No More Food, Thanks," *American Demographics,* August 1998, p. 59.
18. "Consumer Expenditures in 2002," U.S. Department of Labor, Bureau of Labor Statistics, February 2004, pp. 1–4; and "Spending on Necessities," *Monthly Labor Review,* U.S. Department of Labor, Bureau of Labor Statistics, June 24, 2003.
19. John Carey, "Tiny Smart Bombs vs. Cancer?" *BusinessWeek,* March 1, 2004, p. 115; Stephen H. Wildstrom, "Get Ready for an Innovative New Year," *BusinessWeek,* December 29, 2003, p. 28; Herve Gallaire, "Can New Technology Recharge Xerox?" *BusinessWeek,* December 22, 2003, p. IM2; and Fred Vogelstein, "10 Tech Trends to Bet On," *Fortune,* February 23, 2004, pp. 75–88.
20. Michael Krauss, "Young Net Entrepreneurs Leverage Web Anew," *Marketing News,* February 1, 2004, p. 6.
21. Leon Jaroff, "Smart's the Word in Detroit," *Time,* February 6, 1995, pp. 50–52.
22. Clint Willis, "25 Cool Things You Wish You Had and Will," *Forbes ASAP,* June 1, 1998, pp. 49–60.
23. Chris Anderson, "The Wi-Fi Revolution," *Unwired,* supplement to *Wired,* 2003.
24. Henry Goldblatt, "The End of the Long Distance Club," *Fortune,* May 26, 1997, p. 30; and "Wheel of Fortune," *The Economist,* November 21, 1998, p. 53.
25. DeAnn Welmer, "Don't Be Shocked by Surges in the Price of Power," *BusinessWeek,* July 27, 1998, p. 33.
26. Jay Greene, "Microsoft: First Europe, Then. . . ?" *BusinessWeek,* March 22, 2004, p. 86.
27. "Small Business Resources for Faculty, Students, and Researchers: Answers to Frequently Asked Questions," Small Business Administration, Office of Advocacy, March 2004.
28. "A New Copyright Law?" *BusinessWeek,* August 3, 1998, p. 45.
29. "Highlights of Food Labeling," *Marketing News,* March 15, 2004, p. 14.
30. Dorothy Cohen, "Trademark Strategy Revisited," *Journal of Marketing,* July 1991, pp. 46–59.
31. Maxine L. Retsky, "Review Int'l Filing Process for Marks," *Marketing News,* September 29, 2003, p. 8.
32. Paul Barrett, "High Court Sees Color as Basis for Trademarks," *The Wall Street Journal,* March 29, 1995, p. A6; Paul Barrett, "Color in the Court," *The Wall Street Journal,* January 5, 1995, p. A1; and David Kelly, "Rainbow of Ideas to Trademark Color," *Advertising Age,* April 24, 1995, pp. 20, 22.
33. Maxine L. Retsky, "Dilution of Trademarks Hard to Prove," *Marketing News,* May 12, 2003, p. 6.
34. Dick Mercer, "Tempest in a Soup Can," *Advertising Age,* October 17, 1994, pp. 25–29.
35. Catherine Arnold, "Law Gives Industry a Buzz," *Marketing News,* February 1, 2004, p. 11; Maxine L. Retsky, "New National 'Do Not Call' Law Becomes Effective, Enforceable," *Marketing News,* August 4, 2003, p. 6; "Who Buys That Stuff?" *Marketing News,* February 1, 2004, p. 11; Arundhati Parmar, "We Said, Do-Not-Call," *Marketing News,* March 15, 2004, p. 4; and Deborah L. Vence, "Less Ringing in the Ear," *Marketing News,* December 8, 2003, p. 14.
36. Maxine L. Retsky, "Stakes Are High for Direct Mail Sweepstakes Promotions," *Marketing News,* July 3, 2000, p. 8; Catherine Arnold, "Picky, Picky, Picky" *Marketing News,* February 15, 2004, p. 17; Catherine Arnold, "No Can Spam," *Marketing News,* January 15, 2004, p. 3; Arundhati Parmar, "Can't Say You Weren't Warned," *Marketing News,* February 15, 2004, p. 4; and James Heckman, "Laws That Take Effect—and Some Likely to Return in 1999 Mean Marketers Must Change Some Policies," *Marketing News,* December 7, 1998, p. 1, 16.
37. Mark McFadden, "The BBB on the WWW," *HP Professional,* September 1997, p. 36.

Flyte Time Productions, Inc.: This case was written by William Rudelius based on personal interviews with Jimmy Jam and Terry Lewis and the following sources: Don Campbell, "In Groove We Trust," *NWA World Traveler,* February 2004, pp. 29–33; Jon Bream, "Flyte Tyme Is Still Ticking after 20 Years of Hits," *Star Tribune,* April 29, 2001, pp. F1, F7; and "Jimmy Jam and Terry Lewis Make Flyte Tyme Studios No. 1," *Business Wire,* August 21, 2001.

CHAPTER 4

1. www.beeresponsible.com, downloaded May 2, 2005; www.beerinstitute.org, downloaded March 1, 2004; Mike Beirne, "In the Name of Responsibility," *BrandWeek,* May 12, 2003, pp. 32–36.
2. "Honorable?" *Business 2.0,* February 2000, p. 92.
3. Ray O. Werner, "Marketing and the Supreme Court in Transition, 1982–1984," *Journal of Marketing,* Summer 1985, pp. 97–105; and Jane Bryant Quinn, "Computer Program Deceives Consumers," *Dallas Morning News,* March 2, 1998, p. B3.
4. *The 2003 National Business Ethics Survey* (Washington, DC: Ethics Resource Center, 2003); "Image Issue," *Advertising Age,* December 9, 2002, p. 18; and Patrick J. Gnazzo and George R. Wratney, "Are You Serious about Ethics?" *Across the Board,* July–August 2003, pp. 47–50.
5. "Levi Only Comfortable Dealing with Countries That Fit Its Image," *Dallas Morning News,* January 9, 1995, p. D2.
6. These statistics were obtained from Recording Industry Association of America (www.riaa.com), Motion Picture Association of America (www.mpaa.com), and the Business Software Alliance (www.bsa.com).
7. *Internet Piracy on Campus* (IPSOS: Washington, DC, September 16, 2003).
8. Vern Terpstra and Kenneth David, *The Cultural Environment of International Business,* 3rd ed. (Cincinnati: South-Western Publishing, 1991), p. 12.
9. "Carnivore in the Cabbage Patch," *U.S. News & World Report,* January 20, 1997, p. 69.
10. Timothy Muris, "Protecting Consumers' Privacy: 2002 and Beyond," www.ftc.gov, downloaded January 3, 2004.
11. "FBI Chief Puts Cost of Economic Espionage at $200 Million," *Bloomberg News,* June 21, 2003.
12. "P&G Expected to Get about $120 Million in Settlement of Chewy-Cookie Lawsuit," *The Wall Street Journal,* September 11, 1989, p. B10.
13. These examples are highlighted in Thomas W. Dunfee, N. Craig Smith, and William T. Ross, Jr., "Social Contracts and Marketing Ethics," *Journal of Marketing,* July 1999, pp. 14–32; and Andy Pasztor, *When the Pentagon Was for Sale: Inside America's Biggest Defense Scandal* (New York: Scribner, 1995).
14. www.transparency.org, downloaded May 4, 2005.
15. Thomas Donaldson, "The Corporate Ethics Boom: Significant, or Just for Show?" Knowledge.Wharton.upenn.edu, downloaded February 25, 2001; and "Doing Well by Doing Good," *The Economist,* April 22, 2000, pp. 65–67.
16. "Coca-Cola Unit Head Resigns after Rigged Test," www.forbes.com, downloaded August 25, 2003.
17. *The 2003 National Business Ethics Survey.*
18. "3M's Big Cleanup," *BusinessWeek,* June 5, 2000, pp. 96–98.

19. Alix M. Freedman, "Bad Reaction: Nestlé's Bid to Crash Baby-Formula Market in U.S. Stirs a Row," *The Wall Street Journal,* February 16, 1989, pp. A1, A6; and Alix Freedman, "Nestlé to Drop Claim on Label of Its Formula," *The Wall Street Journal,* March 13, 1989, p. B5.
20. Harvey S. James and Farhad Rassekh, "Smith, Friedman, and Self-Interest in Ethical Society," *Business Ethics Quarterly,* July 2000, pp. 659–74.
21. "Cost of Living," *The Economist,* March 1, 2003, p. 60.
22. "Perrier—Overresponding to a Crisis," in Robert F. Hartley, *Marketing Mistakes and Successes,* 9th ed. (New York: John Wiley & Sons, 2004), pp. 153–64.
23. "The Great Firestone/Ford Explorer Tire Disaster," in Hartley, *Marketing Mistakes and Successes,* pp. 139–52.
24. "More about Pollution Prevention Pays," www.3M.com, downloaded April 22, 2005; "Xerox Steps up Successes of Environment, Health, Safety Programs," www.xerox.com/environment, downloaded February 25, 2004; "Boise Cascade Turns Green," *The Wall Street Journal,* September 3, 2003, p. B6; and "FedEx and Brown Are Going Green," *BusinessWeek,* August 11, 2003, pp. 60, 62.
25. For an extended discussion on this topic, see P. Rajan Varadarajan and Anil Menon, "Causes-Related Marketing: A Coalignment of Marketing Strategy and Corporate Philanthropy," *Journal of Marketing,* July 1988, pp. 58–74. The examples are found in Susan Orenstein, "The Selling of Breast Cancer," *Business 2.0,* February 2003, pp. 88–94; and Christine Bittar, "Seeking Cause and Effect," *BrandWeek,* September 11, 2002, pp. 19–23.
26. "Cause Marketing," *Advertising Age,* June 13, 2005, pp. 31–36; "Cause and 'Affect,'" *BrandWeek,* October 7, 2002, p. 16; and Bittar, "Seeking Cause and Effect."
27. These steps are adapted from J. J. Carson and G. A. Steiner, *Measuring Business Social Performance: The Corporate Social Audit* (New York: Committee for Economic Development, 1974). See also Sandra Waddock and Neil Smith, "Corporate Responsibility Audits: Doing Well by Doing Good," *Sloan Management Review,* Winter 2000, pp. 75–84.
28. "Sweatshops: Finally, Airing the Dirty Linen," *BusinessWeek,* June 23, 2003, pp. 100–1.
29. "A Survey of Corporate Social Responsibility," *The Economist,* January 22, 2005, special section.
30. This discussion is based on Wayne D. Hoyer and Deborah J. MacInnis, *Consumer Behavior,* 3rd ed. (New York: Houghton Mifflin Company, 2004), pp. 535–37; "Factoids," *Research Alert,* December 8, 2002, p. 5; and "Penny for Your Thoughts," *American Demographics,* September 2000, pp. 8–9.
31. "A Pirate and His Penance," *Time,* January 26, 2004, p. 60.
32. "A Lighter Shade of Green," *American Demographics,* February 2000, p. 24.
33. "Schism on the Green," *BrandWeek,* February 26, 2001, p. 18.

Starbucks Corporation: This case is based on information on the company website (www.starbucks.com) and the following sources: "Living Our Values," *2003 Corporate Social Responsibility Annual Report;* "Starbucks Annual Shareholder Meeting," Starbucks press release, March 30, 2004; Ranjay Gulati, Sarah Huffman, and Gary Neilson, "The Barista Principle: Starbucks and the Rise of Relational Capital," *Strategy and Business,* 3rd Quarter 2002, pp. 58–69; and Andy Serwer, "Hot Starbucks to Go," *Fortune,* January 12, 2004, pp. 52ff.

CHAPTER 5

1. "This Volvo Is Not a Guy Thing," *BusinessWeek,* March 15, 2004, pp. 84–86; and "Volvo for Wife," www.forbes.com, downloaded April 1, 2004.
2. Roger D. Blackwell, Paul W. Miniard, and James F. Engel, *Consumer Behavior,* 9th ed. (Mason, OH: South-Western Publishing, 2001).
3. For thorough descriptions of consumer expertise, see Joseph W. Alba and J. Wesley Hutchinson, "Knowledge Calibration: What Consumers Know and What They Think They Know," *Journal of Consumer Research,* September 2000, pp. 123–57.
4. For in-depth studies on external information search patterns, see Sridhar Moorthy, Brian T. Ratchford, and Debabrata Tulukdar, "Consumer Information Search Revisited: Theory and Empirical Analysis," *Journal of Consumer Research,* March 1997, pp. 263–77; Joel E. Urbany, Peter R. Dickson, and William L. Wilkie, "Buyer Uncertainty and Information Search," *Journal of Consumer Research,* March 1992, pp. 452–63; and Sharon E. Beatty and Scott M. Smith, "External Search Effort: An Investigation across Several Product Categories," *Journal of Consumer Research,* June 1987, pp. 83–95.
5. "CD Players—Portable," *Consumer Reports 2003 Buying Guide* (Yonkers, NY: Consumers Union, 2003), pp. 225–27.
6. John A. Howard, *Buyer Behavior in Marketing Strategy,* 2nd ed. (Englewood Cliffs, NJ: Prentice Hall, 1994), pp. 101, 128–89. For an extended discussion on consumer choice sets, see Allan D. Shocker, Moshe Ben-Akiva, Bruno Boccara, and Prakesh Nedungadi, "Consideration Set Influences on Consumer Decision Making and Choice: Issues, Models, and Suggestions," *Marketing Letters,* August 1991, pp. 181–98.
7. William J. McDonald, "Time Use in Shopping: The Role of Personal Characteristics," *Journal of Retailing,* Winter 1994, pp. 345–66; Robert J. Donovan, John R. Rossiter, Gillian Marcoolyn, and Andrew Nesdale, "Store Atmosphere and Purchasing Behavior," *Journal of Retailing,* Fall 1994, pp. 283–94; and Eric A. Greenleaf and Donald R. Lehman, "Reasons for Substantial Delay in Consumer Decision Making," *Journal of Consumer Research,* September 1995, pp. 186–99.
8. Jagdish N. Sheth, Banwari Mitral, and Bruce Newman, *Consumer Behavior* (Fort Worth: Dryden Press, 1999), p. 22.
9. For an overview of research on involvement, see John C. Mowen and Michael Minor, *Consumer Behavior,* 5th ed. (Upper Saddle River, NJ: Prentice Hall, 1998), pp. 64–68; and Wayne D. Hoyer and Deborah J. MacInnis, *Consumer Behavior,* 3rd ed. (Boston: Houghton Mifflin, 2004), pp. 57–59.
10. For an overview on the three problem-solving variations, see Del J. Hawkins, Roger J. Best, and Kenneth A. Coney, *Consumer Behavior,* 9th ed. (Burr Ridge, IL: McGraw-Hill/Irwin, 2004), pp. 500–4.
11. Russell Belk, "Situational Variables and Consumer Behavior," *Journal of Consumer Research,* December 1975, pp. 157–63.
12. A. H. Maslow, *Motivation and Personality* (New York: Harper & Row, 1970). Also see Richard Yalch and Frederic Brunel, "Need Hierarchies in Consumer Judgments of Product Design: Is It Time to Reconsider Maslow's Hierarchy?" in Kim Corfman and John Lynch, eds., *Advances in Consumer Research* (Provo, UT: Association for Consumer Research, 1996), pp. 405–10.
13. Joel B. Cohen, "An Interpersonal Orientation to the Study of Consumer Behavior," *Journal of Marketing Research,* August 1967, pp. 270–78; and Rena Bartos, *Marketing to Women around the World* (Cambridge, MA: Harvard Business School, 1989).
14. Myron Magnet, "Let's Go for Growth," *Fortune,* March 7, 1994, p. 70.
15. This example provided in Michael R. Solomon, *Consumer Behavior,* 5th ed. (Upper Saddle River, NJ: Prentice Hall, 2002).
16. For further reading on subliminal perception, see Anthony G. Greenwald, Sean C. Draine, and Richard L. Abrams, "Three Cognitive Markers of Unconscious Semantic Activation," *Science,* September 1996, pp. 1699–701; Dennis L. Rosen and Surendra N. Singh, "An Investigation of Subliminal Embedded Effect on Multiple Measures of Advertising Effectiveness," *Psychology & Marketing,* March–April 1992, pp. 157–73; and Kathryn T. Theus, "Subliminal Advertising and the Psychology of Processing Unconscious Stimuli: A Review of the Research," *Psychology & Marketing,* May–June 1994, pp. 271–90.
17. August Bullock, *The Secret Sales Pitch* (San Jose, CA: Norwich Publishers, 2004); "GOP Commercial Resurrects Debate on Subliminal Ads," *The Wall Street Journal,* September 13, 2000, p. B10; "I Will Love This Story," *U.S. News & World Report,* May 12, 1997, p. 12; and "Firm Gets Message Out Subliminally," *Dallas Morning News,* February 2, 1997, pp. 1H, 6H.

18. Martin Fishbein and I. Aizen, *Belief, Attitude, Intention and Behavior: An Introduction to Theory and Research* (Reading, MA: Addison-Wesley 1975), p. 6.
19. Richard J. Lutz, "Changing Brand Attitudes through Modification of Cognitive Structure," *Journal of Consumer Research,* March 1975, pp. 49–59. See also Mowen and Minor, *Consumer Behavior,* pp. 287–88.
20. "The VALS™ Types," www.sric-bi.com/VALS, downloaded May 10, 2005.
21. This discussion is based on Ed Keller and Jon Berry, *The Influentials* (New York: Simon and Schuster, 2003).
22. "Have you Heard?" *Business 2.0,* December 2004, p. 37.
23. Gerg Frost, "Didja Hear...?" *Marketing News* (September 1, 2005), pp. 12-14ff; Linda Tischler, "What's the Buzz?" *Fast Company,* May 2004, pp. 76–77; Melanie Wells, "Kid Nabbing," *Forbes,* February 2, 2004, pp. 84–87; and Marion Salzman, Ira Matathia, and Ann O'Reilly, *Buzz: Harness the Power of Influence and Create Demand* (New York: John Wiley & Sons, 2003).
24. For an extensive review on consumer socialization of children, see Deborah Roedder John, "Consumer Socialization of Children: A Retrospective Look at Twenty-Five Years of Research," *Journal of Consumer Research,* December 1999, pp. 183–213.
25. This discussion is based on "Marriage Drain's Big Cost," *American Demographics,* April 2004, pp. 40–41; James Morrow, "A Place for One," *American Demographics,* November 2003, pp. 25–31; and J. Paul Peter and Jerry C. Olson, *Consumer Behavior and Marketing Strategy,* 7th ed. (Burr Ridge, IL: McGraw Hill/Irwin, 2005), pp. 342–44.
26. "Co-Masters of Their Domain," *BrandWeek,* September 8, 2003, p. 20; and Eric Arnould, Linda Price, and George Zinkhan, *Consumers,* 2nd ed. (Burr Ridge, IL: McGraw-Hill/Irwin, 2004).
27. "He's in Fashion," *American Demographics,* November 2002, p. 10; and "Look Who's Shopping," *Progressive Grocer,* January 2001, p. 18; "Kids Gaining Voice in How Home Looks," *Advertising Age,* March 29, 2004, p. S4; "Coming of Age in Consumerdom," *American Demographics,* April 2004, p. 14; and www.teenresearch.com, downloaded February 14, 2005.
28. Selig Center for Economic Growth, www.selig.uga.edu, downloaded January 31, 2005.
29. For a summary of representative research on African American consumers, see Christine Bittar, "The New Face of Beauty," *BrandWeek,* January 19, 2004, pp. 24–28; William H. Frey, "Revival," *American Demographics,* October 2003, pp. 27–31; and "Race, Ethnicity, and the Way We Shop," *American Demographics,* February 2003, pp. 30–33.
30. "Hispanic Nation," *BusinessWeek,* March 15, 2004, pp. 58–68; "P&G, Sears, GM Top Hispanic Ad Spending Survey," *Advertising Age,* April 19, 2004, pp. 1, 60; Laurel Wentz, "Cross Over," *Advertising Age,* July 7, 2003, pp. S1–S6; "Campbell Looks to Make Splash with Hispanics," *BrandWeek,* December 8, 2003, p. 22; and "Pick Up the Pieces," *Marketing News,* March 15, 2005, pp. 13–14.
31. "Hispanics Wanted," *BrandWeek,* April 12, 2004, p. 22.
32. Allison Stein Wellner, "Diversity in America" supplement to *American Demographics,* November 2002; and "Race, Ethnicity, and the Way We Shop."

Ken Davis Products, Inc. This case was written by William Rudelius and is based on interviews with Barbara Jo Davis and the company's website (www.kendavis-bbq.com) and newsletters.

CHAPTER 6

1. Interview with Kim Nagele, JCPMedia, September 19, 2005.
2. This figure is based on *Statistical Abstract of the United States: 2004,* 124th ed. (Washington, DC: U.S. Census Bureau, 2004).
3. "FAA Announces Contract for New Workstations," *Dallas Morning News,* April 30, 1999, p. 16H.
4. *2002 NAICS United States Manual* (Washington, DC: Office of Management and Budget, 2002).
5. This listing and portions of the following discussion are based on F. Robert Dwyer and John F. Tanner, Jr., *Business Marketing,* 3rd ed. (Burr Ridge, IL: McGraw-Hill/Irwin, 2006); Michael D. Hutt and Thomas W. Speh, *Business Marketing Management,* 8th ed. (Mason, OH: South-Western, 2004); and Frank G. Bingham, Jr., Roger Gomes, and Patricia A. Knowles, *Business Marketing,* 3rd ed. (Burr Ridge, IL: McGraw-Hill/Irwin, 2005).
6. "Latin Trade Connections," *Latin Trade,* June 1998, p. 72.
7. "The Super-Jumbo of all Gambles," *The Economist,* January 22, 2005, pp. 55–56; and "Battle for the Sky," *Time,* March 2005, B17–B18.
8. These and other examples are found in "The Business Case for Diversity," www.diversity.com, downloaded on February 28, 2004; and "Boise Cascade Turns Green," *The Wall Street Journal,* September 3, 2003, p. B6. Also see Minette E. Drumwright, "Socially Responsible Organizational Buying: Environmental Concern as a Noneconomic Buying Criterion," *Journal of Marketing,* July 1994, pp. 1–18.
9. For a study of buying criteria used by industrial firms, see Daniel H. McQuiston and Rockney G. Walters, "The Evaluation Criteria of Industrial Buyers: Implications for Sales Training," *Journal of Business & Industrial Marketing,* Summer–Fall 1989, pp. 65–75. Also see Dwyer and Tanner, *Business Marketing,* chap. 2.
10. Michael R. Leenders and David L. Blenkhorn, *Reverse Marketing: The New Buyer–Supplier Relationship* (New York: Free Press, 1996).
11. This example is found in Sandy D. Jap and Jakki J. Mohr, "Leveraging Internet Technologies in B2B Relationships," *California Management Review,* Summer 2002, pp. 24–38.
12. "America's Most Admired Companies," *Fortune,* March 8, 2004, pp. 80ff; Brian Milligan, "Medal of Excellence: Harley-Davidson Wins by Getting Suppliers on Board," *Purchasing,* September 2000, pp. 52–65; and "Harley-Davidson Company," *Purchasing Magazine Online,* September 4, 2003.
13. "IBM Plans New Supercomputers," *Dallas Morning News,* November 19, 2002, p. 8D.
14. "EDS Jars Rivals, Wins Big Defense Deal," *The Wall Street Journal,* October 9, 2000, p. A4; and "HP Finalizes $3 Billion Outsourcing Agreement to Manage Procter & Gamble's IT Infrastructure," Hewlett-Packard news release, May 6, 2003.
15. This discussion is based on James C. Anderson and James A. Narus, *Business Market Management,* 2nd ed. (Upper Saddle River, NJ: Prentice Hall, 2004); and Joseph P. Cannon and Christian Homburg, "Buyer–Supplier Relationships and Customer Firm Costs," *Journal of Marketing,* January 2001, pp. 29–43.
16. Thomas V. Bonoma, "Major Sales: Who Really Does the Buying?" *Harvard Business Review,* May–June 1982, pp. 11–19. For recent research on buying centers, see Morry Ghingold and David T. Wilson, "Buying Center Research and Business Marketing Practices: Meeting the Challenge of Dynamic Marketing," *Journal of Business & Industrial Marketing* 13, no. 2 (1998), pp. 96–108; and Philip L. Dawes, Don Y. Lee, and Grahame R. Dowling, "Information Control and Influence in Emerging Buying Centers," *Journal of Marketing,* July 1998, pp. 55–68.
17. These definitions are adapted from Frederick E. Webster, Jr., and Yoram Wind, *Organizational Buying Behavior* (Englewood Cliffs, NJ: Prentice Hall, 1972), p. 6.
18. "Can Corning Find Its Optic Nerve?" *Fortune,* March 19, 2001, pp. 148–50.
19. Representative studies on the buy-class framework that document its usefulness include Erin Anderson, Wujin Chu, and Barton Weitz, "Industrial Purchasing: An Empirical Exploration of the Buy-Class Framework," *Journal of Marketing,* July 1987, pp. 71–86; Morry Ghingold, "Testing the 'Buy-Grid' Buying Process Model," *Journal of Purchasing and Materials Management,* Winter 1986, pp. 30–36; P. Matthyssens and W. Faes, "OEM Buying Process for New Components: Purchasing and Marketing Implications," *Industrial Marketing Management,* August 1985, pp. 145–57; and Thomas W. Leigh and Arno J. Ethans, "A Script-Theoretic Analysis of Industrial Purchasing Behavior," *Journal of Marketing,* Fall 1984, pp. 22–32. Studies not

supporting the buy-class framework include Joseph A. Bellizi and Philip McVey, "How Valid Is the Buy-Grid Model?" *Industrial Marketing Management,* February 1983, pp. 57–62; and Donald W. Jackson, Janet E. Keith, and Richard K. Burdick, "Purchasing Agents' Perceptions of Industrial Buying Center Influences: A Situational Approach," *Journal of Marketing,* Fall 1984, pp. 75–83.

20. "B2B E-Commerce Headed for Trillions," www.clickz.com, downloaded May 2, 2005.
21. This discussion is based on Jennifer Reinhold, "What We Learned in the New Economy," *Fast Company,* March 4, 2004, pp. 56ff; Mark Roberti, "General Electric's Spin Machine," *The Industry Standard,* January 22–29, 2001, pp. 74–83; "Grainger Lightens Its Digital Load," *Industrial Distribution,* March 2001, pp. 77–79; and www.boeing.com/procurement, downloaded February 6, 2004.
22. This discussion is based on Robert J. Dolan and Youngme Moon, "Pricing and Market Making on the Internet," *Journal of Interactive Marketing,* Spring 2000, pp. 56–73; and Ajit Kambil and Eric van Heck, *Marking Markets: How Firms Can Benefit from Online Auctions and Exchanges* (Boston: Harvard Business School Press, 2002).
23. Sandy Jap, "An Exploratory Study of the Introduction of Online Reverse Auctions," *Journal of Marketing,* July 2003, pp. 96–107.

Lands' End: This case is based on information available on the company website (www.landsend.com) and the following sources: Robert Berner, "A Hard Bargain at Lands' End?" *BusinessWeek,* May 28, 2001, p. 14; Rebecca Quick, "Getting the Right Fit—Hips and All—Can a Machine Measure You Better than Your Tailor?" *The Wall Street Journal,* October 18, 2000, p. B1; Stephanie Miles, "Apparel E-Tailers Spruce Up for Holidays," *The Wall Street Journal,* November 6, 2001, p. B6; and Dana James, "Custom Goods Nice Means for Lands' End," *Marketing News,* August 14, 2000, p. 5.

CHAPTER 7

1. Lisa Bannon and Carlta Vitzthum, "One-Toy-Fits-All: How Industry Learned to Love the Global Kid," *The Wall Street Journal,* April 29, 2003, pp. A1, A4; "Mattel, Inc.," *Hoover's Online,* www.hoovers.com, downloaded March 25, 2004; and "Mattel Recharges Its Batteries," *NYSE Magazine,* www.nyse.com, downloaded July 3, 2003.
2. The discussion on protectionism is based on Dennis R. Appleyard and Alfred J. Field, Jr., *International Economics,* 4th ed. (Burr Ridge, IL: McGraw-Hill/Irwin, 2001), chap. 15; "A Fruit Peace," *The Economist,* April 21, 2001, pp. 75–76; and Gary C. Hufbauer and Kimberly A. Elliott, *Measuring the Cost of Protection in the United States* (Washington, DC: Institute for International Economics, 1994).
3. This discussion is based on information provided by the World Trade Organization, www.wto.org, downloaded May 21, 2005.
4. "A Survey of EU Enlargement," *The Economist,* November 22, 2003, special section; and www.europa.eu.int, downloaded April 2, 2005.
5. "Free Trade on Trial," *The Economist,* January 3, 2004, pp. 13–15.
6. Johnny K. Johansson and Ilkka A. Ronkainen, "The Brand Challenge," *Marketing Management,* March–April 2004, pp. 54–55.
7. Kevin Lane Keller, *Strategic Brand Management,* 2nd ed. (Upper Saddle River, NJ: Prentice Hall, 2003), p. 693.
8. "Golden Boys and Girls," *The Economist,* February 14, 2004, pp. 37–38; Elissa Moses, *The $100 Billion Allowance: Accessing the Global Teen Market* (New York: Wiley, 2000); and www.mtv.com/company, downloaded March 22, 2004.
9. "The Net's Second Superpower," *BusinessWeek,* March 15, 2004, pp. 54–56; "B2B E-Commerce Headed for Trillions," www.clickz.com, downloaded March 27, 2004; and "EU B2B Expected to Explode," www.clickz.com, downloaded March 27, 2004.
10. For comprehensive references on cross-cultural aspects of marketing, see Paul A. Herbig, *Handbook of Cross-Cultural Marketing* (New York: Halworth Press, 1998); Jean-Claude Usunier, *Marketing across Cultures,* 2nd ed. (London: Prentice Hall Europe, 1996); and Philip R. Cateora and John L. Graham, *International Marketing,* 12th ed. (Burr Ridge, IL: McGraw-Hill/Irwin, 2005). Unless otherwise indicated, examples found in this section appear in these excellent sources.
11. "Greeks Protest Coke's Use of Parthenon," *Dallas Morning News,* August 17, 1992, p. D4.
12. "Japanese Products Are Popular in the U.S.," *Research Alert,* November 17, 2000, p. 8.
13. "Betting on a New Label: Made in Russia," *BusinessWeek,* April 12, 1999, p. 122; "Russia and Central-Eastern Europe: Worlds Apart," *BrandWeek,* May 4, 1998, pp. 30–31; and "We Will Bury You . . . with a Snickers Bar," *U.S. News & World Report,* January 26, 1998, pp. 50–51.
14. www.wto.com, downloaded February 15, 2005.
15. "Mattel Plans to Double Sales Abroad," *The Wall Street Journal,* February 11, 1998, pp. A3, A11.
16. For an extensive and recent examination of these market entry options, see, for example, Johnny K. Johansson, *Global Marketing: Foreign Entry, Local Marketing, and Global Management,* 4th ed. (Burr Ridge, IL: McGraw Hill/Irwin, 2006); and Warren J. Keegan and Mark C. Green, *Global Marketing,* 4th ed. (Upper Saddle River, NJ: Prentice Hall, 2005).
17. Based on an interview with Pamela Viglielmo, director of international marketing, Fran Wilson Creative Cosmetics; and "Foreign Firms Think Their Way into Japan," www.successstories.com/nikkei, downloaded March 24, 2001.
18. This discussion is based on Keller, *Strategic Brand Management,* pp. 709–10; "Machines for the Masses," *The Wall Street Journal,* December 9, 2003, pp. A19, A20; "The Color of Beauty," *Forbes,* November 22, 2000, pp. 170–76; "It's Goo, Goo, Goo, Goo Vibrations at the Gerber Lab," *The Wall Street Journal,* December 4, 1996, pp. A1, A6; Donald R. Graber, "How to Manage a Global Product Development Process," *Industrial Marketing Management,* November 1996, pp. 483–98; and Herbig, *Handbook of Cross-Cultural Marketing.*
19. Jagdish N. Sheth and Atul Parvatiyar, "The Antecedents and Consequences of Integrated Global Marketing," *International Marketing Review* 18, no. 1 (2001), pp. 16–29. Also see D. Szymanski, S. Bharadwaj, and R. Varadarajan, "Standardization versus Adaptation of International Marketing Strategy: An Empirical Investigation," *Journal of Marketing,* October 1993, pp. 1–17.
20. This discussion is based on John Fahy and Fuyuki Taguchi, "Reassessing the Japanese Distribution System," *Sloan Management Review,* Winter 1995, pp. 49–61; and Edward Tse, "The Right Way to Achieve Profitable Growth in the Chinese Consumer Market," *Strategy & Business,* Second Quarter 1998, pp. 10–21.
21. "Stores Told to Lift Prices in Germany," *The Wall Street Journal,* September 11, 2000, pp. A27, A30.
22. "Rotten Apples," *Dallas Morning News,* April 7, 1998, p. 14A.

CNS Breathe Right Strips: This case was prepared by Mary L. Brown based on interviews with Kevin McKenna, vice president, International and Nick Naumann, Sr. Marketing Services Manager of CNS, Inc., September 2004.

CHAPTER 8

1. John Horn, "Studios Play Name Games," *Star Tribune,* August 10, 1997, p. F11; and "Flunking Chemistry," *Star Tribune,* April 11, 2003, p. E13.
2. U.S. Entertainment Industry: 2003 MPA Market Statistics; Worldwide Market Research; Motion Picture Association of America, p. 17.
3. Willow Bay, "Test Audiences Have Profound Effect on Movies," *CNN Newsstand & Entertainment Weekly,* September 28, 1998; see www.cnn.com/SHOWBIZ/Movies/9809/28/screen.test.
4. Helene Diamond, "Lights, Camera . . . Research!" *Marketing News,* September 11, 1989, pp. 10–11; and "Killer!" *Time,* November 16, 1987, pp. 72–79.
5. Desa Philadelphia, "Dark Side Rising," *Time,* May 9, 2005, pp. 52–57.
6. Richard Schiekel, "A Look Back in Wonder," *Time,* May 9, 2005, pp. 61–62.
7. For a lengthier, expanded 2004 definition, consult the American Marketing Association's website at www.marketingpower.com; for a researcher's comments on this and other definitions of marketing

research, see Lawrence D. Gibson, "Quo Vadis, Marketing Research?" *Marketing Research,* Spring 2000, pp. 36–41.

8. John Cloud, "How the Furby Flies," *Time,* November 30, 1998, pp. 84–85; Joseph Pereira, "To These Youngsters, Trying Out Toys Is Hardly Kids' Play," *The Wall Street Journal,* December 17, 1997, pp. A1, A11; and "Toy of the Year Awards, 2000," *Family Fun,* November 2000; see www.family.go.com/entertain/toys/feature/famf1000toymethod–led/famf1000toymethod–led.html.
9. Lawrence D. Gibson, "Defining Marketing Problems," *Marketing Research,* Spring 1998, pp. 4–12.
10. *Overview of the American Community Survey,* February 2005, www.census.gov.
11. "What TV Ratings Really Mean," Nielsen Media Research website, pp. 1–8; see www.nielsenmedia.com/whatratingsmean.
12. Network Primetime Averages: week of 9/27/04–10/03/04; see www.nielsenmedia.com.
13. Emily Nelson and Martin Peers, "As Technology Scatters Viewers, Networks Go Looking for Them," *The Wall Street Journal,* November 21, 2003, pp. A1, A6; Emily Nelson and Sarah Ellison, "Nielsen's Feud with TV Networks Shows Scarcity of Marketing Data," *The Wall Street Journal,* October 29, 2003, pp. A1, A6; "Nielsen Adapts Its Methods as TV Evolves," *The Wall Street Journal,* September 29, 2003, pp. B1, B10; and Jim Kite, "Too Early to Think in Minutes," *Advertising Age,* February 7, 2005, p. 23.
14. Robert Frank, "How to Live Large, and Largely for Free, Jennifer Voitle's Way," *The Wall Street Journal,* June 9, 2003, pp. A1, A8.
15. Mark Maremont, "New Toothbrush Is Big-Ticket Item," *The Wall Street Journal,* October 27, 1998, pp. B1, B6; and Emily Nelson, "P&G Checks Out Real Life," *The Wall Street Journal,* May 17, 2001, pp. B1, B4.
16. For a more complete discussion of questionnaire methods, see David A. Aaker, V. Kumar, and George S. Day, *Marketing Research,* 8th ed. (New York: John Wiley & Sons, Inc., 2004), pp. 188–272.
17. Jyoti Thottam, "How Kids Set the (Ring) Tone," *Time,* April 4, 2005, pp. 40–45.
18. Jonathan Eig, "Food Industry Battles for Moms Who Want to Cook—Just a Little," *The Wall Street Journal,* March 7, 2001, pp. A1, A10; and Susan Feyder, "It Took Tinkering by Twin Cities Firms to Saver Some Sure Bets," *Minneapolis Star Tribune,* June 9, 1982, p. 11A.
19. Constance Gustke, "Built to Last," *Sales & Marketing Management,* August 1997, pp. 78–83.
20. "Focus on Consumers," *General Mills Midyear Report,* Minneapolis, MN, January 8, 1998, pp. 2–3.
21. Michael J. McCarthy, "Stalking the Elusive Teenage Trendsetter," *The Wall Street Journal,* November 19, 1998, pp. B1, B10; and "Teens Spend $155 Billion in 2000," Teenage Research Unlimited press releases, January 25, 2001.
22. Roy Furchgott, "For Cool Hunters, Tomorrow's Trend Is the Trophy," *The New York Times,* June 28, 1998, p. 10; Patrick Goldstein, "Untangling the Web of Teen Trends," *Los Angeles Times,* November 21, 2000, p. F1; and Lev Grossman, "The Quest for Cool," *Time,* September 8, 2003, pp. 48–54.
23. Joshua Grossnickle and Oliver Raskin, "What's Ahead on the Internet," *Marketing Research,* Summer 2001, pp. 9–13; and Gordon A. Wyner, "Life (on the Internet) Imitates Research," *Marketing Research,* Summer 2000, pp. 38–39.
24. Wendy Zellner, "Look Out, Supermarkets—Wal-Mart Is Hungry," *BusinessWeek,* September 14, 1998, pp. 98–100; Richard McCattery, "Wal-Mart Rumbles in the Supermarket Jungle," The Motley Fool, March 7, 1998, www.fool.com/news/foth/2000/foth000307; and "Our 1,000 Supercenter," Wal-Mart news release, August 22, 2001.
25. William M. Bulkeley, "Mayo, IBM Join to Mine Medical Data," *The Wall Street Journal,* August 4, 2004, pp. B1, B9.
26. Information obtained from the websites of Information Resources, Inc. (www.infores.com) and AC Nielsen (www.acnielsen.com).
27. Joe Schwartz, "Back to the Source," *American Demographics,* January 1989, pp. 22–26; and Felix Kessler, "High-Tech Shocks in Ad Research," *Fortune,* July 7, 1986, pp. 58–62.
28. Dale Buss, "The Race to RFID," *CEO Magazine,* November 2004, pp. 32–36.
29. The step 4 discussion was written by David Ford and Don Rylander of Ford Consulting Group, Inc.; the Tony's Pizza example was provided by Teré Carral of Tony's Pizza.

Ford Consulting Group, Inc.: This case was written by David Ford of Ford Consulting Group, Inc.

CHAPTER 9

1. Rick Thomaselli, "Nike Finds a Way to Go to Wal-Mart," *Advertising Age,* March 21, 2005, p. 1; Stanley Holmes, "The Machine of a New Sole," *BusinessWeek,* March 14, 2005, pp. 99–100; and Seth Stevenson, "How to Beat Nike," *The New York Times Magazine,* January 5, 2003, pp. 29–33.
2. Nadira A. Hira, "America's Hippest CEO," *Fortune,* October 17, 2005, pp. 110–122.
3. Joseph Pereira and Stephanie Kang, "Phat News: Rappers Choose Reebok Shoes," *The Wall Street Journal,* November 14, 2003, pp. B1, B4.
4. Material on sneakers is based on the SGMA Report 2002, "The U.S. Athletic Footwear Market Today," which is published annually by the Sporting Goods Manufacturers Association (www.sgma.com) based on a study by the NPD Group (www.npd.com), which polls 35,000 consumers weekly and collects data from over 3,500 retailers to provide this information; and April Y. Pennington "Heeling Art," *Entrepreneur Magazine,* May 2002, www.entrepreneur.com.
5. Information obtained from press releases from www.reebok.com, www.nike.com, www.vans.com, www.footlocker-inc.com, and Thomas Howard, "Sneaker Makers Picky about Really Big Shoes," *USA Today,* November 1, 2004, p. 4B.
6. Devin Leonard, "Nightmare on Madison Avenue," *Fortune,* June 28, 2004, pp. 93–108; and Anthony Bianco, "The Vanishing Mass Market," *BusinessWeek,* July 12, 2004, pp. 61–65.
7. Carol Memmott, "Potter's Print-Run Record Goes 'Poof!'" *USA Today,* March 30, 2005, p. 10.
8. "Special Report on Mass Customization: A Long March," *The Economist,* July 14, 2001, pp. 63–65.
9. Amy Merrick, "Once a Bellwether, Ann Taylor Fights Its Stodgy Image," *The Wall Street Journal,* July 12, 2005, pp. A1, A8.
10. "Will the U.S. Chicken Out on Russia," *Fortune,* November 23, 1998, pp. 52–53.
11. The discussion of fast-food trends and market share is based on: Patronage of Fast-Food Restaurants by Adults 18 Years and Older: Simmons Market Research Bureau NCS/NHCS Spring 2004 Adult Full-Year Choices System Crosstabulation Report based on visits within the past 30 days.
12. Jennifer Ordonez, "Taco Bell Chef Has New Tactic: Be Like Wendy's," *The Wall Street Journal,* February 23, 2001, pp. B1, B4; and Jennifer Ordonez, "An Efficiency Drive: Fast-Food Lanes Are Getting Even Faster," *The Wall Street Journal,* May 18, 2000, pp. A1, A10.
13. Kate MacArthur, "Big Mac's Back," *Advertising Age,* December 13, 2004, pp. S1–S8; and "Big Mac's Makeover," *The Economist,* October 16, 2004, pp. 63–65.
14. The discussion of Apple's segmentation strategies through the years is based on information from its website, www.apple-history.com/history.html.
15. Dennis Sellers, "Business Journal: Digital Hub Plan Just Might Work," *MacCentral,* January 16, 2001, Mac Publishing, LLC.
16. "The iPod's Big Brother," *BusinessWeek,* September 13, 2004, p. 46.
17. Nicholas Zamiska, "How Milk Got a Major Boost by Food Panel," *The Wall Street Journal,* August 30, 2004, pp. B1, B5.
18. Rebecca Winters, "Chocolate Milk," *Time,* April 30, 2001, p. 20.
19. Patricia R. Olsen, "Adding Fizz to the Dairy Case," *The New York Times,* November 2, 2003, p. BU1.

Nokia: This case was written by Michael J. Vessey based on personal and telephone interviews with Keith Nowak of Nokia and David

Linsalata of IDC, company data, and the following sources: Information obtained from press releases and other resources from Nokia's website, www.nokiausa.com; Worldwide Mobile Phone Shipments by Region, 2003–2008; Worldwide Mobile Phone 2004–2008 Forecast Update: July 2004, Doc #31640, IDC, Mobile Devices, www.idc.com; Sumner Lemmon, "Chinese Mobile Phone Users Top 310 Million," *The Industry Standard,* August 24, 2004, www.theindustrystandard.com; "Cracks in the Armor: The Strengths and Weaknesses of the Mobile Phone Market," IDC Telebriefing Report #TB20040930 PowerPoint presentation, September 2004, information courtesy of David Linsalata IDC, Mobile - Devices—Associate Analyst, www.idc.com; "Wireless Industry Posts Winning Numbers," Cellular Telecommunications & Internet Association (CTIA) Semi-Annual Wireless Data Survey, March 22, 2004, www.ctia.org; and Kim Tae-gyu, "4G Forum Offers Glimpse of New Telecom Tech," *Korea Times,* August 22, 2004, www.koreatimes.co.kr.

CHAPTER 10

1. Personal interview with Dr. George Dierberger, 3M, April 2004 and October 2005.
2. Michael Arndt, "3M's Rising Star," *BusinessWeek,* April 12, 2004, pp. 62–74.
3. Personal interview with Matt Kornberg, Little Remedies, May 2004.
4. Matthew L. Meuter, Amy L. Ostrom, Robert I. Roundtree, and Mary Jo Bitner, "Self-Service Technologies: Understanding Customer Satisfaction with Technology-Based Service Encounters," *Journal of Marketing,* July 2000, pp. 50–64.
5. Michael Gibb, "Inject New Life into Nonprofits' Marketing Program," *Marketing News,* October 23, 2000, p. 47.
6. Joan Oleck, "Cookies and High Tech," *BusinessWeek,* March 12, 2001, p. 16; and Ani Hadjian, "Follow the Leader," *Fortune,* November 27, 1995, p. 96.
7. "Nonprofit Activities," *Nikkei Weekly,* October 30, 2000; and Paul Magnusson, "It's Open Season on Nonprofits," *Journal of Marketing,* July 3, 1995, p. 31.
8. Greg A. Stevens and James Burley, "3,000 Raw Ideas = 1 Commercial Success!" *Research–Technology Management,* May–June 1997, pp. 16–27.
9. R. G. Cooper and E. J. Kleinschmidt, "New Products—What Separates Winners from Losers?" *Journal of Product Innovation Management,* September 1987, pp. 169–84; Robert G. Cooper, *Winning at New Products,* 2nd ed. (Reading, MA: Addison-Wesley, 1993), pp. 49–66; and Thomas D. Kuczmarski, "Measuring Your Return on Innovation," *Marketing Management,* Spring 2000, pp. 25–32.
10. Julie Fortser, "The Lucky Charm of Steve Sanger," *BusinessWeek,* March 26, 2001, pp. 75–76.
11. John Gilbert, "To Sell Cars in Japan, U.S. Needs to Offer More Right-Drive Models," *Star Tribune,* May 27, 1995, p. M1.
12. Clayton M. Christensen and Michael E. Raynor, *The Innovator's Solution: Creating and Sustaining Successful Growth* (Cambridge, MA: Harvard Business School Press, 2003); Clayton M. Christensen, *The Innovator's Dilemma: When Technologies Cause Great Firms to Fail* (Cambridge, MA: Harvard Business School Press, 1997); Clayton M. Christensen and Michael Overdorf, "Meeting the Challenge of Descriptive Change," *Harvard Business Review,* March–April 2000, pp. 67–76; and Clayton M. Christensen and Michael E. Raynor, "Creating a Killer Product," *Forbes,* October 13, 2003, pp. 82–84.
13. See Productscan Online at www.productscan.com.
14. The Avert Virucidal Tissues and Hey! There's A Monster in My Room spray examples are adapted from Robert M. McMath and Thom Forbes, *What* Were *They Thinking*? (New York: Random House, Inc., 1998).
15. Amy Merrick, "As 3M Chief, McNerney Wastes No Time Starting Systems Favored by Ex-Boss Welch," *The Wall Street Journal,* June 5, 2001, pp. B1, B4; see General Electric's website (www.ge.com) for an in-depth explanation of Six Sigma that 3M and other Fortune 500 companies use to improve quality: "The Road to Customer Impact: What Is Six Sigma?"
16. Morgan L. Swink and Vincent A. Mabert, "Product Development Partnerships: Balancing Needs of OEMs and Suppliers," *Business Horizons,* May–June 2000, pp. 59–68.
17. C. K. Prahalad and Venkat Ramswamy, *The Future of Competition* (Boston: Harvard Business School Press, 2004); and Steve Hamm, "Adding Customers to the Design Team," *BusinessWeek,* March 1, 2004, pp. 22–23.
18. Anthony W. Ulwick, "Turn Customer Input into Innovation" *Harvard Business Review,* January 2002, pp. 91–97.
19. Sarah Ellison, "P&G Chief's Turnaround Recipe: Find Out What Women Want," *The Wall Street Journal,* June 1, 2005, pp. A1, A16.
20. Adam Aston and Gail Edmonson, "This Volvo Is Not a Guy Thing," *BusinessWeek,* March 15, 2004, pp. 84–86.
21. "The Device That Ate Everything?" *The Economist,* March 12, 2005, p. 16; Roger O. Crockett, "iPod Killers?" *BusinessWeek,* April 25, 2005, pp. 58–66; Pui-Wing Tam, "How One Hot Product Helped Resuscitate a Troubled Company," *The Wall Street Journal,* October 27, 2004, pp. B1, B8; "The Giant in the Palm of Your Hand," *The Economist,* February 12, 2005, pp. 67–69; and Roger O. Crockett, "Motorola Sharpens the Razr Edge," *BusinessWeek,* January 31, 2005, p. 34.
22. Dennis Berman, "Now Tennis Balls Are Chasing Dogs," *BusinessWeek,* July 23, 1998, p. 138.
23. Steve Hoeffler, "Measuring Preferences for Really New Products," *Journal of Marketing Research,* November 2003, pp. 406–20.
24. Leila Abboud, "The Truth about Trans Fats: Coming to a Label Near You," *The Wall Street Journal,* July 10, 2003, pp. D1, D3; Betsey McKay, "Frito-Lay Puts 'Smart Snack' Label on Baked Chips," *The Wall Street Journal,* August 6, 2003, p. D3; and Bruce Horovitz, "Under Fire, Food Giants Switch to Healthier Fare," *USA Today,* July 1, 2003, pp. 1A, 2A.
25. Thomas Lee, "Culture of Success," *Star Tribune,* March 25, 2005, pp. D1, D2; Jonathan Eig, "General Mills Intends to Reshape Doughboy in Its Own Image," *The Wall Street Journal,* July 18, 2000, pp. A1, A8; and Julie Forster, "The Lucky Charm of Steve Sanger," *BusinessWeek,* March 26, 2001, pp. 75–76.
26. Gray Hammel, "Innovation's New Math," *Fortune,* July 9, 2001, pp. 130–31.
27. Thomas M. Burton, "By Learning from Failures, Lilly Keeps Drug Pipeline Full," *The Wall Street Journal,* April 21, 2004, pp. A1, A12.
28. Danny Hakim, "Change Coming for Car Safety," *Star Tribune,* December 4, 2003, pp. A1, A8; Jayne O'Donnell, "Automakers Plan to Make Trucks Less of a Threat," *USA Today,* November 28, 2003, p. B1; and Dee-Ann Durbin, "Safety Official Softens Stance on SUVs," *Star Tribune,* February 27, 2003, p. A11.
29. Jack Neff, "White Bread, USA," *Advertising Age,* July 9, 2001, pp. 1, 12, 13.
30. Ben Elgin, "Can Google Hit It out of the Park Again?" *BusinessWeek,* April 19, 2004, pp. 38–39.
31. Yuhong Wu, Sridhar Balasubramanian, and Vijay Mahajan, "When Is a Preannounced New Product Likely to Be Delayed?" *Journal of Marketing,* April, 2004, pp. 101–13.
32. Jennifer Ordonez, "How Burger King Got Burned in Quest to Make the Perfect Fry," *The Wall Street Journal,* January 16, 2001, pp. A1, A8.
33. Youngme Moon, "Break Free from the Product Life Cycle," *Harvard Business Review,* May, 2005, pp. 87–94.
34. Ben Elgin, "Can HP's Printer Biz Keep Printing Money?" *BusinessWeek,* July 14, 2003, pp. 68–70.

3M Greptile Grip Golf Glove: This case was written by Michael J. Vessey based on interviews with Dr. George Dierberger, 3M personnel, and these other published sources: "3M Introduces 3M Golf Glove with Greptile Grip," 3M press release, May 5, 2004; "Who We Are," National Golf Foundation, www.ngf.org; "The Golf 20/20 Vision for the Future" industry report for 2003, published June 8, 2004, www.golf2020.com; "Core Golfers Gain Ground in 2003," National Golf Foundation press release, May 21, 2004, www.ngf.org; National Sporting Goods Association e-mail newsletter received June 21, 2004, www.nsga.org; and 3M Golf Greptile Grip business plan.

CHAPTER 11

1. "X-Factor Marks the Spot as Gatorade Boosts Flavors," *BrandWeek,* February 28, 2004, p. 5; "Gatorade Sweats the Visual Details to Refresh Connection with Consumers," *BrandWeek,* March 3, 2003, p. 4; and "Gatorade Works on Endurance," *The Wall Street Journal,* March 21, 2005, p. B6.
2. Glenn Rifkin, "Mach3: Anatomy of Gillette's Latest Global Launch," *Strategy & Business,* 2nd Quarter 1999, pp. 34–41.
3. Portions of this discussion on the fax machine industry are based on "Brother Wins Gamble in Shifting to Faxes," *The Wall Street Journal,* June 24, 2004, p. B6; "When Your Time Has Come—and Gone," www.edn.com, November 27, 2003; "Electronics: 2004 Market Share Report by Category," *Reed Business Information,* March 8, 2005; and "Atlas Electronics Corporation," in Roger A. Kerin and Robert A. Peterson, *Strategic Marketing Problems: Cases and Comments,* 8th ed. (Upper Saddle River, NJ: Prentice Hall, 1998), pp. 494–506.
4. "Population Explosion" www.clickz.com, downloaded April 24, 2004; and "Last Gasp of the Fax Machine," www.economist.com, downloaded September 16, 2004.
5. "Why Coke Indulges (the Few) Fans of Tab," *The Wall Street Journal,* April 13, 2001, pp. B1, B4.
6. "Gillette Creates a Little Buzz with its New Razor," www.boston.com, downloaded January 16, 2004.
7. "How to Separate Trends from Fads," *BrandWeek,* October 23, 2000, pp. 30, 32.
8. Everett M. Rogers, *Diffusion of Innovations,* 4th ed. (New York: Free Press, 1995).
9. Jagdish N. Sheth, Banwasi Mitral, and Bruce Newman, *Consumer Behavior* (Fort Worth: Dryden Press, 1999).
10. "When Free Samples Become Saviors," *The Wall Street Journal,* August 14, 2001, pp. B1, B4.
11. "Hurdles on the Road to Hog Heaven" *BusinessWeek,* November 19, 2003, pp. 96–98.
12. "Mass-Market Brands See More Upscale Heads," *Advertising Age,* September 25, 2000, p. S16.
13. www.newbalance.com, downloaded May 15, 2005.
14. "St. Joseph: From Babies to Baby Boomers," *Advertising Age,* July 9, 2001, pp. 1, 38.
15. "The Shrink Wrap," *Time,* June 2, 2003, p. 81; "Don't Raise the Price, Lower the Water Award," *BrandWeek,* January 8, 2001, p. 19; and "More for Less," *Consumer Reports,* August 2004, p. 63.
16. Jennifer L. Aaker, "Dimensions of Brand Personality," *Journal of Marketing Research,* August 1997, pp. 347–56. See also, Susan Fournier, "Consumers and Their Brands: Developing Relationship Theory in Consumer Research," *Journal of Consumer Research,* March 1998, pp. 343–73.
17. This discussion is based on Kevin Lane Keller, *Strategic Brand Management,* 2nd ed. (Upper Saddle River, NJ: Prentice Hall, 2003).
18. This discussion is based on Kevin Lane Keller, "Building Customer-Based Brand Equity" *Marketing Management,* July–August, 2001, pp. 15–19.
19. This discussion is based on John Deighton, "How Snapple Got Its Juice Back," *Harvard Business Review,* January 2002, pp. 47–53; and "Breakfast King Agrees to Sell Bagel Business," *The Wall Street Journal,* September 28, 1999, pp. B1, B6.
20. "Hummer Markets Shoes for Offroad Set," *Advertising Age,* January 12, 2004, pp. 3, 40; Bruce Orwell, "Disney's Magic Transformation?" *The Wall Street Journal,* October 4, 2000, pp. A1, A15; and Keller, *Strategic Brand Management.*
21. "A Good Name Should Live Forever," *Forbes,* November 16, 1998, p. 88.
22. Rob Osler, "The Name Game: Tips on How to Get It Right," *Marketing News,* September 14, 1998, p. 50; and Keller, *Strategic Brand Management.* Also see Pamela W. Henderson and Joseph A. Cote, "Guidelines for Selecting or Modifying Logos," *Journal of Marketing,* April 1998, pp. 14–30; and Chiranjeev Kohli and Douglas W. LaBahn, "Creating Effective Brand Names: A Study of the Naming Process," *Journal of Advertising Research,* January–February 1997, pp. 67–75.
23. "When Brand Extension Becomes Brand Abuse," *BrandWeek,* October 26, 1998, pp. 20, 22.
24. This discussion is based on David Aaker, *Brand Portfolio Strategy* (New York: Free Press, 2004); and "To Lure Older Girls, Mattel Brings in Hip-Hop Crowd," *The Wall Street Journal,* July 18, 2003, pp. A1, A6.
25. Matthew Boyle, "Brand Killers," *Fortune,* August 11, 2003, pp. 89–100.
26. www.pez.com, downloaded May 22, 2005; David Welch, *Collecting Pez* (Murphysboro, IL: Bubba Scrubba Publications, 1995); "Pez Dispense with Idea It's Just for Kids," *BrandWeek,* September 26, 1996, p. 10; and "Put Some Pizzazz in Your Packaging," *BrandWeek,* January 17, 2005, p. 17.
27. "Just the Facts," *Research Alert,* January 2004, p. 2.
28. "L'eggs Hatches a New Hosiery Package," *BrandWeek,* January 1, 2001, p. 6.
29. "Packaging Is the Capper," *Advertising Age,* May 5, 2003, p. 22; Theresa Howard, "Frito-Lay's New Stax to Take a Stand," *USA Today,* August 14, 2003, p. 12B; and "Asian Brands Are Sprouting English Logos in Pursuit of Status, International Image," *The Wall Street Journal,* August 7, 2001, p. B7C.
30. This discussion is based on Valarie A. Zeithaml, Mary Jo Bitner, and Dwayne D. Gremler, *Services Marketing: Integrating Customer Focus Across the Firm,* 4th ed. (Burr Ridge, IL: McGraw-Hill/Irwin, 2006).
31. Kent B. Monroe, *Pricing: Making Profitable Decisions,* 3rd ed. (Burr Ridge, IL: McGraw-Hill/Irwin, 2003).
32. Philip Kutler, Thomas Hayes, and Paul N. Bloom, *Marketing Professional Services,* 2nd ed. (Englewood Cliffs, NJ: Prentice Hall, 2000).

Philadelphia Phillies: This case was prepared by William Rudelius based on interviews with David Montgomery, David Buck, Marisol Lezeano, and Scott Brandreth; internal company materials: and the Phillies website (www.phillies.com).

CHAPTER 12

1. Wendy Zellner, "Where the Net Delivers: Travel," *BusinessWeek,* June 11, 2001, pp. 142–43.
2. Ibid.
3. Michael V. Marn, Eric V. Roegner, and Craig C. Zawanda, "The Power of Pricing," *McKinsey Quarterly,* no. 1 (2003), pp. 27–39; and Timothy Matanovich, Gary L. Lillien, and Arvind Rangaswamy, "Engineering the Price-Value Relationship," *Marketing Management,* Spring 1999, pp. 48–53.
4. Lisa Gubernick, "The Little Extras That Count (Up)," *The Wall Street Journal,* July 12, 2001, pp. B1, B4; and Donald V. Potter, "Discovering Hidden Pricing Power," *Business Horizons,* November–December 2000, pp. 41–48.
5. www.bugatti-cars.de.
6. Numerous studies have examined the price–quality–value relationship. See, for example, Jacob Jacoby and Jerry C. Olsen, eds., *Perceived Quality* (Lexington, MA: Lexington Books, 1985); William D. Dodds, Kent B. Monroe, and Dhruv Grewal, "Effects of Price, Brand, and Store Information on Buyers' Product Evaluations," *Journal of Marketing Research,* August 1991, pp. 307–19; and Roger A. Kerin, Ambuj Jain, and Daniel Howard, "Store Shopping Experience and Consumer Price–Quality–Value Perceptions," *Journal of Retailing,* Winter 1992, pp. 235–45. For a thorough review of the price–quality–value relationship, see Valerie A. Ziethaml, "Consumer Perceptions of Price, Quality, and Value," *Journal of Marketing,* July 1998, pp. 2–22.
7. Roger A. Kerin and Robert A. Peterson, "Carrington Furniture (A)," *Strategic Marketing Problems: Cases and Comments,* 10th ed. (Englewood Cliffs, NJ: Prentice Hall, 2004), pp. 279–89.
8. "Nintendo GameCube Set at Mass Market Price of $199.95"; "Dedicated Gameplay System Launches November 5, 2001, with Six First-Party Titles Priced at $49.95," Nintendo of America, Inc., press release, May 21, 2001.

9. For the classic description of skimming and penetration pricing, see Joel Dean, "Pricing Policies for New Products," *Harvard Business Review,* November–December 1976, pp. 141–53. See also, Reed K. Holden and Thomas T. Nagle, "Kamikaze Pricing," *Marketing Management,* Summer 1998, pp. 31–39.
10. "Premium AA Alkaline Batteries," *Consumer Reports,* March 21, 2001, p. 54; Kemp Powers, "Assault and Batteries," *Forbes,* September 4, 2000, pp. 54, 56; and "Razor Burn at Gillette," *BusinessWeek,* June 18, 2001, p. 37.
11. "Why That Deal Is Only $9.99," *BusinessWeek,* January 10, 2000, p. 36. For further reading on odd-even pricing, see Robert M. Schindler and Thomas M. Kilbarian, "Increased Consumer Sales Response through Use of 99-Ending Prices," *Journal of Retailing,* Summer 1996, pp. 187–99; Mark Stiving and Russell S. Winer, "An Empirical Analysis of Price Endings with Scanner Data," *Journal of Consumer Research,* June 1997, pp. 57–67; and Robert M. Schindler, "Patterns of Rightmost Digits Used in Advertised Prices: Implications for Nine-Ending Effects," *Journal of Consumer Research,* September 1997, pp. 192–201.
12. For an overview on target pricing, see Stephan A. Butscher and Michael Laker, "Market Driven Product Development," *Marketing Management,* Summer 2000, pp. 48–53.
13. Thomas T. Nagle and Reed K. Holden, *The Strategy and Tactics of Pricing,* 3rd ed. (Englewood Cliffs, NJ: Prentice Hall, 2002), pp. 243–49.
14. Kent B. Monroe, *Pricing: Making Profitable Decisions,* 3rd ed. (McGraw-Hill/Irwin, 2003), pp. 420–30.
15. Robert J. Dolan and Hermann Simon, *Power Pricing: How Managing Price Transforms the Bottom Line* (New York: Free Press, 1996), p. 249.
16. Peter M. Noble and Thomas S. Gruca, "Industrial Pricing: Theory and Managerial Practice," *Marketing Science* 18, no. 3 (1999), pp. 435–54.
17. George E. Belch and Michael A. Belch, *Introduction to Advertising and Promotion,* 5th ed. (New York: Irwin/McGraw-Hill, 2004), p. 98.
18. "Is the Music Store Over?" *Business 2.0,* March 2004, pp. 115–19.
19. Frank Bruni, "Price of Newsweek? It Depends," *Dallas Times Herald,* August 14, 1986, pp. S1, S20.
20. For an extended discussion on product complements and substitutes, see Allan D. Shocker, Barry L. Bayus, and Namwoon Kim, "Product Complements and Substitutes in Real World: The Relevance of Other Products," *Journal of Marketing,* January 2004, pp. 28–40.
21. Tammo H. A. Bijmolt, Harald J. Van Heerde, and Rik G. M. Pieters, "New Empirical Generalizations on the Determinants of Price Elasticity," *Journal of Marketing Research,* May 2005, pp. 141–56.
22. "Why Gas Won't Get Cheaper," *Time,* May 9, 2005, pp. 40–41.
23. Suzanne P. Nimocks, Robert L. Rosiello, and Oliver Wright, "Managing Overhead Costs," *McKinsey Quarterly,* no. 2 (2005), pp. 107–17.
24. Brian Bremner, "The China Price," *BusinessWeek,* December 6, 2004, pp. 102–12.
25. Linda Himelstein, "Webvan Left the Basics on the Shelf," *BusinessWeek,* July 23, 2001, p. 43.
26. Mike Dodd, "Cards Hold 50 Years of Memories," *USA Today,* March 27, 2001, pp. 1A, 2A; and J. C. Conklin, "Don't Throw Out Those Old Sneakers, They're a Gold Mine," *The Wall Street Journal,* September 21, 1998, pp. A1, A20.
27. Bid prices as of September 29, 2005, from www.eBay.com.
28. Akshay R. Rao, Mark E. Bergen, and Scott Davis, "How to Fight a Price War," *Harvard Business Review,* March–April 2000, pp. 107–16.
29. "How Dell Fine-Tunes Its PC Pricing to Gain Edge in a Slow Market," *The Wall Street Journal,* June 8, 2001, pp. A1, A8.
30. Jane Spencer, "Cracking the Code: How Not to Pay Retail," *The Wall Street Journal,* November 27, 2002, pp. D1, D2; Bob Tedeschi, "Specifically Priced Retail Goods," *The New York Times,* September 2, 2002, pp. F1.8; and www.spotlightsolutions.com.
31. For an extensive discussion on discounts, see Monroe, *Pricing,* chaps. 16 and 17.
32. Kenneth C. Manning, William O. Bearden, and Randall L. Rose, "Development of a Theory of Retailer Response to Manufacturers' Everyday Low Cost Programs," *Journal of Retailing,* Spring 1998, pp. 107–37; "Everyday Low Profits," *Harvard Business Review,* March–April 1994, pp. 13; Stephen J. Hoch, Xavier Dreze, and Mary E. Purk, "EDLP, Hi-Lo, and Margin Arithmetic," *Journal of Marketing,* October 1994, pp. 16–27; and Tibbett Speer, "Do Low Prices Bore Shoppers?" *American Demographics,* January 1994, pp. 11–13. Also see Philip Zerillo and Dawn Iacobucci, "Trade Promotions: A Call for a More Rational Approach," *Business Horizons,* July–August 1995, pp. 69–76; and Barbara E. Kahn and Leigh McAlister, *The Grocery Revolution: The New Focus on the Consumer* (Reading, MA: Addison-Wesley Educational Publishers, 1996).

Stuart Cellars: This case was prepared by Professor Linda Rochford based on information from the company website (www.stuartcellars.com) and the following sources: Dana Nigro, "What's Behind the Bottle Price?" *Wine Spectator,* December 15, 2002, pp. 24–28; and Cyril Penn, ed., "The Hottest Small Brands of 2003," *Wine Business Monthly,* February 1, 2004, p. 8.

CHAPTER 13

1. "Show Time!" *BusinessWeek,* February 2, 2004, pp. 56ff: www.ifoapplestore.com/stores, downloaded May 28, 2005; and Jonah Bloom, "Apple, Song, Hershey Ring Up More than Sales at Their Shops," *Advertising Age,* February 2, 2004, p. 16.
2. See Peter D. Bennett, ed., *Dictionary of Marketing Terms,* 2nd ed. (Chicago: American Marketing Association, 1995).
3. PepsiCo. Inc., *Annual Report* 1997.
4. This discussion is based on Bert Rosenbloom, *Marketing Channels: A Management View,* 7th ed. (Cincinnati, OH: South-Western College Publishing, 2004).
5. www.generalmills.com, downloaded May 15, 2005; www.nestle.com, downloaded May 15, 2005.
6. For an overview of vertical marketing systems, see Lou Pelton, David Strutton, and James R. Lumpkin, *Marketing Channels,* 2nd ed. (Burr Ridge, IL: McGraw-Hill/Irwin, 2002), chap. 11.
7. For an extensive discussion on channel conflict, see Anne T. Coughlan, Erin Anderson, Louis W. Stern, and Adel I. El-Ansary, *Marketing Channels,* 6th ed. (Upper Saddle River, NJ: Prentice Hall, 2001).
8. Ethan Smith, "Why a Grand Plan to Cut CD Prices Went off the Track," *The Wall Street Journal,* June 4, 2004, pp. A1, A6; and "Feud with Seller Hurts Nike Sales, Shares," *Dallas Morning News,* June 28, 2003, p. 30.
9. "Black Pearls Recast for Spring," *Advertising Age,* November 13, 1995, p. 49.
10. Studies that explore the dimensions and use of power and influence in marketing channels include the following: Gul Butaney and Lawrence H. Wortzel, "Distributor Power versus Manufacturer Power: The Customer Role," *Journal of Marketing,* January 1988, pp. 52–63; Kenneth A. Hunt, John T. Mentzer, and Jeffrey E. Danes, "The Effect of Power Sources on Compliance in a Channel of Distribution: A Causal Model," *Journal of Business Research,* October 1987, pp. 377–98; John F. Gaski, "Interrelations among a Channel Entity's Power Sources, Impact of the Exercise of Reward and Coercion on Expert, Referent, and Legitimate Power Sources," *Journal of Marketing Research,* February 1986, pp. 62–67; Gary Frazier and John O. Summers, "Interfirm Influence Strategies and Their Application within Distribution Channels," *Journal of Marketing,* Summer 1984, pp. 43–55; Sudhir Kale, "Dealer Perceptions of Manufacturer Power and Influence Strategies in a Developing Country," *Journal of Marketing Research,* November 1986, pp. 387–93; George H. Lucas and Larry G. Gresham, "Power, Conflict, Control, and the Application of Contingency Theory in Channels of Distribution," *Journal of the Academy of Marketing Science,* Summer 1985, pp. 27–37; and F. Robert Dwyer and Julie Gassenheimer, "Relational Roles and Triangle Dramas: Effects on Power Play and Sentiments in Industrial Channels," *Marketing Letters* 3 (1992), pp. 187–200.

11. David Simchi-Levi, Philip Kaminsky, and Edith Simchi-Levi, *Designing and Managing the Supply Chain,* 2nd ed. (Burr Ridge, IL: McGraw-Hill/Irwin, 2003), p. 6.
12. This discussion is based on Robyn Meredith, "Harder than the Hype," *Forbes,* April 16, 2001, pp. 188–94; Jeffry McCracken, "Ford Seeks Big Savings by Overhauling Supply System," *The Wall Street Journal,* September 29, 2005, pp. A1, A11; and Robert B. Handfield and Earnest Z. Nichols, *Introduction to Supply Chain Management* (Upper Saddle River, NJ: Prentice Hall, 1998), chap. 1.
13. Major portions of this discussion are based on Sunil Chopra and Peter Meindl, *Supply Chain Management: Strategy, Planning, and Operations,* 2nd ed. (Upper Saddle River, NJ: Prentice Hall, 2004), chaps. 1–3; and Marshall L. Fisher, "What Is the Right Supply Chain for Your Product?" *Harvard Business Review,* March–April 1997, pp. 105–17.
14. David Drickhamer, "Supply-Chain Superstars," *Industry Week,* May 1, 2004, pp. 5–7; "Big Blue Flips 'On' New Global Effort," *BrandWeek,* May 24, 2004, p. 15; Brian T. Fek and Murry Mitchell, "Transformation at IBM," *Supply Chain Management,* November–December 2003, pp. 56–62; Damel Lyons, "Back on the Chain Gang," *Forbes,* October 13, 2003, pp. 114–23; and "Experience: Order for Supply Chains," www.informationweek.com, downloaded February 9, 2004.
15. This discussion is based on Kathryn Jones, "The Dell Way," *Business 2.0,* February 2003, pp. 61–66; and Charles Fishman. "The Wal-Mart You Don't Know," *Fast Company,* December 2003, pp. 68–80.
16. Douglas M. Lambert, James R. Stock, and Lisa Ellram, *Fundamentals of Logistics Management* (Burr Ridge, IL: McGraw-Hill/Irwin, 1998).
17. Michael Levy and Barton A. Weitz, *Retailing Management,* 5th ed. (Burr Ridge, IL: McGraw-Hill/Irwin, 2004), pp. 325–26.
18. Fisher, "What Is the Right Supply Chain for Your Product?"

Golden Valley Microwave Foods: This case was written by Thomas J. Belich, Mark T. Spriggs, and Steven W. Hartley based on personal interviews with Jack McKeon and Frank Lynch, company data they provided, and the following sources: "Snagging a Pop Fly," *Snack Food and Wholesale Bakery,* May 2004, p. 48; "Choosing the Right Growth Strategy," *PR Newswire,* November 13, 2003; and "Company Information," from www.actii.com/company.

CHAPTER 14

1. Gene G. Marcial, "The Knot: Here Come the Brides," *BusinessWeek,* April 11, 2005, p. 110; "Thomas O'Brien Brings Sophisticated Modern Design to Target," Target Corporation press release, June 6, 2005; "Target and Yahoo! Debut a Full-Featured Digital Photo Resource," Target Corporation press release, April 21, 2005; "Reinventing the Store," *The Economist,* November 22, 2003, pp. 65–68; "25 New Targets Aim for the Bull's Eye," *HFN,* April 12, 2004, p. 1; Larry Armstrong, "E-Tune Shopping," *BusinessWeek,* March 29, 2004, p. 108; Robert Berner, "Target: The Cool Factor Fizzles," *BusinessWeek,* February 24, 2003, p. 42; Laura Heller, "Target Gets Mod in Manhattan," *DSN Retailing Today,* August 20, 2001, p. 2; Alice Z. Cuneo, "On Target," *Advertising Age,* December 11, 2000, p. 1; "Target Lets Ads onto the Bag," *HFN,* August 20, 2001, p. 58; and "Target and MJC: Sweet Game Plan," *DSN Retailing Today,* August 20, 2001, p. A4.
2. Kate Betts, "So You Want to Be a Designer," *Time,* May 17, 2004, p. 85.
3. "Fortune 1000 Ranked within Industries," *Fortune,* April 18, 2005, p. F46.
4. *Statistical Abstract of the United States,* 123rd ed. (Washington, DC: U.S. Department of Commerce, Bureau of the Census, 2003), pp. 657–74.
5. "Fortune Global 500," *Fortune,* July 21, 2003, p. 106.
6. "Retail Trade-Establishments, Employees, and Payroll," *Statistical Abstract of the United States,* 123rd ed. (Washington, DC: U.S. Department of Commerce, Bureau of the Census, 2003), p. 660.
7. Daniel Thomas, "Suppliers Will Meet RFID Deadline," *Computer Weekly,* May 11, 2004, p. 14; Laurie Sullivan and Darrell Dunn, "HP, Sun Ramp up RFID Services," *Information Week,* May 10, 2004, p. 16; Irene M. Nunii and Adam Aston, "Radio ID Tags So Cheap They'll Be Everywhere," *BusinessWeek,* October 20, 2003, p. 147; and "Target's RFID Goal Is to Have All Vendors Tagging by 2007," *HFN,* March 22, 2004, p. 26.
8. "Franchise 500," *Entrepreneur,* January 2004; and Scott Shane and Chester Spell, "Factors for New Franchise Success," *Sloan Management Review,* Spring 1998, pp. 43–50.
9. Don DeBolt, "Franchises Are Key Segment of Nation's Economy," *Franchising Today,* April 2004; also see "Franchise 500" at www.entrepreneur.com.
10. Charles Haddad, "Delta's Flight to Self-Service," *BusinessWeek,* July 7, 2003, p. 92; "At Your Self-Service," *Hotels,* December 1, 2003, p. 12; and Larry Armstrong, "Digital Photos, on the Double," *BusinessWeek,* June 23, 2003, p. 118.
11. Robert Berner, "Retail: This Rising Tide Won't Lift All Boats," *BusinessWeek,* January 12, 2004, p. 114.
12. Aixa M. Pascual, "Can Office Depot Get Back On Track?" *BusinessWeek,* September 18, 2000, p. 74.
13. Keith Reed, "Staples Installs Vending Machines at Boston Airport, College Campuses," *Boston Globe,* April 22, 2004; Simone Kaplan, "Earthlink Offices Sprout DVD Vending Machines," *Video Business,* April 12, 2004, p. 8; and "2004 State of the Vending Industry Report," *Automatic Merchandiser,* August 2004, p. 4.
14. Kwan Weng Kin, "Vending Machines in Japan Get 'Smart,'" *The Strait Times* (Singapore), October 26, 2003; and Andy Reinhardt, "A Machine-to-Machine 'Internet of Things,'" *BusinessWeek,* April 26, 2004, p. 102.
15. "U.S. Catalog Sales to Top $175 bn," *Precision Marketing,* May 14, 2004, p. 9; Vito Pilieci, "The IKEA Catalog: It's Bigger than the Bible," *Ottawa Citizen,* August 27, 2003, p. A1; *U.S. Direct and Interactive Marketing Today,* 6th ed. (New York: Direct Marketing Association, October 2000); *Statistical Fact Book 2000* (New York: Direct Marketing Association, 2000); and Ellen Neuborne, "Coaxing with Catalogs," *BusinessWeek,* August 6, 2001, p. EB6.
16. Monica Roman, "You Gotta Have a Catalog," *BusinessWeek,* May 14, 2001, p. 56; and Beth Viveiros, "Catalog and Internet Sales Grow More Quickly than Retail," *Direct,* July 2001.
17. Shayn Ferriolo, "Home Shopping Network Tunes into Cataloging," *Catalog Age,* November 2002, p. 12; Matt Stump, "Open TV Activates Sports, Shopping Apps," *Multichannel News,* May 3, 2004, p. 129; and Carole Nicksin, "QVC Opens Up in Mall Space," *HFN,* August 20, 2001, p. 6.
18. Heather Green, "Where Did All the Surfers Go?" *BusinessWeek,* August 6, 2001, p. 35; Steve Hamm, David Welch, Wendy Zellner, Faith Keenan, and Peter Engardio, "E-Biz: Down but Hardly Out," *BusinessWeek,* March 26, 2001, pp. 126–30; Lewis Braham, "E-Tailers Are Clicking," *BusinessWeek,* July 23, 2001, p. 73; "Will Wal-Mart Get It Right This Time?" *BusinessWeek,* November 6, 2000, p. 104; and Raymond R. Burke, "Do You See What I See? The Future of Virtual Shopping," *Journal of the Academy of Marketing Science,* Fall 1997, pp. 352–60.
19. "Former Cendant Marketing Chief Will Help Company Leverage Core Media Products while Broadening Member Benefit Offerings," *PR Newswire,* February 21, 2001; Tim Mullaney, "And All the Price Trimmings," *BusinessWeek,* December 18, 2000, p. 68; Mary J. Cronin, "Business Secrets of the Billion-Dollar Website," *Fortune,* February 2, 1998, p. 142; Robert D. Hof, Ellen Neuborne, and Heather Green, "Amazon.com: The Wild World of E-Commerce," *BusinessWeek,* December 14, 1998, pp. 106–19; "Future Shop," *Forbes ASAP,* April 6, 1998, pp. 37–52; Chris Taylor, "Cybershop," *Time,* November 23, 1998, p. 142; Stephen H. Wildstrom, " 'Bots' Don't Make Great Shoppers," *BusinessWeek,* December 7, 1998, p. 14; and Jeffrey Ressner, "Online Flea Markets," *Time,* October 5, 1998, p. 48.
20. Roger O. Crocket, "Let the Buyer Compare," *BusinessWeek,* September 3, 2001, p. EB10.

21. "Economic Impact: U.S. Direct Marketing Today Executive Summary—2003," Direct Marketing Association, New York; and Kelly Shermach, "Outsourcing Seen as a Way to Cut Costs, Retain Service," *Marketing News,* June 19, 1995, pp. 5, 8.
22. Catherine Arnold, "Law Gives Industry a Buzz," *Marketing News,* February 1, 2004, p. 11; Scott Reeves, "Back to (Old) School, 'Do-Not-Call' Revives Door-to-Door Sales," *Marketing News,* December 8, 2003, p. 13; and "Direct Marketing," *Marketing News,* January 15, 2004, p. 16.
23. Nanette Byrnes, "The New Calling," *BusinessWeek,* September 18, 2000, pp. 137–48.
24. Bill Vlasic and Mary Beth Regan, "Amway II: The Kids Take Over," *BusinessWeek,* February 1, 1998, pp. 60–70.
25. Mathew Schifrin, "Okay, Big Mouth," *Forbes,* October 9, 1995, pp. 47–48; Veronica Byrd and Wendy Zellner, "The Avon Lady of the Amazon," *BusinessWeek,* October 24, 1994, pp. 93–96; and Ann Marsh "Avon Is Calling on Eastern Europe," *Advertising Age,* June 20, 1994, p. 116.
26. Francis J. Mulhern and Robert P. Leon, "Implicit Price Bundling of Retail Products: A Multiproduct Approach to Maximizing Store Profitability," *Journal of Marketing,* October 1991, pp. 63–76.
27. Marc Vanhuele and Xavier Dreze, "Measuring the Price Knowledge Shoppers Bring to the Store," *Journal of Marketing,* October 2002, pp. 72–85.
28. Gwen Ortmeyer, John A. Quelch, and Walter Salmon, "Restoring Credibility to Retail Pricing," *Sloan Management Review,* Fall 1991, pp. 55–66.
29. William B. Dodds, "In Search of Value: How Price and Store Name Information Influence Buyers' Product Perceptions," *Journal of Consumer Marketing,* Spring 1991, pp. 15–24.
30. Leonard L. Berry, "Old Pillars of New Retailing," *Harvard Business Review,* April 2001, pp. 131–37.
31. Eric Anderson and Duncan Simester, "Mind Your Pricing Cues," *Harvard Business Review,* September 2003, pp. 96–103.
32. Julie Baker, A. Parasuraman, Dhruv Grewal, and Glenn B. Voss, "The Influence of Multiple Store Environment Cues on Perceived Merchandise Value and Patronage Intentions," *Journal of Marketing,* April 2002, pp. 120–41.
33. Neil Gross, "On beyond Shoplifting Prevention," *BusinessWeek,* October 2, 2000, p. 170; and "A Time to Steal," *BrandWeek,* February 16, 1999, p. 24.
34. Rita Koselka, "The Schottenstein Factor," *Forbes,* September 28, 1992, pp. 104, 106.
35. Barry Brown, "Edmonton Makes Size Pay Off in Down Market," *Advertising Age,* January 27, 1992, pp. 4–5.
36. James R. Lowry, "The Life Cycle of Shopping Centers," *Business Horizons,* January–February 1997, pp. 77–86; Eric Peterson, "Power Centers! Now!" *Stores,* March 1989, pp. 61–66; and "Power Centers Flex Their Muscle," *Chain Store Age Executive,* February 1989, pp. 3A, 4A.
37. Robert A. Peterson and Sridhar Balasubramanian, "Retailing in the 21st Century: Reflections and Prologue to Research," *Journal of Retailing,* Spring 2002, pp. 9–16.
38. Jim Carter and Norman Sheehan, "From Competition to Cooperation: E-Tailing's Integration with Retailing," *Business Horizons,* March–April 2004, pp. 71–78.
39. Pierre Martineau, "The Personality of the Retail Store," *Harvard Business Review,* January–February 1958, p. 47.
40. Julie Baker, Dhruv Grewal, and A. Parasuraman, "The Influence of Store Environment on Quality Inferences and Store Image," *Journal of the Academy of Marketing Science,* Fall 1994, pp. 328–39; Howard Barich and Philip Kotler, "A Framework for Marketing Image Management," *Sloan Management Review,* Winter 1991, pp. 94–104; Susan M. Keaveney and Kenneth A. Hunt, "Conceptualization and Operationalization of Retail Store Image: A Case of Rival Middle-Level Theories," *Journal of the Academy of Marketing Science,* Spring 1992, pp. 165–75; James C. Ward, Mary Jo Bitner, and John Barnes, "Measuring the Prototypicality and Meaning of Retail Environments," *Journal of Retailing,* Summer 1992, p. 194; and Dhruv Grewal, R. Krishnan, Julie Baker, and Norm Burin, "The Effect of Store Name, Brand Name and Price Discounts on Consumers' Evaluations and Purchase Intentions," *Journal of Retailing,* Fall 1998, pp. 331–52. For a review of the store image literature, see Mary R. Zimmer and Linda L. Golden, "Impressions of Retail Stores: A Content Analysis of Consumer Images," *Journal of Retailing,* Fall 1988, pp. 265–93.
41. Mary Jo Bitner, "Servicescapes: The Impact of Physical Surroundings on Customers and Employees," *Journal of Marketing,* April 1992, pp. 57–71.
42. Jans-Benedict Steenkamp and Michel Wedel, "Segmenting Retail Markets on Store Image Using a Consumer-Based Methodology," *Journal of Retailing,* Fall 1991, p. 300; and Philip Kotler, "Atmospherics as a Marketing Tool," *Journal of Retailing* 49 (Winter 1973–74), p. 61.
43. Carole Nicksin, "Sears' New Ad Campaign to Stress Brand Image, Shopping Convenience," *HFN,* August 27, 2001, p. 4.
44. Kusum L. Ailwadi and Bari Harlam, "An Empirical Analysis of the Determinants of Retail Margins: The Role of Store-Brand Share," *Journal of Marketing,* January 2004, pp. 147–65; Joseph Tarnowski, "And the Awards Went to . . ." *Progressive Grocer,* April 15, 2004; Betsy Spethmann, "Shelf Sets," *Promo,* May 1, 2004, p. 6; and "Study Shows Continued Support for Category Management," *CSNews Online,* March 17, 2004.
45. The wheel of retailing theory was originally proposed by Malcolm P. McNair, "Significant Trends and Development in the Postwar Period," in A. B. Smith, ed., *Competitive Distribution in a Free, High-Level Economy and Its Implications for the University* (Pittsburgh: University of Pittsburgh Press, 1958), pp. 1–25; also see Stephen Brown, "The Wheel of Retailing—Past and Future," *Journal of Retailing,* Summer 1990, pp. 143–49; and Malcolm P. McNair and Eleanor May, "The Next Revolution of the Retailing Wheel," *Harvard Business Review,* September–October 1978, pp. 81–91.
46. Kenneth Hein, "Upfront 2004—The Advertisers: Fast Food," www.adweek.com, April 26, 2004; "McDonald's Tests In-Store McCafes," www.ddimagazine.com, November 14, 2003; and "New McDonald's Ad Pushes Health," www.restaurantbiz.com, May 12, 2004.
47. Peter Kiekmeyer, "McDonald's Bet Heavily on McCafe," *Montreal Gazette,* August 28, 2001, p. D2; "McDonald's Adds Sourdough Line and Cheesecake to Revolving Menu Offerings," *PR Newswire,* August 9, 2001; and David Farkas, "Drive-Thru in the Fast Lane," *Chain Leader,* July 2001, p. 40.
48. Bill Saporito, "What's for Dinner?" *Fortune,* May 15, 1995, pp. 51–64.
49. William R. Davidson, Albert D. Bates, and Stephen J. Bass, "Retail Life Cycle," *Harvard Business Review,* November–December 1976, pp. 89–96.

Mall of America: This case was written by David P. Brennan and is based on an interview with Maureen Cahill and materials provided by Mall of America.

CHAPTER 15

1. Wayne Friedman, "Brand Management," *Daily Variety,* April 29, 2005, p. 22; "Disney's Visa Card Brings Magical Moments to the 'Happiest Celebration on Earth,'" *PR Newswire,* May 5, 2005; "For McD's 'Happy Summer,'" *Brandweek.com,* June 6, 2005; "Kodak Snaps Disneyland Sweepstakes," *Promo Online,* May 19, 2005; T. L. Stanley, "Disney Hopes Virtual Park Delivers Real-World Results," *Advertising Age,* January 3, 2005, p. 4; Maria Matzer Rose, "Disney Special: Big Birthday Is a Ticket for Tie-ins," *Amusement Business,* May 2, 2005; "New England Patriots Quarterback Tom Brady Joins NFL Greats by Being Featured in 2nd Commercial Proclaiming 'I'm Going Back to Disney World!'" *PR Newswire,* February 2, 2004; Rod Taylor, "Beanie Madness," *Promo,* April 1, 2004, p. 4; "Finding Frito," *Promo,* May 1, 2003, p. 6; "Disney's Toontown Online

Lauches in Japan," Disney Online press release, April 19, 2004, see www.psc.disney.go.com; and Ian W. Mitchell, "Tokyo DisneySea: How It Translates," *Chicago Sun-Times,* July 27, 2003, p. 1.

2. Wilbur Schramm, "How Communication Works," in Wilbur Schramm, ed., *The Process and Effects of Mass Communication* (Urbana, IL: University of Illinois Press, 1955), pp. 3–26.
3. E. Cooper and M. Jahoda, "The Evasion of Propaganda," *Journal of Psychology* 22 (1947), pp. 15–25; H. Hyman and P. Sheatsley, "Some Reasons Why Information Campaigns Fail," *Public Opinion Quarterly* 11 (1947), pp. 412–23; and J. T. Klapper, *The Effects of Mass Communication* (New York: Free Press, 1960), chap. VII.
4. Cynthia L. Kemper, "Biting Wax Tadpole, Other Faux Pas," *Denver Post,* August 3, 1997, p. G4.
5. Rik Pieters and Michel Wedel, "Attention Capture and Transfer in Advertising: Brand Pictorial, and Text-Size Effects," *Journal of Marketing,* April 2004, pp. 36–50.
6. Adapted from *Dictionary of Marketing Terms,* 2nd ed., Peter D. Bennett, ed. (Chicago: American Marketing Association, 1995), p. 231.
7. Dick Martin, "Gilded and Gelded: Hard-Won Lessons from the PR Wars," *Harvard Business Review,* October 2003, pp. 44–54.
8. Kusum L Ailawadi, Scott A. Neslin, and Karen Gedenk, "Pursuing the Value-Conscious Consumer: Store Brands versus National Brand Promotions," *Journal of Marketing,* January 2001, pp. 71–89.
9. B. C. Cotton and Emerson M. Babb, "Consumer Response to Promotional Deals," *Journal of Marketing* 42 (July 1978), pp. 109–13.
10. Robert George Brown, "Sales Response to Promotions and Advertising," *Journal of Advertising Research* 14 (August 1974), pp. 33–40.
11. Adapted from *Economic Impact: U.S. Direct Marketing Today* (New York: Direct Marketing Association, 1998), p. 25.
12. Siva K. Balasubramanian and V. Kumar, "Analyzing Variations in Advertising and Promotional Expenditures: Key Correlates in Consumer, Industrial, and Service Markets," *Journal of Marketing,* April 1990, pp. 57–68.
13. Don E. Schultz, "Include SIMM in Modern Media Ad Plans," *Marketing News,* May 15, 2004, p. 6; Don E. Schultz, "TV Advertisers Defy Logic, Pay More for Less," *Marketing News,* June 9, 2003, p. 14; Catherine Arnold, "Tech Design," *Marketing News,* January 15, 2004, p. 4; Gail Edmondson and Michael Eidam, "The Mini Just Keeps Getting Mightier," *BusinessWeek,* April 5, 2004, p. 26; Don E. Schultz, "Consumer Marketing Changed by Advent of 29.8/7 Media Week," *Marketing News,* September 24, 2001, pp. 13, 15; Pamela Paul, "Getting Inside Gen Y," *American Demographics,* September 2001, pp. 43–49; Charles Pappas, "Ad Nauseam," *Advertising Age,* July 10, 2000, pp. 16–18; and Dan Lippe, "It's All in Creative Delivery," *Advertising Age,* June 25, 2001, pp. S8, S9.
14. James M. Olver and Paul W. Farris, "Push and Pull: A One-Two Punch for Packages Products," *Sloan Management Review,* Fall 1989, pp. 53–61.
15. Fusun F. Gonul, Franklin Carter, Elina Petrova, and Kannan Srinivasan, "Promotion of Prescription Drugs and Its Impact on Physicians' Choice Behavior," *Journal of Marketing,* July 2001, pp. 79–90.
16. Robert J. Lavidge and Gary A. Steiner, "A Model for Predictive Measurement of Advertising Effectiveness," *Journal of Marketing,* October 1961, p. 61.
17. "49th Annual Report: 100 Leading National Advertisers," *Advertising Age,* June 28, 2004, p. S2.
18. Don E. Schultz and Anders Gronstedt, "Making Marcom an Investment," *Marketing Management,* Fall 1997, pp. 41–49; and J. Enrique Bigne, "Advertising Budget Practices: A Review," *Journal of Current Issues and Research in Advertising,* Fall 1995, pp. 17–31.
19. John Philip Jones, "Ad Spending: Maintaining Market Share," *Harvard Business Review,* January–February 1990, pp. 38–42; and Charles H. Patti and Vincent Blanko, "Budgeting Practices of Big Advertisers," *Journal of Advertising Research* 21 (December 1981), pp. 23–30.
20. James A. Schroer, "Ad Spending: Growing Market Share," *Harvard Business Review,* January–February 1990, pp. 44–48.
21. James E. Lynch and Graham J. Hooley, "Increasing Sophistication in Advertising Budget Setting," *Journal of Advertising Research* 30 (February–March 1990), pp. 67–75.
22. Jimmy D. Barnes, Brenda J. Muscove, and Javad Rassouli, "An Objective and Task Media Selection Decision Model and Advertising Cost Formula to Determine International Advertising Budgets," *Journal of Advertising* 11, no. 4 (1982), pp. 68–75.
23. Don E. Schultz, "Olympics Get the Gold Medal in Integrating Marketing Event," *Marketing News,* April 27, 1998, pp. 5, 10.
24. Cornelia Pechman, Guangzhi Zhao, Marvin E. Goldberg, and Ellen Thomas Reibling, "What to Convey in Antismoking Advertisements for Adolescents: The Use of Protection Motivation Theory to Identify Effective Message Themes," *Journal of Marketing,* April 2003, pp. 1–18.
25. Jill Kipnis, "Picture This: New Line Breaks Ground with HD Promos," *Billboard,* May 29, 2004; David Finnigan, "The Biz," *BrandWeek,* October 14, 2002; "The Fellowship of the New Line," *Promo,* September 2001, p. 84; and "Sneak Preview of Trailer for New Line Cinema's 'The Lord of the Rings: The Fellowship of the Ring,'" *PR Newswire,* September 21, 2001.
26. Claire Atkinson, "Coke Catapults Starcom Media Vest," *Advertising Age,* February 9, 2004, p. S6.
27. Kate Fitzgerald, "Beyond Advertising," *Advertising Age,* August 3, 1998, pp. 1, 14; Curtis P. Johnson, "Follow the Money: Sell CFO on Integrated Marketing's Merits," *Marketing News,* May 11, 1998, p. 10; and Laura Schneider, "Agencies Show That IMC Can Be Good for Bottom Line," *Marketing News,* May 11, 1998, p. 11.
28. *Economic Impact: U.S. Direct Marketing Today* (New York: Direct Marketing Association, 2000), pp. 24–30.
29. *Statistical Fact Book '98* (New York: Direct Marketing Association, 1998).
30. Robert Berner, "Going that Extra Inch," *BusinessWeek,* September 18, 2000, p. 84.
31. Adapted from *Economic Impact: U.S. Direct Marketing Today* (New York: Direct Marketing Association, 1998), pp. 25–26.
32. Carol Krol, "Club Med Uses E-Mail to Pitch Unsold, Discounted Packages," *Advertising Age,* December 14, 1998, p. 40.
33. "Rising to the Top," *Promo,* September 2001, pp. 46–62.
34. Jean Halliday, "Taking Direct Route," *Advertising Age,* September 7, 1998, p. 17.
35. Julie Tilsner, "Lillian Vernon: Creating a Host of Spin-offs from Its Core Catalog," *BusinessWeek,* December 19, 1994, p. 85; and Lisa Coleman, "I Went Out and Did It," *Forbes,* August 17, 1992, pp. 102–4.
36. Alan K. Gorenstein, "Direct Marketing's Growth Will Be Global," *Marketing News,* December 7, 1998, p. 15; Don E. Schultz, "Integrated Global Marketing Will Be the Name of the Game," *Marketing News,* October 26, 1998, p. 5; and Mary Sutter and Andrea Mandel-Campbell, "Customers Are Eager, Infrastructure Lags," *Advertising Age International,* October 5, 1998, p. 12.
37. Juliana Koranten, "European Privacy Rules Go into Effect in 15 EU States," *Advertising Age,* October 26, 1998, p. S31; and Rashi Glazer, "The Illusion of Privacy and Competition for Attention," *Journal of Interactive Marketing,* Summer 1998, pp. 2–4.
38. LaToya Deann Rembert, "Will CAN-SPAM Affect You?" *Marketing Research,* Spring 2004, p. 8; Douglas Wood and David Brosse, "Mulling E-Mail Options," *Promo,* September 2001, p. 18; Kathleen Cholewka, "Making E-Mail Matter," *Sales and Marketing Management,* September 2001, pp. 21, 22; "$2.1 Billion Will Be Spent on E-Mail Marketing by Year-End 2001," *Direct Marketing,* August 2001, p. 7; Arlene Weintraub, "When E-Mail Ads Aren't Spam," *BusinessWeek,* October 16, 2000, p. 112; "Opting Out of E-Mail Ads Isn't So Easy to Do," *BusinessWeek,* November 6, 2000, p. 20; and "With E-Mail Marketing, Permission Is Key," eStatNews, www.emarketer.com, September 2001.

UPS: This case was written by Steven Hartley based on taped interviews of company personnel and the following sources: Dean Foust, "Big

Brown's New Bag," *BusinessWeek,* July 19, 2004, p. 54; David Rynecki, "Does This Package Make Sense?" *Fortune,* January 26, 2004, p. 132; "The UPS Store and Mail Boxes Etc. Expand to 5000 Worldwide Locations," *Business Wire,* September 13, 2004; Charles Haddad, "The Websmart 50," *BusinessWeek,* November 24, 2003, p. 92; and information contained on the UPS website (www.ups.com).

CHAPTER 16

1. Kris Oser, "WildTangent, Massive, IGN Stake Claims on Frontier of $900M Market," *Advertising Age,* April 18, 2005, p. 6; "Advergaming Set to Surge," *O'Dwyer's PR Services Report,* December 2004, p. 9; "Jeep Brand and Oakley to Sponsor'Snowboard Super Jam' First Downloadable Game to Feature Dynamic In-Game Ad Serving and Product Placement Reaching Millions of Gamers," *PR Newswire,* April 19, 2005; Devin Leonard, "Nightmare on Madison Avenue," *Fortune,* June 28, 2004, pp. 92–108; Gregory Solman, "Wow Factor about to Spike for Ads in Online Games," www.adweek.com, May 24, 2004; Catherine Arnold, "The New Game in Advergaming," *Marketing News,* June 1, 2004, p. 6; "Virtual Advertising: Digitopia," *New Media Age,* March 18, 2004, p. 25; Nancy Coltun Webster, "Now Down To Business: Counting Gamer Thumbs," *Advertising Age,* May 24, 2004, p. S6; and Christine Y. Chen, "TiVo Is Smart TV," *Fortune,* March 19, 2001, p. 124.
2. David A. Aaker and Donald Norris, "Characteristics of TV Commercials Perceived as Informative," *Journal of Advertising Research* 22, no. 2 (April–May 1982), pp. 61–70.
3. Larry D. Compeau and Dhruv Grewal, "Comparative Price Advertising: An Integrative Review," *Journal of Public Policy & Marketing,* Fall 1998, pp. 257–73; and William Wilkie and Paul W. Farris, "Comparison Advertising: Problems and Potentials," *Journal of Marketing,* October 1975, pp. 7–15.
4. Jennifer Lawrence, "P&G Ads Get Competitive," *Advertising Age,* February 1, 1993, p. 14; Jerry Gotlieb and Dan Sorel, "The Influence of Type of Advertisement, Price, and Source Credibility on Perceived Quality," *Journal of the Academy of Marketing Science,* Summer 1992, pp. 253–60; and Cornelia Pechman and David Stewart, "The Effects of Comparative Advertising on Attention, Memory, and Purchase Intentions," *Journal of Consumer Research,* September 1990, pp. 180–92.
5. Bruce Buchanan and Doron Goldman, "Us vs. Them: The Minefield of Comparative Ads," *Harvard Business Review,* May–June 1989, pp. 38–50; Dorothy Cohen, "The FTC's Advertising Substantiation Program," *Journal of Marketing,* Winter 1980, pp. 26–35; and Michael Etger and Stephen A. Goodwin, "Planning for Comparative Advertising Requires Special Attention," *Journal of Advertising* 8, no. 1 (Winter 1979), pp. 26–32.
6. Lewis C. Winters, "Does It Pay to Advertise to Hostile Audiences with Corporate Advertising?" *Journal of Advertising Research,* June–July 1988, pp. 11–18; and Robert Selwitz, "The Selling of an Image," *Madison Avenue,* February 1985, pp. 61–69.
7. Jean Halliday, "Of Hummers and Zen," *Advertising Age,* August 6, 2001, p. 29.
8. "Claritin Springs into Allergy Season with New Consumer Programs," *PR Newswire,* February 20, 2001.
9. Ira Teinowitz, "Self-Regulation Urged to Prevent Bias in Ad Buying," *Advertising Age,* January 18, 1999, p. 4.
10. Bob Donath, "Match Your Media Choice and Ad Copy Objective," *Marketing News,* June 8, 1998, p. 6.
11. "TBWA/Chiat/Day Wins the $100,000 Grand Prize Kelly Award for Apple's iPod 'Silhouettes' Magazine Campaign," Magazine Publishers of America press release, June 10, 2004.
12. Kate Maddox, "ARF Forum Examines Internet Research Effectiveness," *Advertising Age,* January 11, 1999, p. 28.
13. "The Week: Dodge Reintroduces Muscle-car Charger," *Advertising Age,* May 23, 2005, p. 20; and Jean Halliday, "Entry-Lux Gears Up," *Advertising Age,* June 23, 2003, p. S4.
14. Michael S. LaTour and Herbert J. Rotfeld, "There Are Threats and (Maybe) Fear-Caused Arousal: Theory and Confusions of Appeals to Fear and Fear Arousal Itself," *Journal of Advertising,* Fall 1997, pp. 45–59.
15. Cornelia Pechmann, Guangzhi Zhao, Marvin E. Goldberg, and Ellen Thomas Reibling, "What to Convey in Antismoking Advertisements for Adolescents: The Use of Protection Motivation Theory to Identify Effective Message Themes," *Journal of Marketing,* April, 2003, pp. 1–18; Jeffrey D. Zbar, "Fear!" *Advertising Age,* November 14, 1994, pp. 18–19; John F. Tanner, Jr., James B. Hunt, and David R. Eppright, "The Protection Motivation Model: A Normative Model of Fear Appeals," *Journal of Marketing,* July 1991, pp. 36–45; and Michael S. LaTour and Shaker A. Zahra, "Fear Appeals as Advertising Strategy: Should They Be Used?" *Journal of Consumer Marketing,* Spring 1989, pp. 61–70.
16. Stuart Elliot, "Can Beer Ads Extol Great Taste in Good Taste?" *The New York Times,* April 16, 2004, p. C2; and "Operating Strategy," bebe website, www.bebe.com.
17. Eric Gillin and Greg Lindsay, "The New Puritanism," *Advertising Age,* April 5, 2004, pp. 1, 34; Bruce Horvitz, "Risque May Be Too Risky for Ads," *USA Today,* April 16, 2004, p. 1B; and Rich Thomaselli, "NFL Stops the Music," *Advertising Age,* March 15, 2004, p. 78.
18. Theresa Howard, "Thinking Outside the TV Box Ads Get Creative in Midst of New Media Choices," *USA Today,* June 22, 2004, p. 4B; Anthony Vagnoni, "Best Awards," *Advertising Age,* May 28, 2001, pp. S1–18; Dana L. Alden, Wayne D. Hoyer, and Chol Lee, "Identifying Global and Culture-Specific Dimensions of Humor in Advertising: A Multinational Analysis," *Journal of Marketing,* April 1993, pp. 64–75; and Johny K. Johansson, "The Sense of 'Nonsense': Japanese TV Advertising," *Journal of Advertising,* March 1994, pp. 17–26.
19. *2003 Television Production Cost Survey,* American Association of Advertising Agencies, 2003, p. 5; and Jean Halliday, "Exotic Ads Get Noticed," *Advertising Age,* April 9, 2001, p. S4.
20. Matthew Creamer, "Crispin Ups the Ante," *Advertising Age,* January 10, 2005, p. S1–2.
21. R. Craig Endicott, "50th Annual Report: 100 Leading National Advertisers," *Advertising Age,* June 27, 2005, p. S21.
22. Giles D'Souza and Ram C. Rao, "Can Repeating an Advertisement More Frequently than the Competition Affect Brand Preference in a Mature Market?" *Journal of Marketing,* April 1995, pp. 32–42.
23. Vicki R. Lane, "The Impact of Ad Repetition and Ad Content on Consumer Perceptions of Incongruent Extensions," *Journal of Marketing,* April 2000, pp. 80–91.
24. Katherine Barrett, "Taking a Closer Look," *Madison Avenue,* August 1984, pp. 106–9.
25. Joe Mandese, "Out-of-Home TV: Does It Count?" *Advertising Age,* January 18, 1993, p. 53.
26. Claire Atkinson, "TV Buyers Bow Before Fox's 'Idol'," *Advertising Age,* September 19, 2005, pp. 1, 50.
27. Surendra N. Singh, Denise Linville, and Ajay Sukhdial, "Enhancing the Efficacy of Split Thirty-Second Television Commercials: An Encoding Variability Application," *Journal of Advertising,* Fall 1995, pp. 13–23; Scott Ward, Terence A. Oliva, and David J. Reibstein, "Effectiveness of Brand-Related 15-Second Commercials," *Journal of Consumer Marketing,* no. 2 (1994), pp. 38–44; and Surendra N. Singh and Catherine Cole, "The Effects of Length, Content, and Repetition on Television Commercial Effectiveness," *Journal of Marketing Research,* February 1993, pp. 91–104.
28. Cara Beardi, "Radio's Big Bounce," *Advertising Age,* August 27, 2001, p. S2.
29. Kate Fitzgerald, "Launches Crowd Already Tough Field," *Advertising Age,* April 5, 2004, p. S2; Catherine Arnold, *Marketing News,* May 1, 2004, p. 3; Jon Fine, "Silicon Valley Spawns New Nascar Lifestyle Magazine," *Advertising Age,* January 12, 2004, p. 8; Jon Fine, "Magazine of the Year: Lucky," *Advertising Age,* October 20, 2003, p. S1; "A Magazine for Everyone," *The Magazine Handbook,* Magazine

Publishers Association, 2003, p. 6; R. Craig Endicott, "Past Performance Is Not a Guarantee of Future Returns," *Advertising Age,* June 18, 2001, pp. S1, S6; and George R. Milne, "A Magazine Taxonomy Based on Customer Overlap," *Journal of the Academy of Marketing Science,* Spring 1994, pp. 170–79.

30. Julia Collins, "Image and Advertising," *Harvard Business Review,* January–February 1989, pp. 93–97.

31. Lisa Sanders, "Major Marketers Turn to Yellow Pages," *Advertising Age,* March 8, 2004, p. 4; "Yellow Pages Still 'Gold Standard' for Searches," *USA Today,* February 16, 2004, p. 10A; Avery M. Abernethy and David N. Laband, "The Impact of Trademarks and Advertisement Size on Yellow Page Call Rates," *Journal of Advertising Research,* March 2004, pp. 119–25; and "Yellow Pages and the Media Mix," Yellow Pages Publishers Association, Troy, MI.

32. Pierre Berthon and James M. Hulbert, "Marketing in Metamorphosis: Breaking Boundaries," *Business Horizons,* May–June 2003, pp. 31–40.

33. Sandeep Krishnamurthy, "Deciphering the Internet Advertising Puzzle," *Marketing Management,* Fall 2000, pp. 35–39; Judy Strauss and Raymond Frost, *Marketing on the Internet: Principles of Online Marketing* (Englewood Cliffs, NJ: Prentice Hall, 1999), pp. 196–249; and Maricris G. Briones, "Rich Media May Be Too Rich for Your Blood," *Marketing News,* March 29, 1999, p. 4.

34. Arch G. Woodside, "Outdoor Advertising as Experiments," *Journal of the Academy of Marketing Science* 18 (Summer 1990), pp. 229–37.

35. Ed Brown, "Advertisers Skip to the Loo," *Fortune,* October 26, 1998, p. 64; John Cortex, "Growing Pains Can't Stop the New Kid on the Ad Block," *Advertising Age,* October 12, 1992, pp. 5–28; Allen Banks, "How to Assess New Place-Based Media," *Advertising Age,* November 30, 1992, p. 36; and John Cortex, "Media Pioneers Try to Corral On-the-Go Consumers," *Advertising Age,* August 17, 1992, p. 25.

36. "It's An Ad, Ad, Ad, Ad World," *Time,* July 9, 2001, p. 17; "Triton, Secora in Alliance for Advertising on ATMs," *Marketing News,* June 5, 2000, p. 12; and Joan Oleck, "High-Octane Advertising," *BusinessWeek,* November 29, 1999, p. 8.

37. Rob Norton, "How Uninformative Advertising Tells Consumers Quite a Bit," *Fortune,* December 26, 1994, p. 37; and "Professor Claims Corporations Waste Billions on Advertising," *Marketing News,* July 6, 1992, p. 5.

38. The discussion of posttesting is based on William F. Arens, *Contemporary Advertising,* 6th ed. (Burr Ridge, IL: Richard D. Irwin, 1996), pp. 181–82.

39. David A. Aaker and Douglas M. Stayman, "Measuring Audience Perceptions of Commercials and Relating Them to Ad Impact," *Journal of Advertising Research* 30 (August–September 1990), pp. 7–17; and Ernest Dichter, "A Psychological View of Advertising Effectiveness," *Marketing Management* 1, no. 3 (1992), pp. 60–62.

40. David Kruegel, "Television Advertising Effectiveness and Research Innovation," *Journal of Consumer Marketing,* Summer 1988, pp. 43–51; and Laurence N. Gold, "The Evolution of Television Advertising Sales Measurement: Past, Present, and Future," *Journal of Advertising Research,* June–July 1988, pp. 19–24.

41. "Upward Bound," *Promo,* April 2004, p. AR5.

42. Magid M. Abraham and Leonard M. Lodish, "Getting the Most out of Advertising and Promotion," *Harvard Business Review,* May–June 1990, pp. 50–60; Steven W. Hartley and James Cross, "How Sales Promotion Can Work for and against You," *Journal of Consumer Marketing,* Summer 1988, pp. 35–42; Robert D. Buzzell, John A. Quelch, and Walter J. Salmon, "The Costly Bargain of Trade Promotion," *Harvard Business Review,* March–April 1990, pp. 141–49; and Mary L. Nicastro, "Break-Even Analysis Determines Success of Sales Promotions," *Marketing News,* March 5, 1990, p. 11.

43. Natalie Schwartz, "Clipping Path," *Promo,* April 1, 2004, p. 4; Mathew Kinsman, "The Hard Sell," *Promo's 11th Annual Source Book,* 2004, p. 19; Betsy Spethmann, "Going for Broke," *Promo,* August 2001, pp. 27–31; and Mathew Kinsman, "Bad Is Good," *Promo,* April 2001, pp. 71–74.

44. Karen Holt, "Coupon Crimes," *Promo,* April 2004, pp. 23–26, 70.

45. "McD Has Happy Recipe for Kids Meals," www.brandweek.com, March 29, 2004; Carrie MacMillan, "Creature Features," *Promo,* October 2001, p. 11; and Dan Hanover, "Not Just for Breakfast Anymore," *Promo,* September 2001, p. 10.

46. Matthew Kinsman, "Riding High," *Promo's 11th Annual Source Book,* 2004, p. 26.

47. Lorraine Woellert, "The Sweepstakes Biz Isn't Feeling Lucky," *BusinessWeek,* March 22, 1999, p. 80.

48. Edward Kabak, "Staking out the States," *Promo,* October 2001, p. 11; Maxine Lans Retsky, "Stakes Are High for Direct Mail Sweepstakes Promotions," *Marketing News,* July 3, 2000, p. 8; Richard Sale, "Sweeping the Courts," *Promo,* May 1998, pp. 42–45; and Fred C. Allvine, Richard D. Teach, and John Connelly, Jr., "The Demise of Promotional Games," *Journal of Advertising Research* 16 (October 1976), pp. 79–84.

49. Lorin Cipolla, "Instant Gratification," *Promo,* April 1, 2004, p. 4; "Best Activity Generating Brand Awareness/Trial," *Promo,* September 2001, p. 51; and "Brand Handing," *Promo's 9th Annual Sourcebook,* 2002, p. 32.

50. Kathleen Joyce, "Keeping the Faith," *Promo,* April 2004, p. AR23; and Kelly Shermack, "CPG Marketers Are Developing Loyalty Programs That Benefit Both Manufacturers and Retailers," *Marketing News,* November 10, 2003, p. 13.

51. Cyndee Miller, "P-O-P Gains Followers as 'Era of Retailing' Dawns," *Marketing News,* May 14, 1990, p. 2.

52. See www.fordcollegegrad.com.

53. Marvin A. Jolson, Joshua L. Wiener, and Richard B. Rosecky, "Correlates of Rebate Proneness," *Journal of Advertising Research,* February–March 1987, pp. 33–43.

54. M. Ellen Peebles, "And Now, a Word from Our Sponsor," *Harvard Business Review,* October 2003, pp. 31–42; Karl Greenberg, "Tie-Ins: Jaguar Goes Hollywood," www.brandweek.com, May 31, 2004; "Samsung Remaps the Matrix," *Promo,* April 1, 2004, p. 4; Paula Lyon Andruss, "Survivor Packages Make Real-Life Money," *Marketing News,* March 26, 2001, p. 5; Wayne Friedman, "Eagle-Eye Marketers Find Right Spot, Right Time," *Advertising Age,* January 22, 2001, p. S2; David Goetzl, "TBS Tries Virtual Advertising," *Advertising Age,* May 21, 2001, p. 8; and James Poniewozik, "This Plug's for You," *Time,* June 18, 2001 p. 76–77.

55. This discussion is drawn particularly from John A. Quelch, *Trade Promotions by Grocery Manufacturers: A Management Perspective* (Cambridge, MA: Marketing Science Institute, August 1982).

56. Michael Chevalier and Ronald C. Curhan, "Retail Promotions as a Function of Trade Promotions: A Descriptive Analysis," *Sloan Management Review* 18 (Fall 1976), pp. 19–32.

57. G. A. Marken, "Firms Can Maintain Control over Creative Co-op Programs," *Marketing News,* September 28, 1992, pp. 7, 9.

58. Scott Hue, "Free 'Plugs' Supply Ad Power," *Advertising Age,* January 29, 1990, p. 6.

59. Mike Harris, "Earnhardt's Lap Belt Was Broken," www.safetyforum.com, February 23, 2001; and Marc Weinberger, Jean Romeo, and Azhar Piracha, "Negative Product Safety News: Coverage, Responses, and Effects," *Business Horizons,* May–June 1991, pp. 23–31.

Fallon Worldwide: This case was written by Mark T. Spriggs, William Rudelius, and Linda Rochford based on interviews with Fallon personnel and materials on the Citi and BMW promotional campaigns provided by Citi, BMW, and Fallon.

CHAPTER 17

1. "The Best Managers of 2004: Anne Mulcahy," *BusinessWeek Online,* January 10, 2005; "Turning the Page," *Business 2.0,* July 2005, pp. 98–100; and "Anne Mulcahy Has Xerox by the Horns," *BusinessWeek Online,* May 29, 2003.

2. "Leading CEOs: A Statistical Snapshot of S&P 500 Leaders," www.spencerstuart.com, downloaded January 25, 2005.
3. "America's 25 Best Sales Forces," *Sales & Marketing Management,* July 2000, pp. 57–85.
4. Mark W. Johnston and Greg W. Marshall, *Relationship Selling and Sales Management* (Burr Ridge, IL: McGraw-Hill/Irwin, 2005).
5. "Increasing Face Time," *Sales & Marketing Management,* January 2004, p. 12; and Barton A. Weitz, Stephen B. Castleberry, and John F. Tanner, Jr., *Selling: Building Partnerships,* 5th ed. (Burr Ridge, IL: McGraw-Hill/Irwin, 2004), p. 10.
6. "The Cost of a Sales Call," *Research Alert,* May 10, 2005, p. 9.
7. "Stop Calling Us," *Time,* April 29, 2003, pp. 56–58.
8. Carol J. Loomis, "Have You Been Cold-Called?" *Fortune,* December 16, 1991, pp. 109–15.
9. Jim Edwards, "Dinner, Interrupted," *BrandWeek,* May 26, 2003, pp. 28–32.
10. Paul A. Herbing, *Handbook of Cross-Cultural Marketing* (New York: Holworth Press, 1998); and "Japanese Business Etiquette," *Smart Business,* August 2000, p. 55.
11. This discussion is based on Rolph E. Anderson and Alan J. Dubinsky, *Personal Selling: Achieving Customer Satisfaction and Loyalty* (Boston: Houghton Mifflin, 2004).
12. Jeff Golterman, "Strategic Account Management in the Age of the Never Satisfied Customer," *Velocity* 2 (2000), pp. 13–16.
13. For an extensive discussion of objections, see Charles M. Futrell, *Fundamentals of Selling,* 8th ed. (Burr Ridge, IL: McGraw-Hill/Irwin, 2004), chap. 12.
14. Theodore Levitt, *The Marketing Imagination* (New York: Free Press, 1983), p. 111.
15. *Management Briefing: Sales and Marketing* (New York: Conference Board, October 1996), pp. 3–4.
16. Steve Atlas and Elise Atlas, "Team Approach," *Selling Power,* May 2000, pp. 126–28; and Neil Rackman, Lawrence Friedman, and Richard Ruff, *Getting Partnering Right* (New York: McGraw-Hill, 1996), pp. 47–48.
17. Several variations of the account management policy grid exist. See, for example, Mark W. Johnston and Greg W. Marshall, *Churchill/Ford/Walker's Sales Force Management,* 7th ed. (Burr Ridge, IL: McGraw-Hill/Irwin, 2003).
18. Douglas J. Dalrymple, William L. Cron, and Thomas E. DeCarlo, *Sales Management,* 8th ed. (New York: John Wiley & Sons, 2004).
19. *Statistical Abstract of the United States,* 124th ed. (Washington, DC: U.S. Department of Commerce, 2004). Also see Lucette B. Comer, J. A. F. Nicholls, and Leslie J. Vermillion, "Diversity in the Sales Force: Problems and Challenges," *Journal of Personal Selling & Marketing,* Fall 1998, pp. 1–20; and *Occupational Outlook Quarterly* (Washington, DC: U.S. Department of Labor, Fall, 2005).
20. This discussion is based on Johnston and Marshall, *Churchill/Ford/Walker's Sales Force Management.*
21. www.marykay.com/recognition, downloaded June 1, 2005.
22. "Measuring Sales Effectiveness," *Sales & Marketing Management,* October 2000, p. 136; and "Quota Busters," *Sales & Marketing Management,* January 2001, pp. 59–63.
23. "Tools of the Trade," *Sales & Marketing Management,* October 2003, pp. 46–51.
24. www.toshiba.com/technology, downloaded May 15, 2005.
25. "Supercharged Sell," *Inc.Tech,* November 1998, pp. 42–50.
26. "Intranets Grow Up," *Sales & Marketing Management,* December 2000, p. 105.

Reebok: This case was written by Giana Eckhardt.

CHAPTER 18

1. www.sevencycles.com, downloaded June 8, 2005; Scott Mowbray, "The $5,000 Bike," *Fortune,* November 12, 2001, p. 62; and Lori Valigra, "Why Seven Cycles Is Racing Ahead: The Net," *Business-Week e-biz,* June 22, 1999, pp. 32–33.
2. "U.S. E-Commerce Growth to Significantly Outpace Total Retail Spending," www.emarketer.com, downloaded April 19, 2005; and "Online Retail Growth Robust," www.clickz.com, downloaded May 24, 2005.
3. "E-Commerce: 2005," www.jupiterresearch.com, downloaded June 1, 2005; and "Electronic Commerce," www.wto.org, downloaded June 5, 2005.
4. "Statistics: U.S. Online Shoppers," www.shop.org, downloaded June 26, 2004.
5. Rafi A. Mohammed, Robert J. Fisher, Bernard J. Jaworski, and Gordon J. Paddison, *Internet Marketing: Building Advantage in a Networked Economy,* 2nd ed. (Burr Ridge, IL: McGraw-Hill/Irwin, 2004).
6. Adrian J. Slywotzky, "The Age of the Choiceboard," *Harvard Business Review,* January–February 2000, pp. 40–41.
7. For a description of collaborative filtering and similar types of systems, see Ward Hanson, *Principles of Internet Marketing,* 2nd ed. (Cincinnati: South-Western College Publishing, 2005), pp. 215–30.
8. Michael Grebb, "Behavioral Science," *Business 2.0,* March 2000, p. 112.
9. "Consumers Worried about Online Privacy," Jupiter Media Matrix press release, downloaded June 15, 2003.
10. This discussion is drawn from Jeffrey F. Rayport and Bernard J. Jaworski, *e-Commerce,* 2nd ed. (Burr Ridge, IL: McGraw-Hill/Irwin MarketspaceU, 2004); and Mohammed et al., *Internet Marketing.*
11. These figures are found in "Crowded at Last: A Survey of Consumer Power," *The Economist,* April 2, 2005, special section.
12. "The 90/20 Rule of E-Commerce: Nearly 90% of Online Sales Accounted for by 20% of Consumers," Cyber Dialogue press release, September 25, 2000.
13. "New Study Reveals Internet Is the Medium Moms Rely on Most," Disney Online news release, March 8, 2004; and "On a Mission: The New Internet Mom," FC NOW: The Fast Company Weblog, May 25, 2004.
14. "Branding on the Net," *BusinessWeek,* November 2, 1998, pp. 78–86.
15. "Jupiter Market Forecast Report," Jupiter Research, New York, January 3, 2003, and January 5, 2006.
16. Yoram Wind, Vijay Mahajan, with Robert E. Gunther, *Convergence Marketing,* (Upper Saddle River, NJ: Prentice Hall, 2002), chap. 3.
17. "Stopping Spam," *The Economist,* April 26, 2003, p. 58.
18. This discussion is based on Lev Grossman, "Meet Joe Blog," *Time,* June 21, 2004, pp. 67–70; "ISP's Band Together to Fight Spam," *Advertising Age,* June 28, 2004, p. 8; and Mohammed et al., *Internet Marketing.*
19. "Pass It On," *The Wall Street Journal,* January 14, 2002, pp. R6, R7; Renée Dye. "The Buzz on Buzz," *Harvard Business Review,* November–December 2000, pp. 139–46; and "Buzz Marketing." *BusinessWeek,* July 30, 2001, pp. 50–56.
20. "The Price Is Right," *BusinessWeek,* March 31, 2003, pp. 62–68.
21. "Branding on the Net," *BusinessWeek.*
22. "Consumers Worried about Online Privacy"; "Online Privacy and You," www.cyberdialogue.com, downloaded June 10, 2004; and Daniel Roth and Stephanie Mehta, "The Great Data Heist," *Fortune,* May 16, 2005, pp. 66–72.
23. "Marketers Seek to Make Cookies More Palatable," *The Wall Street Journal,* June 17, 2005, pp. B1, B2.
24. "Shop Around the Clock," *American Demographics,* September 2003, p. 18; and Nick Wingfield, "The Rise and Fall of Web Shopping at Work," *The Wall Street Journal,* September 27, 2002, pp. B1, B4.
25. "NPD e-Visory Report Shows Offline Sales Benefit from Online Browsing," NPO Group press release, downloaded May 15, 2004.
26. "Eddie Bauer's Banner Time of Year," *Advertising Age,* October 1, 2001, p. 55.
27. For an extended discussion on leveraging multiple channels with multichannel marketing, see Ranjay Gulati and Jason Garino, "Get the Right Mix of Bricks and Clicks," *Harvard Business Review,*

May–June 2000, pp. 107–14; and Chao Xiong, "Online Stores Try New Pitch: Fetch It Yourself," *The Wall Street Journal,* November 19, 2003, pp. D1, D4.

28. Michael Krantz, "Click Till You Drop," *Time,* July 20, 1998, pp. 34–39.
29. *Statistical Fact Book 2004* (New York: Direct Marketing Association, 2004); and *Multi-Channel Integration: The New Retail Battleground* (Columbus, OH: PricewaterhouseCoopers, March 2001).
30. *Fighting Fire with Water—from Channel Conflict to Confluence* (Cambridge, MA: Bain & Company, July 1, 2000).
31. *The Next Chapter in Business-to-Consumer E-Commerce: Advantage Incumbent* (Boston: The Boston Consulting Group, March 2001); and Timothy J. Mullaney, "E-Biz Strikes Again," *BusinessWeek,* May 10, 2004, pp. 80–90.
32. "Multichannel Shopping—Projections," www.Forrester.com, downloaded June 2, 2004; and "The State of Retailing Online 8.0," www.shop.org, downloaded May 24, 2005.

McFarlane Toys: This case was written by Steve Hartley and Roger Kerin. Sources: "McFarlane Toys Launches ToyFest Winter 2003 Online-Only Toy Fair Event Debuting 18 New Lines," *PR Newswire,* February 18, 2003; Bruce Handy, "Small Is Beautiful," *Vanity Fair,* December 2003, p. 208; Wes Orshoski, "McFarlane Adds Hendrix, Elvis to Action-Figure Series," *Billboard,* December 20, 2003, p. 65; Todd McFarlane and Tom Conley, "Toy Fair 2003: Buyers' Market or PR Expense?" *Kidscreen,* February 1, 2003, p. 60; and *World Toy Facts and Figures: 2003,* New York: International Council of Toy Industries, 2003.

APPENDIX B

1. Denny E. McCorkle, Joe F. Alexander, and Memo F. Diriker, "Developing Self-Marketing Skills for Student Career Success," *Journal of Marketing Education,* Spring 1992, pp. 57–67.
2. Joanne Cleaver, "Find a Job through Self-Promotion," *Marketing News,* January 31, 2000, pp. 12, 16; and James McBride, "Job-Search Strategies to Begin the Next Millenium," *Planning Job Choices: 1999,* 42nd ed. (Bethlehem, PA: National Association of Colleges and Employers, 1998), pp. 14–18.
3. Julie Rawe, "What Will Be the 10 Hottest Jobs?" *Time,* May 22, 2000, pp. 70–71; and "Five 'New Economy' Careers for Liberal Arts Majors," *Job Choices in Business: 2002,* 45th ed. (Bethlehem, PA: National Association of Colleges and Employers, 2001), pp. 11–13.
4. Paula Lyon Andruss, "So You Want to Be a CEO?" *Marketing News,* January 29, 2001, pp. 1, 10.
5. "Average Yearly Salary Offers," *Salary Survey* (Bethlehem, PA: National Association of Colleges and Employers, 2004), p. 4.
6. Elaine L. Chao and Kathleen P. Utgoff, "Tomorrow's Jobs," *Occupational Outlook Handbook* (Indianapolis: JIST Works, 2004), p. 5.
7. Linda M. Gorchels, "Traditional Product Management Evolves," *Marketing News,* January 30, 1995, p. 4; "Focus on Five Stages of Category Management," *Marketing News,* September 28, 1992, pp. 17, 19; and Sandy Gillis, "On the Job: Product Manager," *BusinessWeek's Guide to Careers,* April–May 1988, pp. 63–66.
8. Robin T. Peterson, "Wholesaling: A Neglected Job Opportunity for Marketing Majors," *Marketing News,* January 15, 1996, p. 4.
9. "Advertising," *Career Guide to America's Top Industries* (Indianapolis: JIST Works, 1994), pp. 142–45.
10. "The Climb to the Top," *Careers in Retailing,* January 1995, p. 18.
11. "Playing the Retail Career Game," *Careers in Retailing 2001* (New York: DSN Retailing Today, January 2001), pp. 4, 6.
12. Christine Galea, "The 2004 Compensation Survey," *Sales & Marketing Management,* May 2004, p. 29.
13. Robin T. Peterson, "Startup Careers through Rep Firms," *Marketing News,* August 4, 1997, p. 8.
14. William Keenan, Jr., "America's Best Sales Forces: Six at the Summit," *Sales & Marketing Management,* June 1990, pp. 62–72.
15. Michael R. Wukitsch, "Should Research Know More about Marketing?" *Marketing Research,* Winter 1993, p. 50.
16. "Market Research Analyst," in Les Krantz, ed., *Jobs Rated Almanac,* 3rd ed. (New York: Wiley, 1995).
17. Joshua Grossnickle and Oliver Raskin, "What's Ahead on the Internet," *Marketing Research,* Summer 2001, pp. 9–13.
18. Susan B. Larsen, "International Careers: Reality, Not Fantasy," *CPC Annual: A Guide to Employment Opportunities for College Graduates,* 36th ed. (Bethlehem, PA: College Placement Council, 1992), pp. 78–85; and Hal Lancaster, "Global Managers Need Boundless Sensitivity, Rugged Constitutions," *The Wall Street Journal,* October 13, 1998, p. B1.
19. John W. Buckner, "Working Abroad at Home," *Managing Your Career,* Spring 1992, pp. 16–17.
20. "Your Job Search Starts with You," *Job Choices: 1996,* 39th ed. (Bethlehem, PA: National Association of Colleges and Employers, 1995), pp. 6–9; Hugh E. Kramer, "Applying Marketing Strategy and Personal Value Analysis to Career Planning: An Experiential Approach," *Journal of Marketing Education,* Fall 1988, pp. 69–73; Alan Deutschman, "What 25-Year-Olds Want," *Fortune,* August 27, 1990, pp. 42–50; and Dawn Richerson, "Personality and Your Career," *Career Woman,* Winter 1993, pp. 46–47.
21. Arthur F. Miller, "Discover Your Design," in *CPC Annual,* vol. 1 (Bethlehem, PA: College Placement Council, 1984), p. 2.
22. Diane Goldner, "Fill In the Blank," *The Wall Street Journal,* February 27, 1995, pp. R5, R11.
23. Barbara Kiviat, "The New Rules of Web Hiring," *Time,* November 24, 2003, p. 57; Karen Epper Hoffman, "Recruitment Sites Changing Their Focus," *Internet World,* March 15, 1999; Pamela Mendels, "Now That's Casting a Wide Net," *BusinessWeek,* May 25, 1998; and James C. Gonyea, *The Online Job Search Companion* (New York: McGraw-Hill, 1995).
24. Ronald B. Marks, *Personal Selling* (Boston: Allyn & Bacon, 1985), pp. 451–62.
25. Leonard Felson, "Undergrad Marketers Must Get Jump on Networking Skills," *Marketing News,* April 8, 2001, p. 14; and Wayne E. Baker, *Networking Smart* (New York: McGraw-Hill, 1994).
26. John L. Munschauer, "How to Find a Customer for Your Capabilities," in 1984–1985 *CPC Annual,* vol. 1 (Bethlehem, PA: College Placement Council, 1984), p. 24.
27. C. Randall Powell, "Secrets of Selling a Résumé," in *The Honda How to Get a Job Guide,* ed. Peggy Schmidt (New York: McGraw-Hill, 1984), pp. 4–9.
28. Joyce Lain Kennedy, "Computer-Friendly Résumé Tips," *Planning Job Choices: 1999,* 42nd ed. (Bethlehem, PA: National Association of Colleges and Employers, 1998), p. 49; and Joyce Lain Kennedy and Thomas J. Morrow, *Electronic Résumé Revolution* (New York: Wiley, 1994).
29. Arthur G. Sharp, "The Art of the Cover Letter," *Career Futures* 4, no. 1 (1992), pp. 50–51.
30. Perri Capell, "Unconventional Job Search Tactics," *Managing Your Career,* Spring 1991, pp. 31, 35.
31. Julie Griffin Levitt, *Your Career: How to Make It Happen* (Cincinnati: South-Western Publishing, 1985).
32. Deborah Vendy, "Drug Screening and Your Career," *CPC Annual* (Bethlehem, PA: College Placement Council, 1992), pp. 61–62.
33. Dana James, "A Day in the Life of a Corporate Recruiter," *Marketing News,* April 10, 2000, pp. 1, 11.
34. Marks, *Personal Selling,* p. 469.
35. Terence P. Pare, "The Uncommitted Class of 1989," *Fortune,* June 5, 1989, pp. 199–210.
36. Robert M. Greenberg, "The Company Visit—Revisited," *NACE Journal,* Winter 2003, pp. 21–27.
37. Bob Weinstein, "What Employers Look For," in *The Honda How to Get a Job Guide,* ed. Peggy Schmidt (New York: McGraw-Hill, 1985), p. 10.

CREDITS

CHAPTER 1

p. 4, ©M. Hruby; p. 6 (top left), ©M. Hruby; p. 6 (top right), ©M. Hruby; p. 6 (bottom), ©2005 3M; p. 7, ©M. Hruby; p. 10 (top left), Courtesy New Product Works; p. 10 (top right), Courtesy Nestlé USA. HOT POCKETS® brand is a registered trademark of Société des Produits Nestlé SA. Vevey, Switzerland; p. 10 (bottom left), Photo by Scott Olson/Getty Images; p. 10 (bottom right), ©M. Hruby; p. 13 (left), Courtesy Costco; p. 13 (right), Courtesy Starbucks Coffee Company (2004); p. 15 (top), ©2005 3M; p. 15 (bottom), ©M. Hruby; p. 18, Courtesy Arizona Highways; p. 21, Courtesy Rollerblade, Inc.

CHAPTER 2

p. 22, Courtesy Ben & Jerry's; p. 24, AP Photo/Dawn Villella; p. 26, Courtesy Medtronic; p. 28, Courtesy Rick Armstrong; p. 29 (all), Courtesy Eastman Kodak Company; Agency: Ketchum Communications; p. 30 (all), Courtesy Eastman Kodak Company; Agency: Ketchum Communications; p. 33 (top left), Courtesy Ben & Jerry's; p. 33 (top right), Courtesy Ben & Jerry's; p. 33 (bottom right), ©M. Hruby; p. 36, Courtesy Medtronic; p. 39, Courtesy Eastman Kodak Company; Agency: Ketchum Communications; p. 42, Courtesy British Petroleum.

APPENDIX A

p. 48, ©1996 Paradise Kitchens, Inc. All photos & ads reprinted with permission; p. 51, ©1996 Paradise Kitchens, Inc. All photos & ads reprinted with permission; p. 53, ©1996 Paradise Kitchens, Inc. All photos & ads reprinted with permission; p. 54, ©1996 Paradise Kitchens, Inc. All photos & ads reprinted with permission; p. 55, ©1996 Paradise Kitchens, Inc. All photos & ads reprinted with permission.

CHAPTER 3

p. 58, Courtesy Apple Computer; p. 62 (left), ©The Procter & Gamble Company. Used by permission; p. 62 (center), The Donna Karan Company, 2001; p. 62 (right), ©Motorola, Inc. 2003; p. 67, Courtesy Cunard Line Limited/ Carnival Corporation; p. 68 (left), TravelDrive™ ad provided courtesy of Memorex Products, Inc. ©2004 All Rights Reserved; p. 68 (center), Mapster ad is copyright 2004, Napster lLC and reprinted with Napster's permission; p. 68 (right), Courtesy LG Electronics U.S.A., Inc; p. 69, Courtesy T-Mobile; Agency: Publicis Agency/Seattle; p. 71, ©M. Hruby; p. 74, Courtesy of Better Business Bureau, Inc; p. 76, Courtesy Flyte Time; p. 77, Courtesy Flyte Time.

Figure 3-3, Reprinted with permission from the November 2002 issue of American Demographics. Copyright Crain Communications Inc. 2004.

CHAPTER 4

p. 78, Courtesy Anheuser-Busch Companies, Inc; p. 83, ©2001 Michelle Delsol; p. 85, ©M. Hruby; p. 88, Courtesy Susan G. Komen Breast Cancer Foundation; p. 89, Getty Images/Photodisc Blue (DIL); p. 90, Courtesy McDonald's Corporation; p. 91, Paula Bronstein; p. 94, Michael Newman/Photo Edit.

CHAPTER 5

p. 98, Courtesy Volvo of North America; p. 102, Monica Lau/Getty Images (DIL); p. 106, The Secret Sales Pitch: An Overview of Subliminal Advertising. Copyright ©2004 by August Bullock. All Rights Reserved. Used with permission SubliminalSex.com; p. 107 (left), FRESH STEPS® is a registered trademark of The Clorox Pet Products Company. Used with permission; p. 107 (right), ©2001 Mary Kay, Inc. Photos by: Grace Huang/for Sarah Laird; p. 109 (left), Courtesy Colgate-Palmolive Company; p. 109 (right), The Bayer Company; p. 110, Courtesy SRI Consulting Business Intelligence (SRIC-B1), Menlo Park/CA. VALS™ is a trademark of SRI Consulting Business Intelligence. Reprinted with permission; p. 111 (left), Courtesy Omega S.A.; p. 111 (right), Courtesy Omega S.A.; p. 112, Courtesy BzzAgent, LLC; p. 114, Courtesy of Haggar Clothing Co. ©2004. Haggar Clothing Co; p. 115 (top), Courtesy Bonne Bell, Inc; p. 115 (bottom), Courtesy The Hershey Company; p. 118, Courtesy of Ken Davis Products, Inc; p. 119, ©2005 Rick Armstrong.

Figure 5-2, "MP-3 capable Portable CD Players" ©2002 by Consumers Union of U.S., Inc. Yonkers, NY 10703-1057, a nonprofit organization. Reprinted with permission from the September 2002 issue of Consumer Reports® for educational purposes only. No commercial use or reproduction permitted. www.ConsumerReports.org®.

CHAPTER 6

p. 120, Courtesy JCPenney; p. 123, Courtesy U.S. Department of Commerce/Bureau of the Census; p. 126, Courtesy Airbus; p. 127, Lluis Gene/AFP/Getty Images; p. 130, Dan Bosler/Stone/Getty Images; p. 136, ©2004 Lands' Ends, Inc. Used with permission.

CHAPTER 7

p. 138, ©M. Hruby; p. 143, Courtesy ALMA/BBDO São Paulo; p. 144, Courtesy Bartle Bogle Hegarty/Singapore; p. 145, Courtesy McDonald's Corporation; p. 147 (left), Travelpix/FPG International; p. 147 (right), Antonio Rosario/The Image Bank; p. 149, Courtesy The Coca-Cola Company; p. 151, Courtesy of Sanyu Boh, Ltd.; p. 152, Courtesy of Nestlé S.A.; p. 154 (all), Courtesy The Gillette Company; p. 158, Courtesy CNS, Inc.

CHAPTER 8

p. 162, Photo by Andreas Rentz/Getty Images; p. 164, Photo by Bill Pugliano/Getty Images; p. 165, Fisher-Price, Inc. a subsidiary of Mattel, Inc. East Aurora, NY 14052 U.S.A. ©2006 Mattel, Inc. All rights reserved; p. 166, ©M. Hruby; p. 167, Fisher-Price, Inc. a subsidiary of Mattel, Inc. East Aurora, NY 14052 U.S.A. ©2006 Mattel, Inc. All rights reserved; p. 171, AP Photo/ Kevork Djansezian; p. 172, Macduff Everton/ The Image Bank/Getty Images; p. 173 (left), Courtesy The Gillette Company; p. 173 (center), Courtesy 3M; p. 173 (right), Courtesy Skechers USA; p. 173 (bottom), ©2005 Karen Moskowitz; p. 174, Courtesy Teen Research Unlimited; p. 176, Photo by Cancan Chu/Getty Images; p. 177, ©Brent Jones; p. 178, Courtesy The Schwan Food Company; p. 181, Courtesy Wilson Sporting Goods Co., Copyright 2005.

Figure 8-3, Nielsen ratings of the top 10 national television programs. Used by permission of Nielsen Media Research; Figure 8-4, Nielsen/ NetRatings of top 10 internet websites. Used by permission of Nielsen/NetRatings.

CHAPTER 9

p. 186, Photo by Reebok via Getty Images; p. 187, ©Brent Jones; p. 188, Photo by Sam Forencich/NBAE via Getty Images; p. 191, Photo by David Silverman/Getty Images; p. 192, Courtesy of Street & Smith's Sports Annuals; p. 192, Courtesy of Street & Smith's Sports Annuals; p. 192, Courtesy of Street & Smith's Sports Annuals; p. 192, Courtesy of Street & Smith's Sports Annuals; p. 193, © The McGraw-Hill Companies/Jill Braaten Photographer (DIL); p. 195, Courtesy Mac-Gray; p. 197, Courtesy Xerox Corporation; p. 199, Courtesy Wendy's International, Inc; p. 200 (both), Courtesy Apple Computer; p. 202 (all), Courtesy Apple Computer; p. 203, ©M. Hruby; p. 204, ©M. Hruby; p. 206, Courtesy Nokia.

Figure 9-4, Comparison of various kinds of users and nonusers for Wendy's, Burger King, and McDonald's restaurants

CHAPTER 10

p. 210, Courtesy 3M; p. 211, Courtesy 3M; p. 213, Courtesy Vetco, Inc. Consumer Healthcare; p. 215, Courtesy Raymond Weil; p. 217 (left), Photo by Junko Kimura/Staff/Getty Images; p. 217 (right), Courtesy Microsoft Corporation; p. 218, Courtesy New Product Works;

p. 219 (left), Courtesy Canon U.S.A.; Agency: DCA Advertising, Inc; p. 219 (second from left), Courtesy Palm, Inc; p. 219 (second from right), Courtesy Intuit, Inc; p. 219 (right), Courtesy Swatch USA; p. 220 (top), Courtesy of The Original Pet Drink; p. 220 (bottom), Courtesy New Product Works; p. 221, Courtesy New Product Works; p. 222, Courtesy Volvo of North America; p. 223, ©M. Hruby; p. 224, ©M. Hruby; p. 225 (all), ©M. Hruby; p. 226, Jose Azel/Aurora Photos; 229 (top), ©M. Hruby; p. 229 (bottom), Courtesy of Hewlett-Packard Company; p. 232, Courtesy 3M.

CHAPTER 11

p. 234, Courtesy Element 79 Partners; p. 236, ©M. Hruby; p. 239 (left), Courtesy American Honda Motor Co; Agency: Rubin Postaer & Associates; p. 239 (right), Courtesy Casio, Inc; p. 244, Courtesy of the National Fluid Milk Processor Promotion Board; Agency: Bozell/ Chicago; p. 246 (left), Courtesy Advanced Research Labs; p. 246 (right), Courtesy Liz Claiborne; Agency: Avrett Free & Ginsberg; Models: Roberto Sanchez & Nadja Scantamburlo; Photographer: J. Westley Jones; p. 248, Courtesy Roper Footwear & Apparel; p. 251 (left), Courtesy of Black & Decker (U.S.), Inc; p. 251 (right), Courtesy of DeWalt Industrial Tool Company; p. 252, Courtesy of Pez Candy, Inc; p. 253 (top), ©M. Hruby; p. 253 (bottom), ©2001 Susan G. Holtz; p. 254, Used with permission from McDonald's Corporation; p. 255, Trademarks and copyrights used herein are properties of the United States Postal Service and are used under license to McGraw-Hill. All Rights Reserved; p. 257, Courtesy The Phillies/Citizens Bank Way; p. 258, Courtesy The Phillies; Photographer: Rosemary Rahn.

CHAPTER 12

p. 260, Courtesy Priceline.com; p. 262, Courtesy Bugatti; p. 265 (top), ©Terry McElroy; p. 265 (bottom), Photo by Nintendo/Getty Images; p. 266, Courtesy Sears Roebuck and Co; p. 267, Courtesy of The Caplow Company; p. 269, ©M. Hruby; p. 273, ©M. Hruby; p. 276, Courtesy Alexander Global Promotions; p. 278 (top), ©Kim Brewster; p. 278, (bottom), Photo by James Leynse/Corbis; p. 279, Courtesy Payless ShoeSource, Inc; p. 282, Stuart Cellars; p. 283, Stuart Cellars.

CHAPTER 13

p. 284, © The McGraw-Hill Companies/Jill Braaten Photographer (DIL); p. 291, Courtesy CPW; p. 292 (left), ©M. Hruby; p. 292 (right), © The McGraw-Hill Companies/Jill Braaten Photographer (DIL); p. 295 (left), Courtesy Jiffy Lube International, Inc; p. 295 (right), ©Amy Etra; p. 299 (left), Courtesy Dell, Inc; p. 299 (right), Courtesy Wal-Mart Stores, Inc; p. 300, Courtesy IBM; p. 305, Courtesy Golden Valley; p. 306 (left), Photo by MarkWilson/Getty Images; p. 306 (center), Photo by Justin Sullivan/ Getty Images; p. 306 (right), Photo by Justin Sullivan/Getty Images.

CHAPTER 14

p. 308, Reprinted with pemission by Target Corporation; p. 311 bottom, Courtesy PPR Group; p. 313, Reprinted with permission of Tandy Corporation; p. 315, Courtesy Marconi Commerce Systems; p. 316 (top), Courtesy L.L.Bean; p. 316 (bottom), Courtesy of QVC Network; p. 317, Courtesy CNET; p. 323, Courtesy Taco Bell; p. 328, Courtesy Mall of America; p. 329, Courtesy Mall of America.

CHAPTER 15

p. 330, AP Photo/Peter Cosgrove; p. 333, 2005 General Motors Corporation. Used with permission of HUMMER and General Motors; p. 335, Courtesy Best Buy; p. 336, ©M. Hruby; p. 338 (top), Courtesy Fence Magazine; p. 338 (bottom), ©2005. Used with permission MINI Cooper USA; p. 339, ©M. Hruby; p. 340, CRESTOR® is a registered trademark of the AstraZeneca group of companies. ©2005 AstraZeneca Pharmaceuticals LP. All rights reserved; p. 343 (top), ©2005 Hilton Hotels Corporation; p. 343 (bottom), ©M. Hruby; p. 345, ©M. Hruby; p. 346, ©1999 Hertz System, Inc. Hertz is a registered service mark and trademark of Hertz System, Inc; p. 347, Courtesy of Porsche Cars North America, Inc; p. 350, McGraw-Hill IMC 2nd Edition Educational Video.

CHAPTER 16

p. 352, Courtesy Wildtangent Online Video Game, Snowboard Super Jam; p. 354 (center), ©2005 SmithGlaxoKline. Reproduced with permission; p. 354 (right), Courtesy of 1-800-Flowers.com; p. 355, Courtesy National Fluid Milk Processor Promotion Board; Agency: Lowe Worldwide, Inc; p. 356, Courtesy Pepsi Cola Company; p. 358, Courtesy Virgin Atlantic Airlines Limited; p. 359, Courtesy Speed Channel 2004; p. 361 (top), TEEN PEOPLE ©2005 Time Inc. All rights reserved; p. 361 (bottom), Courtesy Yellow Pages Association; p. 362 (top), ©James Leynse/CORBIS; p. 363 (bottom), ©Beach 'N Billboard; p. 364, Courtesy of Roper Starch Worldwide, Inc; p. 365, Courtesy Cox Target Media, provider of Valpak® products; p. 366 (left), Nestle USA/ Nestle Crunch Brand; p. 366 (right), Courtesy CIT Group, Inc; p. 368 (left), ©Shooting Star; p. 368 (center), AP Photo; p. 368 (right), Photo by Kevin Winter/Getty Images; p. 372, Courtesy CIT Group, Inc; p. 373, Courtesy Fallon McElligott.

CHAPTER 17

p. 374, Courtesy Xerox Corporation; p. 376, ©John Madere; p. 378, Mitch Kezar/Stone/Getty Images; p. 381, Einzig Photography; p. 382, CB Productions/Corbis; p. 384, Richard Pasley/Stock Boston LLC; p. 386, Courtesy Xerox Corporation; p. 389, Courtesy of Mary Kay; p. 390, Courtesy of Toshiba America Medical Systems and Interactive Media; p. 390, Courtesy of Toshiba America Medical Systems and Interactive Media; p. 391, ©Jose Peleaz; p. 394, Courtesy of Reebok International Ltd.

CHAPTER 18

p. 396, ©tom white.images; p. 399, Courtesy Godiva Chocolatier; p. 404 ©Paul Barton/ CORBIS; p. 407, Courtesy Diamond Trading Company; Agency: J. Walter Thompson; p. 408, ©The Procter & Gamble Company. Used by permission; p. 409, ©Matt Mahurin, Inc.

APPENDIX B

p. 417, ©Paul Elledge; p. 418, Courtesy The May Department Stores Company; p. 419, Courtesy Xerox Corporation; p. 420, Reprinted from Job Choices 2002 with permission of the National Association of Colleges and Employers, copyright holder; p. 421, Courtesy Monster; p. 424 (top), White Packert/Getty Images; p. 424 (bottom), Thatch Cartoon by Jeff Shesol; Reprinted with permission of Vintage Books.

Figure B-1, Careers in Marketing by David W. Rosenthal and Michael A. Powell © 1984, pp. 352–54. Reprinted by permission.

NAME INDEX

T

U

V

W

Y

Z

COMPANY/PRODUCT INDEX

Q

R

S

SUBJECT INDEX

C

N

O

P

T

U

V

W

Y